American Foreign Policy

Second Edition

American Foreign Policy

The Dynamics of Choice
in the 21st Century

SECOND EDITION

BRUCE W. JENTLESON

Duke University

W. W. NORTON & COMPANY
NEW YORK • LONDON

W. W. Norton & Company has been independent since its founding in 1923, when William Warder Norton and Mary D. Herter Norton first published lectures delivered at the People's Institute, the adult education division of New York City's Cooper Union. The Nortons soon expanded their program beyond the Institute, publishing books by celebrated academics from America and abroad. By mid-century, the two major pillars of Norton's publishing program— trade books and college texts—were firmly established. In the 1950s, the Norton family transferred control of the company to its employees, and today—with a staff of four hundred and a comparable number of trade, college, and professional titles published each year—W. W. Norton & Company stands as the largest and oldest publishing house owned wholly by its employees.

Manufacturing by the Maple-Vail Book Group, Binghamton.
Book design by Jack Meserole and Rubina Yeh.
Production manager: Ben Reynolds.
Drawn art by John McAusland.
Composition by TSI Graphics.

Library of Congress Cataloging-in-Publication Data

Jentleson, Bruce W., 1951–
    American foreign policy: the dynamics of choice in the 21st century / Bruce W.
Jentleson.—2nd ed.
        p. cm.
    Includes bibliographical references and index.

ISBN 0-393-97934-2 (pbk.)

    1. United States—Foreign relations—1989– 2. United States—Foreign relations—1989–
—Forecasting. 3. United States—Foreign relations—21st century. I. Title.

E840.J46 2003
327.73—dc21   2003048787

W. W. Norton & Company, Inc., 500 Fifth Avenue, New York, N.Y. 10110
www.wwnorton.com

W. W. Norton & Company Ltd., 10 Castle House, 75/76 Wells Street, London W1T 3QT

3 4 5 6 7 8 9 0

To my students, and those of my colleagues,
with whom the choices have begun to lie

Contents

PART **I** *The Context of*
U.S. Foreign Policy:
Theory and History

1 *The Strategic Context: Foreign Policy Strategy and the Essence of Choice*   2

Supplemental Readings for Part I: The Context of U.S. Foreign Policy

PART II *American Foreign Policy in the Twenty-First Century: Choices and Challenges*

List of Maps and Boxed Features

Perspectives

Dynamics of Choice

Additional Figures, Tables, and Boxed Features

Preface to the Second Edition

When we went to bed on the night of September 10, 2001, the world already was going through a historic transition. The Cold War had ended, raising hopes for the future. War, though, had not ended, as the 1990s bore tragic witness in Bosnia, Rwanda, and all too many other deadly conflicts. New forces of globalization were sweeping the world, bringing their own combination of progress and problems. Democracy had spread but now was facing the challenges of consolidation and institutionalization. All this, and more, made for quite a full foreign policy agenda for the United States.

And then came September 11. Most of us always will remember where we were when we first heard the news of the terrorist attacks on the World Trade Center and the Pentagon. The images were piercing. The American psyche was shaken. And the foreign policy agenda was further transformed as the war on terrorism was launched.

We thus now had to deal with both the September 10 agenda and the September 11 one. Such are the challenges and opportunities confronting American foreign policy as we move further into this new era and new century, for those who make it—and for those who teach and study it.

American Foreign Policy: The Dynamics of Choice in the 21st Century, Second Edition, is intended to help those of us who are professors and students take advantage of those opportunities and meet those challenges. The book is designed as a primary text for courses on American foreign policy. Its scope encompasses both key issues of *foreign policy strategy,* of what the U.S. national interest is and which policies serve it best, and key questions of *foreign policy politics,* of which institutions and actors within the American political system play what roles and have how much influence. Formulating foreign policy strategy is the "essence of choice," the means by which goals are established and the policies that are the optimal means of achieving them are forged. Foreign policy politics is the "process of choice," the making of foreign policy through the political institutions and amid the societal influences of the American political system.

Part I of this book provides the theory (Chapters 1 and 2) and history (Chapter 3 for 1789–1945, Chapters 4 and 5 on the Cold War) for establishing the framework of the dynamics of choice. The theory chapters draw on the international relations and American foreign policy literatures to introduce core concepts, pose debates over alternative explanations, and frame the analytic approach to foreign policy strategy and foreign policy politics. The history chapters help ensure that expressions like "break with the past" are not taken too literally. Not only must we still cope with the legacies of the Cold War, but many current issues are contemporary versions of long-standing "great debates" with lengthy histories in U.S. foreign policy. These chapters follow closely with the First Edition, with revisions and elaborations drawing on the helpful feedback from reviewers, instructors and students.

Part II (Chapters 6–10) applies the framework to the post–Cold War foreign policy agenda and the major choices the United States faces today. This section begins with a new Overview chapter (6), laying out the overarching debate over foreign policy strategy and examining general patterns in the dynamics of post–Cold War foreign policy politics. Chapters 7 through 10 are revised and expanded from the First Edition, focusing in on key sets of issues across the foreign policy agenda. What policies should the United States pursue in this post–Cold War era? What threats do we face, what interests do we have, where do our democratic values fit in? How well is the process for making our foreign policy working? The chapters are highly comprehensive, providing students with a broad survey of the post–Cold War foreign policy agenda. A wide range of issues is covered in a manner that both provides an initial understanding and lays the foundation for further reading and research.

Throughout the book a number of special pedagogical features are included: *Dynamics of Choice,* charts that illustrate and highlight key aspects of the analytic framework; *At the Source,* primary source materials such as major speeches and policy documents; *Perspectives,* providing insightful and often controversial views on major issues; a number of maps, tables, and other boxed elements; and a Web site Bibliography providing a helpful guide for research and further reading using Web sites from the U.S. government, the United Nations and other international organizations, foreign governments, think tanks, nongovernmental organizations (NGOs), and media sources.

This edition also offers the text and reader in a single volume. Supplemental readings are keyed to each chapter. These readings help to develop more fully theories and concepts introduced in the text and to delve more deeply into major policy debates. They include works both by major policy figures such as Henry Kissinger, Mikhail Gorbachev, and Kofi Annan and by scholars such as Hans Morgenthau, Walter LaFeber, Alexander George, and Samuel Huntington.

This book reflects my own belief in a "multi-integrative" approach to teaching about American foreign policy. By that I mean three things: an approach that breaks through the levels-of-analysis barriers and integrates international policy and domestic process; one that encompasses the full range of post–Cold War foreign policy issue areas (e.g., diplomacy, defense, international economic policy, global democratization, global environment); and one that "bridges the gap" between theory and practice by drawing on both perspectives. With regard to this last point, I have sought to incorporate the perspectives and experiences gained through my own work in the policy world (at the State Department on the Policy Planning Staff, in Congress as a Senate foreign policy aide, and in other capacities) as well as from more than twenty years as a professor.

My interest in writing this book is a manifestation of my commitment to teaching. Throughout my university education I was fortunate to have some exceptional teachers. I was among the thousands of undergraduates at Cornell University who were first captivated by the study of foreign policy through Walter LaFeber's courses on diplomatic history. The late Bud Kenworthy, a superb and caring teacher in his own right, was instrumental in my realization as a senior that I wanted to pursue an academic career. When I went back to Cornell for my Ph.D., I was just as fortunate as a graduate student. Anyone who knows Theodore Lowi knows his intensity and passion for his work; these are especially evident in his teaching. Peter Katzenstein was my dissertation chair and a mentor in many ways, including in showing how commitments to superior scholarship and excellent teaching can be combined.

In my years as a professor my good fortune has continued. In both his approach and his persona, Alexander George has been a much-valued mentor and colleague. Thanks also to Larry Berman, Ed Costantini, Emily Goldman, Alex Groth, Miko Nincic, and Don Rothchild, and other colleagues at the University of California at Davis who were partners of many years in trying to make our political science and international relations majors as rich and rewarding for our students as possible. And to Peter Feaver, Ole Holsti, Bob Keohane, Judith Kelley, Anirudh Krishna, Fritz Mayer, and many other valued colleagues here at Duke with whom I have been sharing similar pursuits over the past four years.

Rebecca Britton, Alexandra Pass, Kim Cole, and Sara Johnson were able research assistants on the First Edition, Seth Weinberger on the Second. Librarians Jean Stratford at U.C. Davis and Jim Cornelius at the U.S. Institute of Peace helped greatly in accessing sources and checking citations. Melody Johnson, Lori Renard, Fatima Mohamud, and especially Barbara Taylor-Keil provided tremendous support on the First Edition; Susanne Borchardt was of enormous help on the Second Edition. I owe many thanks to them all. Thanks also to U.C. Davis, Duke, and the U.S. Institute of Peace for research support.

Special thanks to colleagues whose feedback as reviewers has been so helpful: Loch Johnson, Jim Lindsay, Dan Caldwell and his students, and others on the First Edition; John Barkdull, Colin Dueck, Todd Eisenstadt, Margaret Karns,

Roy Licklider, Peter Loedel, F. Ugboaja Ohaegbulam, and Jon Western on the Second Edition.

At W. W. Norton, Roby Harrington has been there from the inception of the project and has provided the steady hand to see it through to initial completion and now a Second Edition. Authors know that we can count on Roby to be supportive and enthusiastic yet also committed to quality and focused on getting the book done. Thanks are due also to Sarah Caldwell and Rob Whiteside on the First Edition and to Avery Johnson, Andrea Haver and especially Aaron Javsicas on the Second. Traci Nagle's and Patterson Lamb's copyediting was extremely helpful; the reader has them to thank for the book's reading as well as it does.

Special thanks to my family: Adam and Katie, children and now young adults who continue to bring so much to my life; Barbara, who once again has been consistently supportive and encouraging of a husband too often too long in his study; and my mother, Elaine, and the memory of my father, Ted, for their love and understanding.

B.W.J.
June 2003
Durham, North Carolina

The World

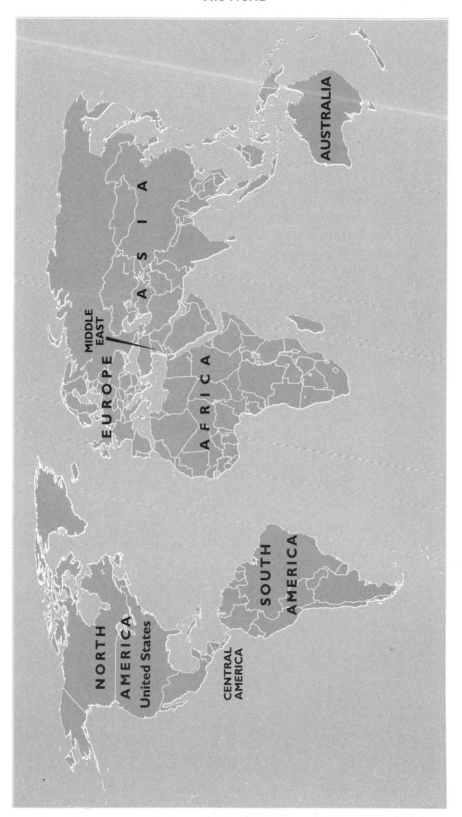

Africa, 2003

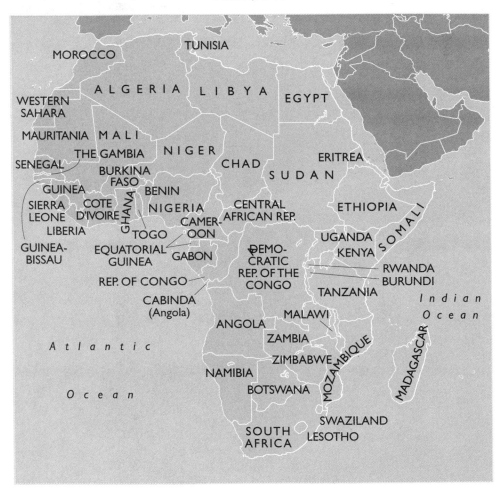

MOROCCO

TUNISIA

ALGERIA   LIBYA   EGYPT

WESTERN
SAHARA

MAURITANIA   MALI

SENEGAL   THE GAMBIA   NIGER

BURKINA   CHAD   ERITREA
FASO

GUINEA   BENIN   SUDAN

SIERRA   COTE   NIGERIA   CENTRAL   ETHIOPIA
LEONE   D'IVOIRE   AFRICAN REP.

LIBERIA   GHANA   TOGO   CAMER-   OON

GUINEA-   EQUATORIAL   GABON   UGANDA   SOMALI
BISSAU   GUINEA   DEMO-   KENYA
CRATIC
REP. OF CONGO   REP. OF THE   RWANDA
CONGO   BURUNDI

CABINDA   TANZANIA   Indian
(Angola)   Ocean

MALAWI

ANGOLA

Atlantic   ZAMBIA

ZIMBABWE   MOZAMBIQUE   MADAGASCAR

NAMIBIA

Ocean   BOTSWANA

SWAZILAND
SOUTH   LESOTHO
AFRICA

Asia, 2003

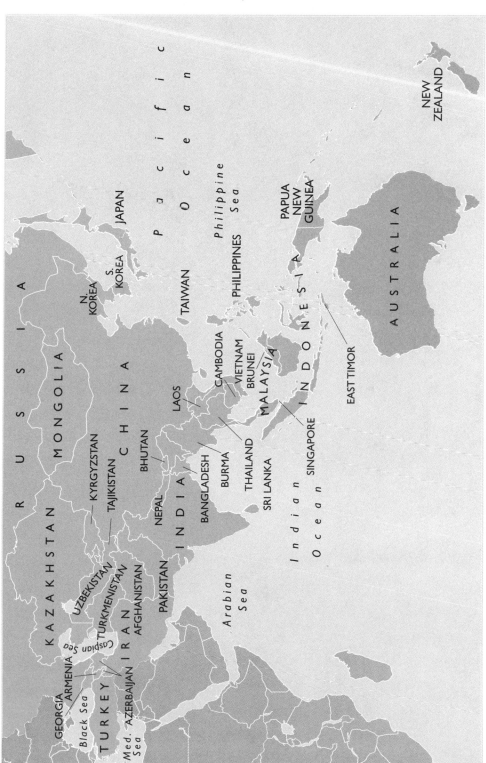

Europe, 2003

The Western Hemisphere, 2003

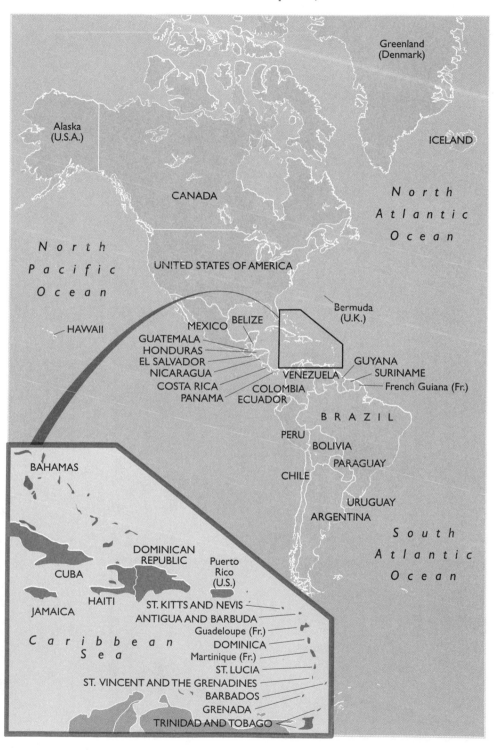

Greenland (Denmark)

Alaska (U.S.A.)

ICELAND

CANADA

North Atlantic Ocean

North Pacific Ocean

UNITED STATES OF AMERICA

Bermuda (U.K.)

HAWAII

MEXICO
BELIZE
GUATEMALA
HONDURAS
EL SALVADOR
NICARAGUA
COSTA RICA
PANAMA
ECUADOR
COLOMBIA
VENEZUELA
GUYANA
SURINAME
French Guiana (Fr.)

BRAZIL

PERU
BOLIVIA
PARAGUAY
CHILE

URUGUAY
ARGENTINA

South Atlantic Ocean

BAHAMAS

DOMINICAN REPUBLIC
Puerto Rico (U.S.)

CUBA

HAITI
ST. KITTS AND NEVIS
ANTIGUA AND BARBUDA
Guadeloupe (Fr.)
DOMINICA
Martinique (Fr.)
ST. LUCIA

JAMAICA

Caribbean Sea

ST. VINCENT AND THE GRENADINES
BARBADOS
GRENADA
TRINIDAD AND TOBAGO

The Middle East, 2003

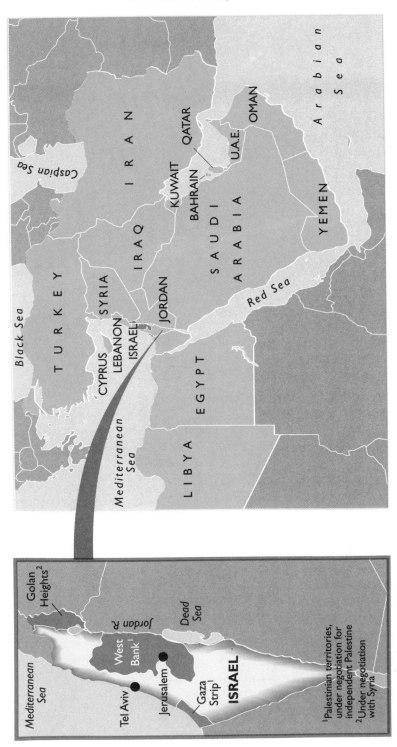

Black Sea

Caspian Sea

TURKEY

CYPRUS
LEBANON
ISRAEL
Mediterranean Sea

SYRIA

IRAQ

IRAN

JORDAN

KUWAIT
BAHRAIN
QATAR
U.A.E.
OMAN

Arabian Sea

SAUDI ARABIA

Red Sea

YEMEN

EGYPT

LIBYA

Golan Heights²

Jordan R.

Dead Sea

Mediterranean Sea

West Bank¹

Tel Aviv

Jerusalem

Gaza Strip¹

ISRAEL

¹Palestinian territories, under negotiation for independent Palestine
²Under negotiation with Syria

PART I *The Context of U.S. Foreign Policy: Theory and History*

1 *The Strategic Context: Foreign Policy Strategy and the Essence of Choice*

Introduction: Foreign Policy in a Time of Transition

It was October 22, 1962, 7:00 P.M. A young boy sat on his living room floor watching television. President John F. Kennedy came on to warn the American public of an ominous crisis with the Soviet Union over nuclear missiles in Cuba. The boy's parents tried to look calm, but the fear in their eyes could not be masked. It seemed that the United States was on the brink of nuclear war.

The Cuban missile crisis ended up being settled peacefully, and the Cold War ultimately ended without nuclear war. For a while it seemed that the post–Cold War era was going to be a peaceful one. Indeed, when the Berlin Wall came down in 1989, and then the Soviet Union fell apart in 1991, a sense of near euphoria enveloped the West. We won. They lost. President George H.W. Bush (1989–93) spoke of the end of the Cold War as "a time of great promise," an "unparalleled opportunity . . . to work toward transforming this new world into a new world order, one of governments that are democratic, tolerant and economically free at home and committed abroad to settling differences peacefully, without the threat or use of force" (see At the Source, p. 4). Articles and books proclaimed "the end of history," the triumph of democracy, the "obsolescence" of war.

To be sure, the significance of families freed of the worry of an all-out nuclear war is not to be underestimated. In that sense the end of the Cold War left the world more secure. All too soon, however, we saw that the end of the Cold War did not mean the end of war. The 1990s will be remembered for peace agreements and the advance of democracy—but also for ethnic "cleansings," civil wars, and genocide. It was a decade of strides toward peace and order, but also stumbles toward anarchy and chaos. For American foreign policy, it was a decade of great successes, but also dismal failures.

The 1990s also saw the emergence of the "globalization" agenda. Globalization has been hailed by many for bringing such benefits as the spread of capitalism and economic freedom to the former communist bloc and the Third World, and the closer linking through technology and markets of all corners of the globe, and for building the basis for global prosperity. President Bill Clinton spoke of "the train of globalization" that "cannot be reversed" and of how global trade could "lift hundreds of millions of people out of poverty." But he also warned that globalization needed "a more human face," that it needed to address issues such as the global environment, the global AIDS crisis, and the widening gap between rich and poor nations. Indeed a powerful anti-globalization movement emerged in the 1990s: first in Seattle at the 1999 summit of the World Trade Organization and then at international economic meetings in ensuing years in various cities around the world, this movement mounted the most extensive and violent foreign policy protests since those of the anti–Vietnam War movement in the 1960s and 1970s. On this issue agenda as well, the euphoria of the immediate post–Cold War years faded and the 1990s ended with a mixed sense of progress and problems.

Then came the tragic and shocking terrorist assault of September 11, 2001. "U.S. ATTACKED," the *New York Times* headline blared the next day in the large print used for only the most momentous events. It described "a hellish storm of ash, glass, smoke and leaping victims" as the World Trade Center towers crashed down.[1] In Washington, D.C., the Pentagon, the fortress of American defense, was literally ripped open by the impact of another hijacked jetliner. The death tolls were staggering. The shock ran deep. A new sense of insecurity set in, for it soon became clear that this was not an isolated incident. President George W. Bush declared a "war on terrorism," which started in October 2001 in Afghanistan against Osama bin Laden, his Al Qaeda terrorist network, and the Taliban regime in Afghanistan. But it did not end there: "It will not end," President Bush declared, "until every terrorist group of global reach has been found, stopped and defeated."

Any one of these sets of changes—the end of the Cold War, deadly ethnic conflicts, globalization, struggles over democratization and human rights, the war on terrorism—would be profound by itself. Dealing with the combined effects of all five truly makes these times of historic transition. One era and one century ended; a new era and a new century have begun.

At the Source

THE UNITED STATES IN THE POST–COLD WAR WORLD

As Seen by President George H.W. Bush (1993)

❝ The end of the Cold War . . . is a time of great promise. . . . But this does not mean that there is no specter of war, no threats to be reckoned with. And, already, we see disturbing signs of what this new world could become if we are passive and aloof. We would risk the emergence of a world characterized by violence, characterized by chaos, one in which dictators and tyrants threaten their neighbors, build arsenals brimming with weapons of mass destruction, and ignore the welfare of their own men, women and children. And we could see a horrible increase in terrorism with American citizens more at risk than ever before.

We cannot and we will not allow this to happen. Our objective must be to exploit the unparalleled opportunity presented by the Cold War's end to work toward transforming this new world into a new world order, one of governments that are democratic, tolerant and economically free at home and committed abroad to settling differences peacefully, without the threat or use of force. ❞

As Seen by President Bill Clinton (2000)

❝ The train of globalization cannot be reversed, but it has more than one possible destination. If we want America to stay on the right track, if we want other people to be on that track, and have the chance to enjoy peace and prosperity, we have no choice but to try to lead that train. . . . We want global trade to lift hundreds of millions of people out of poverty, from India to China to Africa. We know if it happens, it'll create a big market for everything American, from corn to cars to computers. And it will give all of us new ideas, new innovation, and we'll all help each other in constructive competition.

But the gap between rich and poor nations could continue to widen and bring more misery, more environmental destruction, more health

(*Continued on page 5*)

(Post–Cold War World *Continued from page 4*)

problems, more and more young people in poor countries just checking out of wanting to be part of a global system, because they think there's nothing in it for them.

We should be for more open trade, but we have to build a global economy with a more human face. "

As Seen by President George W. Bush (2001, 2002)

" On September the 11th, enemies of freedom committed an act of war against our country. Americans have known wars—but for the past 136 years, they have been wars on foreign soil, except for one Sunday in December 1941. Americans have known the casualties of war—but not at the center of a great city on a peaceful morning. Americans have known surprise attacks—but never before on thousands of civilians. All of this was brought upon us in a single day—and night fell on a different world, a world where freedom itself is under attack. . . .

Our war on terror begins with Al Qaeda, but it does not end there. It will not end until every terrorist group of global reach has been found, stopped and defeated. "

* * *

" Our nation will continue to be steadfast and patient and persistent in the pursuit of two great objectives. First, we will shut down terrorist camps, disrupt terrorist plans and bring terrorists to justice. And, second, we must prevent the terrorists and regimes who seek chemical, biological or nuclear weapons from threatening the United States and the world. . . .

States like these [Iraq, Iran, and North Korea] and their terrorist allies constitute an axis of evil, arming to threaten the peace of the world. "

Sources: George H.W. Bush, "Remarks at the United States Military Academy in West Point, New York," January 5, 1993, *Public Papers of the Presidents: George Bush,* Vol. 2 (Washington, D.C.: Office of the Federal Register, National Archives and Records Administration, 1993), 2228–32; Bill Clinton, "Speech at the University of Nebraska," December 8, 2000, *Public Papers of the Presidents: William J. Clinton 2000–2001,* Vol. 3 (Washington, D.C.: U.S. Government Printing Office, 2002), 2653–61; George W. Bush, "Address to a Joint Session of Congress and the American People," September 20, 2001, and "2002 State of the Union Address," January 29, 2002, available at www.whitehouse.gov.

Just as each of the three most recent presidents has given different emphases to the U.S. role in this new era, so too have prominent scholars and analysts offered a range of views on the nature of this new era. Back in 1989, amid the sense of political and ideological triumph over communism, the conservative intellectual Francis Fukuyama envisioned "the end of history . . . and the universalization of Western liberal democracy as the final form of human government." A few years later Harvard University professor Samuel Huntington offered a much less optimistic view of a "clash of civilizations," particularly between the West and Islam, with prospects for political and military conflicts. *New York Times* columnist Thomas Friedman pointed more to economics as the driving dynamic, to liberalism, clashing civilizations, and power politics as "the old system," and to globalization as "the new system." The Rockefeller Brothers Fund stressed the importance of "nonmilitary threats to peace and security," especially global poverty and environmental degradation, and advocated a conception of "social stewardship" for addressing these issues "before they metastasize into larger threats." Columbia University professor Richard Betts was stressing the threat of nuclear, chemical, and biological weapons of mass destruction, including those in the hands of terrorists who might "decide they want to stun American policymakers by inflicting enormous damage," even before the events of September 11, 2001, and the anthrax-tainted letters that followed.

Whatever the differences among these perspectives, they all share a common view of the importance of foreign policy. For too long too many voices have been claiming that the United States can and should turn inward and can afford to care less about and do less with the rest of the world. But for five fundamental reasons, the importance of foreign policy must not be underestimated.

First are the security threats. September 11 drove these home all too dramatically. No longer was the threat "over there" in some distant corner of the globe; it had arrived right here at home. Moreover, regions such as the Middle East, South Asia (India, Pakistan), and East Asia (the Korean Peninsula, China, Taiwan), in which the United States still has significant interests and long-standing commitments to allies, are still at serious risk of war. Furthermore, although no great power threatens the United States today, that doesn't mean an adversary will not emerge in the future. Relations with Russia and China are vastly improved but cannot be taken for granted, given both the policy differences that still exist and the political uncertainties and potential instabilities these giant countries face.

Second, the American economy is more internationalized than ever before. Whereas in 1970 foreign trade accounted for less than 15 percent of the U.S. gross domestic product (GDP), it now amounts to more than 30 percent. Exports fund a larger and larger number of American jobs. When the Federal Reserve Board sets interest rates, in addition to domestic factors like inflation, it increasingly also has to consider international ones, such as foreign-currency exchange rates and the likely reactions of foreign investors. Private financial markets also have become increasingly globalized. So when Asian stock markets plunged in late 1997, and when Russia's economy collapsed in mid-1998, middle-class America felt the effects, as mutual funds, college savings, and retirement nest eggs plummeted in value.

Third, many other areas of policy that used to be considered "domestic" also have been internationalized. The environmental policy agenda has extended from the largely domestic issues of the 1960s and 1970s to international issues such as global warming and biodiversity. The "just say no" drug policy of the 1980s is insufficient as a policy when thousands of tons of drugs come into the United States every day from Latin America, Asia, and elsewhere. Whereas the Federal Bureau of Investigation's "Ten Most Wanted" fugitives list included mostly members of U.S.-based crime syndicates when it first started in 1950, by 1997 eight of the ten fugitives on the list were international criminals. Public-health problems like the spread of AIDS have to be combated globally. In these and other areas the distinctions between foreign and domestic policy have become increasingly blurred, as international forces impact in more and more ways on spheres of American life that used to be considered domestic.

Fourth, the increasing racial and ethnic diversity of the American people has produced a larger number and wider range of groups with personal bases for interest in foreign affairs. Some forms of "identity politics" can be traced all the way back to the nineteenth century, and some were quite common during the Cold War. But more and more Americans trace their ancestry and heritage to different countries and regions and are asserting their interests and seeking influence over foreign policy toward those countries and regions.

Fifth, it is hard for the United States to uphold its most basic values if it ignores grievous violations of those values that take place outside its national borders. It is not necessary to go so far as to take on the role of global missionary or world police. But it also is not possible to claim to stand for democracy, freedom, and justice, yet say "not my problem" to genocide, repression, torture, and other horrors.

PERSPECTIVES
PERSPECTIVES
PERSPECTIVES

THE NATURE OF THE NEW ERA

What we may be witnessing is not just the end of the Cold War, or the passing of a particular period of postwar history, but the end of history as such: that is, the end point of mankind's ideological evolution and the universalization of Western liberal democracy as the final form of human government.

Francis Fukuyama, *The End of History*

The fundamental source of conflict in this new world will not be primarily ideological or primarily economic. The great divisions among humankind and the dominating source of conflict will be cultural. . . . The clash of civilizations will dominate global politics. The fault lines between civilizations will be the battle lines of the future. . . . The paramount axis of world politics will be the relations between "the West and the Rest."

Samuel Huntington, *The Clash of Civilizations*

If you want to understand the post–Cold War world you have to start by understanding that a new international system has succeeded it— globalization. . . . Globalization is not the only thing influencing events in the world today, but to the extent that there is a North Star and a worldwide shaping force, it is this system. What is new is the system; what is old is power politics, chaos, clashing civilizations and liberalism. And what is the drama of the post–Cold War world is the interaction between this new system and these old passions.

Thomas Friedman, *The Lexus and the Olive Tree*

Today, weapons of mass destruction (WMD) present more and different things to worry about than during the Cold War. For one, nuclear arms are no longer the only concern, as chemical and biological weapons have come to the fore. . . . If terrorists decide that they want to stun American policymakers by inflicting enormous damage, WMD become more attractive at the same time that they are becoming more accessible.

Richard Betts, *The New Threat of Mass Destruction*
(*Continued on page 9*)

(The Nature of the New Era   *Continued from page 8)*
In a world made smaller by global commerce and communication, cooperative engagement is more possible—and more necessary—than ever
before.... "Social stewardship" is increasingly recognized as a component
of national—and global—security. With the end of the Cold War, there is
a growing understanding of nonmilitary threats to peace and security.
International problems, such as resource scarcities and wide gaps
between rich and poor, have the potential to destabilize nations and even
precipitate military aggression. Successful social stewardship can address
intranational problems before they metastasize into larger threats.

Rockefeller Brothers Fund Report

Sources: Francis Fukuyama, "The End of History?" *National Interest* 16 (Summer 1989), 4;
Samuel P. Huntington, "The Clash of Civilizations?" *Foreign Affairs* 72:3 (Summer 1993),
22, 28; Thomas L. Friedman, *The Lexus and the Olive Tree: Understanding Globalization*
(New York: Farrar, Straus and Giroux, 1999), xviii; Richard K. Betts, "The New Threat of
Mass Destruction," *Foreign Affairs* 77:1 (January/February 1998), 26, 29; Laurie Ann
Mazur and Susan E. Sechler, *Global Interdependence and the Need for Social Stewardship*
(New York: Rockefeller Brothers Fund, 1997), 9–10.

Foreign policy thus continues to press upon us, as individuals and as a nation. The choices it poses are just as crucial for the twenty-first century as the
Cold War choices were for the second half of the twentieth century.

This book has two principal purposes: (1) to provide a framework, grounded
in international relations theory and U.S. diplomatic history, for foreign
policy analysis; and (2) to apply that framework to the agenda for U.S. foreign policy in the post–Cold War world.

The analytic framework, as reflected in the book's subtitle, is *the dynamics
of choice*. It is structured by two fundamental sets of questions that, whatever
the specific foreign policy issues involved, and whatever the time period being
discussed, have been at the center of debate:

- questions of *foreign policy strategy*—of what the national interest is and
  how best to achieve it; and
- questions of *foreign policy politics*—of which institutions and actors
  within the American political system play what roles and have how
  much influence.

Setting foreign policy strategy is the *essence of choice,* establishing the goals to be achieved and forging the policies that are the optimal means for achieving them. Foreign policy politics is the *process of choice*, the making of foreign policy through the political institutions and amid the societal influences of the American political system.

Part I of this book provides the theory (in this chapter and Chapter 2) and history (Chapters 3, 4, and 5) for establishing the framework of the dynamics of choice in U.S. foreign policy. Part II then applies the framework to the major foreign policy choices the United States faces as it enters this new post–Cold War era and a new century.

The Context of the International System

The United States, like all states, makes its choices of foreign policy strategy within the context of the international system. Although extensive study of international systems is more the province of international relations texts, three points are important to our focus on American foreign policy.

Quasi-anarchy

One of the fundamental differences between the international system and domestic political systems is the absence of a recognized central governing authority in the international system. This often is referred to as the *anarchic* view of international relations. Its roots go back to the seventeenth-century English political philosopher Thomas Hobbes and his classic treatise, *Leviathan.* Hobbes saw international affairs as a "war of all against all." Unlike in domestic affairs, where order was maintained by a king or other recognized authority figure, no such recognized authority existed in the international sphere, according to Hobbes. Others since have taken a more tempered view, pointing to ways in which international norms, laws, and institutions have provided some order and authority and stressing the potential for even greater progress in this regard. Yet even in our contemporary era, although we have progressed beyond the "nasty, brutish," unadulterated Hobbesian world by developing international institutions like the United Nations and the International Monetary Fund, as well as a growing body of international law, the world still has nothing at the international level as weighty and authoritative as a constitution, a legislature, a president, or a supreme court. The prevailing sense thus is that what makes international relations "unique and inherently different from relations within states" is that "no ultimate authority exists to govern the international system. . . . As a result the existence of a 'quasi-anarchy' at the international level conditions state-to-state relations."[2]

System Structure

System structure is based on the distribution of power among the major states in the international system. "Poles" refer to how many major powers there are—one in a unipolar system, two in a bipolar system, three or more in a multipolar system. In multipolar systems the key is a *balance of power* among the three or more states that are the major powers in the system, such that none of them can safely calculate that it can achieve dominance. The international system of the nineteenth century, when the United States was not yet a global power and the old European powers still dominated, is a frequent example of a balance-of-power system. In bipolar systems, such as the one that existed during the Cold War, peace and stability rest heavily on *deterrence*. The general definition of deterrence is the prevention of war by fear of retaliation. In the Cold War the United States and the Soviet Union were particularly concerned with nuclear deterrence and the avoidance of nuclear war because of fear on both sides that even if one launched a first strike, the other would still have enough nuclear weaponry to strike back. In a unipolar system peace and stability depend on the *primacy* of a major power, and whether that major power uses its dominant position for the common international good or exploits it for its own benefit. As we will see in Part II, one of the central debates about the post–Cold War system is the extent to which the system has become unipolar, with the United States holding primacy, and whether the United States should pursue more unilateral rather than multilateral foreign policy strategies.

State Structural Position

Where a state ranks in the international system structure affects what it can do in foreign policy terms. Theorists such as Kenneth Waltz see system structure as very deterministic, making "[states'] behavior and the outcomes of their behavior predictable."[3] To know a state's structural position is thus to know its foreign policy strategy. Yet such claims can go too far, taking too rigid a view of how much is fixed and determined at the system level. For example, we know the Cold War went on for almost fifty years and that it ended peacefully.

Waltz argues that this proves the stability of bipolarity and justifies the deterrence policies as successful. Yet it is worth asking whether the Cold War had to go on for fifty years: could it have been ended sooner had leaders on one or both sides pursued different policies? Or consider the Cuban missile crisis of 1962 (discussed in more detail in Chapter 4): the bipolar system structure raised the possibility of such a crisis but did not make either its occurrence or its successful resolution inevitable. The same logic applies to the end of the Cold War (Chapter 5) and leads us to ask whether it might have gone on longer had there been different leaders and policies on one or both sides in the 1980s and 1990s. Although it is important to take system structure into account, it should be as a context for, not a determinant of, choices of foreign policy strategy.

This debate often is conveyed through the metaphor of a game of billiards. The essence of billiards is the predictability of how a ball will move once it has been struck; hit the cue ball at a certain angle from a certain distance with a certain force, and you can predict exactly where on the table the target ball will go, regardless of whether it is solid or striped. In international systems theory the "hitting" is done by external threats and the "angles set" by the state's position in the structure of the international system, and the "path" the state's foreign policy takes is predictable regardless of the "stripes or solids" of its foreign policy priorities, domestic politics, or other characteristics. In reality, states are not like "crazy balls," bouncing wherever their domestic whims might take them, although they are not strictly reactive, either. Their foreign policy choices are constrained by the structure of the international system but are not determined by it. Domestic politics and institutions matter a great deal, as we discuss in Chapter 2.

The National Interest: The 4 Ps Framework

The national interest: all of us have heard it preached. Many of us may have done some of the preaching ourselves—that U.S. foreign policy must be made in the name of the national interest. No one would argue with the proposition that following the national interest is the essence of the choices to be made in a nation's foreign policy. But defining what the national interest is and then developing policies for achieving it have rarely been as easy or self-evident as such invocations would imply. Political scientists Alexander George and Robert Keohane capture this dilemma in a jointly authored article. They note the

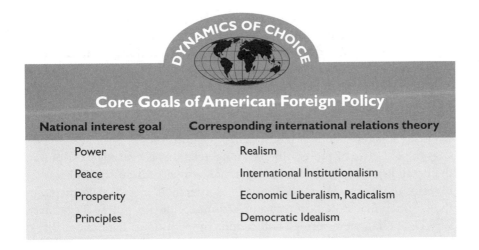

DYNAMICS OF CHOICE

Core Goals of American Foreign Policy

National interest goal	Corresponding international relations theory
Power	Realism
Peace	International Institutionalism
Prosperity	Economic Liberalism, Radicalism
Principles	Democratic Idealism

problems that have been encountered because the concept of the national interest has "become so elastic and ambiguous . . . that its role as a guide to foreign policy is problematical and controversial." Yet they also stress the importance that the national interest can have, and needs to have, to help "improve judgments regarding the proper ends and goals of foreign policy."[4]

Our approach in this book is to establish in general analytic terms the four core goals that go into defining the U.S. national interest: power, peace, prosperity, and principles. Dynamics of Choice above, depicts the "four Ps" framework and indicates the major "school" of international relations theory to which each is most closely linked. These distinctions are not strict categories in which this policy goes in one box and that one in another. Reality is never that neat. The national interest almost always combines one or more of the 4Ps. Indeed, although sometimes all four core goals are complementary and can be satisfied through the same policy, more often they pose trade-offs and tensions, and sometimes fundamental contradictions. The 4 Ps framework helps us see this complexity and especially to analyze how priorities get set and to locate the corresponding debates over what American foreign policy *is* and what it *should be*—what we earlier called "the essence of choice" in foreign policy strategy.

Power

Power is the key requirement for the most basic goal of foreign policy, self-defense and the preservation of national independence and territory. It is also essential for deterring aggression and influencing other states on a range of issues. "Power enables an actor to shape his environment so as to reflect his interests," Professor Samuel Huntington states. "In particular it enables a state to protect its security and prevent, deflect or defeat threats to that security."[5] To the extent that a state is interested in asserting itself, advancing its own interests and itself being aggressive, it needs power. "The strong do what they have the power to do," the ancient Greek historian Thucydides wrote, "and the weak accept what they have to accept."[6]

Realism is the school of international relations theory that most emphasizes the objective of power. "International relations is a struggle for power," the noted Realist scholar Hans Morgenthau wrote; "statesmen think and act in terms of interest defined as power."[7] Morgenthau and other Realists view the international system in terms of a competition for power. They take a very Hobbesian view, seeing conflict and competition as the basic reality of international politics. The "grim picture" is painted by University of Chicago professor John Mearsheimer: "International relations is not a constant state of war, but it is a state of relentless security competition, with the possibility of war always in the background. . . . Cooperation among states has its limits, mainly because it is constrained by the dominating logic of security competition, which no amount of cooperation can eliminate. Genuine peace, or a world where states do not compete for power, is not likely."[8] States thus ultimately can rely only on themselves for security. It is a "self-help" system—and power is critical to the self-help states need to be secure.

For Realists, consequently, four points are central. First, states pursue interests, not peace per se. If their interests are better served by war, aggression, and other such coercive means, appeals to peace as an objective won't work very well. Peace is best served by using power to affect the calculations states make. Second, political and military power remain the major currencies of power. They are crucial to a strong national defense, to credible deterrence, and to other effective means of statecraft. The requirements of each of these strategies have changed with the change in the nature of threats, but the need for the basic strategies remains. Third, economic power and other aspects of prosperity are valued by Realists less as their own international currency than as the "bullion" on which military power ultimately rests. The American economy has to be kept strong and competitive primarily so that the advanced technologies needed for next-generation weapons can be provided, and so that the political support for a large defense budget and other global commitments can be maintained. Fourth, although principles such as democracy and human rights are important, they rarely should be given priority over considerations of power.

---

*Icons in the margin indicate that a related reading is available (readings are located at the ends of Part I and II.

The principal foreign policy strategies that follow from this line of reasoning are largely *coercive* ones. "Covenants without the sword," to go back to Hobbes, "are but words, and of no strength to secure a man at all. The bonds of words are too weak to bridle men's ambitions, avarice, anger and other passions, without the fear of some coercive power."[9] The ultimate coercive strategy of course, is *war*—"the continuation of policy by other means," in the words of the great nineteenth-century Prussian strategist Karl von Clausewitz, "an act of violence intended to compel our opponent to fulfill our will." Starting with its own Revolutionary War and then through the nineteenth century (e.g., the War of 1812, the Mexican-American War, the Civil War, the Spanish-American War) and the twentieth century (e.g., World Wars I and II, the Korean War, the Vietnam War, the Persian Gulf War) and into the twenty-first century with the war on terrorism, the wars fought by the United States have had varying success in achieving the Clausewitzian objective of "compel[ling one's] opponent to fulfill [one's] will." *Military interventions* are the "small wars," the uses of military force in a more limited fashion, as in the overthrow of governments considered hostile to U.S. interests and the protection or bringing to power of pro-U.S. leaders, of which there also are numerous historical as well as contemporary examples.

Power is also key to maintaining a strong *defense* and credible *deterrence*. The particular requirements to provide the United States with defense and deterrence have varied dramatically over time with changes in the identity of the potential aggressor—Great Britain in early U.S. history, Germany in the two world wars, the Soviet Union during the Cold War, terrorism today—and the nature of weaponry—from muskets and a few warships to nuclear weapons, submarines, and supersonic bombers to suicide bombers and anthrax letter "bombs." But the basic strategy always has been essentially the same: to deter aggression and, if deterrence fails, to ensure the defense of the nation.

Alliances against a mutual enemy are a key component of both defense and deterrence strategies. For most of American history, alliances were formed principally in wartime: for example, with France in 1778 when twelve thousand French troops came over to help the Americans fight for independence against the shared enemy, Britain; with Britain and France in World War I; with Britain and the Soviet Union in World War II; with twenty-six other nations in the 1990–91 Persian Gulf War; with an even wider coalition in the 2001 Afghanistan war; but with a less broadly based coalition in the 2003 Iraq war. During the Cold War (officially, peacetime), the United States set up a global network of alliances, including multilateral ones like the North Atlantic Treaty Organization (NATO), the Southeast

Asia Treaty Organization (SEATO), and the Rio Treaty (with Latin American countries), as well as bilateral agreements with Japan, South Korea, Taiwan, Israel, Iran, and others. A related strategy is the provision of *military assistance,* such as weapons, advisers, financing, and other forms of aid, to a pro-American government or rebel group.

Power can be exerted through more than just military force. Diplomacy also can be used coercively. *Coercive statecraft* takes a number of forms, from such low-level actions as the filing of an official protest or issuing a public condemnation, to withdrawing an ambassador and suspending diplomatic relations, to imposing *economic sanctions* and other, tougher measures. Then there is *covert action,* the secret operations of intelligence agencies conducted, as former secretary of state Henry Kissinger put it, to "defend the American national interest in the gray areas where military operations are not suitable and diplomacy cannot operate."[10] Although they have been especially associated with the Cold War and now with the war on terrorism, covert actions go back to early U.S. history, as when Benjamin Franklin secretly bought arms from France during the Revolutionary War, or when President Thomas Jefferson secretly arranged the overthrow of the Pasha of Tripoli (in today's Libya).

Peace

In a certain sense, all four of the national interest objectives ultimately are about *peace*—for that is what power is supposed to safeguard, what prosperity is supposed to contribute to, what principles are supposed to undergird. But in this particular analytic category, we specifically have in mind theories of *International Institutionalism* and two types of foreign policy strategy.

International Institutionalism views world politics as "a cultivable 'garden,'" in contrast to the Realist view of a global "'jungle.'"[11] Although they stop well short of world government, these theories emphasize both the possibility and the value of reducing the chances of war and of achieving common interests sufficiently for the international system to be one of *world order.* International Institutionalists recognize that tensions and conflicts among nations do exist, but they see cooperation among nations as more possible and more beneficial than Realists do. Pursuing cooperation thus is neither naïve nor dangerous, but rather a rational way to reduce risks and make gains that even the most powerful state could not achieve solely on its own. To be sure, as Professor Inis Claude acknowledges, "the problem of power is here to stay; it is, realistically, not a problem to be eliminated, but"—the key point for International Institutionalists—"a problem to be managed."[12] International

Institutionalists have their own conception of power, which in contrast to that of Realists stresses diplomatic over military and other coercive means. To the extent that treaties and international institutions constrain potential aggressors, they contribute to "the general capacity of a state to control the behavior of others," which is how one international relations textbook defines power. When peace brokering is effective, it adds to the ability of the United States' "to overcome obstacles and prevail in conflicts," which is another text's definition of power.[13]

Consistent with this sense that peace is achievable but not automatic, theorists such as Keohane stress the importance of creating international institutions as the basis for "sustained cooperation." Anarchy cannot be eliminated totally, but it can be tempered or partially regulated. Indeed, it is precisely because the power and interests that Realists stress do generate conflicts that "international institutions . . . will be components of any lasting peace."[14] This also is true with regard to relations among allies. States may have friendly relations and share common interests but still have problems of collective action or even just coordination. International institutions provide the structure and the commitments to facilitate, and in some instances require, the fulfillment of commitments to collective action and coordination. "Institutions can provide information, reduce transaction costs, make commitments more credible, establish focal points for coordination and, in general, facilitate the operation of reciprocity."[15] In so doing international institutions help states overcome the difficulties of collective action, which can persist even when states have common interests. This is a very rational argument, much more pragmatically grounded than classical Wilsonian idealism. The world envisioned is not one strictly free of tensions and conflicts. But it is one in which the prospects for achieving cooperation are greater than Realism and other power-based theories foresee. International Institutionalists also see the constraints on a state's own freedom of action that come with multilateralism as less than the capacity gained to achieve shared objectives and serve national interests in ways that would be less possible unilaterally.

International institutions may be formal bodies like the United Nations, but they also can be more informal, in what are often called "international regimes." Keohane defines international institutions both functionally and structurally, as "the rules that govern elements of world politics and the organizations that help implement those rules."[16] This definition encompasses norms and rules of behavior, procedures for managing and resolving conflicts, and the organizational bases for at least some degree of global governance, albeit well short of full global government.

We can identify five principal types of international institutions: (a) *global*, such as the League of Nations (an unsuccessful example) and the United Nations (a more successful one); (b) *regional*, such as the Cold War–era Conference on Security and Cooperation in Europe (CSCE), or the Pan American Conference of the late nineteenth century; (c) *international legal*, such as the long-standing World Court and the newly created International Criminal Court; (d) *arms control and nonproliferation*, such as the International Atomic Energy Agency and the Organization for the Prohibition of Chemical Weapons; and (e) *economic*, particularly global ones such as the International Monetary Fund, the World Bank, and the World Trade Organization, and also regional ones such as the Asia-Pacific Economic Cooperation forum and the newly proposed Free Trade Area of the Americas. In none of these cases has the United States been the only state involved in establishing the institutions and organizations. But in most, if not all, the United States has played a key role.

The other type of foreign policy strategy that fits here is the *"peace broker"* role the United States has played in wars and conflicts to which it has not been a direct party. Familiar contemporary examples include the 1973–75 "shuttle diplomacy" in the Middle East by Henry Kissinger, the 1978 Camp David accord between Egypt and Israel brokered by President Jimmy Carter, and the Clinton administration's role in the 1995 Dayton accord ending the war in Bosnia. But this role, too, traces back historically, as with the peace treaty brokered by President Theodore Roosevelt ending the Russo-Japanese War, for which "TR" was awarded the 1906 Nobel peace prize.

Prosperity

Foreign policies motivated by the pursuit of *prosperity* are those which place the economic national interest above other concerns. They seek gains for the American economy from policies that help provide reliable and low-cost imports, growing markets for American exports, profitable foreign investments, and other international economic opportunities. Some of these involve policies that are specifically *foreign economic* ones, such as trade policy. Others involve general relations with countries whose significance to U.S. foreign policy is largely economic, as with an oil-rich country like Saudi Arabia. Most generally they involve efforts to strengthen global capitalism as the structure of the international economy.

Among those theories that stress the economic factor in American foreign policy, there are two principal schools of thought. These schools share the emphasis on economics but differ on whether the prime motivator of policy is to serve the general public interest or the more particular interests of the economic elite. The first school of thought, often referred to as *Economic Liberalism*, emphasizes the pursuit through foreign policy of general economic benefits to the nation: a favorable balance of trade, strong economic growth, a healthy macroeconomy.[17] The ultimate goal is collective prosperity, in which the interests served are those of the American people in general. This was said to have been a major part of U.S. foreign policy in the nineteenth century, when about 70 percent of the treaties and other international agreements the United States signed were on matters related to trade and international commerce.[18] It was the basis for the creation after World War II of the General Agreement on Tariffs and Trade (GATT), the International Monetary Fund (IMF), and the World Bank as the key international economic institutions of an open, market-based free trade system. It also has been evident in recent years, as in the 1995 statement by Secretary of State Warren Christopher that whereas other secretaries of state put their main emphasis on arms control, "I make no apologies for putting economics at the top of [the U.S.] foreign policy agenda."[19]

Radicalism includes a number of theories, most notably theories of imperialism and neocolonialism, that see such policies as dominated by and serving the interests of the capitalist class and other elites, such as multinational corporations and major banks.[20] The prosperity that is sought is more for the private benefit of special interests, and the ways in which it is sought are highly exploitative of other countries. The basics of this theory go back to the British economist John Hobson and his 1902 book *Imperialism*. Because the unequal distribution of wealth leaves the lower classes with limited purchasing power, capitalism creates for itself the twin problems of underconsumption and overproduction. It thus needs to find new markets for its products if it is to avoid recession and depression. Although Hobson's own Britain and its colonialism were his primary focus, his arguments also were applicable to the United States and its more indirect "neocolonialism" in Latin America and parts of Asia (see Chapter 3).

Vladimir Ilyich Lenin, while still in exile in Switzerland in 1916, the year before he would return to Russia to lead the communist revolution, wrote his most famous book, *Imperialism: The Highest Stage of Capitalism*. Lenin's version of imperialist theory differed from Hobson's in rejecting the possibility that capitalism could reform itself.* One reason was that, in addition to the

---

*Hobson believed that liberal domestic reforms were possible and would help capitalism break out of the underconsumption and overproduction cycle. Such reforms would create a more equitable distribution of wealth, bringing an increase in consumption, in the process both making the home society more equitable and alleviating the need for colonies, thus making foreign policy less imperialistic.

underconsumption/overproduction problem, Lenin emphasized the pursuit of inexpensive and abundant supplies of raw materials as another key motive for capitalist expansionism. Giving the working class more purchasing power would not do anything about the lust for the iron ore, foodstuffs, and later, oil that were so much more plentiful and so much cheaper in the colonial world (later called the Third World). Moreover, the essence of Lenin's theory was the belief that the capitalist class so dominated the political process and defined the limits of democracy that it never would allow the kinds of re-forms Hobson advocated. Lenin's theories and their spin-offs became the basis for many highly critical views of U.S. foreign policy during the Cold War, particularly in the Third World.

In sum, their differences notwithstanding, Economic Liberalism and Radicalism share an emphasis on economic goals as driving forces behind U.S. foreign policy. They differ over whose prosperity is being served, but they agree on the centrality of prosperity among the 4 Ps.

Principles

The fourth core goal, principles, involves the values, ideals, and beliefs that the United States has claimed to stand for in the world. As a more general theory, this emphasis on principles is rooted in *Democratic Idealism*.

Democratic Idealists hold to two central tenets about foreign policy. One is that when trade-offs have to be made, "right" is to be chosen over "might." This is said to be particularly true for the United States because of the ostensibly special role bestowed on it—to stand up for the principles on which it was founded and not be just another player in global power politics. We find assertions of this notion of "American exceptionalism" throughout U.S. history. Thomas Jefferson, the country's first secretary of state and its third president, characterized the new United States of America as such: "the solitary republic of the world, the only monument of human rights . . . the sole depository of the sacred fire of freedom and self-government, from hence it is to be lighted up in other regions of the earth, if other regions shall ever become susceptible to its benign influence."[21] And then there was President Woodrow Wilson's famous declaration that U.S. entry into World War I was intended "to make the world safe for democracy": "We shall fight for the things which we have always carried nearest our hearts—for democracy, for the right of those who submit to authority to have a voice in their own government, for the rights and liberties of small nations, for a universal dominion of right by such a concert of free peoples as shall bring peace and

safety to all nations and make the world in itself at last free." Idealism was
also claimed by many a Cold War president, from Democrats such as John
Kennedy with his call in his inaugural address to "bear any burden, pay any
price" to defend democracy and fight communism, to Republicans such as
Ronald Reagan and his crusade against "the evil empire." It also was part of
President George W. Bush's launching of the war on terrorism as not only a
matter of security but also a war against "evil . . . the fight of all who believe
in progress and pluralism, tolerance and freedom."

The other key tenet of Democratic Idealism is that in the long run
"right" makes for "might," that in the end interests like peace and power are
well served by principles. One of the strongest statements of this view is the
democratic peace theory, which asserts that by promoting democracy we
promote peace because democracies do not go to war against each other. To
put it another way, the world could be made safe *by* democracy. For all the
attention the democratic peace theory has gotten in the post–Cold War era,
its central argument and philosophical basis trace back to the eighteenth-
century political philosopher Immanuel Kant and his book *Perpetual Peace*.
"If . . . the consent of the citizenry is required in order to decide that war
should be declared," Kant wrote, "nothing is more natural than that they
would be very cautious in commencing such a poor game. . . . But, on the
other hand, in a constitution which is not republican, and under which the
subjects are not citizens, a declaration of war is the easiest thing to decide
upon, because war does not require of the ruler . . . the least sacrifice of the
pleasure of his table, the chase, his country houses, his court functions and
the like."[22]

As to serving the goal of power, Professor Joseph Nye of Harvard University coined the term "soft power" to refer to the ways in which the values for
which a nation stands, its cultural attractiveness, and other aspects of its reputation can have quite practical value as sources of influence.[23] This is not just
a matter of what American leaders claim in their rhetoric, but of whether
other governments and peoples perceive for themselves a consistency between
the principles espoused and the actual policies pursued by the United States. It
also depends on how well America is deemed to be living up to its ideals
within its own society on issues such as race relations, protection of the environment, and crime and violence.

Given its strong and exceptionalist claims to principles, American foreign policy often has been criticized at home and abroad for not living up to
these values. We are seeing this in the post–September 11 "why do they hate
us?" debates over America's image in the Muslim world. Such contentions

also arose during the Cold War especially in the Third World (see Chapters 4 and 5), and indeed at various times throughout American history (see Chapter 3). Precisely because of the arguments that right should be chosen over might and that in the long run right makes for might, debates over how true American foreign policy is to its principles matter as more than just idealistic questions.

Dynamics of Choice, below, summarizes the 4 Ps of foreign policy strategy, highlighting differences among core national-interest goals, schools of international relations theory, principal conceptions of the international system, and principal types of policies pursued. It is important to emphasize again that these are distinctions of degree and not inflexible one-or-the-other categorizations. They provide a framework for analyzing foreign policy strategy in ways that push deeper into general conceptions of the national interest and get at the "essence of choice" over what American foreign policy is and should be.

DYNAMICS OF CHOICE

A Foreign Policy Strategy Typology

Core national interest goals	International relations theory	Conception of the international system	Main types of policies
Power	Realism	Competition for power	Coercive
Peace	International Institutionalism	World order	Diplomatic
Prosperity	Economic Liberalism, Radicalism	Global capitalism	Economic
Principles	Democratic Idealism	Global democracy	Political

Dilemmas of Foreign Policy Choice: 4 Ps Complementarity and Trade-offs

4 Ps Complementarity: Optimal, but Infrequent

To the extent that all 4 Ps can be satisfied through the same strategy—i.e., they are complementary—the dilemmas of foreign policy choice are relatively easy. No major trade-offs have to be made, no strict priorities set. This does happen sometimes, as the following two cases illustrate.

THE 1990–91 PERSIAN GULF WAR   The Persian Gulf War was a great victory for American foreign policy in many respects. The invasion of Kuwait by Iraq, led by Saddam Hussein, was a blatant act of aggression—one of the most naked acts of aggression since World War II. Furthermore, the Iraqis were poised to keep going, straight into Saudi Arabia, an even more strategic country and a close U.S. ally.

But through U.S. leadership, the *peace* was restored. "This will not stand," President George H.W. Bush declared. Resolutions were sponsored in the United Nations (UN) Security Council, demanding an Iraqi withdrawal and then authorizing the use of military force to liberate Kuwait. A twenty-seven-nation diplomatic coalition was built, including most of western Europe, Japan, and much of the Arab world. A multinational military force went to war under the command of General Norman Schwarzkopf of the U.S. Army.

Operation Desert Storm, as it was named, was also a formidable demonstration of American *power*. It is important to recall how worried many military analysts were at the outset of Desert Storm about incurring high casualties, and even about the possibility that Saddam would resort to chemical or biological weapons. That the military victory came so quickly and with so few U.S. and allied casualties was testimony to the military superiority the United States had achieved. Striding tall from its Gulf War victory, American power was shown to be second to none.

Of course, this was not just about helping Kuwait. *Prosperity* also was at risk, in the form of oil. Twice before in recent decades war and instability in the Middle East had disrupted oil supplies and sent oil prices skyrocketing. The parents of today's college students still have memories of waiting in gasoline lines and watching prices escalate on a daily basis during the 1973 Arab-Israeli War and the 1979 Iranian Revolution. This time, though, because the

Gulf War victory came so swiftly, disruptions to the American and global economies were minimized.

Although Kuwait couldn't claim to be a democracy, other important *principles* were at issue. One was the right of all states to be free from aggression. Another was the moral imperative of standing up to a dictator as brutal as Saddam Hussein. Comparisons to Adolf Hitler went too far, but Saddam was a leader who left a trail of torture, repression, and mass killings.

THE MARSHALL PLAN, 1947   The Marshall Plan was the first major U.S. foreign aid program; it provided about $17 billion to Western Europe for economic reconstruction following World War II.* This was an enormous amount of money, equivalent to $60 billion today. Yet the Marshall Plan passed Congress by overwhelming majorities, 69 to 17 in the Senate and 329 to 74 in the House. Compare these figures to total U.S. foreign economic aid today, which is less than one-quarter as much and barely gets a congressional majority.

The key reason for such strong support was that the Marshall Plan was seen as serving the full range of U.S. foreign policy goals. The communist parties in France, Italy, and elsewhere in Western Europe were feeding off the continuing economic suffering and dislocation, making worrisome political gains. The Marshall Plan thus was a component of the broader strategy of containment of communism to keep the *peace* in Western Europe. It also asserted American *power*, for with the foreign aid came certain conditions, some explicit and some implicit. And in a more general sense, the United States was establishing its global predominance and leadership. The glorious nations of the Old World were now dependent on the New World former colony.

American *prosperity* was also well served. The rebuilding of European markets generated demand for American exports and created opportunities for American investments. Thus, although its motives were not strict altruism, the Marshall Plan was quite consistent with American *principles:* the stability of fellow Western democracies was at stake.

In both of these cases, peace, power, prosperity, and principles fit together quite effectively. But while optimal, such complementarity of core goals is infrequent. Much more common are cases in which one or more of the 4 Ps pull in competing directions, and choices have to be made among core national interest goals.

---

*The Marshall Plan is named for Secretary of State George Marshall, who made the initial public proposal in a commencement speech at Harvard University.

4 Ps Trade-offs: More Frequent, More Problematic

Not only are cases with competing tensions more common, they require much tougher choices. Trade-offs have to be made; priorities have to be set. The following two examples illustrate such choices.

CHINA, 1989: POWER AND PROSPERITY VS. PRINCIPLES   In 1989, hundreds of Chinese students staged a massive pro-democracy sit-in in Tiananmen Square in Beijing, China's capital city. As one expression of their protest, they constructed a plaster replica of the American Statue of Liberty. The Communist government ordered the students to leave. They refused. The Chinese army then moved in with tanks and troops. An estimated 1,000 students were killed, and tens of thousands of students and other dissidents were arrested that night and in the ensuing months.

In reaction to the Chinese crackdown, many in the United States called for the imposition of economic sanctions. The focus of these efforts was on revoking China's most-favored-nation (MFN) status. Essentially MFN status limits tariffs on a country's exports to the United States to a standard, low level; without MFN status, a country's exports to the United States are much less competitive, and that country's international trade will be adversely affected.* The pro-sanctions argument, which came from a bipartisan coalition in Congress and from human-rights groups, was based on *principles:* How could the United States conduct business as usual with a government that massacred its own people? These pro-democracy Chinese protesters had turned to America for inspiration. How could the United States not now stand up for what it says are values and beliefs it holds dear?

The George H.W. Bush administration, which was in office at the time, was willing to impose only limited economic sanctions; it would not revoke China's MFN status. Its main argument was based on *power*. The administration still considered the U.S.-Soviet rivalry to be the central issue in its foreign relations and thus gave priority to its geopolitical interests—namely, continued good relations with China. Among President Bush's critics was Democratic presidential candidate Bill Clinton, who castigated his opponent for coddling "the butchers of Beijing." Yet as president, Clinton also refused to revoke China's MFN status. His reasons, however, were based more on

---

*It is not that the country receiving MFN is favored over others, but rather that all countries receiving MFN get the same "most favored" tariff treatment. In 2000 this terminology was changed from MFN to PNTR, or permanent normal trade relations.

economic considerations—*prosperity*—and the calculation of billions of dollars in potential trade and investment losses for the American economy.

Both Bush and Clinton claimed that they were not abandoning principles, that other steps were being taken to try to protect human rights and promote democracy in China. But although this justification was partly true, debate still raged over fundamentally competing definitions of the national interest. The requisites of power and prosperity pointed to one set of policies, principles to another. Trade-offs were inevitable; choices had to be made.

GUATEMALA, 1954: PROSPERITY AND POWER VS. PRINCIPLES In 1945, Guatemala, the Central American country just south of Mexico, had ended a long string of military dictatorships by holding free elections. A progressive new constitution was written, freedoms of the press and of speech were guaranteed, and workers and peasants were encouraged to organize. A number of military coups were attempted, but they were put down. In 1951, Colonel Jacobo Arbenz Guzman, a pro-reform military officer, was elected president.

One of Arbenz's highest priorities was land reform. Only 2 percent of the population owned 70 percent of the land in Guatemala. The largest of all landholders was the United Fruit Company (UFCO), a U.S.-owned banana exporter. In March 1953, Arbenz's government included about 230,000 acres of UFCO holdings in the land being expropriated for redistribution to the peasantry. Most of this land was uncultivated, but that didn't matter to the UFCO. The compensation offered to the company by the Guatemalan government was deemed inadequate, even though it was the same valuation rate (a low one) that the UFCO had been using to limit the taxes it had to pay.

This wasn't just a UFCO problem, its corporate president declared: "From here on out it's not a matter of the people of Guatemala against the United Fruit Company. The question is going to be communism against the right of property, the life and security of the Western Hemisphere."[24] It was true that Arbenz had members of the Guatemalan Communist Party in his government. He also was buying some weapons from Czechoslovakia, which was a Soviet satellite. Might this be the beginning of the feared Soviet "beachhead" in the Western Hemisphere?* In defending the anti-Arbenz coup d'état that it engineered in 1954 through covert CIA action, the Eisenhower administration

---

*Fidel Castro had not yet come to power in Cuba. That would happen in 1959.

stressed the *power* concerns raised by this perceived threat to containment. The evidence of links to Soviet communism was not that strong, but the standard that needed to be met was only what an earlier U.S. ambassador to Guatemala had called the "duck test": "Many times it is impossible to prove legally that a certain individual is a communist; but for cases of this sort I recommend a practical method of detection—the 'duck test.' The duck test works this way: suppose you see a bird walking around in a farmyard. The bird wears no label that says 'duck.' But the bird certainly looks like a duck. Also, he goes to the pond and you notice that he swims like a duck. Well, by this time you have probably reached the conclusion that the bird is a duck, whether he's wearing a label or not."[25]

An argument can be made that, given the Cold War, the duck test was sufficient from a power perspective. Even so, the anti-Arbenz coup was something of a "joint venture" strikingly consistent with Imperialist critiques of U.S. foreign policy (*prosperity*). The UFCO had close ties to the Eisenhower administration; the historical record shows evidence of collaboration between the company and the government; and one of the first acts of the new regime of General Carlos Castillo Armas, who was a graduate of the military-intelligence training school at Fort Leavenworth, Kansas, and whom the CIA installed in power after the coup, was to give land back to the UFCO.

The critical tension here was with *principles*. The Arbenz government had come to power through elections that, while not perfectly free and fair, were much more fair than those in most of Latin America. And the military governments that ruled Guatemala for the thirty-five years following the U.S.-engineered coup showed extreme brutality and wanton disregard for human rights, killing and persecuting tens of thousands of their own people. The U.S. role was hidden for decades but was pointedly revealed in 1999 in a shocking report by a Guatemalan historical commission, which estimated that two hundred thousand people had been killed by the U.S.-supported military regimes and provided strong evidence of U.S. complicity.[26]

These examples show the difficulties that ensue when choices need to be made among different core goals of the national interest. Other examples could be cited to show other lines of competing tensions; we will see many such situations in later chapters. And, as noted earlier, 4 Ps trade-offs are much more common in American foreign policy than 4 Ps complementarity.

Summary

Whatever the issue at hand, and whether past, present, or future, American foreign policy has been, is, and will continue to be about the *dynamics of choice*.

One set of these choices is about *foreign policy strategy*. It is easy to preach about the national interest, but much harder to assess what that interest is in a particular situation. One or more of the four core goals—*power, peace, prosperity, and principles*—may be involved. Not only may basic analyses differ, but more often than not trade-offs have to be made and priorities set among these four Ps. Views on this reflect different schools of international relations theory, carry with them alternative policy approaches, and can result in fundamentally different foreign policy strategies. This is the *essence of choice* that is inherent to every major foreign policy issue.

We will use this framework for analyzing U.S. foreign policy strategy historically (Chapter 3), during the Cold War (Chapters 4 and 5), and most especially in our current post–Cold War era (Part II, Chapters 6–10). First, though, we turn in Chapter 2 to foreign policy politics and lay out an analytic framework for this other key dimension of American foreign policy, the *process of choice*.

Notes

[1]Serge Schmemann, "U.S. Attacked: President Vows to Exact Punishment for 'Evil,'" *New York Times,* September 12, 2001, A1.

[2]Robert J. Lieber, *No Common Power: Understanding International Relations* (Boston: Scott, Foresman, 1988), 5.

[3]Kenneth N. Waltz, *Theory of International Politics* (Reading, Mass.: Addison-Wesley, 1979), 72.

[4]Alexander L. George and Robert O. Keohane, "The Concepts of National Interests: Uses and Limitations," in Alexander L. George, ed., *Presidential Decisionmaking in Foreign Policy: The Effective Use of Information and Advice* (Boulder, Colo.: Westview, 1980), 217–18.

[5]Samuel Huntington, "Why International Primacy Matters," *International Security* 17:4 (Spring 1993), 69–70.

[6]Thucydides, *History of the Peloponnesian War,* trans. R. Warner (New York: Penguin, 1972), 402.

[7]Hans J. Morgenthau, *Politics among Nations: The Struggle for Power and Peace* (New York: Knopf, 1948), 5.

[8]John J. Mearsheimer, "The False Promise of International Institutions," *International Security* 19:3 (Winter 1994/95), 9.

[9]Caleb Carr, *The Lessons of Terror* (New York: Random House, 2002), 81.

[10]Cited in Loch K. Johnson, *America as a World Power: Foreign Policy in a Constitutional Framework* (New York: McGraw-Hill, 1991), 239.

[11]Michael W. Doyle, *Ways of War and Peace* (New York: Norton, 1997), 19.

[12]Claude, cited in Mearsheimer, "False Promise of International Institutions," 26–27.

[13]Bruce Russett and Harvey Starr, *World Politics: The Menu for Choice* (New York: Freeman, 1996), 117; K. J. Holsti, *International Politics: A Framework for Analysis* (Englewood Cliffs, N.J.: Prentice-Hall, 1988), 141.

[14]Robert O. Keohane and Lisa L. Martin, "The Promise of Institutionalist Theory," *International Security* 20:1 (Summer 1995), 50.

[15]Keohane and Martin, "The Promise of Institutionalist Theory," 42.

[16]Robert O. Keohane, "International Institutions: Can Interdependence Work?" *Foreign Policy* 110 (Spring 1998), 82.

[17]See, for example, Joan E. Spero and Jeffrey A. Hart, *The Politics of International Economic Relations* (New York: St. Martin's, 1997); and Richard N. Gardner, *Sterling-Dollar Diplomacy: The Origins and Prospects of Our International Economic Order* (New York: Columbia University Press, 1980)

[18]James M. McCormick, *American Foreign Policy and Process* (Itasca, Ill.: F. E. Peacock, 1992), 15–16.

[19]Michael Hirsh and Karen Breslau, "Closing the Deal Diplomacy: In Clinton's Foreign Policy, the Business of America Is Business," *Newsweek,* March 6, 1995, 34.

[20]See, for example, V. I. Lenin, *Imperialism: The Highest Form of Capitalism* (New York: International Publishers, 1939); John A. Hobson, *Imperialism* (London: George Allen and Unwin, 1954); and Richard J. Barnet and Ronald E. Muller, *Global Reach: The Power of the Multinational Corporations* (New York: Simon and Schuster, 1974).

[21]Cited in Robert W. Tucker and David C. Hendrickson, "Thomas Jefferson and Foreign Policy," *Foreign Affairs* 69:2 (Spring 1990), 136.

[22]Immanuel Kant, "Perpetual Peace," cited in Michael W. Doyle, "Kant, Liberal Legacies and Foreign Affairs," in Michael E. Brown et al., eds., *Debating the Democratic Peace* (Cambridge, Mass.: MIT Press, 1997), 24–25.

[23]Joseph S. Nye, Jr., *Bound to Lead: The Changing Nature of American Power* (New York: Basic Books, 1990).

[24]Cited in James A. Nathan and James K. Oliver, *United States Foreign Policy and World Order* (Boston: Little, Brown, 1985), 176. See also Stephen Schlesinger and Stephen Kinzer, *Bitter Fruit: The Untold Story of the American Coup in Guatemala* (Garden City, N.Y.: Doubleday, 1982).

[25]Cited in Walter LaFeber, *Inevitable Revolutions: The United States in Central America,* 2d ed. (New York: Norton, 1993), 115–16.

[26]Mireya Navarro, "Guatemalan Army Waged 'Genocide', New Report Finds," *New York Times,* February 26, 1999, A1, A8. See also "Documents on U.S. Policy in Guatemala," at the Web site of the National Security Archive, http://www.seas.gwu.edu/nsarchive.

CHAPTER 2

The Domestic Context: Foreign Policy Politics and the Process of Choice

Introduction: Dispelling the "Water's Edge" Myth

When it comes to foreign policy, according to an old saying, "politics stops at the water's edge." In other words, partisan and other political differences that characterize domestic policy are to be left behind—"at the water's edge"— when entering the realm of foreign policy, so that the country can be united in confronting foreign threats.

The example most often cited by proponents of this ideal is the consensus of the early Cold War era, that "golden age of bipartisanship." Here is "a story of democracy at its finest," as one famous book portrayed it, "with the executive branch of the government operating far beyond the normal boundaries of timidity and politics, the Congress beyond usual partisanship, and the American people as a whole beyond selfishness and complacency. All three . . . worked together to accomplish a national acceptance of world responsibility."[1] That's how foreign policy politics is supposed to be, the "water's edge" thinking goes.

In three key respects, though, this notion of politics' stopping at the water's edge is a myth that needs to be dispelled. First, *historically, the domestic consensus that characterized the Cold War era was more the exception than the rule.* The common view is that divisive foreign policy politics started with the Vietnam War. But although Vietnam did shatter the Cold War consensus, it was hardly the first time that foreign policy politics hadn't stopped at the water's edge. In the years leading up to World War II, President Franklin

Roosevelt had his own intense political battles with an isolationist Congress. In the years following World War I, President Woodrow Wilson suffered one of the worst foreign policy politics defeats ever when the Senate refused to ratify the Treaty of Versailles. We can even go back to 1794 and President George Washington, the revered "father" of the country, and his battles with Congress over a treaty with Great Britain called the Jay Treaty. The bitter and vociferous attacks on the Jay Treaty for "tilting" toward Britain in its war with France were a rhetorical match for any of today's political battles. "Ruinous . . . detestable . . . contemptible," editorialized one major newspaper of the day, excoriating a treaty "signed with our inveterate enemy and the foe of human happiness." The Senate did ratify the treaty, but by a margin of only one vote. Indeed the whole Jay Treaty controversy was a key factor in President Washington's decision to retire to Mount Vernon instead of seeking a third term as president.

Second, *consensus has not always been a good thing.* It surely can be, in manifesting national solidarity behind the nation's foreign policy. But national solidarity is one thing, the delegitimization of dissent quite another. The most virulent example was the anticommunist witch-hunt spurred by the McCarthyism of the 1950s, during which accusations of disloyalty were hurled at government officials, playwrights, professors, scientists, and average citizens, often on the flimsiest of evidence. Dissent was also criminalized during both world wars, when domestic consensus was often crucial to meeting the wartime challenges; nevertheless, many Americans paid a severe price in civil liberties and individual rights during the wars. The Espionage and Sedition Acts passed during World War I permitted such repressive measures as banning postal delivery of any magazine that included views critical of the war effort—restrictions "as extreme as any legislation of the kind anywhere in the world."[2] During World War II the national security rationale was invoked to uproot 120,000 Japanese Americans and put them in internment camps, on the basis only of their ethnicity. During Vietnam, shouts of "America, love it or leave it" were aimed at antiwar critics and protesters. Consensus is not a particularly good thing when it equates dissent with disloyalty. These issues have arisen again in the context of the war on terrorism.

Third, *domestic political conflict is not necessarily always bad for foreign policy.* Debate and disagreement can facilitate a more thorough consideration of the issues. They can subject questionable assumptions to serious scrutiny. They can bring about constructive compromises around a policy that serves the national interest better than anything either side originally proposed. As former House Foreign Affairs Committee chair Lee Hamilton wrote, "debate, creative tension and review of policy can bring about decisions and actions that stand a better chance of serving the interests and values of the American people."[3] A good example of this was the outcome of the debate about the U.S. role in helping restore democracy in the Philippines in the mid-1980s. The policy preferred by President Ronald Reagan was to continue supporting the dictator Ferdinand Marcos, even after his forces had assassinated the democratic opposition leader, Benigno Aquino, and even amid mounting evidence of rampant corruption in the Marcos regime. But the U.S. Congress, led by a bipartisan coalition of Democrats and Republicans, refused to go along with a continued unconditional embrace of Marcos. It pushed for support for the pro-democracy forces led by Corazon Aquino, widow of the slain opposition leader. Democracy was restored, and an important U.S. ally was made more stable. This might not have been achieved, however, had it not been for the good that can sometimes come out of conflictual foreign policy politics.

Thus the realities of *foreign policy politics,* the process by which foreign policy choices are made, are more complex than the conventional wisdom holds. Our purpose in this chapter is to provide a framework for understanding the dynamics of foreign policy politics. We do so by focusing on five sets of domestic actors: the president and Congress, and the "Pennsylvania Avenue diplomacy" that marks (and often mars) their interbranch relationship; the policy- and decision-making processes within the executive branch; the pressures brought to bear by major interest groups; the impact of the news media; and the nature and influence of public opinion. In the next three chapters, we will examine key historical cases of foreign policy politics.

The President, Congress, and "Pennsylvania Avenue Diplomacy"

They stare at each other down the length of Pennsylvania Avenue. The White House and the Capitol: connected by the avenue, but also divided by it. The avenue: a path for cooperation, but also a line of conflict. The president and Congress: a relationship very much in need of its own "diplomacy."

Historically, and across various issue areas, presidential-congressional relations in the making of foreign policy have been characterized by four patterns: *cooperation,* when Congress has either concurred with or deferred to the president and a largely common, coordinated policy has been pursued;

constructive compromise, when the two branches have bridged conflicts and come to a policy that proved better than either's original position (as in the 1980s Philippines case cited above); *institutional competition,* in which the conflicts have been less over the substance of policy than over institutional prerogatives and the balance between the need for executive accountability and congressional oversight; and *confrontation,* in which the policy positions have been in substantial conflict and Pennsylvania Avenue diplomacy has shown its greatest tensions.

Which pattern prevails on what issues and, more broadly, during any particular presidential administration depends in part on politics, especially when there is "divided government," wherein one political party controls the White House and the other party holds the majority in one or both houses of Congress. Fundamentally, though, the dynamic is a structural one. Despite all the theories expounded, political positions taken, legal briefs filed, no one has come up with a definitive answer to the question of constitutional intent and design for presidential-congressional relations in the making of foreign policy. The Constitution left it, in one classic statement, as "an invitation to struggle for the privilege of directing American foreign policy."[4] Indeed, although we usually are taught to think of the relationship between the president and Congress as a "separation of powers," it really is much more "separate institutions sharing powers."[5] A separation of powers would mean that the president has power *a,* Congress power *b,* the president power *c,* Congress power *d,* and so on. But the actual relationship is more one in which both the president and Congress have a share of power *a,* a share of power *b,* a share of power *c,* and so on—that is, the separate institutions *share powers.* This basic structural relationship is evident in five key areas of foreign policy politics (see Dynamics of Choice, 34).

War Powers

No domain of foreign policy politics has been debated more hotly nor more recurringly than war powers. The Constitution designates the president as "commander in chief" but gives Congress the power to "declare war" and "provide for the common defense"—not separate powers, but each a share of the same power.

Both sides support their claims for the precedence of their share of the war power with citations from the country's founders. Presidentialists invoke the logic, developed by Alexander Hamilton in the Federalist Papers, that the need for an effective foreign policy was one of the main reasons the young

DYNAMICS OF CHOICE

Principal Foreign Policy Provisions of the Constitution

	Power granted to:	
	President	**Congress**
War power	Commander in chief of armed forces	Provide for the common defense; declare war
Treaties	Negotiate treaties	Ratification of treaties, by two-thirds majority (Senate)
Appointments	Nominate high-level government officials	Confirm president's appointments (Senate)
Foreign commerce	No explicit powers, but treaty negotiation and appointment powers pertain	Explicit power "to regulate foreign commerce"
General powers	Executive power; veto	Legislative power; power of the purse; oversight and investigation

nation needed an "energetic government" (Federalist no. 23); that "energy in the executive" was "a leading character in the definition of good government" (no. 70); and that "in the conduct of war . . . the energy of the executive is the bulwark of national security" (no. 75). Congressionalists, on the other hand, cite the proceedings of the Constitutional Convention. At James Madison's initiative, the original wording of the proposed constitution, which would have given Congress the power to "make war," was changed to "declare war." This is explained by congressionalists as intended to recognize that *how* to use military force ("make war") was appropriately a power for the commander in chief, whereas *whether* to use military force ("declare war") was for the Congress. Furthermore, as Madison stated in a letter to Thomas Jefferson, "the Constitution supposes what the history of all governments demonstrates, that the executive is the branch of power most interested in war, and most prone to it. It has accordingly with studied care vested the question of war in the legislature."[6]

Nor is the weight of historical precedent strictly on one side or the other. One of the favorite statistics of proponents of the presidency's war powers is that of the more than two hundred times that the United States has used military force, only five—the War of 1812, the Mexican War (1846–48), the Spanish-American War (1898), World War I (1917–19), and World War II (1941–45)—have been through congressional declarations of war. Perhaps another eighty-five or ninety (e.g., the 1991 Persian Gulf War, the 2001 Afghanistan war, and the 2003 Iraq war) have been through some other legislative authority. All the others have been by presidents acting on their own, which is taken as evidence of both the need for and the legitimacy of presidents' having such freedom of action.

This statistic, though, is somewhat deceptive. Many of the cases of presidents acting on their own involved minor military incidents generally regarded as the business of a commander in chief. Besides that, defenders of Congress's share of the war powers interpret this gross disproportion—many uses of military force yet few declarations of war—not as legitimizing the arrangement, but as emphasizing the problem. They put less emphasis on the overall numbers than on key cases like Vietnam, in which undeclared war had devastating consequences.

We will take war powers up again as a historical issue in Chapter 3, as an early Cold War–era issue in Chapter 4, as a Vietnam-era controversy over the 1973 War Powers Resolution in Chapter 5, and as a continuing debate in Chapters 7 and 8.

Treaties and Other International Commitments

The basic power-sharing arrangement for treaties vests negotiating power in the president but requires that treaties be ratified by a two-thirds majority of the Senate. On the surface this appears to have worked pretty well: of the more than 1,700 treaties signed by presidents in U.S. history, only about 20 have been voted down by the Senate. But here, too, simple statistics can be misleading.

One reason is that although it may not happen often, Senate defeat of a treaty can have a huge impact—as with the 1919–20 defeat of the Treaty of Versailles, on which the post–World War I peace was to be based, and the 1999 defeat of the Comprehensive Test Ban Treaty, which dealt with nuclear weapons. Another reason is that Congress has alternative ways to influence treaties other than by defeating them. For example, it can offer advice during negotiations through the official "observer groups" that often accompany State Department negotiators. It also can try to amend or attach a "reservation" to alter the terms of a treaty, an action that can be quite controversial, since it may require the reopening of negotiations with the other country or countries.

On the other hand, presidents also have an array of strategies at their disposal to circumvent Senate objections. In particular, they can resort to mechanisms other than treaties, such as *executive agreements,* for making international commitments. Executive agreements usually do not require congressional approval, let alone the two-thirds Senate majority that treaties do. Although in theory executive agreements are supposed to be used for minor government-to-government matters, leaving major aspects of relations to treaties, the line between the two has never been particularly clear. In addition, sometimes the most important foreign policy commitments do not come from treaties or executive agreements or any other written or legal form. Such *declaratory commitments* come from speeches and statements by presidents. This was the case, for example, with the Monroe Doctrine, which sprang from a speech by President James Monroe in 1823 to become the bedrock of U.S. foreign policy in the Western Hemisphere. So, too, with the Truman Doctrine (1947): its clarion call "to support free peoples who are resisting attempted subjugation by armed minorities or by outside pressures" became a basis for the containment strategy pursued in U.S. policy for the next 40–50 years.

Some presidents also have claimed authority to withdraw from existing treaties without going to the Senate for approval, as President George W. Bush did in 2001 in withdrawing from the 1972 Anti–Ballistic Missile (ABM) Treaty. His action was different from that of President John Adams, who in 1798 terminated treaties with France but did so through an act of Congress, or that of President James Polk, who in 1846 sought congressional approval for withdrawing from the Oregon Territory Treaty with Great Britain. At least a partial precedent came from President Jimmy Carter, who did not go to Congress for approval when in 1978 he ended the U.S. mutual defense treaty with Taiwan as part of the normalization of diplomatic relations with the People's Republic of China. All told, who has exactly what share of the shared powers in this area remains disputed.

Appointments of Foreign Policy Officials

The standard process as reflected in Dynamics of Choice on p. 34 is that the president nominates and the Senate confirms (by a simple majority) the appointments of Cabinet members, ambassadors, and other high-level foreign policy officials. In pure statistical terms the confirmation rate for presidential foreign policy nominees is higher than 90 percent. Yet here, too, we need to look past the numbers.

First of all, these numbers don't include nominations withdrawn before a formal Senate vote. When White House congressional-liaison aides come back from Capitol Hill reporting that "the vote count doesn't look good," a president often decides to avoid the embarrassment of a vote and instead withdraw the nomination. This happened to President Carter in 1977 when his original nominee as Central Intelligence Agency (CIA) director (Theodore Sorensen) was met with vocal opposition in Congress, and also to President Clinton in 1997 with his CIA director nominee (Anthony Lake). Second, precisely because it is often assumed that nominees will be confirmed, when they are not the political impact can be substantial. Thus, for example, in 1989 far less attention was given to all of the Bush administration's other foreign policy nominations combined than to the one case of former senator John Tower, Bush's nominee for secretary of defense, who ended up being voted down. The Senate also has left its mark on some nominees even in the process of confirming them. This was the fate of William Colby, confirmed as President Nixon's CIA director in 1973 amid controversies over Vietnam and covert action by the CIA, and of Paul Warnke, Carter's choice to head the Arms Control and Disarmament Agency, who was excoriated by conservatives as too "dovish": neither of these officials ever fully recovered from the wounds of their confirmation battles.

None of these legislative tactics, however, applies to foreign policy officials who do not require Senate confirmation. This in particular includes the assistant to the president for national security affairs (called the national security adviser, for short) and the staff of the National Security Council (NSC). Thus such major figures as Henry Kissinger, Zbigniew Brzezinski, and Condoleezza Rice, who served as national security advisers to Presidents Nixon, Carter, and George W. Bush, respectively, did not need Senate confirmation for that position. (When Kissinger was nominated by Nixon to also be secretary of state, however, Senate approval was required.)

"Commerce with Foreign Nations"

In the area of foreign commerce the Constitution is more explicit than in others. Congress is very clearly granted the power "to regulate commerce with foreign nations" and "to lay and collect . . . duties." Presidential authority over trade policy thus has been more dependent than in other areas on what and how much authority Congress chooses to delegate.[7] For about 150 years, Congress actually decided each tariff, item by item; one result of this was the infamous Smoot-Hawley Tariff Act of 1930, which set tariffs for more than 20,000 items—and moved almost all of them higher, the classic example of protectionism. The Reciprocal Trade Agreements Act of 1934, which arose from the Smoot-Hawley disaster, delegated to the president extensive authority to cut tariffs on his own by as much as 50 percent if he could negotiate reciprocal cuts with other countries. Both institutions were generally happy with this arrangement, especially under the international free trade system set up after World War II by the General Agreement on Tariffs and Trade (GATT). But beginning again in the mid-1970s, as trade became more politically controversial, the power-sharing pulls and tugs along Pennsylvania Avenue on international trade issues grew more frequent and more wrenching.

General Powers

The president and Congress both also bring to the foreign policy struggle their general constitutional powers.

EXECUTIVE POWER   The Constitution states that "the executive power shall be vested in the President," and roughly defines this power as to ensure "that the laws be faithfully executed." In itself this is a broad and vague mandate, which presidents have invoked as the basis for a wide range of actions taken in order to "execute" foreign policy, such as executive agreements, as already discussed, and executive orders, which are directives issued by the president for executive-branch actions not requiring legislative approval. Sometimes executive orders are issued just to fill in the blanks of legislation passed by Congress. But they also can be used by presidents as a way of getting around Congress. Thus, for example, President Truman racially integrated the armed forces by issuing Executive Order No. 9981 on July 26, 1948, because he knew the segregationists in Congress would block any integration legislation.

Then there is the veto, the most potent executive power the Constitution gives the president. The authority to block legislation unless Congress can pass it a second time, by a two-thirds majority in both chambers, is a formidable power. It is especially so in foreign policy, where the president can tap both patriotism and fear to intimidate potential veto overrides. Thus even amid the congressional activism and partisan battles of the 1970s and 1980s, presidential vetoes on foreign policy legislation were overridden only twice: President Nixon's veto of the 1973 War Powers Resolution and President Reagan's veto of the 1986 Anti-Apartheid Act.

In many respects even more important than a president's formal executive powers are the informal political powers of the office and the skills of being a practiced politician. Stories are legion of deal-making with members of Congress to get that one last vote to ratify a treaty or pass an important bill. President Lyndon Johnson was especially well known for this. So was President Reagan, who to get Senate approval of a major 1981 arms sale to Saudi Arabia doled out funds for a new hospital in the state of one senator, a coal-fired power plant for another, and a U.S. attorney appointment for a friend of another.[8]

The most significant political power a president has may well be what Teddy Roosevelt called the "bully pulpit." As Roosevelt once put it, "people used to say to me that I was an astonishingly good politician and divined what the people are going to think. . . . I did not 'divine' how the people were going to think, I simply made up my mind what they ought to think, and then did my best to get them to think it." And that was before television!

LEGISLATIVE POWER   Professor Louis Henkin of Columbia University goes so far as to claim that there is no part of foreign policy "that is not subject to legislation by Congress."[9] That may be an overstatement, as demonstrated by some of the examples of executive power just cited. But it is true that the legislative power gives Congress a great deal of influence over foreign policy.

The distinction made by James Lindsay between *substantive* and *procedural* legislation is a useful one for understanding that Congress has a number of ways of exerting its foreign policy influence.[10] Substantive legislation is policy-specific, spelling out what the details of foreign policy should or should not be. Disapproval of the 1919 Treaty of Versailles, approval of the 1947 Marshall Plan, ratification of the 1972 SALT arms-control treaty with the Soviet Union, approval of the 1993 North American Free Trade Agreement (NAFTA), approval of annual defense budgets—all are examples of substantive legislation.

Procedural legislation is a bit more subtle and requires more elaboration. It deals more with "the structures and procedures by which foreign policy is made. The underlying premise is that if Congress changes the decision-making process it will change the policy."[11] The 1973 War Powers Resolution is one example; it was an effort to restructure how decisions on the use of military force are made. The War Powers Resolution involved the use of the *legislative veto,* a procedure by which certain actions taken and policies set by the president can be overridden by Congress through a resolution rather than through a bill. The key difference is that whereas bills generally must be signed by the president to become law and thus give the president the opportunity to exercise a veto, congressional resolutions do not. For this very reason, the

Supreme Court severely limited the use of the legislative veto in its 1983 decision in the case *INS v. Chadha,* to be discussed in the next section.

Among Congress's other powers are its oversight and investigative powers and, most especially, its *power of the purse:* "no money shall be drawn from the Treasury but in Consequence of Appropriation made by Law." This power gives Congress direct influence over decisions on how much to spend and what to spend it on. In addition to stipulating the total budget of, for example, the Defense Department, Congress can use its appropriations power directly to influence more basic policy decisions, such as by setting "conditionalities" as to how the money can or cannot be spent, or "earmarking" it for specific programs or countries.

The Supreme Court as Referee?

It is not that often that the Supreme Court gets involved in foreign policy politics. When the Court does become involved, it is usually because it has been turned to as a "referee" to resolve presidential-congressional conflicts over foreign policy power-sharing. But the Court generally has been unable and unwilling to take on this role.

It has been unable to do so in the sense that different Court rulings seem to lend support to each side. For example, a very strong statement of presidential prerogatives in foreign policy was made in the 1936 case *United States v. Curtiss-Wright Export Corp.* Although the specific case was over whether an embargo could be imposed against an American company's arms sales, the significance of the Court's ruling was in the general principle that the president could claim greater powers in foreign than in domestic policy because of "the law of nations" and not just the Constitution: "In this vast external realm, with its important, complicated, delicate and manifold problems, the President alone has the power to speak or listen as a representative of the nation. . . . The President is the sole organ of the nation in its external relations, and its sole representative with foreign nations. . . . It is quite apparent that . . . in the maintenance of our international relations . . . [Congress] must often accord to the President a degree of discretion and freedom from statutory restriction which would not be admissible were domestic affairs alone involved."[12]

Yet the 1952 case *Youngstown Sheet and Tube Co. v. Sawyer* in many respects became the counterpart to *Curtiss-Wright,* establishing some limits on executive power. In this case, involving a labor-union strike in the steel industry during the Korean War, the Court ruled against President Truman's claim that he could break the strike in the name of national security. Going beyond the specifics of the case, the Court focused on the problems of "zones of twi-light," situations for which Congress had neither explicitly authorized the president to take a certain action nor explicitly prohibited the president from doing so. In these situations the president "and Congress may have concurrent authority, or . . . its distribution is uncertain," and thus "any actual test of power is likely to depend on the imperatives of events and contemporary im-ponderables rather than on abstract theories of law." On these types of issues, while stopping well short of asserting congressional preeminence, the Court did not accept nearly as much presidential preeminence as it had in 1936 in its *Curtiss-Wright* decision.[13]

In other instances the Supreme Court and other federal courts have been unwilling even to attempt to adjudicate presidential-congressional foreign policy disputes. In the 1970s and 1980s members of Congress took the presi-dent to court a number of times over issues of war and treaty powers.[14] In most of these cases the courts refused to rule definitively one way or the other. Although there were differences in the specifics of the rulings, the cases gener-ally were deemed to fall under the "political question" doctrine, meaning that they involved political differences between the executive and legislative branches more than constitutional issues, and thus required a political resolu-tion between the branches, rather than a judicial remedy. In other words, the Supreme Court essentially told the president and Congress to work the issues out themselves.

Another key case was the 1983 case *INS v. Chadha,* mentioned briefly ear-lier. In striking down the legislative veto as unconstitutional, the Court stripped Congress of one of its levers of power. Even so, within a year and a half of the *Chadha* decision, Congress had passed more than fifty new laws that sought to accomplish the same goals as the legislative veto while avoiding the objections raised by the Court. The constitutionality of some of these laws remains untested, but they still cast a sufficient shadow for the president not to be able to assume too much freedom of action.

Executive-Branch Politics

There was a time when books on foreign policy didn't include sections on executive-branch politics. Foreign policy politics was largely seen as an *inter-*branch phenomenon, not an *intra-*branch one. The executive branch, after all, was the president's own branch. Its usual organizational diagram was a pyramid: the president sat atop it, the various executive-branch departments and agencies fell below. Major foreign policy decisions were made in a hierarchical, structured, and orderly manner. It was believed to be a highly *rational* process, often called a "rational actor" model.

Analytically speaking, five principal criteria need to be met for an executive-branch policy process to be considered rational: (1) adequate and timely *information* must be provided through intelligence and other channels, so that policy-makers are well informed of the nature of the issues on which they need to make decisions; (2) thorough and incisive *analysis* must be made of the nature of the threats posed, the interests at stake, and other key aspects of the issues; (3) the *range of policy options* must be identified, with an analysis of the relative pros and cons of each; (4) *implementation* strategies must be spelled out for how to proceed once the policy choice is made; and (5) a *feedback "loop"* must be established to evaluate how the policies are working in practice and to make adjustments over time.[15]

Yet, as we will see throughout this book, the executive branch's foreign policy process often has not met these criteria. The dynamics of decision-making and policy implementation have tended to be less strictly hierarchical, less neatly structured, and much more disorderly than as portrayed in the rational-actor model. To put it more directly, the executive branch also has its own politics.

Presidents as Foreign Policy Leaders

For all the other executive-branch actors that play major foreign policy roles, the president remains the key decision-maker. How well the president fulfills that role depends on a number of factors.

One factor is the extent of foreign policy experience and expertise that a president brings to the office. Experience was an advantage for President George H.W. Bush, who had been CIA director, ambassador to the United Nations, and chief of the U.S. liaison office in China. Yet, surprisingly, it was much more common in the eighteenth and nineteenth centuries than in the twentieth for presidents to have had substantial prior foreign policy experience. Four of the first six presidents had served previously as secretary of state (Thomas Jefferson, James Madison, James Monroe, and John Quincy Adams). So had two other presidents in the nineteenth century (Martin Van Buren and James Buchanan). But no president since has had that experience. And of the seven war heroes who became president, only one (Dwight Eisenhower) was in this century; the others were in the eighteenth (George Washington) and nineteenth (Andrew Jackson, William Henry Harrison, Zachary Taylor,

Ulysses Grant, and Benjamin Harrison). Many attribute some of the foreign policy problems that presidents like Ronald Reagan, Bill Clinton, and George W. Bush had initially to their prior foreign policy inexperience.

A second set of factors influencing foreign policy decision-making are characteristics of the president as an individual. As with any individual in any walk of life, the president's personality affects how and how well the job gets done. Although personality is rarely the sole determinant of behavior, in some cases it does have a very strong bearing. Woodrow Wilson's unwillingness to compromise with Senate opponents on the Treaty of Versailles has been traced in part to his self-righteousness and other deep-seated personality traits. Richard Nixon's personality significantly affected his policy-making, particularly with regard to Vietnam. The consistent image of Nixon that comes through both in his own writing and that of biographers is of a pervasive suspiciousness: Nixon viewed opponents as enemies and political setbacks as personal humiliations, had an extreme penchant for secrecy, and seemed obsessed with concentrating and guarding power. These personality characteristics help explain the rigidity with which Nixon kept the Vietnam War effort going despite the evidence that it was failing, and the virtual paranoia he exhibited by putting antiwar figures on an "enemies list" and recruiting former CIA operatives to work in secret as "plumbers" to "plug" supposed leaks—actions that, like those of the self-destructive figures of ancient Greek tragedies, led to Nixon's own downfall through the Watergate scandal.

A more cognitive approach focuses on the president's worldview, or what a number of authors have called a *belief system*. No president comes to the job "tabula rasa," with a cognitive clean slate; quite to the contrary, as Robert Jervis states, "it is often impossible to explain crucial decisions and policies without reference to the decision-maker's beliefs about the world and their images of others."[16] Belief systems can be construed in terms of three core components:

1. the analytic component of the *conception of the international system:* What is the president's view of the basic structure of the international system? Who and what are seen as the principal threats to the United States?
2. the normative component of the *national interest hierarchy:* How are the core objectives of power, peace, prosperity, and principles prioritized?
3. the instrumental component of a basic *strategy:* Given both the conception of the international system and the national interest hierarchy, what is the optimal strategy to be pursued?

Dynamics of Choice, below, illustrates the importance of belief systems by contrasting those of Jimmy Carter and Ronald Reagan. The differences in their worldviews are quite pronounced, and the connections to their respective foreign policies are clear. In 1977 when he took office, Jimmy Carter was convinced that the Cold War was virtually over and that the rigid structures of bipolarity had given way to a "post-polar" world. His 4 Ps hierarchy of the national interest put principles and peace at the top. His basic foreign policy strategy was noninterventionist. All these characteristics were evident in many if not most of his foreign policies. In contrast, Ronald Reagan saw the world in bipolar terms and focused much of his 1980 presidential campaign against President Carter on Cold War themes. He put power more than peace at the top of his national-interest hierarchy, and although he too stressed principles his conception was defined largely by anticommunism, in contrast to President Carter's emphasis on human rights. In addition, President Reagan's strategy was decidedly interventionist, militarily as well as in other respects.

Presidents of course are also politicians, so another important factor affecting presidential foreign policy leadership is one of *political calculations*. This can work in different ways. Presidents in trouble at home may turn more to foreign policy to try to draw on the prestige of international leadership to bolster their domestic standing. At other times presidents feel pressured to give

DYNAMICS OF CHOICE

Presidential Belief Systems

	Carter	Reagan
Conception of the international system	Post-polar	Bipolar
National interest hierarchy	Principles, peace	Power, principles
Strategy	Noninterventionist	Interventionist

Source: Bruce W. Jentleson, "Discrepant Responses to Falling Dictators: Presidential Belief Systems and the Mediating Effects of the Senior Advisory Process," *Political Psychology* 11:2 (June 1990), 353–84.

less emphasis to foreign policy to respond to criticisms about not paying enough attention to the domestic front. The election cycle also enters in, with foreign policy tending to get more politicized during election years. And outside the election cycle there is the steady flow of public-opinion polls, which get factored in along with the intelligence analyses and other parts of the decision-making process.

Roles of Senior Foreign Policy Advisers

In looking at presidential advisers, we need to ask two sets of questions. The first concerns who among the "big four"—the national security adviser, the secretary of state, the secretary of defense, and the CIA director—has the most influential role? The answer depends on a number of factors, including respective relationships of these advisers with the president and their own prominence and bureaucratic skills. Henry Kissinger, who became so well known as to take on celebrity status, is everyone's major example. A Harvard professor, Kissinger served as national security adviser in President Nixon's first term. When President Nixon appointed him secretary of state in 1973, Kissinger also kept the national security adviser position, a highly unusual step that accorded him unprecedented influence. He continued to hold both positions under President Gerald Ford, until pressured in 1975 to give one up (national security adviser). All told, we find far more references in books on the foreign policy of that period to "Kissingerian" doctrines than to "Nixonian" or, especially, "Fordian" ones.

The other analytic question is whether *consensus or conflict* prevails among the senior advisers. Consensus does not necessarily mean perfect harmony, but it does mean a prevailing sense of teamwork and collegiality. President George H.W. Bush's team of advisers was a good example of consensus. Secretary of State James Baker, National Security Adviser Brent Scowcroft, Secretary of Defense Dick Cheney, and Chair of the Joint Chiefs of Staff Colin Powell knew each other well and had worked together in previous administrations. We thus saw much less of the end runs, get-the-other-guy leaks to the press, and bureaucratic infighting than were evidenced in some other administrations.

A possible negative aspect of consensus, though, is that too much consensus among senior advisers can lead to *"groupthink,"* a social-psychology concept that refers to the pressures within small groups for unanimity that work against individual critical thinking.[17] Group cohesion is a good thing, but too much of it can be stifling. The result can be the kinds of decisions about which in retrospect the question gets asked, How did so many smart people make such a dumb decision? The Kennedy administration's decision-making on the disastrous 1961 Bay of Pigs invasion of Cuba is an oft-cited example, one we will discuss in Chapter 4.

As to conflict among senior advisers, we come back to Kissinger as a classic example. While he was President Nixon's national security adviser, Kissinger clashed repeatedly with Secretary of State William Rogers, and while he was President Ford's secretary of state, with Defense Secretary James Schlesinger. Kissinger won many of these battles, adding to his prominence. But the impact of these disagreements on foreign policy often was quite negative. Such high-level divisiveness made broader domestic consensus-building much more difficult. Moreover, with so much emphasis on winning the bureaucratic warfare, some ideas that were good on their merits, but that happened to be someone else's, were dismissed, buried, or otherwise condemned to bureaucratic purgatory.

Bureaucratic Politics and Organizational Dynamics

Politics in the executive branch do not occur only at the senior advisory level. Political battles go on daily at every level of the bureaucracy. "Where you stand depends on where you sit" is the basic dynamic of *bureaucratic politics*—i.e., the positions taken on an issue by different executive-branch departments and agencies depend on the interests of that particular department or agency. On economic sanctions, for example, the Commerce and Agriculture Departments, with their trade-promotion missions, often have opposed the Departments of State and Defense. This can be disaggregated even further to bureaus within the same department or agency, which may also "stand" differently depending on where they "sit." Within the State Department, the Bureau of Human Rights and the East Asia–Pacific Bureau disagreed over the linkage of MFN renewal with human rights progress in China in the early 1990s. And within the military, inter-service rivalry often breaks out as the Army, Navy, and Air Force compete for shares of the defense budget, higher profiles in military actions, and other perceived advantages.

On top of these interest-based dynamics are the problems inherent in any large, complex bureaucracy: simply getting things done. The nineteenth-century German political philosopher Max Weber first focused on the problems inherent in large bureaucracies in government as well as other complex organizations. Often, instead of using rational processes consistent with the criteria noted earlier, bureaucracies proceed according to their own standard operating procedures and in other cumbersome ways that remind us why the term "bureaucracy" has the negative connotations that it does.

As Figure 2.1 shows, the foreign affairs bureaucracy is vast and complex. We depict it here in five tiers:

- the departments and agencies with principal foreign affairs responsibility (National Security Council, State, Defense, and Homeland Security);
- those most involved in foreign economic policy (Commerce, Treasury, Agriculture, State's Bureau of Economic Affairs, U.S. Trade Representative, International Trade Commission);
- agencies that deal with political democratization and economic development (Agency for International Development, State's Bureau of Democracy, Human Rights, and Labor);
- intelligence agencies (the CIA, National Security Agency, Defense Intelligence Agency); and
- those agencies and offices that, while primarily focused on domestic policy, also have important foreign policy involvement: the Environmental Protection Agency on global environmental issues, the Office of National Drug Control Policy on international narcotics policy, the Department of Labor on international policies regarding employment practices.

Most of this discussion has been about normal foreign policy decision-making. When the situations faced are international crises, the challenges for meeting the criteria for a rational executive-branch decision-making process are even greater. The key characteristics of crises are a high level of threat against vital interests, a short time frame for decision-making, and usually a significant element of surprise that the situation arose. Such situations tend to give presidents more power, since they require fast, decisive action. They also often lead presidents to set up special decision-making teams, drawing most heavily on the most trusted advisers. The crisis most often cited as a model of effective decision-making is the Cuban missile crisis, which we will discuss further in Chapter 4.

In sum, a rational executive-branch policy-making process is desirable but difficult. The sources of executive-branch politics are many, and the dynamics can get quite intricate. We will see these played out in ways that show both striking similarities and sharp differences over time.

FIGURE 2.1   The Foreign Affairs Bureaucracy

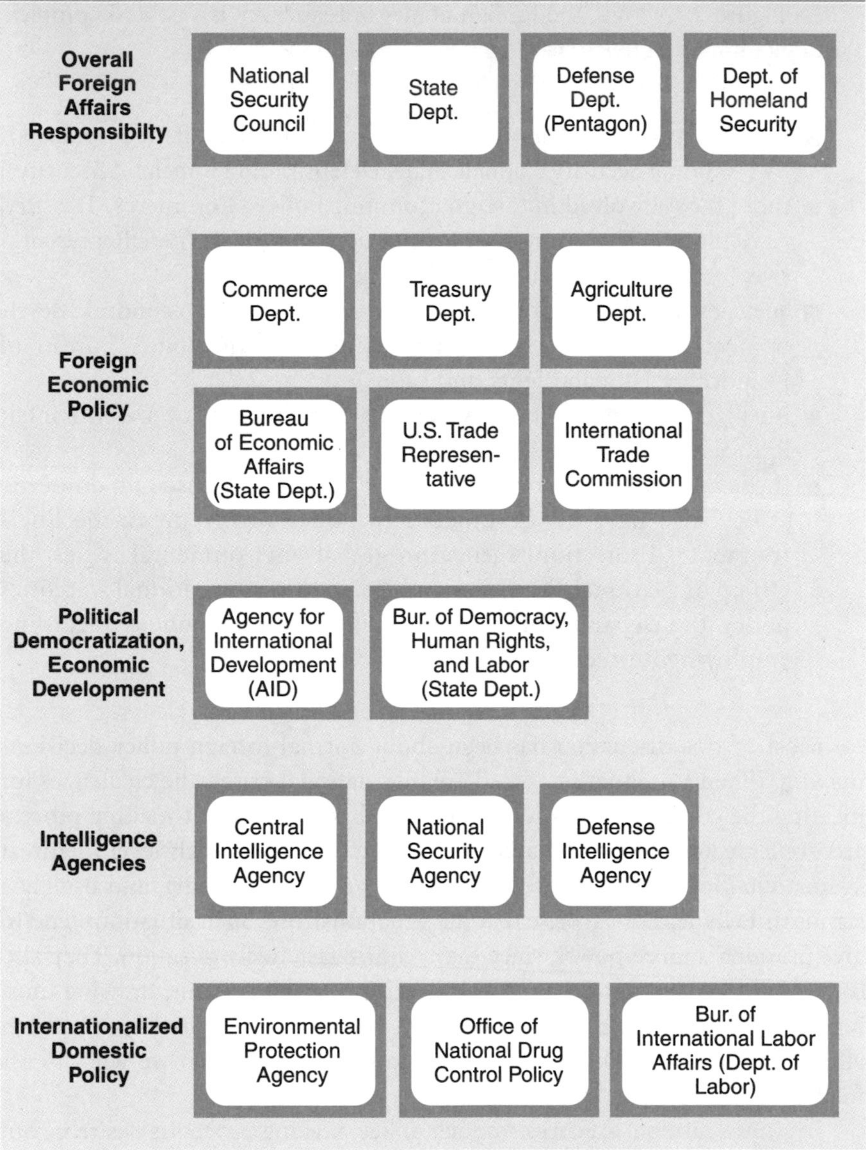

Overall Foreign Affairs Responsibilty	National Security Council	State Dept.	Defense Dept. (Pentagon)	Dept. of Homeland Security

Foreign Economic Policy	Commerce Dept.	Treasury Dept.	Agriculture Dept.	
	Bureau of Economic Affairs (State Dept.)	U.S. Trade Representative	International Trade Commission	

Political Democratization, Economic Development	Agency for International Development (AID)	Bur. of Democracy, Human Rights, and Labor (State Dept.)

Intelligence Agencies	Central Intelligence Agency	National Security Agency	Defense Intelligence Agency

Internationalized Domestic Policy	Environmental Protection Agency	Office of National Drug Control Policy	Bur. of International Labor Affairs (Dept. of Labor)

Interest Groups and Their Influence

Interest groups are "formal organizations of people who share a common out-look or social circumstance and who band together in the hope of influencing government policy."[18] Three questions are central to understanding the for-eign policy role of interest groups: (1) What are the principal types of foreign policy interest groups? (2) What are the main strategies and techniques of in-fluence used by interest groups? (3) How much influence do interest groups have, and how much should they have?

A Typology of Foreign Policy Interest Groups

Distinctions can be made among five main types of foreign policy interest groups based on differences in the nature of the interests that motivate their activity and in their forms of organization. Dynamics of Choice on p. 50 pre-sents the typology, with some general examples.

ECONOMIC INTEREST GROUPS   This category includes multinational cor-porations (MNCs) and other businesses, labor unions, consumers, and other groups whose lobbying is motivated principally by how foreign policy affects the economic interests of their members. These groups are especially active on trade and other international economic policy issues. Take the infamous 1930 Smoot-Hawley Act, which raised so many tariffs so high that it helped deepen and globalize the Great Depression. Some wondered how such a bill ever could have passed. Very easily, according to one senator who "brazenly admit-ted that the people who gave money to congressional campaigns had a right to expect it back in tariffs."[19] In the South Africa case of the 1980s many Ameri-can businesses actively opposed the anti-apartheid sanctions as threatening their economic interests by damaging trade, endangering investments, and hurting profits. With the spread of globalization, in recent years there have been even more groups whose interests have been affected, one way or the other, by trade and other international economic issues.

IDENTITY GROUPS   These groups are motivated less by economic interests than by ethnic or religious identity. Irish Americans, Polish Americans, African Americans, Greek Americans, Cuban Americans, Vietnamese Ameri-cans—these and other ethnic identity groups have sought to influence U.S. re-lations with the country or region to which they trace their ancestry or

DYNAMICS OF CHOICE

A Typology of Foreign Policy Interest Groups

Type	General examples
Economic groups	AFL-CIO (organization of trade unions) National Association of Manufacturers Consumer Federation of America Major multinational corporations (MNCs)
Identity groups	Jewish Americans Cuban Americans Greek Americans African Americans
Political issue groups	Anti–Vietnam War movement Committee on the Present Danger Amnesty International World Wildlife Fund Refugees International
State and local governments	Local Elected Officials for Social Responsibility California World Trade Commission
Foreign governments	Washington law firms, lobbyists, public-relations companies (hired to promote interests of foreign governments in Washington)

heritage. The group most often pointed to as the most powerful ethnic lobby is Jewish Americans and their principal organization, the American-Israel Public Affairs Committee (AIPAC); indeed, one book on AIPAC was titled *The Lobby*. But while the Jewish lobby unquestionably has been quite influential, it is not nearly as all-powerful or always-winning as it is often portrayed. It has lost, for example, on some Arab-Israeli issues in part because major oil companies and arms exporters with key interests in the Arab world (i.e., economic interest groups) have pressured more strongly for the opposite policy. The Jewish-American community itself at times has been split, reflecting Israel's own deep political splits on issues like the Arab-Israeli peace process. Moreover, the politics of the Jewish-American lobby are not solely responsible for pro-Israel U.S. policy; both power (the geostrategic benefits of a reliable ally in a region known for its anti-Americanism) and principles (Israel is the only democracy in the entire Middle East region) have also been served.

POLITICAL ISSUE GROUPS   This third category includes groups that are organized around support or opposition to a political issue that is not principally a matter of their economic interests or group identity. Among these are antiwar groups and movements, such as the anti–Vietnam War movement; the America First Committee, which tried to keep the United States out of World War II; and the Anti-Imperialist League, which opposed the Spanish-American War of 1898. During the Cold War, groups such as the Council for a Livable World and the nuclear freeze movement pushed for ratcheting down the levels of armaments and greater efforts at U.S.-Soviet accommodation. On the other hand, quite a few groups have been strong advocates of more assertive foreign policies, such as the American Legion, the Veterans of Foreign Wars, and the tellingly named Committee on the Present Danger.

Other sub-areas of foreign policy also have their sets of political issue groups. There are environmental groups (the World Wildlife Federation, the Sierra Club), human rights groups (Amnesty International, Human Rights Watch), women's rights groups, advocates of the rights of refugees (InterAction, Refugees International), and many others. Groups such as these are most commonly called *nongovernmental organizations* (NGOs) and have been playing increasingly important roles in influencing American foreign policy, as we will see in detail in Chapter 9.

STATE AND LOCAL GOVERNMENTS   Although they do not fit the term "interest groups" in the same way, state and local governments increasingly seek to influence foreign policy as it affects their interests.[20] In the early 1980s, for example, they pressured the federal government to end the arms race through groups such as the Local Elected Officials for Social Responsibility and by proclamations and referendums by more than 150 cities and counties declaring themselves "nuclear-free zones" or otherwise opposing the nuclear arms race. Conversely, states and cities with large defense industries have pressured the federal government not to cut defense spending. Local activism has been even greater on trade issues. The California World Trade Commission, part of the state government, sent its own representative to the GATT trade talks in Geneva, Switzerland. Many state and local governments actually led the effort to combat apartheid in South Africa. In fact the pressure on Congress to pass economic sanctions legislation was strengthened because so many state and local governments, including California and New York City, already had imposed their own sanctions by prohibiting purchases and divesting pension-fund holdings from companies still doing business with South Africa.

FOREIGN GOVERNMENTS   It is of course normal diplomacy for governments to have embassies in each others' capitals. The reference here is to the American law firms, lobbyists, and public relations companies hired by foreign governments to lobby for them. These foreign lobbyists often are former members of Congress (both Republican and Democratic), former Cabinet members, other former top executive-branch officials, and other "big guns." Indeed by the early 1990s there were well over one thousand lobbyists in Washington who were representing foreign countries. Major controversies have arisen over foreign lobbying; one high-profile case involved Japan and, as claimed in a book provocatively titled *Agents of Influence,* its "manipulation" of U.S. policy through lobbyists to the point where "it threatens our national sovereignty."[21] Another striking case was that of Angola in the mid-1980s, in which American lobbyists were hired both by the Angolan guerrillas, to try to improve their image and otherwise win support for military aid, and by the Angolan government, to try to block the aid to the guerrillas. More than $2 million was paid out by the rebels and almost $1 million by the government in just one year—a hefty sum for a country so poor.

   Not all issues have all five types of interest groups involved. But all have at least some of these groups seeking to exert their influence.

Strategies and Techniques of Influence

Interest groups seek to influence foreign policy according to many different strategies aimed at the various foreign policy actors.

INFLUENCING CONGRESS   Foreign policy legislation generally needs to pass through five principal stages within Congress: the writing of a bill, hearings and mark-up by the relevant committees, votes on the floors of the House of Representatives and the Senate, reconciliation of any differences between the House and Senate bills in a conference committee, and the appropriations process, in which the actual amounts of money are set for defense spending, foreign aid, and other items. Lobbyists will seek to influence legislation at each of these stages. Much, of course, also goes on behind the scenes. Lobbyists regularly meet privately with senators and representatives who are allies to set strategy, count votes, and in some cases even to help write the legislation.

Interest groups also try to go even more to the source by influencing who wins elections. Defense industry political action committees (PACs), for example, are major campaign contributors, especially for members of Congress who serve on defense-related committees. A 1982 study showed that almost half of the PAC contributions made by the nation's twelve largest defense contractors went to members of Congress's armed services committees and defense and military-construction subcommittees.

INFLUENCING THE EXECUTIVE BRANCH   Interest groups also try to directly influence executive-branch departments and agencies as they formulate and implement foreign policy on a day-to-day basis. In the 1980s, AIPAC broadened its efforts from being heavily focused on Capitol Hill to also work with mid-level officials in the State and Defense Departments who were working on U.S.-Israeli relations. In trade policy there is a whole system of advisory committees through which the private sector can channel its influence to executive-branch officials who negotiate trade treaties.

Another strategy is to try to influence who gets appointed to important foreign policy positions. One case in which interest groups were able to have significant influence over an executive appointment involved the ability of the conservative Cuban-American National Foundation (CANF) in 1992–93 to block the nomination of Mario Baeza, a Cuban American whose views on how to deal with Fidel Castro were seen as too moderate, as assistant secretary of state for inter-American affairs. In another case Ernest LeFever, President Reagan's nominee for assistant secretary of state for human rights, was not confirmed because of opposition by pro–human rights groups who viewed him as more a critic than an advocate of their cause.

INFLUENCING PUBLIC OPINION   Groups also take their efforts to influence foreign policy outside the halls of Congress and the executive branch, mobilizing protests and demonstrations to show "shoulder-to-shoulder" support for their causes. This is an old tradition, going back to peace movements in the early twentieth century, as well as to such nineteenth-century events as the Civil War veterans' march on Washington to demand payment of their pensions. The anti–Vietnam War movement was particularly known for its demonstrations on college campuses as well as in Washington. In the spring of 1970, for example, college campuses around the country were shut down (and final exams were even canceled on many campuses) and almost half a million protesters descended on Washington. An even larger demonstration was staged in 1990 on the twentieth anniversary of "Earth Day" to pressure the government for stronger and more forward-looking policies on global environmental issues.

Especially in recent years, foreign policy interest groups have become quite astute at using the media as a magnifying glass to enlarge their exposure and as a megaphone to amplify their voice. For all the econometric models that were run and other studies that were conducted to show the damage done to the American auto industry by Japanese auto imports in the 1970s and 1980s, for example, none had nearly the impact of the televised image of two members of Congress smashing a Toyota with a sledgehammer in front of the Capitol. Members of the anti-apartheid movement dramatized their cause by handcuffing themselves to the fence around the South African embassy in Washington, D.C., and staging other civil disobedience protests, a major objective of which was to get on the nightly television news. The anti-globalization movement of recent years has tried to use similar tactics, but the violence in the streets of many of these protests at times has backfired by alienating the support of broad swaths of the public.

CORRUPTION   Popular images of suitcases stuffed with $100 bills, exorbitant junkets, and other corruption at times get grossly exaggerated. Nevertheless, there have been sufficient instances of corrupt efforts to influence foreign policy that to not include it as a technique of influence would be a glaring omission. For example, Koreagate was a 1976 scandal over alleged South Korean influence-peddling in Congress. Another example was the 1980s Pentagon defense-contract scandals involving bribes, cover-ups, and cost overruns that led to the purchase of "specially designed" $600 toilet seats and $1,000 coffee machines.

The Extent of Interest-Group Influence: Analytic and Normative Considerations

"The friend of popular governments never finds himself so much alarmed for their character and fate," James Madison warned back in Federalist no. 10, "as when he contemplates their propensity to . . . the violence of faction." Madison defined a "faction" not just as a group with a particular set of interests but as one whose interests, or "common impulse of passion," were "adverse to the rights of other citizens, or to the permanent and aggregate interests of the community."

Madison's general political concern with what we now call the extent of interest-group influence bears particularly on foreign policy, for three principal reasons. First, if there is even the slightest sense that the nation is asking its citizens to make the ultimate sacrifice of war for interests that are more group-specific than collectively national, the consequences for national morale and purpose can be devastating. Even in more ongoing, less dramatic areas of policy the effects of such an impression on the overall state of democracy and conceptions of public authority can be deeply corrosive.

Second, this "capturing" by interest groups of areas of policy makes change much more difficult because of the many vested interests that get ensconced.[22] This is especially a problem in foreign policy, given the many threats and challenges to which the United States must respond, including the rigors of staying competitive in the international economy. The work of political scientist Mancur Olson asserts that throughout history it has been the sapping of capacity for change and adaptation brought on by too many vested interests that has brought down one empire and major power after another—and into which, he warned in 1982, the United States was sinking.[23]

Third is the highly emotionally charged nature of so many foreign policy issues. The "impulses of passion" Madison warned about can be quite intense. The stakes tend to be seen not as just winning or losing, but as tests of morality and even of patriotism.

One of the examples most often cited of excessive interest-group influence is the *military-industrial complex.** Consider the warning sounded in a famous speech in 1961 (see At the Source on p. 56). Sound like something that might have come from Nikita Khrushchev? Fidel Castro? Or maybe Abbie Hoffman or some other 1960s radical? None of the above. It is from the farewell address of President (and former general) Dwight D. Eisenhower.

Some of the statistics on the Cold War military-industrial complex really are staggering. By 1970 the Pentagon owned 29 million acres of land (almost the size of New York State) valued at $47.7 billion, and had "true wealth" of $300 to $400 billion, or about six to eight times greater than the annual after-tax profits of all U.S. corporations.[24] During the Reagan defense buildup in the mid-1980s, "the Pentagon was spending an average of $28 million *an hour.*" One out of every sixteen American workers as well as 47 percent of all

---

*The formal political science definition of the military-industrial complex is a social and political subsystem that integrates the armament industry, the military-oriented science community, the defense-related parts of the political system, and the military bureaucracies. David Skidmore and Valerie M. Hudson, eds., *The Limits of State Autonomy: Societal Groups and Foreign Policy Formation* (Boulder, Colo.: Westview, 1992), 36.

> ▶ **At the Source** ◀

BEWARE THE MILITARY-INDUSTRIAL COMPLEX

❝ The conjunction of an immense military establishment and a large arms industry is new in the American experience. The total influence—economic, political, even spiritual—is felt in every city, every statehouse, every office of the federal government. . . . We must not fail to comprehend its grave implications. Our toil, our resources and livelihood all are involved; so is the very structure of our society.

In the councils of government, we must guard against the acquisition of unwarranted influence, whether sought or unsought, by the *military-industrial complex* [emphasis added]. The potential for the disastrous rise of misplaced power exists and will persist.

We must never let the weight of this combination endanger our liberties or democratic processes. ❞

Source: Dwight D. Eisenhower, "Farewell Address," January 1961, *Public Papers of the Presidents of the United States, Dwight D. Eisenhower*, Vol. 8 (Washington, D.C.: U.S. Government Printing Office, 1962), 1035–41.

---

aeronautical engineers, more than 30 percent of mathematicians, and 25 percent of physicists either worked directly for or drew grants from the defense sector.[25]

One of the best examples of how the military-industrial complex was set up involved the B-1 bomber, a highly capable but expensive new strategic bomber whose production President Carter sought to cancel but was unable to, largely because of the "gerrymandered subcontracting" depicted in Figure 2.2. The main contractor for the B-1 was Rockwell International, based in California. In subcontracting out the various parts of the plane, Rockwell astutely ensured that contracts would go to companies in forty-eight states: the defensive avionics to a firm in New York, the offensive avionics to one in Nebraska, the tires and wheels to Ohio, the tail to Maryland, the wings to Tennessee, etc. To make sure they knew the score, Rockwell spent $110,000 on a study delineating the B-1's economic benefits on a state-by-state, district-by-district basis. Thus when President Carter did not include funding for the B-1 in his version of the annual

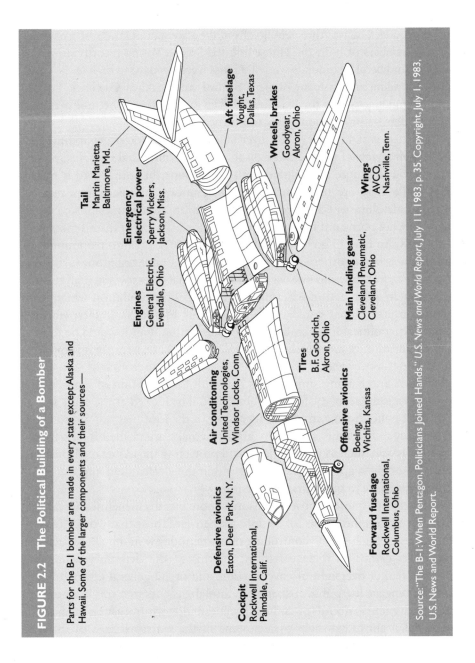

FIGURE 2.2 The Political Building of a Bomber

Parts for the B-1 bomber are made in every state except Alaska and Hawaii. Some of the larger components and their sources—

Tail
Martin Marietta,
Baltimore, Md.

Aft fuselage
Vought,
Dallas, Texas

Emergency electrical power
Sperry Vickers,
Jackson, Miss.

Wheels, brakes
Goodyear,
Akron, Ohio

Engines
General Electric,
Evendale, Ohio

Wings
AVCO,
Nashville, Tenn.

Air conditoning
United Technologies,
Windsor Locks, Conn.

Main landing gear
Cleveland Pneumatic,
Cleveland, Ohio

Tires
B.F. Goodrich,
Akron, Ohio

Defensive avionics
Eaton, Deer Park, N.Y.

Offensive avionics
Boeing,
Wichita, Kansas

Cockpit
Rockwell International,
Palmdale, Calif.

Forward fuselage
Rockwell International,
Columbus, Ohio

Source: "The B-1: When Pentagon, Politicians Joined Hands," *U.S. News and World Report,* July 11, 1983, p. 35. Copyright, July 1, 1983, U.S. News and World Report.

defense budget, he was threatening jobs in the states and districts of a majority of the members of both the House and the Senate. Voting records show that even many liberal Democrats who otherwise were opposed to high levels of defense spending and in favor of arms control voted against Carter and added enough funding to keep the B-1 alive.[26] When Ronald Reagan became president in 1981, the B-1 production spigot was turned on full force.

Yet there is significant debate over how extensive interest-group influence is. In their review of the literature on the military-industrial complex, professors David Skidmore and Valerie Hudson conclude that the record is mixed, that while there are numerous cases of significant influence, especially in weapons development and procurement, the more sweeping claims of dominance are not borne out by the empirical research.[27] Moreover, and more generally, we also have to go back to Madison for a note of caution about efforts to somehow ban or otherwise "remove the causes" of interest groups: "It could never be more truly said than of [this] remedy that it was worse than the disease. Liberty is to faction what air is to fire, an aliment without which it instantly expires. But it could not be a less folly to abolish liberty, which is essential to political life, because it nourishes faction than it would be to wish the annihilation of air, which is essential to animal life, because it imparts to fire its destructive agency."[28]

Others argue along similar lines that with the exception of issues of the utmost national security, foreign policy should be looked at the same way as domestic policy, with a much broader sense of the legitimacy of group interests. Many of the issues pushed by groups actually are in the broad national interest as well, such as human rights and protecting the global environment, but are not given appropriate priority within the government and thus need outside pressure to bring them to the fore.

In his work quoted above, Madison is more positively inclined toward efforts "to control the effects" of factions than toward those that would "remove their causes." Such effects-controlling measures today would include such initiatives as campaign-finance reform, reforms of the defense-procurement process, tighter oversight of covert action, and broad general efforts to educate and engage the public. Experience, though, teaches that this is a problem for which there is no full or enduring solution. Reform measures such as the ones noted above can help correct some of the worst excesses of interest-group influence. But this is one of those dilemmas for which, as American government scholars Theodore Lowi and Benjamin Ginsberg write, "there is no ideal answer. . . . Those who believe that there are simple solutions to the issues of political life would do well to ponder this problem."[29]

The Impact of the News Media

It was just a few hours short of prime time, on the evening of January 16, 1991, when American bombers started attacking Iraq, live on CNN. A war was starting, and Americans and much of the world could see it (at least some of it) right there on their living-room TVs. The Persian Gulf War made the foreign policy role of the news media more graphic and more evident than ever before. So, more recently, did the war in Afghanistan and then the war in Iraq with the "embedded" journalists. Here, too, though, as with much of what we have discussed in this chapter, the key questions debated were not totally new: (1) What role should the news media play? (2) How much influence do they actually have? (3) How is the balance to be struck between freedom of the press and national security?

Role of the Media: Cheerleader or Critic?

In 1916, in an effort to ensure support for a just-launched military intervention into Mexico, President Woodrow Wilson stated, "I have asked the several news services to be good enough to assist the Administration in keeping this view of the expedition constantly before both the people of this country and the distressed and sensitive people of Mexico."[30] The president was asking newspapers to be his "cheerleaders." The matter-of-fact tone of his statement, made in a public speech, not just leaked from some secret memo, conveys the expectation that although the press could muckrake all it wanted in domestic policy, in foreign policy, especially during wars or other crises, it was to be less free and more friendly.

Grandparents can tell you about World War II and how strongly the media supported the war effort. Foreign correspondents filled the newspapers, and newsreels played in the movie theaters, with stories and pictures of American and allied heroism, and Nazi and Japanese evil and atrocities. This was "the good war," and there generally was a basis for positive reporting. It did get intentionally manipulative, however. A book called *Hollywood Goes to War* tells the story of how "officials of the Office of War Information, the government's propaganda agency, issued a constantly updated manual instructing the studios in how to assist the war effort, sat in on story conferences with Hollywood's top brass, . . . pressured the movie makers to change scripts and even scrap pictures when they found objectionable material, and sometimes wrote dialogue for key speeches."[31]

Even in the early days of U.S. involvement in Vietnam, the media were largely supportive. But as the war went on, and went bad, the media sent back reports that were much more critical of the conduct of the war and that contradicted the official versions being put out by the Johnson and Nixon administrations. In one telling incident a reporter who had written critical stories was dressed down by a military commander for "not getting on the team."

Similar issues were raised during the 1990–91 Persian Gulf War. During the buildup of Operation Desert Shield and especially once Operation Desert Storm was launched and war began, the Bush administration and the military sought to manage the news coverage with two principal goals: to limit the independence of the media coverage and to shape it to be as positive as possible. War correspondents were confined to "pools" of limited numbers and restricted to designated locations. Film footage released for TV was carefully screened so as to give the impression of a near-flawless bombing campaign—"smart" bombs going through ventilation shafts, high "target-kill" ratios, very few civilian sites hit. General Norman Schwarzkopf, commanding officer of the U.S. and allied forces in the Persian Gulf, proved to be not only an excellent military strategist but also a whiz at media briefings and TV communication, and became a new folk hero.

The media protested that, while certain restrictions were understandable during war, the measures taken to control the coverage "go far beyond what is required to protect troop safety and mission security."[32] *Newsweek* called it "the propaganda war. . . . In theory, reporters in democratic societies work independent of propaganda. In practice they are treated during war as simply more pieces of military hardware to be deployed."[33] The military essentially was saying to the media that, with the nation at war, our intention is to limit and direct your role to the cheerleader one, not the critic one. In pursuit of cheerleader coverage, the military limited the amount and accuracy of information provided to the media. It was later learned that in fact the air campaign had not been nearly as successful as portrayed. Later information revealed that only 7 percent of the bombs were precision-guided munitions, and while these did hit their targets 90 percent of the time, more than 90 percent of the bombs were "dumb" conventional ones that missed their targets 75 percent of the time. Data such as these sharply contrasted with "the high-tech, never-miss image that the Pentagon carefully cultivated during the war."[34]

Cheerleader or critic? Which role have the media played? And which role should they play? These long have been and continue to be crucial questions. We return to them in Chapter 6 with reference to the 2003 Iraq war.

Modes of Influence

Three main distinctions are made as to the modes of influence the media have on foreign policy politics. First is *agenda setting*. "The mass media may not be successful in telling people what to think," one classic study put it, "but the media are stunningly successful in telling their audience what to think about."[35] Television in particular has a major agenda-setting impact. Studies by media scholar Shanto Iyengar and others show that when people are asked to identify the most significant problem facing the nation, they name something that has been on television news recently. Mass starvation was plaguing many parts of Africa in the mid-1980s, but the outside world, the United States included, was paying little attention. Yet once NBC News went to Ethiopia and broadcast footage of ravaged children and emaciated adults to millions of television viewers back in the United States, suddenly the Ethiopian famine was on the foreign policy agenda.

Of course, the equally tragic famines elsewhere in Africa, where the TV cameras did not go, did not make it onto the U.S. national agenda. Such discrepancies raise a troubling question for policy makers: If a tree falls in the woods and television doesn't cover it, did it really fall? The media play a crucial role in determining which issues get focused on and which do not. Some issues do force their way onto the agenda, and the media are largely reactive and mirroring. But there are many other issues that would get much less policy attention if it were not for major media coverage. Conversely, there are foreign policy issues that despite their importance don't get media coverage and thus don't get on the agenda—whole "forests" may fall down with no television cameras in sight.

As to *shaping public opinion,* in terms of its substantive content, the main impact of the media is in what researchers call "framing" and "priming" effects.[36] The stakes involved in a particular foreign policy issue are not necessarily self-evident or part of a strictly objective reality. How an issue is cast ("framed") affects the substantive judgments people make—and the media play a key role in this framing. The media also influence ("prime") the relative priority the public gives to one issue over another, as well as the criteria by which the public makes its judgments about success and failure. These framing and priming effects occur both directly through the general public's own exposure to the media and indirectly through "opinion leaders"—i.e., political, business, community, educational, celebrity, and other leaders to whom the public often looks for cues.

To the extent that the media's substantive impact goes beyond these framing and priming effects, it tends to be on two kinds of foreign policy issues.

One set comprises those for which the public has little prior information and few sources other than the media. The other set includes those issues that have strong symbolic significance and are heavily emotionally charged, such as the 1979–81 Iranian hostage crisis and the 2001 terrorist attacks. The intense media coverage of the Iranian hostage crisis made sure this issue stayed front-and-center on the agenda, which, given the nature of the issue, also influenced the substance of public opinion.* Even this didn't compare to the saturation coverage of the September 11, 2001, terrorist attacks. Virtually all Americans were transfixed to their television sets for days, arguably as much for the sense of community as for the information they were obtaining.

A third type of influence is directly on *policy-makers.* "What will the press think?" is a common question inside the White House and the State Department. It is asked in an anticipatory manner and thus can affect policy as it is formulated. The concern with how a policy will be perceived comes into play as part of the plans for pursuing a policy, with strategies for press conferences, special briefings, and "political spin" at times almost as detailed as military battle plans. Also, in a more informational sense, smart policy-makers draw on dispatches and analyses by the more prominent foreign-affairs journalists as additional and independent sources of information to supplement even their own intelligence sources.

Freedom of the Press vs. National Security

How to strike the balance between freedom of the press and national security has been a recurring issue in American politics. The First Amendment guarantees freedom of the press. Yet situations can arise when the nation's security would be endangered if certain information became public. This national-security rationale can be, and has been, very real; it also can be, and has been, abused.

Historical precedents cut both ways. For example, in 1961 the *New York Times* had uncovered information on the secret Bay of Pigs invasion of Cuba being planned by the Kennedy administration. Under some pressure from the White House, but primarily as their own self-censorship based on the national-security rationale, the *Times*'s publisher and editors decided not to

---

*Ted Koppel's *Nightline*, which went on to become one of the top-rated news shows ever, started out as nightly coverage of just the hostage crisis. Every show would be introduced as "Day 1 of the Hostage Crisis," "Day 2 . . . ," "Day 50 . . . ," "Day 100 . . . ," all the way through "Day 444," when on January 20, 1981, the last hostages were finally released.

print the information. The Bay of Pigs invasion went ahead, and it failed disastrously—leaving many to question whether national security would have been better served had the story been run and the plan unmasked.[37] On the other hand, in 1962, during the Cuban missile crisis, the press again restrained some of its reporting. An ABC correspondent even served as a secret intermediary for some tense negotiations between President Kennedy and Soviet leader Nikita Khrushchev. This time the outcome was more positive: the crisis was resolved, and many concluded that the restraint on full freedom of the press was justified.

With the Cuban missile crisis especially in mind, historian Michael Beschloss stresses the value in times of crisis of "a cocoon of time and privacy."[38] He speculates as to how differently the Cuban missile crisis might have turned out if the media coverage had been as intrusive and intense as it is today. What if TV network satellites had discovered the Soviet missiles on their own and broke the story on the evening news, sparking congressional and public outcry and increasing pressure on President Kennedy to take immediate but precipitous and potentially escalating action like an air strike? Could ExCom have deliberated over so many days without leaks? Kennedy was able to shape his own story rather than being caught on the defensive; today his position would have been much tougher to sell, and he probably could not have gotten away with a number of gambits that balanced toughness with understanding of Khrushchev's situation if every move had been independently and immediately reported and discussed on radio talk shows.

In other instances, though, the restrictions imposed on the freedom of the press in the name of national security have been questioned for their impact both on foreign policy and on civil liberties. The Vietnam War "get on the team" view noted earlier in this chapter came to a head as a freedom of the press issue in the "Pentagon Papers" case. In mid-1967, at a point when the war was going very badly, Defense Secretary Robert McNamara set up a comprehensive internal review of U.S. policy. By the end of the Johnson administration the forty-seven-volume *History of the United States Decision-Making Process on Vietnam Policy,* which came to be called the "Pentagon Papers," had been completed. It was given highly classified status, to be kept secret and for high-level government use only. But in March 1971, Daniel Ellsberg, who had been one of the researchers and authors of the Pentagon Papers but now was a critic and opponent of the war, leaked a copy to a *New York Times* reporter. On June 13, 1971, the *Times* began publishing excerpts. The Nixon administration immediately sued to stop publication, claiming potential damage to national security. (The administration also had a political agenda, fearing that already-eroding public support for the war would crumble even more.) On June 30 the Supreme Court ruled 6 to 3 against the Nixon administration. The Court did not totally disregard the national-security justification but ruled that the standard had not been met in this case, and that therefore First Amendment freedom of the press rights took precedence.[39] The *Times* continued its stories on the Pentagon Papers, as did other newspapers.*

Freedom of the press and national-security issues also have been heated in the war on terrorism, as we will see in Chapter 7.

The Nature and Influence of Public Opinion

With respect to public opinion and foreign policy, our concern is with two principal questions: (1) What is its nature? (2) How much influence does it have?

Ignorant or Sensible? The Nature of Public Opinion about Foreign Policy

2.2

To read some of the commentaries on American public opinion and foreign policy, one would think that Americans believe much more in government *for* the people than in government *by* and *of* the people. Walter Lippmann, the leading U.S. foreign-affairs journalist of the first half of the twentieth century, disparaged public opinion as "destructively wrong at critical junctures . . . a dangerous master of decision when the stakes are life and death."[40] Nor was the traditional view taken by leading scholars any more positive. "The rational requirements of good foreign policy," wrote the eminent Realist Hans Morgenthau, "cannot from the outset count upon the support of a public whose

---

*It was in reaction to the Pentagon Papers leak that President Nixon set up the special White House unit known as the "plumbers" to "plug" any further leaks. Among the operations carried out by the "plumbers" was an illegal break-in to the offices of Daniel Ellsberg's psychiatrist, seeking information with which to discredit Ellsberg, and the 1972 June break-in at the headquarters of the Democratic National Committee in the Watergate building. These events and actions, and others later uncovered, ultimately led to an impeachment investigation against President Nixon and on August 9, 1974, his resignation as president.

preferences are emotional rather than rational."[41] Gabriel Almond, in his *The American People and Foreign Policy*, a 1950 study long considered the classic in the field, stressed the "inattentiveness" of the vast majority of the public to foreign policy, an inattentiveness he attributed to the lack of "intellectual structure and factual content." [42] Others took this even further, positing a historical pattern of reflexively alternating "moods" of introversion and extroversion, sort of a societal biorhythm by which every two decades or so the public shifted between internationalism and isolationism.[43]

These criticisms are built around a basic distinction between the "mass public," prone to all of the above and more, and the better-informed, more thoughtful, and more sophisticated "elites." The general public consistently has shown very little knowledge about foreign affairs. The following facts illustrate general public ignorance:

- Only 58 percent of the public in 1964 knew that the United States was a member of NATO, and 38 percent thought the Soviet Union was.[44]
- In 1986, despite the extreme attention being given to the conflict in Nicaragua by the Reagan administration, only 38 percent of Americans could correctly identify whether the United States was supporting the contras or the Sandinistas.
- Only four months after the dramatic ceremony held on September 13, 1993, on the White House lawn with President Clinton, Israeli Prime Minister Yitzhak Rabin, and Palestine Liberation Organization leader Yasir Arafat, 56 percent of Americans could not identify the group that Arafat headed.[45]
- A 1989 study by the National Geographic Society found Americans able to correctly identify only 8 of 16 locations on a world map, achieving no better than sixth place out of ten countries surveyed. Broken down by age, American eighteen- to twenty-four-year-olds came in last.[46]

Other critics point to overreactive tendencies in the mass public. Take the "rally 'round the flag" pattern in times of crisis. On the one hand this can be quite positive in helping build consensus and national solidarity when the nation faces a serious threat. It also can be politically helpful to presidents whose popularity gets boosted as part of the rallying effect. But often it becomes blind "followership," and in extremes can pose dangers to democracy by adding to the forces equating dissent with disloyalty.

An alternative view of the public sees it as much more sensible about foreign policy than it gets credit for. Elmo Roper, who founded a trailblazing public-opinion-polling firm, observed back in 1942 that "during my eight years of asking the common man questions about what he thinks and what he wants . . . I have often been surprised and elated to discover that, despite his lack of information, the common man's native intelligence generally brings him to a sound conclusion."[47]

Two key points are made by those who share the "sensible public" view. One is that rather than being wildly and whimsically fluctuating, public opinion has been quite stable over time. Take, for example, basic attitudes toward isolationism ("stay out of world affairs") vs. internationalism ("play an active role"). For the entire period since World War II, as illustrated in Figure 2.3, despite some ups and downs the overall pro-internationalism pattern holds. We can see a definite narrowing of the gap, but even then the pattern holds.

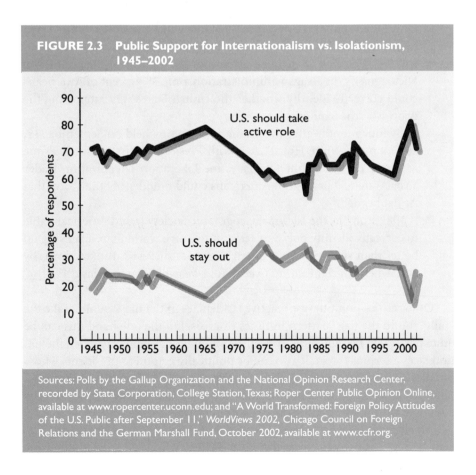

FIGURE 2.3   Public Support for Internationalism vs. Isolationism, 1945–2002

Sources: Polls by the Gallup Organization and the National Opinion Research Center, recorded by Stata Corporation, College Station, Texas; Roper Center Public Opinion Online, available at www.ropercenter.uconn.edu; and "A World Transformed: Foreign Policy Attitudes of the U.S. Public after September 11," *WorldViews 2002*, Chicago Council on Foreign Relations and the German Marshall Fund, October 2002, available at www.ccfr.org.

The second point made by those who view public opinion positively is that to the extent that public views on foreign policy have changed over time, it has been less a matter of moodiness and much more a rational process. A study of the fifty-year period 1935–85 concludes that "virtually all the rapid shifts [in public opinion] . . . were related to political and economic circumstances or to significant events which sensible citizens would take into account. In particular, most abrupt foreign policy changes took place in connection with wars, confrontations or crises in which major policy changes in the actions of the United States or other nations quite naturally affect preference about what policies to pursue."[48] This is termed an "event-driven" process; that is to say, when the threats facing the United States or other aspects of the international situation have changed, in an altogether rational way so too has public opinion.

What, for example, was so feckless about the public's turning against the Vietnam War when many people believed at the time, and now former defense secretary Robert McNamara's memoirs have confirmed, that even those at the highest levels did not believe the war could be won? "It is difficult to fault the American people," wrote Army major Andrew F. Krepinevich, Jr., "when, after that long a period of active engagement, the Joint Chiefs of Staff could only offer more of the same for an indefinite period with no assurance of eventual success."[49] Indeed, had the public stayed supportive of such an ill-conceived war effort, we might *then* really have wondered about its rationality.

We thus get two very different views of the nature of public opinion. The analytic challenge is that neither holds all the time, and both hold some of the time.

The Influence of Public Opinion on Foreign Policy

Political scientist Bruce Russett characterizes the basic public opinion–foreign policy dynamic as an *interactive* one. Leaders do not control the public; they cannot "persuade the populace to support whatever the leaders wish to do." Nor is the public controlling, having so much impact that foreign policy basically "obeys [its] dictates." Instead "each influences the other."[50]

Public opinion influences foreign policy in five principal ways. The first is by *parameter setting,* which means that public opinion imposes limits on the range of the president's policy options via assessments made by presidential advisers of what has any chance of being made "to fly" with the public and what options are "nonstarters." A good example is U.S. policy toward Saddam Hussein in the 1980s, the period before he became Public Enemy #1 during the Persian Gulf War. During Saddam's war with Iran, which lasted from 1980 to 1988, the Reagan administration gave Iraq extensive support on the grounds that "the enemy of my enemy is my friend." Once the Iran-Iraq War was over, and Saddam then attacked the Iraqi Kurds with chemical weapons and showed other signs of aggression in the region, some in the State Department began to question whether the United States should continue aiding Iraq. But with the Iran-contra affair still in the political air, the Reagan administration flatly ruled out any shift from the pro-Saddam policy as risking being seen by the public as "soft on Iran." Consequently, when the internal State Department paper proposing such a shift in policy was leaked to the press, Secretary of State George Shultz "called a meeting in his office, angrily demanding to know who was responsible for the paper. . . . [The paper] was dismissed less by any analytic refutation of its strategic logic than on political grounds. . . . On the cover page, in big letters, [Shultz] had written 'NO.'"[51]

A second way that public opinion influences policy is through *centripetal pull* toward the center on presidents who need to build supportive coalitions. This centering pull has worked both on presidents whose tendencies were too far to the left and on those too far to the right to gain sufficient political support. With President Jimmy Carter, whose foreign policy reputation generally raised doubts as to whether he was "tough" enough, the public sought to balance this concern by expressing low levels of approval of Carter's Soviet policy when it was in its conciliatory phases (1977–78, most of 1979), and higher levels of support when Carter got tough (mid-1978, 1979–80). President Ronald Reagan's foreign policy reputation, in contrast, was plenty tough but raised concerns among a substantial segment of the public as to whether it was reckless and risked war. Thus public approval of President Reagan's Soviet policy fell when it was most strident and confrontational (1981–83), and then increased only in late 1985 once it started to become more genuinely open to cooperation, peaking at 65 percent following Reagan's first summit with Soviet leader Mikhail Gorbachev in November 1985.[52]

The third influence of public opinion is its *impact on Congress.* Congress is very sensitive, arguably too sensitive, to public opinion on foreign policy. It responds both to polls on specific issues and to more general assessments of whether the public really cares much about foreign policy at all. Often this translates into Congress's paying the most attention to the groups that are the most vocal and are the most politically potent, and caring less about broader opinion-poll trends. Former senator Hubert H. Humphrey, a leading figure from the late 1940s to his death in 1978, excoriated many of his colleagues for being "POPPs," or what he called "public opinion poll politicians," on foreign policy.[53]

Fourth, public opinion can *affect diplomatic negotiations.* Public opinion does not just come into play once a treaty or other diplomatic agreement is reached; it also can affect the actual diplomatic negotiations themselves, because U.S. diplomats need to know while still at the table what terms of agreement are politically viable back home.[54] This kind of influence is not necessarily a bad thing. It can be, to the extent that it ties the negotiators' hands in ways that are politically popular but unsound in policy terms. But public opinion also can strengthen negotiators' hands, as part of a "good cop–bad cop" dynamic. "I'd be more than willing to consider your proposal," a U.S. negotiator might say to his Japanese or Russian counterpart, "but the American public would never accept it."

The fifth avenue for public opinion's influence is *through presidential elections.* Voting analysts identify three factors as key to attributing significant electoral impact to a foreign policy issue: the issue must be demonstrated through survey questions to be highly salient; there must be significant differences between the positions of the Republican and Democratic candidates; and the public's awareness of these differences must be evident.[55] Recent examples of the strong impact of foreign policy issues in elections were in the 1952 (Dwight Eisenhower vs. Adlai Stevenson), 1972 (Richard Nixon vs. George McGovern), and 1980 (Jimmy Carter vs. Ronald Reagan) presidential contests.[56] In other instances the public has focused less on a specific issue than on a general sense of which candidate generally seems to be a strong leader, or which seems too "soft" to stand up to foreign enemies and otherwise be entrusted with the nation's security. Admittedly these are highly subjective assessments, and harder for pollsters and political scientists to measure precisely. But experience has shown that these difficulties don't make the opinions any less important.

Summary

Foreign policy politics is the *process* by which the choices of foreign policy strategy are made. It is much more complex than the conventional wisdom depicts; as we have seen in this chapter, politics' stopping "at the water's edge" has been more the exception than the rule. The basic patterns are of both consensus and conflict, with positive and negative variations of each in terms of their effects on policy.

The basic framework this chapter has laid out for foreign policy politics is a structural one, focusing on the roles of the principal political institutions involved in the making of foreign policy (the president, Congress, and the executive branch) and the major societal influences (interest groups, the news media, and public opinion).

In the next few chapters we will see how the dynamics of foreign policy politics and the process of choice, as well as Chapter 1's foreign policy strategy and the essence of choice, have played out historically.

Notes

[1] Joseph Marion Jones, *The Fifteen Weeks (February 21–June 5, 1947)* (New York: Harcourt Brace and World, 1955), 8.

[2] James M. McCormick, *American Foreign Policy and Process* (Itasca, Ill.: F. E. Peacock, 1992), 478.

[3] Quoted in Bruce W. Jentleson, "American Diplomacy: Around the World and Along Pennsylvania Avenue," in Thomas E. Mann, ed., *A Question of Balance: The President, the Congress and Foreign Policy* (Washington, D.C.: Brookings Institution Press, 1990), 184.

[4] Edward S. Corwin, *The President: Office and Powers, 1787–1957,* 4th rev. ed. (New York: New York University Press, 1957), 171.

[5] Richard E. Neustadt, *Presidential Power: The Politics of Leadership* (New York: Wiley, 1976), 101.

[6] Cited in Arthur M. Schlesinger, Jr., *The Imperial Presidency* (New York: Atlantic Monthly Press, 1974), 17.

[7] Excellent books on the executive-legislative politics of trade policy are I. M. Destler, *American Trade Politics,* 3d ed. (Washington, D.C.: Institute for International Economics, 1995); and Robert A. Pastor, *Congress and the Politics of Foreign Economic Policy, 1929–1976* (Berkeley: University of California Press, 1980).

[8] James M. Lindsay, *Congress and the Politics of U.S. Foreign Policy* (Baltimore: Johns Hopkins University Press, 1994), 90.

[9] Cited in McCormick, *American Foreign Policy and Process,* 268.

[10] Lindsay, *Congress and the Politics of U.S. Foreign Policy,* chaps. 4 and 5.

[11] Lindsay, *Congress and the Politics of U.S. Foreign Policy,* 99.

[12] *United States v. Curtiss-Wright Export Corp.* (1936), quoted in Thomas M. Franck and Michael J. Glennon, eds., *Foreign Relations and National Security Law: Cases, Materials and Simulations* (St. Paul, Minn.: West Publishing, 1987), 32–37.

[13] *Youngstown Sheet and Tube Co. v. Sawyer* [the *Steel Seizure* case] (1952), quoted in Franck and Glennon, eds., *Foreign Relations and National Security Law,* 5–28.

[14] One of these cases was *Goldwater et al. v. Carter* (1979), in which Republican senator Barry Goldwater led a suit challenging the constitutionality of President Carter's decision to terminate the Mutual Defense Treaty with Taiwan as part of his policy of normalizing relations with the People's Republic of China. The others were four suits brought by Democratic members of Congress in the Reagan and Bush administrations on war powers issues: *Crockett v. Reagan* (1984), on U.S. military aid and advisers in El Salvador; *Conyers v. Reagan* (1985), over the 1983 invasion of Grenada; *Lowry v. Reagan* (1987), over the reflagging and naval operations in

the Persian Gulf during the Iran-Iraq War; and *Dellums v. Bush* (1990), over the initial Operation Desert Shield deployment following the Iraqi invasion of Kuwait.

[15]Alexander L. George, *Presidential Decisionmaking in Foreign Policy: The Effective Use of Information and Advice* (Boulder, Colo.: Westview, 1980), 10.

[16]Robert Jervis, *Perception and Misperception in International Politics* (Princeton: Princeton University Press, 1976), 28.

[17]See Irving L. Janis, *Groupthink: Psychological Studies of Policy Decisions and Fiascos* (Boston: Houghton Mifflin, 1982).

[18]Larry Berman and Bruce Murphy, *Approaching Democracy* (Englewood Cliffs, N.J.: Prentice-Hall, 1996), 408.

[19]Quoted in Pastor, *Congress and the Politics of Foreign Economic Policy,* 79.

[20]Earl H. Fry, *The Expanding Role of State and Local Governments in U.S. Foreign Policy* (New York: Council on Foreign Relations Press, 1998); also Chadwick Alger, "The World Relations of Cities: Closing the Gap between Social Science Paradigms and Everyday Human Experience," *International Studies Quarterly* 34:4 (1990), 493–518; and Michael H. Shuman, "Dateline Main Street: Local Foreign Policies," *Foreign Policy* 65 (1986/87), 154–74.

[21]Pat Choate, *Agents of Influence: How Japan's Lobbyists in the United States Manipulate America's Political and Economic System* (New York: Knopf, 1990), xiv.

[22]Theodore J. Lowi, *The End of Liberalism: Ideology, Policy, and the Crisis in Public Authority* (New York: Norton, 1969).

[23]Mancur Olson, *The Rise and Decline of Nations: Economic Growth, Stagflation, and Social Rigidities* (New Haven: Yale University Press, 1982).

[24]Sidney Lens, *The Military-Industrial Complex* (Philadelphia: Pilgrim, 1970), 12.

[25]Charles W. Kegley, Jr., and Eugene R. Wittkopf, *American Foreign Policy: Pattern and Process,* 5th ed. (New York: St. Martin's, 1996), 302.

[26]"The B-1: When Pentagon, Politicians Join Hands," *U.S. News and World Report,* July 1, 1983, 34. See also Nick Kotz, *Wild Blue Yonder: Money, Politics and the B-1 Bomber* (New York: Pantheon, 1988).

[27]David Skidmore and Valerie M. Hudson, eds., *The Limits of State Authority: Societal Groups and Foreign Policy Formation* (Boulder, Colo.: Westview, 1992), 36–38

[28]James Madison, "Federalist no. 10," in Clinton Rossiter, ed., *The Federalist Papers* (New York: New American Library, 1961), 78.

[29]Theodore J. Lowi and Benjamin Ginsberg, *American Government: Freedom and Power,* 3d ed. (New York: Norton, 1993), 540.

[30]Quoted in Will Friedman, "Presidential Rhetoric, the News Media and the Use of Force in the Post–Cold War Era," paper presented to the Annual Conference of the American Political Science Association, New York, September 1994, 9.

[31]Clayton R. Koppes and Gregory D. Black, *Hollywood Goes to War: How Politics, Profits and Propaganda Shaped World War II Movies* (New York: Free Press, 1987), vii.

[32]John T. Rourke, Ralph G. Carter, and Mark A. Boyer, *Making American Foreign Policy,* 2d ed. (Dubuque, Iowa: Brown and Benchmark, 1996), 362.

[33]"The Propaganda War," *Newsweek,* February 25, 1991, 38.

[34]Jerel A. Rosati, *The Politics of United States Foreign Policy* (New York: Harcourt, Brace, 1993), 507.

[35]Bernard C. Cohen, *The Press and Foreign Policy* (Princeton: Princeton University Press, 1963), cited in Kegley and Wittkopf, *American Foreign Policy,* 310.

[36]See Shanto Iyengar, *Is Anyone Responsible? How Television Frames Political Issues* (Chicago:

University of Chicago Press, 1991); and Shanto Iyengar and Donald R. Kinder, *News That Matters: Television and American Opinion* (Chicago: University of Chicago Press, 1987).

[37]James Aronson, *The Press and the Cold War* (New York: Bobbs Merrill, 1970), chap. 11.

[38]Michael R. Beschloss, *Presidents, Television, and Foreign Crises* (Washington, D.C.: Annenberg Washington Program, 1993).

[39]*New York Times Co. v. United States* (1971), cited in Franck and Glennon, eds., *Foreign Relations and National Security Law,* 863–78.

[40]Walter Lippmann, *Essays in the Public Philosophy* (Boston: Little, Brown, 1955), 20.

[41]Hans J. Morgenthau, *Politics among Nations: The Struggle for Power and Peace* (New York: Knopf, 1955), 20.

[42]Gabriel Almond, *The American People and Foreign Policy* (New York: Harcourt, Brace, 1950), 69.

[43]Frank L. Klingberg, "The Historical Alternation of Moods in American Foreign Policy," *World Politics* 4:2 (January 1952), 239–73.

[44]Lloyd A. Free and Hadley Cantril, *The Political Beliefs of Americans* (New York: Simon and Schuster, 1968), 60.

[45]Kegley and Wittkopf, *American Foreign Policy,* 265.

[46]Gilbert S. Grosvenor, "Superpowers Not So Super in Geography," *National Geographic,* December 1989, 816.

[47]Cited in Miroslav Nincic, *Democracy and Foreign Policy: The Fallacy of Political Realism* (New York: Columbia University Press, 1992), 48.

[48]Benjamin I. Page and Robert Y. Shapiro, "Changes in Americans' Policy Preferences, 1935–1979," *Public Opinion Quarterly* 46:1 (1982), 34.

[49]Andrew F. Krepinevich, Jr., *The Army and Vietnam* (Baltimore: John Hopkins University Press, 1986), 270.

[50]Bruce M. Russett, *Controlling the Sword* (Cambridge, Mass.: Harvard University Press, 1990), chap. 4.

[51]Bruce W. Jentleson, *With Friends Like These: Reagan, Bush and Saddam, 1982–1990* (New York: Norton, 1994), 90–91.

[52]Miroslav Nincic, "The United States, the Soviet Union and the Politics of Opposites," *World Politics* 40:4 (July 1988), 452–75.

[53]Interview by author, July 20 and 22, 1977, published in Bruce W. Jentleson, ed., *Perspectives 1979* (Washington, D.C.: Close Up Foundation, 1979), 273–79.

[54]Robert Putnam, "Diplomacy and Domestic Politics: The Logic of Two-Level Games," *International Organization* 42:3 (Summer 1988), 427–60.

[55]John H. Aldrich, John L. Sullivan, and Eugene Borgida, "Foreign Affairs and Issue Voting: Do Presidential Candidates 'Waltz Before a Blind Audience'?" *American Political Science Review* 83 (March 1989), 123–42.

[56]In the 1952 election, with the Korean War mired in stalemate, the public had much more confidence in the Republican candidate, General Dwight D. Eisenhower, the triumphant World War II commander of U.S. forces in Europe, than in the Democratic candidate, Illinois governor Adlai Stevenson. In the 1972 election, foreign policy was crucial in the Democratic presidential nomination process; Senator George McGovern (D–S.D.) won the nomination largely on the basis of being the candidate most strongly opposed to the Vietnam War. But McGovern lost to President Richard Nixon in the general election. Although the Vietnam War was highly unpopular, McGovern was seen as too "dovish," whereas Nixon countered some of

the sense of his responsibility for the war with announcements in the month before the election that "peace [was] at hand." In the 1980 election, data show that whereas only 38.3 percent of the public could articulate the differences between Jimmy Carter and Ronald Reagan on inflation and unemployment, 63.5 percent could on defense spending and 58.8 percent could on relations with the Soviet Union. Moreover, the taking of American hostages in Iran was for many Americans "a powerful symbol of American weakness and humiliation," and, whether fairly or unfairly, the dominant view was "that an inability to bring the hostages home reflected directly on [Carter's] competence." Samuel L. Popkin, *The Reasoning Voter* (Chicago: University of Chicago Press, 1991), 111.

3
The Historical Context: Great Debates in American Foreign Policy, 1789–1945

Introduction: "The Past Is Prologue"

The words "The past is prologue" are inscribed on the base of the National Archives in Washington, D.C. For all the ways that today's world is new and different, there is much to be learned from history. The particular choices debated for U.S. foreign policy in the twenty-first century clearly differ in many ways from past agendas. But for all the changes, we still wrestle with many of the same core questions of foreign policy strategy and foreign policy politics that have been debated for more than two hundred years of American history.

To provide part of this important historical context, this chapter examines the "great debates" from pre–Cold War history (1789–1945) that are most relevant to U.S. foreign policy in the post–Cold War era. Six of these "great debates" deal with foreign policy strategy:

- the overarching debate over isolationism vs. internationalism, encompassing considerations of power, peace, principles, and posterity;
- power and peace debates over how big a military the United States should have and how much to spend on defense;
- how true U.S. foreign policy has been to its democratic principles;
- whether U.S. foreign policy has been imperialistic (prosperity);
- relations with Latin America as a key case exemplifying the competing tensions among the 4 Ps; and
- U.S. emergence as a Pacific power and its relations with the countries of Asia as another key case.

The National Archives building in Washington, D.C., bears the inscription "The past is pro-logue" at its base (*courtesy the National Archives*).

Three others deal with foreign policy politics:

- recurring "Pennsylvania Avenue diplomacy" struggles between the president and Congress over going to war;
- tensions between considerations of national security and the constitutional guarantees of civil liberties; and
- interest-group pressures and other political battles over free trade vs. protectionism.

Great Debates over Foreign Policy Strategy

Isolationism vs. Internationalism

Should the United States seek to minimize its involvement in world affairs, to "isolate" itself from the rest of the world? Or should it take an active, "internationalist" role? Which strategy would best serve the national interest in all of its 4 Ps components?

Contrary to many traditional historics, the United States never really was fully isolationist. From the very beginning the founders knew that this new nation needed a foreign policy, needed to find foreign support where it could, needed to be able to trade, generally needed to have at least some involvement in the world. Their strategy, though, was to stay out of the "Old World" European rivalries, machinations, and wars. This was what President

At the Source

GEORGE WASHINGTON'S FAREWELL ADDRESS

66 . . . History and experience prove that foreign influence is one of the most baneful foes of republican government. . . . Excessive partiality for one foreign nation and excessive dislike of another cause those whom they actuate to see danger only on one side and serve to veil and even second the arts of influence on the other. . . .

The great rule of conduct for us in regard to foreign nations is, in extending our commercial relations to have as little political connection as possible. So far as we have already formed engagements let them be fulfilled with perfect good faith. Here let us stop.

Europe has a set of primary interests which to us have none or a very remote relation. Hence she must be engaged in frequent controversies, the causes of which are essentially foreign to our concerns. Hence, therefore, it must be unwise for us to implicate ourselves by artificial ties in the ordinary vicissitudes of her politics or the ordinary combinations and collisions of her friendships or enmities.

Our detached and distant situation invites and enables us to pursue a different course. . . . Why forego the advantages of so peculiar a situation? . . . Why, by interweaving our destiny with that of any part of Europe, estrange our peace and prosperity in the toils of European ambition, rivalship, interest, humor or caprice?

It is our true policy to steer clear of permanent alliances with any portion of the foreign world, so far, I mean, as we are at liberty to do it. . . .

Taking care always to keep ourselves to suitable establishments on a respectable defensive posture, we may safely trust to temporary alliances for extraordinary emergencies. . . .

There can be no greater error than to expect or calculate upon real favors from nation to nation. It is an illusion which experience must cure, which a just pride ought to discard. . . . 99

Source: George Washington, "Farewell Address," September 17, 1796, reprinted in *Congressional Record*, 106th Cong., 1st sess., February 22, 1999, p. S1673.

George Washington articulated in his famous 1796 farewell address. "Steer clear of permanent alliances with any portion of the foreign world," he urged the young nation as he left office and handed the reins to President John Adams (see At the Source on p. 76 for extended excerpts). Temporary alliances were fine—Washington knew how important the alliance with France had been to winning the Revolutionary War against Britain. French loans had kept the new nation solvent and French military support was so extensive that at the decisive Battle of Yorktown there actually were more French soldiers than Americans fighting against the British. But the best way for the United States to preserve its own peace, according to its first president, was to avoid getting "entangled" in the affairs of Europe. "Europe has a set of primary interests which to us have none or a very remote relation," Washington stated. Those interests lead its nations to "be engaged in frequent controversies, the causes of which are essentially foreign to our concerns." Moreover, "foreign influence is one of the most baneful foes of republican government," Washington cautioned with regard to the impact on the principles of the nascent American democracy. So the United States should take advantage of its "detached and distant situation" across the Atlantic Ocean, which made it physically possible to avoid such entanglements.

As far as foreign trade was concerned, Washington and his successors pursued it to the extent that it contributed to prosperity, but to develop these commercial relations with as little political connection as possible. In his first inaugural address in 1801, President Thomas Jefferson reaffirmed "entangling alliances with none" while also calling for "peace, commerce and honest friendship with all nations." The goal was to extend commercial relations (prosperity) more than political ones. About 70 percent of the treaties and other international agreements the United States signed in the nineteenth century were on matters related to trade and commerce.[1] Nor did isolationism preclude assertions of U.S. power and interests in its own hemisphere, as through the Monroe Doctrine. What it did mean most essentially, and what the United States did do, was to stay out of the various wars Europe fought in the nineteenth century.

Many view the Spanish-American War of 1898 as marking the beginning of the emergence of the United States as a world power. The Americans won the war, defeating a European power, and for the first time gained a far-flung colony of their own: the Philippines. Theodore Roosevelt, as a "Rough Rider" during the Spanish-American War and as president from 1901 to 1908, embodied the new and more muscular spirit of internationalism. Isolationism was no longer in the national interest, as Roosevelt saw it. "The increasing interdependence and complexity of international political and economic relations," he explained, "render it incumbent on all civilized and orderly powers to insist on the proper policing of the world."[2]

President Woodrow Wilson also was inclined to internationalism, although his emphasis was more on principles than on power. Yet the old tradition of noninvolvement in Europe's wars was still strong enough that when World War I broke out in Europe, the Wilson administration tried to stay out. Even the usually sober *New York Times* editorialized as to how the nations of Europe had "reverted to the condition of savage tribes roaming the forests and falling upon each other in a fury of blood and carnage to achieve the ambitious designs of chieftains clad in skins and drunk with mead."[3] It was only after the threat to U.S. interests became undeniably direct that the futility of trying to stay isolated became evident. When the "Zimmermann telegram," a secret German message to Mexico in early 1917 proposing an alliance against the United States, was intercepted, the United States learned that the Germans were offering to help Mexico "reconquer the lost [Mexican] territory in Texas, New Mexico and Arizona." And German U-boats had opened up unrestricted submarine warfare and sank three U.S. merchant ships. Isolation no longer was possible; the world's war had come home for the United States.

However, immediately after the war, isolationism reasserted itself over what role the United States should play in building the peace. The League of Nations would create a "community of power" and provide a structure of peace, the internationalist President Wilson argued, with the collective security commitment embodied in Article X of the League Covenant destroying "the war-breeding alliance system and the bad old balance of power."[4] No, his isolationist opponents argued, it was precisely this kind of commitment that would obligate the United States to go to war to defend other League members and that would entangle Americans in other countries' problems. This was a time not "to make the world safe for democracy," as Wilson aspired, but for a "return to normalcy," back to the way things were before the war. The isolationists prevailed as the Senate refused to ratify U.S. membership in the League of Nations.

For the next two decades, Congress refused to budge from a strongly isolationist foreign policy. Interestingly, although their specific reasons for being isolationist differed, both the left and the right political wings feared the reverberations at home if the United States went to war again. As World War II brewed in Europe, conservatives such as Robert E. Wood, chairman of Sears, Roebuck and Co. and head of the America First Committee, argued that entry into the war against Hitler would give President Franklin Roosevelt the opportunity to "turn the New Deal into a permanent socialist dictatorship."

3.1

At the other end of the political spectrum, socialists like Norman Thomas feared that war would provide justification for repression that "would bring fascist dictatorship to America."[5] Congress even came very close to passing the "Ludlow amendment," a proposed constitutional amendment that would have required a national referendum before any decision to go to war.

FDR tried taking his case directly to the American people, as with his 1937 "quarantine of aggressor nations" speech:

> The very foundations of civilization are seriously threatened. . . . If those things come to pass in other parts of the world, let no one imagine that America will escape, that it will continue tranquilly and peacefully to carry on. . . . When an epidemic of physical disease starts to spread, the community approves and joins in a quarantine of the patients in order to protect the health of the community against the spread of the disease. . . . The peace-loving nations must make a concerted effort in opposition to those violations of treaties and those ignorings of humane instincts which today are creating a state of international anarchy and instability from which there is no escape through mere isolation or neutrality.

His appeal, however, fell flat. The public still did not see the connection between what was happening "over there" and American interests and security. A public-opinion poll taken the week *after* Hitler invaded Poland in September 1939 showed 94 percent of Americans opposed to declaring war.

In 1940, with FDR running for re-election to an unprecedented third term, even the fall of France to Hitler's armies was not enough to break through the isolationist American politics. With Britain also about to fall, and Prime Minister Winston Churchill urging the United States to provide support, FDR resorted to an "end run" around Congress to provide some support through the famous "destroyers-for-bases deal."*[6]

It wasn't until December 7, 1941, when the Japanese launched a surprise attack on Pearl Harbor, that the politics changed and the United States joined the effort to restore world peace. The full national mobilization that ultimately transpired during World War II stands as a monumental example of what the United States is capable of achieving. Even then, however, FDR worried during the closing months of the war that "anybody who thinks isolationism is dead in this country is crazy. As soon as this war is over, it may well be stronger than

---

*Under this agreement, the U.S. Navy provided the British navy with fifty destroyer warships in exchange for the rights to British military bases in the Western Hemisphere. The "end run" came from the deal's being made as an executive agreement, not requiring any congressional approval.

ever."[7] Indeed, once victory was achieved there was a rapid demobilization, another yearning to "bring the boys home" and get back to normal—only to be confronted by the threats of the Cold War.

Power, Peace: How Big a Military, How Much for Defense?

For the United States to maximize its power and to pursue peace, how big a military is required? How much needs to be spent on defense? These issues, which we know very well from recent debates, have been hotly contested throughout American history.

This is evident even in the Constitution. On the one hand the Constitution provides for the creation of an army and a navy. On the other, it dedicates both the Second Amendment, the right of states to have their own militias, and the Third Amendment, the prohibition on "quartering" of troops in private homes without the owner's permission, to checks on the national military. Nor was much done initially with the constitutional provisions authorizing a standing army and navy. Building more than a few naval frigates was too expensive for the young country. And when in 1790 President Washington proposed a permanent peacetime draft, Congress rejected it.

But the risks of a weak military were quickly made evident. By 1798 the United States was on the verge of war with its former ally and patron, France. President John Adams got Congress to authorize increases in the Army and the Navy, and General George Washington came out of retirement to take command. War was avoided through a combination of successful diplomacy and displays of naval strength. Still, though, the British navy utilized its superiority over the next decade to continually harass American merchant ships with blockades and impressment (seizing) of sailors. Tensions escalated in the 1807 *Chesapeake* affair to an attack on an American naval ship. The sense of vulnerability in these years was expressed by Secretary of the Treasury Albert Gallatin, who warned that the British "could land at Annapolis, march to the city [Washington, D.C.], and re-embark before the militia could be collected to repel [them]."[8] Gallatin's warning proved all too prophetic when, during the War of 1812, the British did march on Washington and burned down much of the capital city, the White House included. To fight the War of 1812 the U.S. Army had to be more than tripled in size from its standing level of about 12,000 troops (see Dynamics of Choice on p. 81). Once the war was over, the Army was rapidly demobilized.

The same pattern of small troop levels, massive mobilization, and rapid demobilization was played out even more dramatically during the Civil War.

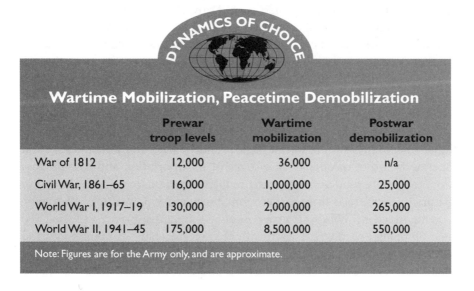

DYNAMICS OF CHOICE

Wartime Mobilization, Peacetime Demobilization

	Prewar troop levels	Wartime mobilization	Postwar demobilization
War of 1812	12,000	36,000	n/a
Civil War, 1861–65	16,000	1,000,000	25,000
World War I, 1917–19	130,000	2,000,000	265,000
World War II, 1941–45	175,000	8,500,000	550,000

Note: Figures are for the Army only, and are approximate.

When the war broke out the Union Army had only about 16,000 troops. President Abraham Lincoln mobilized the state militias and took unilateral action without prior budget approval from Congress to rapidly enlarge both the Army and the Navy. He also instituted the first military draft in U.S. history. Through these and other measures the Union forces grew to almost one million. Then, in the decade following the end of the Civil War in 1865, the Army went back down to 25,000 troops.

In the late nineteenth century the main debate was over building up a larger and more modern Navy. There was general consensus that the Army could be kept small; another direct attack on the United States by Britain or another European power now seemed highly unlikely. The real competition with the Europeans was on the high seas. The greatness of a nation, argued Navy Captain Alfred Thayer Mahan in his seminal book *The Influence of Sea Power upon History* (1890), depends on a strong navy capable not just of its own coastal defense but of command of the seas. Congress was sufficiently persuaded by Mahan and others to fund enough naval construction to make the U.S. Navy the seventh largest in the world by 1893. Yet there also were critics. Some objected to Mahan's naval buildup as draining resources from domestic priorities. Others warned that the new sense of power would make the pull toward the pursuit of empire irresistible.

When World War I came, because of the new Navy buildup, the United States was better prepared on the seas than on land. The United States entered the war with only 130,000 soldiers in its Army. One of the first actions Congress took was passage of the Selective Service Act of 1917, reviving the military draft. At its World War I peak the Army reached over two million soldiers.

Yet President Wilson also realized that "it is not [just] an army that we must shape and train for war, it is a nation—including its economy. Indeed, during World War I Wilson requested and Congress approved powers over the economy that, in the view of noted historians Samuel Eliot Morison and Henry Steele Commager, were "more extensive than those possessed by any other ruler in the Western world."[9] The president was empowered to seize and operate factories, to operate all systems of transportation and communication, to allocate food and fuel, to set industrial production schedules, and to fix prices. To exercise these vast economic regulatory powers for which there was no precedent, Wilson set up a host of new executive-branch agencies. The War Shipping Board was charged with keeping merchant shipping going and with building two ships for each one sunk by German U-boats. The Food Board supervised both food production and consumption, setting rules for "Wheatless Mondays" and "Meatless Tuesdays" to ensure enough food surplus to help feed the allies. The War Industries Board regulated virtually every production and investment decision made by private companies, from the number of automobiles rolling off Henry Ford's assembly lines, to the number of colors on typewriter ribbons (reduced from 150 to 5 to free up carbon and other chemicals for the war effort), to cutting down the length of the upper parts of shoes (to save leather for uniforms and supplies). Wilson was even able to impose new taxes on consumption and to increase existing income, inheritance, and corporate taxes, all with relatively little political opposition.

Yet once the war ended, this vast governmental economic bureaucracy was disbanded, as was the military. The Army came down to 265,000 troops by 1920. As part of the naval arms-control treaties signed at the 1921–22 Washington Naval Conference with the four other major naval powers (Britain, France, Italy, and Japan), the U.S. Navy scrapped, sank, or decommissioned about two million tons of ships, including thirty-one major warships.

The mobilization-demobilization pattern recurred yet again with World War II. The Army started at about 175,000 troops and grew to almost 8,500,000 by 1945. The Navy amassed another 3,400,000 sailors in a fleet of 2,500 warships. President Roosevelt's wartime powers over the economy were even more extensive than his New Deal ones. He created the War Production Board (WPB), which mobilized and allocated industrial facilities and plants; the War Manpower Commission, which had sweeping authority to mobilize labor to meet the WPB's production goals; and the Office of Price Administration, which set prices and rationed goods even for such staples as meat, sugar, tires, and gasoline. The fiats these and other agencies could issue went so far as prohibiting the pleasure driving of automobiles, cutting the production of consumer durable goods by almost 30 percent, imposing wage and price controls, passing major tax increases, and taking other measures deemed necessary for "forging a war economy."[10]

The overall scope of the economic effort involved in World War II dwarfed that of any previous period in American history. The number of civilian employees of the federal government climbed from 1 million to 3.8 million. Annual budget expenditures soared from $9 billion to $98.4 billion. All told, the federal government spent nearly twice as much between 1940 and 1945 as it had in the preceding 150 years. The Manhattan Project, the program that developed the atomic bomb, itself involved expenditures of more than $2 billion, the employment of more than 150,000 people, and the building of new cities in Los Alamos, New Mexico; Oak Ridge, Tennessee; and Hanford, Washington—all with the utmost secrecy, so much so that little was known even by Vice President Harry Truman, let alone Congress.

Once Hitler was defeated and Japan had surrendered, however, the recalculation of how big a military and how much for defense was made anew. By 1948 most of the wartime economic agencies had been dismantled. The Army was down to 550,000 troops. The Navy also was being scaled back. But then the Cold War raised yet again the how big, how much questions for assuring the peace and maintaining U.S. power.

Principles: True to American Democratic Ideals?

The United States often has claimed to be the defender of democracy, a country that defines its national interest very much in terms of principles. But has it been as true to these values historically as it has claimed?

The concept of "American exceptionalism" mentioned in Chapter 1, that the United States has a special role to play in the world, was evoked early on in a poem by David Humphreys, a protégé of George Washington:

All former empires rose, the work of guilt,
On conquest, blood or usurpation built;
But we, taught wisdom by their woes and crimes,
Fraught with their lore, and born to better times;
Our constitutions form'd on freedom's base,
Which all the blessings of all lands embrace;
Embrace humanity's extended cause,
A world of our empire, for a world of our laws . . .[11]

Yes, ours was to be an empire, but it would not be built like the Old World ones on "guilt, . . . conquest, blood or usurpation." It instead would serve "humanity's extended cause."

The same themes were developed further in the mid-nineteenth century in the concept of "manifest destiny." As the term was originally coined in 1845, it referred to the "right" claimed for the United States "to overspread and to possess the whole continent which Providence has given us for the development of the great experiment of liberty and federated self government."[12] The immediate reference was to continental expansion and specific territorial disputes, including the immediate one with Mexico that resulted in the 1846–48 war and the annexation of Texas.

Again, though, this was said not to be just typical self-interested expansionism, but rather based on principles and thus also in the interest of those over whom the United States was expanding, such as Native Americans and Mexicans. Toward the end of the nineteenth century, by which time the United States pretty much had finished its continental territorial expansion, manifest destiny was invoked in a similar spirit as part of the justification for the Spanish-American War and the acquisition of colonies and quasi-colonies in the Pacific and the Caribbean.

For Woodrow Wilson the main reason for fighting World War I was "to make the world safe for democracy." His message to Congress requesting a declaration of war was heavily laden with appeals to principles (see At the Source on p. 85). "Our motive will not be revenge or the victorious assertion of the physical might of the nation," Wilson proclaimed, "but only the vindication of right." And so too was the postwar order to be built on democratic principles and ideals.[13] Many of Wilson's Fourteen Points dealt with self-determination for various central and eastern European peoples and nations that had been subjugated in the Austro-Hungarian and Ottoman (Turkish) empires. Despite some compromises with Britain and France, which had little interest in dismantling their own empires, a "mandate" system was established under the League of Nations that was supposed to begin the process of decolonization in Africa, the Middle East, and Asia.

The case for the values at stake in the war against Hitler and Nazism was about as incontrovertible as is possible. Underlying the political and strategic issues were what FDR called the "Four Freedoms": freedom of religion, freedom of speech, freedom from fear, and freedom from want. The Atlantic Charter, a joint statement by FDR and Churchill even before the United States entered the war (August 1941), pledged to "respect the right of all peoples to choose the form of government under which they will live; and . . . to see

At the Source

MAKING THE WORLD SAFE FOR DEMOCRACY

❝ . . . It is a war against all nations. American ships have been sunk, American lives have been taken, in ways which it has stirred us very deeply to learn of, but the ships and people of other neutral nations have been sunk and overwhelmed in the waters in the same way. There has been no discrimination. The challenge is to all mankind. Each nation must decide for itself how it will meet it. The choice we make for ourselves must be made with a moderation of counsel and a temperateness of judgment befitting our character and our motives as a nation. We must put excited feeling away. Our motive will not be revenge or the physical might of the nation, but only the vindication of right, of human right, of which we are only a single champion. . . .

With a profound sense of the solemn and even tragical character of the step I am taking and of the grave responsibilities which it involves, but in unhesitating obedience to what I deem my constitutional duty, I advise the Congress to declare the recent course of the Imperial German Government to be in fact nothing less than war against the government and people of the United States. . . .

We are accepting this challenge of hostile purpose because we know that in such a government, following such methods, we can never have a friend; and that in the presence of its organized power, always lying in wait to accomplish we know not what purpose, there can be no assured security for the democratic governments of the world. . . . *The world must be made safe for democracy* [emphasis added]. . . .

It is a distressing and oppressive duty, Gentlemen of the Congress, which I have performed in thus addressing you. There are, it may be, many months of fiery trial and sacrifice ahead of us. . . . But the right is more precious than the peace, and we shall fight for the things we have always carried nearest our hearts—for democracy, for the rights and liberties of small nations, for a universal dominion of right by such a concert of free peoples as shall bring peace and safety to all nations and make the world itself at last free. To such a task we can dedicate our lives and our fortunes, everything that we are and everything that we have,

(*Continued on page 86*)

(Making the World Safe for Democracy   *Continued from page 85*)
with the pride of those who know that the day has come when America
is privileged to spend her blood and her might for the principles that
gave her birth and happiness and the peace which she has treasured.
God helping her, she can do no other. "

Source: Woodrow Wilson, "Address to Joint Session of Congress," April 2, 1917, reprinted in Arthur S. Link, ed., *Papers of Woodrow Wilson*, Vol. 41 (Princeton: Princeton University Press, 1966), 519–27.

---

sovereign rights and self-government restored to those who have been forcibly
deprived of them."[14] The latter was a reference to those countries in Europe
overrun by Hitler's Germany. The former was ostensibly about the colonial
world and was something from which Churchill soon backed off, and on
which, although FDR was sincere at the time, with the onset of the Cold War
the United States also did not fully or speedily follow through.

The basis for debate over how true to its principles the United States historically has been is threefold: questions of consistency, of contradictions, and of
cover stories. The question of consistency allows for acknowledgment that
there has been some practicing of what is preached, but less than has been
claimed. We saw this in the Mexican War, in which the U.S. claim to be liberat-
ing Texas was seen quite differently by Mexico. The condemnation by a Mexican leader of "the degenerate sons of Washington" for their "dissimulation,
fraud, and the basest treachery" is a nineteenth-century echo of the "why do
they hate us" question being asked in the twenty-first-century war on terrorism
(see Perspectives, p. 87). Through much of the nineteenth and early twentieth
centuries the United States opposed, not supported, social and political revolutions against undemocratic governments in Latin America. We will see this, for
example, in the discussion later in this chapter of U.S. relations with Latin
America. We can also see it in the case of the Philippines, where after gaining
colonial control 125,000 American troops fought to put down the pro-
independence Filipino forces in what has been called "one of the ugliest wars in
American history," in battles that took a death toll of more than 5,000 Americans and 200,000 Filipinos.[15] The "Manifesto Protesting the United States'
Claim of Sovereignty over the Philippines," issued in 1899 by Emilio Aguinaldo,
leader of the Filipino independence movement, challenges the stated intentions
of the United States in getting involved in the Philippine war in the first place.

PERSPECTIVES
PERSPECTIVES

PERSPECTIVES

THE NINETEENTH-CENTURY "WHY DO THEY HATE US?"

Mexican War, 1846–48

The annexation of the department of Texas to the United States, project-ed and consummated by the tortuous policy of the cabinet of the Union, does not yet satisfy the ambitious desires of the degenerate sons of Wash-ington. The civilized world already has recognized in that act all the marks of injustice, iniquity, and the most scandalous violation of the rights of nations. Indelible is the stain which will forever darken the char-acter for virtue falsely attributed to the people of the United States. . . . To the United States it has been reserved to put into practice dissimulation, fraud and the basest treachery, in order to obtain possession, in the midst of peace, of the territory of a friendly nation, which generously relied upon the faith of promises and the solemnity of treaties.

Mexican general Francisco Mejias

Spanish-American War, 1898, and Philippine War, 1899–1902

It is distinctly stated that the naval and field forces of the United States had come to give us our liberty, by subverting the bad Spanish Govern-ment. And I hereby protest against this unexpected act of the United States claiming sovereignty over these Islands. My relations with the United States did not bring me over here from Hong Kong to make war on the Spaniards for their benefit, but for the purpose of our own liber-ty and independence.

Emilio Aguinaldo

Sources: www.dmwv.org/mexwar/documents/mejia.htm;
www.msc.edu.ph/centennial/ag 990105.html.

Elements of racism found in a number of aspects of U.S. foreign policy also stand in contradiction of the ideals Americans espoused. This racism goes back to the African slave trade and the foreign policy importance given to protecting those trade routes. It also goes to the core of manifest destiny. "White Ameri-cans had not inherited the fabled empty continent," historian Michael Hunt writes with reference to what happened to Native Americans. "Rather, by their presence and policies, they had emptied it."[16] Similarly, the Mexican War was "fought with clear racial overtones."[17] These racial attitudes were captured by the poet James Russell Lowell: "Mexicans wor'nt human beans," just "the sort o'folks a chap could kill an' never dream on't after."[18] In another example, even if one were to concede a degree of benevolence in the paternalism, a sense of racial superiority was undeniable in President William McKinley's justification for making the Philippines a U.S. colony because "we could not leave [the Filipinos] to themselves—they were unfit for self-government, and they would soon have anarchy over there worse than Spain's was . . . [so] there was nothing left for us to do but take them all, and to educate the Filipinos and uplift and civilize them as our fellow-men."[19]

In addition, there have been times when principles have been less a genuine driving force than something of a cover story for other objectives. This was the case, for example, with Panama and the Panama Canal in the early years of the twentieth century. Up until then Panama had been a rebellious province of Colombia. And up until then U.S. efforts to acquire the rights to build a canal across the Panamanian isthmus had been stymied by the unwillingness of the Colombian government to agree to the terms the United States demanded. So although President Theodore Roosevelt could cite the historical basis for Panama's claim to independence, the landing of U.S. troops to support the revolt had far more to do with the willingness of the Panamanian leaders to make a deal for a canal. Less than a month after Panama had declared its independence, Teddy Roosevelt had a treaty with terms even more favorable to the United States than the one the Colombian legislature had rejected the year before.

Prosperity: U.S. Imperialism?

Those who see U.S. foreign policy as historically imperialistic focus particularly on the late nineteenth and early twentieth centuries. An 1898 editorial from the *Washington Post* evoked—indeed, lauded—the temper of the times:

> A new consciousness seems to have come upon us—the consciousness of strength—and with it a new appetite, the yearning to show our strength. . . . Ambition, interest, land hunger, pride, the mere joy of fighting, whatever it may be, we are animated by a new sensation. . . . The taste of Empire is in the mouth of the people. . . . It means an Imperial policy, the Republic, renascent, taking her place with the armed nations.[20]

One gets a different view, however, from Mark Twain's parody of the "Battle Hymn of the Republic":

Mine eyes have seen the orgy of the launching of the sword;
He is searching out the hoardings where the strangers' wealth is stored;
He has loosed his fateful lightning, and with woe and death has scored;
His lust is marching on.[21]

Consistent with theories of Imperialism as examined in Chapter 1, the growing U.S. interest in foreign markets was in part a consequence of the severe economic crises of this period (there were depressions in 1873–78 and 1893–97),
which set off the problems of underconsumption and overproduction. "We have
advanced in manufactures, as in agriculture," Secretary of State William M. Evans
stated in 1880, "until we are being forced outward by the irresistible pressure of
our internal development." The United States needed new markets or, as an economist of the day warned, "we are certain to be smothered in our own grease."[22]

Those new markets were sought out principally in Latin America. U.S. exports to Latin America increased more than 150 percent between 1900 and
1914. Investments in plantations, mining, manufacturing, banking, and other
industries shot up at an even faster pace. And the flag seemed to be following
the dollar. As shown by the map on p. 90, during this era the United States
launched numerous military interventions in Latin America. In many instances these actions clearly were taken in defense of the foreign investments
and other economic interests of American corporations and financiers. By
1913, for example, the United Fruit Company (UFCO) owned more than
130,000 acres of plantations (bananas and other fruits) in Central America—
and it was in significant part to defend the economic interests of the UFCO
that the U.S. Marines went into Nicaragua (1909–10, 1912–25) and Honduras
(1924–25). So too with other American corporations and the military interventions in Haiti (1915–34) and the Dominican Republic (1916–24).

In Cuba, "liberated" from Spain in the Spanish-American War only to be
put under U.S. neocolonial domination, the pattern was even more pronounced. While formally allowing Cuba independence, the United States insisted that the "Platt Amendment" be attached to the Cuban constitution,
granting the United States the right to intervene to, among other things, protect the property of U.S. corporations.* And so the Marines did on a number
of occasions. The Platt Amendment also gave the United States the power to

---

*This amendment was named for its principal congressional sponsor, U.S. Senator Orville Platt.
This was not, however, a case of Congress imposing something the executive branch didn't
want. Secretary of War Elihu Root worked closely with Senator Platt in writing the amendment.
Thomas G. Paterson, J. Gary Clifford, and Kenneth J. Hagan, *American Foreign Relations: A History to 1920*, Vol. 1 (Lexington, Mass.: D. C. Heath, 1995), 254–55.

U.S. Military Interventions in Latin America, Early Twentieth Century

Texas

Gulf of Mexico

Florida

Cuba
1898–1902
1906–9
1912
1917–1922

Dominican Republic
1916–24

Atlantic Ocean

Mexico
1914
1916–17

Belize

Guatemala
El Salvador

Caribbean Sea

Haiti
1915–34

Honduras
1924–25

Costa Rica

V e n e z u e l a

Guyana
Suriname

Nicaragua
1909–10
1912–25
1926–33

Panama
1903 (Canal
Zone acquired)

C o l o m b i a

B r a z i l

Ecuador

P a c i f i c   O c e a n

P e r u

Source: Adapted from Thomas G. Paterson, J. Gary Clifford, and Kenneth J. Hagan, *American Foreign Relations: A History since 1895*, Vol. 2, 4th ed. (Lexington, Mass.: D. C. Heath, 1995), 55.

veto treaties between Cuba and other governments, as another way of giving U.S. interests special status. These measures made conditions as conducive as possible for American business: U.S. investments in Cuba increased from $50 million in 1896 to $220 million in 1913, and Cuban exports to the United States grew from $31 million in 1900 to $722 million in 1920.[23]

The other side of the debate, questioning the Imperialist analysis, makes two principal arguments. One is based on counterexamples that are said to show that U.S. foreign policy has not consistently been geared to the defense of American capitalist interests. One such example is from early in the Mexican Revolution, when Woodrow Wilson refused to recognize the military government of General Victoriano Huerta despite pressures from U.S. corporations with some $1.5 billion in Mexican investments. "I . . . am not the servant of those who wish to enhance the value of their Mexican investments," Wilson declared.[24]

The other argument is based on alternative explanations. This argument doesn't deny that American foreign policy has had its expansionist dimension but attributes it less to prosperity than to other factors, such as power and principles. For example, a power-based alternative explanation of the U.S. military interventions in Latin America accepts that capitalist interests were well served, but emphasizes political and military factors as the driving forces. Similarly, although no question is raised that the Panama Canal had economic value, some would argue that what really was motivating Teddy Roosevelt was linking up the Atlantic and Pacific fleets of the U.S. Navy, and the confirmation of U.S. status as an emerging global power.

Key Case: U.S. Relations with Latin America—Good Neighbor or Regional Hegemon?

U.S. relations with Latin America, mentioned a number of times already, warrant special focus as a historical case providing numerous examples of the competing tensions among the 4 Ps. As the richest and most powerful country in the Western Hemisphere, was the United States to be the regional hegemon—the dominant country lording over its sphere of influence—exerting its power largely as it saw fit, managing hemispheric peace but on its own terms, and dominating economically for the sake of its own prosperity? Or was the United States to be the good neighbor, true to its principles, a benefactor for those in its hemispheric neighborhood who had less and were less powerful, promoting democracy and acting respectfully of their equal rights and privileges as sovereign nations?

For the most part the United States has played the role of regional hegemon. This role goes back to the Monroe Doctrine and its warning to the European powers not to seek to recolonize or in other ways to "extend their system to any position of this hemisphere" (see At the Source on p. 92). Initially, some Latin American countries saw this very positively, as a U.S. pledge to help them maintain their independence, and even proposed "that the Doctrine be transformed into a binding inter-American alliance." But "[Secretary of State John Quincy] Adams said no. He emphasized that the Doctrine was a unilateral American statement and that any action taken under it would be for the United States alone to decide."[25] There was little altruism in this policy,

At the Source

THE MONROE DOCTRINE (1823) AND
THE ROOSEVELT COROLLARY (1904)

Monroe Doctrine

66 . . . The American continents, by the free and independent condition which they have assumed and maintained, are henceforth not to be considered as subjects for future colonization by any European powers. . . .

In the wars of the European powers in matters relating to themselves, we have never taken any part, not does it comport with our policy so to do. It is only when our rights are invaded or seriously menaced that we resent injuries or make preparations for our defense. With the movements in this hemisphere, we are of necessity more immediately connected, and by causes which must be obvious to all enlightened and impartial observers. . . .

We should consider any attempt on [the Europeans'] part to extend their system to any portion of this hemisphere as dangerous to our peace and safety. With the existing colonies or dependencies of any European power, we have not interfered and shall not interfere. But with the Governments who have declared their independence and maintained it, and whose independence we have, on great consideration and on just principles acknowledged, we could not view any interposition for the purpose of oppressing them, or controlling in any other manner their destiny, by any European power in any other light than as the manifestations of an unfriendly disposition toward the United States. 99

Roosevelt Corollary

66 It is not true that the United States feels any land hunger or entertains any projects as regards the other nations of the Western Hemisphere save such as are for their welfare. All that this country desires is to see the neighboring countries stable, orderly and prosperous. Any country whose people conduct themselves well can count upon our hearty friendship. If a nation shows that it knows how to act with reasonable sufficiency and decency in social and political matters, if it keeps order

(*Continued on page 93*)

(The Monroe Doctrine *Continued from page 92)*

and pays its obligations, it need fear no interference from the United States. Chronic wrongdoing, or an impotence which results in the general loosening of the ties of civilized society, may in America, as elsewhere, ultimately require intervention by some civilized nation, and in the Western Hemisphere the adherence of the United States to the Monroe Doctrine may force the United States, however reluctantly, in flagrant cases of such wrongdoing or impotence, to the exercise of an international police power. . . .

It is a mere truism to say that every nation, whether in America or anywhere else, which desires to maintain its freedom, its independence, must ultimately realize that the right of such independence can not be separated from the responsibility of making good use of it. . . . ”

Sources: James Monroe, "Seventh Annual Message," December 2, 1823, *The Writings of James Monroe*, Vol. 6, ed. Stanislaus Murray Hamilton (New York: G. P. Putnam, 1912), 325–42; Theodore Roosevelt, "Fourth Annual Message," December 16, 1904, *A Compilation of the Messages and Papers of the Presidents*, Vol. 14 (New York: Bureau of National Literature, 1923), 6894–930.

or even straightforward good neighborliness; it represented much more the self-interest of a regional power seeking to preserve its dominant position against outside challenges.

For the rest of the nineteenth century there were quite a few outside challenges from the European powers. Britain and the United States contested in the 1840s and 1850s for rights to build a transisthmian canal across Central America. In a particularly bold episode, amid the American Civil War, France sought to install its own handpicked nobleman, Archduke Ferdinand Maximilian, as Napoleon III, emperor of Mexico. The Spanish-American War was in significant part about getting Spain not only out of Cuba but totally out of the hemisphere. Yet the U.S. support for Cuba's effort to end Spain's colonial rule was one thing, support for genuine Cuban independence quite another. U.S. troops stayed in Cuba for four years after the war (1898–1902) and then, as noted earlier, reintervened repeatedly in 1906–9, 1912, and 1917–22. And then there was the Platt Amendment—what clearer manifestation of hegemony could there be than writing oneself into another country's constitution?

In 1904 President Theodore Roosevelt pronounced his "corollary" to the Monroe Doctrine (see At the Source on p. 92). The "Roosevelt Corollary" claimed for the United States the "international police power" to intervene when instability within a Latin American country risked creating the pretext (e.g., to collect debts or protect property) for an Old World power to intervene. This policy became the basis for a bevy of interventions and extended military occupations in Cuba, the Dominican Republic, Haiti, Mexico, and Nicaragua. U.S. troops stayed in Haiti for almost twenty years, and in Cuba and Nicaragua on and off for twenty-five.

President Franklin Roosevelt sought to pursue a much different approach to Latin America than had his cousin Theodore and most of his other predecessors. A few years before becoming president, FDR had written an article in *Foreign Affairs* quite critical of U.S. interventionism in Latin America. "Never before in our history," he wrote, "have we had fewer friends in the Western Hemisphere than we have today. . . . The time has come when we must accept not only certain facts but many new principles of a higher law, a newer and better standard in international relations. . . . [N]either from the argument of financial gain, nor from the sound reasoning of the Golden Rule, can our policy, or lack of policy, be approved."[26] We want to be "the good neighbor," FDR proclaimed once elected, "the neighbor who resolutely respects himself and because he does so, respects the rights of others—the neighbor who respects the sanctity of his agreements in and with a world of neighbors."[27] As part of this new approach FDR repealed the Platt Amendment, withdrew the Marines from Nicaragua and Haiti, settled a long-standing oil dispute with Mexico, signed bilateral trade treaties as well as treaties of nonaggression and conciliation with a number of Latin American countries, and became the first U.S. president to visit South America. As World War II approached FDR also struck a number of mutual security deals, including affirming a Monroe Doctrine–like commitment at the 1938 Pan-American Conference to resist any foreign intervention in the hemisphere.

Regional hegemon or good neighbor? Not only did the historical record feed this debate, but as we will see in the next chapter, the onset of the Cold War made it even more controversial.

Key Case: The United States as a Pacific Power

Trade and commerce (prosperity) first took the United States across the Pacific to Asia. In the 1840s American ships were sailing to China with cotton and returning with tea. The Treaty of Wangxia, the first trade treaty with China, was signed in 1844. Close to a decade later (1853) Commodore Matthew C. Perry sailed into Tokyo Harbor and "opened up" Japan. "Our steamships can go from California to Japan in eighteen days," President Millard Fillmore stated in the letter delivered to Japanese rulers by Commodore Perry. "I am delighted that our two countries should trade with each other, for the benefit both of Japan and the United States."[28]

But it was never really just trade and commerce (prosperity) that the United States was after. America's sense of moral mission (principles) also was at work. Interestingly, it cut both ways. On the one hand was the U.S. desire to liberalize and democratize these societies. "The thirty millions of Japan," wrote one author at the time of Commodore Perry's expedition, "await the key of the western Democrat to open their prison to the sun-light of social interchange."[29] On the other hand was fear and animosity toward the Orient and its culture, the view that "there were in conflict two great types of civilization, . . . Eastern and Western, inferior and superior."[30]

The power motivation was also at work. Historian Thomas Paterson and his colleagues describe it thus: "Perry saw his Japanese expedition as but one step toward a U.S. empire in the Pacific. . . . Eventually, the commodore prophesied, the American people would 'extend their dominion and their power, until they shall have brought within their mighty embrace the Islands of the great Pacific, and place the Saxon race upon the eastern shores of Asia.'"[31] Asia was yet another region for competition with the Europeans, who had the advantage of colonies and experience but who lacked the U.S. geographic advantage of being a Pacific as well as an Atlantic country. Hawaii, Samoa, and other Pacific island territories were acquired by the United States in an effort to further develop that advantage, as later was the Philippines. The United States also began maintaining a military presence in the region, thanks to Captain Mahan's "new Navy." The Open Door policy of the 1890s, contrary to self-justifying claims of being intended to help China against the encroachments of European colonialism, actually was a self-interested demand made on the major European powers that the United States not be closed out of spheres of trade and influence in China.

At the same time that the United States was extending its influence in Asia and the Pacific, so too was Japan. As but one example of the emerging rivalry, Japan initially refused to recognize the U.S. annexation of Hawaii, asserting its own claim based on the larger number of immigrants to Hawaii from Japan than from any other country. The antagonisms subsided somewhat when, in 1904 at the invitation of the Japanese government, President Theodore Roosevelt successfully mediated an end to the Russo-Japanese

War.* Yet when the Japanese didn't get everything they wanted and for reasons of domestic politics and national honor blamed Roosevelt, the first anti-American demonstrations in Japanese history broke out. Relations improved sufficiently by 1908 for the Root-Takahira Agreement to be signed, mutually recognizing the status quo in the Asia-Pacific region.

By World War I suspicions and tensions over commercial competition and naval rivalry again were running high. The wartime alliance against Germany superseded these tensions for a while, and the Washington Naval Conference of 1921–22 worked out naval arms-control agreements (also involving the European powers). But political forces at home were making Japan increasingly militaristic and expansionist. In 1931 it took the bold and provocative step of invading Manchuria, against which neither the United States nor the League of Nations responded effectively. U.S.-Japanese tensions mounted over the rest of the 1930s, culminating on December 7, 1941, in the attack on Pearl Harbor.

U.S. relations with China went through even more extreme fluctuations as China began what would become more than a half-century of revolution. The Chinese revolution in its various stages would be antiforeigner, prodemocracy, anti–indigenous warlords, anti–Japanese occupation, and Marxist. The United States had to grapple with how best to defend American interests and stand up for American ideals as its relationship with China shifted from friendship and even emulation to antipathy. In 1921 Nationalist pro-republic revolutionary leader Sun Yat-sen appealed for assistance to the United States as "the champion of liberalism and righteousness, whose disinterested friendship and support of China in her hour of distress has been demonstrated to us more than once." Three years later, though, Sun expressed his disappointment not only in how little support had come, but in the United States's having joined with other foreign powers in yet another intervention in China over an economic dispute. "We might well have expected that an American Lafayette would fight on our side in this good cause. In the twelfth year of our struggle towards liberty there comes not a Lafayette but an American Admiral with more ships of war than any other nation in our waters."[32] The Nationalists soon thereafter struck their alliance with the Communists of Mao Zedong. This alliance was short-lived and gave way to renewed civil war. But although the United States resumed its friendship with the Nationalists in 1928, the

*For his efforts Roosevelt was awarded the 1905 Nobel Peace Prize; he was the first American president to win that esteemed recognition.

1931 invasion of Manchuria by Japan made the limits of this support abundantly clear.

Thus by the time World War II broke out, American interests in Asia and the Pacific had been developing for close to a century.

Great Debates in Foreign Policy Politics

Going to War

Americans have a tendency to think that it has only been since the trauma of the Vietnam War that political controversy and uncertainty have existed on whether to go to war. Yet as we discussed in Chapter 2, no domain better fits the "invitation to struggle" characterization of the foreign policy provisions of the Constitution than war powers. A closer look at the historical record shows that decisions on going to war rarely have come easily or readily; time and again they have been the subject of intense political debate, in early versions of the contentious Pennsylvania Avenue diplomacy between the president and Congress.

In the War of 1812, for example, it took almost three weeks after President James Madison's request for a declaration of war for Congress to approve it. Even then the votes were far from unanimous—79 to 49 in the House, 19 to 13 in the Senate—and closely followed party and regional lines. Opposition in the New England states was so strong that state leaders initially withheld both money and troops. Although myths later developed about the war being "a glorious triumph," the historian Donald Hickey takes the view that "Mr. Madison's war" was "a futile and costly struggle in which the United States had barely escaped dismemberment and disunion." Hickey also quotes Thomas Jefferson that the War of 1812 "arrested the course of the most remarkable tide of prosperity any nation ever experienced."[33]

Controversy and interbranch maneuvering characterized the politics that led up to the Mexican War of 1846–48. The key issue in this war was the annexation of Texas, the "lone star republic," which in 1836 had declared its independence from Mexico. In the 1840s, knowing that Congress was divided on the issue and thus was not likely to authorize a troop commitment to defend the annexation against the Mexicans, President John Tyler sought to make war secretly. Word leaked, however, prompting Senator Thomas Hart Benton, a leading politician of the day, to denounce President Tyler's actions as "a crime against God and man and our own Constitution . . . a piece of business which belonged to Congress and should have been referred to them." President Tyler next tried the treaty route, proposing a treaty of annexation to the Senate. But the ratification vote in the Senate fell short of the two-thirds margin needed. Tyler then pulled a deft legislative maneuver by which he reintroduced the annexation proposal in the form of a joint resolution. A joint resolution must be approved by both the House and the Senate but requires only a majority vote in each house. Although denounced as "an undisguised usurpation of power and violation of the Constitution," it worked—Texas was annexed as the twenty-eighth state.[34]

Mexico responded by breaking off diplomatic relations with the United States. New president James K. Polk, Jr., who had defeated Tyler in the 1844 elections, "stampeded Congress" into a declaration of war by sending American troops into an area of disputed land where "Mexican units who, operating no doubt on their own theory of defensive war, supposed themselves repelling an invasion of Mexico." Many in Congress "had the uneasy feeling that the President had put something over on them."[35] But political considerations then were no different than today: when forced to vote one way or the other, elected representatives were reluctant to go on record against declaring war on a country whose troops, however provoked, had fired on American troops.

Among those who had that uneasy feeling was a first-term representative from Illinois named Abraham Lincoln. "Allow the President to invade a neighboring nation, whenever he shall deem it necessary," Representative Lincoln wrote at the time, "and you allow him to make war at [his] pleasure. Study to see if you fix *any limit* to his power in this respect."[36] Many a member of Congress would invoke Lincoln's views a century and a quarter later in the context of the Vietnam War.

The Spanish-American War of 1898 did begin with quite a bit of fervor, especially among expansionists in Congress and as whipped up by the "yellow journalism" of newspaper tycoon William Randolph Hearst. The main precipitating incident was the bombing of the battleship U.S.S. *Maine,* allegedly by Spain, killing 266 Americans in Havana Harbor. Spurred by rallying cries like "Remember the *Maine,* To Hell with Spain," Congress declared war and thousands of young men enlisted in what was dubbed "a splendid little war." But although it took only four months of fighting before Spain sued for peace, the death toll was much heavier than expected. For many this was no more "splendid" than other wars, as movingly conveyed in the letter to the editor of the *San Francisco Examiner* from the widow of a fallen soldier, excerpted in Perspectives on p. 99.

PERSPECTIVES
PERSPECTIVES
PERSPECTIVES

ANTIWAR SENTIMENT IN THE SPANISH-AMERICAN WAR

Among those killed in the Spanish-American War was Captain William "Bucky" O'Neill, the mayor of Prescott in the then-territory of Arizona. Mayor O'Neill had been hailed in a newspaper of the day as "the most many-sided man Arizona had produced." He had left to join Teddy Roosevelt's fabled "Rough Riders" and was killed in the battle for Kettle Hill, outside Santiago, Cuba. The sentiments expressed by his wife, Pauline O'Neill, reflected the deep disillusionment shared by many from what turned out to be not so "splendid" a war:

You men who clamored for war, did you know what it would mean to the women of our country, when strife and bloodshed should sweep o'er the land; when the shouts of victory would but ineffectually drown the moans of the women who mourned for the lives of those that were given to make that victory possible? . . .

To you who will celebrate our nation's success, when your spirits are raised in triumph and your songs of thanksgiving are the loudest, remember that we, who sit and weep in our closed and darkened homes, have given our best gifts to our country and our flag.

Patriotism, how many hearts are broken in thy cause?

Source: Pauline O'Neill, letter published in the *San Francisco Examiner*, August 7, 1898, in the collection of the Sharlott Hall Museum, Prescott, Arizona.

As we saw earlier in this chapter, U.S. entry into World War I came almost three years after the war had started, and only after German U-boats and other direct threats to U.S. security drove home the point that isolationism no longer was possible. Germany, as President Wilson made the case, had "thrust" war upon the United States. In this context of a clear and present danger the vote in Congress for approval of a declaration of war was by wide margins, 82 to 6 in the Senate and 373 to 50 in the House. The country pulled together, enlisting in droves under the rallying cry "Johnny Get Your Gun" and doing whatever was necessary for the war effort. Yet what was supposed to be "the war to end all wars" proved not to be so. More people died in this war than had in all the wars of all the world over the preceding century. The American death toll was 116,516, with more than twice that many wounded.

No wonder the pattern of going to war reluctantly repeated itself in World War II. It was only after the direct attack by Japan on Pearl Harbor—a day of "infamy," as FDR called it—that the United States entered a war that already had been raging for more than two years in Europe and even longer than that in Asia. Some historians, noting that the initial declaration of war passed by Congress was only against Japan, still wonder whether the United States would have gone to war against Germany had not Hitler declared war against it a few days later.

Americans came to know World War II as "the Good War," in author Studs Terkel's phrase. But the "Good War" took a heavy toll, including more than one million American soldiers killed or wounded. The belief in the justness and righteousness of the cause against Hitler and Nazism and against Japanese aggression—of peace, power, principles, and prosperity all being at stake—kept public support solid despite such high casualties. Compared with earlier wars and with later wars, however, this was very much the historical exception.

National Security vs. the Bill of Rights

Another major recurring foreign policy politics debate has been over the tension between the demands and exigencies of safeguarding the nation's security, and the guarantees of individual rights and civil liberties ensconced in the Bill of Rights. "Perhaps it is a universal truth," James Madison wrote in a letter to Thomas Jefferson in 1798, "that the loss of liberty at home is to be charged to provisions against danger, real or pretended, from abroad."[37] How far can the justification of national security be taken, even with respect to what Madison meant by "real" danger from abroad, let alone as a rationale for "pretended" ones?

Madison himself fought bitterly against the repressive Alien and Sedition Acts passed by Congress and signed by President John Adams in 1798. On their face these laws were protection against subversive activities by the French and their sympathizers at a time when the United States and France were on the verge of war. But in reality they were intended to silence the opponents of war—the leaders of whom were none other than Madison and Jefferson—by limiting their freedom of speech and of the press. The acts represented a "loss of liberty" in the name of a "danger from abroad" which, while not fully "pretended," also was not as real as it was made out to be.

In the name of saving the Union, over the course of the Civil War, President Lincoln took a number of actions that infringed on the Bill of Rights and other civil liberties. He suspended *habeas corpus* and claimed authority to arrest without warrant persons suspected of "disloyal" practices. He banned "treasonable" correspondence from being delivered by the U.S. Postal Service. He censored newspapers. He seized property. He proclaimed martial law. To those who criticized such actions as going too far, Lincoln responded that "measures otherwise unconstitutional might become lawful by becoming indispensable to the preservation of the Constitution through the preservation of the Nation." Yet he also stressed that these must be temporary powers. "The Executive power itself would be greatly diminished," he stated in 1864, "by the cessation of actual war."[38]

The Espionage and Sedition Acts of 1917–18, passed during World War I, were "as extreme as any legislation of the kind anywhere in the world." They made it illegal to "willfully utter, print, write or publish any disloyal, profane, scurrilous or abusive language about the United States, its form of government, the Constitution, soldiers and sailors, the flag or uniform of the armed forces . . . or by word or act oppose the cause of the United States."[39] Quite the broad prohibition! Ads were placed in the *Saturday Evening Post* and other mass-circulation magazines urging readers to report to the government "the man who spreads pessimistic stories . . . cries for peace or belittles our effort to win the war."[40] The postmaster general refused to deliver any magazine that included critical views. Schools dropped German from their curricula. German books were taken off the shelves of public libraries. Some cities banned dachshunds from their streets. Restaurants and snack bars stopped serving sauerkraut and started calling hamburgers "liberty steaks." All told, about 2,000 people were prosecuted and 800 convicted of violations of the Espionage and Sedition Acts. The most prominent was Eugene V. Debs, leader of the Socialist Party, who as a candidate for president in 1912 had received about 6 percent of the vote. Debs was given a twenty-year prison sentence for giving a speech against the war—and while still in prison during the 1920 presidential election received nearly one million votes!

Supreme Court justices Oliver Wendell Holmes and Louis Brandeis, two of the giants in the Court's history, wrestled with this balance between national security and civil liberties. Justice Holmes defended the constitutionality of the Espionage and Sedition Acts with a famous analogy: "The most stringent protection of free speech," Holmes wrote, "would not protect a man in falsely shouting 'fire' in a theater and causing a panic." Holmes argued that the same general principle applied but the key was to determine in any particular instance "whether the words are used in such circumstance and are of such a nature as to create a clear and present danger that they will bring about the substantive evils that Congress has a right to prevent." Something that might not meet the "clear and present danger" test in times of peace may meet it in times of war: "When a nation is at war many things that might be said in time of peace are such a hindrance to its effort that their utterance will not be endured so long as men fight." Justice Brandeis concurred in his opinion but expressed concerns that the clear and present danger test was too easy to pass. In one case in which a man was convicted for distributing pro-German press reports, Brandeis criticized what he saw as "an intolerant majority, swayed by passion or by fear, . . . prone . . . to stamp as disloyal opinions with which it disagrees." Holmes and Brandeis, however, were in the minority in qualifying their approval of the Acts with these concerns.[41]

World War I ended and the German enemy was defeated, but a new enemy had arisen with the 1917 Communist revolution in Russia. The "Red Scare" of 1919–20 was a period in which the Wilson administration, led by Attorney General A. Mitchell Palmer, grossly overreacted to fears of internal subversion linked to "world communism" with heavy-handed repression and blatant disregard for civil liberties. "The blaze of revolution," Palmer propounded, was "eating its way into the home of the American workman, its sharp tongues of revolutionary heat . . . licking the altars of churches, leaping into the belfry of the school bell, crawling into the sacred corners of American homes, burning up the foundations of society."[42] Claiming the wartime Sedition Act as authority, on the night of January 2, 1920, Palmer sent his agents sweeping into meeting halls, offices, and homes all over the country, arresting about 4,000 people as alleged communists, many even without warrants. The "Palmer raids" were so extreme that Congress almost impeached the attorney general. But it didn't, and he kept up his anticommunist attacks. The Supreme Court largely supported these policies, although with strong dissents from Justice Brandeis. As his biographer recounts, Brandeis felt that restrictions on civil liberties made necessary by war "would be entirely inappropriate in peace . . . when the nation's survival was not at stake. . . . [D]uring a war 'all bets are off'. But not otherwise."[43]

Perhaps the most profound violation of civil liberties in the name of national security came during World War II with the internment of 120,000 Japanese Americans in prison camps. On February 19, 1942, about three months after the Japanese attack on Pearl Harbor, President Franklin Roosevelt issued Executive Order 9066, uprooting people of Japanese ethnicity from their homes, jobs, and communities and banishing them to fenced-in prison camps, in the name of the war effort. "A Jap's a Jap!" proclaimed one general. "It makes no difference whether he's an American or not." In reality, though, not only were the vast majority of Japanese Americans loyal and patriotic citizens of the United States, once they were allowed in 1943 to join the military more than 17,000 Japanese Americans volunteered. "Even though my older brother was living in Japan," one Japanese American stated, "I told my parents that I was going to enlist because America was my country."[44] One unit, the Japanese-American 442nd Regimental Combat Team, fought with such valor as to amass more than 18,000 individual decorations, more than any other unit of its size and duration.[45]

At the time of the Japanese-American internments, but a few voices were raised in protest in government, the media, or society at large. The Supreme Court even ruled that FDR's executive order was constitutional.[46] Not until more than thirty years later was a law passed as an official apology, providing monetary compensation to those Japanese Americans who had been interned and to their families. Although this was an important act of repentance and retribution, it hardly made up for the thousands of lives damaged and destroyed. The Bill of Rights was trampled insofar as it pertained to Japanese Americans, in the name of national security.

Thus, repeatedly, tensions have arisen between considerations of national security and fundamental guarantees provided in the Bill of Rights. Repeatedly, the latter have been overtaken by the former. And, repeatedly, the criticisms and outrage that later followed were quite severe. Yet, as we will see in the next chapter, the pattern was repeated during the Cold War, and as we will see in Chapter 7, has risen again in the context of the war on terrorism.

Free Trade vs. Protectionism

A member of Congress from Detroit smashing a Toyota with a sledgehammer in a photo opportunity in front of the Capitol dome; Ross Perot warning of the "giant sucking sound" that passage of NAFTA (the North American Free Trade Agreement) would set off: recent years have been full of controversies over trade and other international economic policies. But although it is true that this recent discord contrasts with the prevailing pro–free trade consensus of 1945–71, most of the rest of American history has had extensive interest-group pressure and other political conflict over free trade vs. protectionism.

In the first half of the nineteenth century, divisions over the tariff issue largely followed regional lines. Northern industrialists seeking protection from foreign competition for their "infant industries" and Northern and Western farmers who produced primarily for the domestic market favored high tariffs on imported goods. Northeastern merchants, whose economic interests lay in import and export businesses, and Southern plantation owners, whose cotton and tobacco crops were in high demand in Europe, favored low tariffs in order to facilitate international trade. Indeed, while slavery clearly was the most contentious issue, the Civil War also was fed by these fundamental differences over trade policy.

In the late nineteenth century not only was the tariff the primary foreign policy issue of the day, tariff policies were one of the defining differences between the Democratic and Republican parties. In those days the Democrats were predominately in support of free trade, and the Republicans were so protectionist as to proclaim high tariffs as one of the "plain and natural rights of Americans."[47] When President Grover Cleveland, a Democrat, managed to get a tariff reduction bill through the House, the Republican-controlled Senate killed it. The Republicans rode their protectionist position to a major victory in the 1888 elections, with Benjamin Harrison defeating Cleveland for president and Republicans winning majorities in both the House and the Senate.

Yet the Republican-controlled Congress and the new Republican president also fought over trade issues. They did agree on higher tariffs and passed these in the McKinley Tariff Act (named for William McKinley, then-chair of the House Ways and Means Committee). The most significant battle centered on the Harrison administration's proposal for authority to negotiate reciprocity treaties. A reciprocity treaty involves an agreement with another country for mutual reductions in tariffs. The Senate was willing to go along with this since it still would be a player through its treaty-ratification authority. But the House, which has no constitutional authority over treaties, was concerned about being left out of the ball game. It took extensive negotiations—seven days of Republican party caucuses, according to the leading historian of the period—to get the House to agree even to a compromise version.[48]

Politics in those days was extremely volatile. Democrats took control of both the House and the Senate in the 1890 midterm elections, and Grover Cleveland won back the White House in 1892, becoming the only president ever to win two nonconsecutive terms. Since Democratic victories were in large part attributable to the political pendulum having swung back toward antitariff sentiment, President Cleveland made major tariff reductions one of his highest priorities. But with special interests exerting extensive pressure, by the time his antitariff bill passed the Senate it had 634 amendments. It still reduced tariffs, but by much less than the president had wanted.

In 1896, in yet another swing of the political pendulum, Republican William McKinley was elected president and the Republicans regained control of Congress. Ironically, President McKinley now pushed for an even greater congressional delegation of authority to negotiate trade treaties than that which Representative McKinley had opposed as inimical to the Constitution. McKinley won the authority, but although he and his successors would use this authority to negotiate eleven trade treaties over the next decade, not a single one was ever ratified.[49] In 1909 Congress took back the reciprocal trade treaty authority and did not regrant it to the president for another quarter-century, until after the 1930 Smoot-Hawley protectionist tariff had worked its disastrous effects, including contributing to the Great Depression.

Like the reformed alcoholic acknowledging the need to steer clear of the temptations of the liquor store, Congress ceded much of its authority to set tariffs to the president in the Reciprocal Trade Agreements Act (RTAA) of 1934. The RTAA, called "a revolution in tariff making" by one historian,[50] delegated to the president authority to cut tariffs on his own by as much as 50 percent if he could negotiate reciprocal cuts with other countries. This laid the basis for a fundamental shift away from protectionism and toward free trade, a shift that was further manifested following World War II, when the United States played a key role in setting up the General Agreement on Tariffs and Trade as the basis for an international system of free trade.

Summary

In studying history, change often is more readily apparent than continuity. In so many ways the twenty-first century and its foreign policy challenges are vastly different from those of even the recent past, let alone those of the eighteenth, nineteenth, and early twentieth centuries. Yet many of the foreign policy choices we debate today, at their core, are about the same fundamental questions that have been debated over two centuries of U.S. history.

Can the United States best fulfill its national interest in all its components through isolationism or internationalism? How big a military and how much defense spending are needed to ensure U.S. power and assure the peace? How true to its democratic principles does U.S. foreign policy need to be? Are those who criticize U.S. foreign policy as imperialistic right? How is the record of relations in such major regions as Latin America and Asia to be assessed? Every one of these questions of foreign policy strategy has a long history that provides important context for current foreign policy choices.

The same is true with regard to the three historical debates over foreign policy politics examined in this chapter. Struggles between the president and

Congress over decisions to go to war are hardly just a post-Vietnam matter; they go back a long way in U.S. history. The profoundly difficult trade-offs between the demands of national security and the constitutional guarantees of civil liberties have been demonstrated all too many times in U.S. history. The interest-group pressures over free trade vs. protectionism were at least as intense in the late nineteenth century as in the late twentieth century.

It is therefore crucial that as we consider the foreign policy challenges today, we not only seek to understand what is new about our world, but also seek to learn from the prologue that is the past.

In the next chapter we will look at the Cold War and the more recent historical context it provides to our analysis of today's challenges.

Notes

[1] James M. McCormick, *American Foreign Policy and Process* (Itasca, Ill.: F. E. Peacock, 1992), 15–16.

[2] Cited in John Gerard Ruggie, "The Past as Prologue? Interests, Identity and American Foreign Policy," *International Security* 21:4 (Spring 1997), 89–90.

[3] Richard J. Barnet, *The Rockets' Red Glare: War, Politics and the American Presidency* (New York: Simon and Schuster, 1990), 142.

[4] President Woodrow Wilson, "An Address to a Joint Session of Congress," in Ray Stannard Baker and William E. Dodd, eds., *The Public Papers of Woodrow Wilson*, Vol. 5 (New York: Harper and Brothers, 1927), 6–16.

[5] Both cited in Barnet, *Rockets' Red Glare*, 200.

[6] Robert Shogan, *Hard Bargain: How FDR Twisted Churchill's Arm, Evaded the Law, and Changed the Role of the American Presidency* (New York: Scribner's, 1995).

[7] Arthur M. Schlesinger, Jr., "Back to the Womb? Isolationism's Renewed Threat," *Foreign Affairs* 74:4 (July/August 1995), 4.

[8] Quoted in Paul A. Varg, *Foreign Policies of the Founding Fathers* (Baltimore: Penguin, 1970), 192.

[9] Samuel Eliot Morison and Henry Steele Commager, *The Growth of the American Republic*, Vol. 2 (New York: Oxford University Press, 1940), 471.

[10] Richard Polenberg, *War and Society: The United States, 1941–1945* (New York: J. B. Lippincott, 1972), 5.

[11] Cited in Anders Stephanson, *Manifest Destiny: American Expansionism and the Empire of Right* (New York: Hill and Wang, 1995), 19.

[12] The term was first used by John L. O'Sullivan, editor of the *Democratic Review*. O'Sullivan was an interesting character, the descendant of "a long line of Irish adventurers and mercenaries," known among other things for being involved in failed plots to annex Cuba, and said by his friend, the writer Nathaniel Hawthorne, to be a "bizarre" fellow. Stephanson, *Manifest Destiny*, xi–xii.

[13] Woodrow Wilson, "Address to Joint Session of Congress," April 2, 1917, reprinted in Arthur S. Link, ed., *Papers of Woodrow Wilson* (Princeton: Princeton University Press, 1966), 519–27.

[14]"Atlantic Charter," joint statement by President Roosevelt and Prime Minister Churchill, August 14, 1941, in U.S. Department of State, *Foreign Relations of the United States: 1941, Vol. 1: General, the Soviet Union* (Washington, D.C.: U.S. Government Printing Office, 1958), 367–69.

[15]Thomas G. Paterson, J. Gary Clifford, and Kenneth J. Hagan, *American Foreign Relations: A History to 1920* (Lexington, Mass.: D. C. Heath, 1995), 233.

[16]Michael Hunt, *Ideology and U.S. Foreign Policy* (New Haven: Yale University Press, 1987), 53.

[17]Thomas Bortelsmann, "Race and Racism," in Bruce W. Jentleson and Thomas G. Paterson, eds., *Encyclopedia of U.S. Foreign Relations* (New York: Oxford University Press, 1997), Vol. 3, 451–52.

[18]Cited in Alexander DeConde, "Ethnic Groups," in Jentleson and Paterson, eds., *Encyclopedia of U.S. Foreign Relations*, Vol. 2, 111.

[19]Cited in Walter LaFeber, *The American Age: United States Foreign Policy at Home and Abroad*, 2d ed. (New York: Norton, 1994), 213.

[20]Cited in Morison and Commager, *Growth of the American Republic*, 324.

[21]Cited in Paterson, Clifford, and Hagan, *American Foreign Relations*, 229, from Hugh Deane, *Good Deeds and Gunboats* (San Francisco: China Books and Periodicals, 1990), 65.

[22]Both cited in Paterson, Clifford, and Hagan, *American Foreign Relations*, 175.

[23]Paterson, Clifford, and Hagan, *American Foreign Relations*, 254–57.

[24]Quoted in Paterson, Clifford, and Hagan, *American Foreign Relations*, 262–63.

[25]Gaddis Smith, "Monroe Doctrine," in Jentleson and Paterson, eds., *Encyclopedia of U.S. Foreign Relations*, Vol. 3, 159–67.

[26]Franklin D. Roosevelt, "Our Foreign Policy: A Democratic View," *Foreign Affairs* 6:4 (July 1928), 584.

[27]Cited in Peter W. Rodman, *More Precious Than Peace: The Cold War and the Struggle for the Third World* (New York: Scribner's 1994), 38.

[28]Quoted in Paterson, Clifford, and Hagan, *American Foreign Relations*, 133.

[29]Quoted in Akira Iriye, *Across the Pacific: An Inner History of American–East Asian Relations* (New York: Harcourt, Brace, 1967), 23.

[30]Iriye, *Across the Pacific*, 60.

[31]Paterson, Clifford, and Hagan, *American Foreign Relations*, 135.

[32]Both quotes given in Iriye, *Across the Pacific*, 147–48.

[33]Donald R. Hickey, *The War of 1812: A Forgotten Conflict* (Urbana: University of Illinois Press, 1989), 305, 309.

[34]Arthur M. Schlesinger, Jr., *The Imperial Presidency* (New York: Atlantic Monthly Press, 1974), 51–52.

[35]Schlesinger, *The Imperial Presidency*, 53.

[36]Schlesinger, *The Imperial Presidency*, 54, emphasis in original.

[37]S. Padover, ed., *The Complete Madison* (New York: Harper, 1953), 258.

[38]Quoted in Schlesinger, *The Imperial Presidency*, 71, 75.

[39]Morison and Commager, *Growth of the American Republic*, 478.

[40]Cited in Barnet, *Rockets' Red Glare*, 158.

[41]Lewis J. Paper, *Brandeis* (Englewood Cliffs, N.J.: Prentice-Hall, 1983), 282–83.

[42]Paterson, Clifford, and Hagan, *American Foreign Relations*, 324.

[43]Paper, *Brandeis*, 283. On these cases Justice Holmes was much less supportive of Brandeis.

[44]Both quoted in Jerel A. Rosati, *The Politics of United States Foreign Policy* (New York: Harcourt, Brace, 1993), 476–78

45Ronald Smothers, "Japanese-Americans Recall War Service," *New York Times,* June 19, 1995, A8.

46*Korematsu v. United States* (1944), cited in Thomas M. Franck and Michael J. Glennon, eds., *Foreign Relations and National Security Law: Cases, Materials and Simulations* (St. Paul, Minn.: West, 1987), 43–53.

47Tom E. Terrill, *The Tariff, Politics and American Foreign Policy, 1874–1901* (Westport, Conn.: Greenwood, 1973), 199.

48Terrill, *The Tariff,* 172

49Robert A. Pastor, *Congress and the Politics of Foreign Economic Policy, 1929–1976* (Berkeley: University of California Press, 1980), 75.

50Sidney Ratner, cited in Pastor, *Congress and the Politics of Foreign Economic Policy,* 92.

4 *The Cold War Context: Origins and First Stages*

Introduction: "Present at the Creation"

"Present at the Creation" is how Dean Acheson, secretary of state in the early days of the Cold War, titled his memoirs. At the outset of the Cold War, Americans felt they were facing threats as dangerous and challenges as profound as any ever before faced in American history. Moreover, the United States was no longer pursuing just its own foreign policy; it was being looked to as a world leader, a "superpower." It had been a leader in World War II, but only after overcoming isolationism, and even then only for a period that, as dire as it was, lasted less than four years. The Cold War, though, would go on for more than four decades. And so it was that, when years later Acheson wrote his memoirs, he chose a title that reflected his generation's sense of having created their own new era.[1]

During World War II the United States and the Soviet Union had been allies. President Franklin D. Roosevelt, British prime minister Winston Churchill, and Soviet leader Josef Stalin were known as the "Big Three." The Soviets were second only to the British as beneficiaries of American Lend-Lease economic assistance during the war, receiving more than $9 billion worth of food, equipment, and other aid. Even Stalin's image as a ruthless dictator who viciously purged his own people in the 1930s was "spun" more favorably, to the more amiable "Uncle Joe." Yet, fundamentally, the American-Soviet wartime alliance was based on the age-old maxim that *the enemy of my enemy is my friend.* "I can't take communism," was how FDR put it, "but to cross this bridge I'd hold hands with the Devil."[2] After the war was over and the shared common enemy of Nazi Germany had been vanquished, would the alliance continue? Should it?

Different views on these questions are reflected in the debate over the origins of the Cold War. This debate is marked by two main schools of thought, the orthodox and the revisionist. In the *orthodox* view principal responsibility is put squarely on the shoulders of Josef Stalin and the Soviet Union.[3] This view has been strengthened by revelations in recent years from Soviet and other archives. "We now know," historian John Lewis Gaddis contends, that "as long as Stalin was running the Soviet Union, a cold war was unavoidable." The Soviets used the Red Army to make Eastern Europe their own sphere of influence. They sought to subvert governments in Western Europe. They blockaded West Berlin in an effort to force the United States, France, and Britain out. In Asia they supported the Chinese communists and helped start the Korean War. They supported communist parties in Southeast Asia, Latin America, and within African anticolonial movements; indeed, one of the fundamental tenets of Soviet communist ideology was to aid revolution everywhere. And in the United States they ran a major spy ring trying, among other things, to steal the secret of the atomic bomb.

In the *revisionist* view of the origins of the Cold War the United States bears its own significant share of the responsibility.[4] Some revisionists see the United States as seeking its own empire, for reasons of both power and prosperity. Its methods may have been less direct and more subtle, but its objectives nevertheless were for domination to serve American grand ambitions. In citing evidence for U.S. neo-imperialist ambitions, these critics point as far back as the 1918–19 U.S. "expeditionary force" that, along with European forces, intervened in Russia to try to reverse the Russian Revolution. Other revisionists see the problem more as one of U.S. miscalculation. They maintain that the Soviets were seeking little more than to assure their own security by preserving Poland and Eastern Europe as a *cordon sanitaire* to prevent future invasions of Soviet soil. What transpired in those early post–World War II years, these revisionists argue, was akin to the classic "security dilemma," often present in international politics, in which both sides are motivated less by aggression than by the fear that the other side cannot be trusted, and thus see their own actions as defensive while the other side sees them as offensive. Had U.S. policy been more one of reassurance and cooperation, rather than deterrence and containment, there might not have been a Cold War.

With this debate in mind, in this chapter and the next we analyze the dynamics of foreign policy choice for the United States as played out during the Cold War, with regard to both foreign policy strategy and foreign policy politics.

In so doing we will gain a deeper understanding of the Cold War itself and provide the contemporary context to go with the historical one (from Chapter 3) for the challenges and choices that face the United States in the post–Cold War era.

Peace: International Institutionalism and the United Nations

Work on the United Nations (UN) was begun well before World War II was over. One of the primary reasons that World War I had not turned out to be "the war to end all wars," as Woodrow Wilson and other leaders had hoped, was the weakness of the League of Nations. Franklin Roosevelt and other world leaders felt they had learned from that experience, and this time intended to create a stronger global body as the basis for a stable peace.

The Original Vision of the United Nations

The grand hope for the United Nations, as articulated by FDR's secretary of state, Cordell Hull, was that "there would no longer be need for spheres of influence, for alliances, for balance of power, or any other special arrangements through which, in the unhappy past, nations strove to safeguard their security or promote their interests." Their vision was of "one world," and a peace that was broad and enduring.

This was quintessential International Institutionalism, a vision of international relations in which the national interest of the United States, as well as the national interests of other nations, would best be served by multilateral cooperation through international institutions—a world that could be, in the metaphors cited back in Chapter 1, the "cultivable garden" of peace, not necessarily the "global jungle" of power. It was the United States, more than any other country, that saw the world in these terms and pushed for the creation of the UN. It was in San Francisco on June 26, 1945, that the UN Charter was signed (with 51 original signatories). New York City was chosen as the location for UN headquarters.

The lesson drawn from the failure of the League of Nations was not that the International Institutionalist strategy was inherently flawed, but that there were two crucial errors in the post–World War I version of it. One was U.S. nonmembership. FDR knew that American membership was key to the UN and that the UN was necessary in order that the United States not revert to isolationism. U.S. membership in the UN thus was "an institutional tripwire," as John Ruggie calls it, "that would force American policymakers to take positions on potential threats to international peace and security . . . not simply to look the other way, as they had done in the 1930s."[5] FDR was determined not to make the same political mistakes that Woodrow Wilson had made. Roosevelt worked closely with Congress, including giving a major role in the U.S. delegation to the San Francisco Conference to senior Republicans such as Senator Arthur Vandenberg of Michigan. He also used his "fireside chats" and other political techniques to ensure that public opinion supported the UN. All this work paid off: the Senate vote on U.S. membership in the UN was 89 to 2, and public-opinion polls showed that 66 percent of Americans favored U.S. membership and only 3 percent were opposed (31 percent were uncertain).

Following the second lesson drawn from the interwar years, world leaders strove to ensure that the UN would be a stronger institution than the League had been. Having the United States as a member was part of this plan, but so was institutional design. The League had allocated roughly equal powers to its Assembly, comprising all member nations, and to its Council, made up of permanent seats for the four "great powers" who were League members (Britain, France, Italy, and Japan) and four seats to be rotated among other member nations; all seats on the Council were equally powerful. In contrast, the UN gave its Security Council much greater authority than its General Assembly. The UN Security Council could authorize the use of military force, order the severance of diplomatic relations, impose economic sanctions, and take other actions and make them binding on member states. And the five permanent members of the Security Council—the United States, the Soviet Union, Britain, France, and China—were made particularly powerful, as they were given the power to veto any Security Council action.

The UN Charter even envisioned a standing UN military force. Article 43 of the charter had called on "all Members . . . to make available to the Security Council, on its call and with special agreement or agreements . . . [to be] negotiated as soon as possible . . . armed force, assistance and facilities . . . necessary for the purpose of maintaining international peace and security." This standing force was to be directed by a Military Staff Committee, consisting of the chiefs of staff of the armed forces of the permanent members of the Security Council. The Military Staff Committee would directly advise the Security Council and be in operational charge of the military forces. No Article 43 agreements were ever concluded, however. Over the years the UN has raised temporary military forces for particular missions such as peacekeeping, but it has never had a permanent standing military of its own. In this and other respects, the UN did not prove able to provide the institutional infrastructure for a "one world" peace.

The Scaled-Back Reality

One reason the UN was unable to ensure peace was the political ambivalence of a number of countries, including the United States, who wanted an international institution strong enough to help keep the peace but not so strong as to threaten nation-state supremacy or sovereignty. Although Roosevelt and Truman administration officials had helped write the Article 43 provision into the UN Charter, many in Congress saw it as a step too far toward "world government." They supported the UN, but not that much, and had the power of the purse and other legislative authority to ensure that no American troops would be put under any sort of permanent UN command. Congress demonstrated similar relicence with two UN treaties signed in 1948, the Genocide Convention and the Universal Declaration of Human Rights. The goals of preventing genocide and promoting human rights obviously were nonobjectionable. But the U.S. Senate refused for years to ratify either treaty because they ostensibly risked giving the UN and international courts jurisdiction over American domestic affairs in a manner that threatened American sovereignty. We will come back to this issue of international institutions/national sovereignty in Part II of this book, for it has resurfaced as a major debate in post–Cold War foreign policy. The point here is that this issue was there even amid the original grand vision of the UN.

The other, more important reason that the UN fell short of its original vision was the onset of the Cold War and the resultant priority given to considerations of power. Even before the UN Charter was signed, U.S.-Soviet tensions had flared over the future of Poland and other states of Eastern Europe. It also was only weeks after the signing of the UN Charter that the United States dropped the world's first atomic bombs on Japan. President Harry Truman defended his A-bomb decision as the only alternative to a major and risky invasion, but some critics believed it was less about getting Japan to surrender and establishing peace than about demonstrating American military might so as to intimidate the Soviet Union.[6] Whichever interpretation one took, the tensions that arose during this time demonstrated the limits of the UN for managing key international events and actions. This weakness was confirmed by the controversy in 1946 over the Baruch Plan. Named for Truman adviser Bernard Baruch, the plan was a U.S. proposal to the UN Atomic Energy Commission for establishing international control of nuclear weapons. The Soviet Union rejected the Baruch Plan. Some cited this as evidence of Stalin's nonpeaceful intentions. Others assessed the Baruch Plan as one-sided and actually intended to spur a rejection.[7]

In other ways as well, instead of a unifying institution the UN became yet another forum for the competition between the United States and the Soviet Union and their respective allies. They differed over who should be secretary-general. They disagreed on which countries would be admitted to the General Assembly. Each used its veto so much that the Security Council was effectively paralyzed. At one point, following the October 1949 communist triumph in the Chinese civil war, the Soviets boycotted the Security Council in protest against its decision to allow Chiang Kai-shek and his anticommunist Nationalist government, which had fled to the island of Taiwan, to continue to hold China's UN seat. In fact, one of the few times the Security Council did act decisively in these early years was in June 1950, when communist North Korea invaded South Korea, setting off the Korean War: the United States took advantage of the Soviet boycott of the Security Council to get a resolution passed creating a UN-sponsored military force to defend South Korea.

Thus, although for most of this period the UN was more pro-U.S. than pro-Soviet, as an international institution it was not strong enough to end the global game of "spheres of influence . . . alliances . . . balance of power" and make the break with that "unhappy past" as envisioned by Secretary of State Hull and other UN founders. This was not the peace that was supposed to be.

Power: Nuclear Deterrence and Containment

A "one world" peace had its attractiveness, but was unrealistic—power had to be met with power. Some argued that this should have been foreseen even before World War II was over, and that FDR had conceded too much at the Yalta summit on issues such as the future of Poland. Now more than ever, in the classic Realist dictum presented back in Chapter 1, American foreign policy had to be based on interests defined in terms of power.

For all the other differences that emerged over the course of the Cold War, two basic doctrines of power developed in these early years remained the core of U.S. foreign policy. One was *nuclear deterrence*. The standard definition of deterrence is the prevention of attack through the fear of retaliation. On the one hand, deterrence is more than just the capacity to defend oneself sufficiently to prevent defeat. On the other hand, it is less than "compellence," which means getting another state to take a particular action that it otherwise would not.[8] Although the use of deterrence strategy goes way back in history, the nuclear age gave it greater centrality. As devastating as the 1941 Japanese attack on Pearl Harbor had been, the United States managed to absorb it and recover from it. But nuclear weapons, so much more destructive than anything the world had ever seen, changed the world's security landscape. The single atomic bomb dropped on Hiroshima killed instantly 130,000 people, one-third of the city's population; another 70,000 died later of radiation poisoning and other injuries. As the United States thought about its own national security in the nuclear age, its leaders realized that a strong and resilient defense, while still necessary, no longer was sufficient. Any attack with nuclear weapons or that could lead to the use of nuclear weapons had to be deterred before it began. This capacity for deterrence required a strong military, and especially nuclear weapons superiority, and also had political, psychological, and perceptual dimensions. The deterrence "formula" was a combination of capabilities and intentions, both the capacity to retaliate and the will to do so. The requisites for meeting this nuclear deterrence formula changed over time, but the basic strategy of preventing attack through fear of retaliation stayed the same.

Containment was the other basic doctrine developed in the early Cold War. In February 1946, George F. Kennan, then a high-ranking U.S. diplomat in Moscow, sent a "long telegram" back to Washington, in which he sounded the alarm about the Soviet Union. A version of the long telegram later appeared in the prestigious journal *Foreign Affairs* as "The Sources of Soviet Conduct," with authorship attributed to an anonymous "X." Kennan's analysis of Stalin and his Soviet Union was that "there can never be on Moscow's side any sincere assumption of a community of interests between the Soviet Union and powers which are regarded as capitalist." American strategy therefore had to seek the "patient but firm and vigilant containment of Russian expansive tendencies." The Soviet Union was seeking "to make sure that it has filled every nook and cranny available to it in the basin of world power." Kennan recommended a policy of "containment," whereby the United States would counter any attempt by the Soviets to expand their sphere of influence or to spread communism beyond their own borders. Only sustained containment had a chance of bringing about "the gradual mellowing of Soviet power," Kennan argued; it might even reveal the internal contradictions of their system to the point that the Soviet Union would "break up."[9]

At the Source

THE TRUMAN DOCTRINE AND THE MARSHALL PLAN

Truman Doctrine

"At the present moment in world history nearly every nation must choose between alternative ways of life. The choice too often is not a free one.

One way of life is based upon the will of the majority, and is distinguished by free institutions, representative government, free elections, guaranties of individual liberty, freedom of speech and religion, and freedom from political oppression.

The second way of life is based upon the will of a minority forcibly imposed upon the majority. It relies upon terror and oppression, a controlled press and radio, fixed elections, and the suppression of personal freedoms.

I believe that it must be the policy of the United States to support free peoples who are resisting attempted subjugation by armed minorities or by outside pressures. . . .

Should we fail to aid Greece and Turkey in this fateful hour, the effect will be far-reaching to the West as well as to the East. . . . "

Marshall Plan

" In considering the requirements for the rehabilitation of Europe, the physical loss of life, the visible destruction of cities, factories, mines and railroads was correctly estimated, but it has become obvious during recent months that this visible destruction was probably less serious than the dislocation of the entire fabric of European economy.

The truth of the matter is that Europe's requirements for the next three or four years of foreign food and other essential products—principally from America—are so much greater than her present ability to pay that she must have substantial additional help or face economic, social, and political deterioration of a very grave character. The remedy lies in breaking the vicious circle and restoring the confidence of the European people in the economic future of their own countries and of Europe as a whole. . . .

(*Continued on page 117*)

(The Truman Doctrine and the Marshall Plan *Continued from page 116*)
It is logical that the United States should do whatever it is able to do to assist in the return of normal economic health in the world, without which there can be no political stability and no assured peace. Our policy is directed not against any country or doctrine but against hunger, poverty, desperation, and chaos. Its purpose should be the revival of a working economy in the world so as to permit the emergence of political and social conditions in which free institutions can exist. ""

Sources: Harry Truman, "Special Message to the Congress on Greece and Turkey: The Truman Doctrine," March 12, 1947, in *Documents on American Foreign Relations*, Vol. 9 (Princeton, N.J.: Princeton University Press for the World Peace Foundation, 1947), 6–7; George Marshall, "European Initiative Essential to Economic Recovery," speech made June 5, 1947, at Harvard University, reprinted in *Department of State Bulletin* 16 (June 15, 1947), 1159.

The Formative Period, 1947–50

Both these doctrines were evident in Truman administration foreign policies. The Truman Doctrine, proclaimed in March 1947, was essentially a U.S. commitment to aid Greece and Turkey against Soviet and Soviet-assisted threats. The U.S. aid was economic, not military, and it totaled only about $400 million. But the significance, as President Truman stressed in his historic speech to Congress and the nation, was much more sweeping (see At the Source on p. 116). This was not just another foreign policy issue involving a couple of important but minor countries. It was a defining moment in history with significance for the fate of the entire post–World War II world. And the United States was the only country that could provide the necessary leadership.

A few months later the Marshall Plan was announced in a commencement speech at Harvard University by Secretary of State George Marshall (see also At the Source on p. 116). Most of Western Europe still had not recovered economically from the devastation of World War II. In France, Italy, and elsewhere communist parties were gaining support by capitalizing on the economic discontent. To meet this threat to containment the Marshall Plan pledged enormous amounts of money, the equivalent of over $60 billion today, as U.S. economic assistance to the countries of Western Europe. Thus began the first major U.S. Cold War foreign-aid program.

> **At the Source**

THE NORTH ATLANTIC TREATY

❝ The Parties to this Treaty . . . seek to promote stability and well-being in the North Atlantic area. . . .

Art. 3. In order more effectively to achieve the objectives of this Treaty, the Parties, separately and jointly, by means of continuous and effective self-help and mutual aid, will maintain and develop their individual and collective capacity to resist armed attack. . . .

Art. 5. The Parties agree that an armed attack against one or more of them in Europe or North America shall be considered an attack against them all; and consequently they agree that, if such an armed attack occurs, each of them, in exercise of the right of individual or collective self-defense recognized by Article 51 of the Charter of the United Nations, will assist the Party or Parties, [using] such actions as it deems necessary, including the use of armed force, to restore and maintain the security of the North Atlantic area. . . . ❞

Signed in 1949 by twelve founding members: Belgium, Canada, Denmark, France, Iceland, Italy, Luxembourg, the Netherlands, Norway, Portugal, the United Kingdom, and the United States.

Source: *Department of State Bulletin* 20:507 (March 20, 1949).

The creation of the North Atlantic Treaty Organization (NATO) in 1949 marked the first peacetime military alliance in American history. To the Truman Doctrine's political-diplomatic commitments and the Marshall Plan's economic assistance, NATO added the military commitment to keep U.S. troops in Europe and the *collective defense* pledge that the United States would defend its European allies if they were attacked. Article 5 of the NATO treaty affirmed this pledge of collective defense: "The Parties agree that an armed attack against one or more of them in Europe or North America shall be considered an attack against them all" (see At the Source above). This included the commitment to use nuclear weapons against the Soviet Union, even if their attack was on Europe but not directly on the United States. All this was quite a change from earlier American foreign policy, such as George Washington's "beware entangling alliances" and 1930s isolationism. The 82-to-13 Senate vote ratifying the NATO treaty made clear that it was a consensual change.

Yet within months the Soviet threat became even more formidable. Reports emerged in August 1949 that the Soviet Union now also had nuclear weapons. This came as a surprise to the American public and even to the Truman administration. Could the Soviets really have achieved this on their own? Were spies at work stealing America's nuclear secrets? Although the answers to these questions were unclear at the time, what was certain was that the U.S. nuclear monopoly was broken, and thus the requirements of nuclear deterrence were going to have to be recalculated.

At virtually the same time the threat to containment grew worse as the Cold War was extended from Europe to Asia. On October 1, 1949, the People's Republic of China was proclaimed by the Chinese communists, led by Mao Zedong and Zhou Enlai, who had won China's civil war. Now China, the world's most populous country, joined the Soviet Union, the world's largest, as communism's giant powers. "Red China," for many Americans, seemed an even more ominous enemy than the Soviet Union.

These developments prompted a reassessment of U.S. strategy. NSC-68, a seminal security-planning paper developed in early 1950 by President Truman's National Security Council, called for three important shifts in U.S. strategy (see At the Source on p. 120). First, there needed to be a *globalization* of containment. The threat was not just in Europe and Asia, but everywhere: "the assault on free institutions is world-wide now."[10] This meant that U.S. commitments had to be extended to span the globe. Allies needed to be defended, vital sea lanes protected, and access to strategic raw materials maintained. Part of the rationale was also psychological: the concern that a communist gain anywhere would be perceived more generally as the tide turning in their favor and thus would hurt American credibility.

Second, NSC-68 proposed a *militarization* of containment. The Truman Doctrine and the Marshall Plan were largely economic measures. What was needed now was a broad and extensive military buildup: a global ring of overseas military bases, military alliances beyond NATO, and a substantial increase in defense spending. The latter had to be pursued, the NSC-68 strategists stressed, even if it meant federal budget deficits and higher taxes.

The third step called for by NSC-68 was the development of the *hydrogen bomb*. As destructive as the atomic bomb was, a hydrogen bomb (or H-bomb) would be vastly more destructive. Now that the Soviets had developed the A-bomb much sooner than anticipated, the development of the H-bomb was deemed necessary to maintain American nuclear superiority.

```
▶◀ At the Source ▶◀
```

NSC-68

❝ The fundamental design of those who control the Soviet Union and the international communist movement . . . calls for the complete subversion or forcible destruction of the machinery of government and structure of society in the countries of the non-Soviet world and their replacement by an apparatus and structure subservient to and controlled from the Kremlin. To that end Soviet efforts are now directed toward the domination of the Eurasian land mass. The United States, as the principal center of power in the non-Soviet world and bulwark of opposition to Soviet expansion, is the principal enemy whose integrity and vitality must be subverted or destroyed by one means or another if the Kremlin is to achieve its fundamental design.

The Soviet Union is developing the military capacity to support its design for world domination. . . .

A more rapid build-up of political, economic, and military strength and thereby of confidence in the free world than is now contemplated is the only course which is consistent with progress toward achieving our fundamental purpose. The frustration of the Kremlin design requires the free world to develop a successfully functioning political and economic system and a vigorous political offensive against the Soviet Union. These, in turn, require an adequate military shield under which they can develop. It is necessary to have the military power to deter, if possible, Soviet expansion, and to defeat, if necessary, aggressive Soviet or Soviet-directed actions of a limited or total character. . . . Unless our combined strength is rapidly increased, our allies will tend to become increasingly reluctant to support a firm foreign policy on our part and increasingly anxious to seek other solutions, even though they are aware that appeasement means defeat. . . .

The whole success of the proposed program hangs ultimately on recognition by this Government, the American people, and all free peoples, that the cold war is in fact a real war in which the survival of the free world is at stake. ❞

Source: Text of memorandum no. NSC-68, from U.S. Department of State, *Foreign Relations of the United States 1950*, Vol. 1, 237–39.

Some policy-makers believed that the United States should pursue nuclear arms-control agreements with the Soviet Union before crossing this next threshold of a nuclear arms race. But NSC-68 dismissed the prospect of the Soviets' being serious about arms-control negotiations.

NSC-68 was never formally approved. Its recommendations were tough, both strategically and politically, and thus stirred debate within the Truman administration. All that debate became largely moot, though, when a few months later the Korean War broke out. There now could be little doubt that, as President Truman stated it, "communism was acting in Korea just as Hitler, Mussolini, and the Japanese had acted 10, 15, and 20 years earlier."[11] The Korean War lasted three years and ended largely in stalemate. Its lessons were mixed, on the one hand reinforcing the view of the communist threat as globalized, while on the other showing the difficulties of land wars in Asia. It was also during this time that the United States first began getting involved in another part of Asia, Vietnam, sending aid to the French as they sought to maintain their colonial control against nationalist-communist independence forces led by Ho Chi Minh.

Intensification, 1950s to the Early 1960s

Over the rest of the 1950s and into the 1960s the Cold War intensified in virtually every global region. In Europe, West Germany was brought into NATO, not only to strengthen the NATO alliance, but also to address concerns rooted deeply in European historical memories about Germany rising again. In addition to "keeping the Americans in" and "the Soviets out," by integrating Germany into the U.S.-dominated alliance, NATO also was intended to "keep the Germans down."[12] The Soviets' response, though, was to formalize their military alliance in Eastern Europe through the Warsaw Pact. The Soviets also demonstrated their determination to maintain their bloc when in 1956 they invaded Hungary to put down a political revolution that threatened communist control. The Soviet invasion left thousands dead and even more imprisoned. NATO and the United States, despite much rhetoric from Secretary of State John Foster Dulles about not just the containment but the "rollback" of communism, did nothing significant to aid the Hungarian freedom fighters.

In 1952 the United States ended the military occupation it had maintained in Japan since the end of World War II. Defense agreements were signed for U.S. troops and bases to be maintained there, both to help defend Japan and as part of the overall containment strategy in Asia. Japan had by then begun functioning as a democracy under a constitution written largely by U.S. officials and including provisions that renounced war and that permanently limited the size and scope of the Japanese military to "self-defense forces." Thus as with Germany, the U.S. strategy in Japan was to finish the business of World War II and start the business of the Cold War, in which these former U.S. enemies were now U.S. allies against the Soviet Union, China, and world communism.

As mentioned in the preceding section, this period was also when the United States began its involvement in Vietnam. The United States provided some aid to the French, for whom Vietnam was still a colony, and then stepped up its involvement following the French defeat in 1954. The American concern was not only Vietnam itself: Vietnam was the original case on which the domino theory was based. "You have a row of dominoes set up," as President Eisenhower stated at a 1954 press conference. "You knock over the first one, and what will happen to the last one is the certainty that it will go over very quickly. So you could have a beginning of a disintegration that would have the most profound influences."[13] Throughout this period the United States got more and more involved in Vietnam. Also in Asia, the United States and its allies created the Southeast Asia Treaty Organization (SEATO), somewhat modeled after NATO, to be the Asian link in the chain of alliances with which Eisenhower and Dulles sought to ring the globe.

In the Middle East, the Baghdad Pact was set up in 1955; within a year it included Iran, Iraq, Pakistan, Turkey, and Great Britain, with the United States as a de facto but not formal member. Iraq withdrew from the group in 1958 following a radical coup against its monarchy; the rest of the alliance continued, albeit weakened, under the title Central Treaty Organization (CENTO). Containment was also manifested in Iran in 1953 in the U.S.-led covert action to bring the shah of Iran back to power and depose the anti-Western prime minister, Mohammed Mossadegh, and in Lebanon in 1958 with the intervention of U.S. Marines in support of the pro-American government against its more radical domestic foes. The Lebanon case was made into a more general precedent, under the rubric of the Eisenhower Doctrine, of U.S. willingness to provide military support to any state in the Middle East against "overt armed aggression from any nation controlled by international communism."[14]

In Latin America, Cold War opposition to Soviet influence was cast as the contemporary follow-on to the Monroe Doctrine. The major challenge came in Cuba in 1958–59 with the revolution led by Fidel Castro. As in Vietnam and elsewhere, the Cuban revolution was a mix of nationalism, anti-imperialism, and communism. Historians continue to debate whether the absolute antagonism that developed between Castro's Cuba and the United States was inevitable, or whether some modus vivendi could have been worked out. Whatever chance there may have been for something other than adversarial relations was gone after the disastrous 1961 Bay of Pigs invasion. The Eisenhower administration planned and the Kennedy administration launched this covert project, in which the United States trained, supplied, and assisted Cuban exiles in an attempted invasion of Cuba aimed at overthrowing Castro. The invasion failed miserably, embarrassing the United States, leaving Castro in power, and intensifying hatreds and fears on both sides.

As for nuclear-deterrence doctrine, this period saw a number of developments. For a while the Eisenhower administration pursued the doctrine of "massive retaliation," by which it threatened to resort to nuclear weapons to counter any Soviet challenge anywhere of any kind. This doctrine was not very credible, though: If a threat were made and delivered on, there would be nuclear war; if a threat were made and not delivered on, its credibility would be undermined akin to that of the boy who cried wolf. It also was quite risky, especially as the Soviets kept pace with and even seemed poised to overtake the U.S. nuclear program. The Soviets beat the Americans into space in 1957 with the launching of the *Sputnik* satellite. That same year they also tested their first intercontinental ballistic missile (ICBM), which meant that they now had the capacity to overcome the large distances and reach U.S. territory with a nuclear attack. This led to great fears of a "missile gap," a Soviet advantage in nuclear weapons, and prompted a massive U.S. nuclear buildup during the Kennedy administration.

In October 1962 the Cuban missile crisis brought the United States and the Soviet Union to the brink of nuclear war.[15] The Soviet decision to base nuclear missiles in Cuba was a daring and by most accounts reckless move. The Soviets defended it as an attempt to equalize the imbalance caused by the massive U.S. nuclear buildup under Kennedy and by the stationing of U.S. nuclear forces close to Soviet borders at bases in Turkey and other NATO countries in Europe. For its part, Cuba saw this new Soviet commitment as a way to insure itself against another Bay of Pigs invasion. Whatever the claims, the effect was to take the world to the brink of nuclear war.

In the end the crisis ended up being effectively managed.* Nuclear war was averted. And by most assessments, especially at the time, it was the Soviets who were seen as having backed down, the United States as having "won." But the world had come so close, too close, to nuclear war. Thus, while many saw in the Cuban and Soviet actions that started the crisis confirmation for U.S. global-containment and nuclear-deterrence doctrines, the dangerous dynamics of a crisis that could have had catastrophic consequences drove home, like never before, the risks of the Cold War.

---

*See p. 136 for a further discussion of the Cuban missile crisis as an example of successful crisis decision-making.

Principles: Ideological Bipolarity and the Third World "ABC" Approach

One of the primary differences between the Cold War and other historical great-power struggles was that the Cold War was not just between rival nations but also between opposing ideologies. This "ideological bipolarity" can be seen in the Truman Doctrine, the Marshall Plan, and many other official pronouncements. There was not much doubt then, and is even less now, about the evils of communism. Almost immediately after World War II, the Soviets had shown in Poland and elsewhere in Eastern Europe that they had little interest in allowing democracy. In this respect containment was consistent with American principles. The controversy, though, was less about what the United States opposed than whom it supported, and how it did so.

This wasn't so much a problem in Western Europe, where genuinely democratic leaders and political parties emerged (although in countries like Italy, where the Communist Party had major electoral strength, the CIA did covertly seek to manipulate elections). But quite a few Third World dictators were garbed in the rhetoric of freedom and democracy but really fit only an "ABC" definition of democracy—"anything but communism." One doesn't have to be so naive as to expect the United States to support only regimes good of heart and pure in practice. But the ABC rationale was used repeatedly as if there could be only two options, the communists or the other guy, whoever he might be and whatever his political practices. Moreover, the criteria by which leaders, parties, and movements were deemed communist were often quite subjective, if not manipulative.

Support for "ABC Democrats"

Vietnam is a good example of the U.S. support for an "ABC" leadership. There is much historical debate over whether a relationship could have been worked out with Ho Chi Minh, the Vietnamese leader who was both nationalist and communist. Ho had worked with the Allies during World War II against the Japanese occupation of Vietnam, even receiving arms and aid from the United States. After the war he made appeals to Washington for help, based on America's professed anticolonialism, against France's effort to re-establish its own colonial rule. He even cited the American Declaration of Independence in proclaiming Vietnam's independence in 1945. There was no question that Ho was a communist; he believed in social revolution at home and received support from the Soviet Union and the Chinese communists. Yet when it was suggested that as a nationalist, and like Tito in Yugoslavia,* it was not inevitable that Ho would make his country a mere communist satellite, such thinking was patently rejected. It wasn't so much that there was evidence to the contrary as that, as put in a 1949 State Department cable to the U.S. consulate in Hanoi, the "question of whether Ho was as much nationalist as Commie was irrelevant."[16] His communism was all that mattered.

Thus the United States threw its support to one Vietnamese "ABC democrat" after another. In 1949, as their alternative to Ho Chi Minh, the French reinstalled Emperor Bao Dai. He was neither a democrat (he bore the title "emperor") nor a nationalist (having sat on the throne during the Japanese occupation in World War II) and he had little credibility with his own people. Internal State Department documents showed that Bao Dai was recognized as a French colonial puppet, but U.S. support for him was rationalized as the only alternative to "Commie domination."[17]

In 1954 the Vietnamese had won their war for independence and the French were forced to withdraw. Two nations, North and South Vietnam, were established, with Ho and the communists in control of the North and the anti-communists in control of the South. This partition was supposed to be temporary, with unification and general elections to be held within a few years. In searching for someone who could be built up as a nationalist alternative to Ho, the Eisenhower administration came up with Ngo Dinh Diem. Diem was not communist, but his "nationalist" credentials were more made in America than earned in the Vietnamese colonial struggles. He also was a Catholic in a largely Buddhist country. Diem's rule was highly authoritarian— opposing political parties were abolished, press censorship strictly enforced, Buddhists brutally repressed. He gave extensive power to his brother Ngo Dinh Nhu, a shadowy and sinister figure by most accounts. When a seventy-three-year-old Buddhist monk set himself aflame to protest the regime's repression, Nhu's wife made a sneering remark about Buddhist "barbecues."[18] Indeed, by 1963 Diem was so unpopular that the Kennedy administration had a hand in the coup that brought him down and killed him. Thus the cycle of contradicting principles ran its course in this case—support an ally in the

---

*Josip Broz, more famously known as Tito, was a communist who led the Yugoslav Partisans in resistance against Nazi Germany and who became Yugoslavia's dictator after the war. In 1948, however, Tito broke with Stalin and the other members of the Warsaw Pact and began to develop independent ties to the West.

name of democracy who is at best an ABC democrat, but kill him off when he clearly is not the solution, and may even be part of the problem.

In Latin America generally, U.S. policy in the early Cold War was summed up in the comment about support for Nicaraguan dictator Anastasio Somoza: "He may be an S.O.B., but he's our S.O.B."[19] The Alliance for Progress, established in 1961 by the Kennedy administration, initially was heralded as a shift away from this approach and toward promotion of democracy. "Our Alliance for Progress is an alliance of free governments," President Kennedy proclaimed, "and it must work to eliminate tyranny from a hemisphere in which it has no rightful place."[20] While JFK was pointing his rhetorical finger at Cuba and Fidel Castro, the social and economic elites and the militaries in much of the rest of Latin America, seeing their own oligarchic interests threatened by political and economic reforms, undermined "la Alianza." Military coups ousted reformist governments in the early 1960s in Argentina, Brazil, Ecuador, Honduras, and elsewhere. While the coup makers invoked anticommunism and containment, in most cases this was a transparent rationalization. Yet the United States largely bought it. In fact, in the case of Brazil, U.S. "enthusiasm" for the coup "was so palpable that Washington sent its congratulations even before the new regime could be installed."[21] That these regimes were pro-American (power) was a higher priority than their being nondemocratic (principles).

To be sure, there were those who genuinely believed that communism was so bad that support for "anybody but a communist" and "anything but communism" was consistent with American principles, at least in relative terms and given an imperfect world. One of the problems with this defense, however, was the inclusion of more-moderate socialists and nationalists in the "irredeemable communists" category. This attitude no doubt was due in part to the intolerance of ideological biopolarity: it recognized no third way. The ABC attitude also reflected a power calculation that, in the event of conflicts between power and principles in the U.S. national interest, principles were to give way.

CIA Covert Action

Questions about consistency with principles also were raised by CIA covert action seeking the overthrow of anti-American governments, including democratically chosen ones. A commission established by President Eisenhower provided the following recommendation: "Another important requirement is an aggressive covert psychological, political and paramilitary organization more effective, more unique, and if necessary, more ruthless than that employed by the enemy. No one should be permitted to stand in the way of the prompt, efficient and secure accomplishment of this mission. It is now clear that we are facing an implacable enemy. . . . There are no rules in such a game. Hitherto acceptable norms of human conduct do not apply."[22]

One of the cases in which this strategy was applied, in Guatemala in 1954, was discussed in Chapter 1 as an example of 4 Ps tensions and trade-offs. Another case was that of Iran in 1953. In this case, as we saw earlier in this chapter, the target was Iranian prime minister Mohammed Mossadegh, who had begun to both nationalize foreign-owned oil companies (prosperity) and develop closer relations with the Soviet Union (power). The United States supported the exiled shah, and the CIA assisted royalist forces in a plot to return the shah to power. The plot succeeded, albeit with a "wave of repression" and "a purge of the armed forces and government bureaucracy" that "continued for more than a year, silencing all sources of opposition to the new regime." In the years following the coup the CIA helped establish and train the shah's new secret police, known as SAVAK. Over the next 20–25 years, SAVAK "became not just an externally directed intelligence agency but also a powerful, feared and hated instrument of domestic repression"—not exactly a practitioner of democratic principles.[23]

Prosperity: Creation of the Liberal International Economic Order

Along with the dangers of isolationism and appeasement, one of the other lessons that U.S. leaders had learned from the 1920s and 1930s concerned the dangers of trade protectionism and other "beggar-thy-neighbor" economic policies. These policies hurt prosperity globally as well as in the United States. They also contributed to the political instabilities that ultimately led to World War II. Thus one of the other major components of postwar U.S. policy was the creation of the *liberal international economic order* (LIEO). The term "liberal" as used in this context means a relatively open, market-based free-trade system with a minimum of tariffs and other government-initiated trade barriers, and with international economic relations worked out through negotiations. The opposite of liberalism in this context is not conservatism, as in the domestic-policy context, but protectionism.

The Major International Economic Institutions

As set up in the 1940s, the LIEO had three principal components: (1) a free trade system under the rubric of the *General Agreement on Tariffs and Trade* (GATT); (2) an international monetary system, based on fixed exchange rates and the gold standard, and overseen by the *International Monetary Fund* (IMF); and (3) an international lending and aid system under the International Bank for Reconstruction and Development, also known as the *World Bank*.

The establishment of GATT did not bring about instantaneous free trade. Exceptions were made—e.g., for agriculture, which for political and other reasons was much harder to open up to free trade. There were loopholes, as for labor-intensive industries such as shoes and textiles, which were allowed some, albeit not total, protection. And trade disputes continued. The success of GATT was in keeping the arrow pointed in the direction of free trade, in providing a mechanism for managing trade disputes so as to prevent their escalation to trade wars, and in moving the world gradually toward freer trade through periodic "rounds" of negotiations.

Protectionism had generated another insidious practice: the competitive manipulations of currencies. The fixed exchange rates of the IMF system sought to eliminate this form of destructive economic competition and help provide the monetary stability essential for global economic growth. The basic gold-standard exchange rate was set at $36 per ounce of gold. Countries whose international payments were not in balance (i.e., who imported more than they exported) could get some assistance from the IMF but also had to meet stringent IMF guidelines called "conditionalities" for economic and other reforms in order to get that assistance.

The World Bank later would grow into a major source of development aid for Third World countries, but initially it was focused more on European reconstruction. As of 1955, even though the U.S. Marshall Plan had ceased, about half of World Bank loans were going to industrialized countries; by 1965 this was down to one-fourth, and by 1967 virtually all lending was going to Third World development projects. The World Bank itself was chartered to lend only to governments, but over time it added an affiliate, the International Finance Corporation, that made loans to private enterprises involved in development projects.

Critiques: Hegemony? Neo-Imperialism?

While in these and other respects the LIEO did provide broad economic benefits internationally, critics point out that it largely reinforced American economic dominance, or *economic hegemony*. Voting rights in both the IMF and the World

Bank were proportional to capital contributions, which meant that, as the largest contributor of funds, the United States had a correspondingly large voting share. In the GATT negotiations American positions prevailed more often than not. Indeed the whole emphasis on free markets, open trade, and minimal government intervention in the economy also fit American laissez-faire economic ideology. And with Europe and Japan still recovering and rebuilding from World War II, the United States dominated the world economy. Thus, even though other countries benefited from the LIEO, it did also help maintain American economic hegemony to go with American diplomatic dominance and military superiority.

Another critique points to corporate interests as driving U.S. policy. This point is often stressed by revisionists in the debate over the origins of the Cold War. Critics cite cases like Guatemala, where U.S. policy followed the interests of the United Fruit Company, and Iran, where big oil companies were eager to see the shah restored to power, knowing he would return property to them that had been nationalized under Mossadegh. Even in the case of Vietnam, where the intrinsic economic interests were more limited, the fear was said to be of a succession of communist "dominoes" that would undermine global capitalism. So, too, the Marshall Plan is explained as an effort to rebuild European markets in order to generate demand for American exports and investments, thereby overcoming the underconsumption-overproduction dilemma and averting a depression. The deciding factor in the formation of U.S. foreign policy, in this view, was the private interests of multinational corporations, big banks, and the other captains of global capitalism.

Foreign Policy Politics and the Cold War Consensus

The main pattern in U.S. foreign policy politics during this period was the "Cold War consensus." This consensus was marked by three fundamental components: presidential dominance over Congress, a vast expansion of the executive-branch foreign and defense policy bureaucracy, and a fervent anticommunism pervading public opinion, culminating in the scourge of McCarthyism.

Pennsylvania Avenue Diplomacy: A One-Way Street

The term "spirit of bipartisanship" was coined during this period to describe the strong support for the foreign policies of President Truman, a Democrat, from the Republican-majority Congress, led by Senate Foreign Relations Committee Chair Arthur Vandenberg. What made this support especially striking was the extent of the foreign commitments being made—declaring

U.S. willingness "to support free peoples everywhere" (the Truman Doctrine), spending billions of dollars in foreign aid (the Marshall Plan), joining a military alliance during peacetime for the first time in U.S. history (NATO)— all as a matter of consensus and presidential-congressional cooperation.

Before crumbling over the Vietnam War in the Johnson and Nixon administrations, this foreign policy bipartisanship lasted through almost every conceivable Pennsylvania Avenue combination: a Democratic president supported by a Republican Congress (Truman, 1947–48), a Republican president supported by a Democratic Congress (Eisenhower, 1955–60), a Republican president and a Republican Congress (Eisenhower, 1953–54), and Democratic presidents and Democratic Congresses (Truman 1949–52, Kennedy 1961–63, and Johnson 1963 to about 1966). One prominent theory of the day spoke of "one President but two presidencies": the domestic policy one, in which the president succeeded in getting his proposals through Congress only 40 percent of the time, and the foreign policy one, in which the president's success rate was 70 percent.[24]

One of the reasons for this presidential dominance was that, although the Cold War was not a war per se, the fearsome nature of the Soviet threat and the overhanging danger of nuclear war were seen as the functional and moral equivalents of war. Given these exigencies, the presidency had the greater institutional capacity to conduct foreign affairs. Only the presidency possessed the information and expertise necessary for understanding the world, could move with the necessary speed and decisiveness in making key decisions, and had the will and the capacity to guard secrecy. Almost everywhere the president went, the "button" (i.e., the code box for ordering a nuclear attack) went with him—and it was conceivable that he would have less time to make a decision about whether to press it than it typically takes Congress just to have a quorum call. For its part, Congress was seen as too parochial to pay sufficient attention to world affairs, too amateur to understand them, and too slow and unwieldy in its procedures to respond with the necessary dispatch. Even its own foreign policy leaders had expressed strong doubts about its foreign policy competence. Congress "has served us well in our internal life," wrote Senator J. William Fulbright, the longest-serving chair of the Senate Foreign Relations Committee in American history, but "the source of an effective foreign policy under our system is Presidential power." Fulbright went on to propose that the president be given "a measure of power in the conduct of our foreign affairs that we [i.e., the Congress] have hitherto jealously withheld."[25] Fulbright's counterpart, House Foreign Affairs Committee Chair Thomas (Doc) Morgan, went even further, saying that he had a "blanket, all-purpose decision rule: support all executive branch proposals."[26]

Three areas of foreign policy show how the basic relationship of separate institutions sharing powers now had the presidency with the much larger share.

WAR POWERS   In the Korean War, Truman never asked Congress for a declaration of war. He claimed that the resolution passed by the UN Security Council for "urgent military measures . . . to repel the attack" provided him with sufficient authority to commit U.S. troops. Moreover, this wasn't really a war, Truman asserted, just "a police action." There is little doubt that Congress would have supported the president with a declaration of war if it had been asked. But in not asking, Truman set a new precedent for presidential assertion of war powers. This "police action" lasted three years, involved a full-scale military mobilization, incurred more than 50,000 American casualties, and ended in stalemate.

In January 1951 Truman announced his intention to send the first divisions of U.S. ground troops to be stationed in Europe as part of NATO. Here he argued that he was merely fulfilling international responsibilities that Congress had previously approved (in this instance by Senate ratification in 1949 of the NATO treaty) and thus did not need any further congressional approval. Congressional opposition to the NATO deployment was greater than in the Korean War case but still was not strong enough to pass anything more than a nonbinding resolution urging, but not requiring, the president to obtain congressional approval for future NATO deployments.

The trend continued under President Eisenhower, although with some interesting twists. In 1955 a crisis was brewing over threats by China against Taiwan. Unlike Truman, Eisenhower did go to Congress for formal legislative authorization, but he did so with a very open-ended and highly discretionary resolution authorizing him to use military force if and when he deemed it necessary as the situation developed. This kind of anticipatory authorization was very different from declaring war or taking other military action against a specific country. Yet Eisenhower's request was approved by overwhelming margins, 83 to 3 in the Senate and 410 to 3 in the House. House Speaker Sam Rayburn (D-Texas) even remarked, "If the President had done what is proposed here without consulting Congress, he would have had no criticism from me."[27]

In 1957 Eisenhower requested and got a very similar anticipatory authorization for a potential crisis in the Middle East. Here the concern was Soviet gains of influence amid increasing radicalism and instability in a number of Arab countries. Yet once again by lopsided votes, Congress authorized the president "to employ the armed forces of the United States as he deems necessary . . . [against] international communism."[28]

COVERT ACTION   One finds scattered examples of covert action throughout U.S. history. In 1819, for example, President James Monroe took covert action aimed against Spain in the Spanish territory of Florida and kept it secret from Congress. In World War II the Office of Strategic Services (OSS) played a key role in the war effort. But it was only with the onset of the Cold War that the CIA was created as the first permanent intelligence agency in U.S. history and that covert action was undertaken on a sustained, systematic basis.

Here we see another pattern of disproportionate power-sharing, and again as much because of congressional abdication as because of presidential usurpation. It was Congress that created the CIA as part of the National Security Act of 1947 and the Central Intelligence Agency Act of 1949. The latter legislation included a provision authorizing the CIA to "perform such other functions and duties related to intelligence affecting the national security"—i.e., covert operations. The members of congressional oversight committees were charged with responsibility for keeping an eye on these covert operations. But most senators and representatives who served on these committees during the early Cold War saw their roles more as boosters and protectors than as checkers and balancers. The "black budget" procedure, whereby funds are appropriated to the CIA without its having to provide virtually any details of its programs and its accounts, was set up with a congressional wink and nod.

INTERNATIONAL COMMITMENTS   Another manifestation of presidential dominance was the much greater use of executive agreements rather than treaties for making significant international commitments.[29] Consider the statistics in Dynamics of Choice on p. 133 comparing treaties and executive agreements for the Cold War era with the full span of earlier U.S. foreign policy. One obvious trend is the huge overall increase in U.S. international commitments during the Cold War. The skyrocketing number of treaties and executive agreements in the three decades after World War II in itself demonstrates how much more extensive U.S. international involvements had become. But it is the increase in the proportion of U.S. commitments represented by executive agreements—from 64 percent to 94 percent—that shows how much presidents were trying to reduce Congress's role in the making of foreign policy.[30]

It does need to be noted that many executive agreements dealt with technicalities and details of relations and were pursuant to statutes passed by Congress, and thus some of the statistical difference is accounted for simply by the sheer increase in technicalities and details that had to be worked out. But some of the pattern is due to the fact that, the greater the policy significance of the

DYNAMICS OF CHOICE

Executive Agreements vs. Treaties

	Treaties	Executive agreements	Total	Annual average total	Percentage of total represented by executive agreements
1789–1945	843	1,492	2,335	15	64%
1945–1976	437	6,983	7,420	239	94%

Source: Data derived from Michael Nelson, ed., *Congressional Quarterly's Guide to the Presidency* (Washington, D.C.: Congressional Quarterly Press, 1989), 1104.

issue, the more likely were Cold War–era presidents to use executive agreements rather than treaties. Military and diplomatic matters, for example, were more than 50 percent more likely to take the form of executive agreements than were economic, transportation, communications, or cultural-technical matters. Among the significant political-military commitments made by executive agreements were the placement of U.S. troops in Guatemala (1947) and in mainland China in support of Chiang Kai-shek (1948), the establishment of U.S. bases in the Philippines (1947), the sending of military missions to Honduras (1950) and El Salvador (1957), security pledges to Turkey, Pakistan, and Iran (1959), and an expanded security commitment to Thailand (1962).[31]

In sum, Pennsylvania Avenue had pretty much become a one-way street in terms of foreign policy politics during the first half of the Cold War. The arrow pointed down the avenue, away from Capitol Hill and toward the White House.

Executive-Branch Politics and the Creation of the "National Security State"

To exercise his expanded powers the president needed larger, stronger, and more numerous executive-branch departments and agencies. Again, we can draw a parallel with the expansions of the executive branch during World

Wars I and II, only this time the expansion was even more far-reaching and longer-lasting; it created the "national security state."[32]

One of the first steps in this process was the formation in 1947 of the National Security Council (NSC). The original purpose of the NSC was to provide a formal mechanism for bringing together the president's principal foreign policy advisers.* The NSC originally had only a small staff, and the national security adviser was a low-profile position. Few people can even name Truman's or Eisenhower's national security advisers. But beginning in the Kennedy administration, and peaking with Henry Kissinger in the Nixon administration, the national security adviser became even more powerful and prominent than the secretary of state in the making of U.S. foreign policy.

The Department of Defense (DOD) was created in 1949 to combine the formerly separate Departments of War (created in 1789) and the Navy (separated from the Department of War in 1798). During World War II the Joint Chiefs of Staff had been set up to coordinate the military services. In 1947 the position of secretary of defense was created, but each military service still had its own Cabinet-level secretary. But even this proved to be inadequate coordination and consolidation, and DOD was established with the Army, Navy, and Air Force and a newly created chair of the Joint Chiefs of Staff all reporting to the secretary of defense, who by law had to be a civilian. Measured in terms of both personnel and budget, DOD was and is the largest Cabinet department. And its building, the Pentagon, is the largest government office building.

The Central Intelligence Agency (CIA) was also created in this period, as noted earlier in this chapter. In addition, a number of other intelligence agencies were created, including the National Security Agency (1952) and the Defense Intelligence Agency (1961).

The State Department itself was vastly expanded. It grew from pre–World War II levels of about 1,000 employees in Washington and 2,000 overseas to about 7,000 and 23,000, respectively. It also added new bureaus and functions, notably the Policy Planning Staff established in 1949 with George Kennan (Mr. "X") as its first director, charged with strategic planning.

---

*The standing members of the NSC are the president, the vice president, the secretary of state, and the secretary of defense. The national security adviser, the CIA director, and the chair of the Joint Chiefs of Staff are technically defined as advisers. Depending on the issue at hand, other Cabinet officials such as the attorney general and the secretary of the treasury may also be included in NSC meetings. The same is true for political officials such as the White House chief of staff.

A number of other foreign-policy-related agencies were also created during this time: the Economic Cooperation Administration to administer the Marshall Plan; the Agency for International Development (AID), in charge of distributing foreign aid; the Arms Control and Disarmament Agency (ACDA) to monitor and negotiate arms-control agreements; the U.S. Information Agency (USIA) to represent U.S. policies abroad; the U.S. Trade Representative (USTR) to conduct international trade negotiations; and others.

It again is important to stress that this vast expansion of the executive branch was done largely with the consent of Congress. Some presidents did exploit, manipulate, and go beyond the intended congressional mandates. But to appreciate fully the politics of the Cold War era, we need to take into account both seizings by presidential usurpation and cedings by congressional abdication.

FLAWED EXECUTIVE-BRANCH DECISION-MAKING: THE BAY OF PIGS, 1961   The 1961 Bay of Pigs debacle is one of the most often cited cases of flawed executive-branch decision-making.[33] It involved a U.S.-engineered invasion of Cuba by exiled forces seeking to overthrow Fidel Castro (the Bay of Pigs was where they landed on the Cuban coast). Not only did the invasion fail miserably, but major questions were raised about how the Kennedy administration could have believed that it had any chance of succeeding. Many of the assumptions on which the plan was based were exceedingly weak: for example, the cover story that the United States played no role in the invasion had already been contradicted by press reports that anti-Castro rebels were being trained by the CIA; and the planners asserted that the Cuban people were ready to rise up, even though it was less than two years since Castro had come to power and he was still widely seen by his people as a great liberator. Despite these obvious warning signs, the groupthink dynamic dominated the policy-making process. Arthur Schlesinger, Jr., a noted historian and at the time a special assistant to President Kennedy, later explained that he felt that "a course of objection would have accomplished little save to gain me a name as a nuisance."[34]

CIA intelligence failures also contributed to the Bay of Pigs fiasco. A report by the CIA's own inspector general, written in the immediate aftermath but declassified only in 1998, stressed the agency's "failure to subject the project, especially in its latter frenzied stages, to a cold and objective appraisal. . . . Timely and objective appraisal of the operation in the months before the invasion, including study of all available intelligence, would have demonstrated to agency officials that the clandestine paramilitary operation had almost totally failed." The report also criticized the "failure to advise the President, at an appropriate time, that success had become dubious and to recommend that the operation be therefore cancelled."[35]

SUCCESSFUL CRISIS DECISION-MAKING: THE CUBAN MISSILE CRISIS, 1962
On the other hand, the case most often cited as a model of effective decision-making is the 1962 Cuban missile crisis.[36] Having learned from the Bay of Pigs, President Kennedy set up a process and structure that were more deliberate in their pace and deliberative in their consideration of options. He went outside normal bureaucratic channels and established a special crisis decision-making team, called ExCom, with members drawn from his own Cabinet and from former high-ranking foreign policy officials of previous administrations, such as Dean Acheson, secretary of state under Truman. Robert Kennedy also was a key player, an unusual foreign policy crisis role for an attorney general, but a logical one for the brother of the president.

In one sense the reason why the decision-making process worked so well in this case was that formal structures were adapted and modified. The ExCom process ensured a deliberative approach that gets much of the credit for bringing the superpowers back from the brink of nuclear war and for the successful resolution of the crisis. President Kennedy himself also gets an important share of the credit: no structure like ExCom can be established, no decision-making process function effectively, unless the president provides the mandate and the leadership.

It also was out of the Cuban missile crisis that bureaucratic politics and other important theories of intra–executive branch politics were developed. Much of this was based on Graham Allison's 1971 book, *The Essence of Decision: Explaining the Cuban Missile Crisis*.[37] As recounted and analyzed by Allison and others that followed, much of what transpired during the Cuban missile crisis was quite inconsistent with the traditional rational-actor model (described in Chapter 2) of hierarchical, orderly, and structured decision-making and policy implementation. Further research has raised doubts about a number of the case "facts" first stated by Allison.[38] However, as Richard Betts notes, "other chilling examples have turned up" of dangerously dysfunctional bureaucratic politics during this crisis.[39] Bureaucratic problems thus still were there, even if they were not as bad as originally depicted and were ultimately superceded by the effectiveness of the ExCom structure and presidential leadership.

Interest Groups, the Media, and Public Opinion: Benefits and Dangers of Consensus

On the one hand there clearly are benefits to presidents being able to count on public, interest-group, and even media support for their foreign policies. But consensus, when taken too far, also poses dangers and has downsides.

THE MEDIA AS CHEERLEADER   The news media largely carried over its role as uncritical supporter, even cheerleader, for official policy from World War II to the Cold War. To the extent that there was media criticism and pressure, it was for the president to take a tougher stand. Indeed, the news media played a significant role in the shaping of Cold War attitudes. Many give the credit for coining the term "Cold War" to Walter Lippmann, the leading newspaper columnist of the day. Henry Luce, owner and publisher of *Time* and *Life,* the two leading newsmagazines, personally championed South Vietnamese president Diem and ensured favorable, even laudatory coverage for him. Even the *New York Times* followed suit, as in a 1957 editorial titled "Diem on Democracy" in which the editors hailed Diem for being so true to democracy that "Thomas Jefferson would have no quarrel."[40]

In the Bay of Pigs case, the media actually had prior information about the planned invasion but for the most part refrained from publishing it. Most of what appeared in the media about the plan was "designed not to alert the American public to the potentially disastrous course of its own government, but to advance the universally accepted propaganda line that Cuba under Castro was courting disaster."[41] Although some of the postmortems were self-critical, others were more "expressions of sadness that the job was 'bungled,' that it did not 'succeed'—and that a well-meaning President *got caught* and got a 'bloody nose.'"[42] A few weeks after the Bay of Pigs, and despite his other acknowledgements of responsibility, President Kennedy delivered a very strong speech to the American Newspaper Publishers Association broadly construing the national security rationale as a constraint on freedom of the press (see At the Source on p. 138).

INTEREST GROUPS   Foreign policy interest groups were few in number and mostly supportive during the early Cold War. There were some protest movements, such as in the late 1950s in favor of nuclear disarmament. But more common, and more influential, were groups in favor of Cold War policies.

> **At the Source**

"IS IT NEWS?" OR "IS IT IN THE INTEREST OF NATIONAL SECURITY?"

Excerpts from a Speech by President John F. Kennedy

"I do ask every publisher, every editor, and every newsman in the nation to reexamine his own standards, and to recognize the nature of our country's peril. In time of war, the Government and the press have customarily joined in an effort, based largely on self-discipline, to prevent unauthorized disclosure to the enemy. In times of clear and present danger, the courts have held that even the privileged rights of the First Amendment must yield to the public's need for national security.

Today no war has been declared—and however fierce the struggle may be, it may never be declared in the traditional fashion. Our way of life is under attack. . . .

If the press is awaiting a declaration of war before it imposes the self-discipline of combat conditions, then I can only say that no war has ever imposed a greater threat to our security. If you are awaiting a finding of 'clear and present danger,' then I can only say that the danger has never been more clear and its presence has never been more imminent. . . .

It requires a change in outlook, a change in tactics, a change in mission by the Government, by the people, by every businessman and labor leader, and by every newspaper. For we are opposed around the world by a monolithic and ruthless conspiracy that relies primarily on covert means for expanding its sphere of influence—on infiltration instead of invasion, on subversion instead of elections, on intimidation instead of free choice, on guerrillas by night instead of armies by day. . . .

The facts of the matter are that this nation's foes have openly boasted of acquiring through our newspapers information they would otherwise hire agents to acquire through theft, bribery or espionage; that details of this nation's covert preparations to counter the enemy's covert operations have been available to every newspaper reader, friend and foe alike; that the size, the strength, the location, and the nature of our forces and weapons, and our plans and strategy for their use, have

(*Continued on page 139*)

("Is It News?" . . . *Continued from page 138*)
all been pinpointed in the press and other news media to a degree sufficient enough to satisfy any foreign power. . . .

The newspapers which printed these stories were loyal, patriotic, responsible and well-meaning. Had we been engaged in open warfare,
they undoubtedly would not have published such items. But in the absence of open warfare, they recognized only the tests of journalism and
not the tests of national security. And my question tonight is whether
additional tests should not now be adopted. . . .

I am asking the members of the newspaper profession and the industry in this country to reexamine their own responsibilities—to consider the degree and nature of the present danger—and to heed the duty
of self-restraint which that danger imposes upon all of us.

Every newspaper now asks itself with respect to every story: 'Is it
news?' All I suggest is that you add the question: 'Is it in the interest of
national security?' ""

Source: John F. Kennedy, speech to the American Newspaper Publishers Association,
April 27, 1961, from *Public Papers of the Presidents, John F. Kennedy, 1961* (Washington,
D.C.: U.S. Government Printing Office, 1962), 334–38.

If anything, some of these groups were more assertive and more anticommunist than official policy. The "China lobby" strongly sided with Chiang
Kai-shek and Taiwan, criticizing various administrations for not "unleashing"
Chiang to retake mainland China. Another example hails from the early 1960s
when, in the wake of the Cuban missile crisis, Kennedy explored a "mini-
détente" with the Soviets. He was attacked quite stridently when he gave a June
1963 commencement speech at American University proposing that the United
States "re-examine our attitude" toward the Soviet Union. He continued that the
United States should "not be blind to our differences—but let us also direct our
attention to our common interests and to the means by which those differences
can be resolved."[43] When later that year Kennedy announced a $250 million sale
of grain to the Soviet Union, even agricultural interest groups were unwilling to
breach their anticommunism. "We oppose this action," ten Republican members
of the House Agriculture Committee stated, "because we believe the vast majority of American farmers, like the vast majority of all Americans, are unwilling to
sell out a high moral principle, even for solid gold."[44] At the same time a group
called the Committee to Warn of the Arrival of Communist Merchandise on the

Local Business Scene was operating in forty-seven states, harassing merchants who dared to sell Polish hams or other "commie" products.[45]

PUBLIC OPINION   Public opinion was grounded firmly in the Cold War consensus. Internationalism prevailed over isolationism—65 percent to 8 percent in a typical poll. Eighty percent of Americans expressed support for NATO. Containment was ranked second by the public among all national objectives, domestic policy included.[46]

Consensus, though, when taken too far, can breed intolerance, suspicion, and repression. This is what happened in the late 1940s and early 1950s. First, the revealingly named House Un-American Activities Committee (HUAC) launched a series of investigations claiming that communists had infiltrated American government and society. It would be discovered much later, after the fall of the Soviet Union and the opening of Soviet archives, that some of these allegations in fact were true. Soviet spies did steal secrets for building the atomic bomb. They also operated within the State Department and other U.S. government agencies.[47] But the manner in which early Cold War anticommunism was pursued took a profound toll on civil liberties and created an environment inimical to the openness of a democratic society. The standards for the "clear and present danger" test set by Justices Holmes and Brandeis (see Chapter 3) did not require that the danger be all that clear or all that present for national security to be invoked as the basis for limiting—indeed, violating—civil liberties. This was especially the case with McCarthyism.

Senator Joseph McCarthy, until then a relatively unknown junior Republican senator from Wisconsin, became the most rabid spokesperson and instigator in the hunt for "reds under the beds." The essence of the appeal of McCarthyism comes through in a speech the senator gave in Wheeling, West Virginia, in February 1950 (see At the Source on p. 141). "The chips are down," McCarthy warned, not because communists were superior in any way, but because of "traitorous actions" by Americans. He pointed his finger right at the State Department—"the bright young men who are born with silver spoons in their mouths," this heart of America's foreign policy "thoroughly infested with Communists." Nor did McCarthy and his cohort stop there. One member of Congress even charged Secretary of State Dean Acheson with being "on Stalin's payroll." No less a figure than George Marshall—General Marshall, the World War II hero, former secretary of state, former secretary of defense—was accused by one reckless senator of being "a front man for traitors, a living lie."[48]

Nor was it just government that was being purged. Accusations were hurled all over American society. Hollywood blacklisted writers, actors, and directors

> ## ▶◀ At the Source ◀
>
> ## McCARTHYISM
>
> ### Excerpts from a Speech by Senator Joseph McCarthy
>
> 66 Today we are engaged in a final, all-out battle between Communistic atheism and Christianity. The modern champions of Communism have selected this as the time. And, ladies and gentlemen, the chips are down—they are truly down. . . .
>
> Ladies and gentlemen, can there be anyone here tonight who is so blind as to say that the war is not on? Can there be anyone who fails to realize that the Communist world has said, 'The time is now'—that this is the time for the show-down between the democratic Christian world and the Communistic atheistic world?
>
> The reason why we find ourselves in a position of impotency is not because our only powerful potential enemy has sent men to invade our shores, but rather because of the traitorous actions of those who have been treated so well by this Nation. It has not been the less fortunate or members of minority groups who have been selling this Nation out, but rather those who have had all the benefits that the wealthiest nation on earth has had to offer—the finest homes, the finest college education, and the finest jobs in Government we can give. This is glaringly true in the State Department. There the bright young men who are born with silver spoons in their mouths are the ones who have been worst. . . .
>
> In my opinion the State Department, which is one of the most important government departments, is thoroughly infested with Communists.
>
> I have in my hand 57 cases of individuals who would appear to be either card carrying members or certainly loyal to the Communist Party, but who nevertheless are still helping to shape our foreign policy. . . .
>
> However the morals of our people have not been destroyed. They still exist. This cloak of numbness and apathy has only needed a spark to rekindle them. Happily, this spark has finally been supplied. 99
>
> Source: Senator Joseph McCarthy, speech given February 9, 1950, in Wheeling, W.V., from *Congressional Record*, 81st Cong., 2nd sess., February 20, 1954, 58–61.

accused of being communists even though they had not been convicted. Universities fired professors. Scientists who held jobs requiring security clearances lost their jobs. The whole country was consumed with paranoia. Ironically, many of the accusations that were true were discredited by the broader sense of injustice and illegitimacy. And from a foreign policy perspective, McCarthyism's equation of dissent with disloyalty had a chilling effect on those both within government and outside it who might have provided constructive criticisms, alternative policy ideas, and the like. The kind of self-examination that is essential for any successful policy process thus was closed off.

Summary

The early Cold War years were a period of crucial choices for American foreign policy. The policies pursued in these years not only addressed the immediate issues, they became the foundations and framework for the decades that followed. Containment and nuclear deterrence were the central foreign policy doctrines by which American power was exercised. The United Nations was the main political-diplomatic institutional structure for the pursuit of peace. The LIEO was the main institutional structure for the international economy and the pursuit of prosperity. Anticommunism was the dominant set of beliefs by which American principles were said to be manifested. And foreign policy politics was marked by a strong consensus, even as American political institutions underwent major changes in their structure and interrelationship.

A number of questions were raised, however, both at the time and in retrospect. Although Cold War strategy proponents stressed the complementarity among the four core national-interest objectives, critics pointed out tensions and trade-offs that pitted one objective against another: for example, strengthening the United Nations vs. maximizing American power; pursuing containment vs. being true to principles. Concerns also were raised about the domestic political consensus, which, for all its benefits, also had a downside in the expansion of presidential power and violation of civil liberties.

These and other issues would become more difficult and more controversial beginning in the late 1960s and continuing through the 1980s.

Notes

[1] Dean G. Acheson, *Present at the Creation: My Years at the State Department* (New York: Norton, 1969).

[2] Winston Churchill put it in very similar terms: "If Hitler invaded hell, I should at least make a favorable reference to the Devil in the House of Commons." Both quotes cited in Stephen M. Walt, *The Origins of Alliances* (Ithaca, N.Y.: Cornell University Press, 1987), 38.

[3]See, for example, Adam B. Ulam, *The Rivals: America and Russia since World War II* (New York: Viking, 1971); Arthur M. Schlesinger, Jr., "Origins of the Cold War," *Foreign Affairs* 46:1 (October 1967); John Spanier, *American Foreign Policy since World War II* (New York: Praeger, 1968).

[4]See, for example, Walter LaFeber, *America in the Cold War* (New York: Wiley, 1969); Thomas G. Paterson, *Meeting the Communist Threat: From Truman to Reagan* (New York: Oxford University Press, 1988); Melvyn P. Leffler, *A Preponderance of Power: National Security, the Truman Administration, and the Cold War* (Stanford: Stanford University Press, 1992).

[5]John Gerard Ruggie, "The Past as Prologue? Interests, Identity and American Foreign Policy," *International Security* 21:4 (Spring 1997), 100.

[6]Gar Alperovitz, *Atomic Diplomacy: Hiroshima and Potsdam* (New York: Simon and Schuster, 1965); Martin J. Sherwin, "The Atomic Bomb and the Origins of the Cold War: U.S. Atomic Energy Policy and Diplomacy," *American Historical Review* 78:4 (October 1973), 945–68.

[7]Martin J. Sherwin, "Baruch, Bernard Mannes," in Bruce W. Jentleson and Thomas G. Paterson, eds., *Encyclopedia of U.S. Foreign Relations* (New York: Oxford University Press, 1997), Vol. 1, 135–36.

[8]Patrick M. Morgan, "Deterrence," in Bruce W. Jentleson and Thomas G. Paterson, eds., *Encyclopedia of U.S. Foreign Relations* (New York: Oxford University Press, 1997), Vol. 3, 10–16; Thomas Schelling, *The Strategy of Conflict* (Cambridge, Mass.: Harvard University Press, 1960); Alexander L. George, "Coercive Diplomacy: Definition and Characteristics," in Alexander L. George and William E. Simons, eds., *The Limits of Coercive Diplomacy,* 2d ed. (Boulder, Colo.: Westview, 1994), 7–12.

[9]X [George F. Kennan], "The Sources of Soviet Conduct," *Foreign Affairs* 25:4 (July 1947), 572, 575, 582.

[10]"NSC-68, A Report to the President Pursuant to the President's Directive of January 31, 1950," in U.S. Department of State, *Foreign Relations of the United States: 1950,* Vol. 1 (Washington, D.C.: U.S. Government Printing Office, 1977), 240.

[11]Cited in Thomas G. Paterson, "Korean War," in Jentleson and Paterson, eds., *Encyclopedia of U.S. Foreign Relations,* Vol. 3, 30.

[12]Quote from Lord Ismay, cited in David S. Yost, *NATO Transformed: The Alliance's New Role in International Security* (Washington, D.C.: U.S. Institute of Peace Press, 1998), 52.

[13]Jonathan Nashel, "Domino Theory," in Jentleson and Paterson, eds., *Encyclopedia of U.S. Foreign Relations,* Vol. 2, 32–33.

[14]Text of the legislation as passed by Congress, cited in Seyom Brown, *The Faces of Power: Constancy and Change in United States Foreign Policy from Truman to Reagan* (New York: Columbia University Press, 1983), 124.

[15]Graham Allison, *The Essence of Decision: Explaining the Cuban Missile Crisis* (Boston: Little, Brown, 1971); Robert F. Kennedy, *Thirteen Days: A Memoir of the Cuban Missile Crisis* (New York: Norton, 1969); James Blight and David Welch, eds., *On the Brink: Americans and Soviets Re-examine the Cuban Missile Crisis* (New York: Hill and Wang, 1989).

[16]"Telegram, Secretary of State to the Consulate at Hanoi, May 20, 1949," in U.S. Department of State, *Foreign Relations of the United States: 1949,* Vol. 7 (Washington, D.C.: U.S. Government Printing Office, 1973), 29–30.

[17]Secretary of State Dean Acheson, cited in Thomas G. Paterson, J. Gary Clifford, and Kenneth J. Hagan, *American Foreign Relations: A History since 1895* (Lexington, Mass.: D. C. Heath, 1995), 369.

[18]Cited in Paterson, Clifford, and Hagan, *American Foreign Relations,* 405.

[19]Many attribute this quotation to President Franklin Roosevelt. Although there are doubts as to whether he actually said it, few doubt that the statement captures the essence of U.S. policy. See Robert A. Pastor, *Condemned to Repetition: The United States and Nicaragua* (Princeton: Princeton University Press, 1987), 3.

[20]"Address at a White House Reception for Members of Congress and for the Diplomatic Corps of the Latin American Republics, March 13, 1961," in *Public Papers of the Presidents: John F. Kennedy, 1961* (Washington, D. C.: U.S. Government Printing Office, 1962), 170–75.

[21]Abraham F. Lowenthal, *Partners in Conflict: The United States and Latin America* (Baltimore: Johns Hopkins University Press, 1987), 30.

[22]Report of the Hoover Commission, cited in "Get Personal," *New Republic,* September 14 and 21, 1998, 11.

[23]Mark J. Gasiorowski, "Iran," in Jentleson and Paterson, eds., *Encyclopedia of U.S. Foreign Relations,* Vol. 2, 415–16. See also James A. Bill, *The Eagle and the Lion: The Tragedy of American-Iranian Relations* (New Haven: Yale University Press, 1988); Bruce R. Kuniholm, *The Origins of the Cold War in the Near East* (Princeton: Princeton University Press, 1980); and Kermit Roosevelt, *Countercoup: The Struggle for the Control of Iran* (New York: McGraw-Hill, 1979).

[24]Aaron Wildavsky, "The Two Presidencies," *Trans-action* 3 (December 1966), 8.

[25]Senator Fulbright titled the article quoted here "American Foreign Policy in the 20th Century under an 18th-Century Constitution" (*Cornell Law Quarterly* 47 [Fall 1961], 2). He wrote further, "The question we face is whether our basic constitutional machinery, admirably suited to the needs of a remote agrarian republic in the eighteenth century, is adequate for the formulation and conduct of the foreign policy of a twentieth-century nation, pre-eminent in political and military power and burdened with all the enormous responsibilities that accompany such power. . . . My question, then, is whether we have any choice but to modify, and perhaps overhaul, the eighteenth-century procedures that govern the formulation and conduct of American foreign policy" (1–2).

[26]Richard F. Fenno, Jr., *Congressmen in Committees* (Boston: Little, Brown, 1973), 71.

[27]Cited in James M. Lindsay, *Congress and the Politics of U.S. Foreign Policy* (Baltimore: Johns Hopkins University Press, 1994), 22.

[28]Text of the legislation as passed by Congress, cited in Brown, *Faces of Power,* 124.

[29]The main precedent for the use of executive agreements rather than treaties as a way of getting around Congress had actually been set by Franklin Roosevelt in 1940 with the "destroyers for bases" deal with Britain (mentioned in Chapter 3). Even among those who agreed with Roosevelt's objectives, there was some concern at the time about the precedent being set. This also was the view taken in a 1969 report by the Senate Foreign Relations Committee: "Had the president publicly acknowledged his incursion on the Senate's treaty power and explained it as an emergency measure, a damaging constitutional precedent would have been averted. Instead, a spurious claim of constitutionality was made, compounding the incursion on the Senate's authority into a precedent for future incursions." Cited in Loch K. Johnson, *America as a World Power: Foreign Policy in a Constitutional Framework* (New York: McGraw-Hill, 1991), 108–9.

[30]There actually was one major effort in the early 1950s to rein in executive agreements. This was the Bricker Amendment, named for its principal sponsor, Senator John W. Bricker (R-Ohio), which would have amended the Constitution to require congressional approval of all executive agreements. Support for the Bricker Amendment was in part a reflection of McCarthyite distrust of the executive branch, and it too faded with the overall discrediting of McCarthyism. Indeed, until the late 1960s little was heard even about the executive's taking full advantage of the lack of any deadline in the requirement that executive agreements be reported to Congress, reporting very few of these agreements—and even those in a not particularly timely manner.

[31]Loch K. Johnson and James M. McCormick, "Foreign Policy by Executive Fiat," *Foreign Policy* 28 (Fall 1977), 121.

[32]Daniel Yergin, *Shattered Peace: The Origins of the Cold War and the National Security State* (Boston: Houghton Mifflin, 1977).

[33]See, for example, James G. Blight and Peter Kornbluh, eds., *Politics of Illusion: The Bay of Pigs Invasion Re-examined* (Boulder, Colo.: Lynne Rienner, 1997); "A Perfect Failure: The Bay of Pigs," in Irving L. Janis, *Groupthink: Psychological Studies of Policy Decisions and Fiascoes,* 2d ed. (Boston: Houghton Mifflin, 1982), 14–47; Peter Wyden, *Bay of Pigs: The Untold Story* (New York: Simon and Schuster, 1979).

[34]Cited in Janis, *Groupthink,* 39.

[35]Peter Kornbluh, ed., *Bay of Pigs Declassified: The Secret CIA Report on the Invasion of Cuba* (New York: Norton, 1998).

[36]Allison, *Essence of Decision;* Blight and Welch, *On the Brink.*

[37]Allison, *Essence of Decision;* Morton H. Halperin, *Bureaucratic Politics and Foreign Policy* (Washington, D.C.: Brookings Institution Press, 1974); Morton H. Halperin and Arnold Kanter, eds., *Readings in American Foreign Policy: A Bureaucratic Perspective* (Boston: Little, Brown, 1973); David C. Kozak and James M. Keagle, *Bureaucratic Politics and National Security: Theory and Practice* (Boulder, Colo.: Lynne Rienner, 1988). The movie *Thirteen Days,* released in 2000, had some inaccuracies but did provide a clear and vivid portrayal of the strong leadership President Kennedy provided. The movie was based on a book by the same name written by Attorney General Robert F. Kennedy, the president's brother and his main confidante during the Cuban missile crisis. (See Robert F. Kennedy, *Thirteen Days,* New York: W.W. Norton, 1971.)

[38]Dan Caldwell, "A Research Note on the Quarantine of Cuba, 1962," *International Studies Quarterly* 21:2 (December 1978), 625–33; Joseph F. Bouchard, *Command in Crisis: Four Case Studies* (New York: Columbia University Press, 1991); Richard K. Betts, *Soldiers, Statesmen, and Cold War Crises,* 2d ed. (New York: Columbia University Press, 1991); Scott D. Sagan, "Nuclear Alerts and Crisis Management," *International Security* 9:4 (Spring 1985), 99–139; and Graham T. Allison and Philip Zelikow, *Essence of Decision: Explaining the Cuban Missile Crisis,* 2d ed. (New York: Longman, 1999).

[39]Richard K. Betts, "Is Strategy an Illusion?" *International Security* 25:2 (Fall 2000), 34–35; Scott D. Sagan, *The Limits of Safety: Organizations, Accidents, and Nuclear Weapons* (Princeton: Princeton University Press, 1993), chaps. 2–3.

[40]James Aronson, *The Press and the Cold War* (New York: Bobbs Merrill, 1970), 186.

[41]Aronson, *The Press and the Cold War,* 159.

[42]Aronson, *The Press and the Cold War,* 159–60.

[43]"Commencement Address at American University in Washington," June 10, 1963, in *Public Papers of the Presidents: John F. Kennedy, 1963* (Washington, D.C.: U.S. Government Printing Office, 1964), 459–64.

[44]Quoted in Bruce W. Jentleson, *Pipeline Politics: The Complex Political Economy of East-West Energy Trade* (Ithaca, N.Y.: Cornell University Press, 1986), 129.

[45]Jentleson, *Pipeline Politics,* 100.

[46]See Dynamics of Choice on p. 156.

[47]Harvey Klehr, John Earl Haynes, and Kyrill M. Anderson, *The Soviet World of American Communism* (New Haven: Yale University Press, 1998); Ronald Radosh and Joyce Milton, *The Rosenberg File* (New Haven: Yale University Press, 1997).

[48]Cited in Jerel A. Rosati, *The Politics of United States Foreign Policy* (New York: Harcourt, Brace, 1993), 285.

CHAPTER 5 *The Cold War Context: Lessons and Legacies*

Introduction: Turbulent Decades

The 1960s, 1970s, and 1980s were turbulent decades for the United States. Foreign policy was not the only reason—the civil rights movement, the counterculture, economic change, and other forces and factors also were at work. But the setbacks, shifts, and shocks endured by American foreign policy clearly were major factors.

The Vietnam War was the most profound setback American foreign policy had suffered since the beginning of the Cold War, if not in its entire history. Many saw it as the first war the United States had ever lost. The reasons why were hotly debated—and still are. But the profundity of the loss as it affected both foreign policy strategy and foreign policy politics was undeniable.

The fate of détente with the Soviet Union—first its rise and then its fall— marked major shifts. The rise of détente challenged the dominant belief of the first quarter-century of the Cold War that minimal U.S.-Soviet cooperation was possible. This was especially true since the switch to détente was led by President Richard Nixon, who had built his political career on staunch anti-communist credentials. Yet although détente had some successes, its hopes and promises went largely unfulfilled. It engendered major political controversy at home. And when the Soviets invaded Afghanistan in December 1979, détente was pronounced dead.

The United States also endured tremendous economic shocks in the 1970s. Although not as bad as the Great Depression, these shocks were historically unique, for they came from the international economy. In 1971, for the first

146

time since 1893, the American merchandise trade balance was in deficit. Then came the oil embargo and price hikes by the Organization of Petroleum Exporting Countries (OPEC), first in 1973 and again in 1979. The assumption of cheap and reliable supplies of oil, in some respects no less a bed-rock of the post–World War II order than anticommunism, was being called into question. Third World countries tried to capitalize on the OPEC success in bringing the industrialized West to its knees by trying to shift the defining axis of the international system from East-West to North-South. Another major economic blow came as Japan, the country defeated in and occupied after World War II, became the United States' main economic competitor.

The 1980s thus began amid great foreign policy uncertainty, and they, too, proved a turbulent decade. Initially, following the demise of détente and the election of Ronald Reagan, the Cold War resurged. Policies on both sides grew increasingly confrontational, the rhetoric highly antagonistic. Fears of war, even nuclear war, were rising. In 1985 the Soviets selected a leader, Mikhail Gorbachev, who made dramatic changes in Soviet foreign policy. By the end of the decade the Cold War was over. How much credit for the end of the Cold War goes to Gorbachev, and how much to Reagan, has been and continues to be debated. The Cold War did end, though, and it ended peacefully.

In this chapter we examine these and other developments in U.S. foreign policy in the second half of the Cold War, with an eye to the lessons and legacies of the Cold War.

The Vietnam War: America's Most Profound Foreign Policy Setback

In 1995 Robert McNamara, secretary of defense under Presidents Kennedy and Johnson and the official most closely associated with the Vietnam War, published his startling mea culpa memoirs, *In Retrospect*. For almost thirty years McNamara had refused to talk about Vietnam. He had left government and had gone on to be president of the World Bank and to work in the 1980s for nuclear arms control, but he stayed mum on Vietnam. Now, though, he laid out his view of the causes for the U.S. failure in Vietnam (see Perspectives on p. 148). Some were political, such as the failure to maintain congressional and public support. Some were strategic, such as misjudging the geopolitical intentions of U.S. adversaries and exaggerating the actual threats to American interests. Some were diplomatic. Some were military.

 5.1

PERSPECTIVES
PERSPECTIVES
PERSPECTIVES

WHY THE UNITED STATES LOST THE VIETNAM WAR

According to former secretary of defense Robert McNamara

- We misjudged . . . the geopolitical intentions of our adversaries . . . and we exaggerated the dangers to the United States of their actions.
- We viewed the people and leaders of South Vietnam in terms of our own experience. We saw in them a thirst for—and a determination to fight for—freedom and democracy. We totally misjudged the political forces within the country.
- We underestimated the power of nationalism to motivate a people (in this case, the North Vietnamese and Vietcong) to fight and die for their beliefs and values. . . .
- Our misjudgments of friend and foe alike reflected our profound ignorance of the history, culture, and politics of the people in the area and the personalities and habits of their leaders.
- We failed then—as we have since—to recognize the limitations of modern, high-technology military equipment, forces, and doctrine in confronting unconventional, highly motivated people's movements.
- We failed to draw Congress and the American people into a full and frank discussion and debate of the pros and cons of a large-scale U.S. military involvement in Southeast Asia before we initiated the action.
- We did not recognize that neither our people nor our leaders are omniscient. . . .
- We did not hold to the principle that U.S. military action—other than in response to direct threats to our own security—should be carried out only in conjunction with multinational forces supported fully (and not merely cosmetically) by the international community.
- We failed to recognize that in international affairs, as in other aspects of life, there may be problems for which there are no immediate solutions.
- Underlying many of these errors lay our failure to organize the top echelons of the executive branch to deal effectively with the

(*Continued on page 149*)

(Why the United States Lost ... *Continued from page 148*)
extraordinarily complex range of political and military issues, involving the great risks and costs—including, above all else, loss of life—associated with the application of military force under substantial constraints over a long period of time.

Source: Robert S. McNamara, *In Retrospect: The Tragedy and Lessons of Vietnam* (New York: Times Books, 1995), 321–33. Copyright © 1995 by Robert S. McNamara. Reprinted by permission of Times Books, a division of Random House, Inc.

McNamara was not the only former high-level government official to have expressed such doubts and criticisms about Vietnam. Former secretary of state Dean Acheson later acknowledged receiving advice that there was "real danger that our efforts would fail," but nevertheless deciding that "having put our hand to the plow, we would not look back."[1] Dwight Eisenhower wrote of being "convinced that the French could not win" the 1945–54 colonial war, but that nevertheless "the decision to give this aid was almost compulsory. The United States had no real alternative."[2] John Kennedy was said to be "skeptical of the extent of our involvement in Vietnam but unwilling to abandon his predecessor's pledge."[3] And during Lyndon Johnson's "Americanization" of the war, Vice President Hubert Humphrey, Undersecretary of State George Ball, Senator J. William Fulbright, journalist Walter Lippmann, and all other proponents of alternative options were closed out of the decision-making process because of their misgivings. Henry Kissinger himself later described "Vietnamization," the centerpiece of his own policy, as "the operation, conceived in doubt and assailed by skepticism [which] proceeded in confusion"—but proceeded nevertheless.[4]

Some critics argued that Vietnam was a war that should not have been fought, could not have been won, and could and should have been halted at several key junctures. Others vehemently contended that it was right to have fought it, and that it could have been won through tougher policies and more commitment by U.S. policy-makers. The one point on which there has been consensus is that Vietnam was the most profound foreign policy setback the United States suffered during the Cold War era. For American foreign policy strategy, it amounted to failure on all counts: peace was not served, power was eroded, principles were violated, prosperity was damaged. In American foreign policy politics, the Cold War consensus was shattered, in terms of both its institutional structures and its societal underpinnings.

Foreign Policy Strategy: Failure on All Counts

PEACE   American casualities in Vietnam numbered more than two hundred thousand, including almost sixty thousand deaths. Vietnamese casualties numbered in the hundreds of thousands, as well. And rather than keeping the dominoes from falling, communism came to Vietnam, got stronger in Laos, and spread to Cambodia.

Whether peace was achievable through the war effort is one of the main debates between the contending schools noted above. Secretary McNamara believed not, in part because of the inherent "limitations" of modern high-technology warfare when pitted against "the power of nationalism to motivate a people to fight and die for their beliefs and values."[5] Others faulted what was not done more than what was; one general wrote that American strategy violated two of the "time-honored principles of war. . . . We lacked a clear objective and an attainable strategy of a decisive nature."[6]

The sense of the war's unwinnability was not just retrospective. Even while he was intensifying American bombing of the Vietnamese, President Nixon privately acknowledged that "there's no way to win the war. But we can't say that, of course. In fact, we have to seem to say the opposite, just to keep some bargaining leverage." At the peace negotiations with the North Vietnamese in Paris, the ultimate objective was not to win but, as Kissinger stated it, to be able "to withdraw as an expression of policy and not as a collapse."[7] This approach continued after the Treaty of Paris had been signed in 1973. The Ford administration pushed for retaliation against North Vietnamese treaty violations. But it did so less to ensure a peace than to gain a "decent interval" that might convince the global audience that the United States had not lost.[8]

POWER   All along the main factor driving U.S. involvement in Vietnam was the belief that the credibility of American power was being tested there. A 1952 State Department memorandum delineated three reasons for "the strategic importance of Indochina": "its geographic position as key to the defense of mainland Southeast Asia," a somewhat dubious proposition; "its economic importance as a potential large-scale exporter of rice," an interest much closer to trivial than vital; and "*as an example of Western resistance to Communist expansion*" (emphasis added).[9] In 1965, when the decision finally was made to send in American troops, President Johnson quite explicitly articulated the need to demonstrate American credibility, as it pertained to both global allies and adversaries alike: "Around the globe, from Berlin to Thailand, are people whose well-being rests, in part, on the belief that they can count on us if they are attacked. To leave Vietnam to its fate would shake the confidence of all these people in the value of an American commitment and in the value of America's word."[10]

This same precept carried over into the Nixon and Ford administrations. Kissinger stated uncategorically that "the commitment of 500,000 Americans has settled the issue of the importance of Vietnam. For what is involved now is confidence in American promises."[11] If the United States failed this test, President Nixon claimed, it would be perceived as "a pitiful, helpless giant" and "the forces of totalitarianism and anarchy will threaten free nations around the world."[12] On the eve of the American evacuation of Saigon in 1975, President Ford beseeched Congress in similar terms not to cut off aid, arguing that to do so "would draw into question the reliability of the United States and encourage the belief that aggression pays."[13]

Ironically, though, nothing damaged the perception of American power more than these very policies that were supposed to preserve it. No less a figure than Hans Morgenthau, whose books were cited in our original discussion of the Realist paradigm in Chapter 1, had opposed the Vietnam War as early as 1967, precisely because he believed it would be damaging to American power. The interests at stake were not worth the commitments needed. To the contrary, as Morgenthau himself argued, U.S. power could best be served by developing a relationship with Ho Chi Minh that, even without converting him from communism, would "prevent such a communist revolution from turning against the interests of the United States."[14]

PRINCIPLES   In the late 1950s, then-senator John Kennedy tried to make the moral case for American responsibility: "If we are not the parents of little Vietnam, then surely we are the godparents."[15] When American troops were first sent to these distant jungles, LBJ described the action as necessary because "we remain fixed on the pursuit of freedom as a deep and moral obligation that will not let us go."[16] President Nixon turned the principles argument inward with his rebuttal to the antiwar movement: if we withdrew from Vietnam, Nixon claimed, "we would lose confidence in ourselves. . . . North Vietnam cannot defeat or humiliate the United States. Only Americans can do that."[17]

Yet nowhere did Americans feel their foreign policy more violated their principles than in Vietnam. It needs to be acknowledged that among much of the antiwar movement there was a great deal of naiveté, wishful thinking, and rationalization. Ho Chi Minh and the Vietcong hardly were strictly freedom fighters, Jeffersonians, or the like. The horrors that the communist Khmer Rouge inflicted against their own people when they came to power in Cambodia shocked the world. But only according to the Cold War "ABC" definition did the likes of Presidents Ngo Dinh Diem and Nguyen Van Thieu in Vietnam, and Prime Minister Lon Nol in Cambodia, each of whom received staunch U.S. support, qualify as democrats. Moreover, the scenes of peasant villagers fleeing American aircraft spreading napalm, and of incidents like the 1968 My Lai massacre, in which U.S. soldiers killed more than 500 innocent Vietnamese villagers, were deeply disturbing to the American national conscience.

PROSPERITY   Theorists of the military-industrial complex claim that the raging appetite of an economy in which defense industries were so central was a key factor leading to Vietnam. Whether or not that analysis is true, from the more general perspective of the overall American economy, the effects of the war were quite damaging to prosperity. LBJ calculated that cutting domestic spending to finance the war would only further weaken political support, but his "guns and butter" strategy of trying to keep spending up in both areas backfired. The federal budget deficit grew. "Stagflation," meaning simultaneous high unemployment and high inflation, set in. For the first time since 1893, the trade balance went into deficit. The economic situation got so bad that President Nixon, a Republican, imposed wage and price controls and other stringent measures typically identified with liberal, Democratic politicians. But these moves only made the economic situation worse.

Foreign Policy Politics: Shattering the Cold War Consensus

As for politics, here too the effects were paradoxical. "If I did not go into Vietnam," LBJ reflected, "there would follow in this country an endless national debate—a mean and destructive debate—that would shatter my Presidency, kill my administration, and damage our democracy. I knew that Harry Truman and Dean Acheson had lost their effectiveness from the day that the Communists took over China. I believed that the loss of China had played a large role in the rise of Joe McCarthy. And I knew that all these problems, taken together, were chickenshit compared with what might happen if we lost Vietnam."[18] The last part of this statement at least was right, but because LBJ went in, not because he stayed out.

PRESIDENTIAL-CONGRESSIONAL RELATIONS   Recall Senator Fulbright's 1961 statement cited in Chapter 4 about the need to give the president more power. It was the same Senator Fulbright who, as chairman of the Senate Foreign Relations Committee, became one of the leading opponents of the war. More sweepingly he now warned of "presidential dictatorship in foreign affairs. . . . I believe that the presidency has become a dangerously powerful office, more urgently in need of reform than any other institution in government."[19] Similarly, historian and former Kennedy aide Arthur Schlesinger, Jr., attacked "the imperial presidency . . . out of control and badly in need of new definition and restraint."[20]

Now Congress was urged to be more assertive and less deferential. Some of its most ardent supporters even proclaimed the 1970s to be an age of "foreign policy *by* Congress."[21] Many of its members were now less parochial and more worldly, some having served earlier in their careers as State or Defense Department officials or Peace Corps members or even as political science and international relations professors. Greater expertise also was available from the expanded and more-professional staffs of congressional committees. For example, between 1960 and 1975, the staff of the Senate Foreign Relations Committee increased from 25 to 62 members, and the House Foreign Affairs Committee staff grew from 14 to 54.[22] Moreover, as Senator Fulbright wrote, only partially in jest, "whatever may be said against Congress . . . there is one thing to be said for it: It poses no threat to the liberties of the American people."[23]

Congress relied heavily on procedural legislation (defined in Chapter 2) in seeking to redress the imbalance of foreign policy powers. The *War Powers Resolution (WPR) of 1973* was among the most central and controversial of these procedural initiatives. No declaration of war had ever been passed for the military action in Vietnam. Presidents Johnson and Nixon both justified their actions on the basis of the 1964 Tonkin Gulf Resolution, which Congress did pass by overwhelming margins, with an open-ended authorization to use military force.* For Vietnam itself Congress tried a number of ways to end the war, eventually using the power of the purse to cut off funds. The WPR was intended to increase Congress's share of the war powers for the next Vietnam. President Nixon vetoed the WPR, claiming it was unconstitutional as an infringement of his presidential powers as commander in chief. But with Republicans joining Democrats in a show of bipartisanship, the necessary two-thirds margin was reached in both the House and the Senate to override his veto.

---

*It later was revealed that at least one of the two alleged incidents of North Vietnamese attacks on U.S. naval ships, which were the ostensible bases for the Tonkin Gulf Resolution, never actually occurred.

The WPR limited presidential power through two sets of provisions. One set sought to tighten up requirements for the president to consult with Congress before, or at least soon after, committing U.S. troops in any situation other than a genuine national emergency. This stipulation was intended to give Congress more say in whether initial troop commitments were made. The other established the "sixty-day clock," by which the president would have to withdraw U.S. forces unless Congress explicitly allowed an extension. As things have turned out in practice, the WPR has not worked very well, as we will discuss later in this chapter. But at the time it seemed like a significant rebalancing of the war powers.

Congress also tried to stake its claims to a larger share of other aspects of shared foreign policy powers. With respect to treaties and other international commitments, it passed legislation trying to clamp down on the excessive use of executive agreements. It used its investigative and oversight powers to tighten the reins on executive-branch departments and agencies, most notably on the CIA. It made frequent use of the legislative veto in policy areas such as arms sales, nuclear nonproliferation, foreign aid, and trade. All told, it was a period in which Congress was trying to make Pennsylvania Avenue more of a two-way street.

EXECUTIVE-BRANCH POLITICS   It was from Vietnam that the "credibility gap" arose. The Johnson and Nixon administrations kept trying to put the best face on the war by holding back from the public some information and distorting other information, and by outright lying. The public was left doubting the credibility of its leaders. Not only did this sense of skepticism, if not cynicism, cause the public to lose faith in the truthfulness of its leaders about Vietnam, it was applied increasingly to all high-level officials in all arenas of government, and thus became the more generalized problem of the credibility gap.

SHATTERING THE COLD WAR CONSENSUS   During the Cold War a few protest movements had emerged, but none that had any significant impact. The anti–Vietnam War movement marked a major change in this pattern. Hundreds of thousands of demonstrators marched on Washington, not just once but repeatedly. "Teach-ins" spread on college campuses, as did sit-ins and in some instances more violent demonstrations. In one particularly tragic incident in the spring of 1970, National Guard troops fired on antiwar protesters at Kent State University in Ohio, killing four students. Although some of its excesses worked against its very goals, overall the antiwar movement was an important influence on U.S. policy in Vietnam.

As for the news media, the old "cheerleader" role that had prevailed for much of the early Cold War was supplanted by the media as "critic." This, too, was born in Vietnam, where it was the media that first brought home to Americans news of how badly the war was going and how much of a credibility gap there was between official accounts and the reality on the ground. In one telling encounter a reporter posed a tough question to an American official at a press conference. The official asked the reporter his name. "Malcolm Browne of the Associated Press," he said. "So you're Browne," the official responded, revealing a knowledge of Browne's critical reporting. "Why don't you get on the team?"[24]

The Watergate scandal took media-government antagonism further. President Johnson and his administration had done quite a bit of shading of the truth, but Watergate revealed that President Nixon and his cronies had lied, covered up, and even committed crimes. Had it not been for the media, none of this may have been known. Moreover, even though Watergate wasn't a foreign policy scandal per se, among its revelations was President Nixon's "enemies list," which included some journalists as well as leaders of the antiwar movement.

Dynamics of Choice on p. 156 shows the sharp contrasts in public opinion between the Cold War consensus and the new mindset of "the Vietnam trauma." Whereas only 24 percent considered the Vietnam War a mistake when the United States first sent troops in 1965, by 1971 61 percent did. More generally, the public had become much less internationalist and much more isolationist, as can be seen in its low ranking of the importance of containment as a national objective, and its reduced willingness to use American troops to defend non-American territory, even in Western Europe.

These shifts reflected the differences between the "Munich–Pearl Harbor generation," which came of age during World War II, and the "Vietnam generation," which came of age during the Vietnam War. The lessons of Munich and Pearl Harbor were about the folly of isolationism, the dangers of appeasement, the risks of being unprepared—mistakes that led to World War II and that then became the core lessons for U.S. Cold War strategy. In sending the first U.S. troops to Vietnam in 1965, Defense Secretary McNamara cited a speech by a Vietnamese communist leader as "a speech that ranks with Hitler's *Mein Kampf*"; a Senate supporter flat out stated that "the situation in Vietnam today bears many resemblances to the situation just before Munich."[25] The experience of the Vietnam War, however, left the next generation with what Graham Allison has called a "militant disbelief in the older axioms."[26] Whatever lessons had been drawn from Munich and Pearl Harbor about what should have been done in the 1930s and early 1940s were seen by this new generation as having been misapplied in or inapplicable to the Vietnam War. The Vietnam experience was a searing one; it destroyed the Cold War consensus and left the country deeply divided and for years opposed to almost any use of military force.

DYNAMICS OF CHOICE

Public Opinion from Cold War Consensus to Vietnam Trauma

	Cold war consensus	Vietnam trauma
a. Percentage who support internationalism	65%	41%
b. Percentage who support isolationism	8%	21%
c. Rank of containment as a national objective	2nd	7th
d. Percentage supporting troops to defend Western Europe	80%	39%
e. Percentage supporting troops to defend the Western Hemisphere	73%	31%
f. Percentage responding yes to, "Was the Vietnam War a mistake?"	24%	61%

Sources: (a, b) William Watts and Potomac Associates, presented in Charles W. Kegley, Jr., and Eugene R. Wittkopf, *American Foreign Policy: Pattern and Process*, 3d ed. (New York: St. Martin's, 1987), 292; (c) Lloyd A. Free and Hadley Cantril, *The Political Beliefs of Americans* (New York: Simon and Schuster, 1968), 52; Michael Mandelbaum and William Schneider, "The New Internationalisms: Public Opinion and American Foreign Policy," in *Eagle Entangled: U.S. Foreign Policy in a Complex World*, ed. Kenneth A. Oye, Donald Rothchild, and Robert J. Lieber (New York: Longman, 1979), 41–42; (d) Eugene R. Wittkopf, "Elites and Masses: Another Look at Attitudes toward America's World Role," *International Studies Quarterly* 31:7 (June 1987), 131–59; Mandelbaum and Schneider, "New Internationalisms," 82; (e) Wittkopf, "Elites and Masses"; (f) Barry B. Hughes, *The Domestic Context of American Foreign Policy* (San Francisco: Freeman, 1978), 38–40.

Clearly, a lot had changed. The shift wasn't just because of Vietnam; there were other issues as well on which questions were increasingly being asked about foreign policy strategy and in foreign policy politics. But Vietnam in particular stood as a profound setback for American Cold War strategy and shattered the political patterns of the Cold War.

The Rise and Fall of Détente: Major Foreign Policy Shifts

Détente literally means a "relaxation of tensions." It was the principal term used to characterize efforts in the 1970s to break out of the Cold War and improve relations between the United States and the Soviet Union. But whereas at the beginning of the decade détente was heralded as the dawn of a new era, by the end of the decade these hopes had been dashed and the Cold War had resumed.

Nixon, Kissinger, and the Rise of Détente

What made the rise of détente possible were shifts in all 4 Ps, as well as in foreign policy politics.

Peace was a driving force behind détente for both the Americans and the Soviets. Both sides shared interests in stabilizing Europe, which is where the Cold War had originated and where it had been waged for nearly a quarter-century. It thus was important both substantively and symbolically that one of the first détente agreements achieved (1971) was on Berlin, the divided German city that had been the locus of recurring Cold War crises. Berlin's status as a divided city was not ended, but new agreements did allow increased contact between West and East Berlin, and West and East Germany more generally.

Other important agreements created the Conference on Security and Co-operation in Europe (CSCE) and adopted the Helsinki Accords of 1975. The CSCE was the first major international organization other than the UN to include countries of both Eastern and Western Europe, both NATO allies (including the United States and Canada) and Warsaw Pact members; it also included neutral countries like Sweden and Switzerland. The Helsinki Accords were something of a trade-off. On the one hand they gave the Soviets the recognition they long had wanted of territorial borders in central and Eastern Europe as drawn after World War II. On the other hand they established human rights and other democratic values as basic tenets that CSCE members agreed to respect. Although this provision was not fully binding on Moscow or other communist governments, it provided a degree of legitimization and protection for dissidents that, as we will see later, nurtured the seeds of what would become the great anticommunist revolutions of 1989.

The United States and the Soviet Union also increasingly had come to recognize, especially in the wake of the Cuban missile crisis, their shared interest in working together to reduce the risks of nuclear war. This interest was clearly stated in the "Basic Principles of Relations," a charter-like document signed by Nixon and Soviet leader Leonid Brezhnev at their 1972 summit (see At the Source on p. 159). Underlying this recognition was an important shift in nuclear deterrence doctrine (power). One of the reasons noted in Chapter 4 that the Soviets put nuclear missiles in Cuba was to pose a threat close to American territory as a counterweight to the overall American nuclear superiority. Even though this didn't succeed, or, arguably, precisely because it didn't succeed, the Soviets came out of the Cuban missile crisis determined to close the nuclear-weapons gap. The nuclear arms race thus got another kick upward. On the U.S. side the rising costs of maintaining nuclear superiority, especially on top of the costs of the Vietnam War, were becoming more burdensome. Moreover, even if nuclear superiority were maintained, the Soviets had increased their own nuclear firepower sufficiently that security would not be assured. The dilemma was laid out in a 1967 speech by Defense Secretary McNamara: "In the larger equation of security, our 'superiority' is of limited significance. . . . Even with our current superiority, or indeed with any numerical superiority realistically attainable, the blunt inescapable fact remains that the Soviet Union could still—with its present forces—effectively destroy the United States, even after absorbing the full weight of an American first strike."[27]

The strategic situation he was describing was one of *mutually assured destruction,* or MAD, as it became known in a fitting acronym. Yet as paradoxical as it might sound, MAD was seen as potentially stabilizing. Since neither side could launch a "first strike" without risking getting devastated itself in a "second strike"—i.e., with destruction assured to be mutual—the chances were slim that either side would resort to using nuclear weapons. Trying to break out of this situation could make the arms race endless. Both sides thus had an interest in nuclear arms control.

Prior to the détente era there had been only a few U.S.-Soviet nuclear arms-control agreements.[*] Thus the signing in 1972 of the first *Strategic Arms Limitation Treaty* (SALT I) was highly significant as recognition that peace and

---

[*]One was the Antarctic Treaty of 1959, prohibiting the testing or deployment of nuclear weapons in the South Pole area. Another was the Limited Test Ban Treaty of 1963, with Great Britain and France also signees, prohibiting nuclear-weapons testing in the atmosphere, under water, or in outer space, and imposing some limits on underground testing.

U.S.-SOVIET DÉTENTE

❝The United States of America and the Union of Soviet Socialist Republics . . . have agreed as follows:

First. They will proceed from the common determination that in the nuclear age there is no alternative to conducting their mutual relations on the basis of peaceful coexistence. Differences in ideology and in the social systems of the USA and the USSR are not obstacles to the bilateral development of normal relations based on the principles of sovereignty, equality, non-interference in internal affairs and mutual advantage.

Second. The USA and the USSR attach major importance to preventing the development of situations capable of causing a dangerous exacerbation of their relations. Therefore, they will do their utmost to avoid military confrontations and to prevent the outbreak of nuclear war. They will always exercise restraint in their mutual relations, and will be prepared to negotiate and settle differences by peaceful means. Discussions and negotiations on outstanding issues will be conducted in a spirit of reciprocity, mutual accommodation and mutual benefit.

Both sides recognize that efforts to obtain unilateral advantage at the expense of the other, directly or indirectly, are inconsistent with these objectives. The prerequisites for maintaining and strengthening peaceful relations between the USA and the USSR are the recognition of the security interests of the Parties based on the principle of equality and the renunciation of the use or threat of force. . . .

Sixth. The Parties will continue their efforts to limit armaments on a bilateral as well as on a multilateral basis. They will continue to make special efforts to limit strategic armaments. Whenever possible, they will conclude concrete agreements aimed at achieving these purposes.

The USA and the USSR regard as the ultimate objective of their efforts the achievement of general and complete disarmament and the establishment of an effective system of international security in accordance with the purposes and principles of the United Nations.

Seventh. The USA and the USSR regard commercial and economic ties as an important and necessary element in the strengthening of their

(*Continued on page 160*)

(U.S.-Soviet Détente   *Continued from page 159)*
bilateral relations and thus will actively promote the growth of such
ties....

Ninth. The two sides reaffirm their intention to deepen cultural ties
with one another and to encourage fuller familiarization with each
other's cultural values. They will promote improved conditions for cultural exchanges and tourism. "

Source: "Basic Principles of Relations," signed by the United States and the Soviet Union,
May 1972, in *American Foreign Relations, 1972: A Documentary Record* (New York: New
York University Press for the Council on Foreign Relations, 1976), 75–78.

stability were not achievable only through arms but also required arms control.
SALT I set limits on strategic nuclear weapons according to a formula known
as "essential equivalence," whereby the Soviets were allowed a larger quantity of
missiles because the United States had technological advantages that allowed it
to put more bombs on each missile.* The idea was that if the Soviets had a
quantitative edge and the United States a qualitative one, both would be assured of deterrence. SALT I also severely limited anti–ballistic missile (ABM)
defense systems, on the grounds that such defensive systems were destabilizing:
if one side knew it could defend itself against nuclear attack, then mutual destruction no longer would be assured and that side might be more likely to
launch a first strike.

Trade was also a major component of détente, both for economic reasons
(prosperity) and because of its utility for peace and power objectives. With respect to the latter two, as stated in one Nixon administration report, "our purpose is to build in both countries a vested economic interest in the maintenance
of a harmonious and enduring relationship. . . . If we can create a situation in
which the use of military force would jeopardize a mutually profitable relationship, I think it can be argued that security will have been enhanced."[28] The linkages between prosperity and peace and power were evident both in the grain deal
the United States offered the Soviets in 1971 at cut-rate prices, in part to induce

---

*The technical term is MIRVs, or multiple independently targeted re-entry vehicles. Think of
missiles as delivery vehicles on which nuclear bombs are put. A MIRVed missile is one that can
hold multiple bombs, each aimed at its own target.

them to agree to SALT I, and in the pressure the Soviets put on North Vietnam in late 1972 to sign the Paris peace treaty in order to keep U.S. trade flowing.*

In terms of economic benefits for the United States, interests were strongest in two sectors. One was agriculture. Up until the 1970s the Soviets had been largely self-sufficient in grain. The only prior major grain deal with the United States was in 1963. But for reasons of both bad weather and bad planning, Soviet grain harvests now were falling far short of their needs. Ironically, their first purchases of American grain were so huge and transacted through such clever manipulation of the markets that they garnered low prices for themselves while leaving U.S. domestic grain markets with short supplies and high inflation. The Nixon and Ford administrations worked out trade agreements for future purchases that tried to lock in the export benefits from the grain sales while insulating American markets from further inflationary effects. By 1980, American exporters supplied 80 percent of Soviet grain imports.

The other key sector was energy. The Soviet Union was second only to Saudi Arabia in the size of its oil reserves, and it was first in the world in natural-gas reserves. Even before the OPEC shocks hit in late 1973, the Nixon administration assessed that "with the tremendous increases that are projected in our energy requirements by the end of this century, it may be very much in our interest to explore seriously the possibility of gaining access to, and in fact to aid in the development of energy fields as rich as those possessed by the Soviet Union."[29] After the OPEC shocks there was even more basis for this economic calculus, not least because while supporting the OPEC embargo against the United States and the Netherlands in their rhetoric, the Soviets had undercut it by quietly providing both countries with some additional oil.

The role of principles in promoting détente was mixed. The Nixon-Kissinger approach was to give limited emphasis in their "high politics" to Soviet political and human rights dissidents and other such issues. "The domestic practices of the Soviet Union are not necessarily related to détente," which was primarily related to foreign policy, Kissinger stated in testimony to Congress. Such a position was not "moral callousness" but rather a recognition of the "limits on our ability

---

*According to the *Wall Street Journal*, when President Nixon announced stepped-up bombing of North Vietnam and mining of its harbors, Soviet trade minister Nikolai Patolichev was meeting with U.S. commerce secretary Peter G. Peterson. "After hearing Mr. Nixon's tough words, he [Patolichev] turned to his host [Peterson] and said: 'Well, let's get back to business.' And a couple of days later he posed happily with the President, a clear signal to Hanoi that Moscow put its own interests first." Cited in Bruce W. Jentleson, "The Political Basis for Trade in U.S.-Soviet Relations," *Millennium: Journal of International Studies* 15 (Spring 1986), 31.

to produce internal change in foreign countries."[30] A particularly contentious issue in this regard was the linkage between most-favored-nation (MFN) status and other trade benefits for the Soviet Union and U.S. pressures for increased emigration rights for Soviet Jews. In keeping with his view of détente as more about Soviet foreign policy than its domestic policy, Kissinger preferred to leave the Soviet Jewry issue to "quiet diplomacy." Congress, however, saw it differently, and in 1974 passed the Jackson-Vanik Amendment linking MFN status to a prescribed increase in emigration visas for Soviet Jews.

The Carter administration put much more emphasis on human rights in its détente strategy, in two respects. One was directly vis-à-vis the Soviet Union, as when President Carter personally met with Aleksandr Solzhenitsyn, the renowned Soviet author and dissident who had been exiled in 1974 after decades in prison camps (gulags), and with whom President Ford and Secretary Kissinger had refused to meet. Also in a radical departure from the policies of his predecessors, President Carter championed human rights with respect to the Third World. Declaring in his 1977 inaugural address that "our commitment to human rights must be absolute," President Carter cut or withdrew support from such traditional "ABC" allies as the Somozas in Nicaragua and the shah of Iran.[31]

As for foreign policy politics, initially it seemed that détente might provide the basis for a new consensus. It may have seemed ironic that Richard Nixon, who had launched his political career as a staunch anticommunist, was now the one both to pursue détente with the Soviet Union and to visit "Red" China. But there was a political logic to this seeming reversal, as someone with impeccable anticommunist credentials could be insulated from charges of being soft on communism. In any case, the public was captivated by images of President Nixon in China sharing champagne toasts with Mao Zedong, and of Soviet leader Leonid Brezhnev donning a cowboy hat and giving a bear hug to the star of a popular American television series.

Even so, détente encountered some opposition from both ends of the political spectrum. Liberals supported its overall thrust but were critical on issues like the Nixon-Kissinger de-emphasis of human rights. Conservatives, while Nixon's longtime political comrades, were not yet ready to admit that anything other than confrontation was possible with the Soviets. They were skeptical of arms control in general and of SALT I in particular. Their main criticism of SALT I was that it gave the Soviets a potential advantage once they developed the MIRV technology, breaking out of essential equivalence and gaining true superiority. And on China, Mao was still the subversive who wrote that "little red book," and conservatives' real passion was to stop the "abandonment" of Taiwan.

Executive-branch politics was marked more by the personality of Henry Kissinger than by the policy of détente. Kissinger's biographers paint a picture of a man whose ego often got in the way of his brilliance.[32] Many examples can be drawn from Kissinger's penchant for bureaucratic warfare. As President Nixon's national security adviser, he tried to confine Secretary of State William Rogers to minor issues only. When President Nixon in his second term made Kissinger secretary of state, he allowed him to keep the national security adviser title as well. When Kissinger did give up the NSC post once Gerald Ford became president, he ensured that the position went to his former deputy Brent Scowcroft. Kissinger also fought major bureaucratic battles with Defense Secretary James Schlesinger, who tended to be more hawkish on arms control and defense issues. To be sure, Kissinger won more rounds of executive-branch politics than he lost. And there is something to be said for a take-charge approach that avoids bureaucratic bogs. But some of the flaws in his policies were due to his resistance to input from other top officials, and some of the enemies he made engendered political problems that in turn hampered his effectiveness.

Executive-branch politics during this period was also marred by a number of scandals. The CIA was especially hard hit, both in congressional hearings and in the media, with revelations and allegations ranging from assassination plots concocted against Fidel Castro and other foreign leaders, to illegal spying on U.S. citizens at home, including monitoring and intercepting the mail of members of Congress. Covert actions, in the words of the Senate Select Committee on Intelligence Activities (known as the Church Committee, after its chair, Senator Frank Church, a Democrat from Idaho), had been intended only as "exceptional instruments used only in rare instances," but "presidents and administrations have made excessive, and at times self-defeating, use of covert action."[33]

No doubt the greatest political scandal during these years was Watergate. The Watergate break-in occurred in June 1972, only a little more than a month after President Nixon's first major summit in Moscow. As it built up over the next two years, the Watergate scandal dominated the media and public opinion, crowding out most other news stories. And it precluded any chance President Nixon had of converting his 1972 landslide re-election victory into a mandate for foreign or domestic policy. Ultimately, on August 9, 1974, it led to President Nixon's resignation. Although Nixon didn't take détente down with him, his political self-destruction surely added to the political problems détente faced.

Reasons for the Fall of Détente

The December 1979 Soviet invasion of Afghanistan is the event most often cited as marking the end of détente. President Carter called it "a clear threat to peace" and warned the Soviets that unless they withdrew "this will inevitably jeopardize the course of United States–Soviet relations throughout the world."[34] Even more than the Soviet presence in Afghanistan, the U.S. government's main concern was that the Soviets would not stop in Afghanistan but would continue on into the oil-rich Persian Gulf region. The Carter Doctrine, proclaimed in January 1980, echoed the Truman Doctrine and other cornerstones of the early Cold War: "Let our position be clear," President Carter declared. "An attempt by any outside force to gain control of the Persian Gulf region will be regarded as an assault on the vital interests of the United States of America, and such an assault will be repelled by any means necessary, including military force."[35] This was much tougher talk and a more centrist policy than President Carter originally articulated and pursued.

Yet Afghanistan wasn't solely responsible for détente's fall. There were two deeper reasons. One was that all along, and for both sides, the relaxation of tensions and increased cooperation of détente did not put an end to continued competition and rivalry. The 1972 Basic Principles of Relations agreement cited earlier (see At the Source on p. 159) may have stated that "both sides recognize that efforts to obtain unilateral advantage at the expense of the other, directly or indirectly, are inconsistent" with the objectives of détente. This statement, though, was an example of papering over rather than resolving fundamental differences. The differences are well stated by Raymond Garthoff, a scholar and former State Department official:

> The U.S. conception of détente . . . called for U.S. manipulation of incentives and penalties in bilateral relations in order to serve other policy interests . . . a strategy for managing the emergence of Soviet power by drawing the Soviet Union into the existing world order through acceptance of a code of conduct for competition that favored the United States.
>
> The Soviet conception of détente was one of peaceful coexistence, which would set aside direct conflict between the two superpowers, in order to allow socialist and anti-imperialist forces a free hand. The Soviet leadership thus saw their task as maneuvering the United States into a world no longer marked by U.S. predominance.
>
> This discrepancy led to increasing friction.[36]

For both sides the main objective still was power much more than peace. This fact was evident in the different ways each side tried to use its relations with

China as leverage in great-power politics. The Soviets were trying to get U.S. support in their split with China. The Soviet-Chinese split long had been much worse than generally was realized in the United States. In 1969 military skirmishes took place along the Soviet-Chinese border. The Soviets even tried to find out what the U.S. reaction would be if they went to war with China. Not only was this inquiry rebuffed, but one of the strategic calculations for Nixon and Kissinger in their surprise opening to China (see At the Source, p. 166) was to use this new relationship as leverage in U.S.-Soviet relations. They were "playing the China card," as it was dubbed, beginning the "careful search for a new relationship" and shifting emphasis from the twenty-odd most recent years of animosity to the longer "history of friendship" between the Chinese and American people. Nor were Nixon and Kissinger particularly subtle in playing the China card: it was no coincidence that their trip to China came a few months earlier in 1972 than their trip to Moscow.

The clashing conceptions of the purposes of détente also were evident in the limits of what was achieved through arms control. The best that could be said for SALT I and SALT II (the follow-on agreement) was that they somewhat limited the growth of nuclear arsenals. No cuts were made by either side, just limits on future growth, and there was plenty of room within those limits for new and more destructive weapons. In addition, the Soviets were discovered to have cheated in certain areas. It took seven years after SALT I was signed until Carter and Brezhnev signed SALT II. American conservatives were strongly opposed to the new treaty, and they raised the specter of the Soviets' gaining nuclear superiority and the United States' facing a "window of vulnerability." Liberals were more supportive, although some only begrudgingly so, as they did not think the treaty went far enough. SALT II never was ratified by the Senate, because Carter withdrew it in response to the Soviet invasion of Afghanistan.

Nor was it just in Afghanistan that U.S.-Soviet Third World rivalries intensified and expanded. The U.S. expectation had been that détente amounted to Soviet acceptance of containment, that the Soviets would step back from spreading Marxist-Leninist revolution. The Soviets, though, as Garthoff indicated, saw détente mainly as a way to avoid escalation to superpower conflict while global geopolitical competition went on. Thus in Vietnam the Soviets helped pressure North Vietnam to sign the 1973 Paris peace treaty, but then aided the North's military victory and takeover in 1975. They also became much more active in Africa, supporting Marxist coups and guerrilla wars in places like Angola and Ethiopia.

U.S. Third World policy was still mired in confusion and contradiction. On the one hand, the Nixon and Ford administrations were still intent on

At the Source

THE OPENING OF RELATIONS WITH CHINA

Excerpts from a Speech by President Richard Nixon

❝ The following considerations shaped this Administration's approach to the People's Republic of China.

■ Peace in Asia and peace in the world require that we exchange views, not so much despite our differences as because of them. A clearer grasp of each other's purposes is essential in an age of turmoil and nuclear weapons.
■ It is in America's interest, and the world's interest, that the People's Republic of China play its appropriate role in shaping international arrangements that affect its concerns. Only then will that great nation have a stake in such arrangements; only then will they endure.
■ No one nation shall be the sole voice for a bloc of states. We will deal with all countries on the basis of specific issues and external behavior, not abstract theory.
■ Both Chinese and American policies could be much less rigid if we had no need to consider each other permanent enemies. Over the longer term there need be no clashes between our fundamental national concerns.
■ China and the United States share many parallel interests and can do much together to enrich the lives of our peoples. It is no accident that the Chinese and American peoples have such a long history of friendship.

On this basis we decided that a careful search for a new relationship should be undertaken. ❞

Source: President Richard M. Nixon, "U.S. Foreign Policy for the 1970s: The Emerging Structure of Peace," report to Congress, February 9, 1972, reprinted in *Department of State Bulletin* 66:1707 (March 13, 1972), 327.

containment. In Chile, for example, the CIA was heavily involved in 1970–73 efforts to overthrow socialist (but freely elected) president Salvador Allende. In Angola, CIA and military aid were started for the pro-American faction battling the pro-Soviet one, but then Congress passed legislation prohibiting further aid. On these and other issues, the essence of the debate was over which "lessons of Vietnam" were the right ones—that communism really did have to be contained, or that such efforts ended up as costly quagmires.

Another, related part of the debate was over President Carter's emphasis on human rights. In Nicaragua, where the dictatorship of the Somoza family had a long record of human rights violations, the Carter administration cut back support and brought pressure for reform. Although this had some positive effects, the ensuing revolution that deposed Anastasio Somoza brought to power the Sandinistas, who initially were a mix of nationalists, socialists, Marxist-Leninists, and anti-Americans. Even though the history of U.S. imperialist domination was more the cause of the revolution than was the Carter human rights policy, the Carter policy got much of the blame. The same dynamic played out in Iran, with the fall of the shah to the virulently anti-American Islamic fundamentalist revolution led by Ayatollah Ruhollah Khomeini. Not only did the United States lose a strategically located ally when the shah fell, but the whole American psyche was deeply shaken by the November 1979 seizure of the U.S. embassy in Tehran and the taking of more than seventy Americans as hostages. Ayatollah Khomeini justified the hostage-taking as action against "this great Satan—America" (see At the Source, p. 168). These developments were quite traumatic for Americans, unaccustomed to the sense of vulnerability that the Iranian hostage crisis evoked. Those shock waves were still being felt—strategically, politically, and psychologically—when barely a month later the Soviets launched their invasion of Afghanistan.

Amid all this, the divisiveness of domestic politics grew worse and worse. President Carter had a Democratic Congress, but that mattered only marginally in getting congressional support. His executive branch was stricken by bitter internal politics, with National Security Adviser Zbigniew Brzezinski and Secretary of State Cyrus Vance waging their own bureaucratic warfare. Conservatives, now led by an organization called the Committee on the Present Danger, became increasingly active in opposition to détente. President Carter also felt pressure from agricultural interest groups when he imposed grain sanctions as part of his response to the Soviet invasion of Afghanistan. General public opinion was deeply split, and increasingly confused.

Disparagements of "the decade of so-called détente" were staples of candidate Ronald Reagan's speeches. "We are blind to reality," he said on the campaign

> ## At the Source

AMERICA HELD HOSTAGE

A Speech by Ayatollah Khomeini

66 In this revolution, the big Satan is America, which is clamoring to gather other Satans around it; this includes both the Satans inside and outside Iran. You know that during the rule of these two devils [presumably the shah and his father], whose rule was in contravention of the law, Iran was in turn enslaved by Britain and then America. This great Satan—America—is clamoring and gathering around it other Satans because its hand has been cut off from our resources. It is afraid this amputation may become permanent. Therefore, it is plotting.

As for that center [the U.S. embassy in Tehran] occupied by our young men, I have been informed that it has been a lair of espionage and plotting. America expects to take the shah there, engage in plots, create a base in Iran for these plots, and our young people are expected simply to remain idle and witness all these things.

The rotten roots have become active, hoping we would mediate and tell the young people to leave this place. Our young people resorted to this action because they saw that the shah was allowed in America.

America expects our nation, our young people, our university and our young religious people to sit idle and see the blood of the nearly 100,000 martyrs shed in vain. Obviously, had it not been for the plots, sabotage and all those corrupt acts, everyone could have remained here in freedom. However, when we face plots, our young people cannot wait and see their country return to the past and everything go with the wind. Our young people must foil all these plots with all their might. Today we cannot simply remain idle and watch things; today we are facing underground treason, treason devised in these same embassies, mainly by the great Satan, America. They must bear in mind that Iran is still in a state of revolution; a revolution greater than the first one. They must be put in their place and return this criminal to us as soon as possible. 99

Source: Ayatollah Khomeini, speech broadcast in Persian on Tehran Domestic Service, November 5, 1979, reported in "Khomeini on Occupation," Foreign Broadcast Information Service: Middle East/North Africa, November 6, 1979, R2–R3.

trail, "if we refuse to recognize that détente's usefulness to the Soviets is only as a cover for their traditional and basic strategy for aggression.[37] In November 1980 Ronald Reagan was elected president. The Cold War would be renewed, and then ultimately start to end, during the Reagan presidency.

1970s Economic Shocks

The 1970s were the decade during which the myth of assured prosperity was shattered. The American economy, and the economic psyche of the American people, endured a series of shocks that recast the international economy and the U.S. position in it as less hegemonic and more uncertain than it had been in generations. Some of the fundamental sources of these new economic problems actually were rooted in U.S. domestic and economic policies: such as LBJ's "guns and butter" and the stagflation that ensued, and President Nixon's overstimulation of the economy as part of his 1972 re-election strategy. But the focus was more on external (foreign) sources.

The Nixon Shock, 1971

On August 15, 1971, with the value of the dollar at its lowest point since World War II, President Nixon announced that the United States was unilaterally devaluing the dollar, suspending its convertibility to gold, and imposing a 10 percent special tariff on imports. These moves, which came to be known as the "Nixon shock," were targeted principally at Europe and Japan, who were still strategic allies, but increasingly had also become economic competitors. "Foreigners are out to screw us," Treasury Secretary John Connally rather indelicately put it, "and it's our job to screw them first."[38]

In more analytical terms the principal significance was threefold. First, whereas for the previous quarter-century the United States had been willing to grant economic concessions to its allies to help them with their economic reconstruction and ensure their political stability as part of containment, now it was projecting onto them responsibility for its own economic problems. The United States was coming close, as Kissinger and others warned, to economic war with its own allies.

Second, one of the key pillars of the liberal international order (LIEO), the international monetary system based on fixed exchange rates and the gold standard, had crumbled with the U.S. abandonment of the gold standard. The

world risked descending back into competitive devaluations and other monetary manipulations. Some efforts were made to prevent such moves, first with
a system of "floating" exchange rates and then "flexible" ones, but the new reality fell well short of the stability and multilateralism of the old system.

Third, the free trade vs. protectionism debate was reopened in U.S. domestic politics. Labor unions such as the AFL-CIO had been generally
supportive of free trade in the 1950s and 1960s. They had lobbied for loopholes for industries facing the toughest competition from imports (textiles,
for instance) but had supported most free-trade bills. As long as the United
States was running a trade surplus, more jobs were being created by exports
than were being lost to imports. But with the United States running a merchandise trade balance for the first time since 1893, labor unions shifted their
politics accordingly, becoming much more protectionist.

The OPEC Shocks, 1973 and 1979

The American automobile culture was built on a steady and inexpensive supply of oil. American suburban families and college students alike took for
granted driving to a nearby gas station and filling up at prices of about thirty-
three cents per gallon. That all changed in October 1973 when Americans had
to learn a new acronym: OPEC.

OPEC had been founded back in 1960. It had tried oil embargoes and oil
price hikes before, but they hadn't succeeded. In 1967, during the Arab-Israeli
Six-Day War, two factors undermined the embargo that OPEC instituted to
weaken international support for Israel. One was that some of OPEC's non-
Arab members, such as Iran (a Muslim but non-Arab country) and Venezuela,
didn't go along, and even stepped up their oil production. The other was that
the United States at that time was still the world's largest oil producer and was
able to compensate by increasing its own production by a million barrels per
day. In 1973, though, the cartel held together, with all OPEC members agreeing to 25 percent production cuts, full oil embargoes targeted at the United
States and the Netherlands for their support of Israel in the Yom Kippur War,
and a worldwide price increase of 325 percent. U.S. oil production had been
falling since 1970, and this time only a meager increase of one hundred thousand barrels per day could be mustered.

Economically the OPEC embargo was, as they say, like pouring fuel onto
a fire. The stagflation, the trade imbalance, and other economic problems
plaguing the American economy were made much worse. No commodity
was as central to industry as oil, and no commodity was as essential to the

consumer culture. Moreover, beyond the material impact, the psychological shocks were highly disorienting. The easy-in/easy-out of gas stations gave way to gas lines miles long. For a while gas was rationed, with fill-ups alternated daily for even-numbered and odd-numbered license plates. The ultimate insult was that it wasn't even the Soviet Union or a European great power that was revealing American vulnerabilities—it was weaker, less-developed, not even "modern" countries of sheiks and shahs. That type of thinking may be condemned as arrogant, but it is important to any understanding of the trauma of the OPEC oil shock.

In case there were doubts or hopes that this may have been a one-time thing, the second OPEC oil shock hit in 1979 with the Iranian Revolution. Oil supplies again were disrupted. Prices were hiked. Gas lines returned, unemployment was fed, inflation skyrocketed, interest rates hit double digits, trade deficits shot up. By the mid-1980s, oil prices actually started to come down in real terms, but the marks left by the OPEC shocks were permanent.

The North-South Conflict and Demands for an "NIEO"

Despite having 74 percent of the world's population, as of the early 1970s Third World countries accounted for only 17 percent of the global gross national product (GNP). So when OPEC was so successful in bringing the industrialized world to heel, many Third World countries saw an opportunity to redefine international economic relations toward greater equity and justice for the developing-world "South" against the industrialized "North." They criticized the LIEO for giving inadequate attention to issues of development and for perpetuating inequalities in the global distribution of wealth. The General Agreement on Tariffs and Trade may have been opening markets, but the terms of trade tended to favor the industrial exports of the developed countries over the raw materials and foodstuffs exported by the developing world. The IMF and the "conditionalities" it attached to its loans (i.e., economic, social, and other policy changes required of Third World debtor countries in exchange for receiving IMF financial assistance) were under so much fire as to be the target of protests and riots in Third World cities. So, too, with foreign aid, criticized as too little and not the right kind of development assistance.

In May 1974, at a special session of the UN General Assembly, the South put forward a "Declaration of a New International Economic Order" (see At the Source, p. 172). This NIEO was intended to replace the LIEO. For the United States, this proposal threatened both its economic interests and its free-market ideology. The American economy depended on cheap commodities and raw

At the Source

THE DECLARATION OF A NEW
INTERNATIONAL ECONOMIC ORDER

❝ *We, the Members of the United Nations,*
Having convened a special session of the General Assembly to study for the first time the problems of raw materials and development, devoted to the consideration of the most important economic problems facing the world community...

Solemnly proclaim our united determination to work urgently for the establishment of a new international economic order based on equity, sovereign equality, interdependence, common interest and co-operation among all States, irrespective of their economic and social systems which shall correct inequalities and redress existing injustices, make it possible to eliminate the widening gap between the developed and the developing countries and ensure steadily accelerating economic and social development and peace and justice for present and future generations, and to that end declare ...

It has proved impossible to achieve an even and balanced development of the international community under the existing international economic order. The gap between the developed and the developing countries continues to widen in a system which was established at a time when most of the developing countries did not even exist as independent States and which perpetuates inequality. . . .

The developing world has become a powerful factor felt in all fields of international activity. These irreversible changes in the relationship of forces in the world necessitate the active, full and equal participation of the developing countries in the formulation and application of all decisions that concern the international community. . . .

The prosperity of the international community as a whole depends upon the prosperity of its constituent parts. International co-operation for development is the shared goal and common duty of all countries. Thus the political, economic and social well-being of present and future generations depends more than ever on co-operation between all members of the international community on the basis of sovereign equality

(*Continued on page 173*)

(New International Economic Order *Continued from page 172)*
and the removal of the disequilibrium that exists between them.

The new international economic order should be founded on full respect for the following principles: . . .

The broadest co-operation of all the State members of the international community, based on equity, whereby the prevailing disparities in the world may be banished and prosperity secured for all; . . .

The necessity to ensure the accelerated development of all the developing countries, while devoting particular attention to the adoption of special measures in favour of the least developed. . . .

The right [of] every country to adopt the economic and social system that it deems to be the most appropriate for its own development and not to be subjected to discrimination of any kind as a result; . . .

Regulation and supervision of the activities of transnational corporations by taking measures in the interest of the national economies of the countries where such transnational corporations operate on the basis of the full sovereignty of those countries; . . .

Just and equitable relationship between the prices of raw materials, primary products, manufactured and semi-manufactured goods exported by developing countries and the prices of raw materials, primary commodities, manufactures, capital goods and equipment imported by them with the aim of bringing about sustained improvement in their unsatisfactory terms of trade and the expansion of the world economy; . . .

Giving to the developing countries access to the achievements of modern science and technology, and promoting the transfer of technology and the creation of indigenous technology for the benefit of the developing countries in forms and in accordance with procedures which are suited to their economies. "

Source: "Declaration on Establishment of a New International Economic Order," *Annual Review of UN Affairs 1974* (New York: Oceana Publications, 1976), 208–12.

materials, yet the NIEO demanded higher prices for raw materials and commodities in the name of "justice and equity." American multinational corporations had substantial investments in the Third World, yet the NIEO called for some form of international "regulation and supervision." The NIEO even demanded that modern science and technology be "given" to developing countries.

Among proposals for "special measures in favor of the least developed" and the "full and equal participation" of developing countries in setting international economic policy were direct and indirect accusations that the United States was the source of much that was wrong with the international economy.

The NIEO declaration was formally adopted by the UN General Assembly, and some of its measures were initiated. However, it was mostly a symbolic vote. Actual economic changes were limited, and many Third World countries fell even further behind economically. For the United States, though, here was yet another external source of disruption and challenge. Anti-UN, anti–foreign aid, and anti–Third World sentiments grew ever stronger in the U.S. Congress and among the American public.

Trade with Japan and the Rest of the World

In the 1950s and 1960s, an American child whose parent came back from a business trip might be told, "I got you just a little something as a present; it's a toy made in Japan." By the 1970s and 1980s, though, any child told that a present had come from Japan would think it was a stereo, or television, or VCR—not exactly a "little" something. And his or her parents might be thinking "automobile."

In 1960 Japan's per capita income was only 30 percent of the U.S. level, about equal to that of Mexico. But between 1960 and 1970 its real gross national product (GNP) grew at an average of more than 10 percent per year. Its merchandise exports grew even faster, and its share of world exports doubled between the mid-1960s and the mid-1980s. U.S. trade with Japan went from surplus to deficit. Indeed, the deficit with Japan was the single largest component of the overall U.S. trade deficit.

The United States had had trade disputes with allies before. In the 1960s, for example, it fought "chicken wars" and "pasta wars" with the Europeans. But the trade tensions with Japan threatened to rise to an even more intense level. Some of the criticism of Japan was little more than protectionism. Some was more legitimate, as Japan did have higher trade barriers and more unfair trade practices than the United States did. The two sets of issues that these discrepancies generated, closing U.S. import markets to Japanese exports and opening Japanese markets to U.S. exports, were distinct but interconnected, especially in their politics.

Things started to come to a head in the late 1970s over the issue of Japanese auto imports. Toyota, Nissan, and other Japanese car companies were beating Ford, General Motors, and Chrysler on both price and reputation for quality. Chrysler was losing so much money that the Carter administration and Congress put together a bail-out package for the company. However, when the American auto companies and unions took their case to the International Trade Commission (ITC), the main U.S. regulatory agency on import-relief cases, the ITC ruled that the main problem was of the Big Three's own creation and denied the requests to restrict Japanese auto imports. Pressure nevertheless continued in Congress. Numerous protectionist and retaliatory bills were introduced. Some members of Congress even took to smashing a Toyota with a sledgehammer in front of the Capitol. In 1981 the Reagan administration negotiated a "voluntary" agreement with Japan for some limits on Japanese auto imports. Voluntary is in quotes because in reality, Japan had little choice.

In part as a reflection of Japan's more prominent position in world trade, the 1970s round of GATT global trade negotiations was initiated in Tokyo, Japan's capital. Like the previous six GATT rounds of negotiations, going back to 1945, the Tokyo Round was intended to promote free trade. It went further than its predecessors, however, not only lowering tariffs but also bringing down "nontariff barriers"—various governmental policies and practices that discriminated against imports and thus impeded free trade. Examples of nontariff barriers include government procurement regulations that require that purchases be made only from domestic suppliers, or government subsidies (such as aid and tax breaks) to exporters to make their products more competitive in global markets. Such policies were not just limited to the United States; many other countries had nontariff barriers higher than those of the United States, Japan in particular. Like all GATT agreements the strategy in the Tokyo Round was to set new rules for the whole international economic system, with all countries both making their own concessions and benefiting from those of others.

With trade politics having become so much more contentious at home over the course of the 1970s, a new U.S. legislative mechanism called *fast-track* was developed to help ensure passage of the Tokyo Round. In Chapter 2 we saw that the Constitution was unusually explicit in granting authority over trade to Congress, with presidential trade authority heavily subject to the limits of what Congress chooses to delegate. Fast-track authority gets its name from the guarantee that any trade agreements the president negotiates and submits to Congress will receive expedited legislative consideration within ninety days, and under a special procedural rule the vote on that agreement will be "up or down," yea or nay, with no amendments allowed. In this way Congress could allow free trade to go forward while "protecting itself," as

Professor I. M. Destler insightfully put it, from interest-group pressures demanding special protection.[39] With fast-track, representatives or senators could avoid having to respond to particular concerns from lobbyists, because Congress can only deal with the package as a whole. Such concerns would therefore be deflected on to the president—and become the president's potential political liability. This worked for the Tokyo Round, which Congress passed in 1979 with large majorities in both the House and the Senate. By the mid-1990s, though, as we'll see in Chapter 9, fast-track unraveled amid the increased pressures of trade politics.

Reagan, Gorbachev, and the End of the Cold War

The 4 Ps under Reagan

Ronald Reagan came into office firmly believing that American foreign policy had to be reasserted along all four dimensions of the national interest.

PEACE   Détente not only had failed to bring about peace, but as far as President Reagan and his supporters were concerned it had been used by the Soviets "as a cover for their traditional and basic strategy of aggression." President Reagan pulled few rhetorical punches: the Soviets "lie and cheat"; they had been "unrelenting" in their military buildup; indeed, "the Soviet Union underlies all the unrest that is going on. If they weren't engaged in this game of dominoes, there wouldn't be any hot spots in the world."[40] The reference to the early Cold War domino theory was intentional, and it was telling. The Soviets hadn't changed one iota as far as President Reagan was concerned. Democrats like President Carter, and even Republicans like Nixon, Ford, and Kissinger, had been deluding themselves, and endangering the country, to think the Soviets had changed.

With Reagan, then, peace was not going to be achieved through negotiations. It could be achieved only through strength. "Peace through strength" was the Reagan motto.

POWER   American power had to be reasserted, in a big way, and in all its aspects. The *Reagan Doctrine* developed as the basis not only for taking a harder line on global containment, but going further than every before toward rollback—i.e., ousting communists who had come to power. Unlike Secretary of

State John Foster Dulles, who failed to deliver on rollback against the 1956 Soviet invasion of Hungary, the Reagan administration provided extensive military aid, weapons, and covert action for the Afghan mujahideen fighting against the Soviets and the puppet government they set up in the Afghan capital, Kabul. The struggle was a protracted one, as Afghanistan became the Soviets' Vietnam. They suffered their own decade of defeat and demoralization, and in 1989 were forced to withdraw from Afghanistan.

Another Reagan Doctrine target was Nicaragua, where the communist-nationalist Sandinistas had triumphed. They were being opposed by the Nicaraguan contras (in Spanish, "those against"), to whom the Reagan administration supplied extensive military aid, CIA assistance, and other support. For the Reagan administration the Nicaragua issue embodied all that was wrong with the Vietnam syndrome and Carterite moralism. The Sandinistas professed Marxism-Leninism as their ideology. They were Soviet and Cuban allies. They were running guns to comrades in El Salvador and other neighboring countries. Their heritage as a movement was rooted in anti-American songs, slogans, and versions of history. But even more than that, their very existence was deemed a challenge to the credibility of American power. "If the United States cannot respond to a threat near our own borders," Reagan asked, "why should Europeans or Asians believe that we are seriously concerned about threats to them? . . . Our credibility would collapse, our alliances would crumble."[41]

Opponents of the Reagan Nicaragua policy also invoked analogies to Vietnam, but as a quagmire to be avoided, not a syndrome to be overcome. They did not necessarily embrace the Sandinistas or deny that the United States had vital interests in the region; instead they stressed the possibilities for a negotiated settlement establishing viable terms for coexistence. As to the credibility issue, they saw this as a matter more of judgment than of resolve; what would truly be impressive would be a demonstration that the United States could distinguish a test from a trap.

The Reagan administration also had to contend with its disastrous 1982–84 military intervention in Lebanon. American troops were originally sent to Lebanon as part of a multilateral peacekeeping force following the June 1982 Israeli military invasion of that country. Although some initial success was achieved in stabilizing the situation, the United States increasingly was pulled into the still-raging Lebanese civil war. In October 1983 the Islamic Jihad, a fundamentalist terrorist group, bombed the barracks in which the U.S. Marine Corps was stationed in Beirut, killing 241 Marines and other personnel. Within months the Reagan administration withdrew the remaining

American troops. "Redeployment offshore" was the euphemism used in official pronouncements, but this could not mask the reality of retreat.

The Lebanon failure prompted Defense Secretary Caspar Weinberger in November 1984 to give a speech laying out six criteria that needed to be met for future uses of U.S. military force (At the Source, p. 179). The "Weinberger criteria" set a high threshold for when and how to use military force. The lesson being drawn from Lebanon, and indeed going back to Vietnam, was that these failures resulted because too many military commitments had been made too half-heartedly with objectives that were too vague and with too little political support, or that in other ways were inconsistent with the criteria laid out by Weinberger. The pronouncement of this new doctrine brought on some intrabranch tension, with Secretary of State George Shultz arguing for a more flexible approach and still being willing in certain situations to use force on a more limited basis. The Weinberger approach, though, largely prevailed. It also was the basis for the doctrine of "decisive force" developed in 1990–91 by Colin Powell, then chair of the Joint Chiefs of Staff, for U.S. strategy in the Persian Gulf War following Iraq's invasion of Kuwait (see Chapter 7).

Power considerations also were the basis for the Reagan nuclear buildup. That "window of vulnerability" that the Reaganites believed had opened up because of the combined effects of the Soviet nuclear buildup and the Carter "defense neglect" needed to be closed, and quickly. Overall defense spending went up 16 percent in 1981, and another 14 percent in 1982. Major new nuclear-weapons systems, such as the B-1 bomber, the Trident submarine, and the MX missile, whose development had been shelved and slowed by President Carter, were revived and accelerated. The go-ahead was given for deployment in Europe of the Pershing and cruise missiles, modern and more capable intermediate-range nuclear missiles. And with great fanfare the Strategic Defense Initiative (SDI), also known as "Star Wars," was announced as an effort to build a nationwide defense umbrella against nuclear attack.

Guiding the Reagan nuclear buildup were two main shifts in nuclear deterrence doctrine. First, this administration was much more skeptical of arms control than were the Nixon, Ford, or Carter administrations. Security had to be guaranteed principally by one's own defense capabilities, the Reaganites believed. They did not write off arms-control prospects totally, but at minimum they wanted more bargaining chips to bring to the table. Second, they doubted the security and stability of the MAD doctrine. Thus they advocated replacing MAD with NUTS(!), which stood for "nuclear utilization targeting strategy" and which constituted a nuclear war-fighting capability. Only by having the capacity to fight a "limited" nuclear war would deterrence be

> **At the Source**

THE "WEINBERGER CRITERIA" FOR
THE USE OF MILITARY FORCE (1984)

❝ Under what circumstances, and by what means, does a great democracy such as ours reach the painful decision that the use of military force is necessary to protect our interests or to carry out our national policy? . . .

Some reject entirely the question of whether any force can be used abroad. They want to avoid grappling with a complex issue because, despite clever rhetoric disguising their purpose, these people are in fact advocating a return to post–World War I isolationism. While they may maintain in principle that military force has a role in foreign policy, they are never willing to name the circumstances or the place where it would apply.

On the other side, some theorists argue that military force can be brought to bear in any crisis. Some of the proponents of force are eager to advocate its use even in limited amounts simply because they believe that if there are American forces of *any* size present they will somehow solve the problem.

Neither of these two extremes offers us any lasting or satisfying solutions. The first—undue reserve—would lead us ultimately to withdraw from international events that require free nations to defend their interests from the aggressive use of force. . . .

The second alternative—employing our forces almost indiscriminately and as a regular and customary part of our diplomatic efforts—would surely plunge us headlong into the sort of domestic turmoil we experienced during the Vietnam War, without accomplishing the goal for which we committed our forces. . . .

I believe the postwar period has taught us several lessons, and from them I have developed *six* major tests to be applied when we are weighing the use of U.S. combat forces abroad. . . .

First, the United States should not commit forces to *combat* overseas unless the particular engagement or occasion is deemed vital to our national interest or that of our allies. . . .

Second, if we decide it *is* necessary to put *combat* troops into a given situation, we should do so wholeheartedly, and with the clear intention

(*Continued on page 180*)

(The "Weinberger Criteria" (1984)   *Continued from page 179)*
of winning. If we are *un*willing to commit the forces or resources necessary to achieve our objectives, we should not commit them at all. . . .

    Third, if we *do* decide to commit to combat overseas, we should have
clearly defined political and military objectives. And we should know
precisely how our forces can accomplish those clearly defined objectives.
And we should have and send the forces needed to do just that. . . .

    Fourth, the relationship between our objectives and the forces we
have committed—their size, composition and disposition—must be
continually reassessed and adjusted if necessary. Conditions and objectives invariably change during the course of a conflict. When they do
change, so must our combat requirements. . . .

    Fifth, before the U.S. commits combat forces abroad, there must be
some reasonable assurance that we will have the support of the American people and their elected representatives in Congress. . . .

    Finally, the commitment of U.S. forces to combat should be a last
resort. "

Source: Speech by Secretary of Defense Caspar Weinberger to the National Press Club,
November 28, 1984, included in Richard N. Haass, *Intervention: The Use of American Military Force in the Post–Cold War Era* (Washington, D.C.: Carnegie Endowment for International Peace Press, 1994), App. C, 173–81.

strengthened—and would the United States be in a position to "win" should it
come to that. Their defensive strategy involved SDI, which reopened the question, presumably settled with SALT I and the ABM Treaty, of the desirability
and feasibility of building a defensive shield against nuclear attacks.

    However, just as a president who was perceived as pursuing peace at the ex-
pense of power (Carter) was pulled from the left toward the center, now a president perceived as excessively risking peace in pursuit of power (Reagan) was
pulled from the right back toward the center.[42] In the early 1980s the "nuclear
freeze" movement gathered strength. A rally in New York City attracted some
seven hundred thousand people. Large demonstrations also were held in Western Europe, protesting the Pershing and cruise missile deployments. *The Day
After,* a made-for-television movie about a nuclear war actually occurring, was
both indicative of and a further contributor to a widespread fear that the

buildup was going too far and that things might be careening out of control. These developments slowed the Reagan nuclear buildup, but they did not stop it.

PRINCIPLES   They were "the focus of evil in the modern world," headed for "the ash bin of history." President Reagan didn't mince words in how he saw the Soviet Union (see At the Source, p. 182). In one of the television debates during his 1984 re-election campaign, he accused his Democratic opponent, Walter Mondale, of being so misguided as to believe that the "Soviets were just people like ourselves." Reagan matched this demonic view of the enemy with classic American exceptionalism. America was "a shining city on a hill," the "nation of destiny," the "last best hope of mankind." Even the Vietnam War (especially the Vietnam War) had been "a noble cause."[43]

In Nicaragua and elsewhere, the ostensibly principled human rights policies of the Carter administration came in for scathing attacks as having their own "double standards." Jeane Kirkpatrick, then a political science professor, wrote an article in 1979 strongly making this argument, which led to her appointment as Reagan's UN ambassador. How morally defensible was it, she questioned, to have cut support for Somoza in Nicaragua and the shah in Iran when the regimes that came to power in their wake (the Marxist-Leninist Sandinistas, Ayatollah Khomeini and his Islamic fundamentalists) were not just authoritarian but totalitarian? While authoritarians weren't democratic, at least they largely limited their repression to the political sphere; totalitarian regimes sought "total" domination of the personal as well as the political spheres of life. Therefore, Kirkpatrick contended, there *was* a moral basis to the "ABC" rule, as communists often were far more repressive than other leaders, however imperfect those others may be. This argument resquared the circle, casting principles and power as complementary once again. The contras were freedom fighters, nothing less than the "moral equal of our Founding Fathers."[44]

This view was hard to reconcile, though, with the U.S. support for the military regime in El Salvador, which tacitly supported the mass murder of its citizens. The Salvadoran "death squads" were brutal in their tactics and sweeping in whom they defined as a communist—as but one example, they assassinated Roman Catholic archbishop Oscar Romero in his cathedral while he was saying Mass. It was Congress, over Reagan administration objections, that attached human rights conditions to U.S. aid to El Salvador. A few years later the Salvadoran defense minister conceded that Congress's insistence on these human rights conditions made the Salvadoran military realize that "in order to receive U.S. aid, we had to do certain things."[45] Among those "certain things" was cracking down on the death squads.

At the Source

FREEDOM VS. "TOTALITARIAN EVIL"

Excerpts from a 1982 Speech by President Ronald Reagan

❝ We're approaching the end of a bloody century plagued by a terrible political invention—totalitarianism. Optimism comes less easily today, not because democracy is less vigorous, but because democracy's enemies have refined their instruments of repression. Yet optimism is in order, because day by day democracy is proving itself to be a not-at-all fragile flower. From Stettin on the Baltic to Varna on the Black Sea, the regimes planted by totalitarianism have had more than 30 years to establish their legitimacy. But none—not one regime—has yet been able to risk free elections. . . .

The decay of the Soviet experiment should come as no surprise to us. Wherever the comparisons have been made between free and closed societies—West Germany and East Germany, Austria and Czechoslovakia, Malaysia and Vietnam—it is the democratic countries that are prosperous and responsive to the needs of their people. And one of the simple but overwhelming facts of our time is this: Of all the millions of refugees we've seen in the modern world, their flight is always away from, not toward the Communist world. Today on the NATO front line our forces face east to prevent a possible invasion. On the other side of the line, the Soviet forces also face east to prevent their people from leaving. . . .

The objective I propose is quite simple to state: to foster the infrastructure of democracy, the system of a free press, unions, political parties, universities, which allows a people to choose their own way to develop their own culture, to reconcile their differences through peaceful means. . . .

No, democracy is not a fragile flower. Still it needs cultivating. If the rest of this century is to witness the gradual growth of freedom and democratic ideals, we must take action to assist the campaign for democracy. . . .

This is not cultural imperialism, it is providing the means for genuine self-determination and protection for diversity. Democracy already flourishes in countries with very different cultures and historical experi-

(*Continued on page 183*)

(Freedom vs. "Totalitarian Evil" *Continued from page 182*)
ences. It would be cultural condescension, or worse, to say that any people prefer dictatorship to democracy. Who would voluntarily choose not to have the right to vote, decide to purchase government propaganda handouts instead of independent newspapers, prefer government to worker-controlled unions, opt for land to be owned by the state instead of those who till it, want government repression of religious liberty, a single political party instead of a free choice, a rigid cultural orthodoxy instead of democratic tolerance and diversity? "

Source: Ronald Reagan, "Address to Members of the British Parliament," June 8, 1982, *Public Papers of the Presidents: Ronald Reagan, 1982* (Washington, D.C.: U.S. Government Printing Office, 1983), 742–48.

PROSPERITY   It often is forgotten that in the early 1980s the American economy was so mired in the deepest recession since the Great Depression that Ronald Reagan's popularity fell as low as 35 percent. So, too, is the fact often forgotten that for all the attacks on Democrats for deficit spending, the Reagan administration ran up greater budget deficits during its eight years than the total deficits of every previous president from George Washington to Jimmy Carter combined. And the U.S. trade deficit, which had caused alarm in the 1970s when it was running around $30 billion, went over $100 billion in 1984, and over $150 billion in 1986.

Nevertheless the Reagan years became prosperous ones. Inflation was tamed, brought down from more than 20 percent in 1979 to less than 10 percent in 1982. The economy boomed at growth rates of over 7 percent per year. The increases in defense spending were in part responsible for this prosperity. One of candidate Reagan's most effective lines in the 1980 presidential campaign was the question posed in his closing statement in one of the debates with President Carter: "Are you better off now than you were four years ago?" With inflation and unemployment both running so high then, most Americans answered "no." In 1984, with the economic recovery racing along, voters seemed to answer "we are now," as the revived prosperity contributed significantly to Reagan's landslide re-election victory.

Confrontational Foreign Policy Politics

Pennsylvania Avenue diplomacy really broke down during the Reagan years. The dominant pattern of presidential-congressional relations was confrontational.

CONTRA AID   The politics of aid to the contras and other aspects of the Nicaragua issue were the most glaring example. The debate was extremely bitter. The National Conservative Political Action Committee circulated a letter to all senators before one crucial vote on aid to the contras, threatening that "should you vote against Contra aid, we intend to see that a permanent record is made—a roll of dishonor, a list of shame, for all to see—of your failure of resolve and vision at this crucial hour."[46] For their part, liberal groups had no less harsh words for contra supporters, making for a virulent and vitriolic debate.

The contra-aid issue also got caught in "backward" institutional power-sharing arrangements. Each branch coveted the policy instruments of the other. The policy instrument the executive branch needed most—money—was controlled by Congress. The Reagan administration did get Congress to appropriate contra aid in 1983. But the aid was defeated in 1984, then passed again in 1985 but with restrictions, increased and de-restricted in 1986, cut back and re-restricted in 1987, and cut back and restricted further in 1988.

On the other side, for its preferred policy objective of a negotiated regional peace plan, Congress needed diplomatic authority and negotiating instruments of its own. But that remained the nearly exclusive authority of the executive branch, and the Reagan administration preferred to merely appear to support peace negotiations than to seriously pursue them. At one point House Speaker Jim Wright actually launched his own "alternative-track diplomacy," meeting with Nicaraguan president Daniel Ortega. Irrespective of the ends being pursued, this was a serious breach, for the costs and risks are substantial when any member of Congress tries to become an alternative negotiating partner for a foreign leader to circumvent the president.

The greatest breach of all was the Iran-contra scandal, which combined the potent Nicaragua issue with U.S. Middle East policy, particularly the problem of the American hostages taken by Iranian-supported fundamentalist terrorists in Lebanon. The basic deal, as worked out by National Security Council aide Colonel Oliver North and other Reagan administration officials, was that the United States would provide arms to Iran in exchange for Iran's help in getting the American hostages in Lebanon released; the profits from the arms sales would be used to fund the Nicaraguan contras, thereby circumventing congressional prohibitions on funding for the contras. The scheme fell apart

for a number of reasons, not the least of which was that at its core it was an illegal and unconstitutional effort to get around Congress. When the cover was
broken and the scheme was revealed, Congress launched its most significant
investigation since Watergate. "Secrecy, deception and disdain for the law,"
were among the findings of the congressional investigative committees. "The
United States Constitution specifies the processes by which laws and policies
are to be made and executed. Constitutional process is the essence of our
democracy and our democratic form of Government is the basis of our
strength. . . . The Committees find that the scheme, taken as a whole . . . violated cardinal principles of the Constitution. . . . Administration officials holding no elected office repeatedly evidenced disrespect for Congress' efforts to
perform its constitutional oversight role in foreign policy."[47]

WAR POWERS   The failings of the 1973 War Powers Resolution (WPR) also
became increasingly apparent. As discussed earlier in this chapter, when originally passed with an override of President Nixon's veto, the WPR was regarded
as finally settling the war powers issue. In practice, though, the resolution
ended up being ignored far more than invoked. This was true in the Ford and
Carter administrations, although the cases then were few and minor, such as
the 1975 *Mayaguez* incident involving the limited use of force against Cambodia to rescue an American merchant ship and its crew, and the 1980 attempt to
rescue American hostages in Iran. It was especially true in the Reagan administration, when the uses of force were more frequent and of greater magnitude. In addition to the 1982–84 Lebanon case these included the 1983
invasion of Grenada, which the Reagan administration defined as a rescue
mission to protect endangered American medical students but which congressional critics claimed was an effort to overthrow the Marxist government
there; the 1986 bombing of Libya in retaliation for Libyan leader Muammar
Qaddafi's involvement in terrorism against Americans; and the 1987–88 naval
"reflagging" operations in the Persian Gulf during the Iran-Iraq War to protect Kuwait, help Iraq, and maintain safe passage for oil tankers.

One of the problems inherent in the WPR that these cases made more apparent was that it ran against institutionally rooted attitudes in both branches.
For presidents, opposition to the WPR has been almost an institutionally in-
stinctual response. The WPR's very existence, let alone its specific provisions,
has been seen as an infringement on the role of the commander in chief and
other aspects of the presidency's constitutional share of war powers. This was
true for Presidents Ford and Carter but was especially so for President Reagan,
who took a generally more assertive approach to the presidency.

The WPR's fundamental problem lies in the ambiguity of its legal and legislative language. Take the 1987–88 reflagging case as an example. The mission of the U.S. Navy in that case was defined as a defensive one: protecting oil tankers. This was not strictly a neutral act, however; it was taking the side of Kuwait and Iraq against Iran. Sure enough, Iran launched a series of attacks, and the American naval forces counterattacked. More than just one incident occurred, and there were casualties on both sides. Section 2 of the WPR, the law's statement of purpose, states that it is to apply to situations in which "imminent involvement in hostilities is clearly indicated." Yet there is no clear definition in the law of what level of attack was necessary to be considered not just "skirmishes" but actual "hostilities." Thus Congress had no definitive basis for challenging the Reagan administration's claim that the Kuwaiti re-flagging operation was below the threshold of "hostilities," and thus did not fall under the strictures of the WPR.

Ambiguity also is inherent in Section 3 of the WPR and its provision for consultation with Congress "in every possible instance . . . before introducing U.S. armed forces into hostilities or into situations where imminent involvement in such is clearly indicated." When is consultation "possible"? Does it meet the requirement of being "before" if, as in 1986 when attacks were launched against Libya, congressional leaders are called in once the planes are on their way, but before they have dropped their bombs?

One doesn't have to be a linguist or a lawyer to see the problems that arise when these terms are left open to interpretation. It is true that the option was there when the law was written in 1973–74, and is there today for those who would rewrite it, to use tighter and more precise language. One could, for example, define "hostilities" as the firing of any first shot at a U.S. soldier, or "imminent involvement" as a U.S. solider being within range of an enemy's weapon—say 50 feet for a gun, 10 miles for a bomb, 100 miles for a missile. Clearly, though, such language-tightening can present its own problems by taking too much discretion away from a president, straitjacketing the president's ability to formulate strategy.

With the WPR not resolving much, members of Congress resorted to lawsuits as a means of trying to rein the president in. In 1982 eleven House members filed suit claiming that the commitment of U.S. military advisers to El Salvador without congressional consent violated the Constitution. A similar claim was made about the October 1983 Grenada intervention. A third suit involved the 1987–88 Persian Gulf naval "reflagging" case. Yet in all three cases the courts refused to rule and dismissed the suits. These were some of the cases referred to in Chapter 2 as falling under the "political question" doctrine and therefore to be "nonjusticiable," meaning that they involved political differences between the executive and legislative branches more than constitutional issues, and thus required a political resolution directly between those two branches rather than a judicial remedy. In other words, the courts were telling the president and Congress to go work the issues out themselves.

There were other issues on which President Reagan and Congress had less conflict, and some on which they even cooperated. The number of these common-ground issues increased in the second Reagan term, especially as the Cold War began to thaw.

The End of the Cold War: Why Did the Cold War End, and End Peacefully?

Just as we couldn't say precisely when the Cold War began, no specific date can be pinpointed for its end. The year 1989 was truly revolutionary, as one East European Soviet-satellite regime after another fell (see Table 5.1). Some point to November 9, 1989, the day the Berlin Wall came down, as the Cold War's end. Others cite December 25, 1991, the day the Soviet Union officially was disbanded. Others place it on other dates.

But whatever the precise dating, few if any academics, policy-makers, intelligence analysts, journalists, or other "experts" predicted that the Cold War would end when it did, or as peacefully as it did. As with the origins of the Cold War, different theories have been put forward to explain the end of the Cold War. Here we group them into two principal categories.[48]

U.S. TRIUMPHALISM　This theory gives the United States, and particularly President Reagan, the credit for having pursued a tough and assertive foreign policy that pushed the Soviets into collapse. In one sense, the credit is shared by every administration from President Truman's on; they all sustained deterrence and containment and generally pursued tough Cold War strategies (which for triumphalists meant some administrations more than others). The cumulative effects of those policies over the decades laid the groundwork. The pressure ratcheted up by the Reagan administration in the 1980s turned the tide. In this view, the domestic and foreign policy changes undertaken by Mikhail Gorbachev, who became the leader of the Soviet Union in 1985, were more reactions to the limited options the Reagan policies left him than bold new peace initiatives of his own.

The Soviets simply couldn't match American power, as it had been rebuilt and reasserted by Reagan. SDI was a good example. For all the questioning by

TABLE 5.1   1989: Eastern Europe's Year of Revolution

Date	Event
January 11	Hungarian parliament permits independent political parties for the first time under communist rule
April 5	Ban repealed on Solidarity movement in Poland
May 2	Hungary takes major steps to further open its borders with Austria, providing a route for thousands of East Germans to emigrate to West Germany
June 3	Solidarity candidates for parliament win by huge margin in Poland
July 21	General Wojciech Jaruzelski, who had led the imposition of martial law in Poland in 1981, has no choice but to invite Solidarity to form a coalition government
October 18	Hungary adopts a new constitution for multiparty democracy
October 18	Longtime East German Communist leader Erich Honecker is forced to resign, and is replaced by another, much weaker, Communist
November 3	Czechoslovakia opens border for East Germans seeking to go to the West
November 9	Amid mounting protests, East Germany opens the Berlin Wall and promises free elections in 1990
November 10	Unrest in Bulgaria forces resignation of Communist Party leader Todor Zhivkov
November 24	Peaceful mass protests, dubbed the "velvet revolution" and led by former political prisoner Vaclav Havel, overthrow the communist government of Czechoslovakia
December 6	East German government resigns
December 22–25	Protests turn violent in Romania, leading to execution of Communist leader Nicolae Ceausescu

critics within the United States of whether it was technologically feasible, SDI sure worried the Soviets. The Kremlin feared that the Soviet economy couldn't finance the huge expenditures necessary to keep up and doubted its scientists could master the new technologies needed. So when Gorbachev showed new interest in arms control, it was less because of his heralded "new thinking" than because he finally had to admit that his country couldn't win an arms race with the United States. So too with the Intermediate Nuclear Forces treaty in 1987, eliminating major arsenals of nuclear weapons stationed in Europe.* This was the first U.S.-Soviet arms control treaty ever to actually reduce nuclear weapons, not just limit their future growth (as with the SALT treaties). Yet in the triumphalist view, the INF treaty never would have happened if the Reagan administration had not withstood the political pressures of the nuclear freeze movement at home and the peace movements in Western Europe and gone ahead with the Pershing and cruise missile deployments.

The Reagan Doctrine, with its rollback as well as containment components, stopped the tide of Soviet geopolitical gains in the Third World. In Nicaragua the Sandinistas were forced to agree to elections as part of a peace agreement; sure enough, when elections were held in 1990 they lost. In El Salvador a peace accord was reached that included elections, and the pro-American side also won these elections. Most of all, the Red Army was forced to beat a retreat out of Afghanistan, with politically wrenching and demoralizing consequences back in the Soviet Union.

The triumph also was of American principles. The fall of communism in Eastern Europe was a revolution from below, brought about by masses of people who wanted freedom and democracy. When Vaclav Havel, a playwright who had been a human rights activist and political prisoner under the communists in Czechoslovakia, became the new democratically elected president of that country, he quoted Thomas Jefferson in his inaugural speech. Lech Walesa, the courageous Polish shipyard worker and leader of the Solidarity movement who was arrested when martial law was imposed in 1981 at Moscow's behest, now was elected president of Poland. Throughout most of the former Soviet bloc, and ultimately in most of the former Soviet Union itself, new constitutions were written, free elections held, an independent and free press established, and civil societies fostered. The "campaign for democracy" that Reagan had heralded in his 1982 speech (see At the Source, p. 182) had been successful; "man's instinctive drive for freedom and self-determination" that throughout history "surfaces again and again" had done so, again.

---

*Intermediate-range nuclear missiles were those with attack ranges of between 500 and 5,500 kilometers (320 to 34,000 miles). This included most of the nuclear missiles stationed in NATO countries and those in the Soviet Union that could attack Western Europe. It did not include either long-range missiles the United States and the Soviets had aimed at each other, or shorter-range and battlefield nuclear weapons in the European theater.

Capitalism and its perceived promise of prosperity also were part of the appeal. Back in the late 1950s when Soviet leader Nikita Khrushchev had threatened the West that "we will bury you," he was speaking in part about the economic competition and the sense that socialism was in the process of demonstrating its superiority. The Soviet system at that time had piled up impressive rates of economic growth. But this simply reflected the suitability of command economies for the initial stages of industrialization concentrated in heavy industries like steel; over the ensuing three decades the inefficiencies of the Soviet economy both in itself and as a model had become glaringly clear. Meanwhile, for all its economic problems in the 1970s, capitalism was on the rebound in the 1980s. The postcommunist governments were quick to start selling off state enterprises, opening their economies to Western foreign investment, and taking other measures to hang out the sign "open for business," capitalist style. The results were not uniformly positive—growth rates were lower than expected, unemployment was higher, and corruption was more rampant in a number of countries. But there was no going back to communist economic systems.

Overall this view confirms the validity of the U.S. Cold War position and policies. "We now know," as historian John Lewis Gaddis argues, that the Soviets and their leaders really did bear most of the responsibility for the Cold War. Stalin *was* an evil megalomaniac with aspirations to global domination. Marxism-Leninism *was* an ideology with limited appeal that declined even more over time. The Soviet Union was, as Gaddis puts it, "a state uniquely configured to the Cold War—and it has become a good deal more difficult, now that that conflict has ended, to see how it could have done so without the Soviet Union itself having passed from the scene."[49]

SOVIET REFORMISM AND OTHER REVISIONIST THEORIES   Just as revisionist theories of the origins of the Cold War put more blame on the United States, revisionist theories of the end of the Cold War give the United States less credit. Much greater credit in these explanations goes to Gorbachev. In 1982, after eighteen years in power, Soviet leader Leonid Brezhnev died. He was replaced first by Yuri Andropov, the former head of the KGB (the Soviet spy agency), but Andropov died in 1984. His successor, Konstantin Chernenko, an old *apparatchik* (party bureaucrat) in the Brezhnev mold, was very ill most of the time he was leader and died barely a year later. Gorbachev was a relative unknown when he came to power in 1985 but immediately was billed by no less a figure than conservative British prime minister Margaret Thatcher as "a man we can do business with." And she didn't just mean business deals, she meant the whole foreign policy agenda.

At age 51, Gorbachev was of a different generation than his predecessors. He quickly proclaimed a "new thinking" based on *glasnost* (openness) and *perestroika* (restructuring). In terms of Soviet domestic policy *glasnost* meant greater political freedoms, including a degree of freedom of the press, the release of such leading dissidents as Andrei Sakharov,* and an end to the Communist Party's "leading role" in society. *Perestroika* meant changes in the Soviet economy allowing for more open markets with some private enterprise and foreign investment. In Soviet foreign policy the "new thinking" was manifest in numerous initiatives aimed at reducing tensions and promoting cooperation. Under Gorbachev the Soviets became much more amenable to arms control. They signed the INF treaty in 1987 and moved forward with negotiations in the Strategic Arms Reduction Talks (START), which were the successor to SALT. While there were doubts as to whether it was more than rhetoric, Gorbachev declared the goal of eliminating all nuclear weapons by 2000. It was also Gorbachev who agreed in 1988 to the UN-mediated accord under which the Soviets withdrew their military forces from Afghanistan. And whereas Nikita Khrushchev had crushed the 1956 Hungarian Revolution and Brezhnev had done the same against the "Prague Spring" in Czechoslovakia in 1968, Gorbachev did not send a single tank into any East European country as the people in one country after another overthrew their communist governments.

So at least part of the answer to the question of why the Cold War ended when it did, and especially to the question of why it ended peacefully, is Gorbachev. While the triumphalists contend that U.S. pressures and strengths left Gorbachev with little choice other than to do what he did, revisionists argue that this is too simplistic. How many other times in history have leaders responded to crises at home and declining strength abroad by choosing repression and aggression? The central concept of foreign policy choice that frames our entire discussion of U.S. foreign policy in this book also applies to other countries. Gorbachev had choices: he could have sought to put down the rebellions in Eastern Europe. This may not have worked but it could have been tried. The popular revolutions still may have prevailed, and the Cold War still may have come to an end—but it would have been a much less peaceful end.

---

*Andrei Sakharov was known around the world for his courageous opposition to the Soviet regime. He actually was the physicist who, earlier in his career, had developed the Soviet hydrogen bomb. But he became a leading advocate of arms control and, later, of human rights and political freedom. He was awarded the Nobel Peace Prize in 1973, but was denied permission to leave the country to go to Stockholm, Sweden, to receive it. He was harassed by the KGB and, following his opposition to the Soviet invasion of Afghanistan, was put under house arrest. That was where and how he was forced to stay until Gorbachev freed him in 1986.

The same argument applies to many other aspects of the Gorbachev foreign policy. The choices he made were not the only ones he had. Gorbachev not only received the Nobel Peace Prize, but was deemed by one leading American scholar "the most deserving recipient in the history of the award."[50]

Nor was it just Gorbachev. Credit is also given to American and European peace movements.[51] They tempered the Reagan hard-line policies, keeping him, for example, from spending even more on SDI and possibly from a direct military intervention in Nicaragua. With the Reagan policies moved back toward the center, there was more of a basis for finding common ground with the Soviets. Peace activists also built relationships over many years with intellectuals, activists, scientists, and others within the Soviet Union. Even in some of the dark days of the early 1980s, Reagan's "evil empire" rhetoric notwithstanding, various groups kept up efforts to exchange ideas, maintain communications, and try to find common ground with colleagues, counterparts, and friends within the Soviet Union. Many of these counterparts came into positions of influence under Gorbachev; even those who did not were important as sources of support and expertise for Gorbachev's liberalizing policies.[52]

Other international actors also get some of the credit. European leaders for many years had pushed more strongly for détente than the United States wanted. West German chancellor Helmut Kohl was instrumental in the reunification of Germany following the fall of the Berlin Wall. The United Nations played such a key role in helping bring peace in Afghanistan and elsewhere that its peacekeeping units won the 1988 Nobel Peace Prize. Another Nobel Peace Prize went to Oscar Arias, president of Costa Rica, whose peace plan was the basis for the settlements in Nicaragua and El Salvador. Principal focus on the two superpowers is warranted, but the roles of these other key international actors are not to be ignored.

A further point concerns nuclear weapons and nuclear deterrence. Some revisionists take issue with any suggestion that nuclear weapons ultimately were part of the solution to the Cold War, seeing them more as a major part of the problem, causing close calls like the Cuban missile crisis and the overhanging specter of the arms race. Others give some credit to nuclear deterrence as having ensured the avoidance of a major-power war, but still argue that the ratcheting up of the nuclear arms race to ever higher levels prolonged the Cold War.

A final point distinguishes between the Soviets' having lost the Cold War and the United States' having "won." The assessment of the victory needs to be more nuanced, or the wrong lessons can get drawn. Containment in Europe can be assessed as a successful policy, whereas aspects of Third World containment like the

Vietnam War and support for the Nicaraguan contras were misguided and failed. So too with various CIA covert actions, which even when they accomplished their objectives in the field had some dangerous domestic political reverberations. And some short-term successes turned out to have longer-term negative consequences—for example, in "failed states" like Somalia and Zaire, where corrupt dictators took advantage of their "ABC" credentials to rob and repress their people, knowing that U.S. support would continue in the same name of global containment; or in Afghanistan, where the void left by the Soviet defeat and the American decision to disengage once the Soviets had left was filled by the Taliban and by Osama bin Laden and his Al Qaeda terrorist organization.

This is one of those debates in which there is no single right answer. And just as we still debate the origins of the Cold War, so too will the debate over its end continue.

What must be acknowledged is how humbling the end was, or should have been, for "experts." It was not uncommon in the mid-1980s for professors to assume that any student who imagined a post–Cold War world was just young, naive, and idealistic. The Cold War was with us and, students were told, apt to have its ups and downs, its thaws and freezes, but it was not about to go away. Yet it did.

We need to bear this lack of certainty in mind as we consider our new era in the twenty-first century and think about what the possibilities may be.

Summary

Dynamics of Choice, p. 194, summarizes the main characteristics of U.S. foreign policy strategy in the early Cold War period, the Vietnam-détente–economic shocks period, and the Reagan-Gorbachev period. We can see elements of both continuity and change in both the emphasis placed on and the strategies chosen for each of the 4 Ps:

- *Peace:* pursued first principally by creating the multilateral structure of the United Nations, then in the 1970s through the bilateral superpower diplomacy of détente, then under President Reagan by reverting more to unilateral assertion of peace through strength.
- *Power:* containment starting in Europe and then extending to Asia and more globally, the 1970s dominated by the debate over the lessons of Vietnam, the 1980s pushing for rollback through the Reagan Doctrine;

DYNAMICS OF CHOICE

A Summary of U.S. Cold War Foreign Policy Strategy

	Early Cold War	Vietnam, détente, economic shocks	Reagan-Gorbachev era
Peace	United Nations	Détente	Peace through strength
Power	Containment, arms race	Lessons of Vietnam, arms control	Reagan doctrine, arms race–arms control
Principles	Ideological bipolarity, Third World "ABC"	Human rights	Evil empire, "ABC"
Prosperity	LIEO	OPEC, NIEO, Japan shocks	Boom and deficits

deterrence first seen as a matter of U.S. nuclear superiority to be maintained by winning the arms race, then to be assured through arms control, then requiring a renewed arms race as a prerequisite to more effective arms control.

■ *Principles:* the original conception of the Cold War as not just typical great-power politics but also deeply ideological, and the attendant equation of "ABC" with democracy in the Third World; the 1970s shift to human rights and questioning of the ABC rationale; the 1980s "evil empire" ideological warfare and reversion to ABC.

■ *Prosperity:* to be assured by the LIEO; then shaken by OPEC, the NIEO, and other 1970s economic shocks; and restored in the 1980s boom albeit amid massive trade and budget deficits.

We also saw varying patterns in the foreign policy politics of the different sub-periods (Dynamics of Choice, p. 195). As long as the Cold War consensus held, Pennsylvania Avenue was largely a one-way street in the White House's favor, making for an imperial presidency. This was as much because of congressional deference as presidential usurpation. The executive branch grew dramatically

DYNAMICS OF CHOICE

A Summary of U.S. Cold War Foreign Policy Politics

	Early Cold War	Vietnam, détente, economic shocks	Reagan-Gorbachev era
Presidency	Imperial	Imperiled	Resurgent
Congress	Deferential	Assertive	Confrontational
Executive branch	Expanding	Bureaucratic warfare	Bureaucratic warfare
Interest groups	Supportive	Oppositional	Proliferating
News media	Cheerleader	Critic	Critic
Public opinion	Consensus, McCarthyism	"Dissensus"	Polarized

in the size, scope, and number of foreign and defense policy agencies. Societal influences were limited and mostly supportive of official policy, the media included; they also included the extremism of McCarthyism. But the consensus was shattered by the Vietnam War. Other issues and factors also came into play, with the net effect of more conflictual Pennsylvania Avenue diplomacy, with a more assertive Congress, in the eyes of some a less imperial and more imperiled presidency, more divisive intra–executive branch politics, more interest-group pressures, much more critical media, and more "dissensus" than consensus in public opinion. Foreign policy politics in the 1980s became even more contentious, to the point where many questioned whether, as one prominent book put it, we had become "our own worst enemy."[53]

We now have a picture of the dynamics of foreign policy choice during the entire Cold War era, both the foreign policy strategy choices that were its essence (drawing on the Chapter 1 framework) and the foreign policy politics that were its process (Chapter 2). Chapter 3 gave us the historical context. And looking toward Part II, Chapters 4 and 5 have provided us with the contemporary context for the foreign policy choices that the United States faces in the post–Cold War era.

Notes

[1] Dean G. Acheson, *Present at the Creation: My Years at the State Department* (New York: Norton, 1969), 674.

[2] Dwight D. Eisenhower, *Mandate for Change* (New York: Doubleday, 1963), 372–73.

[3] Theodore C. Sorensen, *Kennedy* (New York: Harper and Row, 1965), 639.

[4] Cited in Stanley Karnow, *Vietnam: A History* (New York: Viking, 1983), 629.

[5] Robert S. McNamara, *In Retrospect: The Tragedy and Lessons of Vietnam* (New York: Times Books, 1995), 322.

[6] Statement by General Bruce Palmer, Jr., cited in Bruce W. Jentleson, "American Commitments in the Third World: Theory vs. Practice," *International Organization* 41:4 (Autumn 1987), 696.

[7] Both cited in Col. Harry G. Summers, Jr., "How We Lost," *New Republic,* April 29, 1985, 22.

[8] Frank Snepp, *Decent Interval: An Insider's Account of Saigon's Indecent End* (New York: Random House, 1977); Arnold Isaacs, *Without Honor: Defeat in Vietnam and Cambodia* (Baltimore: Johns Hopkins University Press, 1983).

[9] William Appleman Williams, Thomas McCormick, Lloyd Gardner, and Walter LaFeber, *America in Vietnam: A Documentary History* (Garden City, N.Y.: Anchor Books, 1985), 122.

[10] "Address at Johns Hopkins University: Peace Without Conquest," April 7, 1965, *Public Papers of the Presidents: Lyndon B. Johnson, 1965,* Vol. 1 (Washington, D.C.: U.S. Government Printing Office, 1966), 395.

[11] Henry A. Kissinger, "The Vietnam Negotiations," *Foreign Affairs* 47:2 (January 1969), 218–19.

[12] "Address to the Nation on the Situation in Southeast Asia," *Public Papers of the Presidents: Richard M. Nixon, 1970* (Washington, D.C.: U.S. Government Printing Office, 1971), 409.

[13] Cited in Snepp, *Decent Interval,* 175.

[14] Hans J. Morgenthau, "To Intervene or Not Intervene," *Foreign Affairs* 45:3 (April 1967), 434.

[15] Cited in James A. Nathan and James K. Oliver, *United States Foreign Policy and World Order,* 2d ed. (Boston: Little, Brown, 1981), 322.

[16] "Telephone Remarks to the Delegates to the AFL-CIO Convention," December 9, 1965, *Public Papers of the Presidents: Lyndon B. Johnson, 1965,* Vol. 2 (Washington, D.C.: U.S. Government Printing Office, 1966), 1149.

[17] "Address to the Nation on the War in Vietnam," November 3, 1969, *Public Papers of the Presidents: Richard M. Nixon, 1969* (Washington, D.C.: U.S. Government Printing Office, 1970), 908–9.

[18] Cited in Doris Kearns, *Lyndon Johnson and the American Dream* (New York: New American Library, 1976), 264. See also Larry Berman, *Planning a Tragedy: The Americanization of the War in Vietnam* (New York: Norton, 1982); and Berman, *Lyndon Johnson's War* (New York: Norton, 1989).

[19] J. William Fulbright, "Congress and Foreign Policy," in Murphy Commission, *Organization of the Government for the Conduct of Foreign Policy,* Vol. 5, App. L (Washington, D.C.: U.S. Government Printing Office, 1975), 59.

[20] Arthur M. Schlesinger, Jr., *The Imperial Presidency* (New York: Atlantic Monthly Press, 1974), 11–12.

[21] Thomas M. Franck and Edward Weisband, *Foreign Policy by Congress* (New York: Oxford University Press, 1979).

[22] I. M. Destler, Leslie H. Gelb, and Anthony Lake, *Our Own Worst Enemy: The Unmaking of American Foreign Policy* (New York: Simon and Schuster, 1984), 137.

[23] Fulbright, "Congress and Foreign Policy," 60.

[24]James Aronson, *The Press and the Cold War* (New York: Bobbs-Merrill, 1970), 195.

[25]Michael Roskin, "From Pearl Harbor to Vietnam: Shifting Generational Paradigms and Foreign Policy," *Political Science Quarterly* 89:3 (1974), 569.

[26]Graham Allison, "Cool It: The Foreign Policy of Young America," *Foreign Policy* 1 (Winter 1970–71), 156.

[27]Speech by Secretary of Defense Robert S. McNamara, October 1967, reprinted in Bruce W. Jentleson, *Documents in American Foreign Policy: A Reader* (Davis: University of California at Davis, 1984), 48–53.

[28]Peter G. Peterson, *U.S.-Soviet Commercial Relations in a New Era* (Washington, D.C.: U.S. Government Printing Office, 1972), 3–4.

[29]Peterson, *U.S.-Soviet Commercial Relations,* 14.

[30]Cited in Bruce W. Jentleson, *Pipeline Politics: The Complex Political Economy of East-West Energy Trade* (Ithaca, N.Y.: Cornell University Press, 1986), 142.

[31]"Inaugural Address of President Jimmy Carter," January 20, 1977, in *Public Papers of the Presidents: Jimmy Carter, 1977* (Washington, D.C.: U.S. Government Printing Office, 1977), 1–4.

[32]Walter Isaacson, *Kissinger: A Biography* (New York: Simon and Schuster, 1992). See also the three volumes of Kissinger's memoirs: *White House Years* (Boston: Little, Brown, 1979); *Years of Upheaval* (Boston: Little, Brown, 1982); and *Years of Renewal* (New York: Simon and Schuster, 1999).

[33]Cited in James M. McCormick, *American Foreign Policy and Process,* 2d ed. (Itasca, Ill.: F. E. Peacock, 1992), 414.

[34]Quoted in Gaddis Smith, *Morality, Reason and Power: American Diplomacy in the Carter Years* (New York: Hill and Wang, 1986), 223.

[35]"State of the Union Address Delivered Before a Joint Session of the Congress," January 23, 1980, *Public Papers of the Presidents: Jimmy Carter, 1980–1981* (Washington, D.C.: U.S. Government Printing Office, 1981), 194–200.

[36]Raymond L. Garthoff, "Détente," in *Encyclopedia of U.S. Foreign Relations,* ed. Bruce W. Jentleson and Thomas G. Paterson (New York: Oxford University Press, 1997), Vol. 2, 10–11.

[37]Cited in Bruce W. Jentleson, "Discrepant Responses to Falling Dictators: Presidential Belief Systems and the Mediating Effects of the Senior Advisory Process," *Political Psychology* 11:2 (June 1990), 371.

[38]Quoted in Seymour Hersh, *The Price of Power: Kissinger in the Nixon White House* (New York: Summit Books, 1983), 462.

[39]I. M. Destler, *American Trade Politics,* 2d ed. (Washington, D.C.: Institute of International Economics, 1992).

[40]Cited in Jentleson, "Discrepant Responses to Falling Dictators," 371.

[41]Cited in Bruce W. Jentleson, "American Diplomacy: Around the World and Along Pennsylvania Avenue," in *A Question of Balance: The President, the Congress and Foreign Policy,* ed. Thomas E. Mann (Washington, D.C.: Brookings Institution Press, 1990), 149.

[42]Miroslav Nincic, "The United States, the Soviet Union and the Politics of Opposites," *World Politics* 40:4 (July 1988), 452–75.

[43]Cited in Jentleson, "Discrepant Responses," 372.

[44]Jentleson, "Discrepant Responses," 372.

[45]Cited in Jentleson, "American Diplomacy," 179.

[46]Cited in Jentleson, "American Diplomacy," 151.

[47]U.S. Congress, *Report of the Congressional Committees Investigating the Iran-Contra Affair,* 100th Congr., 1st sess., November 1987, 11, 411, 19.

[48]See, for example, Richard Ned Lebow and Thomas Risse-Kappen, eds., *International Relations Theory and the End of the Cold War* (New York: Columbia University Press, 1995); Richard K. Betts, ed., *Conflicts after the Cold War: Arguments on Causes of War and Peace* (New York: Macmillan, 1994); Raymond L. Garthoff, *The Great Transition: American-Soviet Relations and the End of the Cold War* (Washington, D.C.: Brookings Institution Press, 1994); and Jay Winik, *On the Brink: The Dramatic Saga of How the Reagan Administration Changed the Course of History and Won the Cold War* (New York: Simon and Schuster, 1997).

[49]John Lewis Gaddis, "The New Cold War History," lecture published by Foreign Policy Research Institute, *Footnotes* 5 (June 1998), 1–2. See also John Lewis Gaddis, *We Now Know: Rethinking Cold War History* (New York: Oxford University Press, 1997).

[50]Michael Mandelbaum, *The Ideas That Conquered the World* (New York: Public Affairs, 2002), 121.

[51]Thomas Risse-Kappen, "Did 'Peace through Strength' End the Cold War?" *International Security* 16: 1 (Summer 1991), 162–88.

[52]Matthew Evangelista, *Unarmed Forces: The Transnational Movement to End the Cold War* (Ithaca: Cornell University Press, 1999).

[53]Destler, Gelb, and Lake, *Our Own Worst Enemy.*

Readings for Part I
The Context of
U.S. Foreign Policy:
Theory and History

Power

1.1

HANS J. MORGENTHAU

The Mainsprings of American Foreign Policy

Wherever American foreign policy has operated, political thought has been divorced from political action. Even where our long-range policies reflect faithfully, as they do in the Americas and in Europe, the true interests of the United States, we think about them in terms that have at best but a tenuous connection with the actual character of the policies pursued. We have acted on the international scene, as all nations must, in power-political terms; but we have tended to conceive of our actions in non-political, moralistic terms. This aversion to seeing problems of international politics as they are, and the inclination to view them in non-political and moralistic terms, can be attributed both to certain misunderstood peculiarities of the American experience in foreign affairs and to the general climate of opinion in the Western world during the better part of the nineteenth and the first decades of the twentieth centuries. Three of these peculiarities of the American experience stand out: the uniqueness of the American experiment; the actual isolation, during the nineteenth century, of the United States from the centers of world conflict; and the humanitarian pacifism and anti-imperialism of American ideology.

* * *

The fundamental error that has thwarted American foreign policy in thought and action is the antithesis of national interest and moral principles. The equation of political moralizing with morality and of political realism with immorality is itself untenable. The choice is not between moral principles and the national interest, devoid of moral dignity, but between one set of moral principles divorced from political reality, and another set of moral principles derived from political reality.

The moralistic detractors of the national interest are guilty of both intellectual error and moral perversion. The nature of the intellectual error must be obvious from what has been said thus far, as it is from the record of history: a foreign policy guided by moral abstractions, without consideration of the national interest, is bound to fail; for it accepts a standard of action alien to the nature of the action itself. All the successful

From *In Defense of the National Interest* (New York: Knopf, 1951), chaps. 1 and 8.

statesmen of modern times from [Cardinal] Richelieu to [Winston] Churchill have made the national interest the ultimate standard of their policies, and none of the great moralists in international affairs has attained his goals.

The perversion of the moralizing approach to foreign policy is threefold. That approach operates with a false concept of morality, developed by national societies but unsuited to the conditions of international society. In the process of its realization, it is bound to destroy the very moral values it sets out to promote. Finally, it is derived from a false antithesis between morality and power politics, thus arrogating to itself all moral values and placing the stigma of immorality upon the theory and practice of power politics.

There is a profound and neglected truth hidden in [Thomas] Hobbes's extreme dictum that the state creates morality as well as law and that there is neither morality nor law outside the state. Universal moral principles, such as justice or equality, are capable of guiding political action only to the extent that they have been given concrete content and have been related to political situations by society. What justice means in the United States can within wide limits be objectively ascertained; for interests and convictions, experiences of life and institutionalized traditions have in large measure created a consensus concerning what justice means under the conditions of American society. No such consensus exists in the relations between nations. For above the national societies there exists no international society so integrated as to be able to define for them the concrete meaning of justice or equality, as national societies do for their individual

members. In consequence, the appeal to moral principles by the representative of a nation vis-à-vis another nation signifies something fundamentally different from a verbally identical appeal made by an individual in his relations to another individual member of the same national society. The appeal to moral principles in the international sphere has no concrete universal meaning. It is either so vague as to have no concrete meaning that could provide rational guidance for political action, or it will be nothing but the reflection of the moral preconceptions of a particular nation and will by that same token be unable to gain the universal recognition it pretends to deserve.

Whenever the appeal to moral principles provides guidance for political action in international affairs, it destroys the very moral principles it intends to realize. It can do so in three different ways. Universal moral principles can serve as a mere pretext for the pursuit of national policies. In other words, they fulfill the functions of those ideological rationalizations and justifications to which we have referred before. They are mere means to the ends of national policies, bestowing upon the national interest the false dignity of universal moral principles. The performance of such a function is hypocrisy and abuse and carries a negative moral connotation.

The appeal to moral principles may also guide political action to that political failure which we have mentioned above. The extreme instance of political failure on the international plane is national suicide. It may well be said that a foreign policy guided by universal moral principles, by definition relegating the national interest to the background, is under contemporary conditions of foreign policy and warfare a policy of national suicide, actual or potential. Within a national society the individual can at times afford, and may even be required, to subordinate his interests and even to sacrifice his very existence to a supra-individual moral principle—for in national societies such principles exist, capable of providing concrete standards for individual action. What is more important still, national societies take it upon themselves within certain limits to protect and promote the interests of the individual and, in particular, to guard his existence against violent attack. National societies of this kind can exist and fulfill their functions only if their individual members are willing to subordinate their individual interests in a certain measure to the common good of society. Altruism and self-sacrifice are in that measure morally required.

The mutual relations of national societies are fundamentally different. These relations are not controlled by universal moral principles concrete enough to guide the political actions of individual nations. What again is more important, no agency is able to promote and protect the interests of individual nations and to guard their existence—and that is emphatically true of the great powers—but the individual nations themselves. To ask, then, a nation to embark upon altruistic policies oblivious of the national interest is really to ask something immoral. For such disregard of the individual interest, on the part of nations as of individuals, can be morally justified only by the existence of social institutions, the embodiment of concrete moral principles, which are able to do what otherwise the individual would have to do. In the absence of such institutions it would be both foolish

and morally wrong to ask a nation to forego its national interests not for the good of a society with a superior moral claim but for a chimera. Morally speaking, national egotism is not the same as individual egotism because the functions of the international society are not identical with those of a national society.

The immorality of a politically effective appeal to moral abstractions in foreign policy is consummated in the contemporary phenomenon of the moral crusade. The crusading moralist, unable in the absence of an integrated national society to transcend the limits of national moral values and political interests, identifies the national interest with the manifestation of moral principles, which is, as we have seen, the typical function of ideology. Yet the crusader goes one step farther. He projects the national moral standards onto the international scene not only with the legitimate claim of reflecting the national interest, but with the politically and morally unfounded claim of providing moral standards for all mankind to conform to in concrete political action. Through the intermediary of the universal moral appeal the national and the universal interest become one and the same thing. What is good for the crusading country is by definition good for all mankind, and if the rest of mankind refuses to accept such claims to universal recognition, it must be converted with fire and sword.

There is already an inkling of this ultimate degeneration of international moralism in [Woodrow] Wilson's crusade to make the world safe for democracy. We see it in full bloom in the universal aspirations of Bolshevism. Yet to the extent that the West, too, is persuaded that it has a holy mission, in the name of whatever moral principle, first to save the world and then to remake it, it has itself fallen victim to the moral disease of the crusading spirit in politics. If that disease should become general, as well it might, the age of political moralizing would issue in one or a series of religious world wars. The fanaticism of political religions would, then, justify all those abominations unknown to less moralistic but more politically-minded ages and for which in times past the fanaticism of other-worldly religions provided a convenient cloak.

In order to understand fully what these intellectual and moral aberrations of a moralizing in foreign policy imply, and how the moral and political problems to which that philosophy has given rise can be solved, we must recall that from the day of Machiavelli onward the controversy has been fought on the assumption that there was morality on one side and immorality on the other. Yet the antithesis that equates political moralizing with morality and political realism with immorality is erroneous.

* * *

In our time the United States is groping toward a reason of state of its own—one that expresses our national interest. The history of American foreign policy since the end of the Second World War is the story of the encounter of the American mind with a new political world. That mind was weakened in its understanding of foreign policy by half a century of ever more complete intoxication with moral abstractions. Even a mind less weakened would have found it hard to face with adequate understanding and successful action the unprecedented novelty and magnitude of the new political world. American foreign policy in that period presents itself as a slow, painful, and incomplete process of emancipation from deeply ingrained error, and of rediscovery of long-forgotten truths.

* * *

FORGET AND REMEMBER!

FORGET *the sentimental notion that foreign policy is a struggle between virtue and vice, with virtue bound to win.*

FORGET *the utopian notion that a brave new world without power politics will follow the unconditional surrender of wicked nations.*

FORGET *the crusading notion that any nation, however virtuous and powerful, can have the mission to make the world over in its own image.*

REMEMBER *that the golden age of isolated normalcy is gone forever and that no effort, however great, and no action, however radical, will bring it back.*

REMEMBER *that diplomacy without power is feeble, and power without diplomacy is destructive and blind.*

REMEMBER *that no nation's power is without limits, and hence that its policies must respect the power and interests of others.*

REMEMBER *that the American people have shown throughout their history that they are able to face the truth and act upon it with courage and resourcefulness in war, with common sense and moral determination in peace.*

And, above all, remember always that it is not only a political necessity but also a moral duty for a nation to follow in its dealings with other nations but one guiding star, one standard for thought, one rule for action:

THE NATIONAL INTEREST.

Peace

1.2

INIS L. CLAUDE, JR.

International Organization and World Order

* * *

In functional terms, the process of international organization has brought greater progress toward a governed world than has been generally recognized, and certainly more than is acknowledged by those who adhere to the doctrinaire view that government and anarchy are the two halves of an absolute either-or formula.

The last century, and particularly the last generation, has been an era of continuous development of patterns and techniques for managing the business of the international community. The old story of the sociological lag emphasizes the important truth that mankind has far to go, but it tends to obscure the fact that we are living in a period of adventurous experiment and flourishing inventiveness in the field of international relations. The creation of such institutional innovations as the general international organization, the international secretariat, the international conference of the parliamentary type, the international field commission for investigation and supervision, the peace-keeping force, the in-

ternational technical assistance mission, the multilateral defense machinery of the NATO type, and the supranational functional agency of the kind recently developed in the European Community testifies to the significance of that fact. Moreover, fruitful improvisation is being increasingly supplemented by more systematic activities. The invention of invention is not exclusively a phenomenon of the scientific world; the international community is now equipped as never before with the analytical tools, professional staff, and organizational framework for designing and instituting new instruments to meet its needs.

The achievements of international organization include notable gains in the field of noncoercive regulatory devices. The agencies of the United Nations system exercise substantial influence and control—in short, *power*—over the behavior of states through the exploitation of a variety of methods: consultation and advice; inquiry, debate, and criticism of both public and private varieties; examination of reports and conduct of inspections; granting and with-

From *Swords into Plowshares: The Problems and Progress of International Organizations,* 4th ed. (New York: Random House, 1984), introduction and chap. 19.

drawal of subsidies and other forms of assistance; and recommendation followed by evaluation of response to this sort of pressure and possibly by insistent reiteration.

International institutions provide, above all, opportunities for states, singly and collectively, to influence each other. The facilities that they offer and the processes that they set in motion make it possible for states to exercise power in new ways, to utilize capabilities that have never before counted for much in international relations. Such factors as voting power, parliamentary skill, persuasiveness in debate, capacity to influence the content and ordering of agenda, and ability to affect the definition of issues and the wording of proposals become important elements of political power in international organizations. These agencies have not, of course, rendered the conventional varieties of power irrelevant to international relations, nor have they made these new varieties decisive, but they have significantly expanded the list of resources and methods available to states for affecting the policies and actions of other states.

International organization has made no such significant progress, nor has it demonstrated great promise, in the realm of coercive control of state behavior. True, the League [of Nations] engaged in a half-hearted effort to suppress Italian aggression in Ethiopia, and the United Nations sponsored the mobilization of collective resistance to Communist attack upon South Korea, with successful if not satisfactory results. More recently, the Untied Nations has attempted to use diplomatic and economic sanctions as instruments for breaking down the resistance of white-dominated regimes in Southern Africa, most notably that of Rhodesia, to demands for fundamental alteration of the racial and colonial status quo. At the regional level, the Organization of American States has shown some capacity for organized coercive activity against aberrant members. Nevertheless, international coercion of states determined to pursue their objectives or defend their policies by all necessary means, including the use of force, has not become, in any general sense, a reliable expectation or even a meaningful possibility. The United Nations has offered states no substitute for their own strength or that of allies as a resource for deterring or defeating their enemies. It is not, in reality or in evident potentiality, a synthetic superpower, able to protect all states by subduing any assailant. Its major contribution to the security of its members must be a product of its eligibility to serve as a neutral element in international relations, a kind of collective Switzerland, helping states to avoid clashes that their prudence commands them to avoid. While it cannot fight its members' battles for them, it can reinforce their efforts to remain at peace.

The primary resources for regulation of state behavior which have been discovered and developed by the League and the United Nations fall into the category of persuasion and influence rather than edict and compulsion. The question of the implications to be drawn from this factual situation is of central importance for the evaluation of international organization.

* * *

In short, the conception of government as an agency that maintains order simply by commanding and compelling, prohibiting and punishing, has little relevance to a pluralistic national society and still less to a global society chiefly characterized by the depth of its divisions, the simplicity of its pluralistic pattern, and the underdevelopment of its capacity to superimpose a universal allegiance upon national loyalties. Given this kind of international community, the realization of the theoretical ideal of subjecting the world to unchallengeable authority would require the creation of an inordinately powerful world government; the fulfillment of the practical task of maintaining order in such a world involves the assiduous application of methods of compromise and adjustment. Here is a real paradox: the international community is so deficient in consensual foundations that it must theoretically be held together more by force than by consent, but it is marked by such decentralization of the resources of political and physical power that it must in practice be managed by agencies, whether they be called instruments of international organization or of world federation, that operate more by persuasion than by coercion. In the world as it is, there is no real alternative to efforts to achieve regulation of state behavior by noncoercive methods, and no more appropriate collective task than the provision of international services which may ultimately prove conducive to the breaking down of those features of the community structure which make reliance upon consent rather than coercion at once so necessary and so precarious. The regulatory methods and functional emphases of international organization may not conform to the image of government con-

cocted by those who are impatient to abolish the problem of war by creating an entity which can, by definition, knock any and all national heads together, but they do correspond closely to the actual approach to the problem of maintaining order in a pluralistic society that the federal government of the United States has found essential. It is less significant that international organization is not a federal world government than that it is engaged in the effort to do the sort of thing that must be done, by the sort of method that can be used, to produce the sort of community that can, with proper management, sustain a peaceful existence.

The Prospects of International Organization

To say that international organization does not represent a fundamentally mistaken approach to the problem of world order is not to assert that it is destined to succeed. The tough reality of the national divisions of world society makes the quest for agreed solutions of international problems a necessary enterprise, but the conflicting interests and purposes of national entities also make that quest a difficult one. Mankind is blessed by no cosmic guarantee that all its problems are soluble and all its dangers are avoidable.

The danger of violent conflict among states possessing vast power is the overwhelming reality of our time. Only the coldest of comfort is to be derived from the observation that the existence of this danger is attributable to the nature of the international community rather than to the nature of the international architecture contrived in 1945. In this situation, it is all too clear that the United Nations can offer no guarantee of peace and security; at best, it can facilitate the balancing of power against power, and mobilize the resources of political adjustment. In the long run, international organization may transform the working of the multi-state system. In the short run, it is inevitably more affected by the circumstances of international relations than effective in alerting those circumstances.

There can be no guarantee that international machinery will in fact be utilized for the high purposes to which it may be formally dedicated. The establishment of an international organization does not involve the creation of an autonomous will, inexorably set upon the pursuit of the ideal of peace in a prescribed manner. Rather, it involves the creation of a mechanism to be placed at the disposal of states, which may use it for whatever purposes their agreements or their disagreements dictate. In practice, international organization may serve as the institutional framework for the joint exploration of approaches to peace, but it is also capable of serving as an arena for the conduct of international political warfare, or as an instrument for the advancement of the political objectives of a particular state or group of states.

International organization does not emancipate the world from dependence upon the quality of its statesmanship. Structural apparatus cannot generate its own supply of political decency, discretion, wisdom, and moderation. In the final

analysis, both the possibilities and the limitations of international organization are set by political forces operative within and among member states. The deficiencies of the United Nations indicate a greater need for review and revision of national policies than of the Charter itself.

The most casual observer of the international scene can see that the problem of world order has not been solved. The most careful student of international organization can see that no world-saving miracles have been wrought, no infallible formula for solution of fundamental problems has been drafted, and no glorious certainty of a brave new world has been projected before the troubled eyes of modern man. But there is more to be seen than unsolved problems, unresolved conflicts, and unparalleled dangers of chaos and destruction. Fallibility is not the same as futility; limited achievement is not the same as unlimited failure; danger is not the same as doom.

The development of international organization represents both a realistic response to the requirements of doing national business in an increasingly complex international setting and an idealistic attempt to modify the operation of the multi-state system so as to make civilized living possible in an increasingly interdependent world.

*   *   *

The long-range effects of international organization upon the multi-state system cannot be confidently predicted. It may be regarded as a process of evolutionary unification; yet, it functions now to support the fragmentation of empires into groups of newly independent states. It may be regarded as a process of gradual replacement of national governments as the major agencies for the management of human affairs; yet, it operates now less to deprive governments of their domestic functions than to assist them in acquiring the competence to do their jobs more effectively. It may be regarded as a process leading to the eventual transcendence of the multi-state system; yet, its immediate function is to reform and supplement the system, so as to make the maintenance of legal, political, and administrative pluralism compatible with the requirements of an interdependent world.

It is perhaps necessary to stress again the distinction between international *organizations* and international *organization*. Particular organizations may be nothing more than playthings of power politics and handmaidens of national ambitions. But international organization, considered as an historical process, represents a secular trend toward the systematic development of an enterprising quest for political means of making the world safe for human habitation. It may fail, and peter out ignominiously. But if it maintains the momentum that it has built up in the twentieth century, it may yet effect a transformation of human relationships on this planet which will at some indeterminate point justify the assertion that the world has come to be governed—that mankind has become a community capable of sustaining order, promoting justice, and establishing the conditions of that good life which Aristotle took to be the supreme aim of politics.

Prosperity

1.3

GABRIEL KOLKO

The United States and World Economic Power

* * *

To understand the unique economic interests and aspirations of the United States in the world, and the degree to which it benefits or loses within the existing distribution and structure of power and the world economy, is to define a crucial basis for comprehending as well as predicting its role overseas.

* * *

The United States and Raw Materials

The role of raw materials is qualitative rather than merely quantitative, and neither volume nor price can measure their ultimate significance and consequences. The economies and technologies of the advanced industrial nations, the United States in particular, are so intricate that the removal of even a small part, as in a watch, can stop the mechanism. The steel industry must add approximately thirteen pounds of manganese to each ton of steel, and though the weight and value of the increase

is a tiny fraction of the total, a modern diversified steel industry *must* have manganese. The same analogy is true of the entire relationship between the industrial and so-called developing nations: The nations of the Third World may be poor, but in the last analysis the industrial world needs their resources more than these nations need the West, for poverty is nothing new to peasantry cut off from export sectors, and trading with industrial states has not ended their subsistence living standards. In case of a total rupture between the industrial and supplier nations, it is the population of the industrial world that proportionately will suffer the most.

* * *

It is extraordinarily difficult to estimate the potential role and value of these scarce minerals to the United States, but certain approximate definitions are quite sufficient to make the point that the future of American economic power is too deeply involved for this nation to permit the rest of the world to take its own political and revolutionary course in a manner that imperils

From *The Roots of American Foreign Policy* (Boston: Beacon Press, 1969), chap. 3.

the American freedom to use them. Suffice it to say, the ultimate significance of the importation of certain critical raw materials is not their cost to American business but rather the end value of the industries that *must* employ these materials, even in small quantities, or pass out of existence. And in the larger sense, confident access to raw materials is a necessary precondition for industrial expansion into new or existing fields of technology, without the fear of limiting shortages which the United States' sole reliance on its national resources would entail. Intangibly, it is really the political and psychological assurance of total freedom of development of national economic power that is vital to American economic growth. Beyond this, United States profits abroad are made on overseas investments in local export industries, giving the Americans the profits of the suppliers as well as the consumer. An isolated America would lose all this, and much more.

* * *

World Trade and World Misery

If the postwar experience is any indication, the nonsocialist developing nations have precious little reason to hope that they can terminate the vast misery of their masses. For in reality the industrialized nations have increased their advantages over them in the world economy by almost any standard one might care to use.

The terms of trade—the unit value or cost of goods a region imports compared to its exports—have consistently disfavored the developing nations since 1958, ignoring altogether the fact that the world prices of raw materials prior to that time were never a measure of equity. Using 1958 as a base year, by 1966 the value of the exports of developing areas had fallen to 97, those of the industrial nations had risen to 104. Using the most extreme example of this shift, from 1954 to 1962 the terms of trade deteriorated 38 percent against the developing nations, for an income loss in 1962 of about $11 billion, or 30 percent more than the financial aid the Third World received that year. Even during 1961–66, when the terms of trade remained almost constant, their loss in potential income was $13.4 billion, wiping away 38 percent of the income from official foreign aid plans of every sort.

* * *

In fact, whether intended or otherwise, low prices and economic stagnation in the Third World directly benefit the industrialized nations. Should the developing nations ever industrialize to the extent that they begin consuming a significant portion of their own oil and mineral output, they would reduce the available supply to the United States and prices would rise. And there has never been any question that conservative American studies of the subject have treated the inability of the Third World to industrialize seriously as a cause for optimism in raw materials planning. Their optimism is fully warranted, since nations dependent on the world market for the capital to industrialize are unlikely to succeed, for when prices of raw materials are high they tend to concentrate on selling more raw materials, and when prices are low their earnings are insufficient to raise capital for diversification. The United States especially gears its investments, private and public, to increasing the output of exportable minerals and agricultural commodities, instead of balanced economic development. With relatively high capital-labor intensive investment and feeding transport facilities to port areas rather than to the population, such investments hardly scratch the living standards of the great majority of the local peasantry or make possible the large increases in agricultural output that are a precondition of a sustained industrial expansion.

*   *   *

United States Investment and Trade

*   *   *

American foreign investments are unusually parasitic, not merely in the manner in which they use a minimum amount of dollars to mobilize maximum foreign resources, but also because of the United States' crucial position in the world raw-materials price structure both as consumer and exporter. This is especially true in the developing regions, where extractive industries and cheap labor result in the smallest permanent foreign contributions to national wealth. In Latin America in 1957, for example, 36 percent of United States manufacturing investments, as opposed to 56 percent in Europe and 78 percent in Canada, went for plant and equipment. And wages as a percentage of operating costs in United States manufac-

turing investments are far lower in Third World nations than Europe or Canada.[1]

*   *   *

Seen in this light, United States foreign aid has been a tool for penetrating and making lucrative the Third World in particular and the entire nonsocialist world in general. The small price for saving European capitalism made possible later vast dividends, the expansion of American capitalism, and ever greater power and profits. It is this broader capability eventually to expand and realize the ultimate potential of a region that we must recall when short-term cost accounting and a narrow view make costly American commitments to a nation or region inexplicable. Quite apart from profits on investments, during 1950–60 the United States allocated $27.3 billion in nonmilitary grants, including the agricultural disposal program. During that same period it exported $166 billion in goods on a commercial basis, and imported materials essential to the very operation of the American economy.[2] It is these vast flows of goods, profits, and wealth that set the fundamental context for the implementation and direction of United States foreign policy in the world.

The United States and the Price of Stability

Under conditions in which the United States has been the major beneficiary of a world economy geared to serve it, the continued, invariable American opposition to basic innovations and reforms in world economic relations is entirely predictable.

Not merely resistance to stabilizing commodity and price agreements, or non-tied grants and loans, but to every imperatively needed structural change has characterized United States policy toward the Third World. In short, the United States is today the bastion of the *ancient regime,* of stagnation and continued poverty for the Third World.

* * *

The numerous American interventions to protect its investors throughout the world, and the United States ability to use foreign aid and loans as a lever to extract required conformity and concessions, have been more significant as a measure of its practice. The instances of this are too plentiful to detail here, but the remarkable relationship between American complaints on this score and the demise of objectionable local political leaders deserves more than passing reference.

* * *

In today's context, we should regard United States political and strategic intervention as a rational overhead charge for its present and future freedom to act and expand. One must also point out that however high that cost may appear today, in the history of United States diplomacy specific American economic interests in a country or region have often defined the national interest on the assumption that the nation can identify its welfare with the profits of some of its citizens—whether in oil, cotton, or bananas. The costs to the state as a whole are less consequential than the desires and profits of specific class strata and their need to operate everywhere in a manner that, collectively, brings vast prosperity to the United States and its rulers.

Today it is a fact that capitalism in one country is a long-term physical and economic impossibility without a drastic shift in the distribution of the world's income. Isolated, the United States would face those domestic backlogged economic and social problems and weaknesses it has deferred confronting for over two decades, and its disappearing strength in a global context would soon open the door to the internal dynamics which might jeopardize the very existence of liberal corporate capitalism at home.

The existing global political and economic structure, with all its stagnation and misery, has not only brought the United States billions but has made possible, above all, a vast power that requires total world economic integration not on the basis of equality but of domination. And to preserve this form of world is vital to the men who run the American economy and politics at the highest levels.

Notes

[1] Department of Commerce, *U.S. Business Investments,* 43, 65–66; *The Economist,* July 10, 1965, 167; Allan W. Johnstone, *United States Direct Investment in France* (Cambridge, 1965), 48–49; *Le Monde,* January 14–15, July 23, 1968; *Wall Street Journal,* December 12, 1967; Committee on Foreign Relations, *United States–Latin American Relations,* 388; *New York Times,* April 16, 1968.

[2] Department of Commerce, *Balance of Payments,* 120, 150–51.

Principles

1.4

TONY SMITH

The United States and the
Global Struggle for Democracy

If the United States had never existed, what would be the status in world affairs of democracy today? Would its forces based in France, Britain, the Low Countries, and Scandinavia have survived the assaults of fascism and communism, or would one of these rival forms of mass political mobilization have instead emerged triumphant at the end of the twentieth century?

The answer is self-evident: we can have no confidence that, without the United States, democracy would have survived. To be sure, London prepared the way for Washington in charting the course of liberal internationalism; and the United States was slow to leave isolationism after 1939, while the Red Army deserves primary praise for the defeat of Nazi Germany. Yet it is difficult to escape the conclusion that since World War I, the fortunes of democracy worldwide have largely depended on American power.

The decisive period of the century, so far as the eventual fate of democracy was concerned, came with the defeat of fas-cism in 1945 and the American-sponsored conversion of Germany and Japan to democracy and a much greater degree of economic liberalism. Here were the glory days of American liberal democratic internationalism (and not the 1980s, however remarkable that decade, as some believe). American leadership of the international economy—thanks to the institutions created at Bretton Woods in 1944, its strong backing for European integration with the Marshall Plan in 1947 and support for the Schuman Plan thereafter, the formation of NATO in 1949, the stability of Japanese political institutions after 1947 and that country's economic dynamism after 1950 (both dependent in good measure on American power)—created the economic, cultural, military, and political momentum that enabled liberal democracy to triumph over Soviet communism. Except perhaps for NATO, all of these developments were the product of the tenets of thinking first brought together in modern form by Woodrow Wilson, before being

From *America's Mission: The United States and the Worldwide Struggle for Democracy in the 20th Century* (Princeton: Princeton University Press, 1994), chap. 1 and appendix.

adapted to the world of the 1940s by the Roosevelt and Truman administrations.

In the moment of triumph, it should not be forgotten that for most of this century, the faith in the future expansion of democracy that had marked progressive thinking in Europe and America at the turn of the century seemed exceedingly naive. By the 1930s, democracy appeared to many to be unable to provide the unity and direction of its totalitarian rivals. Indeed, again in the 1970s, there was a resurgence of literature predicting democracy's imminent demise: its materialism, its individualism, its proceduralism (that is, the elaborate sets of rules and institutions needed to make it function), its tolerance, not to say its permissiveness—the list could be extended indefinitely—seemed to deprive it of the toughness and confidence necessary to survive in a harsh world of belligerent, ideologically driven fascist and communist states.

Fascism was essentially undone by its militarism and its racism; Soviet communism by its overcentralized economic planning and its failure to provide a political apparatus capable of dealing with the tensions of nationalism not only within the Soviet empire but inside the Soviet Union itself. By contrast, however varied the forms of government may be that rightly call themselves democratic, they have demonstrated a relative ability to accommodate class, gender, and ethnic diversity domestically through complicated institutional forms centering on competitive party systems and representative governments. As importantly, the democracies have shown an ability to cooperate internationally with one another through a variety

of regimes managing the complex issues of their interdependence, despite the centrifugal force of rival state interests and nationalism. Hence, at the end of the twentieth century, democracy is unparalleled for its political flexibility, stability, legitimacy, and ability to cooperate internationally.

* * *

The most important statement on the uniqueness of American liberalism remains Alexis de Toqueville's *Democracy in America* published in 1835 (a second volume appeared in 1840). Commenting that the United States was "born free," that "the social state of the Americans is eminently democratic . . . even the seeds of aristocracy were never planted," Toqueville continues:

> There society acts by and for itself. There are no authorities except within itself; one can hardly meet anybody who would dare to conceive, much less to suggest, seeking power elsewhere. The people take part in the making of the laws by choosing the lawgivers, and they share in their application by electing the agents of the executive power; one might say that they govern themselves, so feeble and restricted is the part left to the administration, so vividly is that administration aware of its popular origin, and obedient to the fount of power. The people reign over the American political world as God rules over the universe. It is the cause and the end of all things; everything rises out of it and it absorbed back into it.[1]

Toqueville was correct to see how democratic the United States was by contrast with other countries in the 1830s, for with Andrew Jackson's election in 1828 it could rightfully call itself the first modern democracy. Yet it should be recalled that at the time of American independence there were property qualifications for the vote and that certain religious denominations, as well as women and slaves, were disfranchised. Had Toqueville arrived a decade earlier, his account might not have been so perspicacious.

* * *

It is inevitable that the meaning of liberal democracy in domestic American life should deeply mark the conduct of its foreign policy. When their policy intends to promote democracy abroad, Americans rather naturally tend to think in terms of a weak state relative to society. The result for others is a paradoxical form of "conservative radicalism": radical in that for many countries, democracy has meant an abrupt and basic political change away from the narrow-based authoritarian governments with which these people are familiar; conservative in that in fundamental ways, the Americans have not meant to disturb the traditional social power relations based on property ownership.

Here was the genius, and also the tragedy, of the American sponsorship of democracy abroad: it was genuinely innovative politically, but it was not profoundly upsetting socioeconomically. The genius of the approach was that it could be attractive to established elites abroad (provided that they had the wit to try to adapt), for whatever the hazards of introducing democracy, it promised to mod-ernize and stabilize those regimes that could reform enough to be called democratic. The tragedy, especially in lands that were predominantly agrarian, was that these political changes (where they were accepted) were often not enough to create the cultural, economic, and social circumstances that could reinforce a democratic political order. As a result, American efforts either failed completely (as in Central America and the Caribbean during Wilson's presidency) or created narrowly based and highly corrupt elitist forms of democracy (as in the Philippines or more recently in the Dominican Republic).

It was different when the United States occupied Japan and Germany to promote democracy in 1945. But the men and women who undertook this mission were not liberal democrats of the traditional American sort. Instead, many of them were New Dealers, for whom the prerequisites of democracy included strong labor unions, land reform, welfare legislation, notions of racial equality, and government intervention in the economy. Moreover, they had the good fortune to be working with societies that already had centralized political institutions, diversified industrial economies, and (at least in Germany) many convinced democrats awaiting deliverance from fascism and communism alike. The Americans who conceived of the Alliance for Progress in Latin America were for the most part cut of the same cloth as the New Dealers. But their power in Latin America was not nearly so great as their predecessors' had been in Germany and Japan, and the socioeconomic structures of South and Central America lacked the inherent advantages for democratizers that the former fascist powers possessed. Hence the Alliance's failure.

This New Deal outlook was not typical of the Americans who took the Philippines in 1898 or who were in power under what was deservedly called the "progressive" presidency of Woodrow Wilson. These Franklin Roosevelt Democrats were also different from liberal reformers like Jimmy Carter, who favored a strictly human-rights approach to democratization. The most interesting contrast comes with Ronald Reagan, however, whose insistence on the contribution free markets could make to democratic government shared with the New Dealers the notion that political life depends in good measure on the structure of power socioeconomically (even if the two approaches differed on the need for governmental regulation and social redistribution).

As these cases suggest, American liberal democratic internationalism varied in its agenda over time. The continuity was such, however, that we can speak of a tradition in American foreign policy, one with an agenda for action abroad tied to a firm notion of the national interest that was to have momentous consequences for world affairs in the twentieth century.

* * *

In different countries, American influence has counted in different ways. For example, Czechs and Slovaks today often gratefully acknowledge the American contribution to the establishment of their democracy in 1918–9 and consider Woodrow Wilson to be virtually a founding father of their re-public. Nevertheless, Czechoslovak democracy during the interwar period was almost entirely the doing of its own people. So too, Germany might well have become a democracy even without the American occupation after 1945, though the character of its political order without Allied supervision might have made it less liberal than it is today, and the pace of European economic integration might have been altogether slower, with dramatic consequences for political stability on the continent. By contrast, Japanese democracy bears a more indelible American mark due to General Douglas MacArthur's assertive role in the establishment of its postwar order.

When we turn to the pre-industrial world, the impact of American policy changes dramatically. Thus, the Philippines is a fragile democracy, the American-inspired political institutions not having resolved fundamental issues of class power in this predominately agrarian country. So too in Latin America, the American contribution to democracy has been problematic, as in the case of Chile, or decidedly negative, as in Guatemala or in the Dominican Republic (before 1978, when for the first time a positive intervention occurred). Indeed, whatever its intentions, American policy on balance may have done substantially more to shore up dictatorships in the region than to advance the cause of democracy: the emergence of the Somoza and Trujillo tyrannies as the fruits of American interventions beginning with Wilson illustrates this clearly.

However, country studies alone do not tell us enough. After both the First and Second world wars, and again today in the aftermath of the cold war, America has formulated frameworks for world order in which the promotion of democracy play a conspicuous role. The emphasis on global security, the world market, and international law and organizations figure prominently alongside the call for national, democratic self-determination. The administrations of Wilson, Roosevelt, Truman, and Reagan emerge as particularly important in this context, where the focus is on the ability of democratic countries to cooperate internationally.

Historical watersheds, such as we are now passing through, are moments when the study of the past is especially invigorating. The past is now securely the past: the actors and the consequences of their policies have less claim on the present and so can be studied with some dispassion. Simultaneously, the present is in search of its future and must take stock of how it arrived at its current position.

As Americans ponder the challenges of world affairs at the end of the cold war, they may think back to other times when Washington's decisions were critical: not only to the end of the world wars in 1918 and 1945, but to the end of the Spanish-American War in 1898 and the Civil War in 1865 as well. What they will find is that in the aftermath of victory, Washington determined to win the peace by promoting a concept of national security calling ultimately for democratic government among those with whom the United States would work most closely.

Just how to achieve this end was never a clear matter, to be sure. As the North debated what to do with its victory over the South in 1865, so in 1898 American leaders were somewhat unsure what to do with their new role in the Far East and the Caribbean. The national debate in 1918–9 over Wilson's vision of a "peace without victory" so as "to make the world safe for democracy" was likewise raucous and uncertain. Only in the 1940s, in its planning for the postwar order, did Washington appear relatively clear in its thinking (and here too there were debates, contradictions, improvisations, and accidents aplenty as policy was made). Thus, when President Clinton, like Presidents Bush and Reagan before him, speaks of his conviction that no feature of U.S. foreign policy is more critical at the end of the cold war than helping the democratic forces in Russia, he may often be at a loss on how best to proceed. But he is articulating his concerns for peace in a recognizable way that stretches back across the generations, to American leaders in other times who have speculated on what to do in the aftermath of victory and who rightly concluded that the answer consisted in promoting the fortunes of democracy for others for the sake of American national security.

* * *

Notes

[1] Alexis de Toqueville, *Democracy in America* (New York: Harper and Row, 1966), pt. 1, chaps. 2–3. For a modern restatement of Toqueville's insistence on American egalitarianism, see Gordon S. Wood, *The Radicalism of the American Revolution* (New York: Knopf, 1992).

The President and Congress

2.1

ARTHUR M. SCHLESINGER, JR.

What the Founding Fathers Intended

* * *

In drafting the Constitution, [the Founding Fathers] were, of course, concerned to correct the deficiencies of the Articles of Confederation, under which the rebellious colonies had been governed during the Revolution. The Articles had bestowed executive as well as legislative authority on Congress, establishing in effect parliamentary government without a prime minister. Article VI gave Congress control over the conduct of foreign affairs, and Article IX gave it "the sole and exclusive right and power of determining on peace and war." But the Constitution was founded on the opposite principle of the separation of power. The men of Philadelphia therefore had to work out a division of authority between the legislative and executive branches. In domestic policy, this division was reasonably clear. In foreign affairs, it was often cryptic, ambiguous and incomplete.

Their experience under the Articles led the Founding Fathers to favor more centralization of executive authority than they

had known in the Confederation. Many of them probably agreed with [Alexander] Hamilton's statement in the 70th Federalist [paper] that "energy in the Executive is a leading character in the definition of good government." Those who disagreed were reassured by the expectation that Washington would be the first head of state. At the same time, their experience under the British crown led the Founding Fathers to favor less centralization of authority than they perceived in the British monarchy. As victims of what they considered a tyrannical royal prerogative, they were determined to fashion for themselves a Presidency that would be strong but still limited.

Nothing was more crucial for the new nation than the successful conduct of its external relations. There was broad agreement that national safety could best be assured through the development of equal trading relations with the states of Europe. America's "plan is commerce," Thomas Paine wrote in *Common Sense,* "and that, well attended to, will secure us the peace and friendship of all Europe, because it is

---

From Arthur M. Schlesinger, Jr., *The Imperial Presidency* (Boston: Houghton Mifflin, 1973), chap. 1.

the interest of all Europe to have America as a free port."[1] Washington summed up the policy in his Farewell Address: "The great rule of conduct for us in regard to foreign nations is, in extending our commercial relations to have with them as little political connection as possible." Given the clear priority the Founding Fathers assigned to commercial over political relations, it is significant that the Constitution vested control over this primary aspect of foreign policy in Congress, assigning it the definite and unqualified power "to regulate Commerce with foreign Nations."

The Constitution also brought Congress into the treaty-making process, withholding from the President the exclusive authority enjoyed by European monarchs to make treaties. Where the British King, for example, could conclude treaties on his own, the American President was required to win the consent of two-thirds of the Senate. "The one can do alone," said Hamilton, "what the other can do only with the concurrence of a branch of the legislature."[2] And Congress received other weighty powers related to the conduct of foreign affairs: the power to make appropriations, to raise and maintain the armed forces and make rules for their government and regulation, to control naturalization and immigration, to impose tariffs, to define and punish offenses against the law of nations and, above all, "to declare War, grant Letters of Marque and Reprisal, and make Rules concerning Captures on Land and Water."

II

This last clause—in Article I, Section 8, of the Constitution—was of prime impor-

tance. The Founders were determined to deny the American President what Blackstone had assigned to the British King— "the sole prerogative of making war and peace."[3] Even Hamilton, the most consistent advocate of executive centralization, proposed in the [Constitutional] Convention that the Senate "have the sole power of declaring war" with the executive to "have the direction of war when authorized or begun."[4]

In an early draft, the Constitution gave Congress the power to "make" war. Every scholar knows the successful intervention by [James] Madison and [Elbridge] Gerry—

> M.[r] MADISON and M.[r] GERRY Moved to insert "*declare*," striking out "*make*" war; leaving to the Executive the power to repel sudden attacks.

—but no one really quite knows what this exchange meant.

*   *   *

What does seem clear is that no one wanted either to deny the President the power to respond to surprise attack or to give the President general power to initiate hostilities. The first aspect—the acknowledgment that Presidents must on occasion begin defensive war without recourse to Congress—represented the potential breach in the congressional position and would have the most significance in the future. But the second aspect gained the most attention and brought the most comfort at the time. James Wilson, next to Madison the most penetrating political thinker at the Convention, thus portrayed the constitutional solution: this system "will not hurry us into war; it is calculated to guard against it. It will not be in the power of a single man, or a single body of men, to involve us in such distress."[5]

The Founding Fathers did not have to give unconditional power to declare war to Congress. They might have said, in language they used elsewhere in the Constitution, that war could be declared by the President with the advice and consent of Congress, or by Congress on the recommendation of the President.[6] But they chose not to mention the President at all in connection with the war-making power. Nor was this because they lacked realism about the problems of national security. In a famous passage in the 23rd Federalist [paper], Hamilton said that the powers of national self-defense must "exist without limitation, *because it is impossible to foresee or define the extent and variety of national exigencies. . . .* The circumstances that endanger the safety of nations are infinite, and for this reason no constitutional shackles can wisely be imposed on the power to which the care of it is committed. This power ought to be co-extensive with all the possible combinations of such circumstances." The Founding Fathers were determined that the national government should have all the authority required to defend the nation. But Hamilton was not asserting these unlimited powers for the Presidency, as careless commentators have assumed. He was asserting them for the national government *as a whole*—for, that is, Congress and the Presidency combined.

The resistance to giving a "single man," even if he were President of the United States, the unilateral authority to decide on war pervaded the contemporaneous literature. Hamilton's observations on the treaty-making power applied all the more forcibly to the war-making power: "The history of human conduct does not warrant that exalted opinion of human virtue which would make it wise to commit interests of so delicate and momentous a kind, as those which concern its intercourse with the rest of the world, to the sole disposal of a magistrate created and circumstanced as would be a President of the United States."[7] As Madison put it in a letter to [Thomas] Jefferson in 1798: "The constitution supposes, what the History of all Govts demonstrates, that the Ex. is the branch of power most interested in war, & most prone to it. It has accordingly with studied care vested the question of war in the Legisl."[8]

III

At the same time, the Constitution vested the command of the Army and Navy in the President, which meant that, once Congress had authorized war, the President as Commander in Chief had full power to conduct military operations. "Of all the cares or concerns of government," said the Federalist, "the direction of war most peculiarly demands those qualities which distinguish the exercise of power by a single hand."[9] The designation of the President as Commander in Chief also sprang from a concern to assure civilian control of the military establishment. By making the Commander in Chief a civilian who would be subject to recall after four years, the Founders doubtless hoped to spare American tribulations of the sort that the unfettered command and consequent political power of a Duke of Marlborough had brought to England.

There is no evidence that anyone supposed that his office as Commander in Chief endowed the President with an independent source of authority. Even with Washington in prospect, the Founders emphasized their narrow and military definition of this presidential role. As Hamilton carefully explained in the 69th Federalist [paper], the President's power as Commander in Chief

> would be nominally the same with that of the king of Great Britain, but in substance much inferior to it. It would amount to nothing more than the supreme command and direction of the military and naval forces . . . while that of the British king extends to the *declaring* of war and to the *raising* and *regulating* of fleets and armies,—all which, by the Constitution under consideration, would appertain to the legislature.

As Commander in Chief the President had no more authority than the first general of the army or the first admiral of the navy would have had as professional military men. The President's power as Commander in Chief, in short, was simply the power to issue orders to the armed forces within a framework established by Congress. And even Congress was denied the power to make appropriations for the support of the armed forces for a longer term than two years.

In addition to the command of the armed forces, the Constitution gave the President the power to receive foreign envoys and, with the advice and consent of the Senate, to appoint ambassadors as well as to make treaties. Beyond this, it had nothing specific to say about his authority in foreign affairs. However, Article II gave him general executive power; and, as the 64th and 75th Federalist Papers emphasized, the structural characteristics of the Presidency—unity, secrecy, decision, dispatch, superior sources of information—were deemed especially advantageous to the conduct of diplomacy.

The result was, as Madison said, "a partial mixture of powers." Madison indeed argued that such mingling was indispensable to the system, for unless the branches of government "be so far connected and blended as to give to each a constitutional control over the others, the degree of separation which the maxim requires, as essential to a free government, can never in practice be duly maintained." Particularly in the case of war and peace—the war-making and treaty-making powers—it was really a matter, in Hamilton's phrase, of "joint possession."[10]

In these areas the two branches had interwoven responsibilities and competing opportunities. Moreover, each had an undefined residuum of authority on which to draw—the President through the executive power and the constitutional injunction that "he shall take Care that the Laws be faithfully executed," Congress through the constitutional authorization "to make all Laws which shall be necessary and proper for carrying into Execution . . . all . . . Powers vested by this Constitution in the Government of the United States." In addition, the Constitution itself was silent on certain issues of import to the conduct of foreign affairs: among them, the recognition of foreign governments, the authority to proclaim neutrality, the role of executive agreements, the control of information essential to intelligent decision. The result, as Edward S. Corwin remarked 40 years ago, was to make of the Constitution "an invitation to struggle for the privilege of directing American foreign policy."[11]

IV

One further consideration lingered behind the words of the Constitution and the debates of the Convention. This was the question of emergency. For the Founding Fathers were more influenced by Locke than by any other political philosopher; and, as students of Locke, they were well acquainted with Chapter 14, "Of Prerogative," in the *Second Treatise of Government*. Prerogative was the critical exception in Locke's rendition of the social contract. In general, the contract—the reciprocal obligation of ruler and ruled within the frame of law—was to prevail. In general, the authority of government was to be limited. But in emergency, Locke argued, responsible rulers could resort to exceptional power. Legislatures were too large, unwieldy and slow to cope with crisis; moreover, they were not able "to foresee, and so by laws to provide for, all accidents and necessities." Indeed, on occasion "a strict and rigid observation of the laws may do harm." This meant that

there could be times when "the laws themselves should . . . give way to the executive power, or rather to this fundamental law of nature and government, viz., that, as much as may be, all the members of society are to be preserved."

Prerogative therefore was the exercise of the law of self-preservation. It was "the people's permitting their rulers to do several things of their own free choice, where the law was silent, and sometimes, too, against the direct letter of the law, for the public good, and their acquiescing in it when so done." The executive, Locke contended, must have the reserve power "to act according to discretion for the public good, without the prescription of law and sometimes even against it." If emergency prerogative were abused, the people would rebel; but, used for the good of the society, it would be accepted. "If there comes to be a question between the executive power and the people about a thing claimed as prerogative, the tendency of the exercise of such prerogative to the good or hurt of the people will easily decide that question."[12]

Locke's argument, restated in more democratic terms, was that, when the executive perceived what he deemed an emergency, he could initiate extralegal or even illegal action, but that he would be sustained and vindicated in that action only if his perception of the emergency were shared by the legislature and by the people. Though prerogative enabled the executive to act on his individual finding of emergency, whether or not his finding was right and this was a true emergency was to be determined not by the executive but by the community.

The idea of prerogative was *not* part of presidential power as defined in the Constitution. The Founding Fathers had lived with emergency, but they made no provision in the Constitution, except in relation to *habeas corpus,* for the suspension of law in the case of necessity (and even here they did not specify whether the power of suspension belonged to the executive). The argument of the Federalist Papers, in the words of Clinton Rossiter, was in effect that the Constitution was "equal to any emergency."[13]

Yet there is reason to believe that the doctrine that crisis might require the executive to act outside the Constitution in order to save the Constitution remained in the back of their minds. Even in the Federalist Papers Hamilton wrote of "that original right of self-defence which is paramount to all positive forms of government" and Madison thought it "vain to oppose constitutional barriers to the impulse of self-preservation."[14]

* * *

Notes

[1] Felix Gilbert, *The Beginnings of American Foreign Policy: To the Farewell Address* (Harper Torchbook, 1965), 42–43.

[2] 69th Federalist.

[3] E. S. Corwin, *The President: Office and Powers* (New York, 1940), 154

[4] C. C. Tansill, ed., *Documents Illustrative of the Formation of the Union of the American States* (Washington, 1927), 224.

[5] Charles A. Lofgren, "War-Making Under the Constitution: The Original Understanding," *Yale Law Review,* March 1972 (81 Yale L.J.), 685.

[6] Cf. James Grafton Rogers, *World Policing and the Constitution* (Boston, 1945), 21.

[7] 75th Federalist.

[8] Madison to Jefferson, April 2, 1798, Madison, *Writings,* Gaillard Hunt, ed. (New York, 1906), VI, 312–13.

[9] 73rd Federalist.

[10] The quotations are from the 47th, 48th, and 75th Federalist Papers.

[11] Corwin, *President,* 200.

[12] John Locke, *Second Treatise of Government,* Ch. 14.

[13] Clinton Rossiter, *Constitutional Dictatorship* (Princeton, 1948), 212.

[14] 28th and 41st Federalist Papers.

Public Opinion

2.2

Ole R. Holsti

Public Opinion and Foreign Policy: Challenges to the Almond-Lippmann Consensus

*   *   *

The Post–World War II Consensus

The availability after World War II of growing sets of polling data and the institution of systematic studies of voting behavior, combined with the assumption of a leadership role in world affairs by the United States, served to stimulate a growth industry in analyses of public opinion. The consensus view that developed during this period of some fifteen or twenty years after the end of World War II and just prior to the Vietnam escalation centered on three major propositions:

- ▪ Public opinion is highly volatile and thus it provides very dubious foundations for a sound foreign policy.
- ▪ Public attitudes on foreign affairs are so lacking in structure and coherence that they might best be described as "non-attitudes."
- ▪ At the end of the day, however, public opinion has a very limited impact on the conduct of foreign policy.

PUBLIC OPINION IS VOLATILE As noted earlier, Walter Lippmann's books of the interwar period described the mass public as neither sufficiently interested nor informed to play the pivotal role assigned to it by classical democratic theory. At the height of the Cold War thirty years later, Lippmann had become even more alarmed, depicting the mass public as not merely uninterested and uninformed, but as a powerful force that was so out of synch with reality as to constitute a massive and potentially fatal threat to effective government and policies.

> The unhappy truth is that the prevailing public opinion has been destructively wrong at the critical junctures. The people have impressed a critical veto upon the judgments of informed and responsible officials. They have compelled the govern-

From *International Studies Quarterly* 36:4 (December 1992).

ment, which usually knew what would have been wiser, or was necessary, or what was more expedient, to be too late with too little, or too long with too much, too pacifist in peace and too bellicose in war, too neutralist or appeasing in negotiations or too intransigent. Mass opinion has acquired mounting power in this country. It has shown itself to be a dangerous master of decision when the stakes are life and death.[1]

Similarly pessimistic conclusions and dire warnings were emerging from disparate other quarters as well. Drawing on a growing body of polling data and fearing that the American public might relapse into a mindless isolationism, because only a thin veneer of postwar internationalism covered a thick bedrock of indifference to the world, Gabriel Almond depicted public opinion as a volatile and mood-driven constraint upon foreign policy: "The undertow of withdrawal is still very powerful. Deeply ingrained habits do not die easy deaths. The world outside is still very remote for most Americans; and the tragic lessons of the last decades have not been fully digested."[2] Consequently, "Perhaps the gravest general problem confronting policy-makers is that of the instability of mass moods, the cyclical fluctuations which stand in the way of policy stability."[3]

* * *

Further support for the critics and skeptics emerged from the growing body of polling data which yielded ample evidence of the public's limited store of factual knowledge about foreign affairs. Innumerable surveys revealed such stunning gaps in informa-

tion as: X percent of the American public are unaware that there is a communist government in China, Y percent believe that the Soviet Union is a member of NATO, or Z percent cannot identify a single nation bordering on the Pacific Ocean. Such data reinforced the case of the critics and led some of them to propose measures to reduce the influence of the public. Thus, Lippmann called for stronger executive prerogatives in foreign affairs, and Bailey wondered whether the requirements of an effective foreign policy might make it necessary for the executive deliberately to mislead the public.[4]

PUBLIC OPINION LACKS STRUCTURE AND COHERENCE   A growing volume of data on public opinion and voting behavior, as well as increasingly sophisticated methodologies, enabled analysts not only to describe aggregate results and trends, but also to delve into the structure of political beliefs. Owing to immediate policy concerns about the U.S. role in the postwar era, many of the early studies were largely descriptive, focusing on such issues as participation in international organizations and alliances, the deployment of troops abroad, security commitments, foreign aid, trade and protectionism, and the like. The underlying premise was that a single internationalist-isolationist dimension would serve to structure foreign policy beliefs, much in the way that a liberal-conservative dimension was assumed to provide coherence to preferences on domestic issues.

In a classic study based on data from the late 1950s and early 1960s, Philip Converse concluded that the political beliefs of the mass public lack a real structure or coherence.[5] Comparing responses across several domestic and foreign policy issues, he found little if any "constraint" or underlying ideological structure that might provide some coherence to political thinking. In contrast, his analyses of elites—congressional candidates—revealed substantially higher correlations among responses to various issues. Moreover, Converse found that both mass and elite attitudes on a given issue had a short half-life. Responses in 1956 only modestly predicted responses two years later, much less in 1960. These findings led him to conclude that mass political beliefs are best described as "non-attitudes." Although Converse's findings were later to become the center of an active debate, it should be emphasized that his was not a lone voice in the wilderness. His data were drawn from the National Election Studies [NES] at the University of Michigan, and his findings were only the most widely quoted of a series of studies from the NES that came to essentially the same conclusion about the absence of structure, coherence, or persistence in the political beliefs of the mass public—especially on foreign affairs.[6]

PUBLIC OPINION HAS LIMITED IMPACT ON FOREIGN POLICY   The driving force behind much of the post–World War II attention to public opinion on foreign policy issues was the fear that an ill-informed and emotional mass public would serve as a powerful constraint on the conduct of American diplomacy, establishing unwise limits on policy makers, creating unrealistic expectations about what was feasible in foreign affairs, otherwise doing serious mischief to American diplomacy and, given the American role in the world, perhaps even to international stability. As Bernard Cohen demonstrated in a critical survey of the literature, however, the constraining role of public opinion was often asserted but rarely demonstrated—or even put to a systematic test.[7]

By the middle of the 1960s a consensus in fact seemed to emerge on a third point: Public opinion has little if any real impact on policy. Or, as the point was made most pithily by one State Department official: "To hell with public opinion. . . . We should lead, and not follow."[8] The weight of research evidence cast doubt on the potency of public opinion as a driving force behind, or even a significant constraint upon, foreign policy-making. For example, a classic study of the public-legislator relationship revealed that constituents' attitudes on foreign policy had less impact on members of the House of Representatives than did their views on domestic issues.[9] Cohen's research on the foreign policy bureaucracy indicated that State Department officials had a rather modest interest in public opinion, and to the extent that they even thought about the public, it was as an entity to be "educated" rather than a lodestar by which to be guided.[10] The proposition that the president has "almost a free hand" in the conduct of foreign affairs received support from other analysis, including Lipset, LaFeber, Levering, Paterson, and Graebner.[11]

*   *   *

The Renaissance of Interest in Public Opinion and Foreign Policy

Just as World War II and fears of postwar isolationism among the mass public gave rise to concern about public opinion and its impact on foreign policy, the war in Vietnam was the impetus for a renewed interest in the subject. It was a major catalyst in stimulating a reexamination of the consensus that had emerged during the two decades after World War II. * * * [D]uring the past two decades analysts have begun to challenge important aspects of the consensus described above.

* * *

[J.E.] Mueller's study of public opinion toward the Korean and Vietnam wars posed [a] challenge to the thesis of mindless changes in public attitudes. To be sure, public support for the U.S. war effort in both conflicts eventually changed, but in ways that seemed explicable and rational, rather than random and mindless. More specifically, he found that increasing public opposition to the conflicts traced out a pattern that fit a curve of rising battle deaths, suggesting that the public used an understandable, if simple, heuristic to assess American policy.[12]

The most comprehensive challenge to the Almond-Lippmann thesis has emerged from studies conducted by Benjamin Page and Robert Shapiro. Their evidence includes all questions that have been posed by major polling organizations since the inception of systematic surveys in the 1930s. Of the more than 6000 questions, almost 20 percent have been asked at least twice, pro-viding Page and Shapiro with a large data set to assess the degree of stability and change in mass public attitudes. Employing a cutoff point of a difference of 6 percent from one survey to another to distinguish between continuity and change, they found that mass opinion in the aggregate is in fact characterized by a good deal of stability and that this is no less true of foreign policy than on domestic issues.[13] More important, when attitude shifts take place, they seem to be neither random nor 180 degrees removed from the true state of world affairs. Rather, changes appear to be "reasonable, event driven" reactions to the real world, even if the information upon which they are based is marginally adequate at best. They concluded that

> virtually all the rapid shifts [in public opinion] we found were related to political and economic circumstances or to significant events which sensible citizens would take into account. In particular, most abrupt foreign policy changes took place in connection with wars, confrontations, or crises in which major changes in the actions of the United States or other nations quite naturally affect preferences about what policies to pursue.[14]

* * *

Similar conclusions, supporting Page and Shapiro and casting doubt on the Almond-Lippmann thesis, have also emerged from other studies. Jentleson found that during the post-Vietnam era, variations in public support for the use of force are best explained by differences between force to coerce foreign policy restraint by others, and force to influence or impose internal political changes within another state; the former goal has received much stronger support than the latter.[15]

An interesting variant of the "rational public" thesis stipulates that the public attempts to moderate American behavior toward the USSR by expressing preferences for a conciliatory stance from hawkish administrations while supporting more assertive policies from dovish ones.[16] To the extent that one can generalize from this study focusing on the Carter and Reagan administrations to other periods or other aspects of foreign policy, it further challenges the Almond-Lippmann thesis—indeed, it turns that proposition on its head—for it identifies the public as a source of moderation and continuity rather than of instability and unpredictability.

It is important to emphasize that none of these challenges to the Almond-Lippmann thesis is based on some newly found evidence that the public is in fact well informed about foreign affairs. Not only do polls repeatedly reveal that the mass public has a very thin veneer of factual knowledge about politics, economics, and geography; they also reveal that it is poorly informed about the specifics of conflicts, treaties, negotiations with other nations, characteristics of weapons systems, foreign leaders, and the like. Because the modest factual basis upon which the mass public reacts to international affairs remains an unchallenged—and unchallengeable—fact, we are faced with a puzzle: If a generally poorly informed mass public does indeed react to international affairs in an events-driven, rational manner, what are

the means that permit it to do so? Recall that a not-insignificant body of research evidence indicated that mass public attitudes lack the kind of ideological structure that would provide some coherence across specific issues and persistence through time.

* * *

CHALLENGE #2: DO PUBLIC ATTITUDES LACK STRUCTURE AND COHERENCE?

* * *

Although the more recent research literature has yet to create a consensus on all aspects of the question, there does appear to be a considerable convergence of findings on two general points relating to belief structures:

1. Even though the general public may be rather poorly informed, attitudes about foreign affairs are in fact structured in at least moderately coherent ways. Indeed, low information and an ambiguous foreign policy environment are actually likely to motivate rather than preclude some type of attitude structure.
2. A single isolationist-to-internationalist dimension inadequately describes the main dimensions of public opinion on international affairs.

An early study, based on the first of the quadrennial Chicago Council on Foreign Relations (CCFR) surveys, employed factor analysis and other methods to uncover three foreign policy outlooks: "liberal internationalism," "conservative internationalism," and "non-internationalism."[17] A comparable trichotomy ("three-headed eagle") emerged from early analyses of the data on opinion leaders generated by the Foreign Policy Leadership Project (FPLP).[18]

Others have questioned the division of foreign policy attitudes into three *types* rather than *dimensions,* and they have offered compelling evidence in support of their critiques. Chittick and Billingsley have undertaken both original and secondary analyses which indicated the need for three *dimensions,* including one that taps unilateralist-multilateralist sentiments, not three *types,* to describe adequately the foreign policy beliefs of both the mass public and leaders.[19]

A major set of contributions to the debate about how best to describe foreign policy attitudes has come from Wittkopf's exemplary secondary analyses of the CCFR surveys of both the general public and leaders.[20] His results, developed inductively from the first four CCFR surveys, revealed that with a single exception, two dimensions are necessary to describe foreign policy attitudes: "support-oppose militant internationalism" (MI) and "support-oppose cooperative internationalism" (CI). Dichotomizing and crossing these dimensions yields four types, with the quadrants labeled as *hard-liners* (support MI, oppose CI), *internationalists* (support MI, support CI), *isolationists* (oppose MI, oppose CI), and *accommodationists* (oppose MI, support CI).

Support for Wittkopf's MI/CI scheme also emerges from a reanalysis of the FPLP

data on American opinion leaders.[21] That study put the MI/CI scheme to a demanding test because of three major differences in the data sets: (1) The CCFR surveys were undertaken in 1974, 1978, 1982, and 1986, whereas the four FPLP studies followed two years later in each case; (2) the two sets of surveys have only a few questionnaire items in common; and (3) the MI/CI scheme was developed largely from data on the mass public, whereas the FPLP surveys focused solely on opinion leaders.

* * *

CHALLENGE #3: IS PUBLIC OPINION REALLY IMPOTENT?

* * *

Several recent quantitative studies have challenged some important foundations of the theory that, at least on foreign and defense issues, the public is virtually impotent. One element of that thesis is that policy makers are relatively free agents on foreign policy questions because these issues pose few dangers of electoral retribution by voters: elections are said to be decided by domestic questions, especially those sometimes described as "pocketbook" or "bread and butter" issues. However, a systematic study of presidential campaigns between 1952 and 1984 revealed that in five of the nine elections during the period, foreign policy issues had "large effects." Or, as the authors put it, when presidential candidates devote campaign time and other resources to foreign policy issues, they are not merely "waltzing before a blind audience."[22]

Recent research on voting behavior has also emphasized the importance of retrospective evaluations of performance on voter choice among candidates, especially when one of them is an incumbent.[23] Because voters are perceived as punishing incumbent candidates or parties for foreign policy failures (for example, the Iran hostage episode) or rewarding them for successes (for example, the invasion of Panama to capture General Noriega), decisions by foreign policy leaders may be made in anticipation of public reactions and the probabilities of success or failure.

* * *

Finally, two major studies have measured the congruence between changes in public preferences and a broad range of policies over extended periods. The first, a study of public opinion and policy outcomes spanning the years 1960–1974, revealed that in almost two-thirds of 222 cases, policy outcomes corresponded to public preferences. The consistency was especially high (92%) on foreign policy issues. Monroe offers three possible explanations for his findings: Foreign policy issues permit more decision-making by the executive, are likely to be the object of relatively less interest and influence by organized interest groups, and are especially susceptible to elite manipulation.[24] The second study covered an even longer span—1935 to 1979—which included 357 significant changes of public preferences.[25] Of the 231 instances of subsequent policy changes, 153 (66%) were congruent with changes in public preferences. There was little difference in the level of congruence for domestic (70%) and foreign policy (62%) issues.

* * *

Among the more difficult cases are those dealing with public opinion as a possible constraint on action. During the 1980s, the Reagan administration undertook a massive public relations campaign of dubious legality to generate public support for assistance to the "contra" rebels in Nicaragua,[26] but a careful analysis of surveys on the issue revealed that a majority of the public opposed American military involvement in Central America.[27] Would the Reagan administration have intervened more directly or massively in Nicaragua or El Salvador in the absence of such attitudes? Solid evidence about contemporary non-events is, to understate the case, rather hard to come by. Case studies seem to be the only way to address such questions, although even this approach is not wholly free of potential problems. Does an absence of documentary references to public opinion indicate a lack of interest by decision-makers? Alternatively, was attention to public attitudes so deeply ingrained in their working habits that it was unnecessary to make constant references to it? Are frequent references to public opinion an indication of a significant impact on decisions—or of a desire on the part of officials to be "on record" as having paid attention to public sentiments?

* * *

Conclusion

The consensus of the mid-1960s on the nature, structure, and impact of public opinion has clearly come under vigorous challenge during the past quarter century.

The Vietnam War, while not the sole causal factor in the reexamination of the conventional wisdom, was certainly a catalyst. If a new consensus has yet to emerge on all of the issues discussed above, at least it seems safe to state that the field is marked by innovative research and active debates on the implications of the results.

*   *   *

Notes

[1]Walter Lippman, *Essays in the Public Philosophy* (Boston: Little, Brown, 1955), 20.

[2]Gabriel Almond, *The American People and Foreign Policy* (New York: Praeger, 1950), 85.

[3]Almond, *The American People,* 239. Almond's use of the term "mood" differs from that of Frank Klingberg. Almond refers to sudden shifts of interest and preferences, whereas Klingberg has used the term to explain American foreign policy in terms of generation-long societal swings between introversion and extraversion.

[4]Lippman, *Essays;* T. A. Bailey, *The Man in the Street: The Impact of American Public Opinion on Foreign Policy* (New York: Macmillan, 1948), 13.

[5]Philip E. Converse, "The Nature of Belief Systems in Mass Publics," in D. E. Apter, ed., *Ideology and Discontent* (New York: Free Press, 1964).

[6]A. Campbell, P. E. Converse, W. E. Miller, and D. E. Stokes, *The American Voter* (New York: Wiley, 1964).

[7]Bernard Cohen, *The Public's Impact on Foreign Policy* (Boston: Little, Brown, 1973).

[8]Quoted in Cohen, *The Public's Impact,* 62.

[9]W. E. Miller and D. E. Stokes, "Constituency Influence in Congress," *American Political Science Review* 57 (1963), 45–46.

[10]Cohen, *The Public's Impact.*

[11]S. M. Lipset, "The President, Polls, and Vietnam," *Transaction,* September/October 1966, 10–24. W. LaFeber, "American Policy-Makers, Public Opinion, and the Outbreak of Cold War, 1945–1950," in Y. Nagai and A. Inye, eds., *The Origins of Cold War in Asia* (New York: Columbia University Press, 1977); R. B. Levering, *The Public and American Foreign Policy, 1918–1978* (New York: Morrow, 1978); T. G. Paterson, "Presidential Foreign Policy, Public Opinion, and Congress: The Truman Years," *Diplomatic History* 3 (1979), 1–18; and N. A. Graebner, "Public Opinion and Foreign Policy: A Pragmatic View," in D. C. Piper and R. J. Tercheck, eds., *Interaction: Foreign Policy and Public Policy* (Washington, D.C.: American Enterprise Institute, 1983).

[12]J. E. Mueller, *War, Presidents, and Public Opinion* (New York: Wiley, 1973). During the summer of 1965, as the Johnson administration was moving toward fateful decisions regarding Vietnam, George Ball warned: "We can't win," he said, his deep voice dominating the Cabinet Room. "The war will be long and protracted, with heavy casualties. The most we can hope for is a messy conclusion. We must measure this long-term price against the short-term loss that will result from withdrawal." Producing a chart that correlated public opinion with American casualties in Korea, Ball predicted that the American public would not support a long and inconclusive war. * * *

[13]Benjamin Page and Robert Shapiro, "Foreign Policy and the Rational Public," *Journal of Conflict Resolution* 32 (1988), 211–470.

[14]Benjamin Page and Robert Shapiro, "Changes in Americans' Policy Preferences, 1935–1979," *Public Opinion Quarterly* 46 (1982), 24–42.

[15]B. W. Jentleson, "The Pretty Prudent Public: Post-Post Vietnam American Opinion on the Use of Military Force," *International Studies Quarterly* 36 (1992) 48–73.

[16]M. Nincie, "The United States, the Soviet Union, and the Politics of Opposites," *World Politics* 40 (1988), 452–750.

[17]M. Mandelbaum and W. Schneider, "The New Internationalisms," in K.A. Oye et al., eds., *Eagle Entangled: U.S. Foreign Policy in a Complex World* (New York: Longman, 1979).

[18]O. R. Holsti, "The Three-Headed Eagle: The United States and the System Change," *International Studies Quarterly* 23 (1979), 339–59; O. R. Holsti and J. N. Rosenau, "Vietnam, Consensus, and the Belief Systems of American Leaders,"

World Politics 32 (1979), 1–56; O. R. Holsti and J. N. Rosenau, *American Leadership in World Affairs: Vietnam and the Breakdown of Consensus* (London: Allen and Unwin, 1984).

[19]W. Chittick and K. R. Billingsley, "The Structure of Elite Foreign Policy Beliefs," *Western Political Quarterly* 42 (1989), 201–24. See also B. A. Barde and R. Oldendick, "Beyond Internationalism: The Case for Multiple Dimensions in Foreign Policy Attitudes," *Social Science Quarterly* 59 (1978), 732–42; and W. Chittick, K. R. Billingsly, and R. Travis, "Persistence and Change in Elite and Mass Attitudes toward U.S. Foreign Policy," *Political Psychology* 11 (1990), 385–402.

[20]E. R. Wittkopf, "On the Foreign Policy Beliefs of the American People: A Critique and Some Evidence," *International Studies Quarterly* 30 (1986), 425–45; E. R. Wittkopf, *Faces of Internationalism: Public Opinion and Foreign Policy* (Durham: Duke University Press, 1990).

[21]O. R. Holsti and J. N. Rosenau, "The Structure of Foreign Policy Attitudes among American Leaders," *Journal of Politics* 52 (1990), 94–125.

[22]J. H. Aldrich, J. I. Sullivan, and E. Bordiga, "Foreign Affairs and Issue Voting: Do Presidential Candidates 'Waltz before a Blind Audience?'" *American Political Science Review* 83 (1989), 123–41.

[23]M. Fiorina, *Retrospective Voting in American National Elections* (New Haven: Yale University Press, 1981); P. Abramson; J. H. Aldrich, and J. Rhode, *Change and Continuity in the 1988 Election* (Washington, D.C.: Congressional Quarterly, 1990).

[24]A. D. Monroe, "Consistency between Public Preferences and National Policy Decisions," *American Politics Quarterly* 7 (1979), 3–19.

[25]Benjamin Page and Robert Shapiro, "Effects of Public Opinion on Policy," *American Political Science Review* 77 (1983), 175–90.

[26]R. Parry and P. Kornbluh, "Iran-Contra's Untold Story," *Foreign Policy* 72 (1988), 3–30.

[27]R. Sobel, "Public Opinion about United States Intervention in El Salvador and Nicaragua," *Public Opinion Quarterly* 53 (1989), 114–28. See also R. H. Hinckley, *People, Polls, and Policy-Makers* (New York: Lexington, 1992).

Isolationism vs. Internationalism

3.1

HENRY KISSINGER

Franklin D. Roosevelt and the Coming of World War II

For contemporary political leaders governing by public opinion polls, Roosevelt's role in moving his isolationist people toward participation in the war serves as an object lesson on the scope of leadership in a democracy. Sooner or later, the threat to the European balance of power would have forced the United States to intervene in order to stop Germany's drive for world domination. The sheer, and growing, strength of America was bound to propel it eventually into the center of the international arena. That this happened with such speed and so decisively was the achievement of Franklin Delano Roosevelt.

All great leaders walk alone. Their singularity springs from their ability to discern challenges that are not yet apparent to their contemporaries. Roosevelt took an isolationist people into a war between countries whose conflicts had only a few years earlier been widely considered inconsistent with American values and irrelevant to American security. After 1940, Roosevelt convinced the Congress, which had overwhelmingly passed a series of

Neutrality Acts just a few years before, to authorize ever-increasing American assistance to Great Britain, stopping just short of outright belligerency and occasionally even crossing that line. Finally, Japan's attack on Pearl Harbor removed America's last hesitations. Roosevelt was able to persuade a society which had for two centuries treasured its invulnerability of the dire perils of an Axis victory. And he saw to it that, this time, America's involvement would mark a first step toward permanent international engagement. During the war, his leadership held the alliance together and shaped the multilateral institutions which continue to serve the international community to this day.

No president, with the possible exception of Abraham Lincoln, has made a more decisive difference in American history. Roosevelt took the oath of office at a time of national uncertainty, when America's faith in the New World's infinite capacity for progress had been severely shaken by the Great Depression. All around him, democracies seemed to be

From *Diplomacy* (New York: Simon and Schuster, 1994), chap. 15.

faltering and anti-democratic governments on both the Left and the Right were gaining ground.

* * *

America's journey from involvement in the First World War to active participation in the Second proved to be a long one—interrupted as it was by the nation's about-face to isolationism. The depth of America's revulsion toward international affairs illustrates the magnitude of Roosevelt achievement. A brief sketch of the historical backdrop against which Roosevelt conducted his policies is therefore necessary.

In the 1920s, America's mood was ambivalent, oscillating between a willingness to assert principles of universal applicability and a need to justify them on behalf of an isolationist foreign policy. Americans took to reciting the traditional themes of their foreign policy with even greater emphasis: the uniqueness of America's mission as the exemplar of liberty, the moral superiority of democratic foreign policy, the seamless relationship between personal and international morality, the importance of open diplomacy, and the replacement of the balance of power by international consensus as expressed in the League of Nations.

All of these presumably universal principles were enlisted on behalf of American isolationism. Americans were still incapable of believing that anything outside the Western Hemisphere could possibly affect their security. The America of the 1920s and 1930s rejected even its own doctrine of collective security lest it

lead to involvement in the quarrels of distant, bellicose societies. The provisions of the Treaty of Versailles were interpreted as vindictive, and reparations as self-defeating. When the French occupied the Ruhr, America used the occasion to withdraw its remaining occupying forces from the Rhineland. That Wilsonian exceptionalism had established criteria no international order could fulfill, made disillusionment a part of its very essence.

Disillusionment with the results of the war erased to a considerable extent the distinctions between the internationalists and the isolationists. Not even the most liberal internationalists any longer discerned an American interest in sustaining a flawed postwar settlement. No significant group had a good word to say about the balance of power. What passed for internationalism was being identified with membership in the League of Nations rather than with day-to-day participation in international diplomacy. And even the most dedicated internationalists insisted that the Monroe Doctrine superseded the League of Nations, and recoiled before the idea of America's joining League enforcement measures, even economic ones.

* * *

The Kellogg-Briand Pact turned into another example of America's tendency to treat principles as self-implementing. Although American leaders enthusiastically proclaimed the historic nature of the treaty because sixty-two nations had renounced war as an instrument of national policy, they adamantly refused to endorse any machinery for applying it, much less for enforcing it. President Calvin Coolidge, waxing effusive before the Congress in December 1928, asserted: "Observance of this Covenant . . . promises more for the peace of the world than any other agreement ever negotiated among the nations."[1]

Yet how was this utopia to be achieved? Coolidge's passionate defense of the Kellogg-Briand Pact spurred internationalists and supporters of the League to argue, quite reasonably, that, war having been outlawed, the concept of neutrality had lost all meaning. In their view, since the League had been designed to identify aggressors, the international community was obliged to punish them appropriately. "Does anyone believe," asked one of the proponents of this view, "that the aggressive designs of Mussolini could be checked merely by the good faith of the Italian people and the power of public opinion?"[2]

The prescience of this question did not enhance its acceptability. Even while the treaty bearing his name was still in the process of being debated, Secretary of State Kellogg, in an address before the Council on Foreign Relations, stressed that force would never be used to elicit compliance. Reliance on force, he argued, would turn what had been intended as a long stride toward peace into precisely the sort of military alliance that was so in need of being abolished.

* * *

To prevent America from once again being lured into war, the Congress passed three so-called Neutrality Acts between 1935 and 1937. Prompted by the Nye Report, these laws prohibited loans and any other financial assistance to belligerents (whatever the cause of war) and imposed an arms embargo on all parties (regardless of who the victim was). Purchases of nonmilitary goods for cash were allowed only if they were transported in non-American ships.[3] The Congress was not abjuring profits so much as it was rejecting risks. As the aggressors bestrode Europe, America abolished the distinction between aggressor and victim by legislating a single set of restrictions on both.

* * *

After his landslide electoral victory of 1936, Roosevelt went far beyond the existing framework. In fact, he demonstrated that, though preoccupied with the Depression, he had grasped the essence of the dictators' challenge better than any European leader except Churchill. At first, he sought merely to enunciate America's moral commitment to the cause of the democracies. Roosevelt began this educational process with the so-called Quarantine Speech, which he delivered in Chicago on October 5, 1937. It was his first warning to America of the approaching peril, and his first public statement that America might have to assume some responsibilities with respect to it. Japan's renewed military aggression in China, coupled with the previous year's announcement of the Berlin-Rome Axis, provided the backdrop, giving Roosevelt's concerns a global dimension:

> The peace, the freedom and the security of ninety percent of the population of the world is being jeopardized by the remaining ten percent who are threatening a breakdown of all international order and

law. . . . It seems to be unfortunately true that the epidemic of world lawlessness is spreading. When an epidemic of physical disease starts to spread, the community approves and joins in a quarantine of the patients in order to protect the health of the community against the spread of the disease.[4]

Roosevelt was careful not to spell out what he meant by "quarantine" and what, if any, specific measures he might have in mind. Had the speech implied any kind of action, it would have been inconsistent with the Neutrality Acts, which the Congress had overwhelmingly approved and the President had recently signed.

Not surprisingly, the Quarantine Speech was attacked by isolationists, who demanded clarification of the President's intentions. They argued passionately that the distinction between "peace-loving" and "warlike" nations implied an American value judgment which, in turn, would lead to the abandonment of the policy of non-intervention, to which both Roosevelt and the Congress had pledged themselves. Two years later, Roosevelt described the uproar that resulted from the speech as follows: "Unfortunately, this suggestion fell upon deaf ears—even hostile and resentful ears. . . . It was hailed as war mongering; it was condemned as attempted intervention in foreign affairs; it was even ridiculed as a nervous search 'under the bed' for dangers of war which did not exist."[5]

Roosevelt could have ended the controversy by simply denying the intentions being ascribed to him. Yet, despite the critical onslaught, Roosevelt spoke ambiguously enough at a news conference to keep open the option of collective defense of some kind. According to the journalistic practice of the day, the President always met with the press off-the-record, which meant that he could either be quoted nor identified, and these rules were respected.

*   *   *

Munich seems to have been the turning point which impelled Roosevelt to align America with the European democracies, at first politically but gradually materially as well. From then on, his commitment to thwarting the dictators was inexorable, culminating three years later in America's entry into a second world war. The interplay between leaders and their publics in a democracy is always complex. A leader who confines himself to the experience of his people in a period of upheaval purchases temporary popularity at the price of condemnation by posterity, whose claims he is neglecting. A leader who gets too far ahead of his society will become irrelevant. A great leader must be an educator, bridging the gap between his visions and the familiar. But he must also be willing to walk alone to enable his society to follow the path he has selected.

There is inevitably in every great leader an element of guile which simplifies, sometimes the objectives, sometimes the magnitude, of the task. But his ultimate test is whether he incarnates the truth of his society's values and the essence of its challenges. These qualities Roosevelt possessed to an unusual degree. He deeply believed in America; he was convinced that Nazism was both evil and a threat to American security, and he was extraordinarily guileful. And he was prepared to shoulder the burden of lonely decisions. Like a tightrope walker, he had to move, step by careful, anguishing step, across the chasm between his goal and his society's reality in demonstrating to it that the far shore was in fact safer than the familiar promontory.

On October 26, 1938, less than four weeks after the Munich Pact, Roosevelt returned to the theme of his Quarantine Speech. In a radio address to the Herald-Tribune Forum, he warned against unnamed but easily identifiable aggressors whose "national policy adopts as a deliberate instrument the threat of war."[6] Next, while upholding disarmament in principle, Roosevelt also called for strengthening America's defenses:

> ... we have consistently pointed out that neither we, nor any nation, will accept disarmament while neighbor nations arm to the teeth. If there is not general disarmament, we ourselves must continue to arm. It is a step we do not like to take, and do not wish to take. But, until there is general abandonment of weapons capable of aggression, ordinary rules of national prudence and common sense require that we be prepared.[7]

In secret, Roosevelt went much further. At the end of October 1938, in separate conversations with the British air minister and also with a personal friend of Prime Minister Neville Chamberlain, he put forward a project designed to circumvent the Neutrality Acts. Proposing an outright evasion of legislation he had only recently signed, Roosevelt suggested setting up British and French airplane-assembly plants in Canada, near the American border. The United States would supply all the components, leaving only the final assembly to Great Britain and France. This arrangement would technically permit the project to stay within the letter of the Neutrality Acts, presumably on the ground that the component parts were civilian goods. Roosevelt told Chamberlain's emissary that, "in the event of war with the dictators, he had the industrial resources of the American nation behind him."[8]

Roosevelt's scheme for helping the democracies restore their air power collapsed, as it was bound to, if only because of the sheer logistical impossibility of undertaking an effort on such a scale in secret. But from then on, Roosevelt's support for Britain and France was limited only when the Congress and public opinion could neither be circumvented nor overcome.

* * *

Isolationists observing Roosevelt's actions were deeply disturbed. In February 1939, before the outbreak of the war, Senator Arthur Vandenberg had eloquently put forward the isolationist case:

> True, we do live in a foreshortened world in which, compared with Washington's day, time and space are relatively annihilated. But I still thank God for two insulating oceans; and even though they be foreshortened, they are still our supreme benediction if they be widely and prudently used. ...

> We all have our sympathies and our natural emotions in behalf of the victims of national or international outrage all around the globe; but we are not, we cannot be, the world's protector or the world's policeman.[9]

When, in response to the German invasion of Poland, Great Britain declared war on September 3, 1939, Roosevelt had no choice but to invoke the Neutrality Acts. At the same time, he moved rapidly to modify the legislation to permit Great Britain and France to purchase American arms.

*   *   *

Roosevelt had for many months been acting on the premise that America might have to enter the war. In September 1940, he had devised an ingenious arrangement to give Great Britain fifty allegedly overage destroyers in exchange for the right to set up American bases on eight British possessions, from Newfoundland to the South American mainland. Winston Churchill later called it a "decidedly unneutral act," for the destroyers were far more important to Great Britain than the bases were to America. Most of them were quite remote from any conceivable theater of operations, and some even duplicated existing American bases. More than anything, the destroyer deal represented a pretext based on a legal opinion by Roosevelt's own appointee, Attorney General Francis Biddle—hardly an objective observer.

Roosevelt sought neither Congressional approval nor modification of the Neutrality Acts for his destroyer-for-bases deal. Nor was he challenged, as inconceivable as that seems in the light of contemporary practice. It was the measure of Roosevelt's concern about a possible Nazi victory and of his commitment to bolstering British morale, that he took this step as a presidential election campaign was just beginning. (It was fortunate for Great Britain and for the cause of American unity that the foreign policy views of his opponent, Wendell Willkie, were not significantly different from Roosevelt's.)

Concurrently, Roosevelt vastly increased the American defense budget and, in 1940, induced the Congress to introduce peacetime conscription. So strong was lingering isolationist sentiment that conscription was renewed by only one vote in the House of Representatives in the summer of 1941, less than four months before the outbreak of the war.

*   *   *

Few American presidents have been as sensitive and perspicacious as Franklin Delano Roosevelt was in his grasp of the psychology of his people. Roosevelt understood that only a threat to their security could motivate them to support military preparedness. But to take them into a war, he knew he needed to appeal to their idealism in much the same way that Wilson had. In Roosevelt's view, America's security needs might well be met by control of the Atlantic, but its war aims required some vision of a new world order. Thus "balance of power" was not a term ever found in Roosevelt's pronouncements, except when he used it disparagingly. What he sought was to bring about a world community compatible with America's democratic and social ideals as the best guarantee of peace.

In this atmosphere, the president of a technically neutral United States and Great Britain's quintessential wartime leader, Winston Churchill, met in August 1941 on a cruiser off the coast of Newfoundland. Great Britain's position had improved somewhat when Hitler invaded the Soviet Union in June, but England was far from assured of victory. Nevertheless, the joint statement these two leaders issued reflected not a statement of traditional war aims but the design of a totally new world bearing America's imprimatur. The Atlantic Charter proclaimed a set of "common principles" on which the President and Prime Minister based "their hopes for a better future for the world."[10] These principles enlarged upon Roosevelt's original Four Freedoms by incorporating equal access to raw materials and cooperative efforts to improve social conditions around the world.

*   *   *

When the Atlantic Charter was proclaimed, German armies were approaching Moscow and Japanese forces were preparing to move into Southeast Asia. Churchill was above all concerned with removing the obstacles to America's participation in the war. For he understood very well that, by itself, Great Britain would not be able to achieve a decisive victory, even with Soviet participation in the war and American material support. In addition, the Soviet Union might collapse and some compromise between Hitler and Stalin

was always a possibility, threatening Great Britain with renewed isolation. Churchill saw no point in debating postwar structure before he could even be certain that there would be one.

In September 1941, the United States crossed the line into belligerency. Roosevelt's order that the position of German submarines be reported to the British Navy had made it inevitable that, sooner or later, some clash would occur. On September 4, 1941, the American destroyer *Greer* was torpedoed while signaling the location of a German submarine to British airplanes. On September 11, without describing the circumstances, Roosevelt denounced German "piracy." Comparing German submarines to a rattlesnake coiled to strike, he ordered the United States Navy to sink "on sight" any German or Italian submarines discovered in the previously established American defense area extending all the way to Iceland. To all practical purposes, America was at war on the sea with the Axis powers.[11]

Simultaneously, Roosevelt took up the challenge of Japan. In response to Japan's occupation of Indochina in July 1941, he abrogated America's commercial treaty with Japan, forbade the sale of scrap metal to it, and encouraged the Dutch government-in-exile to stop oil exports to Japan from the Dutch East Indies (present-day Indonesia). These pressures led to negotiations with Japan, which began in October 1941. Roosevelt instructed the American negotiators to demand that Japan relinquish all of its conquests, including Manchuria, by invoking America's previous refusal to "recognize" these acts.

Roosevelt must have known that there was no possibility that Japan would accept. On December 7, 1941, following the pattern of the Russo-Japanese War, Japan launched a surprise attack on Pearl Harbor and destroyed a significant part of America's Pacific fleet. On December 11, Hitler honored his treaty with Tokyo by declaring war on the United States. Why Hitler thus freed Roosevelt to concentrate America's war effort on the country Roosevelt had always considered to be the principal enemy has never been satisfactorily explained.

America's entry into the war marked the culmination of a great and daring leader's extraordinary diplomatic enterprise. In less than three years, Roosevelt had taken his staunchly isolationist people into a global war. As late as May 1940, 64 percent of Americans had considered the preservation of peace more important than the defeat of the Nazis. Eighteen months later, in December 1941, just before the attack on Pearl Harbor, the proportions had been reversed—only 32 percent favored peace over preventing triumph.[12]

Roosevelt had achieved his goal patiently and inexorably, educating his people one step at a time about the necessities before them. His audiences filtered his words through their own preconceptions and did not always understand that his ultimate destination was war, though they could not have doubted that it was confrontation. In fact, Roosevelt was not so much bent on war as on defeating the Nazis; it was simply that, as time passed, the Nazis could only be defeated if America entered the war.

That their entry into the war should have seemed so sudden to the American people was due to three factors: Americans had had no experience with going to war for security concerns outside the Western Hemisphere; many believed that the European democracies could prevail on their own, while few understood the nature of the diplomacy that had preceded Japan's attack on Pearl Harbor or Hitler's rash declaration of war on the United States. It was a measure of the United States' deep-seated isolationism that it had to be bombed at Pearl Harbor before it would enter the war in the Pacific; and that, in Europe, it was Hitler who would ultimately declare war on the United States rather than the other way around.

By initiating hostilities, the Axis powers had solved Roosevelt's lingering dilemma about how to move the American people into the war. Had Japan focused its attack on Southeast Asia and Hitler not declared war against the United States, Roosevelt's task of steering his people toward his views would have been much more complicated. In light of Roosevelt's proclaimed moral and strategic convictions, there can be little doubt that, in the end, he would have somehow managed to enlist America in the struggle he considered so decisive to both the future of freedom and to American security.

Subsequent generations of Americans have placed a greater premium on total candor by their chief executive. Yet, like Lincoln, Roosevelt sensed that the survival of his country and its values was at stake, and that history itself would hold him responsible for the results of his solitary initiatives. And, as was the case with Lincoln, it is a measure of the debt free peoples owe to Franklin Delano Roosevelt that the wisdom of his solitary passage is now, quite simply, taken for granted.

Notes

[1]Selig Adler, *The Isolationist Impulse, Its Twentieth-Century Reaction* (New York: Free Press; London: Collier-Macmillan, 1957), 214.

[2]Quoted in Adler, *The Isolationist Impulse*, 216.

[3]Ruhl J. Bartlett, ed., *The Record of American Diplomacy* (New York: Knopf, 1956), 572–77. The First Neutrality Act, signed by FDR on August 31, 1935: arms embargo; Americans not permitted to travel on ships of belligerents. The Second Neutrality Act, signed by FDR on February 29, 1936 (a week before the reoccupation of the Rhineland on March 7): extended the First Act through May 1, 1936, and added a prohibition against loans or credits to belligerents. The Third Neutrality Act, signed by FDR on May 1, 1937: extended previous acts due to expire at midnight plus "cash and carry" provisions for certain nonmilitary goods.

[4]Address in Chicago, October 5, 1937, in Franklin Roosevelt, *Public Papers* (New York: Macmillan, 1941), 1937 vol., 410.

[5]Introduction, in Roosevelt, *Public Papers*, 1939 vol., xxviii.

[6]Radio address to the Herald-Tribune Forum, October 26, 1938, in Roosevelt, *Public Papers*, 1938 vol., 564.

[7]Radio address, 565.

[8]Donald Cameron Watt, *How War Came: The Immediate Origins of the Second World War, 1938–1939* (London: William Heinemann, 1989), 130.

[9]Vandenberg speech in the Senate, "It Is Not Cowardice to Think of America First," February 27, 1939, in *Vital Speeches of the Day*, vol. v, no. 12 (April 1, 1939), 356–57.

[10]The Atlantic Charter: Official Statement on Meeting Between the President and Prime Minister Churchill, August 14, 1941, in Roosevelt, *Public Papers*, 1941 vol., 314.

[11]Fireside Chat to the Nation, September 11, 1941, in Roosevelt, *Public Papers*, 1941 vol., 384–92.

[12]Adler, *The Isolationist Impulse*, 257.

Imperialism

WALTER LAFEBER

The American "New Empire"

Some intellectuals speak only for them-selves. Theirs is often the later glory, but seldom the present power. Some, however, speak not only for themselves but for the guiding forces of their society. Discovering such men at crucial junctures in history, if such a discovery can be made, is of impor-tance and value. These figures uncover the premises, reveal the approaches, provide the details, and often coherently arrange the ideas which are implicit in the domi-nant thought of their time and society.

The ordered, articulate writings of Frederick Jackson Turner, Josiah Strong, Brooks Adams, and Alfred Thayer Mahan typified the expansive tendencies of their generation. Little evidence exists that Turner and Strong directly influenced ex-pansionists in the business community or the State Department during the 1890's, but their writings best exemplify certain beliefs which determined the nature of American foreign policy. Adams and Mahan participated more directly in the shaping of expansionist programs. It is, of course, impossible to estimate the number of Americans who accepted the arguments of these four men. What cannot be contro-verted is that the writings of these men typ-ified and in some specific instances directly influenced the thought of American policy makers who created the new empire.[1]

Frederick Jackson Turner and the American Frontier

* * *

The importance of the frontier will be as-sociated with the name of Frederick Jack-son Turner as long as historians are able to indent footnotes. Yet as Theodore Roo-sevelt told Turner in a letter of admiration in 1894, "I think you . . . have put into defi-nite shape a good deal of thought which has been floating around rather loosely." As has been amply shown by several scholars, a number of observers warned of the fron-tier's disappearance and the possible con-sequences of this disappearance long before Turner's epochal paper. The acceler-ating communication and transportation

From *The New Empire: An Interpretation of American Expansion, 1860–1898* (Ithaca, N.Y.: Cornell University Press, 1963), chaps. 2 and 7.

revolution, growing agrarian unrest, violent labor strikes, and the problems arising from increasing numbers of immigrants broke upon puzzled and frightened Americans in a relatively short span of time. Many of them clutched the belief of the closing or closed frontier in order to explain their dilemma.[2]

Turner rested the central part of his frontier thesis on the economic power represented by free land. American individualism, nationalism, political institutions, and democracy depended on this power: "So long as free land exists, the opportunity for a competency exists, and economic power secures political power." Stated in these terms, landed expansion became the central factor, the dynamic of American progress. Without the economic power generated by expansion across free lands, American political institutions could stagnate.[3]

Such an analysis could be extremely meaningful to those persons who sought an explanation for the political and social troubles of the period. Few disputed that the social upheavals in both the urban and agrarian areas of the nation stemmed from economic troubles in the international grain markets, from the frequent industrial depressions, or, as the Populists averred, from the failure of the currency to match the pace of ever increasing productivity. This economic interpretation also fitted in nicely with the contemporary measurement of success in terms of material achievement. Perhaps most important, the frontier thesis not only defined the dilemma, but did so in tangible, concrete terms. It offered the hope that Americans could do something about

their problems. Given the assumption that expansion across the western frontier explained past American successes, the solution for the present crisis now became apparent: either radically readjust the political institutions to a nonexpanding society or find new areas for expansion. When Americans seized the second alternative, the meaning for foreign policy became apparent—and immense.

With the appearance and definition of the fundamental problems in the 1880's and 1890's, these decades assumed vast importance. They became not a watershed of American history, but *the* watershed. Many writers emphasized the supremely critical nature of the 1890's, but no one did it better than Turner when he penned the dramatic final sentence of his 1893 paper: "And now, four centuries from the discovery of America, at the end of a hundred years of life under the Constitution, the frontier has gone, and with its going has closed the first period of American history." The American West no longer offered a unique escape from the intractable problems of a closed society. As another writer stated it four years after Turner's announcement in Chicago, "we are no longer a country exceptional and apart." History had finally caught up with the United States.[4]

The first solution that came to some minds suggested the opening of new landed frontiers in Latin America or Canada. Yet was further expansion in a landed sense the answer? Top policy makers, as Secretaries of State James G. Blaine, Thomas F. Bayard, and Walter Quintin Gresham, opposed the addition of noncontiguous territory to the Union. Some

Americans interpreted the labor violence of 1877, 1886, and 1894 as indications that the federal government could no longer harmonize and control the far-flung reaches of the continental empire. Labor and agrarian groups discovered they could not command the necessary political power to solve their mushrooming problems. The sprouting of such factions as the Molly Maguires, Populists, Eugene Debs' Railroad Union, and several varieties of Socialist parties raised doubts in many minds about the ameliorating and controlling qualities which had formerly been a part of the American system.

* * *

Expansion in the form of trade instead of landed settlement ultimately offered the answer to this dilemma. This solution, embodied in the open-door philosophy of American foreign policy, ameliorated the economic stagnation (which by Turner's reasoning led to the political discontent), but it did not pile new colonial areas on an already overburdened governmental structure. It provided the perfect answer to the problems of the 1890's.

* * *

Alfred Thayer Mahan

* * *

The austere, scholarly, arm-chair sailor-turned-prophet constructed a tightly knit historical justification of why and how his country could expand beyond its continental limits.

Mahan grounded his thesis on the central characteristic of the United States of his time: it was an industrial complex which produced, or would soon be capable of producing, vast surpluses. In the first paragraph of his classic, *The Influence of Sea Power upon History, 1660–1783,* Mahan explained how this industrial expansion led to a rivalry for markets and sources of raw materials and would ultimately result in the need for sea power. He summarized his theory in a postulate: "In these three things—production, with the necessity of exchanging products, shipping, whereby the exchange is carried on, and colonies . . .—is to be found the key to much of the history, as well as of the policy, of nations bordering upon the sea." The order is all-important. Production leads to a need for shipping, which in turn creates the need for colonies.[5]

Mahan's neat postulate was peculiarly applicable to his own time, for he clearly understood the United States of the 1890's. His concern, stated in 1890, that ever increasing production would soon make necessary wider trade and markets, anticipated the somber, depression-ridden years of post-1893. Writing three years before Frederick Jackson Turner analyzed the disappearance of the American frontier, Mahan hinted its disappearance and pointed out the implications for America's future economic and political structure. He observed that the policies of the American government since 1865 had been "directed solely to what has been called the first link in the chain which makes sea power." But "the increase of home consumption . . . did not keep up with the increase of forth-putting and facility of distribution offered by steam." The United States would thus have to embark upon a new frontier, for "whether they will or no, Americans must now begin to look outward. The growing production of the country demands it. An increasing volume of public sentiment demands it." The theoretical and actual had met; the productive capacity of the United States, having finally grown too great for its continental container and having lost its landed frontier, had to turn to the sea, its omnipresent frontier. The mercantilists had viewed production as a faculty to be stimulated and consolidated in order to develop its full capabilities of pulling wealth into the country. But Mahan dealt with a productive complex which had been stimulated by the government for years and had been centralized and coordinated by corporate managers. He was now concerned with the problem of keeping this society ongoing without the problems of underemployment and resulting social upheavals.[6]

Reversing the traditional American idea of the oceans as a barrier against European intrigue, Mahan compared the sea to "a great highway; or better, perhaps . . . a wide common, over which men pass in all directions."

* * *

To Mahan, William McKinley, Theodore Roosevelt, and Henry Cabot Lodge, colonial possessions, as these men defined such possessions, served as stepping stones to the two great prizes: the Latin-American and Asian markets. This policy much less resembled traditional colonialism than

it did the new financial and industrial expansion of the 1850–1914 period. These men did not envision "colonizing" either Latin America or Asia. They did want both to exploit these areas economically and give them (especially Asia) the benefits of western, Christian civilization. To do this, these expansionists needed strategic bases from which shipping lanes and interior interests in Asia and Latin America could be protected.

* * *

President William McKinley and the Spanish-American War of 1898

* * *

The President [McKinley] did not want war; he had been sincere and tireless in his efforts to maintain the peace. By mid-March, however, he was beginning to discover that, although he did not want war, he did want what only a war could provide: the disappearance of the terrible uncertainty in American political and economic life, and a solid basis from which to resume the building of the new American commercial empire. When the President made his demands, therefore, he made the ultimate demands; as far as he was concerned, a six-month period of negotiations would not serve to temper the political and economic problems in the United States, but only exacerbate them.

To say this is to raise another question: why did McKinley arrive at this position during mid-March? What were the factors which limited the President's freedom of choice and policies at this particular time? The standard interpretations of the war's causes emphasize the yellow journals and a belligerent Congress. These were doubtlessly crucial factors in shaping the course of American entry into the conflict, but they must be used carefully.

Influences other than the yellow press or congressional belligerence were more important in shaping McKinley's position of April 11. Perhaps most important was the transformation of the opinion of many spokesmen for the business community who had formerly opposed war. If, as one journal declared, the McKinley administration, "more than any that have preceded it, sustains . . . close relations to the business interests of the country," then this change of business sentiment should not be discounted.[7] This transformation brought important financial spokesmen, especially from the Northeast, into much the same position that had long been occupied by pro-interventionist business groups and journals in the trans-Appalachian area. McKinley's decision to intervene placated many of the same business spokesmen whom he had satisfied throughout 1897 and January and February of 1898 by his refusal to declare war.

Five factors may be delineated which shaped this interventionist sentiment of the business community. First, some business journals emphasized the material advantages to be gained should Cuba become a part of the world in which the United States would enjoy, in the words of the New York *Commercial Advertiser,* "full freedom of development in the whole world's interest."

The *Banker's Magazine* noted that "so many of our citizens are so involved in the commerce and productions of the island, that to protect these interests . . . the United States will have eventually to force the establishment of fair and reasonable government." The material damage suffered by investors in Cuba and by many merchants, manufacturers, exporters, and importers, as, for example, the groups which presented the February 10 petition to McKinley, forced these interests to advocate a solution which could be obtained only through force.[8]

A second reason was the uncertainty that plagued the business community in mid-March. This uncertainty was increased by Proctor's powerful and influential speech and by the news that a Spanish torpedo-boat flotilla was sailing from Cadiz to Cuba. The uncertainty was exemplified by the sudden stagnation of trade on the New York Stock Exchange after March 17. Such an unpredictable economic basis could not provide the spring board for the type of overseas commercial empire that McKinley and numerous business spokesmen envisioned.

Third, by March many businessmen who had deprecated war on the ground that the United States Treasury did not possess adequate gold reserves began to realize that they had been arguing from false assumptions. The heavy exports of 1897 and the discoveries of gold in Alaska and Australia brought the yellow metal into the country in an ever widening stream. Private bankers had been preparing for war since 1897. *Banker's Magazine* summarized these developments: "Therefore, while not desiring war, it is apparent that the country now has an ample coin basis for sustaining the credit operations which a conflict would probably make necessary. In such a crisis the gold standard will prove a bulwark of confidence."[9]

Fourth, antiwar sentiment lost much strength when the nation realized that it had nothing to fear from European intervention on the side of Spain. France and Russia, who were most sympathetic to the Spanish monarchy, were forced to devote their attention to the Far East. Neither of these nations wished to alienate the United States on the Cuban issue. More important, Americans happily realized that they had the support of Great Britain. The *rapprochement* which had occurred since the Venezuelan incident now paid dividends. On an official level, the British Foreign Office assured the State Department that nothing would be accomplished in the way of European intervention unless the United States requested such intervention. The British attitude made it easy for McKinley to deal with a joint European note of April 6 which asked for American moderation toward Spain. The President brushed off the request firmly but politely. On an unofficial level, American periodicals expressed appreciation of the British policy on Cuba, and some of the journals noted that a common Anglo-American approach was also desirable in Asia.[10] The European reaction is interesting insofar as it evinces the continental powers' growing realization that the United States was rapidly becoming a major force in the world. But the European governments set no limits on American dealings with Spain. McKinley could take the initiative and make his demands with little concern for European reactions.

Finally, opposition to war melted away in some degree when the administration began to emphasize that the United States enjoyed military power much superior to that of Spain. One possible reason for McKinley's policies during the first two months of 1898 might have been his fear that the nation was not adequately prepared. As late as the weekend of March 25 the President worried over this inadequacy. But in late February and early March, especially after the $50,000,000 appropriation by Congress, the country's military strength developed rapidly. On March 13 the Philadelphia *Press* proclaimed that American naval power greatly exceeded that of the Spanish forces. By early April those who feared a Spanish bombardment of New York City were in the small minority. More representative were the views of Winthrop Chanler who wrote Lodge that if Spanish troops invaded New York "they would all be absorbed in the population . . . and engaged in selling oranges before they got as far as 14th Street."[11]

As the words of McKinley's war message flew across the wires to Madrid, many business spokesmen who had opposed war had recently changed their minds. American military forces were rapidly growing more powerful, banks and the United States Treasury had secured themselves against the initial shocks of war, and the European powers were divided among themselves and preoccupied in the Far East. Business boomed after McKinley signed the declaration of war. "With a hesitation so slight as to amount almost to indifference," *Bradstreet's* reported on April 30, "the business community, relieved from the tension caused by the incubus of doubt and uncertainty which so long controlled it, has stepped confidently forward to accept the situation confronting it owing to the changed conditions. Unfavorable circumstances . . . have hardly excited remark, while the stimulating effects have been so numerous and important as to surprise all but the most optimistic," this journal concluded.[12] A new type of American empire, temporarily clothed in armor, stepped out on the international stage after a half century of preparation to make its claim as one of the great world powers.

*   *   *

By 1899 the United States had forged a new empire. American policy makers and businessmen had created it amid much debate and with conscious purpose. The empire progressed from a continental base in 1861 to assured pre-eminence in the Western Hemisphere in 1895. Three years later it was rescued from a growing economic and political dilemma by the declaration of war against Spain. During and after this conflict the empire moved past Hawaii into the Philippines, and, with the issuance of the Open-Door Notes, enunciated its principles in Asia. The movement of this empire could not be hurried. Harrison discovered this to his regret in 1893. But under the impetus of the effects of the industrial revolution and, most important, *because of the implications for foreign policy which policy makers and businessmen believed to be logical*

corollaries of this economic change, the new empire reached its climax in the 1890's. At this point those who possessed a sense of historical perspective could pause with Henry Adams and observe that one hundred and fifty years of American history had suddenly fallen into place. Those who preferred to peer into the dim future of the twentieth century could be certain only that the United States now dominated its own hemisphere and, as [William] Seward had so passionately hoped, was entering as a major power into Asia, "the chief theatre of events in the world's great hereafter."

Notes

[1] One of the weakest sections in the history of ideas is the relationship between the new intellectual currents and American overseas expansion during the last half of the nineteenth century. The background and some of the general factors may be found in Alfred Kazin, *On Native Grounds: An Interpretation of Modern American Prose Literature* (Garden City, N.Y., 1942, 1956); Henry Steele Commager, *The American Mind: An Interpretation of American Thought and Character since the 1880's* (New Haven, 1950, 1959); Weinberg, *Manifest Destiny;* Julius W. Pratt, "The Ideology of American Expansion," *Essays in Honor of William E. Dodd . . . ,* edited by Avery Craven (Chicago, 1935).

[2] See especially Fulmer Mood, "The Concept of the Frontier, 1871–1898," *Agricultural History,* XIX (January, 1945), 24–31; Lee Benson, "The Historical Background of Turner's Frontier Essay," *Agricultural History,* XXV (April, 1951), 59–82; Herman Clarence Nixon, "The Precursors of Turner in the Interpretation of the American Frontier," *South Atlantic Quarterly,* XXVIII (January, 1929), 83–89. For the Roosevelt letter, see *The Letters of Theodore Roosevelt,* selected and edited by Elting E. Morison *et al.* (Cambridge, Mass., 1951), I, 363.

[3]Frederick Jackson Turner, *The Frontier in American History* (New York, 1947), 32, 30; see also Per Sveaas Andersen, *Westward Is the Course of Empires: A Study in the Shaping of an American Idea: Frederick Jackson Turner's Frontier* (Oslo, Norway, 1956), 20–21; Henry Nash Smith, *Virgin Land: The American West as Symbol and Myth* (New York, 1959), 240.

[4]Turner, *Frontier in American History,* 38; Eugene V. Smalley, "What Are Normal Times?" *The Forum,* XXIII (March, 1897), 98–99; see also Turner, *Frontier in American History,* 311–312. For a brilliant criticism of Turner's closed-space concepts, see James C. Malin, *The Contriving Brain and the Skillful Hand in the United States . . .* (Lawrence, Kan., 1955), the entire essay, but especially ch. xi.

[5]A. T. Mahan, *The Influence of Sea Power upon History, 1660–1783* (Boston, 1890), 53, 28. This postulate is mentioned two more times in the famous first chapter, pages 70 and 83–84.

[6]*Ibid.,* 83–84; Mahan, "A Twentieth-Century Outlook," *The Interest of America in Sea Power, Present and Future* (Boston, 1897), 220–222; Mahan, "The United States Looking Outward," *ibid.,* 21–22. In their work which traces this centralization movement, Thomas C. Cochran and William Miller call the result the "corporate society" (*The Age of Enterprise: A Social History of Industrial America* [New York, 1942], 331).

[7]Chicago *Times-Herald* quoted in Cincinnati *Commercial Tribune,* Dec. 28, 1897, 6:2. The Chicago paper was particularly close to the administration through its publisher's friendship with McKinley. The publisher was H. H. Kohlsaat. Ernest May remarks, regarding McKinley's antiwar position in 1897 and early 1898, "It was simply out of the question for him [McKinley] to embark on a policy unless virtually certain that Republican businessmen would back him" (*Imperial Democracy: The Emergence of America as a Great Power* [New York, 1961], 118). The same comment doubtlessly applies also to McKinley's actions in March and April.

[8]*Commercial Advertiser,* March 10, 1898, 6:3; *Bankers' Magazine,* LVI (April, 1898), 519–520.

[9]*Bankers' Magazine,* LVI (March, 1898), 347–348; LVI (April, 1898), 520; *Pittsburgh Press,* April 8, 1898, 4:1; *Commercial and Financial Chronicle,* April 23, 1898, 786.

[10]Dugdale, *German Documents,* II, 500–502; Porter to Sherman, April 8, 1898, France, Despatches, and Hay to Sherman, March 26, 28, 29, April 1, Great Britain, Despatches, NA, RG 59; *Public Opinion,* March 24, 1898, 360–361.

[11]Margaret Leech, *In the Days of McKinley* (New York, 1969), 176; *Philadelphia Press,* March 13, 1898, 8:3; Garraty, *Lodge,* 191.

[12]*Bradstreet's,* April 9, 1898, 234, also April 30, 1898, 272, 282.

Cold War Revisionist Critique

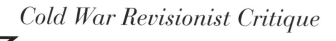

4.1

MELVYN P. LEFFLER

The American Conception of National Security and the Beginnings of the Cold War, 1945–48

* * *

In an interview with Henry Kissinger in 1978 on "The Lessons of the Past," Walter Laqueur observed that during the Second World War "few if any people thought . . . of the structure of peace that would follow the war except perhaps in the most general terms of friendship, mutual trust, and the other noble sentiments mentioned in wartime programmatic speeches about the United Nations and related topics." Kissinger concurred, noting that no statesman, except perhaps Winston Churchill, "gave any attention to what would happen after the war." Americans, Kissinger stressed, "were determined that we were going to base the postwar period on good faith and getting along with everybody."[1]

That two such astute and knowledgeable observers of international politics were so uninformed about American planning at the end of the Second World War is testimony to the enduring mythology of American idealism and innocence in the world of *realpolitik.* * * * American assessments of the Soviet threat were less a consequence of expanding Soviet military capabilities and of Soviet diplomatic demands than a result of growing apprehension about the vulnerability of American strategic and economic interests in a world of unprecedented turmoil and upheaval. Viewed from this perspective, the Cold War assumed many of its most enduring characteristics during 1947–8, when American officials sought to cope with an array of challenges by implementing their own concepts of national security.

* * *

The need to predominate throughout the western hemisphere was not a result of deteriorating Soviet-American relations but a natural evolution of the Monroe Doctrine, accentuated by Axis aggression and new technological imperatives.[2] Patterson, Forrestal, and Army Chief of Staff Dwight D. Eisenhower initially were impelled less

From *American Historical Review* 89 (April 1984).

by reports of Soviet espionage, propaganda, and infiltration in Latin America than by accounts of British efforts to sell cruisers and aircraft to Chile and Ecuador; Swedish sales of anti-aircraft artillery to Argentina; and French offers to build cruisers and destroyers for both Argentina and Brazil.[3] To foreclose all foreign influence and to ensure US strategic hegemony, military officers and the civilian Secretaries of the War and Navy Departments argued for an extensive system of US bases, expansion of commercial airline facilities throughout Latin America, negotiation of a regional defense pact, curtailment of all foreign military aid and foreign military sales, training of Latin American military officers in the United States, outfitting of Latin American armies with US military equipment, and implementation of a comprehensive military assistance program.[4]

*   *   *

From the closing days of the Second World War, American defense officials believed that they could not allow any prospective adversary to control the Eurasian land mass. This was the lesson taught by two world wars. Strategic thinkers and military analysts insisted that any power or powers attempting to dominate Eurasia must be regarded as potentially hostile to the United States.[5] * * * Concern over the consequences of Russian domination of Eurasia helps explain why in July 1945 the joint chiefs decided to oppose a Soviet request for bases in the Dardanelles; why during March and April 1946 they supported a firm stand against Russia in Iran, Turkey,

and Tripolitania; and why in the summer of 1946 Clark Clifford and George Elsey, two White House aides, argued that Soviet incorporation of any parts of Western Europe, the Middle East, China, or Japan into a Communist orbit was incompatible with American national security.[6]

Economic considerations also made defense officials determined to retain American access to Eurasia as well as to deny Soviet predominance over it. Stimson, Patterson, McCloy, and Assistant Secretary Howard C. Peterson agreed with Forrestal that long-term American prosperity required open markets, unhindered access to raw materials, and the rehabilitation of much—if not all—of Eurasia along liberal capitalist lines. * * * But American economic interests in Eurasia were not limited to Western Europe, Germany, and the Middle East. Military planners and intelligence officers in both the army and navy expressed considerable interest in the raw materials of Southeast Asia, wanted to maintain access to those resources, and sought to deny them to a prospective enemy.[7]

*   *   *

During 1946 and 1947, defense officials witnessed a dramatic unravelling of the geopolitical foundations and socioeconomic structure of international affairs. Britain's economic weakness and withdrawal from the eastern Mediterranean, India's independence movement, civil war in China, nationalist insurgencies in Indo-China and the Dutch East Indies, Zionist claims to Palestine and Arab resentment, German and Japanese economic paralysis,

Communist inroads in France and Italy—all were ominous developments. Defense officials recognized that the Soviet Union had not created these circumstances but believed that Soviet leaders would exploit them. Should Communists take power, even without direct Russian intervention, the Soviet Union would gain predominant control of the resources of these areas because of the postulated subservience of Communist parties everywhere to the Kremlin. Should nationalist uprisings persist, Communists seize power in underdeveloped countries, or Arabs revolt against American support of a Jewish state, the petroleum and raw materials of critical areas might be denied the West. The imminent possibility existed that, even without Soviet military aggression, the resources of Eurasia could fall under Russian control. With these resources, the Soviet Union would be able to overcome its chronic economic weaknesses, achieve defense in depth, and challenge American power—perhaps even by military force.[8]

In this frightening postwar environment American assessments of Soviet long-term intentions were transformed. Spurred by the "long telegram" written by George F. Kennan, the US chargé d'affaires in Moscow, it soon became commonplace for policy makers, military officials, and intelligence analysts to state that the ultimate aim of Soviet foreign policy was Russian domination of a Communist world.[9] There was, of course, plentiful evidence for this appraisal of Soviet ambitions—the Soviet consolidation of a sphere of influence in Eastern Europe; Soviet violation of the agreement to withdraw troops from Iran; Soviet relinquishment of Japanese arms to the Chinese Communists; the Soviet mode of extracting reparations from the Russian zone in Germany; Soviet diplomatic overtures for bases in the Dardanelles, Tripolitania, and the Dodecanese; Soviet requests for a role in the occupation of Japan; and the Kremlin's renewed emphasis on Marxist-Leninist doctrine, the vulnerability of capitalist economies, and the inevitability of conflict.

Yet these assessments did not seriously grapple with contradictory evidence. They disregarded numerous signs of Soviet weakness, moderation, and circumspection. During 1946 and 1947 intelligence analysts described the withdrawal of Russian troops from northern Norway, Manchuria, Bornholm, and Iran (from the latter under pressure, of course). Numerous intelligence sources reported the reduction of Russian troops in Eastern Europe and the extensive demobilization going on within the Soviet Union. In October 1947 the Joint Intelligence Committee forecast a Soviet army troop strength during 1948 and 1949 of less than 2 million men. Other reports dealt with the inadequacies of Soviet transportation and bridging equipment and the moderation of Soviet military expenditures. And, as already noted, assessments of the Soviet economy revealed persistent problems likely to restrict Soviet adventurism.[10]

Experience suggested that the Soviet Union was by no means uniformly hostile or unwilling to negotiate with the United States. In April 1946 Ambassador Smith reminded the State Department that the

Soviet press was not unalterably critical of the United States, that the Russians had withdrawn from Bornholm, that Stalin had given a moderate speech on the United Nations, and that Soviet demobilization continued apace. The next month General Lincoln acknowledged that the Soviets had been willing to make numerous concessions regarding Tripolitania, the Dodecanese, and Italian reparations. In the spring of 1946, General Echols, General Clay, and Secretary Patterson again maintained that the French constituted the major impediment to an agreement on united control of Germany. In early 1947 central intelligence delineated more than a half-dozen instances of Soviet moderation or concessions. In April the Military Intelligence Division noted that the Soviets had limited their involvement in the Middle East, diminished their ideological rhetoric, and given only moderate support to Chinese Communists.[11]

In their overall assessments of Soviet long-term intentions, however, military planners dismissed all evidence of Soviet moderation, circumspection, and restraint. In fact, as 1946 progressed, these planners seemed to spend less time analyzing Soviet intentions and more time estimating Soviet capabilities.[12] They no longer explored ways of accommodating a potential adversary's legitimate strategic requirements or pondered how American initiatives might influence the Soviet Union's definition of its objectives.[13] Information not confirming prevailing assumptions either was ignored in overall assessments of Soviet intentions or was used to illustrate that the Soviets were

shifting tactics but not altering objectives. A report from the Joint Chiefs of Staff to the President in July 1946, for example, deleted sections from previous studies that had outlined Soviet weaknesses. A memorandum sent by Secretary Patterson to the President at the same time was designed to answer questions about relations with the Soviet Union "without ambiguity." Truman, Clark Clifford observed many years later, liked things in black and white.[14]

* * *

The dynamics of the Cold War after 1948 are easier to comprehend when one grasps the breadth of the American conception of national security that had emerged between 1945 and 1948. This conception included a strategic sphere of influence within the western hemisphere, domination of the Atlantic and Pacific oceans, an extensive system of outlying bases to enlarge the strategic frontier and project American power, an even more extensive system of transit rights to facilitate the conversion of commercial air bases to military use, access to the resources and markets of most of Eurasia, denial of those resources to a prospective enemy, and the maintenance of nuclear superiority. Not every one of these ingredients, it must be emphasized, was considered vital. Hence, American officials could acquiesce, however grudgingly, to a Soviet sphere in Eastern Europe and could avoid direct intervention in China. But cumulative challenges to these concepts of national security were certain to provoke a firm American response. This occurred initially in 1947–8 when decisions were made in favor of the Truman Doctrine, the Marshall Plan, military assistance, the Atlantic alliance, and German and Japanese rehabilitation. Soon thereafter, the "loss" of China, the Soviet detonation of an atomic bomb, and the North Korean attack on South Korea intensified the perception of threat to prevailing concepts of national security. The Truman administration responded with military assistance to Southeast Asia, a decision to build the hydrogen bomb, direct military intervention in Korea, a commitment to station troops permanently in Europe, expansion of the American alliance system, and a massive rearmament program in the United States. Postulating a long-term Soviet intention to gain world domination, the American conception of national security, based on geopolitical and economic imperatives, could not allow for additional losses in Eurasia, could not risk a challenge to its nuclear supremacy, and could not permit any infringement on its ability to defend in depth or to project American force from areas in close proximity to the Soviet homeland.

To say this, is neither to exculpate the Soviet government for its inhumane treatment of its own citizens nor to suggest that Soviet foreign policy was idle or benign. Indeed, Soviet behavior in Eastern Europe was often deplorable; the Soviets sought opportunities in the Dardanelles, northern Iran, and Manchuria; the Soviets hoped to orient Germany and Austria toward the East; and the Soviets sometimes endeavored to use Communist parties to expand Soviet influence in areas beyond the periphery of Russian military power. But, then again, the Soviet Union had lost

20 million dead during the war, had experienced the destruction of 1,700 towns, 31,000 factories, and 100,000 collective farms, and had witnessed the devastation of the rural economy with the Nazi slaughter of 20 million hogs and 17 million head of cattle. What is remarkable is that after 1946 these monumental losses received so little attention when American defense analysts studied the motives and intentions of Soviet policy; indeed, defense officials did little to analyze the threat perceived by the Soviets. Yet these same officials had absolutely no doubt that the wartime experiences and sacrifices of the United States, though much less devastating than those of Soviet Russia, demonstrated the need for and entitled the United States to oversee the resuscitation of the industrial heartlands of Germany and Japan, establish a viable balance of power in Eurasia, and militarily dominate the Eurasian rimlands, thereby safeguarding American access to raw materials and control over all sea and air approaches to North America.[15]

To suggest a double standard is important only in so far as it raises fundamental questions about the conceptualization and implementation of American national security policy. If Soviet policy was aggressive, bellicose, and ideological, perhaps America's reliance on overseas bases, air power, atomic weapons, military alliances, and the rehabilitation of Germany and Japan was the best course to follow, even if the effect may have been to exacerbate Soviet anxieties and suspicions. But even when one attributes the worst intentions to the Soviet Union, one might still ask whether American presuppositions and apprehensions about the benefits that would accrue to the Soviet Union as a result of Communist (and even revolutionary nationalist) gains anywhere in Eurasia tended to simplify international realities, magnify the breadth of American interests, engender commitments beyond American capabilities, and dissipate the nation's strength and credibility. And, perhaps even more importantly, if Soviet foreign policies tended to be opportunist, reactive, nationalistic, and contradictory, as some recent writers have claimed and as some contemporary analysts suggested, then one might also wonder whether America's own conception of national security tended, perhaps unintentionally, to engender anxieties and to provoke countermeasures from a proud, suspicious, insecure, and cruel government that was at the same time legitimately apprehensive about the long-term implications arising from the rehabilitation of traditional enemies and the development of foreign bases on the periphery of the Soviet homeland. To raise such issues anew seems essential if we are to unravel the complex origins of the Cold War.

Notes

[1] Henry Kissinger, *For the Record: Selected Statements, 1977–80* (Boston, MA, 1980), 123–4.

[2] This evaluation accords with the views of Chester J. Pach, Jr; see his "The Containment of United States Military Aid to Latin America, 1944–1949," *Diplomatic History,* 6 (1982):232–4.

[3] For fears of foreign influence, see, for example, [no signature] "Military Political Cooperation with the Other American Republics," June 24, 1946, RG 18, 092 (International Affairs), box 567; Patterson to the Secretary of State, July 31, 1946, RG 353, SWNCC, box 76; Eisenhower to Patterson, Novem-

ber 26, 1946, RG 107, HCPP, general decimal file, box 1 (top secret); S. J. Chamberlin to Eisenhower, November 26, 1946, ibid.; Minutes of the meeting of the Secretaries of State, War, and Navy, December 11, 1946, ibid., RPPP, safe file, box 3; and Director of Intelligence to Director of P&O, February 26, 1947, RG 319, P&O, 091 France. For reports on Soviet espionage, see, for example, Military Intelligence Service [hereafter MIS], "Soviet-Communist Penetration in Latin America," March 24, 1945, RG 165, OPD 336 (top secret).

[4] See, for example, Craig, "Summary," January 5, 1945; JPS, "Military Arrangements Deriving from the Act of Chapultepec Pertaining to Bases," January 14, 1946, RG 218, ser. CCS 092 (9-10-45), JPS 761/3; Patterson to Byrnes, December 18, 1946; and P&O, "Strategic Importance of Inter-American Military Cooperation" [January 20, 1947].

[5] This view was most explicitly presented in an army paper examining the State Department's expostulation of US foreign policy. See S. F. Giffin, "Draft of Proposed Comments for the Assistant Secretary of War on 'Foreign Policy'" [early February 1946], RG 107, HCPP 092 international affairs (classified). The extent to which this concern with Eurasia shaped American military attitudes is illustrated at greater length below. Here I should note that in March 1945 several of the nation's most prominent civilian experts (Frederick S. Dunn, Edward M. Earle, William T. R. Fox, Grayson L. Kirk, David N. Rowe, Harold Sprout, and Arnold Wolfers) prepared a study, "A Security Policy for Postwar America," in which they argued that the United States had to prevent any one power or coalition of powers from gaining control of Eurasia. America could not, they insisted, withstand attack by any power that had first subdued the whole of Europe or of Eurasia; see Frederick S. Dunn et al., "A Security Policy for Postwar America," NHC, SPD, ser. 14, box 194, A1–2.

The postwar concept of Eurasia developed out of the revival of geopolitical thinking in the United States, stimulated by Axis aggression and strategic decisionmaking. See, for example, the reissued work of Sir Halford F. Mackinder: *Democratic Ideals and Reality* (1919; reprint edn, New York, 1942), and

"The Round World and the Winning of Peace," *Foreign Affairs,* 21 (1943): 598–605. Mackinder's ideas were modified and widely disseminated in the United States, especially by intellectuals such as Nicholas John Spykman, Hans W. Weigert, Robert Strausz-Hupé, and Isaiah Bowman.

[6]For the decision on the Dardanelles, see the attachments to JCS, "United States Policy concerning the Dardanelles and Kiel Canal" [July 1945], RG 218, ser. CCS 092 (7-10-45), JCS 1418/1; for the joint chiefs' position on Iran, Turkey, and Tripolitania, see JCS, "U.S. Security Interests in the Eastern Mediterranean," March 1946, ibid., ser. CCS 092 USSR (3-27-45). JCS 1641 series; and Lincoln, Memorandum for the Record, April 16, 1946, RG 165, ser. ABC 336 Russia (8-22-43); and, for the Clifford memorandum, see Arthur Krock, *Memoirs: Sixty Years on the Firing Line* (New York, 1968), 477–82.

[7]Strategy Section, OPD, "Post-War Base Requirements in the Phillipines," April 23, 195, RG 165, OPD 336 (top secret); MID, "Positive US Action Required to Restore Normal Conditions in Southeast Asia," July 3, 1947, RG 319, P&O, 092 (top secret); and Lauris Norstad to the Director of Intelligence, July 10, 1947, ibid.

[8]See, for example, JCS, "Presidential Request for Certain Facts and Information Regarding the Soviet Union," July 25, 1946, RG 218, ser. CCS 092 USSR (3-27-45), JCS 1696; P&O, "Strategic Study of Western and Northern Europe," May 21, 1947, RG 319, P&O, 092 (top secret); and Wooldridge to the General Board, April 30, 1948.

[9]For Kennan's "long telegram," see *FRUS, 1946* (Washington, DC, 1970), Vol. 4: 696–709; for ominous interpretations of Soviet intentions and capabilities, also see JCS, "Political Estimate of Soviet Policy for Use in Connection with Military Studies," April 5, 1946, RG 218, ser. CCS 092 USSR (3-27-45), JCS 1641/4; and JCS, "Presidential Request for Certain Facts and Information Regarding the Soviet Union," July 25, 1946.

[10]For the withdrawal of Soviet troops, see, for example, MID, "Soviet Intentions and Capabilities in Scandinavia as of 1 July 1946," April 25, 1946, RG 319, P&O, 350.05 (top secret). For reports on reductions of Russian troops in Eastern Europe and demobilization within the Soviet Union, see MID, "Review of Europe, Russia, and the Middle East," December 26, 1945, RG 165, OPD, 350.05 (top secret); Carl Espe, weekly calculations of Soviet troops, May–September 1946, NHC, SPD, ser. 5, box 106, A8; and JIC, "Soviet Military Objectives and Capabilities," October 27, 1947. For references to Soviet military expenditures, see Patterson to Julius Adler, November 2, 1946, RG 107, RPPP, safe file, box 5; and for the Soviet transport system, see R. F. Ennis, Memorandum for the P&O Division, June 24, 1946, RG 165, ser. ABC 336 (8-22-43); Op-32 to the General Board, April 28, 1948, NHC, General Board 425 (ser. 315).

[11]Smith to the Secretary of State, April 11, 1946, RG 165, Records of the Chief of Staff, 091 Russia; and, for Soviet negotiating concessions, see Lincoln, Memorandum for the Chief of Staff, May 20, 1946, USMA; GLP War Dept/files. For the situation in Germany, see OPD and CAD, "Analysis of Certain Political Problems Confronting Military Occupation Authorities in Germany," April 10, 1946, RG 107, HCPP 091 Germany (classified); Patterson to Truman, June 11, 1946, RG 165, Records of the Chief of Staff, 091 Germany. For Clay's references to French obstructionism, see, for example, Smith, *Papers of General Lucius D. Clav,* Vol. 1: 84–5, 88–9, 151–2, 189–90, 212–17, 235–6. For overall intelligence assessments, see Central Intelligence Group [hereafter CIG], "Revised Soviet Tactics in International Affairs," January 6, 1947, HTL, HSTP, PSF, box 254, MID, "World Political Developments Affecting the Security of the United States during the Next Ten Years," April 14, 1947.

[12]My assessment is based primarily on my analysis of the materials in RG 218, ser. CCS.092 USSR (3-27-45); ser. CCS 381 USSR (3-2-46); RG 319, P&O, 350.05 (top secret); and NHC, SPD, central files, 1946–8, A8.

[13]During 1946 it became a fundamental tenet of American policy makers that Soviet policy objectives were a function of developments within the Soviet Union and not related to American actions. See, for example, Kennan's "long telegram," in *FRUS, 1946,* Vol. 4: 696–709; JCS, "Political Estimate of Soviet Policy," April 5, 1946.

[14]Norstad, memorandum, July 25, 1946, RG 319, P&O, 092 (top secret). For references to shifting tactics and constant objectives, see Vandenberg, Memorandum for the President, September 27, 1946, HTL, HSTP, PSF, box 249; ClG, "Revised Soviet Tactics," January 6, 1947; and, for the JCS report to the President, compare JCS 1696 with JIC 250/12. Both studies may be found in RG 218, ser. CCS 092 USSR (3-27-45). For Clifford's recollection, Clark Clifford, HTL, oral history, 170.

[15]For Soviet losses, see Nicholas V. Riasanovsky, *A History of Russia* (3rd edn, New York, 1977), 584–5. While Russian dead totaled almost 20 million and while approximately 25 percent of the reproducible wealth of the Soviet Union was destroyed, American battlefield casualties were 300,000 dead, the index of industrial production in the United States rose from 100 to 196, and the gross national product increased from $91 billion to $166 billion. See Gordon Wright, *The Ordeal of Total War* (New York, 1968), 264–5.

Nuclear Deterrence Doctrine

4.2

BERNARD BRODIE

Strategy in the Missile Age

* * *

We shall be talking about the strategy of deterrence of general war, and about the complementary principle of limiting to tolerable proportions whatever conflicts become inevitable. These ideas spring from the conviction that total nuclear war is to be avoided at almost any cost. This follows from the assumption that such a war, even if we were extraordinarily lucky, would be too big, too all-consuming to permit the survival even of those final values, like personal freedom, for which alone one could think of waging it. It need not be certain that it would turn out so badly; it is enough that there is a large chance that it would.

The conceptions of deterrence and of limited war also take account of the fact that the United States is, and has long been, a status quo power. We are uninterested in acquiring new territories or areas of influence or in accepting great hazard in order to rescue or reform those areas of the world which now have political systems radically different from our own. On the other hand, as a status quo power, we

are also determined to keep what we have, including existence in a world of which half or more is friendly, or at least not sharply and perennially hostile. In other words, our minimum security objectives include not only our own national independence but also that of many other countries, especially those which cherish democratic political institutions. Among the latter are those nations with which we have a special cultural affinity, that is, the countries of western Europe.

* * *

DETERRENCE OLD AND NEW Deterrence as an element in national strategy or diplomacy is nothing new. Since the development of nuclear weapons, however, the term has acquired not only a special emphasis but also a distinctive connotation. It is usually the new and distinctive connotation that we have in mind when we speak nowadays of the "strategy of deterrence."

The threat of war, open or implied, has always been an instrument of diplomacy by which one state deterred another

From *Strategy in the Missile Age* (Princeton: Princeton University Press, 1965), chap. 8.

from doing something of a military or political nature which the former deemed undesirable. Frequently the threat was completely latent, the position of the monitoring state being so obvious and so strong that no one thought of challenging it. Governments, like individuals, were usually aware of hazard in provoking powerful neighbors and governed themselves accordingly. Because avoidance of wars and even of crises hardly makes good copy for historians, we may infer that the past successes of some nations in deterring unwanted action by others add up to much more than one might gather from a casual reading of history. Nevertheless the large number of wars that have occurred in modern times prove that the threat to use force, even what sometimes looked like superior force, has often failed to deter.

We should notice, however, the positive function played by the failures. The very frequency with which wars occurred contributed importantly to the credibility inherent in any threat. In diplomatic correspondence, the statement that a specified kind of conduct would be deemed "an unfriendly act" was regarded as tantamount to an ultimatum and to be taken without question as seriously intended.

Bluffing, in the sense of deliberately trying to sound more determined or bellicose than one actually felt, was by no means as common a phenomenon in diplomacy as latter-day journalistic interpretations of events would have one believe. In any case, it tended to be confined to the more implicit kinds of threat. In short, the operation of deterrence was dynamic; it acquired relevance and strength from its failures as well as its successes.

Today, however, the policy of deterrence in relation to all-out war is markedly different in several respects. For one thing, it uses a kind of threat which we feel must be absolutely effective, allowing for no breakdowns ever. The sanction is, to say the least, not designed for repeating action. One use of it will be fatally too many. Deterrence now means something as a strategic policy only when we are fairly confident that the retaliatory instrument upon which it relies will not be called upon to function at all. Nevertheless, that instrument has to be maintained at a high pitch of efficiency and readiness and constantly improved, which can be done only at high cost to the community and great dedication on the part of the personnel directly involved. In short, we expect the system to be always ready to spring while going permanently unused. Surely there is something almost unreal about all this.

The Problem of Credibility

The unreality is minimal when we are talking about what we shall henceforward call *"basic deterrence,"* that is, deterrence of direct, strategic, nuclear attack upon targets within the home territories of the United States. In that instance there is little or no problem of credibility as concerns our reactions, for the enemy has little reason to doubt that if he strikes us we will try to hit back. But the great and terrible apparatus which we must set up to fulfill our needs for basic deterrence and the sate of readiness at which we have to maintain it create a condition of almost embarrassing availability of huge power. The problem of linking this power to a reasonable conception of its utility has thus far proved a considerable strain.

*   *   *

On the other hand, it would be tactically and factually wrong to assure the enemy in advance (as we tend to do by constantly assuring ourselves) that we would in no case move against him until we had already felt some bombs on our cities and airfields. We have, as we have seen, treaty obligations which forbid so far-reaching a commitment to restraint. It is also impossible for us to predict with absolute assurance our own behavior in extremely tense and provocative circumstances. If we make the wrong prediction about ourselves, we encourage the enemy also to make the wrong prediction about us. The outbreak of war in Korea in 1950 followed exactly that pattern. The wrong kind of prediction in this regard might precipitate that total nuclear war which too many persons have lightly concluded is now impossible.

Deterrence Strategy versus Win-the-War Strategies: The Sliding Scale of Deterrence

To return now to the simpler problem of basic deterrence. The capacity to deter is usually confused with the capacity to win a war. At present, capacity to win a total or unrestricted war requires either a decisive and *completely secure* superiority in strategic air power or success in seizing the initiative. Inasmuch as mere superiority in numbers of vehicles looks like a good thing to have anyway, the confusion between deterring and winning has method in it. But deterrence *per se* does not depend on superiority.

*   *   *

Now that we are in a nuclear age, the potential deterrence value of an admittedly inferior force may be sharply greater than it has ever been before. Let us assume that a menaced small nation could threaten the Soviet Union with only a single thermonuclear bomb, which, however, it could and would certainly deliver on Moscow if attacked. This would be a retaliatory capability sufficient to give the Soviet government pause. Certainly they would not provoke the destruction of Moscow for trivial gains, even if warning enabled the people of the city to save themselves by evacuation or resort to shelters. Naturally, the effect is greater if warning can be ruled out.

Ten such missiles aimed at ten major cities would be even more effective, and fifty aimed at that number of different cities would no doubt work still greater deterrent effect, though of course the cities diminish in size as the number included goes up. However, even when we make allowance for the latter fact, it is a fair surmise that the increase in deterrent effect is less than proportional to the increase in magnitude of potential destruction. We make that surmise on the basis of our everyday experience with human beings and their responses to punishment or deprivation. The human imagination can encompass just so much pain, anguish, or horror. The intrusion of numbers by which to multiply given sums of such feelings is likely to have on the average human mind a rather dull effect—except insofar as the increase in the threatened amount of harm affects the individual's statistical expectation of himself being involved in it.

Governments, it may be suggested, do not think like ordinary human beings, and one has to concede that the *maximum possible deterrence* which can be attained by the threat of retaliatory damage must involve a power which guarantees not only vast losses but also utter defeat. On the other hand, governments, including communistic ones, also comprise human beings, whose departure from the mold of ordinary mortals is not markedly in the direction of greater intellectualism or detachment. It is therefore likely that considerably less retaliatory destruction than that conceived under "maximum possible deterrence" will buy only slightly less deterrence. If we wish to visualize the situation graphically, we will think of a curve of "deterrence effect" in which each unit of additional damage threatened brings progressively diminishing increments of deterrence. Obviously and unfortunately, we lack all the data which would enable us to fill in the values for such a curve and thus to draw it.

If our surmises are in general correct, we are underlining the sharp differences in character between a deterrence capability and strategy on the one hand, and a win-the-war strategy and capability on the other. We have to remember too that since the winning of a war presupposes certain limitations on the quantity of destruction

to one's own country and especially to one's population, a win-the-war strategy could quite conceivably be an utter impossibility to a nation striking second, and is by no means guaranteed to a nation striking first. Too much depends on what the other fellow does—how accessible or inaccessible he makes his own retaliatory force and how he makes his attack if he decides to launch one. However much we dislike the thought, a win-the-war strategy may be impossible because of circumstances outside our control.

Lest we conclude from these remarks that we can be content with a modest retaliatory capability—what some have called "minimum deterrence"—we have to mention at once four qualifying considerations, which we shall amplify later: (a) it may require a large force in hand to guarantee even a modest retaliation; (b) deterrence must always be conceived as a relative thing, which is to say it must be adequate to the variable but generally high degree of motivation which the enemy feels for our destruction; (c) if deterrence fails we shall want enough forces to fight a total war effectively; and (d) our retaliatory force must also be capable of striking first, and if it does so its attack had better be, as nearly as possible, overwhelming to the enemy's retaliatory force. Finally, we have to bear in mind that in their responses to threat or menace, people (including heads of government) do not spontaneously act according to a scrupulous weighing of objective facts. Large forces look more impressive than small ones—for reasons which are by no means entirely irrational—and in some circumstances such impressiveness may be important to us. Human beings, differing widely as they do in temperamental and psychic make-up, nevertheless generally have in common the fact that they make their most momentous decisions by what is fundamentally intuition.

* * *

The Problem of Guaranteeing Strong Retaliation

It should be obvious that what counts in basic deterrence is not so much the size and efficiency of one's striking force before it is hit as the size and condition to which the enemy thinks he can reduce it by a surprise attack—as well as his confidence in the correctness of his predictions. The degree to which the automaticity of our retaliation has been taken for granted by the public, unfortunately including most leaders of opinion and even military officers, is for those who have any knowledge of the facts both incredible and dangerous. The general idea is that if the enemy hits us, we will kill him.

* * *

Deterrence and Armaments Control

We come finally to the question of the political environment favoring the functioning of a deterrence strategy, especially with respect to the much abused and belabored subject of international control of armaments. There is a long and dismal history

of confusion and frustration on this subject. Those who have been most passionate in urging disarmament have often refused to look unpleasant facts in the face; on the other hand, the government officials responsible for actual negotiations have usually been extremely rigid in their attitudes, tending to become more preoccupied with winning marginal and ephemeral advantages from the negotiations than in making real progress toward the presumed objective. There has also been confusion concerning both the objective and the degree of risk warranted by that objective.

Here we can take up only the last point. One must first ask what degree of arms control is a reasonable or sensible objective. It seems by now abundantly clear that total nuclear disarmament is not a reasonable objective. Violation would be too easy for the Communists, and the risks to the non-violator would be enormous. But it should also be obvious that the kind of bitter, relentless race in nuclear weapons and missiles that has been going on since the end of World War II has its own intrinsic dangers.

* * *

The kind of measures in which we ought to be especially interested are those which could seriously reduce on all sides the dangers of surprise attack. Such a policy would be entirely compatible with our basic national commitment to a strategy of deterrence. The best way to reduce the danger of surprise attack is to reduce on all sides the incentives to such attack, an end which is furthered by promoting measures that enhance deterrent rather than aggressive posture—where the two can be distinguished, which, if one is looking for the chance to do so, is probably pretty often. It also helps greatly to reduce the danger of accidental outbreak of total war if each side takes it upon itself to do the opposite of "keeping the enemy guessing" concerning its pacific intentions. This is accomplished not through reiterated declaration of pacific intent, which is for this purpose a worn and useless tactic, but through finding procedures where each side can assure the other through the latter's own eyes that deliberate attack is not being prepared against him.

* * *

Our over-riding interest, for the enhancement of our deterrence posture, is of course in the security of our own retaliatory force. But that does not mean that we especially desire the other side's retaliatory force to be insecure. If the opponent feels insecure, we suffer the hazard of his being more trigger-happy.

* * *

Stability is achieved when each nation believes that the strategic advantage of striking first is overshadowed by the tremendous cost of doing so. If, for example, retaliatory weapons are in the future so well protected that it takes more than one missile to destroy an enemy missile, the chances for stability become quite good. Under such circumstances striking first brings no advantage unless one has enormous numerical superiority. But such a situation is the very opposite of the more familiar one where both sides rely wholly or predominately on unprotected aircraft.

Technological progress could, however, push us rapidly towards a position of almost intolerable mutual menace. Unless something is done politically to alter the environment, each side before many years will have thousands of missiles accurately pointed at targets in the other's territory ready to be fired at a moment's notice. Whether or not we call it "push-button" war is a matter of our taste in phraseology, but there is no use in telling ourselves that the time for it is remote. Well before that time arrives, aircraft depending for their safety on being in the air in time will be operating according to so-called "airborne alert" and "fail-safe" patterns. Nothing which has any promise of obviating or alleviating the tensions of such situations should be overlooked.

The Sources of Containment

4.3

MR. X [GEORGE KENNAN]

The Sources of Soviet Conduct

The political personality of Soviet power as we know it today is the product of ideology and circumstances: ideology inherited by the present Soviet leaders from the movement in which they had their political origin, and circumstances of the power which they now have exercised for nearly three decades in Russia. There can be few tasks of psychological analysis more difficult than to try to trace the interaction of these two forces and the relative rôle of each in the determination of official Soviet conduct.

* * *

[T]remendous emphasis has been placed on the original Communist thesis of a basic antagonism between the capitalist and Socialist worlds. It is clear, from many indications, that this emphasis is not founded in reality. The real facts concerning it have been confused by the existence abroad of genuine resentment provoked by Soviet philosophy and tactics and occasionally by the existence of great centers of military power, notably the Nazi régime in Germany and the Japanese Government of the late 1930's, which did indeed have aggressive designs against the Soviet Union. But there is ample evidence that the stress laid in Moscow on the menace confronting Soviet society from the world outside its borders is founded not in the realities of foreign antagonism but in the necessity of explaining away the maintenance of dictatorial authority at home.

Now the maintenance of this pattern of Soviet power, namely, the pursuit of unlimited authority domestically, accompanied by the cultivation of the semi-myth of implacable foreign hostility, has gone far to shape the actual machinery of Soviet power as we know it today. Internal organs of administration which did not serve this purpose withered on the vine. Organs which did serve this purpose became vastly swollen. The security of Soviet power came to rest on the iron discipline of the party, on the severity and ubiquity of the secret police, and on the uncompromising economic monopolism of the state. The "organs of suppression," in which the Soviet leaders had sought security from rival forces, became in large

From *Foreign Affairs*, July 1947.

measure the masters of those whom they were designed to serve. Today the major part of the structure of Soviet power is committed to the perfection of the dictatorship and to the maintenance of the concept of Russia as in a state of siege, with the enemy lowering beyond the walls. And the millions of human beings who form that part of the structure of power must defend at all costs this concept of Russia's position, for without it they are themselves superfluous.

As things stand today, the rulers can no longer dream of parting with these organs of suppression. The quest for absolute power, pursued now for nearly three decades with a ruthlessness unparalleled (in scope at least) in modern times, has again produced internally, as it did externally, its own reaction. The excesses of the police apparatus have fanned the potential opposition to the régime into something far greater and more dangerous than it could have been before those excesses began.

But least of all can the rulers dispense with the fiction by which the maintenance of dictatorial power has been defended. For this fiction has been canonized in Soviet philosophy by the excesses already committed in its name; and it is now anchored in the Soviet structure of thought by bonds far greater than those of mere ideology.

II

So much for the historical background. What does it spell in terms of the political personality of Soviet power as we know it today?

Of the original ideology, nothing has been officially junked. Belief is maintained in the basic badness of capitalism, in the inevitability of its destruction, in the obligation of the proletariat to assist in that destruction and to take power into its own hands. But stress has come to be laid primarily on those concepts which relate most specifically to the Soviet regime itself: to its position as the sole truly Socialist régime in a dark and misguided world, and to the relationships of power within it.

The first of these concepts is that of the innate antagonism between capitalism and Socialism. We have seen how deeply that concept has become imbedded in foundations of Soviet power. It has profound implications for Russia's conduct as a member of international society. It means that there can never be on Moscow's side any sincere assumption of a community of aims between the Soviet Union and powers which are regarded as capitalist. It must invariably be assumed in Moscow that the aims of the capitalist world are antagonistic to the Soviet régime, and therefore to the interests of the peoples it controls. If the Soviet Government occasionally sets its signature to documents which would indicate the contrary, this is to be regarded as a tactical manœuvre permissible in dealing with the enemy (who is without honor) and should be taken in the spirit of *caveat emptor*. Basically, the antagonism remains. It is postulated. And from it flow many of the phenomena which we find disturbing in the Kremlin's conduct of foreign policy: the secretiveness, the lack of frankness, the duplicity, the wary suspiciousness, and the basic unfriendliness of purpose. These phenomena are there to stay, for the foreseeable future. There can be variations of degree and of emphasis. When there is something the Russians want from us, one or the other of these features of their policy may be thrust temporarily into the background; and when that happens there will always be Americans who will leap forward with gleeful announcements that "the Russians have changed," and some who will even try to take credit for having brought about such "changes." But we should not be misled by tactical manœuvres. These characteristics of Soviet policy, like the postulate from which they flow, are basic to the internal nature of Soviet power, and will be with us whether in the foreground or the background, until the internal nature of Soviet power is changed.

* * *

These considerations make Soviet diplomacy at once easier and more difficult to deal with than the diplomacy of individual aggressive leaders like Napoleon and Hitler. On the one hand it is more sensitive to contrary force, more ready to yield on individual sectors of the diplomatic front when that force is felt to be too strong, and thus more rational in the logic and rhetoric of power. On the other hand it cannot be easily defeated or discouraged by a single victory on the part of its opponents. And the patient persistence by which it is animated means that it can be effectively countered not by sporadic acts which represent the momentary whims of democratic opinion but only by intelligent long-range policies on the part of Russia's adversaries—policies no less steady in their purpose, and no less

variegated and resourceful in their application, than those of the Soviet Union itself.

In these circumstances it is clear that the main element of any United States policy toward the Soviet Union must be that of a long-term, patient but firm and vigilant containment of Russian expansive tendencies. It is important to note, however, that such a policy has nothing to do with outward histrionics: with threats or blustering or superfluous gestures of outward "toughness." While the Kremlin is basically flexible in its reaction to political realities, it is by no means unamenable to considerations of prestige. Like almost any other government, it can be placed by tactless and threatening gestures in a position where it cannot afford to yield even though this might be dictated by its sense of realism. The Russian leaders are keen judges of human psychology, and as such they are highly conscious that loss of temper and of self-control is never a source of strength in political affairs. They are quick to exploit such evidences of weakness. For these reasons, it is a *sine qua non* of successful dealing with Russia that the foreign government in question should remain at all times cool and collected and that its demands on Russian policy should be put forward in such a manner as to leave the way open for a compliance not too detrimental to Russian prestige.

* * *

IV

It is clear that the United States cannot expect in the foreseeable future to enjoy political intimacy with the Soviet régime. It must continue to regard the Soviet Union as a rival, not a partner, in the political arena. It must continue to expect that Soviet policies will reflect no abstract love of peace and stability, no real faith in the possibility of a permanent happy coexistence of the Socialist and capitalist worlds, but rather a cautious, persistent pressure toward the disruption and weakening of all rival influence and rival power.

Balanced against this are the facts that Russia, as opposed to the western world in general, is still by far the weaker party, that Soviet policy is highly flexible, and that Soviet society may well contain deficiencies which will eventually weaken its own total potential. This would of itself warrant the United States entering with reasonable confidence upon a policy of firm containment, designed to confront the Russians with unalterable counterforce at every point where they show signs of encroaching upon the interests of a peaceful and stable world.

But in actuality the possibilities for American policy are by no means limited to holding the line and hoping for the best. It is entirely possible for the United States to influence by its actions the internal developments, both within Russia and throughout the international Communist movement, by which Russian policy is largely determined. This is not only a question of the modest measure of informational activity which this government can conduct in the Soviet Union and elsewhere, although that, too, is important. It is rather a question of the degree to which the United States can create among the

peoples of the world generally the impression of a country which knows what it wants, which is coping successfully with the problems of its internal life and with the responsibilities of a World Power, and which has a spiritual vitality capable of holding its own among the major ideological currents of the time. To the extent that such an impression can be created and maintained, the aims of Russian Communism must appear sterile and quixotic, the hopes and enthusiasm of Moscow's supporters must wane, and added strain must be imposed on the Kremlin's foreign policies. For the palsied decrepitude of the capitalist world is the keystone of Communist philosophy. Even the failure of the United States to experience the early economic depression which the ravens of the Red Square have been predicting with such complacent confidence since hostilities ceased would have deep and important repercussions throughout the Communist world.

By the same token, exhibitions of indecision, disunity and internal disintegration within this country have an exhilarating effect on the whole Communist movement. At each evidence of these tendencies, a thrill of hope and excitement goes through the Communist world; a new jauntiness can be noted in the Moscow tread; new groups of foreign supporters climb on to what they can only view as the band wagon of international politics; and Russian pressure increases all along the line in international affairs.

It would be an exaggeration to say that American behavior unassisted and alone could exercise a power of life and death over the Communist movement and bring about the early fall of Soviet power in Russia. But the United States has it in its power to increase enormously the strains under which Soviet policy must operate, to force upon the Kremlin a far greater degree of moderation and circumspection than it has had to observe in recent years, and in this way to promote tendencies which must eventually find their outlet in either the break-up or the gradual mellowing of Soviet power. For no mystical, Messianic movement—and particularly not that of the Kremlin—can face frustration indefinitely without eventually adjusting itself in one way or another to the logic of that state of affairs.

Thus the decision will really fall in large measure in this country itself. The issue of Soviet-American relations is in essence a test of the over-all worth of the United States as a nation among nations. To avoid destruction the United States need only measure up to its own best traditions and prove itself worthy of preservation as a great nation.

Surely, there was never a fairer test of national quality than this. In the light of these circumstances, the thoughtful observer of Russian-American relations will find no cause for complaint in the Kremlin's challenge to American society. He will rather experience a certain gratitude to a Providence which, by providing the American people with this implacable challenge, has made their entire security as a nation dependent on their pulling themselves together and accepting the responsibilities of moral and political leadership that history plainly intended them to bear.

Vietnam

LESLIE H. GELB

Vietnam: The System Worked

The story of United States policy toward Vietnam is either far better or far worse than generally supposed. Our Presidents and most of those who influenced their decisions did not stumble step by step into Vietnam, unaware of the quagmire. U.S. involvement did not stem from a failure to foresee consequences.

Vietnam was indeed a quagmire, but most of our leaders knew it. Of course there were optimists and periods where many were genuinely optimistic. But those periods were infrequent and short-lived and were invariably followed by periods of deep pessimism. Very few, to be sure, envisioned what the Vietnam situation would be like by 1968. Most realized, however, that "the light at the end of the tunnel" was very far away—if not finally unreachable. Nevertheless, our Presidents persevered. Given international compulsions to "keep our word" and "save face," domestic prohibitions against "losing," and their personal stakes, our leaders did "what was necessary," did it about the way they wanted, were prepared to pay the costs, and plowed

on with a mixture of hope and doom. They "saw" no acceptable alternative.

Three propositions suggest why the United States became involved in Vietnam, why the process was gradual, and what the real expectations of our leaders were:

First, U.S. involvement in Vietnam is not mainly or mostly a story of step by step, inadvertent descent into unforeseen quicksand. It is primarily a story of why U.S. leaders considered that it was vital not to lose Vietnam by force to Communism. Our leaders believed Vietnam to be vital not for itself, but for what they thought its "loss" would mean internationally and domestically. Previous involvement made further involvement more unavoidable, and, to this extent, commitments were inherited. But judgments of Vietnam's "vitalness"—beginning with the Korean War—were sufficient in themselves to set the course for escalation.

Second, our Presidents were never actually seeking a military victory in Vietnam. They were doing only what they thought

From *Foreign Policy* 3 (Summer 1971), 140–67.

was minimally necessary at each stage to keep Indochina, and later South Vietnam, out of Communist hands. This forced our Presidents to be brakemen, to do less than those who were urging military victory and to reject proposals for disengagement. It also meant that our Presidents wanted a negotiated settlement without fully realizing (though realizing more than their critics) that a civil war cannot be ended by political compromise.

Third, our Presidents and most of their lieutenants were not deluded by optimistic reports of progress and did not proceed on the basis of wishful thinking about winning a military victory in South Vietnam. They recognized that the steps they were taking were not adequate to win the war and that unless Hanoi relented, they would have to do more and more. Their strategy was to persevere in the hope that their will to continue—if not the practical effects of their actions—would cause the Communists to relent.

Each of these propositions is explored below.

I. Ends: "We Can't Afford to Lose"

Those who led the United States into Vietnam did so with their eyes open, knowing why, and believing they had the will to succeed. The deepening involvement was not inadvertent, but mainly deductive. It flowed with sureness from the perceived stakes and attendant high objectives. U.S. policy displayed remarkable continuity. There were not dozens of likely "turning points." Each post-war President inherited previous commit-

ments. Each extended these commitments. Each administration from 1947 to 1969 believed that it was necessary to prevent the loss of Vietnam and, after 1954, South Vietnam by force to the Communists. The reasons for this varied from person to person, from bureaucracy to bureaucracy, over time and in emphasis. For the most part, however, they had little to do with Vietnam itself. A few men argued that Vietnam had intrinsic strategic military and economic importance, but this view never prevailed. The reasons rested on broader international, domestic, and bureaucratic considerations.

* * *

The *domestic* repercussions of "losing" Vietnam probably were equally important in Presidential minds. Letting Vietnam "go Communist" was undoubtedly seen as:

- opening the floodgates to domestic criticism and attack for being "soft on Communism" or just plain soft;
- dissipating Presidential influence by having to answer these charges;
- alienating conservative leadership in the Congress and thereby endangering the President's legislative program;
- jeopardizing election prospects for the President and his party;
- undercutting domestic support for a "responsible" U.S. world role; and
- enlarging the prospects for a right-wing reaction—the nightmare of a McCarthyite garrison state.

* * *

II. Means: "Take the Minimal Necessary Steps"

None of our Presidents was seeking total victory over the Vietnamese Communists. War critics who wanted victory always knew this. Those who wanted the U.S. to get out never believed it. Each President was essentially doing what he thought was minimally necessary to prevent a Communist victory during his tenure in office. Each, of course, sought to strengthen the anti-Communist Vietnamese forces, but with the aim of a negotiated settlement. Part of the tragedy of Vietnam was that the compromises our Presidents were prepared to offer could never lead to an end of the war. These preferred compromises only served to reinforce the conviction of both Communist and anti-Communist Vietnamese that they had to fight to the finish in their civil war. And so, more minimal steps were always necessary.

* * *

Our Presidents reacted to the pressures as brakemen, pulling the switch against both the advocates of "decisive escalation" and the advocates of disengagement. The politics of the Presidency largely dictated this role, but the personalities of the Presidents were also important. None were as ideological as many persons around them. All were basically centrist politicians.

Their immediate aim was always to prevent a Communist takeover. The actions they approved were usually only what was minimally necessary to that aim. Each President determined the "minimal necessity" by trial and error and his own judgment.

They might have done more and done it more rapidly if they were convinced that: (1) the threat of a Communist takeover were more immediate, (2) U.S. domestic politics would have been more permissive, (3) the government of South Vietnam had the requisite political stability and military potential for effective use and (4) the job really would have gotten done. After 1965, however, the minimal necessity became the maximum they could get given the same domestic and international constraints.

* * *

III. Expectations: "We Must Persevere"

Each new step was taken not because of wishful thinking or optimism about its leading to a victory in South Vietnam. Few of our leaders thought that they could win the war in a conventional sense or that the Communists would be decimated to a point that they would simply fade away. Even as new and further steps were taken, coupled with expressions of optimism, many of our leaders realized that more— and still more—would have to be done. Few of these men felt confident about how it would all end or when. After 1965, however, they allowed the impression of "winnability" to grow in order to justify their already heavy investment and domestic support for the war.

The strategy always was to persevere. Perseverance, it seemed, was the only way to avoid or postpone having to pay the domestic political costs of failure. Finally, perseverance, it was hoped, would convince the Communists that our will to continue was firm. Perhaps, then, with domestic support for perseverance, with bombing North Vietnam, and with inflicting heavy casualties in the South, the Communists would relent. Perhaps, then, a compromise could be negotiated to save the Communists' face without giving them South Vietnam.

* * *

Most of our leaders saw the Vietnam quagmire for what it was. Optimism was, by and large, put in perspective. This means that many knew that each step would be followed by another. Most seemed to have understood that more assistance would be required either to improve the relative position of our Vietnamese allies or simply to prevent a deterioration of their position. Almost each year and often several times a year, key decisions had to be made to prevent deterioration or collapse. These decisions were made with hard bargaining, but rapidly enough for us now to perceive a preconceived consensus to go on. Sometimes several new steps were decided at once, but announced and implemented piecemeal. The whole pattern conveyed the feeling of more to come.

With a tragic sense of "no exit," our leaders stayed their course. They seemed to hope more than expect that something would "give." The hope was to convince the Vietnamese Communists through perseverance that the U.S. would stay in South Vietnam until they abandoned their struggle. The hope, in a sense, was the product of disbelief. How could a tiny, backward Asian country *not* have a breaking point when opposed by the might of the United States? How could they not relent and negotiate with the U.S.?

And yet, few could answer two questions with any confidence: Why should the Communists abandon tomorrow the goals they had been paying so dear a price to obtain yesterday? What was there really to negotiate? No one seemed to be able to develop a persuasive scenario on how the war could end by peaceful means.

Our Presidents, given their politics and thinking, had nothing to do but persevere. But the Communists' strategy was also to persevere, to make the U.S. go home. It was and is a civil war for national independence. It was and is a Greek tragedy.

* * *

Détente

5.2

ALEXANDER L. GEORGE

Détente: The Search for a "Constructive" Relationship

∗ ∗ ∗

This relationship [détente] did not occur accidentally; it was the result of developments in world politics that U.S. and Soviet leaders recognized and to which they attempted to adapt. Détente—whatever it was intended to be—emerged as a result of policy choices made by the two leaderships, and it was shaped by the way in which they concerted efforts in an attempt to define a new relationship that would replace the acute hostility of the cold war, moderate the conflict potential inherent in their competition, and strengthen cooperation in issue areas in which they believed their interests converged. A mutual desire to move in the direction of détente had been powerfully stimulated by the brush with thermonuclear disaster during the Cuban missile crisis in 1962. Important steps to develop a new relationship were taken during the remainder of the decade of the sixties, but détente was given stronger impetus and moved more steadily in the early seventies during President Nixon's first administration.

It is important to recognize that while both [Richard] Nixon and [Leonid] Brezhnev wanted to develop a more constructive relationship between their countries, they came to the task from different starting points and with expectations that differed in important respects. Soviet leaders wanted to formalize their relationship with the United States in such a way as to encourage that country to accept the emergence of the Soviet Union as a co-equal, with all that they hoped this status would imply for the future. Nixon and [Henry] Kissinger, on the other hand, wanted to draw the Soviet Union into a new relationship that would enable the United States to maintain as much of its declining world position as possible. They were very much aware of changes in the arena of world politics that were eroding the predominant position that the United States had enjoyed during the cold war. As Nixon put it in his annual foreign policy report to Congress of February 25, 1971: "The postwar order in international relations—the configuration of power that

From *Managing U.S.-Soviet Rivalry: Problems of Crisis Prevention* (Boulder, Colo.: Westview, 1983), chap. 2.

emerged from the Second World War—is gone. With it are gone the conditions which have determined the assumptions and practices of United States foreign policy since 1945."[1]

Nixon had in mind the many important changes that had taken place in the international and domestic environments in which U.S. foreign policy had to operate— and to which it had to adjust. Many of the nations that had suffered severe losses and dislocation from World War II had now substantially recovered. New nations had emerged as the major European powers divested themselves of or were deprived of their colonies. Many of these new states displayed an increasing ability to maintain their independence and to avoid becoming battlegrounds for the cold war. U.S. leaders were experiencing increasing limits on the ability of their policies to influence world developments unilaterally (of this limitation, the Vietnam War was only the most obvious and tragic example). U.S. strategic military superiority was giving way to the achievement of strategic parity by the Soviet Union. But, at the same time, the nature of the Communist challenge to the free world had changed with the passing of Moscow's near-monolithic control of the international communist movement and the emergence of competing centers of communist doctrine, power, and practice. In this regard, particularly, the Sino-Soviet split seemed to offer new opportunities for the United States to benefit from the possible emergence of a tripolar balance of power. Finally, U.S. foreign policy had to adjust to the growing constraints on resources available to support the ambitious global role the United States had assumed

during the cold war and to the increasing domestic unwillingness in the United States to continue support of costly commitments abroad.

Accordingly, Nixon and Kissinger sought to introduce a web of incentives into the relationship with the Soviet Union that would give the USSR a stake in a more stable world order and induce it to operate with greater restraint. Thereby, a measure of *self*-containment on the part of Soviet leaders would be introduced that would reduce the need for the United States to rely exclusively on deterrence, as it had in the cold war, to contain the Soviet Union. In time, it was hoped, the new positive relationship with the Soviet Union would become part of a new, more stable international system.

Nixon and Kissinger were intrigued by the possibility of establishing a tripolar balance of power among the United States, the Soviet Union, and the People's Republic of China (PRC). By developing a measure of friendly relations with both of these archrivals, the United States could hope to reduce potential threats to its interests from either side and to induce each to a greater measure of cooperation with U.S. policy. By using its unique middle position in such a triangular relationship, Washington could tilt or threaten to tilt in favor of one or the other of the two Communist rivals, as the situation required, to promote its own interests. Thus, Nixon and Kissinger believed the United States could compensate for the decline of U.S. power by presiding over a tripolar system that, if delicately managed by Washington, would give the United States additional leverage with which to protect and enhance its interests. The immediate, indeed urgent, U.S. objective to be realized by employing this neo-Bismarckian strategy was, of course, to induce both the PRC and the Soviet Union to influence North Vietnam to end the war in Southeast Asia on terms acceptable to the United States.

This is not to say that Nixon and Kissinger viewed the PRC in the same terms as they did the Soviet Union. The major potential threat to U.S. security and worldwide interests was perceived to emanate from the growing power of the USSR. The People's Republic was not a superpower and would not become one for many years. And so the major incentive behind Nixon's improving relations with the PRC was to obtain leverage for developing a more satisfactory relationship with the Soviet Union. The threat of a positive development of U.S. relations with the PRC was supposed to be part of the "stick" that, coupled with the "carrot" of various positive inducements held out to Soviet leaders, would draw the USSR into a more constructive relationship with the United States, one in which the Soviets would restrain themselves from employing the growing power and new global reach of their military forces to make advances at the expense of U.S. interests and the interests of its allies. In seeking an improved relationship with the Soviet Union Nixon and Kissinger did not expect to eliminate competition but merely to moderate it in order to reduce its dangerous potential. What, then, was the grand strategy for achieving the important long-range objective? It had at least four major components.

First, there was Nixon's willingness to acknowledge that the Soviet Union was entitled to the same status of superpower that the United States enjoyed. Aware of the importance that Soviet leaders attached to achieving equality of status, Nixon was willing to recognize this equality symbolically in various ways, via summit meetings and in rhetorical statements. What "equality" was to mean in practice, however, was left undefined and was soon to become a source of fundamental friction in the détente relationship.

A second element in the strategy was Nixon's conditional willingness to recognize and legitimize, as it were, the changes in Eastern Europe that had taken place following World War II. Nixon agreed to go along with the long-standing Soviet desire for a formal document, signed by all European countries as well as by the United States, that would recognize existing borders in Europe and thereby tacitly confirm the dominant role of the Soviet Union in Eastern Europe. This recognition of borders was part of the Helsinki Declaration that finally emerged in 1975 from the Conference on Security and Cooperation in Europe. Nixon agreed to move in this direction at the first summit meeting held in Moscow in May 1972, coupling his acquiescence with a Soviet agreement to regularize the status of West Berlin and to engage in discussions for mutual and balanced force reductions in Europe.

A third element of the strategy called for a variety of formal agreements with the Soviet Union to further mutual cooperation and interdependence. Most important in this connection were to be agreements for limiting the strategic arms race. In this respect the two sides were initially successful, and SALT I [the first

Strategic Arms Limitation Treaty] was signed at the Moscow summit in May 1972. In addition, Nixon offered the prospect of important, continuing economic and technical assistance to the Soviet Union as a major inducement for giving Soviet leaders a strong stake in the evolving constructive relationship. Nixon's willingness to move in this direction was part of the set of understandings developed at the Moscow summit. The trade agreement signed in October, however, was to encounter unexpected difficulties in the Senate and was never carried out, a failure that dealt a major blow to the further development of détente.

The fourth element of their strategy was particularly important to Nixon and Kissinger, even though they recognized its difficulty and elusive character. They hoped that the momentum of détente would lead in time to the development of a new set of norms and rules for regulating and moderating the global competition and rivalry between the two superpowers. A start was made in this direction with some of the provisions of the Basic Principles Agreement (BPA) that Nixon and Brezhnev signed at the Moscow summit. These provisions were characterized as an agreement by the United States and the Soviet Union to cooperate in "crisis prevention," as compared to "crisis management." But neither the objective of crisis prevention nor the means for attempting to achieve it were conceptualized in any useful detail. In fact, the agreement to cooperate in order to prevent dangerous crises contained important ambiguities and unresolved disagreements that were to become a major source of friction.

The Basic Principles Agreement included much more than a vague commitment to crisis prevention. It was described by U.S. and Soviet leaders as a sort of charter for détente. In the document the two sides agreed to adopt the practice of periodical high-level meetings, to continue efforts to limit armaments, and to develop economic, scientific, and cultural ties between their two countries on a long-term basis in order to strengthen their relationship. Nixon tried to clarify the nature of the Basic Principles Agreement for the U.S. public by referring to it as a road map. But terms such as "charter" and "road map" were inadequate designations for what had been accomplished and agreed to in Moscow. So far as the analogy of a road map is concerned, the Basic Principles Agreement was certainly not a Cooks Tour itinerary for a voyage that the two parties had decided to embark upon together; it was more in the nature of Lewis and Clark's rough description of uncharted territory. Perhaps a more apt way of characterizing the Basic Principles Agreement would be to explain it as a contractual arrangement of a very loose and general character, the specifics of which remained to be filled in over time. In the parlance of nineteenth-century European diplomacy, the BPA (together with associated agreements and understandings arrived at in the Moscow summit) was in the nature of a rapprochement (i.e., an arrangement in which both sides express a desire to search for agreements on various issues) but went beyond that to an entente (in which the two sides recognize a similarity of views and interests that, however, are limited to certain issues). In other words, as George Breslauer puts it, U.S. and Soviet leaders set out to develop a new relationship of restrained "collaborative competition" to replace the "confrontational competition" of the cold war. However, important aspects of the collaborative competition, including what has been called the "rules" of détente, remained to be worked out.

* * *

Domestic Constraints on Foreign Policy: The Need for Policy Legitimacy

* * *

To conduct a long-range foreign policy of this kind, a president must find ways of dealing with the special requirements for democratic control of foreign policy. Public opinion, Congress, the media, and powerful interest groups often assert themselves in ways that seriously complicate and jeopardize the ability of an administration to pursue long-range foreign policy objectives in a coherent, consistent manner.

* * *

Policy legitimacy for détente was necessary also in the Soviet Union but, of course, the problem of domestic constraints on the conduct of a long-range foreign policy of this kind arises in a less acute form in a nondemocratic political system. Nixon and Kissinger were acutely aware of the dimensions of the challenge they faced in obtaining and maintaining sufficient domestic support for their détente policy. In

his earlier scholarly study of the Concert of Europe system, Kissinger noted the failure of statesmen of that era to maintain domestic support for their policies. "The acid test of a policy," Kissinger emphasized, ". . . is its ability to obtain domestic support. This has two aspects: the problem of legitimizing a policy within the governmental apparatus . . . and that of harmonizing it with the national experience."[2]

Ironically, in the end Kissinger and the two presidents he served also failed to meet the "acid test" of their policy of détente. The problems they encountered in this respect are sobering and have been discussed elsewhere.[3] Suffice it to say that the erosion of domestic support for their complex détente policy increasingly burdened and eventually crippled the effort to develop détente with the Soviet Union. Critical in this respect was the perception that détente was not effective in dissuading Soviet leaders from embarking on an increasingly assertive policy in third areas. In response to this turn of events, President Ford and Kissinger were forced into making a belated effort to define the rules of détente in such a way as to label assertive Soviet actions as violations or, at least, as contrary to the spirit of détente. . . .

Gradually, as the initial promise of détente proved elusive and concern with Soviet policy in third areas mounted, Kissinger began to redefine détente's objectives. In his major defense of détente in September 1974 he had emphasized, still hopefully, that it entailed "the search for a more *constructive relationship* with the Soviet Union. . . ." Almost a year later, in July 1975, as William Hyland notes, Kissinger's emphasis was shifting: "We consider dé-tente a means to regulate a *competitive re-lationship. . . .*"[4] With a further erosion of domestic support for détente that ex-tended to important elements of the Ford administration and the Republican party, the themes of balance of power and con-tainment began to reappear and to assume new prominence in Kissinger's statements regarding the objectives of the administra-tion's foreign policy. While it would be too much to say that détente foundered on the inability of the two superpowers to man-age their rivalry in third areas, the increas-ingly assertive character of Soviet foreign policy in the mid-seventies contributed to erosion of the legitimacy of the détente policy and became a major issue in the presidential election of 1976, first in the contest for the Republican nomination, in which Reagan mounted a strong challenge to President Ford, and then in the presi-dential contest between Ford and Carter.

President Carter attempted to retain and strengthen what remained of the dé-tente relationship, but the efforts of his ad-ministration in this direction were handicapped by inadequate conceptualiza-tion of a comprehensive policy toward the Soviet Union, poor policy implementa-tion, and divided counsels at the highest policymaking level. If Carter had a clear notion of the type of relationship with the Soviet Union that U.S. policy should seek to bring about, that conception was not ac-companied by a well-developed idea of grand strategy or consistently imple-mented with appropriate tactics. Carter never succeeded in gaining policy legiti-macy and stable domestic support for his policy toward the Soviet Union. Soviet ac-tivities in third areas continued to be of concern in Washington and further eroded domestic support for what remained of détente, a trend that developments in Poland accentuated at the beginning of President Reagan's administration.

Notes

[1]Richard M. Nixon, *U.S. Foreign Policy for the 1970's: Building for Peace* (Washington, D.C.: Government Printing Office, February 25, 1971), p. 3.

[2]Henry Kissinger, *A World Restored* (New York: Houghton Mifflin, 1957), p. 327.

[3]Alexander L. George, "Domestic Constraints on Regime Change in U.S. Foreign Policy: The Need for Policy Legitimacy," in *Change in the Interna-tional System*, ed. Ole R. Holsti, Randolph M. Siver-son, and Alexander L. George (Boulder, Colo.: Westview Press, 1980), pp. 233–262.

[4]Henry Kissinger, "Détente with the Soviet Union," address given September 19, 1974 (*Department of State Bulletin*, October 14, 1974); Kissinger, "The Moral Foundations of Foreign Policy," address given July 15, 1975 (*Department of State Bulletin*, August 4, 1975), as quoted in William G. Hyland, *Soviet-American Relations: A New Cold War?* (Santa Monica, Calif.: RAND Corp., May 1981), pp. 31–32. (Italics added.)

The End of the Cold War

JOHN LEWIS GADDIS

The Unexpected Ronald Reagan

∗　∗　∗

It is difficult, now, to recall how far Soviet-American relations had deteriorated at the time Ronald Reagan entered the White House. Some of the responsibility for this rested with Jimmy Carter: at a time when defeat in Vietnam had severely shaken American self-confidence, when the energy crisis appeared to be demonstrating American impotence, when the military balance seemed to be shifting in the Russians' favor, and when the domestic consensus in favor of detente was rapidly dissolving, he had chosen to launch an unprecedented effort to shift the entire basis of foreign policy from power to principle.[1] Carter's timing was terrible; his implementation was haphazard and inconsistent; only his intentions were praiseworthy, and in the climate of the late 1970s, that was not enough.

But the primary responsibility for the decline of detente must rest with the Soviet Union itself, and its increasingly senescent leader, Leonid Brezhnev. Given the long-term economic and social problems that confronted it, the Kremlin needed detente even more than Washington did. And yet, Brezhnev failed to see that he had, in Carter, an American counterpart who sincerely shared that objective; instead he chose to view the administration's fumbling earnestness as a sinister plot directed against Soviet interests. As if to compound this error, Brezhnev also allowed Soviet foreign policy to get caught up in a pattern of imperial overextension like the one that had afflicted the United States in the 1950s and 1960s. For just as the Americans had felt obliged, during those years, to prevent the coming to power of Third World Marxist governments, so the Russians now believed it necessary to sustain such governments, whatever the effect on the Soviet economy, on relations with the West, or on Moscow's overall reputation in world affairs. By equating expansionism with defense, the Soviet leader made the same mistake Stalin had made in the late 1940s: he brought about what he must have most feared. Brezhnev cannot have found it reassuring to know, as he approached the

---

From *The United States and the End of the Cold War: Implications, Reconsiderations, Provocations* (New York: Oxford University Press, 1992), chap. 7.

end of his life, that the invasion of Afghanistan had tarnished the Soviet image in the Third World; that a new American military buildup was under way with widespread domestic support; that an unusually determined NATO alliance had decided to deploy a new generation of missiles capable of striking Moscow itself; that detente was dead; and, most unsettling of all, that Ronald Reagan had become president of the United States.

* * *

The record of the Reagan years suggests the need to avoid the common error of trying to predict outcomes from attributes.[2] There is no question that the President and his advisers came into office with an ideological view of the world that appeared to allow for no compromise with the Russians; but ideology has a way of evolving to accommodate reality, especially in the hands of skillful political leadership. Indeed a good working definition of leadership might be just this—the ability to accommodate ideology to practical reality—and by that standard, Reagan's achievements in relations with the Soviet Union will certainly compare favorably with, and perhaps even surpass, those of Richard Nixon and Henry Kissinger.

Did President Reagan intend for things to come out this way? That question is, of course, more difficult to determine, given our lack of access to the archives. But a careful reading of the public record would, I think, show that the President was expressing hopes for an improvement in Soviet-American relations from the moment he entered the White

House, and that he began shifting American policy in that direction as early as the first months of 1983, almost two years before Mikhail Gorbachev came to power.[3] Gorbachev's extraordinary receptiveness to such initiatives—as distinct from the literally moribund responses of his predecessors—greatly accelerated the improvement in relations, but it would be a mistake to credit him solely with the responsibility for what happened: Ronald Reagan deserves a great deal of the credit as well.

Critics have raised the question, though, of whether President Reagan was responsible for, or even aware of, the direction administration policy was taking.[4] This argument is, I think, both incorrect and unfair. Reagan's opponents have been quick enough to hold him personally responsible for the failures of his administration; they should be equally prepared to acknowledge his successes. And there are points, even with the limited sources now available, where we can see that the President himself had a decisive impact upon the course of events. They include, among others: the Strategic Defense Initiative, which may have had its problems as a missile shield but which certainly worked in unsettling the Russians; endorsement of the "zero option" in the INF [Intermediate-Range Nuclear Forces] talks and real reductions in START [the Strategic Arms Reduction Talks]; the rapidity with which the President entered into, and thereby legitimized, serious negotiations with Gorbachev once he came into office; and, most remarkably of all, his eagerness to contemplate alternatives to the nuclear arms race in a way no previous president had been willing to do.[5]

Now, it may be objected that these were simple, unsophisticated, and, as people are given to saying these days, imperfectly "nuanced" ideas. I would not argue with that proposition. But it is important to remember that while complexity, sophistication, and nuance may be prerequisites for intellectual leadership, they are not necessarily so for political leadership, and can at times actually get in the way. President Reagan generally meant precisely what he said: when he came out in favor of negotiations from strength, or for strategic arms reductions as opposed to limitations, or even for making nuclear weapons ultimately irrelevant and obsolete, he did not do so in the "killer amendment" spirit favored by geopolitical sophisticates on the right; the President may have been conservative but he was never devious. The lesson here ought to be to beware of excessive convolution and subtlety in strategy, for sometimes simple-mindedness wins out, especially if it occurs in high places.

Finally, President Reagan also understood something that many geopolitical sophisticates on the left have not understood: that although toughness may or may not be a prerequisite for successful negotiations with the Russians—there are arguments for both propositions—it is absolutely essential if the American people are to lend their support, over time, to what has been negotiated. Others may have seen in the doctrine of "negotiation from strength" a way of avoiding negotiations altogether, but it now seems clear

that the President saw in that approach the means of constructing a domestic political base without which agreements with the Russians would almost certainly have foundered, as indeed many of them did in the 1970s. For unless one can sustain domestic support—and one does not do that by appearing weak—then it is hardly likely that whatever one has arranged with any adversary will actually come to anything.

There is one last irony to all of this: it is that it fell to Ronald Reagan to preside over the belated but decisive success of the strategy of containment George F. Kennan had first proposed more than four decades earlier. For what were Gorbachev's reforms if not the long-delayed "mellowing" of Soviet society that Kennan had said would take place with the passage of time? The Stalinist system that had required outside adversaries to justify its own existence now seemed at last to have passed from the scene; Gorbachev appeared to have concluded that the Soviet Union could continue to be a great power in world affairs only through the introduction of something approximating a market economy, democratic political institutions, official accountability, and respect for the rule of law at home.[6] And that, in turn, suggested an even more remarkable conclusion: that the very survival of the ideology Lenin had imposed on Russia in 1917 now required infiltration—perhaps even subversion—by precisely the ideology the great revolutionary had sworn to overthrow.

I have some reason to suspect that Professor Kennan is not entirely comfortable with the suggestion that Ronald Reagan successfully completed the execution of the strategy he originated. But as Kennan the historian would be the first to acknowledge, history is full of ironies, and this one, surely, will not rank among the least of them.

Notes

[1] The best overall treatment of Carter administration foreign policy is Gaddis Smith, *Morality, Reason, and Power: American Diplomacy in the Carter Years* (New York: Hill and Wang, 1986).

[2] See, on this point, Kenneth N. Waltz, *Theory of International Relations* (New York: Random House, 1979), p. 61.

[3] See Lou Cannon's account of a secret Reagan meeting with Soviet Ambassador Anatolii Dobrynin in February, 1983, in *President Reagan: The Role of a Lifetime* (New York: Simon and Schuster, 1991), pp. 311–12.

[4] A typical example is Garry Wills, "Mr. Magoo Remembers," *New York Review of Books,* XXXVII (December 20, 1990), 3–4.

[5] Reagan's most perceptive biographer has pointed out that he was guided "both by extraordinary vision and by remarkable ignorance." [Cannon, *President Reagan,* p. 290]. The implication is that the ignorance may have made possible the vision.

[6] Or so it appeared at the time. Whether these principles will survive the pressures that now threaten to break up the Soviet Union remains to be seen.

The End of the Cold War

MIKHAIL GORBACHEV
The Soviet Union's Crucial Role

* * *

If at the first phase of the invasion into Afghanistan, Soviet leaders could nourish hopes for a favorable outcome, it became clear after two to three years that we would be stuck for a long time without any chances of resolving the matter in our favor. As the United States generously supplied the anti-Kabul opposition groups with money and weapons, Afghanistan turned into a whirlpool, sucking in and crushing our manpower and making the related huge expenditures increasingly unbearable for our country. In general, this war was one of the causes for the economic and political crisis that necessitated *perestroika*.

The situation was further worsened by our society's silent and humble reconciliation with this years-long adventure. Unlike the case of Vietnam for the United States, no strong antiwar movement appeared in the USSR. The reason was not only that the lack of *glasnost* and hard-line political pressure ruled out any massive protest. Our public was not aware of the scale of our spending and losses since it received the strictly rationed and propaganda-processed information on actions of the so-called limited contingent of Soviet troops, "the international assistance to the friendly people of Afghanistan," and so on. Of course, rumors were bringing news about the growing number of zinc coffins with the repatriated remains of Soviet soldiers. But the public reacted limply, without emotions, as if paralyzed by some narcotic.

* * *

German Unification and the Fall of Eastern European Communism

First, let me say that unification did not proceed according to a predesigned plan and following predetermined methods and pace. A lot happened spontaneously. As always, history took its own course, frustrating the designs of politicians and diplomats. However, there was an understanding, or, more precisely, a sense of historical inevitability in the course of events.

From Mikhail Gorbachev et al., *Essays on Leadership* (Washington, D.C.: Carnegie Commission on Preventing Deadly Conflict, 1998).

This grew organically from the transformations that were dictated by the new thinking.

Proceeding from the growing interdependence of countries and peoples and from the fact that a universal disaster can be avoided only through collective efforts that require the balancing of interests, we placed a conscious emphasis on the removal of the military-political bloc confrontation, elimination of the Iron Curtain, and integration of the Soviet Union into European and international economic and political structures. This process was inevitably to result in the change of the political arrangement known as the Yalta agreement, which existed on our continent for half a century. Under the new conditions, East European states gained the possibility for self-determination, and it was logical to assume that sooner or later Germans would use this chance to end the half-century of national division.

Therefore, there are no bases for contending that I did not foresee Germany's unification and the collapse of the Warsaw Pact treaty, that all of that fell upon us unexpectedly, and that the Soviet leadership had to simply reconcile itself since it had neither the power nor the possibility to impede such developments.

This is false. In reality, my colleagues and I were aware of the remote consequences of our actions. Having had sufficiently complete information about the situation in our allied states of East and Central Europe—about their difficulties and the growing influence of the opposition forces—it was not hard to imagine that the weakening of the bloc's discipline and of the political control from the "flagship" would lead to a change in power and then in foreign policy. Under these conditions, it seemed logical for us not to run counter to the inevitable, but to do all we could for the process to take place without huge disturbances and to protect to the maximum the interests of our country.

By the way, to this day, traditionalists fiercely blame me for betrayal, saying that I gave away Poland, Czechoslovakia, Hungary, etc. I always reply with a question: "Gave to whom? Poland to the Poles, Czechoslovakia to the Czechs and Slovaks. . . ." Peoples gained the possibility to decide their own destiny. For us, this was a chance to right a historical wrong and to atone for our attempts to keep these countries forceably in the orbit of our influence (i.e., the suppression of disturbances in the German Democratic Republic (GDR) and Poland in 1953, the uprising of Hungarians in 1956, the Prague Spring of 1968, and finally, the building of the Berlin Wall, which came to symbolize the division of Europe and of the world).

I repeat, we were not naive simpletons caught in the net of our own speeches advocating the new thinking. It was not incidentally or as a result of failures and mistakes, but by intention that we gave the possibility to our allied countries to make a free choice. This was not at all easy. There were plenty of people in the Soviet Union who considered it necessary to use any means in order not to lose the fruits of the victory in the Second World War. These voices were heard not only at home. Ceaucescu was persistently addressing me and the other leaders of the Warsaw Pact countries with a demand to undertake an armed invasion into Poland to prevent the removal of the Communist party from power. One needs only to imagine the consequences of one such punitive expedition in the late 1980s to appreciate the significance of the new thinking and the foreign policy course then taken by Moscow.

*   *   *

Looking back, one can see blemishes and mistakes that could have been avoided. But as the saying goes, "one doesn't shake fists after the fight is over." With all the criticism deserved for the actions of the parties involved in that process, it should be acknowledged that most importantly, they withstood the test. They managed to evade bloodshed, which would have been quite possible under the circumstances, managed not to hamper the new strategic nuclear disarmament, and did not push the world back into the Cold War.

The position of the Soviet Union then played a crucial role.

*   *   *

PART **II** *American Foreign Policy in the Twenty-First Century: Choices and Challenges*

6 *Foreign Policy Strategy and Foreign Policy Politics in a New Era*

Introduction: Crumbling Wall and Crashing Towers

What times these are: Soaring highs like the crumbling of the Berlin Wall, an event many hoped for but few believed would come about peacefully. Traumatic lows like the crashing down of the World Trade Center's twin towers through a terrorist attack that shocked America and much of the world on September 11, 2001. And so much else, uplifting and depressing, foreign policy successes and foreign policy failures, causes for gratification and celebration and for criticism and mourning.

Ours are truly times of historic transition. Their frequent labeling as the "post–Cold War era" is very telling: we know more about what they are not than about what they are. One system ended, another one is in the process of emerging. A number of major global forces are at work. They are creating a new context and posing new challenges for American foreign policy.

In the second part of this book we turn to key issues American foreign policy faces in this new era and this new century. Our framework again encompasses both foreign policy strategy and foreign policy politics—the *essence of choice* as it pertains to the core national interest goals of peace, power, prosperity, and principles, and the *process of choice* in the domestic politics of American foreign policy in each of these issue areas. Despite everything that has changed, is power still the name of the game (Chapter 7)? Can a post–Cold War peace and world order be built (Chapter 8)? What are the key foreign economic and social policy challenges for assuring and enhancing prosperity in this age of globalization (Chapter 9)? Will the twenty-first

Onlookers cheer as a man takes a sledgehammer to the Berlin Wall, the destruction of which symbolized the end of the Cold War. (*AP/Wide World Photos*)
The World Trade Center under terrorist attack on September 11, 2001. (*Chris Collins/Corbis*)

century be a democratic one, an era in which principles can and should play ever greater roles in American foreign policy (Chapter 10)? Our study of these questions takes us into many new issues and debates while staying grounded in the theoretical and historical contexts established in Part I.

This chapter provides an overview prior to getting more deeply into these individual issue areas. The first section of this chapter discusses the major historical forces shaping the international system, and the overarching debate between unilateralism and multilateralism as competing paradigms for U.S. foreign policy. The second section examines general patterns in the dynamics of post–Cold War foreign policy politics.

Foreign Policy Strategy for a New Era

The Nature of the New International System

The international system in which U.S. foreign policy operates is being shaped by five sets of broad historical forces: (1) the geopolitics of the end of the Cold War; (2) the "politics of identity" of ethnic, religious, and related conflicts; (3) globalization; (4) global democratization and human rights; and (5) terrorism as a strategic threat in the wake of September 11.

POST–COLD WAR GEOPOLITICS: RELATIONS WITH OTHER MAJOR POW-
ERS AND PERSISTING REGIONAL CONFLICTS   As discussed in Chapters 4
and 5, the Cold War defined the international system and dominated American foreign policy for most of the half-century following the end of World
War II. The structure of the international system during this time was bipolar,
with the United States and the Soviet Union as the two superpowers at each of
the poles. U.S. relations with most other countries in the world were based in
large part on this bipolarity. With the end of the Cold War the alignments and
dynamics of major-power geopolitics were put in flux. We see this today in
U.S. relations both with its former adversaries Russia and China, and with its
major allies, the countries of western Europe and Japan.

U.S.-Russian relations generally have been much more cooperative in
both tone and substance than were U.S.-Soviet relations. The tone has been
set by cordial summits, even downright chumminess, between American and
Russian leaders. In the waning days of the Cold War it was "Ron and Mikhail"
(President Ronald Reagan and Soviet leader Mikhail Gorbachev), then
"George and Mikhail" (referring to President George H.W. Bush), "Bill and
Boris" (Presidents Bill Clinton and Boris Yeltsin), and "George and Vladimir"
(Presidents George W. Bush and Vladimir Putin).[1] On actual policy issues,
though, there has been a mix of cooperation and conflict. On issues such as
the expansion of the U.S.-led North Atlantic Treaty Organization (NATO) as
well as the termination of the 1972 Anti-Ballistic Missile Treaty and the development of a U.S. national missile defense system, there has been more cooperation than many predicted. So too on some aspects of the war on terrorism.
But there also have been issues on which tensions have been high, such as the
1999 Kosovo war and the 2003 Iraq war. And on other issues, such as the conflict in Chechnya, many have felt there has been too little tension, that the
United States should be more critical of Russian human rights abuses.

The key question in the U.S.-Russian relationship is which of three scenarios will prevail as time goes on: friend, competitor, or adversary. Will relations
continue to improve to the point where Russia genuinely would be considered
a friend or even an ally? Are there limits to U.S.-Russian cooperation based on
differences in national interests and other factors that may lead even a noncommunist, non-Soviet Russia to re-emerge as a great-power competitor to
the United States? Or might foreign policy differences become so great or
Russian domestic politics take such a turn that we will end up again as adversaries?

With regard to China, post–Cold War geopolitics actually do cut both
ways. On the one hand, much common ground and cooperation has been

achieved on a range of diplomatic, security, and economic issues. American and Chinese leaders have regularly held summits accompanied by expressions of friendly spirit. Economic relations have boomed. The war on terrorism generally has provided a further basis of shared interests. On the other hand, the end of the Cold War and the disappearance of the shared Soviet enemy meant that issues such as human rights, on which tensions are greater, have come more to the fore. Some worry about China's own emergence as a global geopolitical challenger to the United States, given the former's size, growing military strength, rapid economic growth and technological modernization, and often assertive diplomacy. And the issue of Taiwan remains unresolved and potentially highly explosive.

Thus the overall U.S. policy debate regarding China has been between strategies of *containment* and *engagement*. Should the emphasis be on China as a rising and assertive geopolitical challenger with which cooperation has significant limits and which must be contained? Or is the optimal strategy to engage China in a web of relations and institutions seeking to ensure that its greater global and regional emergence will be along more cooperative lines?

U.S.-European relations have had their own adjustments to make. "Alliances are against, and only derivatively for, someone or something," according to an old international relations axiom.[2] NATO had been formed principally to counter the threat of an invasion from the Soviet Union and its Warsaw Pact allies. With that threat gone, are there strong enough reasons to keep NATO going? The answer depends principally on three key issues: the expansion of NATO membership to include former Soviet and Soviet-bloc countries; how effective NATO is in European intervention and peacekeeping missions like those in the former Yugoslavia (Bosnia, Kosovo, Macedonia); and whether agreement can be reached within the alliance on NATO's global role, including on the war on terrorism, especially following the divisiveness of the 2003 Iraq war.

Moreover, other tensions have arisen in broader U.S.-European relations since the end of the Cold War. Some have been issue-specific, as on the Israeli-Palestinian conflict, international trade, and global warming. Some have been of a more general nature related to efforts on the part of the European Union (EU) to play a more prominent global foreign policy role and to European-American paradigmatic differences over unilateralism and multilateralism as overarching strategies.

In U.S.-Japan relations the key issues have been a mix of economics and security. Whereas Cold War–era U.S.-Japan relations were "characterized by greater cooperation on the security side and diminishing [cooperation] on the economic side," writes Professor Steven Vogel of the University of California at Berkeley, "that pattern may be about to reverse itself."[3] Although trade and other economic disputes continue to arise between the two countries, Japan's own economic problems have diminished its 1970s–80s image as an economic superpower threatening the U.S. position. Security relations, though, have shown signs of becoming more contentious. The United States and Japan did sign a major new security agreement in 1997 that provides a strong basis for adapting their bilateral relationship to the post–Cold War security context. But Japan is continuing to reassess its global and regional role. With China's military growing stronger and the increased threat from North Korea, and amid some concerns about the long-term reliability of U.S. security guarantees, should Japan loosen up its own constitutional provisions that limit its military to only "self-defense" purposes? What about its long-standing policy prohibition on nuclear weapons?

In sum, the end of the Cold War has forced adjustments and in some instances fundamental changes in U.S. relations with the other major powers, as we will discuss further in Chapter 7. Alignments are changing and the dynamics are shifting as a new geopolitics takes place.

Yet as we also discuss, there is much "old" in the geopolitics, notably three regional conflicts that persist from the Cold War era and that still carry the potential for major war: India and Pakistan, North and South Korea, and the Middle East. Making matters worse than before is the danger that the next war in any of these regions could be a nuclear one, since one or more of the parties to each of these conflicts now possesses nuclear weapons.

THE POLITICS OF IDENTITY   Whereas many of the wars and other violent conflicts of the Cold War were driven in part by differences in ideology, the post–Cold War world has been driven more by differences of identity. The "politics of identity" are about who I am, who you are, and what the differences are between us. To be sure, differences of identity can be and have been sources of strength for a society. This is the spirit of diversity and multiculturalism at its best: I can be me, you can be you, and we can learn and gain from our differences and work to bridge them. Problems arise, however, when conceptions of identity come to be antagonistic: I am me, you are you, and our differences are not bridgeable, indeed they are the bases for conflict. When played out this way identity can leave even less room for compromise and coexistence than does ideology—and can rapidly degenerate from the politics of identity to wars of identity.

Although the politics of identity extend far back in history and were at work in the Cold War as well, extreme mass violence has especially characterized the post–Cold War era. The breakup of Yugoslavia and the wars in Bosnia, Croatia, Kosovo, and Macedonia in the decade that followed left close to a million people dead or wounded and almost two million displaced, and added a new term, *ethnic cleansing*, to the lexicon of warfare. In Rwanda, for all the semantic hoops that the Clinton administration and other international leaders jumped through trying not to use the "g" word, there was no denying that a genocide occurred. In just one month in April 1994, rival ethnic Hutus killed over 700,000 ethnic Tutsis. Nor, sadly, were these isolated cases. The politics of identity also fueled deadly conflicts in Somalia, Liberia, Sierra Leone, Congo, Chechnya, Nagorno-Karabakh, Iraq, Kashmir, and other world hot spots.

The foreign policy debate has revolved around three key sets of questions. First, why have these conflicts been so deadly? One argument, the "ancient hatreds" theory, takes a highly historically deterministic view. The emphasis of this theory is on the deep historical roots of these conflicts—the "Balkan ghosts," as Robert Kaplan called them.[4] The end of the Cold War stripped away the constraining effects of bipolar geopolitics, releasing the "Balkan ghosts" and other historical antagonisms to their "natural" states of conflict. The implication of this analysis is that little can be done by the United States or other outsiders other than to wait until the conflicts burn themselves out; then, perhaps, international efforts can be made at peacekeeping and reconstruction.

A contrasting view sees history as shaping but not determinative. This "purposive" view focuses the analysis on forces and factors that intensify and activate historical animosities into actions and policies reflecting conscious and deliberate choices for war and violence. The dominant dynamic is not the playing out of historical inevitability but "the purposeful actions of political actors who actively create violent conflict" to serve their own domestic political agendas "by selectively drawing on history in order to portray [violent conflict] as historically inevitable." The Carnegie Commission on Preventing Deadly Conflict stressed a similar analysis, that "mass violence invariably results from the deliberately violent response of determined leaders and their groups to a wide range of social, economic and political conditions that provide the environment for violent conflict, but usually do not independently spawn violence."[5] The implication of this analysis is that something *can* be done, that the United States and other international actors can have impact.

The second question that arises in the foreign policy debate is, what policies should be pursued? The most frequent response has been to send peacekeeping missions under the auspices of the United Nations or in some cases through NATO or other regional alliances and coalitions. The record for these peacekeeping missions is mixed: some successes, some on which the jury is still out, some major failures. Yet even many of the successes have been successes only in highly relative terms. In Kosovo and East Timor, for example, peacekeeping forces sent by the international community helped stabilize the situations, but only after mass killings, the ravaging of scores of villages, and the displacement of hundreds of thousands as refugees.

An alternative strategy that has worked in some cases, and that many see as having the most potential, is *preventive diplomacy,* which advocates not waiting—acting early to prevent disputes from escalating, to reduce tensions that if intensified could lead to war, to deal with today's conflicts before they become tomorrow's crises. Part of the problem with preventive diplomacy is that the policy logic and the political imperative are out of kilter. Precisely because conflicts are limited in their early stages, the political pressures for action tend to be less intense. Let's wait to see if we need to really act, the dominant thinking goes—only to find all too often that options are fewer and more difficult the longer one waits.

Third, who should play that role? Particularly, what role should the United Nations play and what role should the United States take on? Each has held its successes, each its failures. Each brings its own strengths to these issues, and each its own weaknesses. We discuss these dilemmas more in Chapter 8.

GLOBALIZATION   "If you want to understand the post–Cold War world," writes Thomas Friedman, a Pulitzer Prize–winning columnist for the *New York Times,* "you have to start by understanding that a new international system has succeeded it—globalization. Globalization is not the only thing influencing events in the world today, but to the extent that there is a North Star and a worldwide shaping force, it is this system."[6] Although Friedman may overstate the case, globalization definitely has its place in our framework as one of the five major forces shaping the international system.

Globalization can be understood in terms of its dynamics, its dimensions, and its dilemmas. The basic *dynamic* of globalization is the increasing interconnectedness of the world across nation-state boundaries—interconnections that affect governments, businesses, communities, and people in their everyday lives. Before even getting into whether globalization is good or bad in policy terms, the analytic reality that globalization exists has to be recognized.

Policies can shape it, but they cannot stop or reverse it. The world is too inter-connected to be disconnected.

One key consequence of this reality is the broadening of the foreign policy agenda through the internationalization of many issues traditionally consid-ered domestic. Take, for example, the environment. Back in the 1960s the en-vironment was seen in the United States largely as an area of domestic policy. When the first "Earth Day" was organized in 1970 it was held principally in American cities and on college campuses. In 2000, on Earth Day's thirtieth an-niversary, mobilizations were held in more than 150 countries around the world. Environmental issues are now part of the international agenda be-cause, when it comes to problems such as global warming, neither the United States nor any other single country can resolve the issue on its own, and envi-ronmental problems arising in one country do not stop at that country's bor-ders. The same point applies to other issues that have a global dimension, such as AIDS and other global public-health issues.

This dynamic is further impetus for the rethinking of traditional concepts of state sovereignty. States are not as insulated or self-contained as traditional conceptions of state sovereignty presume. Even in an economy as large as that of the United States, for instance, when the Federal Reserve Board sets interest rates it has to give greater weight to international factors such as the exchange rate and the expectations of foreign investors holding U.S. Treasury bonds than it ever had to in the past, when monetary policy largely was a domestic matter. For smaller or weaker economies, the external pressures are even greater, often including requirements imposed by the International Monetary Fund or other international institutions. This impinging on sovereignty is the analytic reality, separate from any policy judgments about whether it is a good or a bad thing. Prognostications about the "withering of the nation-state" are overstated, but the powerful forces of globalization belie traditional concep-tions of state sovereignty.

What also make today's era of globalization unique are its many *dimen-sions*. Although this is not the first time in history that international trade and finance have expanded rapidly, economic and financial markets today are in-terconnected in more and deeper ways than ever before. Billions of dollars in investments can be transferred from Wall Street to Frankfurt to Hong Kong in the split second it takes to move the cursor on a financial analyst's computer screen. Multinational firms now run factories and other operations in more countries than ever before. Popular consumer products, be they America's McDonald's hamburgers or Japan's Sony CD players, can be found in stores in major cities in almost every country. As recently as 1970 in the United States trade accounted for less than 15 percent of the country's gross domestic product (GDP), today it constitutes more than 30 percent of GDP.

Globalization also features technological, cultural, political, and human dimensions. Communications technologies bring news instantaneously from one end of the world to the other, be it through the BBC (British Broadcasting Company), CNN (Cable News Network), the Arab satellite network Al-Jazeera, or others in this growth industry. The Internet provides an even more widespread communications link that, even with the developing world on the other side of the "digital divide" and much less networked in, puts all types of information at the fingertips of more and more people. Cultural influences intermix across the globe. American culture at times seems omnipresent: ride a bus in Mexico City, Moscow, Johannesburg, Jakarta, or almost any other major city in the world and you'll see advertisements for Hollywood movies. This cultural influence also flows in reverse: visit a shopping center in an ethnic neighborhood in any major American city and in addition to the omnipresent Blockbuster video store you may also see video stores dealing exclusively in Chinese or Vietnamese or Latin American movies. This is one reflection of the flow of peoples in massive numbers and in multiple directions across borders through international migration.

All of these trends pose a number of major policy *dilemmas.* Although each of these issues has its own specific details, in the broadest sense all are manifestations of the challenges of "governance" amid globalization. For a while in the 1990s there was a sense that the global governance agenda was not that complex, that a ready and largely standard formula could be followed. Dubbed the "Washington consensus," the prevailing view was that countries should give highest priority to reducing barriers to international trade and investment, cutting their own government spending, reducing government regulations, and taking other steps to achieve greater economic efficiency and competitiveness. This policy package is rooted in neoclassical economic theory, tracing back to Adam Smith and his conception of "the invisible hand" that makes markets work and maximizes economic growth, providing a "magic of the marketplace," to the benefit of all.

Some, though, disputed this view all along and more did so over time. The key issues have been threefold. First, why have economies overall not grown as projected? The mid-1990s were heady days for many developing and post-communist countries, but by the late 1990s countries such as Argentina, Brazil, Indonesia, and Hungary were being hit by major economic crises. Was the problem inherent in the Washington consensus, or was it that this policy strategy was sound but these countries had not adhered to it? Second, what about equity and the reduction of poverty? Even when economic growth was going strong, the gaps between rich and poor were not closing, whether measured between countries or within countries. Third, the globalization agenda was broadened to include issues of "sustainable development" and "human security" such as the environment, AIDS and other global public-health issues, workers' rights, and human rights. These issues define an agenda in tension with policies more strictly grounded in the Washington consensus and based primarily on marketplace magic and the invisible hand. We will pick this debate up again in Chapter 9.

The dynamics, dimensions, and dilemmas of globalization have brought into the policy arena a greater array of international actors, particularly nongovernmental organizations (NGOs). These include not only U.S.-based NGOs but also many others with bases in Europe as well as in the developing countries. The role of NGOs is discussed more later in this chapter.

GLOBAL DEMOCRATIZATION AND HUMAN RIGHTS   How captivating was the drama, how exhilarating the joy, how inspiring the sense of hope of those amazing days that marked the beginning of the 1990s. The Berlin Wall, that starkest symbol of the Cold War, crumbled as young Berliners from East and West danced on it. Nelson Mandela, imprisoned for almost thirty years by the apartheid government of South Africa, was set free, and four years later he was elected president of a post-apartheid South Africa. Nicaragua, a country that endured a decade of civil war and had a long history of U.S. intervention and occupation, held its first free elections ever. A coup attempt in the Soviet Union was put down by the Russian people, led by the defiant Russian president, Boris Yeltsin, standing on a tank. Vaclav Havel, among the first democratically elected presidents in postcommunist eastern Europe, quoted Thomas Jefferson in his inaugural address as president of Czechoslovakia. Havel's words (see Perspectives on page 298) conveyed a post–Cold War answer to the "why do they like us" question.

Amid these and other events there was a sense that the world was witnessing "the end of history," as scholar Francis Fukuyama termed it—not just the end of the Cold War but "the universalization of Western liberal democracy as the final form of human government":

> Western liberal democracy seems at its close to be returning full circle to where it started: not to an "end of ideology" or a convergence between capitalism and socialism, as earlier predicted, but to an unabashed victory of economic and political liberalism. . . . The triumph of the West, of the Western *idea,* is evident . . . in the total exhaustion of viable systematic alternatives to Western liberalism.[7]

PERSPECTIVES
PERSPECTIVES

PERSPECTIVES

"WHY THEY LIKE US"

Czechoslovak president Vaclav Havel's speech to the U.S. Congress, 1990

Twice in this century, the world has been threatened by a catastrophe. Twice this catastrophe was born in Europe, and twice Americans, along with others, were called upon to save Europe, the whole world and yourselves. . . .

Thanks to the great support of your President Wilson, our first President, Tomas Garrigue Masaryk, was able to found a modern independent state. He founded it, as you know, on the same principles on which the United States of America had been founded, as Masaryk's manuscripts held by the Library of Congress testify.

At the same time, the United States made enormous strides. It became the most powerful nation on earth, and it understood the responsibility that flowed from this. Proof of this are the hundreds of thousands of your young citizens who gave their lives for the liberation of Europe, and the graves of American airmen and soldiers on Czechoslovak soil. . . .

[You] contributed to the salvation of us Europeans, of the world and thus of yourselves for a third time. You have helped us to survive until today without a hot war this time, merely a cold one. . . . [T]hese revolutionary changes will enable us to escape from the rather antiquated straitjacket of this bipolar view of the world, and to enter . . . into an era in which all of us, large and small, former slaves and former masters, will be able to create what your great President Lincoln called "the family of man." . . .

Wasn't it the best minds of your country, people you could call intellectuals, who wrote your Declaration of Independence, your Bill of Rights and your Constitution and who above all took upon themselves the practical responsibility for putting them into practice? The worker from Branik in Prague, whom your president referred to in his State of the Union message this year, is far from being the only person in Czechoslovakia, let alone in the world, to be inspired by those great documents. They inspire us all. They inspire us despite the fact that they are over 200 years old. They inspire us to be citizens.

(*Continued on page 299*)

("**Why They Like Us**" *Continued from page 298*)

When Thomas Jefferson wrote that "Governments are instituted among Men, deriving their just powers from the Consent of the Governed," it was a simple and important act of the human spirit. What gave meaning to that act, however, was the fact that the author backed it up with his life. It was not just his words, it was his deeds as well.

Source: http://www.hrad.cz/president/Havel/speeches/1990/2102_uk.html.

This excerpt captures the sweeping essence of Fukuyama's thesis. He didn't claim that all conflict is over, or that there won't be a few communist "isolated true believers." But he did see the big issues of world affairs as having been settled once and for all.

As the 1990s went on, however, history came roaring back. In Bosnia, Rwanda, East Timor, Liberia, Sierra Leone, and elsewhere, the world witnessed horrors and inhumanity that many had hoped were part of the past. Politics was once again more about bullets than ballots—indeed, not just bullets but machetes and mass mutilations. In other countries, including China, where the 1989 Tiananmen Square protests were crushed with killings and mass arrests, human rights were trampled. In Latin America, a new wave of military coups showed all too clearly that the past had not gone away. In the Islamic world, although some progress was being made, there still was not a single country that could be pointed to as a full democracy.

A very different view from Fukuyama's was offered by Harvard's Professor Samuel Huntington in his 1993 article "The Clash of Civilizations." "It is my hypothesis," Huntington wrote,

> that the fundamental source of conflict in this new world will not be primarily ideological or primarily economic. The great divisions among humankind and the dominating source of conflict will be cultural. . . . [T]he principal conflicts of global politics will occur between nations and groups of different civilizations. The clash of civilizations will dominate global politics. The fault lines between civilizations will be the battle lines of the future. . . . [T]he paramount axis of world politics will be the relations between "the West and the Rest."

Huntington started with a definition of "civilization" and the reasons for attributing significant causality to it:

> Civilizations are differentiated from each other by history, language, culture, tradition and, most important, religion. The people of different civilizations have different views of God and man, the individual and the group, the citizen and the state, parents and children, husband and wife, as well as differing views of the relative importance of rights and responsibilities, liberty and authority, equality and hierarchy.

These differences, he argued, are even more fundamental than those over political ideologies or economic systems. They are "the product of centuries. They will not soon disappear."[8]

All told, as the world entered what had been proclaimed as the "democratic century," the record was more mixed and the outlook less clear than it had seemed in those heady days of 1989. The policy choices facing the United States thus were more complicated than they had seemed. At one level the issue was how much priority to give to democracy promotion and human rights protection in defining the U.S. national interest (i.e., how much to favor principles over the other Ps). Even to the extent that principles were given priority, the next issue was how to ensure that policies aimed at democracy promotion and human rights protection were effective. The holding of free and fair elections in countries that had never or rarely had them before clearly was an important goal. But the consolidation and institutionalization of democracy and human rights were broader and longer-term challenges. As we will see, U.S. policies under the first Bush, Clinton, and second Bush administrations have had a decidedly mixed record, and there is much to be learned from both their successes and their failures.

One clear lesson is not to overestimate what the U.S. role could be: it is not within American capacity, nor that of any other single country or international institution, to assure the success of democracy or the protection of human rights around the world. The corollary lesson, though, is not to underestimate the American role; democracy is much less likely to spread and deepen without strong and sustained U.S. support.

SEPTEMBER 11 AND TERRORISM   It is true that terrorism goes way back in history, "as far back as does human conflict itself," as historian Caleb Carr has written.[9] It also is true that terrorism has been part of the contemporary U.S. foreign policy agenda since at least the early 1970s. As Table 6.1 shows, numerous terrorist incidents marked the 1970s, 1980s, and 1990s. The peak rate, in fact, was in the 1980s. In the 1990s, although terrorism overall declined, the percentage of incidents involving the United States and its citizens increased.

TABLE 6.1 Terrorism before September 11

	1970s	1980s	1990s
Annual average number of terrorist incidents	405	543	382
Percentage involving U.S.	42	31	35
Number of deaths	277	483	293

Source: Audrey Kurth Cronin, "Rethinking Sovereignty: American Strategy in an Age of Terror," *Survival*, 44:2 (Summer 2002), 124, 126, 128.

Still, most of us always will remember where we were when we first heard the news on September 11, 2001, when we first saw the images, when we first felt the fear. The shock of the crashing twin towers and the gashes in the walls of the Pentagon—symbols of American economic and military strength—seared deeply into the American psyche.

Beyond the immediate shock and crisis, September 11 affected U.S. foreign policy strategy in four fundamental ways. First, more than ever before in its modern history, the United States was proven vulnerable right at home. Foreign policy usually had been about U.S. involvements "over there"—in the Middle East, in the developing world, in Europe, in Asia. Now the threat was "here," on the American side of the oceans. Not since the bloodiest battles of the U.S. Civil War (1861–65) had as many Americans been killed in a single day. Not since the War of 1812, when the British attacked Washington, D.C., and set fire to the White House, had America's own capital been attacked. Even Pearl Harbor was an attack on a military base, not on cities and civilian populations. For Americans, the sense of threat was greater than at any time since the end of the Cold War. And once again, an Enemy had arisen—one with vehement ideological hatred of the United States (see Perspectives on p. 302).

Second, the dangers for the future are even more ominous. Government and nongovermental experts alike increasingly assess the terrorist use of weapons of mass destruction (WMD)—nuclear, chemical, or biological—as a matter of when, not if. A glimpse of this foreboding future came with the "anthrax letter bombs" in the weeks after the September 11 attacks. The actual death toll was only five, but the fear sown and the havoc wreaked by even such a limited incident gave some sense of what more massive WMD terrorism

PERSPECTIVES
PERSPECTIVES

PERSPECTIVES

"WHY THEY HATE US"

Bin Laden and other voices of anti-Americanism

We declared jihad against the U.S. government, because the U.S. government is unjust, criminal, and tyrannical. It has committed acts that are extremely unjust, hideous, and criminal whether directly or through its support of the Israeli occupation of the Prophet's Night Travel Land [Palestine]. And we believe the U.S. is directly responsible for those who were killed in Palestine, Lebanon, and Iraq. . . . The whole Muslim world is the victim of international terrorism, engineered by America at the United Nations.

Osama bin Laden

The state of instability in international relations has widened as a result of unilateral management of international affairs on the basis of the law of brute force. . . . Attempts are escalating to impose certain cultures on the peoples of the world, to heap scorn on their religious beliefs and creeds and their political and social choices, and to preach the clash of civilizations and the launching of new crusades. It was under these circumstances that the events of September 11 took place. . . .

Naji Sabri, Iraqi foreign minister under Saddam Hussein

We should also be aware that much of the world regards Washington as a terrorist regime. In recent years, the U.S. has taken or backed actions in Colombia, Nicaragua, Panama, Sudan and Turkey, to name a few, that meet official U.S. definitions of "terrorism"—that is, when Americans apply the terms to enemies.

Noam Chomsky

Sources: Osama Bin Laden: Interview with Peter Arnett, *CNN,* March 1997
http://news.findlaw.com/cnn/docs/binladen/binladenintvw-cnn.pdf

Naji Sabri: Statement of Naji Sabri, Minister of Foreign Affairs of the Republic of Iraq at the 56th Session of the General Assembly of the United Nations, November 14, 2001, http://www.un.org/webcast/ga/56/statements/011114iraqE.htm

Noam Chomsky: "Drain the Swamp and There Will Be No More Mosquitoes," *Z Magazine Online,* September 10, 2002,
http://www.zmag.org/content/showarticle.cfm?SectionID=11&ItemID=2312

could do. The capabilities existed to cause such havoc—both in the form of conscious efforts made by various states and groups to acquire them, and as an unintended consequence of the spread of technology and information through the broader processes of globalization. The intentions to use those capabilities are likely to continue to exist as well, be they with Al Qaeda or Iraq or some other group or country.

Third, terrorism shifted from being a problem that came and went with this or that incident to becoming the top strategic priority for U.S. foreign policy. Prior to September 11, terrorism had been dealt with largely through limited policy instruments, in terms of both scope (how extensive the uses of force or other coercion) and duration (how long the measures lasted). Economic sanctions were imposed in a number of cases, going back to the Export Administration Act of 1979, which first required the State Department to compile its annual list of state sponsors of terrorism. But economic sanctions, it turned out, were of limited effectiveness. Military force was used in a few cases, such as the Reagan administration's 1986 bombing of Libya in retaliation for Libyan leader Muammar Qaddafi's terrorism against American soldiers stationed in Berlin, Germany; and the Clinton administration's 1998 cruise missile strikes against Osama bin Laden's Al Qaeda bases in Afghanistan and an alleged chemical weapons factory in Sudan in response to the bombing of two U.S. embassies in Africa. But these were limited attacks and they, too, had limited effectiveness. Intelligence operations also had been mounted, but as we learned after September 11, they were not a very high priority, not very well coordinated, and not very well carried out. "We are at war,"

Osama bin Laden, leader of Al Qaeda *(AFP/Corbis)*

President Bush told the nation on October 7, 2001, in announcing the military action against the Taliban regime and Al Qaeda's terrorist network in Afghanistan. And he didn't mean just against Afghanistan. The struggle Bush was referring to was global, and it was for the long term. It was not a classical war, but it was war nevertheless. Other foreign policy issues had to be dealt with, but there was no higher priority than the war on terrorism.

Fourth was a major shift in doctrine on the use of force from an emphasis on deterrence to one on pre-emption. Recall the discussion in Chapter 4 of the logic of containment and deterrence during the Cold War. The view then was that (a) the Soviet threat could be lived with so long as communism and Soviet influence were not allowed to spread (i.e., containment), and (b) U.S. and allied security could be assured against the possibility of a Soviet nuclear attack through the threat of a second strike (deterrence). So long as the Soviets knew that the United States could inflict unacceptable damage even if the Soviets struck first, they were deterred from initiating a first strike.

But in the Bush administration's view this logic of containment and deterrence would not work against terrorism and terrorists. The threat they posed was not one that could be lived with; terrorists were too committed to indiscriminate killing to just be contained. And since terrorists did not have capitals, regular military installations, or major population centers against which to threaten retaliation, there could not be the same confidence in deterrence. The Bush administration thus pushed for a shift to a doctrine of pre-emption, of first and early strikes based on assessments of a likely major threat. President Bush summarized this changed view in a June 2002 speech at West Point:

> For much of the last century, America's defense relied on the Cold War doctrines of deterrence and containment. In some cases, those strategies still apply. But new threats also require new thinking. Deterrence—the promise of massive retaliation against nations—means nothing against shadowy terrorist networks with no nation or citizens to defend. Containment is not possible when unbalanced dictators with weapons of mass destruction can deliver those weapons on missiles or secretly provide them to terrorist allies.[10]

The U.S. doctrine on using force, therefore, would have to shift from relying on after-the-incident retaliations to pre-emptive action. "If we wait for threats to fully materialize, we will have waited too long. . . . [O]ur security will require all Americans to be forward-looking and resolute, to be ready for pre-emptive action when necessary to defend our liberty and to defend our lives."[11] This new doctrine was elaborated in the president's *National Security Strategy of the United States,* issued in September 2002 (see At the Source on p. 306), and was manifested six months later in the Iraq war.

These doctrines and other aspects of the U.S. war on terrorism are hotly debated, as we will go more into in Chapter 7.

In the immediate aftermath of September 11, then, we heard much talk about how "everything had changed." Yet as profound as these changes were, they were not the only forces at work shaping this new era. The other four historical forces discussed in this section—the end of the Cold War, the politics of identity, globalization, and global democratization and human rights—were already at work. They were the agenda as of September 10. And although they were quite understandably superceded for a while amid the shock of September 11, they did not go away. The challenge facing the United States today is dealing with both the September 10 agenda and the September 11 one—a challenge that defies any claims about the "unimportance" of foreign policy and instead defines this new era as among the most complex that the United States ever has faced.

The Unilateralism versus Multilateralism Debate

The debate about the U.S. role in this changing world often is cast in terms of unilateralism vs. multilateralism. *Unilateralism* can be defined as an approach to foreign policy that emphasizes actions taken by a nation largely on its own, or acting with others but largely on its own terms. *Multilateralism* emphasizes acting with other nations through processes that are more consultative and consensual as structured by international institutions, alliances, and coalitions. Although the distinction is one of degree and not a strict dichotomy, this contrast helps frame the debate over how to define the U.S. role in the world.

The contrast also comes through in comparing the foreign policies of the Clinton and second Bush administrations. The Clinton approach was largely multilateralist whenever possible and unilateral only when necessary, whereas the Bush approach is largely unilateralist whenever possible and multilateral only when necessary.

This section will draw on examples from these two administrations as well as from the broader literature to lay out the competing cases for unilateralism and multilateralism as broad frameworks for U.S. foreign policy strategy. We will get more into specific policies in the chapters that follow.

At the Source

PRESIDENT GEORGE W. BUSH'S PRE-EMPTION DOCTRINE

❝ Defending our Nation against its enemies is the first and fundamental commitment of the Federal Government. Today, that task has changed dramatically. Enemies in the past needed great armies and great industrial capabilities to endanger America. Now, shadowy networks of individuals can bring great chaos and suffering to our shores for less than it costs to purchase a single tank. Terrorists are organized to penetrate open societies and turn the power of modern technologies against us.

To defeat this threat we must make use of every tool in our arsenal—military power, homeland defenses, law enforcement, intelligence, and vigorous efforts to cut terrorist financing. . . .

The gravest danger our Nation faces lies at the crossroads of radicalism and technology. Our enemies have openly declared that they are seeking weapons of mass destruction, and evidence indicates that they are doing so with determination. The United States will not allow these efforts to succeed. We will build defenses against ballistic missiles and other means of delivery. We will cooperate with other nations to deny, contain and curtail enemies' efforts to acquire dangerous technologies. And, as a matter of common sense self-defense, America will act against such emerging threats before they are fully formed. We cannot defend America and our friends by hoping for the best. So we must be prepared to defeat our enemies' plans, using the best intelligence and proceeding with deliberation. History will judge harshly those who saw this coming danger but failed to act. In the world we have entered, the only path to peace and security is the path of action. . . .

While the United States will constantly strive to enlist the support of the international community, we will not hesitate to act alone, if necessary, to exercise our right of self-defense by acting pre-emptively against such terrorists, to prevent them from doing harm against our people and our country. . . . ❞

Source: George W. Bush, *National Security Strategy for the United States, 2002,* http://www.whitehouse.gov/nsc, 1, 6.

THE CASE FOR UNILATERALISM   The unilateralist foreign policy strategy is based on six main points.

Realism   Unilateralism is grounded in the Realist paradigm of international relations theory. The end of the Cold War is seen as the closing of a particular era of "power politics," but not the elimination of the struggle and rivalry for power that are the essence of international relations. To think otherwise, as political scientist John Mearsheimer and other leading Realists argue, is ahistorical and dangerously naive.[12] Power politics has been the way of the world for twelve hundred years, through many historical transitions no less sweeping than our own—on what basis would one conclude that our era is so fundamentally different? We must not forget the lessons learned the hard way from the 1920s and 1930s. That was a time when power supposedly didn't matter as much because there was an international institution like the League of Nations and treaties like the 1928 Kellogg-Briand Pact (named in part for the American secretary of state, Frank Kellogg), which simply declared war illegal. Yet, as British scholar Martin Wight wrote, such views were "a chimera. . . . International politics have never revealed, nor do they today, a habitual recognition among states of a community of interest overriding their separate interests, comparable to that which normally binds individuals within the state. . . . The only principle of order is to try to maintain, at the price of perpetual vigilance, an even distribution of power."[13]

Today, no less than then, as far as Realists are concerned, "international institutions have minimal influence on state behavior, and thus hold little promise for promoting stability in the post–Cold War world." Foreign policy competition is an inherently stronger dynamic among states than is foreign policy cooperation. States always have sought and always will seek "opportunities to take advantage of one another" as well as to "work to insure that other states do not take advantage of them."[14]

Power, Unipolarity   "Power matters," wrote Condoleezza Rice, who would just months later become President Bush's national security adviser. The problem, though, as Rice and other Bush strategists saw it, has been that "many in the United States are (and always have been) uncomfortable with the notions of power politics, great powers, and power balances."[15] The Clinton administration in particular and multilateralists in general were the implied targets of this critique. The Bush team billed itself as having no such discomfort. Indeed, now more than ever it felt American foreign policy makers should not have such concerns.

As former secretary of state Henry Kissinger put it in the very first line of a recent book, "the United States is enjoying a pre-eminence unrivaled by even the greatest empires of the past."[16] Scholars Stephen Brooks and William Wohlforth concurred: "There has never been a system of sovereign states that contained one state with this degree of dominance."[17] With the fall of the Soviet Union, the bipolar Cold War system had become a "unipolar" system with the United States as the sole surviving superpower. U.S. military superiority was first demonstrated in the 1991 Persian Gulf War, then in the 2001 Afghanistan war and then the 2003 Iraq war. Its military spending is greater than that of Russia, China, and the next top thirteen military spenders combined. The American economy had outpaced the world in growth and innovation in the 1990s, and even amid the recession that followed still enjoyed unrivaled economic power. The "inescapable reality" of today's world, conservative commentators William Kristol and Robert Kagan asserted, is "American power in its many forms."[18] American foreign policy should be geared to maintaining this "primacy," as some theorists call it, or "preponderance," as others call it,[19] for as we have known since the ancient Greek philosopher Thucydides, "the strong do what they have the power to do, and the weak accept what they have to accept."[20]

Benevolent Hegemony   The United States is a benign superpower, or benevolent hegemon, committed to using its power to preserve peace and promote democratic values. This vision was posed in the Bush 2002 *National Security Strategy* as promoting "a balance of power that favors freedom": "The United States possesses unprecedented—and unequaled—strength and influence in the world. . . . [T]his position comes with unparalleled responsibilities, obligations and opportunity. The great strength of this nation must be used to promote a balance of power that favors freedom."[21] American power and dominance thus are to be feared only by those who oppose peace and freedom.

This outlook in part reflects the Realist view that international order is most possible with a dominant hegemon. It also is rooted in part in the self-conception of American exceptionalism—the view that the United States is different from classical great powers in that it pursues peace and principles as well as power. "The United States would lead the civilized world," as one scholar captures this view, "in the expansion and consolidation of a liberal world order."[22] It thus is in everyone's interest, or at least in the interest of the peace-loving and democratic-spirited, for the United States to assert its power and to maintain its freedom of action with minimal impingements from treaties and other multilateral obligations. It is in this sense that the argument is said to be "hard-headed," not hard-hearted—in effect, American unilateralism is multilateral in function even if not in form.[23]

Some unilateralists have a sharper edge to their hegemonic arguments. Richard Perle, a former Reagan administration official and prominent adviser to the second Bush administration, argued for a largely unilateral approach to the war on terrorism because "the price you end up paying for an alliance is collective judgment, collective decision-making." Perle went on to question whether in this case, and indeed more generally, "the source of enthusiasm for the coalition . . . is a strong desire on the part of those who are promoting the coalition to see the United States restrained."[24] Perle's speech was titled "Next Stop, Iraq," and it was given in November 2001, almost a year and a half before the war with Iraq began.

National, not Global, Interests   Unilateralists stress the distinction between the U.S. national interest and global interests. They criticize multilateralists for thinking too much in terms of "humanitarian interests" and the "international community," and too little in terms of the national interest. "There is nothing wrong with doing something that benefits all humanity," wrote Rice, "but that is, in a sense, a second-order effect" of pursuing the national interest.[25] That is to say, what is good for the world is not a sufficient goal in itself for U.S. foreign policy. Global interests may be satisfied by the pursuit of the national interest but are not on their own a justification for major foreign policy commitments and undertakings.

It was along these lines that the Clinton administration was criticized for its position on international commitments such as the Comprehensive Test Ban Treaty, the International Criminal Court, and the Kyoto global warming treaty for being "so anxious to find multilateral solutions to problems that it has signed agreements that are not in America's interest."[26] This also was the essence of the critique of humanitarian military interventions as "social work" by the Bush administration and others, and not in most cases a sufficiently vital U.S. national interest to warrant the use of force and especially the commitment of U.S. troops.[27]

Inefficacy of Multilateralism   In addition to all these points about the positives of unilateralism, there are the negatives of multilateralism. It doesn't work very well, to put it frankly. Some acknowledgment is granted to the role of international institutions such as the United Nations and the possibilities of international cooperation, but only as partial constraints on international competition and the potential for conflict. This was Mearsheimer's point when he said that "international institutions have minimal influence on state behavior, and thus hold little promise for promoting stability in the post–Cold War world."[28] It also was a main reason that the Bush administration opted for the more unilateral route for the Iraq war.

The inherent problems are ones of both process and impact. The process problem arises out of so many countries with so many national interests trying to act jointly. Making decisions and building consensus among such a large number of states with such disparate interests may hinder prompt action or dilute policies that need to be clear and firm. Moreover, if decisions are made on a one country–one vote basis, the United States is left with the same voting weight as Ecuador, Burkina Faso, Luxembourg, and other small countries. Procedures such as the veto power wielded by the United States on the UN Security Council only partially alleviate this problem.

The problem of impact is rooted in a view of international law, as expressed by Undersecretary of State John Bolton, as "deeply and perhaps irrevocably flawed."[29] Unilateralists have specific critiques of particular institutions such as the UN and particular treaties such as the International Criminal Court and the Kyoto Protocol on global warming, as we will see in later chapters. But even beyond these particulars, unilateralists are highly skeptical even of best-case scenarios of the role of multilateral institutions and treaties in keeping international order and their value for American foreign policy.

Conservative Domestic Politics   Unilateralists raise the specter of America's own constitutional democracy being undermined by the impingements of multilateral institutions and agreements and other aspects of global governance. This debate over safeguarding American sovereignty against multilateralism "fought out at the confluence of constitutional theory and foreign policy," to again quote Bolton, "is *the* decisive issue facing the United States internationally."[30] On issues such as the jurisdiction of the International Criminal Court over American soldiers and other citizens, or U.S. troops under foreign command in UN peacekeeping operations, the debate is said to be a constitutional one, not just a foreign policy one.

Domestic politics also bring more baldly electoral considerations. The noted historian Arthur Schlesinger, Jr., a strong supporter of multilateralism and particularly of the UN, nevertheless notes that "there is no older American tradition in the conduct of foreign affairs" than unilateralism.[31] Unilateralism taps the self-concept of American exceptionalism in ways that have political appeal even if, as in Schlesinger's view, it is a hubris that is bad for the United States as well as for the world. Unilateralists are positioned well politically because they can claim to be more concerned than their multilateralist opponents with "what's good for America" and play to fears and prejudices about the outside world. UN-bashing in particular has great appeal to these groups, many of which are especially influential in the conservative wing of the Republican Party. Right-wing militia groups adhere to an extreme version of this view, with their paranoia about the UN seeking to take over and even invade the United States.

THE CASE FOR MULTILATERALISM   Multilateralism has its own case to be made, which also can be summarized in six main points.

International Institutionalism Liberal Internationalism   Multilateralism is grounded in the International Institutionalist paradigm. The essence of this paradigm, as laid out in Chapter 1, is an emphasis on the building of a system of international institutions, organizations, and regimes that provide the basis for cooperation among states to resolve tensions, settle disputes, and work together in ways that are mutually beneficial and, above all, to avoid war.[32] With reference to the relatively peaceful end that the Cold War came to, International Institutionalist scholars such as John Ruggie contend that "there seems little doubt that multilateral norms and institutions have helped stabilize [the] international consequences." And as to the post–Cold War world, "such norms and institutions appear to be playing a significant role in the management of a broad array of regional and global changes in the world system today."[33] We are entering the post–Cold War era, in this view, with international institutions that, while well short of "world government" and not without their weaknesses, are quite strong and have the potential to be made stronger.

International institutionalists see a Realism of their own in these views. Their Realism takes the system as it is, not as it used to be. The United States is unquestionably the strongest country, but it is neither in the U.S. interest, nor even within the realm of achievability, for the United States to try to maintain peace and security on its own. It often does need to be the lead actor, and at times it needs to act unilaterally, but the greatest power is the power of numbers that comes with effective multilateralism.

This line of thinking characterized much of the Clinton administration's foreign policy:

6.2

International cooperation will be vital for building security in the next century because many of the challenges we face cannot be addressed by a single nation. Many of our security objectives are best achieved—or can only be achieved—by leveraging our influence and capabilities through international organizations, our alliances, or as a leader of an ad hoc coalition formed around a specific objective. Leadership in the United Nations and other international organizations, and durable relationships with allies and friendly nations, are critical to our security.[34]

It also came through in the thinking of the "Powell faction" within the Bush administration. Richard Haass, who as director of the State Department's policy planning staff was a top aide to Secretary of State Colin Powell, laid out a "doctrine of integration" and a strategy of shifting from "a balance of power to a pooling of power":

In the twenty-first century, the principal aim of American foreign policy is to integrate other countries and organizations into arrangements that will sustain a world consistent with U.S. interests and values, and thereby promote peace, prosperity and justice as widely as possible. . . . Integration is about bringing nations together and then building frameworks of cooperation and, when feasible, institutions that reinforce and sustain them even more. . . . With war between great powers almost unthinkable, we can turn our efforts from containment and deterrence to consultation and cooperation. We can move from a balance of power to a pooling of power.[35]

Haass and others claimed that their multilateralism was more "hard-headed" than the Clinton version, but it seemed to share as much if not more with their predecessors than with the unilateralists within their own administration.

Power-Influence Conversion, Soft Power   Second is the distinction between power and influence in measuring international leadership, position, and system structure. Multilateralists acknowledge the huge power advantages the United States has both militarily and economically. But they are less apt to speak of unipolarity, preponderance, and primacy because of their greater emphasis on the difficulties of converting power to influence. In their view, the unilateralists are too quick to assume that the possession of power brings the exertion of influence. It is one thing to have more power than another country, but quite another to get that country to do what you want it to do, and to ensure that outcomes are what you want them to be. The "conversion" of power to influence quite often involves persuasion and the use of what

Harvard professor Joseph Nye calls "soft power." Although coercion and "hard power" remain a key currency in the realm of international politics, persuasion and soft power often can be more effective tools. As Nye wrote,

> Military power remains crucial in certain situations, but it is a mistake to focus too narrowly on the military dimensions of American power. . . . Soft power is also more than persuasion or the ability to move people by argument. It is the ability to entice and attract. And attraction often leads to acquiescence or imitation. . . . If I can get you to *want* to do what I want, then I do not have to force you to do what you do *not* want to do.[36]

Thus, achieving foreign policy objectives is not as simple as Thucydides' dictum about the powerful doing what they want makes it sound. Advantages in military and economic power clearly help but do not always suffice. Moreover, if hard power is wielded in ways that exacerbate tensions or antagonize others, it can be even more difficult to achieve the influence that is key to effective leadership. This more nuanced view of the nature of power and the dynamics of influence is something that, as Nye put it, "unilateralists forget at their and our peril."[37]

Not-So-Benign Hegemony   Third is a questioning of whether other nations generally share the "benevolent hegemon" view that unilateralists claim for the United States. The essence of U.S. Cold War leadership was the overriding sense that others, at least in the noncommunist world, generally did benefit from the U.S. pursuit of its own national interest. It wasn't just that the United States claimed its hegemony to be benign; others generally saw it that way as well. In this era, though, on a number of issues, other countries, including many U.S. allies, see their interests as being hurt rather than helped by the U.S. pursuit of its own interests. The Bush administration sees it as in the U.S. interest to use military force unilaterally, including pre-emptively, when necessary; other nations and the UN not only disagree on specific cases but are concerned about the broader destabilizing effects, such as the undermining of international norms of nonintervention. The Bush administration has opposed the Kyoto global warming treaty as not in U.S. interests; the countries that have signed this treaty see their interests as hurt by the unwillingness of the world's largest producer of the emissions that are causing the problem to be part of the treaty. The Bush administration unilaterally imposed tariffs on steel imports in 2002 and claimed to be acting in accord with the World Trade Organization (WTO) system; those nations whose steel industries bore the costs saw this as U.S. exploitation of its economic power and as contrary to the WTO's multilateral rules. Although the general critique stops short of casting the United States as a malevolent hegemon, it does see it as not so benign.

National and Global Interests   Multilateralists tend to agree that if a choice has to be made, the national interest must come first. But they see the national interest and global interests as much more interconnected. So many of the foreign policy issues we face today simply cannot be solved by one nation acting alone. Even the best national environmental policies would not be sufficient to deal with global warming; global policies are needed for a global problem. Even the tightest homeland security will not be enough to guarantee against the global threat of terrorism; cooperation is needed from as many countries as possible against terrorists wherever they may be. It is basic logic that if the scope of the problem spans national boundaries, the policy strategies for dealing with it must have comparable reach. The national interest and global interests are more complementary and less competing than unilateralists claim. Whatever freedom of action is given up, it is outweighed by the capacity gained to achieve shared objectives and serve national interests in ways that are less possible unilaterally.

Correct, not Reject
Yes, the United Nations and other multilateral institutions have problems. But the optimal strategy is to correct them, not reject them. Professors Robert Keohane and Lisa Martin lay out in functional terms the theoretical basis for why international institutions develop: "Institutions can provide information, reduce transaction costs, make commitments more credible, establish focal points for coordination and, in general, facilitate the operation of reciprocity."[38] In so doing international institutions help states overcome the difficulties of collective action, which as discussed earlier, can persist even when states have common interests. This is a very rational argument, much more pragmatically grounded than classical Wilsonian idealism. The world envisioned is not one strictly free of tensions and conflicts. But it is one in which the prospects for achieving cooperation and the policy benefits of doing so are greater than unilateralists are willing to acknowledge. Substantial progress has been made in recent years in reforming the UN; more needs to be done and can be done if people would just get past bashing the institution. The Kyoto treaty does have its flaws, so shift the debate to amending it, not discarding it. So too with the International Criminal Court, arms control treaties and organizations, and other multilateral measures—correct them, don't reject them.

Liberal Domestic Politics   Multilateralism has broader but less intense domestic political support than does unilateralism. Public-opinion polls show, for example, that support for the United Nations averages around 60 percent. Within that support group are some groups such as the United Nations Association with its chapters across the country; the support of such groups is quite intense. Generally, though, pro-UN groups are less likely to make this their "single-issue vote" than are anti-UN groups. And their seminars and reports manifest a very different approach to seeking political influence than that mounted by right-wing militia groups.

Unilateralists often accuse multilateralists of being "one-worlders," with notions of a world government superceding national governments. This is a distortion, albeit one that works politically. Multilateralists do see the value of greater capacity for global governance in terms of structures and processes for governments to work together, which is very different from being supplanted or superceded. Indeed, multilateralists can make their own claim on American exceptionalism with a vision of the United States as a leader in efforts to bring nations together in common purpose and for common values.

Dynamics of Choice on p. 315 summarizes this unilateralism-multilateralism debate. This is not, as stressed earlier, a strict dichotomy in terms of either theory or policy. Its core contrast, however, does help frame the debate over how to define the U.S. role in the world, and it will be useful as we delve into in greater detail in the chapters that follow.

DYNAMICS OF CHOICE

The Unilateralism-Multilateralism Debate

Unilateralism	Multilateralism
Realism	International institutionalism
Power, unipolarity	Power-Influence conversion, soft power
Benevolent hegemony	Not-so-benevolent hegemony
National, not global, interest	National and global interest
Inefficacy of multilateralism	Correct, not reject
Conservative domestic politics	Liberal domestic politics

Foreign Policy Politics: Diplomacy Begins at Home

"We are about to do a terrible thing to you," a Soviet official quipped toward the end of the Cold War. "We are going to deprive you of an enemy."[39] The Soviet official's remark was an astute observation of U.S. foreign policy politics. Despite all the other dangers that the Soviet Union posed, having an Enemy (capital letter intentional) helped American presidents garner the domestic political support necessary for a strong and active foreign policy. Without the Soviet threat—indeed, without a Soviet Union at all—the U.S. foreign policy debate split wide open.

Some wanted to heed the cry, "Come home, America." Who needs foreign policy anyway? these neo-isolationists asked. Why not just take advantage of the opportunity provided by the end of the Cold War to "put America first"? Reduce our international commitments and, for those commitments the United States does keep, make them more self-centered. Get beyond the old debate about whether politics should "stop at the water's edge"; just stay on our side of the water.

Yet the paradox of the post–Cold War era is that international affairs affect America and Americans at least as much, if not more than, during the Cold War. This was true even before the September 11, 2001, terrorist attacks on the United States. Recall the five major reasons stated at the outset of this book for the continued importance of foreign policy, and which were laid out in our first edition published pre-September 11:

- The United States still faces significant potential threats to its national security.
- The U.S. economy is more internationalized than ever before.
- Many other areas of policy that used to be considered "domestic" also have been internationalized.
- The increasing ethnic diversity of the American people makes for a larger number and wider range of groups with personal bases for interest in foreign affairs.
- It is hard for the United States to claim to be true to its most basic values if it ignores their violation around the world.

Prior to September 11, none of these rationales resonated in tones anything close to the clarion calls of the Truman Doctrine, JFK's 1961 inaugural "Ask not," or Reagan's "tear this wall down." With September 11 and the war on terrorism, there now was a true Enemy. Not just a number of small-e enemies, or the possibility that a major one might emerge down the road. Osama bin Laden, Al Qaeda, and terrorism writ large constituted a capital-e Enemy.

Our new era thus is characterized by a mix of foreign policy politics with and without an Enemy. In the rest of this chapter we focus on broad patterns in post–Cold War foreign policy politics involving the roles and dynamics of the five major sets of actors identified in Chapter 2: the president and Congress, intra–executive branch politics, interest groups, the news media, and public opinion. We then move on to the politics of specific foreign policy issues in each of the succeeding chapters: homeland security (Chapter 7); the United Nations, the Comprehensive Test Ban Treaty, and humanitarian interventions (Chapter 8); trade and other globalization issues (Chapter 9); and global democratization and human rights (Chapter 10).

Presidential-Congressional Relations: Post–Cold War Pennsylvania Avenue Diplomacy

"Divided government," the situation in which one political party controls Congress and the other the White House, has prevailed for most of the post–Cold War era. In 1991–92 there was a Republican president (George H.W. Bush) and a Democratic Congress; from 1995 to 2000 a Democratic president (Clinton) and a Republican Congress; and in 2001–2002 a Republican president (Bush) and Republican House but Democratic Senate.[40] The main exceptions were 1993–94, when Democrats controlled both ends of Pennsylvania Avenue, and after the 2002 elections where the Republicans gained this control. Thus to some extent the tensions in "Pennsylvania Avenue diplomacy" have been an extension of broader partisan politics.

Yet in a more fundamental sense what continues to be manifested is the basic structural problem of *separate institutions sharing power*. As stressed in earlier chapters and as seen historically, the problems created by this sharing of powers are greater than they would be if the presidential-congressional relationship really were a separation of powers. Herein lies the continuity as well as the change. The specifics of many of the issues have changed, and politics seems to have become more of a blood sport. But the basic dynamic remains the same, of separate institutions still trying to figure out how to share powers. We thus continue to see all four patterns of Pennsylvania Avenue diplomacy: conflict, competition, constructive compromise, and cooperation.

CONFLICT Of the many issues that could be cited as examples of inter-branch conflict, *war powers* continues to be the most momentous. We discussed in Chapter 5 how the 1973 War Powers Resolution (WPR) failed to resolve this basic constitutional dilemma. This was again evident in the 1990–91 Persian Gulf War. When President George H.W. Bush first made the Operation Desert Shield commitment of about two hundred thousand troops to Saudi Arabia following Saddam Hussein's invasion of Kuwait, he did report to Congress on the commitment but said that he was doing so only "consistent with," and not as required by, the WPR. His report denied that hostilities were imminent, and the same language game was played a few weeks later in granting higher salaries for the deployed troops according to the Pentagon's pay scale for personnel placed in "imminent danger," not that for "hostilities," even though the Pentagon was busily drawing up war plans and Bush likened Saddam to Hitler. In January 1991, with the deadline given Saddam for withdrawing from Kuwait approaching, Bush indicated that he had no intention of invoking the WPR or asking for congressional approval before moving to military action. He had gone to the United Nations more than a month earlier for a Security Council resolution authorizing "all necessary means" for getting Iraq out of Kuwait. With reference back to President Truman and the Korean War, Bush claimed that the UN Security Council resolution gave him all the authority he needed. Some in his administration however, argued for a middle path of encouraging Congress to vote on some form of a resolution, short of invoking the WPR, to indicate its support. Bush agreed, although he stated up front that if the resolution was defeated he would not consider it binding. Congress did pass the resolution with strong Republican support and enough Democrats to provide the margin of victory.

On January 16 the first Bush administration launched Operation Desert Storm. The war against Iraq was on. We will never know whether the political coalition would have held had the war not gone as well as it did. It wasn't politically difficult to stand behind a war with so few American casualties and such a quick and overwhelming military victory. In fact, those in Congress who voted against the war were the ones who paid politically. The key analytic point, though, was that the American political system showed yet again that it lacked accepted procedures for inter-branch cooperation on the most fundamental issue a democracy must confront.

We will see in Chapter 8 how this problem grew even worse in the 1990s over such issues as Somalia, Bosnia, and Kosovo. The 2001 Afghanistan war and 2003 Iraq war (Chapter 7) were different in some respects but similar in others. Both cases were much more politically consensual than conflictual. The vote on the Afghanistan war was unanimous in the Senate and 420–1 in the House. On the Iraq war it was still by wide margins, 77–23 in the Senate and 296–133 in the House. In both cases, though, the legislation was a use-of-force resolution that sidestepped the War Powers Resolution. The immediate politics of the issues thus were managed while the constitutional issue about when a declaration of war is needed was deferred yet again.

INSTITUTIONAL COMPETITION   An example of executive-legislative institutional competition can be seen in the increased forays of Congress into *direct diplomacy*, where legislators deal directly with foreign heads of state in ways that are not coordinated with and are often inconsistent with official administration policy. This problem has arisen before, as in the 1987 controversy when Speaker of the House Jim Wright (D-Tex.) opened up his own "alternative track" negotiations with Nicaraguan president and Sandinista leader Daniel Ortega. Congressional efforts at direct diplomacy became especially pronounced following the Republican sweep of Congress in the 1994 elections and the return to divided government. In the first six months of 1995, when Speaker of the House Newt Gingrich's power was at its apex, foreign leaders who came to Washington didn't just stop on Capitol Hill for courtesy calls but did a large share of their business there. In January the prime minister of Japan stopped by Gingrich's office. In February the prime minister of Pakistan did. In April the British prime minister did the same. Then, in June 1995, French President Jacques Chirac found himself "pleading with Congress" to support an agreement he and President Clinton had reached for increased funding of the UN Peacekeeping Force (UNPROFOR) in Bosnia. "'It is up to the U.S. Congress to give the green light to the initiative,' the French president said, while the American president stood at his side in a striking scene."[41]

Nor is it only heads of foreign government who have to deal with Congress. In January 1997, shortly after his appointment as the new UN secretary-general, Kofi Annan met with Senator Jesse Helms (R.-N.C.), chairman of the Senate Foreign Relations Committee and an ardent opponent of the UN. "Annan had said earlier in the day he did not think such direct consultations with Congress on UN reform would be proper," the *Washington Post* reported, "because traditionally the secretary general has dealt with member nations through their executive branches rather than legislatures." But he was told by President Clinton, according to a UN official, that "it is necessary to make friends in Congress and sell them on the idea of U.S. support."[42]

A line needs to be drawn separating even the most contentious battles over legislation from direct diplomacy practiced by members of Congress. The ends being pursued by Speaker Gingrich and Senator Helms no more justified their means than did Speaker Wright's. There is nothing wrong with key members of Congress being included by the executive branch as "observers" on U.S. negotiating teams, whether the issues are arms control, trade, the global environment, or others. Where the line gets crossed is if a member of Congress—*any* member of Congress—attempts an alternative track of diplomacy circumventing the president. Battles over U.S. policy through constitutional processes are one thing; raising questions about who is in charge of the actual carrying out of U.S. diplomacy is quite another. The immediate effects and the precedents set when that line is not observed cannot be healthy ones for American foreign policy.

Another example of institutional competition is in the *appointments process* for Cabinet posts and other major foreign policy positions. Whereas in the past a contentious nomination was pretty much the exception, in recent years it has become almost the rule. Presidential nominees still do get confirmed in most instances, but the Senate tends to probe deeper into their pasts, Senate questioning seems more like a cross-examination, and the Senate's agenda more often veers from a nominee's foreign policy qualifications to partisan politics. A pointed example involved the nomination in 1997 of Anthony Lake as CIA director. Lake had been national security adviser in Clinton's first term. While it is fair to say that there were some substantive bases for questioning Lake's CIA nomination, most observers felt these issues were not sufficient to disqualify him. Some leading Republican senators announced their support for Lake, and the votes seemed to be there to confirm him. But Republican senator Richard Shelby of Alabama, chair of the Senate Intelligence Committee, carried on what seemed to many to be a vendetta, repeatedly delaying Lake's confirmation hearings, then dragging them out and bombarding the nominee with questions, demands for documents, and other obstructionism. Lake ultimately asked President Clinton to withdraw his nomination. His letter to President Clinton went beyond his own case to raise the broader concern that "Washington has gone haywire":

> I hope that sooner rather than later, people of all political views beyond our city limits will demand that Washington give priority to policy over partisanship, to governing over "gotcha." It is time that senior officials have more time to concentrate on dealing with very real foreign policy challenges rather than the domestic wounds Washington is inflicting on itself.[43]

CONSTRUCTIVE COMPROMISE   One of the myths noted back in Chapter 2 was that presidential-congressional conflict is necessarily a bad thing. To the contrary, when both branches give a bit they may come together on a policy that proves better than either original position—a "constructive compromise." The dynamic can even be deliberately used in foreign policy negotiations, along the lines of the proverbial "good cop/bad cop." This version of constructive compromise occurs when the president and his diplomats make it known to another government that they really would like to provide certain aid or other benefits, but that the Congress is insistent that the foreign nation meet certain conditions, take certain reciprocating actions, etc. This strategy may be coordinated behind the scenes, with the two branches really sharing the same goal and agreeing that this ploy is the best way to achieve it. Or it may be that the executive really is less insistent on the conditions, or too concerned with not offending the other country, but that Congress has a different sense of the national interest.

Two recent cases exemplify this pattern. One involved Russian troop withdrawal in the early 1990s from Baltic states that used to be part of the Soviet Union, such as Estonia and Latvia. This was a difficult issue because both sides had legitimate claims: the Estonian and Latvian governments to their rights as (newly) independent countries to not have Russian troops on their soil, and Russia for assurances that the rights of the Russian ethnic minorities living in these countries would be protected. The Russian government also was reluctant to lose access to its Baltic Sea naval ports, which are of significant military value. An agreement had been reached setting a deadline for the Russian troop withdrawal and pledging guarantees for the Russian minorities. But as the deadline approached, Russian president Boris Yeltsin was under strong nationalist pressure at home not to withdraw the troops.

The Clinton administration had been trying to mediate, but with little success. Some critics saw the problem as the administration not exerting enough pressure on Russia, and perhaps implying that an arrangement short of full troop withdrawal might be acceptable. Congress, however, issued strong threats to cut off economic aid to Russia if the troops were not withdrawn. And while other factors also came into play in Russia's ultimately fulfilling its troop-withdrawal pledge, the congressional "bad cop" was an important factor.

The 1994 peace treaty between Israel and Jordan is another example. Following the historic 1993 breakthrough of the initial peace agreement between Israel and the Palestine Liberation Organization (PLO), Jordan and Israel had been moving closer to their own peace treaty.* King Hussein of Jordan, however, was being very cautious about moving toward a full and formal peace

---

*See Chapter 8 for a discussion of the Israeli-Palestinian accords.

with Israel. Among the key incentives the United States was offering Jordan was potential forgiveness of its $700 million debt. The executive branch was giving signals that it would grant debt forgiveness for a step short of full peace. But Congress would not. It had been Congress that had cut off aid to Jordan in 1991 when the king sided with Iraq in the Gulf War, and it was Congress that would have to turn aid back on.

Here, too, without overclaiming causal influence, the role of the congressional "bad cop" did have a positive effect. In the July 1994 "Washington Declaration," King Hussein and Israeli prime minister Yitzhak Rabin declared an end to their nations' state of war and their intent to sign a full peace treaty. Hussein and Rabin made an unprecedented appearance before a joint session of Congress. Their speeches "so moved lawmakers of both parties," the *New York Times* reported, "that Representative Bob Michel, the Republican leader, removed his eyeglasses several times to wipe away the tears, and Senator Barbara Boxer, the California Democrat, couldn't put her white handkerchief away."[44] Three days later Congress approved the first tranche of $220 million in debt forgiveness for Jordan. Three months later, Israel and Jordan signed their peace treaty.

COOPERATION   In both the Clinton and the George W. Bush administrations, one of the issues that has elicited the greatest bipartisanship and interbranch cooperation has been NATO expansion. For the forty-plus years of the Cold War, NATO had squared off against the Soviet-led Warsaw Pact. Now with the fall of communism and the dissolution of the Soviet bloc, these former enemy alliance countries were to be considered for membership in NATO. The United States and its NATO allies designated Poland, Hungary and the Czech Republic as the first group eligible to join. Among the issues raised by adding these countries to NATO was that they would fall under the "collective security umbrella" by which an attack on any NATO member is an attack on all. Even though on other issues Congress was resistant to expanding U.S. international commitments, on this one it was not. The 1997 Senate vote on their admission to NATO was 80 to 18, well above the two-thirds margin needed. The 2003 vote on the second round of NATO expansion—seven more Eastern European and former Soviet states, as approved at the 2002 NATO summit—was unanimous, 96–0.

Defense policy is another area in which there has been more cooperation than conflict between the two branches. On some issues, such as national missile defense, there have been some significant differences. But overall the defense budgets passed by Congress have been much closer to those proposed by both Presidents Clinton and George W. Bush than was the case during the Jimmy Carter and Ronald Reagan administrations. In the Carter years, Congress fluctuated from cutting the president's proposed defense budget by 4.2 percent (1977) to increasing his proposal by 10.2 percent (1980). In the Reagan years there were cuts of 6.7 percent (1984), 7 percent (1985), and 4.1 percent (1987). Under Clinton the biggest change had been a 3.3 percent increase by Congress in 1996, with the increases and cuts every other year at less than 3 percent, until Clinton's final year in office, when Congress increased his $277.5 billion proposed budget to $296.3 billion (6.8 percent).

President Bush's first defense budget proposal was as a supplement to the budget already operating when he was inaugurated. His March 2001 proposal to Congress was for an additional $6.15 billion, and Congress passed the full amount. Then following September 11 Bush proposed another $17.2 billion increase, which Congress also fully funded. In 2003 Bush and Congress agreed with very little conflict on a defense budget of $355 billion, almost a 12 percent increase over the previous year. The same pattern continued for 2004, even with defense spending now exceeding $400 billion.

For a while arms control also broke with the past and was marked by cooperation. The first two treaties agreed to in the U.S.-Russian Strategic Arms Reduction Talks (START) were ratified by large margins: START I, signed by President George H.W. Bush in 1991, was ratified 93 to 6 by a Democratic-led Senate; START II, signed by the first President Bush and then pushed by President Clinton, was ratified 87 to 4 by a Republican-led Senate. Clinton also got a Republican-led Senate to ratify the Chemical Weapons Convention, 71 to 29. In 1999, however, old conflictual patterns re-emerged as the Senate defeated the Comprehensive Test Ban Treaty, a case we will examine further in Chapter 8.

Executive-Branch Politics: Issues of Leadership and Bureaucracy

Some initial comparisons can be drawn among the first three post–Cold War presidents: George H.W. Bush (1989–93), Bill Clinton (1993–97), and George W. Bush (2001 –).

EXPERIENCE   George H.W. Bush ranks among the presidents with the most prior relevant foreign policy experience, and Clinton and George W. among those with the least. The first President Bush had served in the military in World War II, the Navy's youngest pilot at the time and recipient of a medal for heroism. He had been a member of the House of Representatives (1966–70), ambassador to the UN in the Nixon administration (1971–73), head of the first U.S. liaison office in the People's Republic of China when diplomatic relations were first established (1974–75), and director of the CIA in the Ford administration (1976–77). He also served eight years as Ronald Reagan's vice president. As president he made foreign policy a higher overall priority than any president had since Richard Nixon. He was known as a "foreign policy president" much more than a domestic policy one. This reputation hurt him politically in the 1992 election, because the public perceived him as not paying enough attention to domestic policy, while Bill Clinton ran on the campaign slogan "It's the economy, stupid."

Clinton, trained as a lawyer, had spent his political career as governor of Arkansas (1978–80, 1982–92), the foreign policy component of which amounted to an overseas trade mission or two. Many attributed the foreign policy failures of his first year as president to his inexperience: "passive and changeable . . . like a cork bobbing on the waves," was one leading journalist's characterization.[45] In addition, the controversies over whether he had dodged the draft during the Vietnam War gave Clinton personal credibility problems as commander in chief.

Over the course of his administration Clinton did gain experience and demonstrated greater foreign policy skills and savvy. In the first eighteen months of his second term he made more foreign trips than in his entire first term. By 1998 the percentage of people rating his foreign policy performance as excellent or good had increased from 31 percent (1994) to 55 percent.[46] Overall he still would be known more for his domestic policy, but he also did have his foreign policy successes.

The second President Bush also had been only a governor (of Texas) with the limited international agenda inherent in that office. There were times during the 2000 presidential campaign in which this hurt Bush's candidacy. So too in his first months in office, there were doubts about his foreign policy competence. The strength of his foreign policy team, seasoned hands who had served in his father's administration, partially compensated. Then the events of September 11 cast Bush in a new light. He was widely praised for helping rally the nation at a time of crisis. For many the 2003 Iraq war reinforced this sense of Bush as a strong foreign policy leader. Others, though, still were critical of his leadership style, as well as of the content of his policies.

BELIEF SYSTEMS   Comparisons of Presidents Bush, Clinton, and Bush in terms of their belief systems also help explain their foreign policy leadership styles. The first President Bush's conception of the international system was of the old bipolar order in transition, with the United States emerging as the most powerful country in the wake of the decline and then collapse of the Soviet Union. Although the United States was needed to lead, others were also needed to contribute to shaping a new world order. His national-interest hierarchy put power first and peace second, not to the exclusion of principles or prosperity but with this ordering of priorities coming through in cases such as the 1989 Tiananmen Square massacre in China. His overall strategy can be characterized as a combination of force and diplomacy, with a preference for acting through coalitions. His active diplomacy was evident in bringing the Cold War to a peaceful end, including the reunification of Germany. In using military force he acted both unilaterally and on a small scale, as in Panama in 1989, and through a broad multilateral coalition and on a much larger scale in the 1990–91 Persian Gulf War. He generally was inclined to build coalitions in which the United States had a leadership role but also benefited from the power and legitimacy that came with having partners.

President Clinton held to a more multilateralist conception of the international system, in which the United States is still the most powerful actor, but other major states and international institutions like the UN play substantially increased roles. His national-interest hierarchy prioritized prosperity and principles, although also not ignoring the other core objectives. His strategy also combined diplomacy and force, although his order of preference was reversed and his uses of force more limited, as in Bosnia and Kosovo. His lawyer's penchant for negotiations led him to peace-brokering activism, notably in the Middle East and also in many other world hot spots.

George W. Bush's belief system is closer to that of his father but more unilateralist and assertive of American military power. In the second President Bush's view the international system has transitioned from bipolarity to unipolarity, with the United States as the sole surviving superpower and with multilateralism at most a partial but not defining characteristic. Even before September 11, his view was that power needed to be put back at the top of the national interest hierarchy. Strategy also needed to shift back to a greater willingness to use force and to do so unilaterally and decisively as necessary, with less concern than his father had for coalitions. The second President Bush also was highly assertive in his diplomatic style, often appearing only begrudgingly willing to turn to negotiations. The war on terrorism, both in its first phase in 2001 in Afghanistan and in the Iraq war, exemplifies his approach, as does his policy on missile defense.

DYNAMICS OF CHOICE

Presidential Cognitive Belief Systems

	Bush 41	Clinton	Bush 43
Conception of the international system	Bipolarity to new world order	Multilateralism with U.S. leadership	Unipolarity, sole surviving superpower
National interest hierarchy	Power, peace	Prosperity, principles	Power, peace
Strategy	Force and diplomacy, coalitions	Diplomacy and force, coalitions	Force and diplomacy, unilateralist
Policy examples	Persian Gulf War	Bosnia, Kosovo	War on terrorism
	Invasion of Panama	Peace brokering (Middle East)	Iraq war
	China after Tiananmen Square	Emphasis on foreign economic policy	Missile defense

THE SENIOR ADVISORY PROCESS: PRESIDENTS AND THEIR TEAMS   Neither the first Bush nor the Clinton administration had anything like the battles that Henry Kissinger fought with other Nixon and Ford administration officials, or those between National Security Adviser Zbigniew Brzezinski and Secretary of State Cyrus Vance in the Carter administration, or between Secretary of State George Shultz and Secretary of Defense Caspar Weinberger in the Reagan administration. We again have seen divisive intra-executive branch politics in the second Bush administration. Table 6.2 lists the key foreign policy officials in all three administrations.

THE FIRST BUSH TEAM   The first President Bush's principal foreign policy appointees had two characteristics in common.[47] They all had prior foreign policy and other relevant government experience, and all were longtime friends or associates of George H.W. Bush. Secretary of State James Baker had

TABLE 6.2   Cabinet and Other Key Foreign Policy Officials in the Past Three Presidential Administrations

	Administration		
Position	Bush (41)	Clinton	Bush (43)
Vice president	Dan Quayle	Al Gore	Dick Cheney
National security adviser	Brent Scowcroft	Anthony Lake Sandy Berger	Condoleezza Rice
Secretary of state	James A. Baker III Lawrence Eagleburger	Warren Christopher Madeleine Albright	Colin Powell
Secretary of defense	Dick Cheney	Les Aspin William Perry William Cohen	Donald Rumsfeld
Chair, Joint Chiefs of Staff	Colin Powell	Colin Powell John Shalikashvili Hugh Shelton	Hugh Shelton Richard Myers
UN ambassador	Thomas Pickering Edward Perkins	Madeleine Albright Richard Holbrooke	John Negroponte
CIA director	William Webster Robert Gates	James Woolsey John Deutch George Tenet	George Tenet
Secretary of the treasury	Nicholas Brady	Lloyd Bentsen Robert Rubin Lawrence Summers	Paul O'Neill John Snow
U.S. trade representative	Carla Hills	Mickey Kantor Charlene Barshevsky	Robert Zoellick

served as White House chief of staff and secretary of the treasury in the Reagan administration, and had been friends with Bush since their early days together in Texas politics. National Security Adviser Brent Scowcroft had served in the same position in the Ford administration, when his friendship with Bush began, and was a retired Air Force lieutenant colonel with a Ph.D. from Columbia University. Secretary of Defense Dick Cheney had been White House chief of staff for Ford, represented Wyoming in Congress for ten years, and had served as a member of the House Intelligence Committee. General Colin Powell, chair of the Joint Chiefs of Staff, emerged during the Reagan years first as a top Pentagon official and then as the national security adviser appointed in the wake of the Iran-contra scandal, a man in uniform who stood for everything that Oliver North did not.

As a team Bush and his top appointees generally were regarded as highly competent and quite cohesive. Even those who disagreed with their policies did not question their capabilities. After all the messy internal fights of prior administrations, the solidarity of the Bush team was a welcome relief. Some critics raised the concern over whether the Bush team was too tightly drawn and too homogeneous. Conservative columnist William Safire remarked on the "absence of creative tension [which] has generated little excitement or innovation. . . . As a result of the Bush emphasis on the appearance of unanimity, we miss the [Franklin] Rooseveltian turbulence that often leads to original thinking."[48] Overall, though, the Bush senior advisory process is seen as having been much more positive than negative.

THE CLINTON TEAM   The Clinton team also was marked more by consensus than by conflict. Illustrative of this was a *New York Times* profile of National Security Adviser Samuel ("Sandy") Berger, full of complimentary quotes from his colleagues. Secretary of Defense William Cohen lauded Berger as an "honest broker." Secretary of State Madeleine Albright dubbed him "the glue for the system." Joint Chiefs of Staff Chair General Hugh Shelton praised his ability to "run a great meeting." Hardly the comments one would have heard about Henry Kissinger in his day! Kissinger, though, did have his own assessment of Berger, portraying him as more of a "trade lawyer" than a "global strategist."[49]

The Clinton team did have its rivalries, however. Les Aspin, Clinton's first secretary of defense, did not even last a year, in part because he ended up with much of the blame for the military failure in Somalia. Warren Christopher will be remembered as a hardworking and gracious secretary of state but not the right man for the nature of the times. Anthony Lake, Clinton's first national security adviser, earlier in his career had worked both for Henry Kissinger and Cyrus Vance. He thus was especially conscious of the damage bureaucratic warfare could cause. Some critics, though, felt he may have learned these lessons too well, and played too low-key a role himself.

Two historic developments during the Clinton administration need to be noted. One was the appointment of Madeleine Albright as the first woman to serve as secretary of state. Albright's appointment was made at the beginning of Clinton's second term, and it brought a sense of historic importance and celebrity-like excitement. The other was the enhanced foreign policy role played by the vice president, Al Gore. Previous occupants of this office, dubbed by its first holder, John Adams, as "the most insignificant office that ever the invention of man contrived," typically had not had much of a substantive foreign policy role. Trips to attend funerals of foreign dignitaries were pretty much the portfolio. Gore, who had earned a reputation for foreign policy expertise in his sixteen years in Congress, took on much greater and more substantive foreign policy responsibilities. The comparable and arguably even greater role being played by Vice President Dick Cheney in the second Bush administration indicates that the role of the vice presidency as an institution is being transformed.

THE SECOND BUSH TEAM   As noted, the effort during the 2000 campaign to provide Governor George W. Bush with credit by association with a strong and experienced foreign policy team was a quite conscious one. Dick Cheney and Colin Powell had served in the first Bush administration, as had Condoleezza Rice, who had been a National Security Council staff specialist on the Soviet Union. So too with U.S. Trade Representative Robert Zoellick, who was a top aide to Secretary of State James Baker in the first Bush administration. Donald Rumsfeld was ambassador to NATO in the Nixon administration and secretary of defense in the Ford administration. This, then, was a new administration but with many familiar faces.

There were definite advantages to a team that began with established credentials and existing working relationships. They were known to the foreign policy community and the diplomatic community, and were expected to be less apt to make the mistakes of learning on the job. They appeared to start with a strong degree of intra-administration consensus.

It wasn't long, though, before questions were raised as to whether there was as much consensus within the Bush team as there originally seemed to be. Within the first few months the Bush team already was showing "two faces," according to a front-page story in the *New York Times,* "an ideologically conservative Pentagon and a more moderate State Department." Although policy debates within an administration can be healthy, the question raised was whether these were becoming "ideological cleavages"—and becoming so quite publicly despite the Bush administration's claims of internal discipline.[50]

One of the earliest and most public intra-administration splits was over North Korea and whether to continue the negotiations over its nuclear weapons program that were initiated by the Clinton administration and South Korean president Kim Dae Jung. On the eve of President Kim's March 2001 visit to Washington, Secretary of State Powell came out largely in support of this strategy. Stories immediately broke in the press about Powell's being out of step with others in the administration, notably Vice President Cheney and Defense Secretary Rumsfeld. Then at a joint press conference with President Kim after their White House meeting, President Bush quite candidly conveyed his own skepticism about negotiations and cooperation with North Korea. Secretary Powell was forced to backtrack and take a tougher line. And President Kim, who had just won the Nobel Peace Prize the previous year for his peace efforts, went home rebuffed by his country's major ally and protector.

Signs of intra-administration splits also have been evident with the war on terrorism and particularly over the war in Iraq. Vice President Cheney and Defense Secretary Rumsfeld were widely viewed as the most hawkish. They held little confidence that negotiations would yield an agreement sufficiently firm and enforceable to address the threat posed by Saddam Hussein's regime, its growing arsenal of weapons of mass destruction, and its other aggressive policies. There was a sense that they saw going to the UN as a box that needed to be checked off for political reasons, but not a genuinely viable policy route. They saw regime change (overthrowing Saddam) as the most viable option and all along were prepared to act unilaterally with massive American military force to achieve it.

Secretary of State Powell largely agreed on the threat but differed on the strategy. He pushed for a strategy that gave negotiations through the UN Security Council a serious shot. He wasn't willing to accept just any new Security Council resolution, to paper over the crisis and then have the agreement erode when world attention had abated. He was realistic about the limits and obstacles of working through the UN but was also concerned about the risks and limits of acting unilaterally. The intra-administration battles periodically leaked into the media, even in some instances planted there as part of bureaucratic battle plans. As the UN route became more problematic and as President Bush's determination to take the largely unilateral route became more apparent, Secretary Powell shifted accordingly. But the splits re-emerged after the war was over on State-Defense roles in Iraqi nation-building as well as on other issues.

Bureaucratic Politics: Assertive New Actors, Troubled Old Ones

THE RISE OF THE FOREIGN ECONOMIC POLICY BUREAUCRACY   The Clinton administration was the first to have consistently brought top foreign economic policy officials onto the foreign policy "first string." But the decision

to include them in the formation of foreign policy introduced two bureaucratic challenges. One was a matter of coordination. Even when policy is reasonably consensual, the multiple foreign economic policy departments and
agencies must be harnessed into a coordinated effort. To help with this task,
one of the bureaucratic innovations of the Clinton administration was the
creation of the National Economic Council (NEC), mandated to do on the
foreign economic policy side what the National Security Council (NSC) does
on the political-diplomatic-military side.

The other challenge arose on issues for which there is no consensus; here,
the strengthening of the economic voice could have made for more divisive
bureaucratic politics. The NEC could compete with the NSC because it, too,
was within the White House, close to the president, and able to speak for a
number of executive-branch departments and agencies. On some foreign policy issues, the Commerce Department, the Agriculture Department, the U.S.
Trade Representative, the Export-Import Bank, and the Overseas Private In
vestment Corporation (OPIC) will be arrayed on one side, and the State Department and the Defense Department will oppose them on the other.

This type of division was seen in 1993–94 when China's most-favored-
nation (MFN) status came up for renewal. Among all the bureaucratic battles
fought over this issue, perhaps the most startling was the display of competitive speech-making in Beijing in early 1994, where a top Commerce Department official gave a strong pro-MFN speech, only to be followed shortly by
Secretary of State Christopher with a "tough on human rights" message. Taking the conflict even further, both sides fed stories to the news media, often
not just advocating their own view but also disparaging their fellow administration colleagues. At times the intrabranch cross-accusations were no less
derogatory than interbranch ones.

The second Bush administration also has had its politically charged and
bureaucratically divisive trade issues. The NEC generally has had less of a role,
with the lead going more to Zoellick at the Office of the U.S. Trade Representative. We look more at this and other aspects of trade policy politics in Chapter 9.

THE STATE DEPARTMENT   During every presidential election season a
flurry of reports are prepared by task forces, commissions, and other groups
outside of government with recommendations for a new administration on
what foreign policy changes it should make. In 2000 many of those focused
not just on policy but also on the bureaucracy: the problem, as one commission put it, is that "the apparatus of U.S. foreign policymaking and

implementation . . . is in a state of serious disrepair."[51] The reference was broad but aimed especially at the State Department.

Upon taking office, Secretary of State Powell pledged to bring the same commitment to the non-uniformed professionals of the Foreign Service as he had to the uniformed military while chair of the Joint Chiefs of Staff. A key to doing so was getting budget increases from Congress. An old joke around the halls of Foggy Bottom is that the State Department budget is equivalent to a rounding error in the Pentagon's budget. The funds available for both foreign policy programs (foreign aid as well as other diplomatic activities and initiatives) and for basic operations, it is felt, are lacking. The State Department cannot be competitive in recruiting and retaining talented people, or protect its embassies, or move up the technology curve without significant increases in its budget. Yet it has not fared very well. Its 2004 budget as proposed by the president was $8.5 billion, up 15 percent from two years earlier, but still disproportionately small compared to the $379.9 billion Pentagon budget.

TROUBLED INTELLIGENCE AGENCIES   The CIA and the FBI have been beset by a series of problems. Each had internal-spy scandals that shook confidence in its ability to keep its own house in order. For the CIA it was Aldrich Ames, who worked as a "mole" for the Soviet Union in the 1980s. Not only did the secrets Ames sold to the Soviets damage national security, but the fact that he was so open about his lavish lifestyle, including driving to work at CIA headquarters in his Jaguar, raised concerns about why the CIA had not discovered him much sooner. Then in 2001 the FBI was hit by its own "mole" scandal involving longtime agent Robert Hanssen, who had also spied for the Soviets and then the Russians for many years.

Other problems arose following exposure of the unsavory relationships the CIA maintained during the Cold War with some of its "ABC" (anything but communist) partners. For example, stories broke in 1994–95 about CIA knowledge and possible involvement in massive human rights violations and killings by the Guatemalan military, including the murders of an American innkeeper living in Guatemala and a leftist guerrilla leader who was married to an American.

Most fundamentally the issues have been about whether the CIA, the FBI, and the rest of the country's myriad intelligence agencies are measuring up to their mission. These questions have been intensified since the September 11 attacks, but they were being asked earlier, as when American intelligence agencies were caught unaware by India's May 1998 nuclear-weapons tests. This was in part a technical matter, arising from the limitations of the CIA's monitoring equipment. But it also revealed shortcomings in the agency's analyses, for the political signals were there, even in the media and other open sources, that the new Hindu nationalist government of India considered development of nuclear weapons as a major part of its political platform. Nor was this episode an isolated instance—a special investigative commission criticized "the underlying mind-set," still too rooted in Cold War threats and scenarios, that hampered the overall quality of intelligence analyses.[52]

The September 11 terrorist attacks took these concerns about mission and performance to a much higher level. Did the attacks have to be a surprise? Were warnings missed? Why, and by whom? We will take these and other questions up in Chapter 7 in our discussion of the politics of homeland security.

Foreign Policy Interest Groups: Proliferation and Intensification

Two main trends have characterized foreign policy interest groups in recent years: *proliferation,* in that there are many more of them than ever before, and *intensification,* in that they are more active not only in seeking to bring pressure on Congress and the executive branch, but also in taking more direct action of their own.

ECONOMIC GLOBALIZATION AND INTEREST GROUPS   As recently as 1970, trade accounted for only 13 percent of the U.S. GDP. Today it amounts to more than 30 percent. And trade now comprises much more than goods and services. Companies scour the world, not just their own country, in deciding where to build factories and make other foreign investments. Millions of dollars in stock investments and other financial transactions flow between New York and Frankfurt, Chicago and London, San Francisco and Tokyo every day. Overall there are now more foreign economic issues on the agenda, and those issues are much more politically salient than they used to be. Whereas during the Cold War most foreign economic policy issues were relegated to "low politics" status in contrast to political and security "high politics" issues, in recent years issues such as the North American Free Trade Agreement (NAFTA), presidential trade promotion authority (previously known as "fast track" authority) funding for the International Monetary Fund, and other international economic issues have been as hotly contested and as prominent as any other foreign policy issues in recent years.

IDENTITY GROUPS   Identity groups—i.e., groups motivated less by material economic interests than by bonds of ethnic or religious identity to other countries—provide another example of the proliferation of interest groups. The increasing racial and ethnic diversity of the American populace, resulting both from new trends in immigration (see Table 6.3) and increasing empowerment of long-present minorities, is making for a larger number and wider range of groups with personal bases for seeking to influence foreign policy.

We discussed the Jewish-American lobby in Chapter 2; it continues to be highly influential on Middle East policy. The various Slavic American groups (e.g., Polish, Lithuanian, Latvian, and Estonian Americans) are another example. Influential during the Cold War in hardening U.S. policy toward the Soviet Union, these groups got a new lease on life with the end of the Cold War in support of policies geared toward helping the former communist states democratize, build their economies, and ensure their security against any future Russian threat through mechanisms such as NATO expansion. For example, in late 1993, when the Clinton administration was "dragging its feet on NATO expansion, Polish lobbying groups flooded the White House with telegrams and telephone calls. The Polish-American Congress put out a 'legislative alert' to its 34 divisions around the country to prevent a 'new Yalta,' political shorthand for the 'betrayal of Poland by the Western allies that occurred after the end of World War II.'" As the head of one lobbying group put it, "there are 23 million Americans who trace their heritage to Eastern Europe," and, even more important, "there are a dozen [U.S.] states—very important states for any presidential election—where they constitute more than 5 percent of the electorate."[53]

African Americans, led by TransAfrica and the Congressional Black Caucus, emerged as a strong foreign policy lobby on the issue of economic sanctions against apartheid South Africa (see Chapter 10). Other groups could be mentioned here as well: Cuban Americans on Cuba, Greek Americans on Cyprus and Macedonia; Irish Americans and the Northern Ireland issue; Arab Americans and their concerns about the Middle East; Pakistani Americans and Indian Americans on issues involving the tensions between Pakistan and India. More will emerge over time, as American politics increasingly reflects the shifts in overall immigration patterns noted in Table 6.3. For just as the proliferation of groups concerned with trade policy reflects the broader economic changes of the internationalization of the American economy, more and more Americans are interested in influencing U.S. relations with the countries from which they or their ancestors came.

THE EXPLOSION OF NGOS   The rise of *non-governmental organizations,* or NGOs, is one of the most important developments of this new era. NGOs

TABLE 6.3 Changing Immigration Patterns		
	Percentage of all immigrants originating in selected areas	
Place of origin	1920	1996
Europe	87%	17%
Canada	8	3
Latin America	4	50
Asia	1	27

Source: U.S. Census Bureau, as reported in the *Washington Post*, May 25, 1998, p. A1.

usually are unofficial, nonprofit organizations whose "business" is some aspect of foreign policy—e.g., promoting human rights, for Amnesty International and Human Rights Watch; building democracy, for the Open Society Institute and the American Bar Association; helping refugees, for Refugees International; protecting the global environment, for the Climate Action Networks; conflict resolution and "track-two diplomacy," for Search for Common Ground and the Carter Center. Although NGOs have been around for a long time, in the post–Cold War era vast numbers of NGOs have been formed. By one estimate there were 20,063 NGOs worldwide in 1989, and 47,098 by 2002.[54]

NGOs fit the "political issue group" category in our Chapter 2 interest-group typology. One of their principal roles is *advocacy*—lobbying, endorsing candidates, mounting media campaigns, etc. Many NGOs operate not only in domestic politics but also in international forums like the United Nations. For example, at the 1995 UN World Conference on Women held in Beijing, China, more than 4,000 NGO delegates were officially accredited, just slightly fewer than the total number of government delegates.

The other major NGO role is *direct action,* in which they themselves are out on the front lines providing humanitarian assistance, monitoring human rights, supervising elections, helping with economic development, and taking on countless other global responsibilities. Proponents such as Jessica Mathews, president of the Carnegie Endowment for International Peace, argue that NGOs "can outperform government in the delivery of many public services," and "are better than governments at dealing with problems that grow slowly and affect society through their cumulative effect on individuals."[55] Others, though, see NGOs as also having their own problems, inefficiencies, and interests that complicate and sometimes conflict with their humanitarian and other liberal missions.[56]

The News Media: New Technologies, Recurring Issues

The most significant change regarding the news media since the end of the Cold War has been in what "the media" are and how they operate. For coverage of foreign policy, first rank still goes to major newspapers (such as the *New York Times* and the *Washington Post*), major television networks (ABC, NBC, and CBS), and major newsmagazines (*Time, Newsweek*). Two newer developments have had their own dramatic effects. One has been the rise of cable and satellite television, led by CNN. CNN made its name for its coverage during the Persian Gulf War. It was on the scene before the traditional networks and its twenty-four-hour news coverage made it a constant presence. In the years since, other cable news channels have entered the business, including both U.S.-based ones such as Fox News and MSNBC and foreign ones such as the Arab world's Al Jazeera.

Although there are many benefits to close and constant news coverage, it does bring intense "real time" pressure. An American soldier gets taken prisoner, and his face flashes on the television time and again, all day, all night. A terrorist incident occurs, and the video plays over and over. Policy-makers often must respond with little prior notice, in some cases actually first hearing about a major event on CNN rather than through official government sources. They also must do so within the immediacy of the churning news cycle. This makes for a very different and more difficult dynamic in television's impact on key foreign policy choices.

The other major development involves the Internet. More and more people also are getting news on the Internet; one study showed a tremendous recent increase in the number of people who went on-line to get their news at least once a week, especially among eighteen to twenty-nine year olds, where the increase was from 7 percent to 30 percent.[57] The Internet also has substantially enhanced the capacity of NGOs, think tanks, and others to become independent sources of information, analysis, and advocacy. Nik Gowing, a journalist with the BBC, calls this development a breaking of the "information dominance" of governments, be they repressive regimes that would prefer to cut their people off from outside communication or democratic governments that must respond to the new dynamics of pressure.[58]

Despite these technological changes, prior to the September 11, 2001, terrorist attacks the overall trend was of declining media coverage of international affairs. Whereas in 1988 each of the major television networks spent about two thousand minutes covering international news over the course of the year, this total had declined by the year 2000 to between eleven hundred and twelve hundred minutes. This amounted to only about 9 percent of each evening news broadcast.[59]

The pattern was similar with the print media, with only some exceptions. By the early 1990s cutbacks were so extensive that only 25 of the top 100 newspapers had at least one full-time foreign correspondent.[60] "Before September 11," wrote *Washington Post* editors Leonard Downie and Robert Kaiser, "most of the American news media gave scant coverage to the fact that the United States was the key participant in an interdependent global society, or that our economic well-being depended on foreigners, or that our population includes millions of people born in foreign lands, more every year."[61] A *Los Angeles Times* reporter expressed his concern that "you don't have editors and staff members who are conversant with the issues and with the world beyond our borders, so foreign news is easy to ignore a lot of the time."[62] Nor was this an isolated view. In a survey of newspaper editors' own views, nearly two-thirds rated post–September 11 foreign news coverage as only fair or poor.[63]

When the media does afford coverage to foreign issues it often is with the klieg-light intensity that has engendered concerns about the ups and downs of the "CNN curve,"[64] meaning television coverage's tendency to raise public awareness of a crisis so much that it brings great pressure on officials, impelling them to precipitate military intervention too quickly and with too little fleshing-out of strategy. On the back end, negative coverage of casualties or other major policy disasters can fuel a steep enough drop in public support to make the political pressure too much to bear without a withdrawal or other major shift in policy, even if such a move is premature or unwise as a matter of strategy.

Although the effect of CNN and other new telecommunications technologies is not to be denied, it also is not to be exaggerated. Warren Strobel, a journalist, provided one of the most insightful analyses of this dynamic. Strobel argued that the power of the media to influence a policy is inversely related to how well grounded the policy itself is:

> It is true that U.S. government policies and actions regarding international conflict are subject to more open public review than previously in history. But policymakers retain great power to frame events and solicit public support—indeed, CNN at times increases this power. Put another way, if officials do not have a firm and well-considered policy or have failed to communicate their views in such a way as to garner the support of the American people, the news media will fill this

6.3

vacuum (often by giving greater time and attention to the criticisms or policy preferences of its opponents).[65]

Strobel bases his argument on two of the cases so often cited as prima facie evidence for the CNN effect: Somalia and Bosnia. His research included more than a hundred interviews with senior policy-makers from both the first Bush and the Clinton administrations, military officers and spokespersons, journalists, and others. He acknowledges that "CNN and its brethren have made leadership more difficult," and that it is television's inherent nature as a visual medium to "feed on conflict, whether political or physical, emphasizing the challenge to policy." But his emphasis is clear, and well supported: "When policy is well grounded, it is less likely that the media will be able to shift officials' focus. When policy is clear, reasonably constant, and well communicated, the news media follow officials rather than lead them."[66]

Media coverage during the 2003 Iraq war was more intensive and instantaneous than anything that had preceded it. In the 1991 Persian Gulf War, journalists were confined to "pools" of limited numbers and restricted to designated locations. In the 2001 Afghanistan war, reporting came mostly from official briefings and a few journalists who managed to get out into the field. The 2003 Iraq war established a new policy of "embedding" journalists within military units and putting them directly in the field and on the march with the combat troops. The 600 "embeds" included reporters not only from the *New York Times* and the *Washington Post,* but also from *People* magazine, MTV, and local news stations; there also were some foreign correspondents. Equipped with the latest in satellite phones and other advanced communications technology, the embeds could air their live television broadcasts and file their stories on the spot and in the moment.

Two main questions have been debated about Iraq war journalism. One is whether it was too critical or too uncritical. Both arguments have been made. Those who saw the reporting as having been too uncritical question whether the journalistic perspective might have been constrained by the natural empathy that developed between the embedded journalists and the troops with whom they were stationed and became their immediate community and also protectors. Those who saw the reporting as too critical accused the press of overdoing the bad news, whether to keep filling that "news hole" created by 24/7 coverage or from doubts about the war policy.

The other main question has been about the quality of press coverage. Even though journalists were on the spot, some felt that the coverage was like "looking through a straw," with the viewer able to see only what was within that defined and delimited field of vision. And although they were outfitted with the latest technologies, the instantaneity of reporting did not leave journalists the time needed for reflection and insight. They were providing a huge amount of information, but they were giving much less emphasis—especially in television coverage—to its context, to whether its importance was brief or of more enduring significance, and to how different pieces of the story fit together.

Howard Kurtz, noted media critic for the *Washington Post*, summarized the key questions: "What did the media accomplish," he asks, "during the most intensively and instantaneously covered war in history? Did the presence of all those journalists capture the harsh realities of war or simply breed a new generation of Scud studs? Were readers and viewers well served or deluged with confusing information? And what does it portend for future wars?"[67]

Nor is it just about war coverage that such questions are asked.

A number of leading scholars stress that the media generally still is too deferential in their treatment of official policy. Reporters still need the government officials who are their sources; government officials know that although good relationships with reporters do not guarantee favorable reporting, they may well help when trying to "spin" a story. Others see the relationship as having become much less symbiotic and more one of "interdependent mutual exploitation."[68] The media and the government still are interdependent, but they have less common ground and make more efforts to manipulate each other. "What will the press think?" is a question regularly asked in executive-branch foreign policy meetings. Editorials and op-ed articles have a remarkable influence. Highly critical opinion pieces in a major paper like the *New York Times* or the *Washington Post* have been known to prompt hastily called State Department meetings or to have made officials forget about whatever else was on their schedule in order to draft a response. Read the minutes of major foreign policy meetings, and you'll see significant attention paid to media-related issues. Check out staff rosters in the State and Defense Departments, and you'll see numerous media advisers. Look at the curriculum taught at the Foreign Service Institute and the National Defense University, and you'll see courses on the role of the media. Given constantly advancing technology, these emphases will only grow with time.

Another recurring issue is the tension between freedom of the press and national security. This has been shaped by three factors. First, in the early part of the post–Cold War era, was the sense of foreign policy politics without an Enemy. With the Cold War over, the security imperatives seemed less imperative. Second was the legacy of past abuses of the national-security rationale for largely political purposes, which left the sense that politics often has more to do with why documents and proceedings get classified than policy does. Is freedom of the press being limited because the issue at hand genuinely requires secrecy in the name of the national interest? Or is secrecy being resorted to more because if the action or policy were known there would be political fallout? Third, though, was September 11 and the return of politics with an Enemy. In the context of the war on terrorism and homeland security, the issues have been not just about journalistic coverage of military operations but more broadly about restrictions on information in an age of terrorism (see Chapter 7).

Public Opinion: Currents and Cross-Currents

What does the public think about foreign policy these days? As befits a period of historic transition, this question as yet has no definitive answer. No new consensus has emerged. The best characterization is of currents flowing in one direction, and cross-currents in the other. In later chapters we will look at public opinion on specific issues; here our focus is on general patterns.

As in other periods, public-opinion analysis starts with general attitudes toward internationalism and isolationism. As Figure 6.1 shows, the former has continued to prevail over the latter. The polls cited never dipped below 57 percent pro-internationalism and went as high as 79 percent in the wake of the Persian Gulf War and to 81 percent following the September 11 attacks and amid the Afghanistan war. By June 2002, after the immediate post–September 11 effects had subsided, the polls still were at 71 percent.

In sticking to its internationalism the American public showed that it had learned the lessons of the twentieth century—of how both world wars inevitably pulled the United States in, and the crucial contributions the United States made to both victories; of the folly of isolationist moves like not joining the League of Nations and passing the 1929 Smoot-Hawley protectionist tariff; of the indispensable role the United States played in the Cold War; of oil crises and the interdependence of the American economy with the global economy. The public fundamentally understood that the United States had come to be so interconnected in so many ways with the rest of the world that isolationism was not just undesirable—it simply was not possible.

However, in the 1990s this was largely an "apathetic internationalism."[69] Take, for example, two polls in a 1998 study by the Chicago Council on Foreign Relations. One showed that the percentage of people who still were internationalist held steady at 61 percent—only 3 percent less than back in

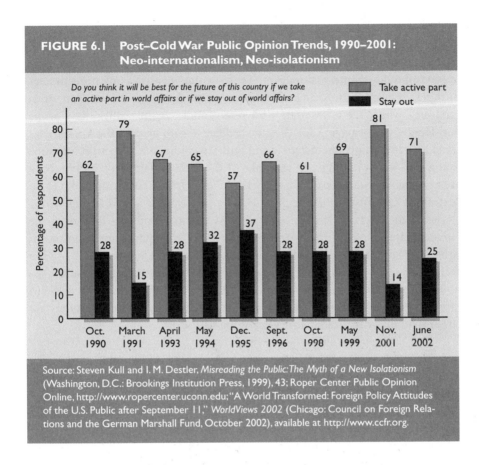

FIGURE 6.1 Post–Cold War Public Opinion Trends, 1990–2001: Neo-internationalism, Neo-isolationism

Do you think it will be best for the future of this country if we take an active part in world affairs or if we stay out of world affairs?

Take active part
Stay out

Source: Steven Kull and I. M. Destler, *Misreading the Public: The Myth of a New Isolationism* (Washington, D.C.: Brookings Institution Press, 1999), 43; Roper Center Public Opinion Online, http://www.ropercenter.uconn.edu; "A World Transformed: Foreign Policy Attitudes of the U.S. Public after September 11," *WorldViews 2002* (Chicago: Council on Foreign Relations and the German Marshall Fund, October 2002), available at http://www.ccfr.org.

1986 during the Cold War. But another poll showed a steep decline in the importance people give to foreign policy.[70]

Moreover, at times and on certain issues the general internationalist current has been swamped by neo-isolationist cross-currents. Part of the dynamic is that the neo-isolationists often are more vocal, more active, and better organized. This can mislead policy-makers who may see the public as more isolationist than it really is. A study by the University of Maryland Program on International Policy Attitudes found that 74 percent of policy-makers believed that the public favored "disengagement," only 32 percent believed that the public wanted the United States to be an international leader, and only 15 percent believed that the public could be convinced to support engagement.[71] These perceptions are quite out of sync with the actual opinion data as seen in Figure 6.1. Yet in political terms perceptions often matter more than the actual numbers. So we end up with perceived public opinion constraining internationalist policies more than the polling data might lead us to believe it would.

Some segments of the American public were not just isolationist but militantly opposed to internationalism. These "antagonistics" constitute smaller numbers but are quite strident in their opposition. They are the "American First-ers," whose views resonate with resentments, against allies like Europe and Japan for not paying for their own defense, and against the United Nations for corruption, inefficiency, and anti-Americanism. The militia groups that got so much publicity in the wake of the 1995 Oklahoma City bombing are a particularly dangerous version of antagonistics. These groups hold to an "extremist catechism" that, as described in *U.S. News and World Report,* includes such tenets as "the United Nations is threatening to take over the United States. . . . [F]oreign troops under UN command are training on American soil, and black helicopters are spying on Americans. . . . [T]he United States is secretly building or supporting 'concentration camps' to house resisters to the new world order. . . . [R]oad signs contain secret codes to direct foreign invaders."[72] These groups are not that large—although they are larger than many realized before Oklahoma City.

FOREIGN-DOMESTIC "NEXUS" ISSUES   One of the polling questions often cited to "show" how little the public cares about foreign policy asks about the biggest problems facing the country. Whereas in the mid-1980s 26 percent cited a foreign policy issue, only 7.3 percent did so in 1998. For social problems the pattern was the reverse, going up from 39 percent to 62 percent.[73] Yet this question is more useful to us as an example of how flawed conclusions can be drawn from poll data than for any major insights into public opinion.

Is it any wonder that more people cite problems close to home as the "biggest" ones? Look at the state of American cities, public education, health care, and the like. Indeed the problem may well have been that during much of the Cold War too little attention was paid to these kinds of problems on the home front. But to say domestic issues are more important is not to say that foreign policy ones are unimportant. What we especially need to get at are those issues at the intersection, or "nexus," of foreign and domestic policy—issues such as jobs, drugs, economic competitiveness, illegal immigration, and oil.

And indeed, it is these issues in which the post–Cold War public is particularly interested (see Table 6.4). As a group they have a 68 percent "top priority" score, a higher average than the 58 percent for global interests and much higher than the 19 percent for global altruism or the various individual scores in the "other" category. Moreover, ranked individually, the nexus issues have

TABLE 6.4 Foreign-Domestic Policy "Nexus" Issues

	Percentage of Americans considering issue to be a top foreign policy priority
Nexus issues	
Protecting the jobs of American workers	80%
Stopping international drug trafficking	75
Strengthening our domestic economy to improve the U.S. international position	67
Stopping illegal immigration into this country	61
Insuring adequate energy supplies for the U.S.	59
Average	68
Global interests	
Reducing the threat of international terrorism	71
Preventing the spread of weapons of mass destruction	68
Improving the global environment	56
Strengthening the United Nations	36
Average	58
Global altruism	
Protecting weaker nations against foreign aggression	21
Promoting and defending human rights in other countries	21
Helping improve living standards in developing nations	16
Promoting democracy in other nations	16
Average	19
Other foreign policy problems	
Better managing our trade and economic disputes with Japan	40
Ending the warfare in Bosnia	32
Helping Mexico become more stable politically and economically	16
Ensuring democracy succeeds in Russia and other former Soviet states	14

Source: Times Mirror survey, June 1995, cited in Alvin Richman, "American and Russian Publics View Global Issues as Top Foreign Policy Goals," U.S. Information Agency report, August 2, 1996.

five of the top seven scores. This type of opinion data shows especially well the basic understanding that the distinctions between foreign and domestic policy have become increasingly blurred, making it impossible to solve such problems without *both* domestic and foreign policy components. Personal security, not just national security, is at stake, and in ways that do not stop at national borders.

SEPTEMBER 11 AND TERRORISM   The domestic consensus in the wake of September 11 was broader and stronger than at any point since the end of the Cold War. It was, once again, foreign policy politics with an Enemy. Polls showed support for the war in Afghanistan at close to 90 percent, for the war in Iraq at 70–80 percent. President Bush's popularity, which had been dipping over the summer of 2001, soared to over 80 percent following September 11, and after a dip in early 2003 it was pushed back over 70 percent by the Iraq war. The public's internationalism index slipped from its initial 81 percent, but still was at 71 percent. Whereas in 1999 only 7 percent had cited foreign policy as one of the biggest problems the United States faces, now 41 percent did. A new sense of patriotism flourished, a sense for many of "recapturing the flag" (see Perspectives on page 345).

This new consensus has its foreign policy benefits, just as it had in the Cold War and other periods in U.S. history. It also has negative aspects for foreign policy politics, just as in the past, raising issues such as the tension between national security and civil liberties and the narrowing of the parameters of policy debate (also taken up in Chapter 7).

Summary

This chapter has provided an overview of foreign policy politics and foreign policy strategy in this new era. We have taken an initial glimpse at the five historical forces shaping the international system in which U.S. foreign policy operates: the end of the Cold War and post–Cold War geopolitics; the "politics of identity" involved in ethnic, religious, and related conflicts; globalization and the social and economic forces it brings into play; global democratization and human rights; and terrorism as a strategic threat in the wake of September 11. We also have laid out the overarching debate between unilateralism and multilateralism as basic approaches to U.S. foreign policy.

PERSPECTIVES
PERSPECTIVES
PERSPECTIVES

"RECAPTURING THE FLAG"

September 11 made it safe for liberals to be patriots. Among the things destroyed with the twin towers was the notion, held by certain Americans ever since Vietnam, that to be stirred by national identity, carry a flag and feel grateful towards someone in uniform ought to be a source of embarrassment. The force of the blows woke us up to the fact that we are part of a national community. This heightened awareness could be the disaster's greatest legacy, one that liberals should not fear but learn to use.

The estrangement of liberal Americans from patriotism is a recent turn. The word "liberal" first came into use among a group of intellectuals who supported Woodrow Wilson taking the country into World War I. In World War II, the anti-fascist war, liberalism and patriotism were still synonymous. My late father, a law professor, quit college to enlist, served on a destroyer and was wounded in action. But by the time I was growing up, on a university campus in the 1960's, too much contrary history had intervened for patriotism to be a part of my moral education: first the McCarthy era, when patriotic slogans were used to target liberals, including my father, and then Vietnam, when American power turned so manifestly unjust. . . .

A strange thing happened after the cold war ended: patriotism all but disappeared from American politics. The right and the left essentially offered a choice between hedonisms: tax cuts or spending. No one asked for sacrifice, no one spoke to common purpose. . . .

September 11 changed that instantly. . . . In the days that followed, we all witnessed an outbreak of civic-mindedness so extreme that it seemed American character had changed overnight. As flags bloomed like flowers, I found that they tapped emotion as quickly as pictures of the missing. . . .

Patriotism is as volatile as any emotion, once released, it can assume ugly forms. "I'm a patriot," said Frank Roque after being arrested for murdering a Sikh in Arizona. But in the past decade, our national disorder has been narcissism, not hysteria. Anyone who wants reform should figure out how to harness the civic passion that rose from the smoking debris. Like jet fuel, it can be used for good or ill. . . .

Source: George Packer, "Recapturing the Flag," *New York Times Magazine,* September 30, 2001, 15–16.

Although foreign policy politics in this new era has its own dynamics, it is structured by the same key domestic political institutions and processes as in earlier eras: president-Congress, intra–executive branch politics, interest groups, the media, and public opinion. All in all, we should not forget that disagreements over issues as important and complex as foreign policy are to be expected. It is precisely because foreign policy issues so often raise such vital concerns and pose choices between such core American values that they take on such political importance. Working those types of debates out is what diplomacy is all about—at home as well as abroad.

Notes

[1]Yeltsin overlapped with the first President Bush for a year but they did not forge a particularly close leader-to-leader relationship. The same was true for Clinton and Putin.

[2]George Liska, *Nations in Alliance: The Limits of Interdependence* (Baltimore: Johns Hopkins University Press, 1962), 12.

[3]Steven K. Vogel, "Final Thoughts: Whither U.S.-Japan Relations?" in Steven K. Vogel, ed., *U.S.-Japan Relations in a Changing World* (Washington, D.C.: Brookings Institution Press, 2002), 264.

[4]Robert D. Kaplan, *Balkan Ghosts: A Journey through History* (New York: St. Martin's Press, 1993).

[5]V. P. Gagnon, Jr., "Ethnic Nationalism and International Conflict: The Case of Serbia," *International Security* 19:3 (Winter 1994–95), 164; Carnegie Commission on Preventing Deadly Conflict, *Final Report* (Washington, D.C.: Carnegie Commission, 1997), 39.

[6]Thomas L. Friedman, *The Lexus and the Olive Tree* (New York: Farrar, Straus and Giroux, 1999), xviii.

[7]Francis Fukuyama, "The End of History?" *National Interest* 16 (Summer 1989), 3.

[8]Samuel P. Huntington, "The Clash of Civilizations," *Foreign Affairs* 72:3 (Summer 1993), 22, 48, 25.

[9]Caleb Carr, *The Lessons of Terror* (New York: Random House, 2002), 6.

[10]President George W. Bush, "West Point Graduation Speech," June 1, 2002, http:/www.whitehouse.gov/news/releases, p. 2.

[11]Ibid., p. 3.

[12]John J. Mearsheimer, "The False Promise of International Institutions," *International Security* 19:3 (Winter 1994–95); Robert J. Art, "A Defensible Defense: America's Grand Strategy after the Cold War," *International Security* 15:4 (Spring 1991); Christopher Layne, "From Preponderance to Offshore Balancing: America's Future Grand Strategy," *International Security* 21:4 (Spring 1997); Samuel P. Huntington, "Why International Primacy Matters," *International Security* 17:4 (Spring 1993).

[13]Martin Wight, "The Balance of Power," in *Diplomatic Investigations: Essays on the Theory of International Politics,* ed. Herbert Butterfield and Martin Wight (Cambridge, Mass.: Harvard University Press, 1966), 150–51.

[14]Mearsheimer, "False Promise of International Institutions," 7, 12.

[15]Condoleezza Rice, "Promoting the National Interest," *Foreign Affairs* 79:1 (January/February 2000), 47.

[16]Henry Kissinger, *Does America Need a Foreign Policy? Towards a Diplomacy for the 21st Century* (New York: Simon and Schuster: 2001).

[17]Stephen G. Brooks and William C. Wohlforth, "American Primacy in Perspective," *Foreign Affairs* 81:4 (July–August 2002), 23.

[18]William Kristol and Robert Kagan, "The Present Danger," *The National Interest* 59 (Spring 2000), 67.

[19]See Layne, "From Preponderance to Offshore Balancing."

[20]Thucydides, *History of the Peloponnesian War,* trans. R. Warner (New York: Penguin, 1972), 402.

[21]George W. Bush, *National Security Strategy 2002,* 3.

[22]Richard K. Betts, "The Soft Underbelly of American Primacy: Tactical Advantages of Terrorism," *Political Science Quarterly* 117:1 (2002), 21.

[23]Richard N. Haass, "Multilateralism for a Global Era," speech on November 14, 2001.

[24]Richard Perle, "Next Stop, Iraq," speech at the Foreign Policy Research Institute (Philadelphia), November 30, 2001, *fpri@fpri.org* e-mail dated November 30, 2001.

[25]Rice, "Promoting the National Interest," 47.

[26]Ibid., 48.

[27]Michael Mandelbaum, "Foreign Policy as Social Work," *Foreign Affairs* 75:1 (January/February 1996), 16–32.

[28]Mearsheimer, "False Promise of International Institutions," 7.

[29]John R. Bolton, "Unilateralism Is not Isolationism," in *Understanding Unilateralism in American Foreign Relations,* ed. Gwyn Prins (London: Royal Institute of International Affairs, 2000), 81.

[30]John R. Bolton, "Should We Take Global Governance Seriously?" paper presented at the American Enterprise Institute conference, "Trends in Global Governance: Do They Threaten American Sovereignty?" April 4–5, 2000, Washington, D.C. (italics in original).

[31]Arthur M. Schlesinger, Jr., "Unilateralism in Historical Perspective," in Prins, *Understanding Unilateralism in American Foreign Relations,* 18.

[32]Among the major works are Robert O. Keohane, *International Institutions and State Power: Essays in International Relations Theory* (Boulder, Colo.: Westview Press, 1989); Robert O. Keohane and Lisa L. Martin, "The Promise of Institutionalist Theory," *International Security* 20:1 (Summer 1995); John G. Ruggie, "Multilateralism: The Anatomy of an Institution," *International Organization* 46:2 (Spring 1992); Ruggie, *Winning the Peace: America and World Order in the New Era* (New York: Columbia University Press, 1996); and Stephen D. Krasner, ed. "International Regimes," special edition of *International Organization* 26:2 (Spring 1982).

[33]Ruggie, "Multilateralism: Anatomy of an Institution," 561.

[34]Bill Clinton, *A National Security Strategy for a New Century* (Washington, D.C.: U.S. Government Printing Office, 1998), 3.

[35]Richard N. Haass, "Defining U.S. Foreign Policy in a Post Post–Cold War World," speech to the Foreign Policy Association, April 22, 2002.

[36]Joseph S. Nye, Jr., *The Paradox of American Power: Why the World's Only Superpower Can't Go It Alone* (New York: Oxford University Press, 2002), 8–9 (italics in original).

[37]Nye, *The Paradox of American Power,* 10.

[38]Keohane and Martin, "Promise of Institutionalist Theory," 42.

[39]Cited in Thomas McCormick, *America's Half-Century: United States Foreign Policy in the Cold War* (Baltimore: Johns Hopkins University Press, 1989), 232.

[40]The Republicans initially controlled the Senate in 2001 based on an even 50–50 split and the

constitutional provision making the vice president the president of the Senate with authority to cast tie-breaking votes. In mid 2001, major differences over domestic policy led Senator James Jeffords, a republican from Vermont, to declare himself an independent and vote with the Democrats. This in effect made for a 51–49 advantage for the Democrats and gave them control of the Senate.

[41]Michael Dobbs and John F. Harris, "French President Chirac Asks Congress to Fund More Peacekeeping in Bosnia," *Washington Post,* June 15, 1995, A34.

[42]John M. Goshko, "In Shift, UN Chief Meets with Helms on Reforms," *Washington Post,* January 24, 1997, A1, A30.

[43]"Text of Lake's Sharply Worded Letter Withdrawing as the CIA Nominee," *New York Times,* March 18, 1997, B6.

[44]Elaine Sciolino, "Old Foes Carve Plowshares before Emotional Congress," *New York Times,* July 27, 1994, A8.

[45]Elizabeth Drew, *On the Edge: The Clinton Presidency* (New York: Simon and Schuster, 1994), 158, 283.

[46]John E. Rielly, ed., *American Public Opinion and U.S. Foreign Policy 1999* (Chicago: Chicago Council on Foreign Relations, 1999), 35.

[47]This section draws on Larry Berman and Bruce W. Jentleson, "Bush and the Post–Cold War World: New Challenges for American Leadership," in *The Bush Presidency: First Appraisals,* ed. Colin Campbell and Bert A. Rockman (Chatham, N.J.: Chatham House, 1991), 93–128.

[48]Cited in Berman and Jentleson, "Bush and the Post–Cold War World," 103.

[49]Elaine Sciolino, "Berger Manages a Welter of Crises in the Post–Cold War White House," *New York Times,* May 18, 1998, A9.

[50]Jane Perlez, "Bush Team's Counsel Is Divided on Foreign Policy," *New York Times,* March 27, 2001, A1, A10.

[51]Council on Foreign Relations Task Force on State Department Reform, www.cfr.org, 3, 7–8.

[52]Tim Weiner, "CIA Study Details Failed Spy System," *New York Times,* June 3, 1998, A1, A8.

[53]Michael Dobbs, "Enthusiasm for Wider Alliance Is Marked by Contradictions," *Washington Post,* July 7, 1995, A1, A24.

[54]Maryann Cusimano Love, "Nongovernmental Organizations: Politics beyond Sovereignty," in Maryann Cusimano Love, ed., *Beyond Sovereignty: Issues for a Global Agenda* (Belmont, Calif.: Wadsworth Thompson, 2003), 75, citing statistics from the *Yearbook of International Organizations.*

[55]Jessica Mathews, "Power Shift," *Foreign Affairs* 76:1 (January/February 1997), 63.

[56]Alexander Cooley and James Ron, "The NGO Scramble: Organizational Insecurity and the Political Economy of Transnational Action," *International Security* 27 (Summer 2002), 5–39.

[57]From a 1998 study by the Pew Center for the People and the Press, available at http://www.people-press.org.

[58]Nik Gowing, presentation at "Managing Information Chaos," conference held at the United States Institute of Peace, Washington, D.C., March 12, 1999.

[59]Ken Auletta, "Annals of Communications: Battle Stations," *The New Yorker,* December 10, 2001, 60–61.

[60]Auletta, "Annals of Communications," 61.

[61]Leonard Downie, Jr., and Robert G. Kaiser, *The News about the News: American Journalism in Peril* (New York: Knopf, 2002), 241.

[62]Cited in Downie and Kaiser, *The News about the News,* 241.

[63]Howard Kurtz, "Despite Sept. 11, Interest Still Low in Foreign News," *Washington Post,* June 10, 2002, A13.

[64]This subsection draws on Bruce Jentleson, "Coercive Prevention: Normative, Political, and Policy Dilemmas," Peaceworks no. 35 (Washington, D.C.: U.S. Institute of Peace, 2000).

[65]Warren P. Strobel, "The Media and U.S. Policies toward Intervention: A Closer Look at the 'CNN Effect'," in Chester A. Crocker and Fen Osler Hampson with Pamela Aall, eds., *Managing Global Chaos* (Washington, D.C.: U.S. Institute of Peace Press, 1996), 358.

[66]Strobel, "The Media and U.S. Policies," 373–74.

[67]Howard Kurtz, "For Media after Iraq, a Case of Shell Shock," *Washington Post,* April 28, 2003, A1.

[68]W. Lance Bennett and David L. Paletz, eds., *Taken by Storm: The Media, Public Opinion and U.S. Foreign Policy in the Gulf War* (Chicago: University of Chicago Press, 1994); Patrick O'Heffernan, "A Mutual Exploitation Model of Media Influence in U.S. Foreign Policy," in Bennett and Paletz, *Taken by Storm,* 232–33.

[69]James M. Lindsay, "The New Apathy: How an Uninterested Public is Reshaping Foreign Policy," *Foreign Affairs 79,* Number 5 (September/October 2000).

[70]John E. Rielly, ed., *American Public Opinion and U.S. Foreign Policy, 1999* (Chicago: Chicago Council on Foreign Relations, 1999), 8, 12.

[71]Steven Kull and I. M. Destler, *Misreading the Public: The Myths of a New Isolationism* (Washington, D.C.: Brookings Institution Press, 1999), 9–32.

[72]Joseph P. Shapiro, "An Epidemic of Fear and Loathing," *U.S. News and World Report,* May 8, 1995, 37–44.

[73]Rielly, ed., *American Public Opinion,* 8.

7 *Power: Still the Name of the Game?*

Introduction: Power in the 21st Century

There is no question that the United States in these opening years of the twenty-first century is the world's most powerful nation. But there are many questions about the strategies for shaping, sustaining, and using that power.

In Chapter 6 we discussed competing conceptions of power in the context of the overarching debates between unilateralism and multilateralism. In this chapter we will delve more into five sets of power-related issues that present themselves for U.S. foreign policy today. The first concerns *the geopolitics of the post–Cold War era.* Russia and China no longer are U.S. enemies, but to what extent are they new friends, and to what extent great-power rivals? What about relations with longtime allies in Europe and Japan? What of the major regional conflicts in South Asia (India–Pakistan), East Asia (North Korea–South Korea) and the Middle East (Arab-Israeli) that have carried over from the Cold War era? The second involves the need for *rethinking military strategy.* Lessons can be drawn from the Persian Gulf War (1990–91) as well as the Kosovo (1999), Afghanistan (2001), and Iraq (2003) wars in this regard. This rethinking also pertains to NATO, regional security, nuclear deterrence, and national missile defense and other aspects of combating the proliferation of weapons of mass destruction. It also raises the latest version of the historical "great debate" on defense spending—how much is enough?

The third set of issues concerns the *war on terrorism.* Prior to September 11, 2001, the post–Cold War agenda featured a number of important issues but no single defining one, in the way anti-communism defined the agenda during the Cold War. After September 11, the war on terrorism became that defining issue for the Bush administration's foreign policy. It posed a range of immediate challenges and also opened up a broad debate over a new doctrine: that of the pre-emptive use of military force. Fourth are *security threats from nonstate actors*. It is necessary not only to bring U.S. power to bear against other states in the international system, but also against terrorists, drug lords, and global crime rings.

The final section focuses on the *domestic politics of homeland security*. The political dynamics of these issues show signs, once again, of foreign policy politics with an Enemy. We see this in the tug-of-war between the president and Congress over war powers, in the executive branch with the bureaucratic politics surrounding the creation of the Department of Homeland Security, and in recurrence of the historical debate over the tensions and trade-offs between national security and civil liberties.

Geopolitics: Major Powers and Regional Conflicts

As discussed in Chapters 4 and 5, the Cold War defined the international system and dominated American foreign policy for most of the half-century following the end of World War II. Its structure was bipolar, with the United States and the Soviet Union at each of the poles. U.S. relations with most other countries in the world were based in large part on Cold War bipolarity. With the end of the Cold War the alignments and dynamics of major power geopolitics were put in flux.

Russia

The great uncertainty about Russia and its future really should not surprise us. Think about it: Russia has not gone through a change just of policy, or of leadership, or ruling party. The Union of Soviet Socialist Republics, proclaimed in 1922 by Vladimir Ilyich Lenin as a new and revolutionary empire setting out to revolutionize the entire world, collapsed and fell apart in 1991. Democracy was proclaimed, capitalism replaced socialism: change swept through every part of Russian society. The first free elections in Russian history were held. A stock market opened in Moscow. Cultural freedom came out of the shadows, and Western influences were let in, including even the Rolling Stones, live and in concert in the summer of 1998 in Moscow (see Perspectives, p. 352).

PERSPECTIVES
PERSPECTIVES
PERSPECTIVES

CHANGE IN RUSSIA SIGNIFIED BY THE ROLLING STONES

MOSCOW, Aug. 12 — Mick Jagger said it all, in Russian. "At last, we are here," the 55-year-old rock star yelled into the microphone, his voice booming across a sports stadium filled with 50,000 cheering Russians. Many had waited 20, even 30 years to see the Rolling Stones, live and in Moscow.

Many fans at tonight's concert—an extravaganza of smoke, lights and special effects dampened only somewhat by a cold rain—had been teenagers when the Stones were at the peak of their popularity. In those days, their records—or copies of their records, ingeniously made on X-ray film—were traded like illicit treasure in Moscow's subway tunnels and dark courtyards, out of sight of the Soviet police. . . .

"I thought I wouldn't live long enough," said Andrei, 42, a Moscow businessman who came to the concert tonight at the Luzhinksi stadium. "For me," echoed Simeon, 40, a television producer who, like Andrei, declined to give his last name, "it is enough if they just walk out on stage. Why? Because for us they are a legend."

The Stones began their concert with "Satisfaction," and the crowd happily joined in, word for word. By trying to keep their youth away from Western mass culture, the Soviet authorities succeeded only in making them commit its lyrics and music to memory. . . .

But it was a local radio station, in a zany talk-show broadcast after the concert, that put the Moscow appearance of the Stones in new historical perspective by staging an imaginary photo linkup between Lenin, the founder of the Soviet state fictitiously resurrected and performing at Carnegie Hall in New York, and Mick Jagger, talking from Moscow, comparing concert notes.

Source: Celestine Bohlen, "For the Rolling Stones' Fans, Satisfaction at Last," *New York Times,* August 12, 1998, p. A4. Copyright © 1998 by the New York Times. Reprinted by permission.

But the process has been a deeply unsettling one in almost every way. There is value to democratic elections having been held, but they have allowed anti-Western demagogues and old-line communists to gain influence in the

Russian Duma (the lower house of the legislature).* Boris Yeltsin held on to the presidency for almost a decade, but at times resorted to means of questionable constitutionality, did not govern very effectively, and periodically lapsed from the scene due to health problems. Russian capitalism has been shaky at best, deeply corrupt at worst, with workers and government employees and even soldiers going months without receiving their paychecks while robber-baron company heads made millions for themselves. The Russian economy shrank by almost 40 percent in the first decade following the breakup of the Soviet Union. International investors have had recurring crises of confidence, and Wall Street and other Western stock markets have felt the shocks from Russian economic instability.

Fundamentally, no matter what the particular nature or pace of ups and downs, the central issue for Russia is, as Stanford University's Gail Lapidus poses it, "defining a new Russian identity and place in the world after the Soviet collapse."[1] Russia "was attempting to come to grips with a profound and traumatic set of losses." It had lost territory, its alliance system, much of its power, and even its superpower status.

> The sudden transformation of a country that had once controlled the fate of millions to a country that perceived itself to have lost control of its own fate created an unaccustomed and radical sense of vulnerability that deeply influenced the ongoing Russian struggle to define its identity and its place in the post–Cold War international system. How to manage the fundamental asymmetry of power, interests and priorities had become and would long remain the central challenge of the Russian-American bilateral relationship.[2]

As Russia deals with these issues, three scenarios are possible for the Russian American foreign policy relationship: Russia as friend, Russia as great-power competitor, or Russia as adversary.

RUSSIA AS FRIEND "Ron and Mikhail," "Bill and Boris," "George and Vladimir"—the end of the Cold War brought quite a bit of chumminess between American and Soviet/Russian leaders. There was much mutual praise, lots of amiable photo ops, plenty of pledges to work together. Andrei Kozyrev, Yeltsin's first foreign minister, spoke in 1992 of Russia becoming "a reliable partner in the community of civilized nations."[3] Warren Christopher, President Clinton's first secretary of state, reciprocated with numerous affirmations of his own about the new Russian-American friendship. The administration of George W. Bush initially was much harsher in its rhetoric and approach, but

---

*See Chapter 10 for further discussion of Russian democratization.

President Bush left his first summit with Russian president Vladimir Putin speaking of a newfound friend.

A number of genuine and substantive areas of foreign policy cooperation have emerged in the first decade-plus of the post–Cold War Russian-American relationship:

U.S. Foreign Aid to Russia and the Other Ex-Soviet States.   American aid to Russia and the other ex-Soviet states exceeded $13 billion in the 1990s. These programs included food aid, medical and health care aid, business development, a first-time Peace Corps presence, funding for the development of the rule of law and other democratization initiatives, military cooperation, and even the construction of housing for former Soviet troops returning from East Germany and elsewhere in Eastern Europe. All this was quite a change from the preceding half-century, when the Soviet threat was the principal rationale for U.S. foreign aid programs to other states during the Cold War. It was somewhat reminiscent of World War II, when as part of the anti-Hitler alliance, Russia was second only to the United Kingdom as a beneficiary of Lend-Lease and other U.S. aid programs.

Nuclear Arms Control.   The first of the post-Cold War U.S.-Soviet nuclear arms-control agreements, known as START (the Strategic Arms Reduction Treaty), was signed in 1991 by President George H.W. Bush and Russian president Mikhail Gorbachev. It cut strategic nuclear weapons from Cold War levels of 13,000 U.S. and 11,000 Soviet warheads to 6,000 on each side. START I was ratified by both the U.S. Senate and the Russian Duma. START II, mandating further cuts of about 50 percent, was signed in 1993 and ratified by the U.S. Senate in 1996 but not by the Russian Duma until 2000. The third major treaty, the Moscow Treaty on Strategic Offensive Reductions, was signed by Presidents George W. Bush and Putin in May 2002. It superceded START II with deeper cuts, to 1,700–2,200 on each side. "This treaty will liquidate the legacy of the Cold War," President Bush declared. "The new era will be a period of enhanced mutual security, economic security and improved relations."[4] Opposition to the Bush-Putin agreement was limited and came mostly from those who felt it achieved too little, not too much, arms control.

Cooperative Threat Reduction.   Many analysts believe that the most serious security threat the United States now faces from Russia is from its "loose nukes." Amid the economic instability and broader societal dislocation that Russia has been going through, concerns have been great about the safety and security of the country's remaining nuclear weapons, of the plutonium and other components from those weapons being dismantled, and from Russian weapons scientists who might be tempted to sell their expertise on the "WMD market" to rogue states or terrorists. The Nunn-Lugar Cooperative Threat Reduction program, named for its key congressional bipartisan sponsors, Senators Sam Nunn (D-Ga.) and Richard Lugar (R-Ind.), has provided U.S. funds, expertise, and other assistance on a cooperative basis with the Russian government to reduce these dangers.

NATO Expansion.   Russian cooperation on the expansion of the North Atlantic Treaty Organization (NATO) to include former Soviet and Soviet bloc states has been greater than many anticipated. Russia has ended up conceding more than opposing, first in 1997 when NATO added three former Warsaw Pact members (Poland, Hungary, and the Czech Republic), and then in 2002 when another seven were offered alliance membership, including four more former Warsaw Pact states (Bulgaria, Romania, Slovakia, Slovenia) and the three Baltic states that formerly were part of the Soviet Union (Estonia, Latvia, Lithuania). Each time, Russia won its own agreement with NATO, giving it enhanced status for consultations and cooperation but not a veto or its own membership. The first of these agreements did not work very well; time will tell on the second.

The War on Terrorism.   Putin was the first foreign leader to phone President Bush with condolences and support following the September 11 terrorist attacks. Russian cooperation was especially important in the war in Afghanistan against the Taliban and Al Qaeda. It included Russian aid to the anti-Taliban Northern Alliance, and agreement not to oppose U.S. military bases set up in the former Soviet republics of Uzbekistan, Tajikistan, and Kyrgyzstan. The significance of Russian consent to an American military presence in these former Soviet republics is not to be underestimated, given the more competitive dynamics on other issues involving the Russian "near abroad." In part, Russia agreed to the U.S. military presence in anticipation of at least a tacit quid pro quo from Washington on Russia's efforts to quell the separatist insurgency in Chechnya, a largely Muslim part of the Russian Federation, which the Russian government portrays as its own war on terrorism.

In sum, the areas of cooperation have been quite substantial. There has been a strong basis for claims of a developing friendship and, as National Security Adviser Condoleezza Rice put it, that "we and the Russians are increasingly moving toward a common security agenda."[5] Yet there have also been signs of tension and issues of contention, indicative of the competition, actual and potential, between the United States and Russia as major powers.

RUSSIA AS GEOPOLITICAL COMPETITOR   When the second Bush administration first came into office, the "geopolitical competitor" view dominated. "In some ways," Secretary of State Colin Powell stated, "the approach to Russia shouldn't be terribly different than the very realistic approach we had to the old Soviet Union in the late '80s. We told them what bothered us. We told them where we could engage on things. We tried to convince them of the power of our values and our system. They argued back."[6] Others in the administration were even more caustic. Secretary of Defense Donald Rumsfeld accused Russia of being "an active proliferator . . . helping Iran and others develop nuclear and other weapons of mass destruction." Paul Wolfowitz, the deputy secretary of defense, was even blunter, saying that the Russians "seem to be willing to sell anything to anyone for money." The Russian response to such statements was to accuse the Bush administration of reverting to "the spirit of the Cold War."[7] The personal rapport between Bush and Putin and the policy of cooperation on the war on terrorism shifted the dynamic more toward friendship, but with no guarantee that the competitive dynamic would not re-emerge. Thus far that competition has had five main bases.

The Balkan Wars.   As fellow Slavs and for their own geopolitical reasons, Russia and Serbia historically have had close relations. Serbia thus had pretty solid Russian support as it aggressively struggled for dominance as Yugoslavia was breaking up. During the war in Bosnia & Herzegovina (1992–95), while the United States sided with the Bosnian Muslims, Russia sided with the Serbs. These differences were bridged following the 1995 Dayton accord, which brought an end to the Bosnian war. The Russian military even was brought into the NATO-led peacekeeping effort that followed.

The Kosovo war, though, was a much greater source of tension. Again, Russian sympathies and political allegiances were with the Serbs; the United States and NATO sided with the Muslim Kosovars. This time, the United States and NATO actually intervened militarily in the conflict, not just after the fact as a peacekeeping force. Although the U.S.-NATO intervention was in reaction to Serbian aggression, from the Russian perspective the key issues were that the military action was taken against a sovereign state (whereas Bosnia was an independent state, Kosovo was a province of Serbia) and without UN Security Council authorization. As Lapidus observed, this "fed into an already heightened sense of Russia's own vulnerability and fueled highly implausible anxieties about Kosovo as a precedent for possible Western intervention in Russia's internal affairs, particularly in Chechnya."[8] When the war reached the point that NATO was about to move from air strikes to ground troops, Russia helped with the diplomacy, convincing Serbian leader Slobodan Milosevic to concede and withdraw. Even then, though, the peacekeeping cooperation was much less than in Bosnia, and the issues raised persisted both directly (as U.S.-Russian tensions over the Balkans) and on the broader multilateral issues of sovereignty and intervention.

Chechnya. Since 1994 Russia has fought two wars against Chechen separatists. The Chechens have been guilty of their own atrocities, but most analysts see the Russians as the aggressors. The United States has been faced with a power-principles tension: between, on the one hand, its strategic interests in maintaining good relations with Russia, and, on the other, the atrocities and other blatant human rights violations the Russian troops have committed in Chechnya. In 1996, during the first Chechen war, President Clinton drew stinging criticism from human rights advocates and others for drawing an analogy to the U.S. Civil War, with Russian president Boris Yeltsin as Russia's Abraham Lincoln seeking to preserve the union. The Clinton administration was a bit more critical of the Russians in the Chechnya war that began in 1999. So too was the Bush administration, initially. But after September 11, the Russians cast Chechnya as their own war on terrorism. National Security Adviser Sergei Ivanov went so far as to cast the Russian war in Chechnya as in the West's interest, with Russia serving as "a front-line warrior fighting international terrorism . . . saving the civilized world [from] the terrorist plague in the same way as it used to save Europe from the Tatar-Mongol invasion in the 12th century."[9]

The Russian Near Abroad. The "near abroad" is the term Russia uses to refer to the other former Soviet republics. To Russia this is its sphere of influence, an area in which it claims a right to exert political pressure and even intervene militarily to protect its interests, as it already has done in Georgia, Moldova, Tajikistan, Armenia, and Azerbaijan. Putin drew his own precedent from the Bush administration's doctrine of pre-emption for asserting Russia's own right to intervene in other states if it determines that terrorism or some other serious threat exists.

The Middle East and Persian Gulf. During the Cold War U.S.-Soviet rivalry was deep and recurring in these regions. In this context, the Russian-American cooperation that was achieved in the early 1990s is quite significant. During the 1990–91 Persian Gulf War, while Russia did not join the U.S.-led military coalition, it did give unprecedented diplomatic cooperation to the war effort. Russia and the United States jointly co-chaired the Middle East multilateral peace negotiations of the 1990s, involving Israel and most Arab countries, on issues ranging from arms control and regional security to regional economic cooperation, water, and the environment.

Iran and Iraq, though, have been more divisive issues. The Clinton and the Bush administrations both have accused Russia of providing Iran with technology and materials for the development of nuclear weapons and ballistic missiles. At one point the United States imposed economic sanctions on Russia to pressure it to end its nuclear assistance to Iran. On Iraq, throughout the 1990s Russia had been a consistent opponent within the UN Security Council of U.S. efforts to tighten economic sanctions and get UN weapons inspectors back into Iraq to uncover Saddam Hussein's weapons of mass destruction. Only in 2002–03 when inspections became the alternative to U.S. military action did Russia shift to being pro-inspections. Russia joined France in threatening to use its UN Security Council veto to try to block American military action. It too was quite critical of the war once it was initiated. Putin labeled it "some new form of colonialism."[10] Russian motivations were in part economic: the $7 billion debt Saddam owed Russia, plus the stakes the rising Russian oil industry had in potential investment opportunities in Iraq. They also were geopolitical, as the balance of power and influence in this crucial region entered yet another period of historic transformation. Both of these sets of factors make it likely that Iraq's future will continue to be a contentious issue in U.S.-Russian relations.

The Global Balance-of-Power.   One of the axioms of international relations is that major powers often seek to balance against whichever state is the most powerful in the international system. Indeed, Russian National Security Adviser Ivanov has spoken in broad terms of "a new architecture of a multipolar world," counterpointed to American hegemony and global dominance, with "the distribution of roles between separate, dynamically developing poles of the international community that will create optimum prerequisites for stable development, ensuring global stability and security."[11] One manifestation of this effort toward "dynamically developing poles" was the Russia-China friendship treaty signed in July 2001, characterized by one Russian commentator as an "act of friendship against America."[12] Another was the Russian-French-German countercoalition that took shape in 2003 against the United States over Iraq.

RUSSIA AS ADVERSARY   In a third possible scenario Russia could become an adversary. Columbia University scholar Robert Legvold has raised concern about an "alienated and combative Russia. . . . It would take only a mishandling of the mounting issues in contention between the United States and Russia to turn Russia into the odd man out among great powers, a spoiler in the sphere of great power cooperation, and a state with a grudge looking for ways to inflict damage on U.S. interests."[13]

This could occur in one of two ways. One would be through the rise of a nationalist leader who might go beyond the normal great-power competition and seek to rebuild an empire and regain global influence through an aggressive and militaristic foreign policy. Expansionism is rooted deep in Russian history, it is argued; it did not just start with Lenin and the communists. Moreover, the instabilities of Russian politics raise concerns that, as with Hitler in Weimar Germany in the 1930s, an aggressively nationalist leader could be brought to power promising to restore the motherland's greatness. The extremist Vladimir Zhirinovsky, with promises to restore the old Russian empire (including taking back Alaska!), caused a scare with the gains he and his party made in the December 1993 Duma elections. The communist Gennadi Zyuganov raised new fears with the political support he was showing leading up to the June 1996 presidential elections. Neither prevailed, but that hasn't alleviated the concern that they or others like them may come to power, whether through elections or nondemocratic means such as a military coup.

The other scenario involves Russia becoming a major threat more out of weakness than of strength. The concern here is of a Russia that is less and less able to govern itself effectively. As Legvold also observed, "Russia alone among the great powers ends [the twentieth] century with unanswered questions about its ability to avoid a basic breakdown of its domestic order and maybe even its demise as a state."[14] The specter raised has many aspects, perhaps most significantly (from a U.S. perspective) the "loose nukes" issue raised earlier: an accidental launching after a false alarm that is not checked out properly amid the breakdown of discipline or of equipment; an intentional but unauthorized launching by disgruntled officers; a terrorist group stealing or buying a nuclear weapon. Such scenarios have been depicted in Hollywood movies and Tom Clancy novels, but any one of them could be all too real.

China

In Chapter 5 we discussed the Nixon-Kissinger opening to China and how the principal basis for it was the geopolitical calculus of the common enemy: the

Soviet Union. Trade and other relations between the United States and China also developed over the 1970s and 1980s. However, four main developments have made the period since the end of the Cold War one of greater U.S.-China differences.

One was greater conflicts over human rights precipitated by the 1989 massacre in Beijing's Tiananmen Square of Chinese students and other pro-democracy demonstrators. This case was examined back in Chapter 1 as an example of tension between power and prosperity vs. principles for U.S. foreign policy. The first Bush administration opted to give priority to power over principles and imposed only limited economic sanctions. The Clinton administration came into office having heavily criticized its predecessor for not championing democracy and human rights, but it too stopped short of serious sanctions against China. Its motivation was more prosperity than power, given its interests in the rapidly growing investment in and trade with China. Both administrations faced strong pro–human rights opposition in Congress and among nongovernmental organizations (NGOs), which ensured that democratization and human rights stayed on the agenda of Chinese-American relations.

Second was that, with the end of the Cold War and the disappearance of the shared Soviet enemy, China and the United States entered the post–Cold War era with their global, geopolitical differences more apparent than their commonalities. Given China's extraordinary economic growth and modernization as well as its assertive style of diplomacy, many analysts believe it may be even more of a possible challenger for global-power status in the coming decades than Russia. Although it is still well below U.S. levels, China has been increasing its military spending and modernizing its military capabilities. On the other hand, from the Chinese perspective there is a long history of having been exploited and dominated by foreign powers because of its weakness. "The emphasis on strength and security," the late scholar Michel Oksenberg argued, "stems from the penetration and perceived exploitation of a weak China by each of the major powers. . . . The demand for respect, dignity and a voice in the councils of nations originates in the humiliations heaped upon China not only in the treaties forced upon its rulers in the nineteenth century but its lack of voice at Versailles at the end of World War I and Yalta at the end of World War II."[15] Oksenberg's point is not to forget that what may seem offensive to the United States may be intended as defensive by China.

Third, China's further emergence as a regional power in East Asia threatens to upset the regional balance of power. Chinese fears of encirclement conflict directly with the fears of Japan and others in the region of Chinese hegemony. This, too, has to be understood from both perspectives. China was invaded by Japan during World War II, it faced strong containment policies during the Cold War from the U.S. Asian alliance system, and it currently shares borders with fourteen different countries. On the other hand Japan, the Philippines, South Korea, and other Asian states feel somewhat intimidated by Chinese military capabilities and hold some doubts about the peacefulness of Chinese intentions. As China grows stronger economically and militarily, the regional balance of power becomes increasingly imbalanced. As a reverse corollary to the point made at the global level, what may be cast as defensive by China may seem offensive to others.

Fourth is the issue of Taiwan. This has been and continues to be the tensest issue in U.S.-China relations. The crux of this issue is the same as it has been since the 1949 Chinese communist victory: Will Taiwan be absorbed into mainland China, or will it retain its separateness and perhaps even become a recognized independent nation? And will the issue be settled peacefully?

The main options for dealing with China as defined in the U.S. policy debate have been containment and engagement. *Containment* is a variation, albeit milder and more limited, of the Cold War strategy toward the Soviet Union. The strategy that follows from this analysis is short of confrontational but is firm, cautious, attentive to threats and relative power—i.e., geared to containment. It rests on the same logic as George Kennan's original 1947 formulation of containment of the Soviet Union (Chapter 4): that the internal changes needed to make China both less of a threat and more of a democracy are more likely to occur if the country's external ambitions are contained and the system is thus forced to fall on its own contradictions. Summits are OK, as they were for Henry Kissinger with the Soviets, but the U.S. posture should be kept strong. Historically the international system has tended to have problems absorbing major new powers, so caution is the watchword.

A number of crises and controversies reinforced the containment posture toward China. In 1998 word spread that China had used contacts developed through military, scientific, and economic cooperation with the United States to steal secrets about American nuclear weapons design and development. Tensions over Taiwan again flared in mid-1999 after the Taiwanese president made pro-independence statements and China responded with barely veiled threats. These controversies heightened concerns about the Chinese military buildup and about Chinese provocations on a number of regional security issues.

Those who support *engagement* take a different view of China, although not a polar opposite. They are wary about Chinese regional interests but assess them as less threatening. China wants the role in the Asia-Pacific to which, based on its size and history, it feels entitled. This does create tensions, and the United States must stand by its allies and its interests, but these issues can be worked out through diplomacy and negotiations. Besides, militarily, China doesn't come close to matching the United States, even with its recent advances. Taiwan is acknowledged as a more contentious issue, although policymakers are cautioned to be careful that the Taiwanese don't exploit U.S. support to be provocative.

This view makes the argument for a strategy that emphasizes integration and diplomacy. China needs to be brought into more multilateral organizations, both economic ones such as the World Trade Organization and strategic ones such as the Missile Technology Control Regime. This integration will provide structured and peaceful mechanisms for dealing with China's own concerns, and will also encourage China to adopt international norms and abide by international rules. On a bilateral basis the United States should continue with periodic summits, other diplomacy, trade, and other areas of engagement. Human rights issues and democratization are not to be ignored, and other approaches pursued, but the explicit sanctions–human rights linkage is strongly rejected. Too many issues are involved to allow overall relations to pivot strictly on this issue. Trade and investment interests are not least among these: American investment in China has grown enormously, and future prospects are for even greater growth.

Whereas the Clinton administration leaned more toward engagement, initially the second Bush administration tilted more toward containment. The Bush administration drew the distinction between the Clinton view of the relationship as a "strategic partnership" and its own view of "strategic competition." This changed outlook was revealed in Secretary of State Powell's first statement on China: "Our challenge with China is to do what we can that is constructive, that is helpful and that is in our interest. . . . A *strategic partner* China is not, but neither is China our inevitable and implacable foe. China is a *competitor,* a potential regional rival but also a trading partner willing to cooperate in areas where our strategic interests overlap. . . . China is all of these things, but China is not an enemy, and our challenge is to keep it that way."[16]

The U.S.-China relationship was seriously tested starting in April 2001. On April 1 an American intelligence-gathering plane flying in international airspace off the coast of China collided with a Chinese air force jet in an accident most attributed to recklessness on the part of the Chinese pilot. The American plane made an emergency landing on a Chinese island. The crew members were held for ten days, until negotiations between the Bush administration and the Chinese government secured their release. Negotiations were tough, at times teetering toward escalation. The terms finally agreed to were for an American partial apology in exchange for the Chinese release of the crew. Despite some criticisms, the Bush administration generally was credited with handling the crisis effectively.

A key debate arose over what lessons to draw from the spy-plane crisis. What did the crisis tell us about China? What did it tell us about U.S. strategies in its relationship with China? One view was that it reinforced the "strategic competitor" conception over the "strategic partner" one, and the need to stress containment over engagement. Fighter-jet harassment at 20,000 feet and holding a crew captive are not the ways "partners" treat each other; what the Chinese understand is toughness and resolve. Another view also took the incident very seriously but drew a more measured assessment for U.S. strategy. The U.S. response succeeded because it was firm without being confrontational. It stopped short of the provocative actions proposed by some hawks, such as moving aircraft carriers and other military forces into the region. Also in this view, it was in part the economic and other ties built through engagement that gave the Chinese leadership the interests and incentives to resolve the crisis cooperatively.

Almost immediately on top of the spy-plane crisis came another over the issue of arms sales to Taiwan. Part of the agreements going back to the 1970s and 1980s for the normalization of U.S.-China relations was that the United States would continue to sell Taiwan defensive weapons but not offensive ones. The line between what is defensive (and therefore stabilizing) and what is offensive (and thus risks being destabilizing) often is not inherently clear in the nature of a weapons system. Moreover, it is not just the particulars of the weapons system but perceptions of intent and message that affect assessments of its potential use. In this instance the Bush administration sought to strike a balance by selling some weapons to Taiwan, but not those most objectionable to China. This issue no doubt will come up again when the next arms package is put together for Taiwan.

The impact of the war on terrorism on Sino-American relations has also been mixed. The bullish view, as articulated in early 2002 by Richard Holbrooke, who was UN ambassador in the Clinton administration and assistant secretary of state for East Asia in the Carter administration, sees a "unique opportunity offered by the fact that China and the United States once again share a common strategic concern—terrorism—on which a revitalized relationship can be based."[17] China has joined the anti-terrorism coalition and cooperated with the United States in a number of ways. A more skeptical view, though, sees this cooperation as limited in scope and significance. As

Princeton professor Aaron Friedberg has argued, "it was not the result of a convergence of basic strategic visions or fundamental values, but rather the product of special circumstances that permitted what will likely prove to have been a partial and fleeting confluence of interests." Friedberg and others further question whether, like with Russia on Chechnya, China is especially interested in justifying its own conflicts with its own Muslim separatists (the Uighurs, a largely Muslim group of about nine million people in the far western province of Xinjiang) under the anti-terrorism umbrella.[18]

The broader containment-engagement debate also continued within the Bush administration, as evidenced by a Pentagon report on the Chinese military leaked to the press in July 2002. The report concluded that the Chinese military threat was still being underestimated. It estimated China's annual military budget at $65 billion per year, not the $20 billion the Chinese government officially claimed. This still was a lot less than the U.S. defense budget, and the military capabilities being developed still would not be enough to invade and conquer Taiwan. The argument, though, was that the emerging Chinese strategy was "coercive over annihilative. . . . Beijing is pursuing the ability to force Taiwan to negotiate on Beijing's terms regarding unification with the mainland."[19] Others raised related concerns about China as a key source of missile proliferation to Iran and Pakistan.

Chinese opposition to the United States in the Iraq war seemed to reinforce the views of the skeptics, although the fact that China kept a lower profile in its opposition than France, Germany, or Russia was taken by some as a tacit nod in the U.S. direction. Different readings also were taken on the nuclear proliferation crisis with North Korea. China long had been North Korea's main ally. Indeed the 1950–53 Korean War came close to escalating to a war also between China and the United States. Some believed China had played a significant role for many years aiding North Korean development of nuclear weapons. The crisis intensified in 2002–03 over new evidence that North Korea had continued developing nuclear weapons, despite being a signatory to the Nuclear Nonproliferation Treaty and in violation of its 1994 agreement with the United States. The Bush administration exerted pressure on China to pressure North Korea. China's own assessments also began to shift toward questioning whether its traditional support for North Korea was still in its own national interest. The issue was positioned as one which could provide either further basis for or impediment to Sino-American cooperation.

Underlying the overall foreign policy debate are mounting concerns about China's domestic situation. Here too the United States has to be concerned about threats that may come from weakness as well as from strength. The Chinese middle class continues to grow; it was estimated in 2002 to comprise about 100 million people and to be growing about 20 percent a year. But China's economic growth has been slowing, and the rising standard of living of the 1980s and early 1990s has stalled. Fully 800 million peasants have largely been left out of the benefits, even when economic growth was rapid. Estimates of the number of unemployed Chinese range as high as 100 million. Some analysts see Chinese membership in the World Trade Organization (WTO) as holding "long-term promise" but bringing "unprecedented economic and political challenges" in the short term, potentially setting off "future shock" that could "increase the pains of reform and pressures on the government."[20] China also faces mounting social problems. Its levels of social investment are low even in comparison to other low-income countries; on education, for example, only 2.6 percent of GDP, below the average of 3.4 percent. Even before the 2003 SARS epidemic (severe acute respiratory syndrome) China's health system was ranked 144th in the world by the World Health Organization, behind India, Indonesia, and Bangladesh. Its incidence of AIDS has been mounting at alarming rates, leading some experts to warn about a crisis equal to or even worse than the one that has occurred in Africa.[21]

These social and economic problems are both causes of and further complications to internal political uncertainties and potential sources of instability. The 2002 leadership succession proved rockier than anticipated. Hu Jintao emerged as the new leader, but only after President Jiang Zemin, who was scheduled to retire from the presidency as well as his other two top leadership posts as head of the Communist Party and chairman of the Central Military Command, pushed to retain at least one of his powerful positions. Human rights and democratization pressures also continued, including the highly public opposition of the Falun Gong, a partly spiritual and partly political-nationalist movement that has staged major political demonstrations and civil disobedience in China and abroad.*

Western Europe

At first glance it might seem that the United States and western Europe have so much else in common that even with the end of the Cold War, relations between the two would be strong. They are a community of democracies. They are highly economically interdependent. They still face common threats, including

---

*See Chapter 10 for further discussion of democratization and human rights in China.

global terrorism. They still have NATO as the most successful peacetime alliance in history. Yet transatlantic geopolitics also have had to make adjustments.

7.1

Even before the Iraq war Robert Kagan, a conservative American analyst and columnist, postulated a deep and fundamental European-American divergence: "It is time to stop pretending that Americans and Europeans share a common view of the world," he wrote. "On major strategic and international questions Americans are from Mars and Europeans from Venus: They agree on little and understand one another less and less."[22] Kagan put most of the blame on the Europeans for naivete about the continuing need for power and force in international affairs, for lapsing further into military weakness, and for not pulling their weight in NATO, especially on global security threats.

Many Europeans see the problems quite differently. In this view the United States has fallen into a "cult of unilateralism," characterized by an "instinctive refusal to admit to any political restraint on its action . . . placing itself above international law, norms and restraints when they do not suit its objectives." There is some acknowledgment of "European legalistic fervour" as going too far in its own right, and both sides contributing to "a dialogue of the deaf."[23] But the driving dynamic is seen as emanating from the United States' side of the Atlantic.

Whatever one's view of the causes, it was clear by 2001–02 that the list of issues on which the United States and western Europe were in conflict had been growing longer. The list included the Kyoto global warming treaty, the International Criminal Court, the multilateral land mines treaty, relations with Iran, the Israeli-Palestinian conflict, and a number of international trade issues. And then came the Iraq war, on which the tensions ran extremely high and the conflicts cut quite deep. Britain was front and center in supporting the United States, as were a number of other European countries. But France and Germany were strongly opposed. Foreign Minister Dominique de Villepin of France went so far as to threaten to use France's veto in the UN Security Council to try to block U.S. military action against Iraq. In Germany, Chancellor Gerhard Schroeder manipulated the Iraq issue to gain crucial support in his 2002 re-election campaign, and pledged not to support military action against Iraq even if the UN Security Council authorized it.

These intra-European differences partly fit with earlier patterns of relations with the United States and partly manifested transitions to post–Cold War foreign policy identities. British-American relations, while not the "special relationship" of Roosevelt and Churchill during World War II, had been close under Clinton as well as Bush. In the Persian Gulf War, the "no-fly zone" 1990s containment strategy against Iraq, the Kosovo war, the Afghanistan war,

and especially in the Iraq war, British and American interests have been sufficiently shared to provide the basis for joint military action.

While the U.S.-French conflict over Iraq was particularly intense, tensions
in this relationship were hardly new. It was right in the middle of the Cold
War that President Charles de Gaulle took France out of the NATO military
command. U.S. leaders often see France as an irksome ally, a country that has-
n't come to grips with its faded imperial status. The French side, in turn, often
views the United States as naive, arrogant, still an upstart. In more specific
terms, policy conflicts have arisen over such issues as relations with Iran and
Iraq, the Arab-Israeli peace process, and a number of African conflicts, particularly in countries that used to be French colonies. A 2002 poll showed 60 percent of French respondents agreeing that "Europe should be more
independent" from the United States in its foreign policy, compared to 51 percent in Germany and 47 percent in the United Kingdom.[24]

As for Germany, one of the old sayings about NATO as cited in Chapter 4
was that, in addition to keeping the Russians out of Europe and the Americans
in, its tacit purpose was also to keep the Germans down. Germany's "traumatic past" and the determination "never again to allow German militarism
and nationalism to threaten European stability," as German scholar Hans
Maull has written, defined the parameters of Germany's foreign policy as that
of a "civilian power."[25] The toughest post–Cold War issues for Germany have
involved military intervention. With the United States and other NATO countries deploying peacekeeping forces in Bosnia and then fighting the war in
Kosovo, yet the former Yugoslavia having been an area of Nazi brutalization
during World War II, how were historical memory and present alliance obligations to be balanced in deciding what role the German military should take
on? German troops did join in the Bosnia peacekeeping effort, and the German air force participated in the Kosovo war, in ways that struck a balance
and marked an evolution of, but not a departure from, the "civilian power"
role. This issue came up again during the 2001 Afghanistan war, when Chancellor Schroeder proposed committing almost 4,000 German troops to the
war effort. The sensitivity and complexity of the issue was evidenced in the
fact that the bill authorizing the participation of the Bundeswehr (the German army) passed the Bundestag (German parliament) by only two votes.
When the Iraq war came up, Schroeder was in the midst of a tough re-election
campaign. He seized on the issue as a way of gaining support from those German voters who had become the most anti-American. This was a striking contrast with how for decades it had been pro-American positions that had been
good politics in Germany.

U.S.-European relations also are being affected by efforts of the European Union (EU) to further develop a "common foreign and security policy" (CFSP). The EU's goal is to establish itself as a stronger and more independent foreign policy player in its own right. The CFSP, however, has been slower to develop than EU economic collaboration. Although most European countries now use the euro, the common European currency that began replacing national currencies in 2002, foreign policy is still made primarily in individual national capitals like London, Paris, and Berlin rather than at EU headquarters in Brussels. The Iraq issue underscored this as well, not only with Britain being on one side and France and Germany on the other, but also in the minor role played by the key EU foreign policy officials Javier Solana and Christopher Patten.

Another key CFSP issue is creation of the Rapid Reaction Force (called the "Eurocorps" by some), a 60,000-troop military force deployable on short notice (sixty days) under EU command, separate from NATO. Proponents stress that this force would be coordinated with and complementary to NATO while giving the EU the capacity to act militarily when NATO chooses not to. Critics question whether competition inevitably would arise that could create EU-U.S. tensions. Here too the issue was hard enough before the Iraq war and even harder after. This was evident at a mini-summit called in April 2003 by France and Germany; the intent was claimed to strengthen NATO rather than counter-maneuver against it, but doubts were raised by Britain and other EU nations that had supported the United States and were excluded from the meeting.

Japan

For U.S.-Japan relations as well, the end of the Cold War has raised new issues and dynamics. The old security concern of a Soviet invasion no longer pertains; Russia and Japan still have some outstanding issues, including territorial disputes dating from World War II, but their relations now are well within the bounds of diplomacy. Nevertheless, the U.S.-Japan security alliance has at least as much if not more importance today for maintaining the Asia-Pacific regional balance of power. "Our security relationship with Japan is the linchpin of United States security policy in Asia," the Pentagon has stated. "It is seen not just by the United States and Japan, but throughout the region, as a major factor for securing stability in Asia."[26] A new U.S.-Japan defense agreement was signed in 1997, and about half of the one hundred thousand American military personnel in the Asia-Pacific region continue to be based in Japan.

Within this basic alliance, however, there are some tensions. One is over trade and other economic issues. The trade disputes that began in the 1970s and grew especially heated in the 1980s have been tempered as Japan's economic problems in recent years have taken away from its image as an economic powerhouse. Still, as long as U.S.-Japanese trade continues to run sharp imbalances, with the U.S. side carrying the deficit, trade will continue to be a point of contention. So too with banking and financial issues. The Japanese government's weakness in dealing with its own economic problems exacerbated the overall Asian financial crisis of the late 1990s and, because of the much greater size of the Japanese economy, reverberated even more than the Russian economic instability on Wall Street.*

A second issue concerns, to borrow from the title of a popular Japanese book, "The Japan that Can Say No." Say "no," that is, to the United States, a sentiment that reflects resentments on that side of the Pacific that mirror the Japan-bashing on this side. Whereas some in the United States have felt that Japan takes advantage of American support, some in Japan feel that the United States is too domineering and that their country needs to show that it can't be taken for granted to always follow the American lead. An issue on which these sentiments have been especially strong has been the presence of U.S. military bases in Japan, especially on the island of Okinawa. Tensions over the continued existence of the Okinawa bases have been exacerbated by a number of incidents in which American soldiers stationed there have been charged with rape and other sexual offenses. Another incident involved a tragic accident off Hawaii in early 2001, in which a U.S. submarine crashed into a Japanese fishing boat that had families and young children aboard, killing nine Japanese and injuring many more. While these are incidents and not policy, they tap deep strands of Japanese political opinion.

Third is Japan's post–Cold War military role. The "peace constitution" written for Japan by the United States during the post–World War II occupation limited Japan's military forces strictly to self-defense. The question now is whether those limits should be loosened somewhat. As with Germany, this reflects pressures to become a more "normal" major power amid a historical legacy of aggression and militarism. This balancing is a concern not just for the United States but also for Japan's regional neighbors. Americans often don't appreciate the extent to which anti-Japan sentiments and fears persist in China, in South Korea, in the Philippines, and elsewhere in the region; these fears draw not only on the World War II experience, but go back further in

---

*We discuss this more in Chapter 9.

history. Many Japanese are themselves concerned that a more active military role would lead to a shift back to militarism and an undermining of Japanese democracy.

As late as the 1990–91 Persian Gulf War, this historical legacy was sufficiently strong that the Japanese Diet (its legislature) rejected a bill even for a limited, noncombat role for the Japanese military in the war; instead, Japan confined its role to providing financial assistance. Some shift came during the 1990s as the Diet passed the International Peace Cooperation Law, which allows Japanese military units to serve in some UN peacekeeping missions, albeit in limited roles. Then in 2001 the war on terrorism posed further challenges. This time the Diet passed a bill permitting Japan to take on a limited noncombat military role. As reported at the time,

> Flying the Rising Sun flag, a destroyer, a minesweeper and a supply ship left Japanese naval bases Sunday headed for the Indian Ocean. . . . Only a few dozen protesters gathered at the Japanese ports with anti-war banners as the ships departed following patriotic speeches from politicians and tearful families waving goodbye. But in a demonstration that not all of the old restrictions have been cast off, Japan decided against deploying a destroyer with an Aegis missile-hunting system after some lawmakers argued that to do so would violate the constitution.[27]

Another aspect of this debate concerns nuclear weapons. Japanese anti-nuclearism has been driven not just by the fears of others; it stems also from the experiences of Hiroshima and Nagasaki, the two Japanese cities on which the United States dropped nuclear bombs in 1945 in the last stages of World War II. Japan's foreign policy had held to three non-nuclear principles: never to own, produce, or permit nuclear weapons on Japanese territory. But with China's military growing stronger, in part through its advanced nuclear weapons programs, with North Korea as an unstable and now nuclear-armed neighbor, with the risks of Russian "loose nukes," and amid concerns about the long-term reliability of U.S. security guarantees, some are asking whether it still is in Japan's interest to be a non-nuclear nation. "You have to wonder," one analyst posed the question, "how long Japan can remain the only non-nuclear power among the major countries in the region."[28]

India-Pakistan

India and Pakistan have fought three wars and endured numerous crises since their independence from British colonial rule in 1947. India was created as a largely Hindu country, Pakistan as a largely Muslim country. In setting the boundaries, though, both sides claimed sovereignty over the state of Kashmir. Pakistan's claim was based on Kashmir's largely Muslim population, India's on the decision by the maharaja (prince) of Kashmir (who was Hindu) to unite with India. Two of the India-Pakistan wars, one at independence in 1947 and the other in 1965, were fought in part over Kashmir. Both of these wars ended with cease-fires and peace plans, but none solved the underlying conflict.

In 1999 India and Pakistan went to the brink of another war over Kashmir. This time the crisis was compounded by both countries having become nuclear weapons powers. Both had been secretly developing nuclear weapons for many years. Nuclear weapons tests, conducted in May 1998 first by India and then by Pakistan, indicated that both now had nuclear weapons capabilities. This development gave the conflict over Kashmir much broader regional and global implications, for the risk now was not just another conventional India-Pakistan war but possibly a nuclear war. The 1999 crisis was defused when the Clinton administration played an important peace-brokering role.

The United States traditionally had had much closer relations with Pakistan than with India. During the Cold War, India was a leader of the Third World–based "non-aligned movement" and also had close ties with the Soviet Union. With the end of the Cold War, however, the United States and India began developing a stronger and more positive relationship. U.S. relations with Pakistan had a somewhat contrasting trajectory, having been quite close for much of the Cold War. Pakistan was part of the U.S. alliance system as a member of the Central Treaty Organization in the 1950s and then through a number of bilateral agreements. Pakistan also was a key ally in the U.S.-supported 1979–88 insurgency against the Soviet invasion of Afghanistan. More recently, though, U.S.-Pakistani relations had been strained by two sets of issues: human rights and democracy concerns prompted by Pakistani military coups, and a bill passed by Congress in 1985 cutting off economic and military aid unless Pakistan ended its nuclear weapons program. The United States also opposed India's nuclear weapons program, but since it didn't give India foreign aid it couldn't bring comparable nonproliferation pressure.

The war on terrorism pushed the United States and Pakistan closer together once again. Pakistan was the crucial front-line state for launching the 2001 war in Afghanistan. Within days of the September 11 attacks, General Pervez Musharraf, who became leader of Pakistan in an October 1999 coup that the United States opposed, pledged to help the United States openly and covertly against the Taliban and Osama bin Laden's Al Qaeda.

Yet in the middle of the war in Afghanistan Kashmir heated up again. The violence intensified in and around Kashmir and also spread to Delhi, the Indian capital, where terrorists attacked the Indian parliament, killing thirteen people. India accused Pakistan of directly supporting these attacks. Pakistan responded with accusations against India for its army's attacks on Pakistani soldiers along the border. Both sides began talking of and making military movements toward war. Neither side was willing to say it would not escalate to nuclear war. For a period in early 2002 the world feared the worst. A nuclear war in the world seemed closer than at any point since the 1962 Cuban missile crisis. The Bush administration engaged diplomatically and played an important role in bringing the crisis under control.

Still, though, the issue of the future of Kashmir remains. The Indians accuse the Pakistanis of terrorism; the Pakistanis call their efforts support for a freedom struggle. The 1999 and 2002 crises added the risk of escalation to nuclear war. New diplomatic overtures in mid-2003 lifted hopes that a lasting solution may be found. The possibility of another crisis, though, could not be dismissed.

North and South Korea

Like Germany, Korea was split into two countries at the end of World War II. North Korea was communist and allied with the Soviet Union and later with China. South Korea was noncommunist, democratic but also for periods ruled by the military, and allied with the United States.

Unlike East and West Germany, however, North and South Korea went to war. The war began in 1950 when the North invaded the South. The United States came to South Korea's defense with endorsement by the UN and support from the militaries of a number of other countries. The war lasted for three years and ended without either side able to claim victory. An armistice was signed, but not a full peace treaty. Neither side recognized the borders of the other. A demilitarized zone (DMZ) was created, separating the two countries. American soldiers have been stationed at the DMZ and at bases in South Korea on an ongoing basis ever since. Even with the Cold War over, about 37,000 American troops remain in South Korea.

Tensions between the two sides have flared periodically over the years. A major crisis stirred in the early 1990s when it was discovered that North Korea was developing nuclear weapons. The prospect of a nuclear-armed North Korea threatened not just South Korea but also Japan, other U.S. allies in the region, and U.S. troops stationed in these countries. There also was concern that North Korea would sell nuclear weapons to other anti-U.S. "rogue states." The Clinton administration pursued a strategy toward North Korea that emphasized negotiations but backed these with measures that threatened military action. The combination helped achieve a crisis-defusing agreement, called the Agreed Framework, in 1994.

A sense of progress also was fed by the first summit ever by the presidents of North and South Korea held in 2000. New policy agreements were announced. Journalists from the South traveled to the North to begin opening lines of communication. Families separated by the DMZ were allowed to meet for the first time since the Korean War. South Korean president Kim Dae Jung was awarded the Nobel Peace Prize for his "sunshine diplomacy" seeking to end the conflict and bring about peaceful reunification of the two Koreas.

The Nobel Prize was premature, though, as problems arose in the subsequent diplomacy. As discussed in Chapter 6, one of the early splits within the Bush administration was over North Korea. President Bush was more standoffish than supportive of South Korean President Kim. This, along with some opposition at home and further incidents raising questions about North Korea's sincerity, offset some progress that continued in family reunifications and some other cooperative measures.

In October 2002 new revelations indicated that North Korea had been cheating on the 1994 Agreed Framework and had continued nuclear weapons development. Reports were that North Korea might already possess some nuclear weapons and was very close to being able to get production lines going that would produce more. North Korea was quite provocative in its reactions, expelling UN inspectors, firing up a nuclear reactor that could produce more plutonium (a key material for nuclear bombs), and renouncing the Nuclear Nonproliferation Treaty. Concerns were over South Korean security, wider concerns for East Asian regional security (for Japan and others), and more global concerns over the prospect of these weapons being sold to other states and terrorists. The sense of crisis was exacerbated by the timing, as the tensions increased during the Iraq war build-up and then the war itself.

U.S.–South Korean tensions built up to the point that anti-American sentiment was a key factor in the 2003 South Korea presidential election victory of Roh Moo Hyun. While the Bush administration saw South Korean opinion as too willing to appease North Korea, many in South Korea saw the Bush administration as too belligerent. The ongoing challenge was how to forge a common position for South Korea and the United States, and optimally China, Japan, and Russia as well, that would strengthen efforts to resolve the crisis peacefully and securely.

The Arab-Israeli Conflict

The Arab-Israeli conflict has gone through five wars (1948, 1956, 1967, 1973, 1982) as well as the two Palestinian "intifadas," or uprisings (1987–93, and since September 2000). The core issue has been "land for peace," meaning recognition by the Arabs of Israel's right to exist and a genuine commitment to peaceful co-existence with Israel, and Israeli return of territories captured in the 1967 war. These terms were achieved in the 1978 Camp David Accord between Israel and Egypt. They were also the basis for the peace process that began with the 1993 Oslo Accord between Israel and the Palestinians, in which the United States has played a major role (see Chapter 8). But while achieving a number of interim and partial agreements, the Oslo peace process fell short of a final Israeli-Palestinian agreement. The negotiations convened by President Clinton at Camp David in July 2000 between Israeli prime minister Ehud Barak and Palestinian leader Yasir Arafat collapsed, and shortly thereafter the Israeli-Palestinian conflict plunged into some of the worst violence in its history. The Palestinians used suicide bombers to attack Israeli soldiers and citizens; the Israelis, under a new prime minister, Ariel Sharon, sent their military in to re-occupy much of the West Bank, often launching their own brutal attacks.

The war on terrorism fed off of and into the Arab-Israeli conflict, for it is the pivotal conflict in the Middle East, to which those asking the "why do they hate us" question most often look. One could argue that it isn't accurate or fair or justified, but the fact is that anti-Americanism has been spreading in the Arab world, in part due to U.S. support for Israel, especially for the Sharon government. Longtime U.S. support for Arab regimes such as Saudi Arabia and Jordan also were factors underlying this anti-Americanism. On the one hand the very instability and radicalism that Islamic fundamentalist and other radical groups manifest has been all the more reason for the United States to support the relatively moderate governments in the region, including with tacit and even at times overt support for anti-democratic practices. On the other hand this very support has been fueling anti-Americanism and risks bringing about the threats and instabilities that the support was intended to prevent. In these and other ways the Middle East has become an even more complex and potentially dangerous place for U.S. policy than it was during the Cold War.

Rethinking Military Strategy

During the Cold War U.S. military planners had a strong sense of who the military enemy was: the Soviet Union. They had a basic strategy for defending the United States, its allies, and its interests: nuclear deterrence, combined with regional deterrence through NATO and other parts of a global network of military alliances and bases. Without the Soviet enemy, and with a number of other emerging threats and challenges, some major rethinking of U.S. defense and military strategy was needed. That process was still in the works when September 11 hit. The rethinking of U.S. defense strategy thus has had to deal both with the issues that already were on the agenda before September 11 and with the war on terrorism.

Waging Post–Cold War Wars

Lessons can be drawn from four major recent wars: the 1990–91 Persian Gulf War, the 1999 Kosovo war, the 2001 Afghanistan war, and the 2003 Iraq war.

THE 1990–91 PERSIAN GULF WAR   The 1990–91 Persian Gulf War against Iraq had four main lessons with regard to both the scope and the limits of American power. The most immediate was that aggression was still a fact of international life. Troops marched and tanks rolled as Iraq took over Kuwait, its smaller and militarily weaker neighbor.

Second was that the twenty-seven-nation international coalition the first Bush administration put together was both a manifestation and a multiplier of American power. That is, the willingness of so many countries to join with the United States demonstrated how much the rest of the world looked to Washington for leadership. Being able to make this not just George H.W. Bush vs. Saddam Hussein, but a coalition of the world's major nations, including some of Saddam's Arab brethren, forged under U.N. auspices made the U.S. position that much stronger.

Third was that the military victory left no doubts about American military power. It is important to recall how dire many of the predictions were of the risks that going to war might bring. But these predictions did not come to pass, and with the help of CNN the whole world watched the vivid images of American military might, particularly of American air power. Bombers took out most Iraqi air defenses and hit targets with a new generation of highly accurate precision-guided munitions. These were part of the heralded "revolution in military affairs" (RMA), through which mastery of electronic and information technologies was giving the United States unprecedented conventional military capabilities. Later studies indicated that the precision was not as great as claimed at the time. Still, the dominant sense was of a new age in which the U.S. military had superiority in the air.

Fourth was an affirmation of the "Powell doctrine" of decisive force. Named for General Colin Powell, who at the time was chair of the Joint Chiefs of Staff, this doctrine advocated that when military force is to be used, it should be used overwhelmingly and decisively. This was a major lesson drawn by General Powell and others from the Vietnam War and its incremental approach to the use of force.

There were, however, limits to the Gulf War's significance. As a military operation, for all the technological innovations the U.S. military displayed, it was fundamentally a classical strategy of armed forces against armed forces on the battlefield. But the nature of this war would prove to be more the exception than the rule. Somalia, Bosnia, Haiti, Kosovo, and the other ethnic conflicts and internal wars in which the United States has been involved were much more politically based uses of military force, and much less battlefield-based—more like Vietnam than Desert Storm, and thus presenting different challenges for the use of military force (these military interventions are discussed further in the next chapter).

Another limitation on the significance of the Gulf War is that it left Saddam in power in Baghdad. A number of factors went into the decision to stop the ground war after only one hundred hours, before potentially reaching Saddam himself; and while in some respects this decision was understandable, the succeeding years would show the problems and threats Saddam still could cause. Moreover, precisely because of how decisive and overwhelming the military victory was, its political limits were all the more striking.

Finally, there were the lessons of the period leading up to Saddam's invasion of Kuwait, during which the United States had tilted toward Iraq in its 1980–88 war with Iran.[29] The policy was based on the greater threat posed by Iran's Islamic fundamentalists and the deep animosity of its anti-American leader, Ayatollah Ruhollah Khomeini. But the Reagan and first Bush administrations failed to see past the old adage "the enemy of my enemy is my friend." Indeed, the enemy of my enemy *may be* my friend, but he also may be my enemy, too. It thus was one thing to feed the Iraqi population while it was at war with Iraq, or to provide some industrial equipment, or even to share military intelligence and to bolster Iraqi defensive military capabilities. It was quite another matter to loosen controls on technology and equipment with "dual uses" (i.e., both commercial and military applications). The United States did this to a degree that, along with Europe and on top of Soviet aid, significantly and substantially contributed to Iraqi development of offensive military capabilities, especially its nuclear, biological, and chemical weapons.

Some argued that these prewar mistakes really didn't matter since the U.S.-led forces won the war. Some even argued that the United States and the world in general were better off that the war had been fought. At best this was a cold power-politics calculus that too readily dismissed the death toll, other human suffering, economic costs, environmental destruction, and further consequences of the war. Yet over time, as the conflicts with Iraq persisted and ultimately led to another war twelve years later, even this strategic logic came into question. Thus, along with the military lessons to be learned from how the war was fought, there were important lessons to be learned about why the war occurred.

THE 1999 KOSOVO WAR   In the Kosovo war, too, the United States was victorious but with mixed lessons. This was the third war in the former Yugoslavia in the 1990s. The first was in Croatia in 1991–92, the second in Bosnia & Herzegovina in 1992–95. The United States and NATO did not get involved militarily in Croatia; they did in Bosnia, with some air strikes but mostly as a peacekeeping force after the war ended. In Kosovo the United States and NATO went to war.

Militarily this proved to be another relatively short and major victory. The war, another display of massive and sophisticated air power, lasted less than three months. No ground troops were used. Casualties were minimal. The United States and NATO won, but they "won ugly."[30]

Serbian leader Slobodan Milosevic and his forces were defeated and forced to withdraw from Kosovo. But this was not until after ethnic violence had taken a heavy toll. One of the points critics raise is that Operation Allied Force could have prevailed more quickly, more overwhelmingly, and with less ethnic killings had the United States been willing to send in ground troops as well as launch air strikes. Concerned that "casualty phobia" would undermine American public support, however, President Clinton had stated from the start that ground troops were "off the table." At minimum, critics argue, the ground troops option should have been left open as a threat for ratcheting up the war effort that could have coerced Milosevic into surrendering sooner.

Similarly mixed lessons came from Kosovo as a case of "war by alliance." This was the first time NATO ever had fought a war. It had trained, prepared, positioned, and strategized for war throughout the Cold War, but had never had to actually fight one. To its credit, NATO did hold together politically and did carry out generally well coordinated and effectively executed military operations in Kosovo. But this was not without political pulling and tugging. As British scholar Michael Cox put it, "friends were politically necessary but militarily problematic."[31] Within a general consensus of common interests in defending Kosovo, different NATO members had different particular interests at stake. Yet NATO decision-making rules required unanimity, or at least no dissenting votes (some states might choose to abstain). Some in the United States saw the internal NATO politics as bothersome and cumbersome, getting in the way of military planning. So while the dominant lesson of Kosovo was that NATO did succeed in its first war, it did have its qualifiers.

The Kosovo war also left much debate about whether NATO had the right to intervene militarily. The 1990–91 Persian Gulf War had two things going for it that the Kosovo war did not: the aggression was pretty clear-cut, one state (Iraq) having invaded another (Kuwait); and the UN Security Council had passed a resolution authorizing the use of force. Neither of these conditions applied in Kosovo. Kosovo was a part of Serbia, not an independent nation-state. Serbia claimed that it had rights of sovereignty within its own borders, in which other states should not intervene. It also cited the lack of UN Security Council authorization for Operation Allied Force. The United States and NATO countered that sovereignty carries responsibilities, not just rights, consistent with humanitarian and other international norms. They also cited some Security Council resolutions and other aspects of international law as partial justification for their military intervention. The ambivalence of these arguments was such that one major international commission concluded that the U.S.-NATO intervention was "legitimate but illegal"—i.e., it had a strong claim on humanitarian grounds of international norms and values but not as a matter of international law.[32]

THE 2001 AFGHANISTAN WAR   The war in Afghanistan, too, was a military victory of major significance but also with substantial limits. The war was launched less than a month after the September 11 terrorist attacks. Its immediate objectives were to remove the Taliban government that had made Afghanistan a safe haven and state sponsor for terrorists, and to destroy the operations of Al Qaeda and its leader, Osama bin Laden. The first of these objectives was accomplished with the fall of the Taliban government and its replacement by a moderate coalition led by U.S.-backed President Hamid Karzai. The second objective was only partially accomplished: Al Qaeda was damaged and disrupted, but was not destroyed. Indeed within a year it again was carrying out terrorist attacks in Afghanistan as well as in neighboring Pakistan and many other parts of the world.

Militarily, the Afghan war showed American air power as having reached even more dominant levels than demonstrated in the Kosovo and Persian Gulf Wars. The accuracy of bombs dropped in the Persian Gulf War had been only 8 percent (the televised bombs-down-the-building-chutes had occurred but were more of an exception than official statements indicated at the time). In Kosovo that figure was 35 percent. In Afghanistan it reached 60 percent. A vast new array of technologies was displayed: JDAMs (joint direct-action munitions) were satellite-guided bombs; Predators were unmanned drones equipped with high-tech sensors and real-time streaming video that enabled commanders to direct warplanes to targets around the clock and with unprecedented precision. Special Operations forces, consisting of Green Berets, other elite units, and CIA agents, infiltrated enemy areas, often riding on horseback in the rugged terrain yet technologically equipped to identify targets and communicate the enemy's exact location to bombers overhead. One U.S. Air Force officer called this basic equation of technology on horseback "21st century air and space power combined with 16th century land forces." The Afghan war showed how much further the RMA had taken military technology and capabilities since the Persian Gulf War. Looking ahead, one report referred to plans for 2020 or earlier in which "pilotless planes and driverless buggies will direct remote-controlled bombers toward targets; pilotless helicopters will coordinate driverless convoys, and unmanned submarines will clear mines and launch cruise missiles. . . . In years to come, once targets are found, chances are good that they will be destroyed by weapons from pilotless vehicles that can distinguish friends from foes without consulting humans."[33]

For all the technological sophistication, though, the Afghan war strategy did have its shortcomings. One was the reliance on local forces as a way of limiting the ground forces that the United States itself had to commit. The Afghan Northern Alliance, the main anti-Taliban group, was a valuable ally in many respects, but not in all. As long as its interests were consonant with those of the United States, it proved a reliable ally. But when it had its own interests it went its own way. An example came in the key battle of Tora Bora in December 2001. Many Al Qaeda leaders, possibly including bin Laden, were holed up in caves in this mountainous region but still managed to escape because the attacks on the caves by the Northern Alliance were poorly executed. The Northern Alliance had achieved its main objective—toppling the Taliban. Capturing Al Qaeda was less important to them than to the United States, so they were less inclined to run the risks inherent in the Tora Bora mission.

Of course, one of the reasons the Northern Alliance was relied on rather than U.S. ground forces was consternation over the U.S. domestic political impact of significant casualties. Ground troops were used more in Afghanistan than in Kosovo but politics still kicked in to self-constrain U.S. military strategy. Here too it was an overcompensation, for reasons we'll get into in Chapter 8. The point here is that even amid the broad consensus on the Afghanistan war, domestic politics was a constraining factor.

Human error also was a problem. Some of this was bureaucratic. One report cited at least ten instances within six weeks at the height of the war in which commanders believed they had top Taliban and Al Qaeda leaders "in [the] cross hairs" but were delayed in getting the attack clearances necessary from U.S. Central Command and the Pentagon.[34] Some was simply the fog of war that even the best technology cannot preclude. On occasion bombs were misguided because of mistakes in identifying targets; such bombs could become "friendly fire," hitting their intended targets—except that the targets were not the enemy. In one incident in December 2001 three U.S. Green Beret soldiers and five Afghan allied fighters were killed. In another, rifle shots fired in celebration at a wedding ceremony in a small village were mistaken for enemy fire, and bombs were brought down on the wedding party, killing a number of people including the bride.

Finally even a victory such as this one can be inconclusive. An FBI-CIA report leaked to the press in June 2002 "concluded that the war in Afghanistan failed to diminish the threat to the United States. . . . Instead the war might have complicated counterterrorism efforts by dispersing potential attackers across a wider geographic area."[35] A few months later, Lt. General Dan McNeil, the U.S. commander in Afghanistan, forecast that it would take up to two more years to eliminate Al Qaeda and build an Afghan army strong enough to deny terrorists a future safe haven.[36]

For there to be an enduring gain for U.S. security, winning the war is not enough; winning the peace is also necessary. This involves ensuring a government stable and moderate enough that Afghanistan will not again become a state sponsor of terrorism or some other form of major security threat.

THE 2003 IRAQ WAR   The Iraq war was an overwhelming military victory. It took just three weeks, less than half the time of the 1991 Persian Gulf War. It achieved victory with about one-third as many troops as the '91 war. And it did what that war stopped short of attempting: removing Saddam Hussein from power.

"Shock and Awe" was the term coined for this military strategy. The idea was to bring so much military power to bear so quickly, inflicting such heavy destruction on their forces as to shock and intimidate the enemy, leaving him so materially weakened and psychologically in awe as to undermine his will to keep fighting. The '91 war's doctrine of decisive and overwhelming force had proceeded sequentially, with six weeks of air power first and then moving into the ground war. The 2003 war strategy was simultaneous rather than sequential, with special operations and ground forces coordinated with and in some aspects even preceding the air war, geared to what strategists called "rapid dominance" of achieving the overwhelming levels of force much more quickly.

Among the lessons and precedents the Iraq war set, five stand out. First is the extraordinary levels American military technology had achieved. In the Persian Gulf War only one in five combat aircraft could drop a bomb sighted by a laser; in the Iraq war all could. In the Persian Gulf War only 9 percent of the attacks used precision-guided munitions; in the Iraq war it was close to 70 percent. In the Persian Gulf War, often two days elapsed between the time a reconnaissance aircraft photographed a target and the target was struck; now with streaming video these events often happened instantaneously. The ground-air coordination of spotters helping with the targeting of air attacks that drew so many kudos in Afghanistan was even more sophisticated and widespread less than two years later in Iraq. Unmanned aircraft like the Predator drone were used much more extensively than ever before. Real-time data flowed by the "trillions of megabytes" to command centers both in the region (in Doha, the capital of neighboring Qatar) and back at the Pentagon. All this had one military expert speculating that "it's possible that in our lifetime we will be able to run a conflict without ever leaving the United States."[37]

Second is the role of special operations. In what was the largest covert military campaign in recent history, special forces were on the ground in Iraq even before the first bombs were dropped. They pursued a number of their own missions such as organizing the Kurdish militia in the north, hunting down Iraqi leaders, scouting out Scud missile launchers in western Iraq, and seizing a major Euphrates River dam to prevent Iraqi soldiers from blowing it up in an effort to block one of the routes to Baghdad for the American forces coming up from the south. They worked jointly with conventional forces in not just target-spotting but guiding in air attacks, even in sandstorms that otherwise would likely have forced the postponement of air operations. They also played a key role in quick response operations like the rescue of American prisoners of war and wounded soldiers.

Third is the degree of "jointness" with which the war was fought. For all the benefits of the organization of the military into separate services of the Army, Navy, Air Force, and Marines, this division also has had its problems. At least since the mid-1980s military reformers have been pushing for greater coordination in planning, budgeting, and operations. The traditional approach often ended up with inter-service rivalries leading to similar weapons systems being developed separately by each of the services, with budgetary waste and little inter-operability. In some instances they have "radios that cannot talk to each other and ordnance that cannot be swapped."[38] Secretary of Defense Donald Rumsfeld, who had been pushing for greater jointness even before the Iraq war, cited the war success as the basis for making coordination even more of a priority.

Fourth is the significance of the Iraq war as the first actual application of the Bush doctrine of pre-emption. One aspect of this bears specifically on Iraq and whether pre-emption was justified in this case. Another revolved around the "who next?" question for U.S. policy, whether the Bush administration would move on to any of the other axis of evil countries (Iran, North Korea) or perhaps others (Syria?). And, more broadly, the debate went to what impact the precedent the United States established in Iraq may have for other world conflicts.

Fifth is the issue of "winning the peace." For all the decisiveness of the military victory, as in Afghanistan as well as Kosovo, here too there is no guarantee that the peace will be won. This poses its own challenges that again come back to peacekeeping, nation-building, and other policies in that category the military refers to as OOTW (operations other than war). Indeed in the immediate aftermath of the military victory, debates raged over the roles of the State Department versus the Defense Department within American policy, and over how much the United States would keep itself in charge versus roles for the UN and other multilateral actors. Whatever else was uncertain, clearly winning the peace would take a lot longer than did winning the war. To the extent that it is not achieved, the lasting impact of having won the war will be greatly lessened.

The Future of NATO

Time and again during the Cold War and at its end, warnings were sounded about the demise and possible death of NATO. But when the Berlin Wall fell, the Warsaw Pact was torn up, and the Soviet Union came asunder, NATO was still standing. Its central goal—to "safeguard the freedom, common heritage and civilization of [its] peoples, founded on the principles of democracy, individual liberty and the rule of law" (see the excerpts from the North Atlantic Treaty in Chapter 4)—had been achieved, and without a single shot having been fired in anger. No wonder NATO has been touted as the most successful peacetime alliance in history.

The ensuing question has been whether NATO's very success would lead to its demise. "Alliances are against, and only derivatively for, someone or something," according to an old international relations axiom.[39] With the

Soviet enemy gone, was there really a strong enough reason to keep NATO going? Given the budgetary costs and other factors, should it just be showered with testimonials, given its "gold watch," and sent into retirement? All these questions boil down to two issues about NATO's future: its membership and its mission.

THE EXPANSION OF NATO MEMBERSHIP   At the end of the Cold War NATO faced a problem that was the fruit of its success: its former adversaries had been defeated. Indeed, their major alliance, the Warsaw Pact, had fallen apart; their major empire, the Soviet Union, had crumbled. Confrontation had ended, and cooperation was now a possibility. The challenge for NATO now was how to build new cooperative relationships with these former adversaries, and with Russia in particular.

The initial transitional strategy started by the first Bush administration and furthered by the Clinton administration was to create new institutional mechanisms linked to NATO but not fully part of it. In 1991 all of the former Soviet and Soviet-bloc states were invited to join the North Atlantic Cooperation Council, later renamed the European-Atlantic Partnership Council. This was to be a mechanism for consultation on political and security issues. Then in 1994 the Partnership for Peace (PFP) was created, also involving most Soviet and Soviet-bloc states and geared toward building cooperation among the members' militaries and defense establishments. The PFP also made possible participation in actual NATO peace operations; for example, thirteen PFP members sent troops to Bosnia as part of the NATO peacekeeping force there. Although these institutional linkages confer the right to consult with NATO if a state feels its security is threatened, this is not the same as the "Article 5" collective-security guarantee that full NATO members give one another. Article 5 of the NATO treaty defines an attack on one state as an attack on all and pledges members to come to each other's defense.

In 1998 the first three ex–Warsaw Pact countries were brought into NATO: Poland, Hungary, and the Czech Republic (see Table 7.1). The expansion process for the second group of prospective members began in late 2002. This group included not only additional ex-Soviet bloc countries but also for the first time countries that had been part of the Soviet Union itself: Bulgaria, Romania, Slovenia, Slovakia, and the Baltic states of Estonia, Latvia, and Lithuania. NATO plans to be open to additional tranches of new members in the coming years.

Three main arguments are made in favor of NATO expansion. The first is based on the concept of a *security community,* defined as an area "in which

TABLE 7.1   NATO: Its Evolution, Cold War to Post–Cold War

	NATO members	
Charter members	Joined during the Cold War	Joined after the Cold War
Belgium	Greece (1952)	Czech Republic (1998)[‡]
Canada	Turkey (1952)	Hungary (1998)[‡]
Denmark	Federal Republic of	Poland (1998)[‡]
France*	Germany (1955)[†]	
Iceland	Spain (1982)	Bulgaria (2002)[‡]
Italy		Estonia (2002)[§]
Luxembourg		Latvia (2002)[§]
Netherlands		Lithuania (2002)[§]
Norway		Romania (2002)[‡]
Portugal		Slovakia (2002)[‡]
United Kingdom		Slovenia (2002)[‡]
United States		

*Withdrew from NATO military command in 1965 but maintained political membership
[†]As a condition of German reunification in 1990, NATO agreed not to station military forces
  in the territory of the former German Democratic Republic (East Germany).
[‡]Former Warsaw Pact members
[§]Formerly part of the Soviet Union

strategic rivalries are attenuated and the use of force within the group is highly unlikely."[40] NATO expansion has been enlarging the area of Europe in which this sense of security and stability prevails. Once a country is a member of NATO, it assures that it will not threaten the security of other members, and it gets the assurance that other countries in the security community will help ensure its security.

Second is the reinforcement of democratization. Free elections and the building of other democratic political institutions and practices, including civilian control of the military, are prerequisites to NATO membership. This provides an incentive to choose and then stay on the democratic path. Czech President Vaclav Havel, who spent many years in prison as a dissident in the communist era, took this concept further, stressing the political, cultural, and even psychological benefits for the countries of eastern Europe of finally becoming genuine and full members of the Western community.

The third main pro-expansion argument stresses the continued, albeit changed, need for deterrence. NATO doctrine still calls for a deterrence posture to ensure collective security against a potential aggressor. The main concern, although it is mostly left implicit, is a resurgent Russia. It is not so much a fear that the Soviet Union may be reconstituted, although this possibility is not totally dismissed. The more salient concerns about Russia run deeper historically—Russia does have a precommunist history of regional expansionism—and grow out of the uncertainties and instabilities of Russia's own postcommunist transition and the possibility of more aggressively nationalist leaders coming to power.

Critics of NATO expansion stress two main points. One is that NATO still has not figured out what to do about Russia. An agreement was signed accompanying the first round of NATO expansion for closer NATO-Russia consultation. Russia was to be given a voice in NATO but not such a strong voice as to be a veto. This agreement was heralded at the time but did not prove very meaningful in actual practice. A similar agreement was reached in 2002 in the prelude to the second round of NATO expansion. It too was vague as to what it meant to have a voice and not a veto, and what it meant to be in a special relationship but not a member of the alliance. With NATO expansion now moving closer to Russia's borders and taking in ex–Soviet states, not just ex–Soviet bloc ones, and amid Russia's uncertain political future, the risks of backlash cannot be dismissed. Time will tell whether the 2002 Russia-NATO Council proves workable, but there is reason to doubt it. If the grand vision of Europe "whole and free" is going to come to fruition, the continent on which the two world wars and the Cold War all started will have to secure a stable peace in which Russia will need to have a firm and foundational place, not a jerry-rigged one. Otherwise NATO expansion may make an aggressive Russia more, rather than less, likely. Antagonistic nationalist forces within Russia may be strengthened in the face of an enlarged NATO, and appeals to traditional Russian fears of encirclement may end up bringing to power leaders much less pro-Western than Yeltsin and Putin.

Second is the concern that adding new members will dilute the cohesion that has made NATO function so effectively. This is less a criticism of any specific new members than a basic organizational precept: as the number of members goes up, making decisions and carrying out policies becomes that much harder. "If one country after another is admitted," a former U.S. ambassador to NATO argued, "it will no longer be today's functioning and cohesive NATO that the new members will be joining but rather a diluted entity, a sort of league of nations."[41] The intra-alliance tensions brought out during the Kosovo war could be even worse with even more members. A bigger NATO may not be a better NATO if one takes seriously the importance of being able to function effectively first and foremost as a military alliance.

NATO'S POST–COLD WAR MISSION   There is a subtle but significant shift in the use of the terms "threats" and "risks" in defining NATO's mission. During the Cold War NATO was focused on deterring and defending against the threat posed by the Soviet Union and the Warsaw Pact. Its central mission was to meet this threat with the necessary forces, weapons, and doctrine. Post–Cold War NATO doctrine recognized that security threats are less likely to come from "classical territorial aggression" than from "the adverse consequences that may arise from the serious economic, social, and political difficulties, including ethnic rivalries and territorial disputes, which are faced by many countries in Central and Eastern Europe."[42] This meant both that deterrence strategy needed to be reformulated and that peace operations needed to be a new and major part of NATO's mission.

The wars in the former Yugoslavia posed the first test of how well NATO would handle this new mission of peace operations. These wars—first in Croatia and Bosnia, and then in Kosovo—posed a number of difficult issues for NATO, and the results were decidedly mixed. The former Yugoslavia was "out of area" in terms of the North Atlantic Treaty's provisions pertaining to attacks on or within the territory of member countries. On the other hand, the underlying purpose of the alliance was to keep the peace in Europe, and these were the most gruesome and destructive wars in Europe since World War II. They also were a different type of conflict than NATO had been formed to fight. NATO doctrine, training, deployments, battle plans, and equipment were geared to conventional warfare against the Warsaw Pact forces, armies against armies, along demarcated battle lines, relying on technology and classical strategy. In Bosnia and Kosovo, though, the wars were marked by ethnic passion more than military professionalism, and they were driven by ethnic cleansing not classical invasion.

From 1992 until late 1995, while the Bosnia war raged, the United States and western Europe mostly hurled accusations and counter-accusations across the Atlantic—"three years of collective buck-passing," as Joseph Lepgold put it.[43] NATO finally did intervene in Bosnia following the signing of the Dayton accord in December 1995. It did so with a 60,000-troop Implementation Force (IFOR), which was followed about a year later with a somewhat smaller Stabilization Force (SFOR). IFOR and SFOR succeeded in restoring stability to Bosnia, and as such demonstrated that NATO could play an important peacekeeping role. Both operated much more efficiently and conveyed much more of a deterrent threat than had the crazy-quilted UN force that had preceded them. They also were noteworthy in including Russian and other former Soviet-bloc troops.

Yet what was the lesson? That NATO would intervene only late in such conflicts, only after ethnic cleansings had run their horrific course? What about initiating earlier peace-making and peace-enforcing operations, which might prevent so many lives from being lost, so many rapes from being committed, so many villages from being plundered? The decision to intervene in Kosovo was made more quickly, but still only after much of the ethnic cleansing had been inflicted. In 2001, when Macedonia, another part of the former Yugoslavia, began sliding into its own ethnic violence, NATO did act sooner and was able to prevent the conflict from escalating or spreading. But it left NATO with the burden of maintaining three simultaneous peacekeeping missions in the former Yugoslavia; it remains to be seen whether the political will will last to see all of them through.

The war on terrorism poses yet another set of issues about NATO's mission. When the United States was attacked on September 11, 2001, its NATO allies invoked Article V of the North Atlantic Treaty and came to its defense with a number of military measures. This was the first time ever that Article V actually had been invoked, and it was by the allies to help the United States rather than the reverse. NATO's action reflected the ways in which terrorism is a shared threat.

Within that general threat perception, though, lie other differences over how best to fight the war on terrorism. The United States chose to conduct the war in Afghanistan with some assistance from European allies in their individual national capacities but outside of NATO in order to have greater control over wartime command and strategy than it had during the Kosovo war. NATO did have a role in the peacekeeping, taking over leadership of the International Security Assistance Force (ISAF) in 2003, in effect further pursuing its new mission of peacekeeping but now very much on an out-of-area basis.

In the Iraq war the Bush administration again opted to fight outside NATO. As in the Afghanistan war, the ad hoc coalition included some NATO members in their individual national capacities (Britain again as the main partner, and this time also Poland, the Czech Republic, and others). Unlike Afghanistan, though, there were major policy differences over the Iraq war, and open and intense confrontations with France and Germany. To be sure, American-French tensions were not new to NATO; French President Charles de Gaulle's withdrawal from the NATO military command in 1966 was a major blow to alliance unity. His action inspired "end of NATO" prognostications at that time, but the alliance survived. Still, combined with the other issues and tensions within U.S.-European relations, the confrontation over Iraq did deepen doubts about NATO's future.

The "Two-MRC" Strategy

"MRC" is the Pentagon acronym for "major regional contingency"—i.e., major regional war. For decades U.S. military doctrine called for the ability to fight two MRCs at any time. American forces in all their aspects—size, force structure, deployment, weaponry—were to be maintained at levels and capabilities sufficient to pose a strong enough deterrent to prevent such wars from happening, but if necessary also to fight and win them quickly and *even simultaneously.* The scenarios on which the two-MRC strategy was based were another war in the Middle East started by Iraq and another Korean war. These were said to be only illustrative, and the Defense Department report announcing the two-MRC doctrine acknowledged that planning assumptions were not based on repeating past experiences. Nevertheless these were the regional deterrence scenarios most often invoked to justify the two-MRC strategy.

In the latter years of the Clinton administration and the start of the second Bush administration, questions were being raised about how applicable the two-MRC strategy still was. One question asked whether forces this large really needed to be maintained. Cold War doctrine had required the capability to fight two and one-half wars, with the "half" war being a guerrilla one. But was a half war all that could be reduced from the planning? Wasn't the assumption of fighting simultaneously a bit improbable? Or was this just being prudent?

Another question raised was about the political viability of the continued global "forward deployment" of U.S. forces at overseas military bases. Japan was not the only place where political problems had arisen over American bases. Key bases in the Philippines had to be shut down because of domestic political opposition. In the Persian Gulf, even after the Gulf War the only governments willing to allow American troops to be based on their soil were Kuwait and Saudi Arabia. A number of other countries have wanted American protection, but have been so fearful of fundamentalist-led anti-Americanism that they concocted such arrangements as floating docks for U.S. forces just off their shores. And in Saudi Arabia there were two major terrorist attacks in 1995–96 against the U.S. forces stationed there.

A third question was whether, by planning for these kinds of large-force conventional wars, U.S. strategy becomes less equipped for dealing with post–Cold War threats. One set of such threats involved peacekeeping, peace enforcement, and other "operations other than war." Another set of such threats involved global terrorism. Thus the shift away from the two-MRC strategy that had begun prior to the September 11 attacks took on added momentum as the war on terrorism became the new central doctrine for U.S. military strategy.

Yet the simultaneity in 2002–03 of the crisis with North Korea over nuclear proliferation and the Iraq war seemed to question again the plausibility of the two-MRC scenario. What would have happened had the North Korea crisis come to a head while the Iraq war was being fought? Would American forces have been stretched too thin? While the military victory in the Iraq war did remove the threat posed by Saddam Hussein, there still were numerous concerns about that region's security. American forces in the region were drawn down somewhat, but an ongoing presence was still to be maintained. Qatar, which was made the central command base for the Iraq war because of Saudi reluctance to house the command within Saudi Arabia, became the locale for a more permanent shift of American forces out of Saudi Arabia. There also was talk of maintaining bases in Iraq over the long term.

Nuclear Strategy

Nuclear deterrence strategy, a centerpiece of U.S. foreign policy throughout the Cold War, remains important but is much less central than in the Cold War era. As a top Clinton National Security Council official put it, "nuclear weapons now play a smaller role in our national security strategy than at any point during the nuclear era." This official went on to stress that "it would be a mistake to think that nuclear weapons no longer matter;" nuclear deterrence does continue to be an integral component of U.S. defense strategy, but a less dominant one than during the Cold War. The basic need to deter aggression remains, and maintaining U.S. nuclear superiority is seen as a crucial component of a credible deterrence posture. "Having the most powerful weapons and deterrent plays an essential role," as one strategist put it, "in attaining the number one security policy objective of the United States, which is to preserve our central interests abroad without involving us in a war. Nuclear weapons are not all that is needed to make war obsolete, but they have no real substitute."[44]

Within this context in May 2002, Presidents Bush and Putin signed the Moscow Treaty on Strategic Offensive Reductions. This treaty, as mentioned earlier in this chapter, mandated that each side cut its arsenal down to 1,700–2,200 nuclear weapons. Although it made cuts two-thirds deeper than any of its predecessors had, it encountered less opposition from hawks than any previous nuclear arms treaty. What opposition there was came from arms control advocates who felt the cuts did not go far enough fast enough; the deadline for achieving these new levels was not until 2012, which some felt was too far away. Furthermore, this agreement called only for dismantling the weapons, rather than the outright destruction of weapons called for by past agreements. The treaty also did not cover short-range nuclear arms, and permitted modernization (which in nuclear weapons parlance means that weapons may be fewer but more lethal and potentially more destabilizing). These issues were not sufficient to cause major opposition to the treaty, but they did cause some doubts as to how significant it would prove to be.

NUCLEAR "ABOLITION"   Serious questioning of this latest version of nuclear deterrence has come from those who believe the end of the Cold War presents a historic opportunity for deeper cuts and even "abolition" of nuclear weapons. Why do the United States and Russia even need 1,700 nuclear weapons each? Surely we can maintain nuclear deterrence with many fewer. Indeed, why not come as close to totally abolishing them as possible?

These questions have not been raised just by "peaceniks." In January 1997 sixty retired generals and admirals from the United States and more than a dozen other countries issued a statement calling for much deeper cuts and a commitment to move toward total elimination of nuclear weapons (see Perspectives, p. 391). Among the most outspoken of this group was retired general George Lee Butler, the former head of the Strategic Air Command (SAC), which is in charge of the major part of the U.S. nuclear force.

Four main arguments are made by General Butler and others who take this position.[45] One is that the United States could make its own deeper cuts unilaterally and actually be more, not less, secure. The American nuclear arsenal still would be well above what is needed for second-strike capacity and to pose a credible deterrent. Such reductions would also help alleviate the risk of Russia turning toward a "first use" doctrine to compensate for the widening U.S. advantage in the face of the disarray and crumbling of Russia's capacity to maintain its nuclear arsenal.

Second is a fundamental questioning of whether nuclear deterrence really still has the credibility it claims. How believable is the threat that the United States would respond to an attack, especially a non-nuclear one, with nuclear weapons? Not very, according to critics: the disproportionality of such a response would make it very difficult to actually carry out.

Third is a concern about accidents. There have been many false alarms for both the United States and Russia over the years, no doubt many more than we know of. In one such incident, in early 1995, a Norwegian research rocket was mistakenly taken by Russia for an incoming U.S. nuclear missile, and

Yeltsin came very close to ordering a counterattack. Both sides still follow a "launch on warning" policy, which can mean that decisions on whether the blip on the screen is an incoming missile or a research rocket or a flock of birds have to be made in a matter of minutes. Here, too, proposals are made

PERSPECTIVES
PERSPECTIVES
PERSPECTIVES

"RETIRED NUCLEAR WARRIOR SOUNDS ALARM ON WEAPONS"

OMAHA, Dec. 4 — Three years ago, Air Force Gen. George Lee Butler commanded a military headquarters on the outskirts of this city with the power to propel the world to a nuclear conflict. At his direction, bombers laden with 2,800 warheads could have raced down runways and flown toward the former Soviet Union or anyplace else Washington targeted for ruin.

Today, Butler is slated to give a lunchtime speech in Washington in which he will make a dramatic departure from the views he publicly espoused as commander in chief of America's nuclear arsenal—the pinnacle of his 37-year career in military uniform. He is to describe U.S. nuclear policy as "fundamentally irrational" on grounds that such arms pose a great threat to mankind.

Butler, who once personally approved thousands of targets for U.S. nuclear weapons, now advocates that Washington urgently pursue the elimination of such arms around the globe. He says taking such an extreme measure is the only way to forestall a horrible nuclear accident and prevent warheads from falling into the hands of rogue states or terrorists. . . .

"Nuclear weapons are inherently dangerous, hugely expensive, militarily inefficient and morally indefensible," Butler says now. He acknowledges that this view is a kind of heresy for a former CINCSAC, or commander in chief of the Strategic Air Command—a job that often has gone to some of the country's most hawkish military leaders, such as Gen. Curtis E. LeMay, the model for Jack D. Ripper in *Dr. Strangelove*. . . .

Butler says those who argue such arms are still needed in the aftermath of the Cold War are victims of the "intellectual smog" that justified the absurd pressures of having to decide in less than 30 minutes whether to order a nuclear retaliatory strike and wipe out an entire nation.

(*Continued on page 392*)

("**Retired Nuclear Warrior**"   *Continued from page 391*)

Today, however, after reflecting more on his experiences, Butler is more angry at what he calls the persistent "terror-filled anesthesia" about nuclear arms. With "the luxury to step back mentally and think about the implications of having spent four trillion dollars producing 70,000 nuclear weapons . . . I realize that the notion nuclear weapons bring security—the idea that somehow we were in charge, that somehow all of this was infallible and manageable and we could make it work—. . . is fatally flawed."

Source: R. Jeffrey Smith, "Retired Nuclear Warrior Sounds Alarm on Weapons," *Washington Post*, December 4, 1996, A1. © 1996, The Washington Post. Reprinted with permission.

for the United States to act unilaterally to take its weapons off hair-trigger alert. This both would reduce the chances of a mistake on the U.S. side and could prompt the Russians to follow suit.

Fourth is a moral argument about having lost sight of what Jonathan Schell, a leading nuclear abolitionist, calls the "singularity" of nuclear weapons. "Their singularity, from a moral point of view, lies in the fact that the use of just a few would carry the user beyond every historical benchmark of indiscriminate mass slaughter. . . . The use of a mere dozen nuclear weapons against, say, the dozen largest cities of the United States, Russia or China, causing tens of millions of deaths, would be a human catastrophe without parallel."[46]

Some of the counterpoints made by defenders of nuclear deterrence can be inferred form the previous discussion. One main point to emphasize is the concern about cheating and "break-out." If cuts go very far, especially if full abolition were to be tried, such that countries have no nuclear weapons or only a very few, a state or perhaps a terrorist organization that "broke out" by having secretly kept or developed some would have an enormous advantage. Moreover, even if every weapon is eliminated from the face of the earth, the knowledge of how to build nuclear weapons would still rest in the minds of humankind.

Nonetheless, the very fact that the debate has gone to this level is yet another example of the profound changes brought by the post–Cold War era. It is a debate that surely will continue.

NATIONAL MISSILE DEFENSE   In stark contrast to nuclear abolitionists, proponents of national missile defense (NMD) see deterrence even at current levels of weapons as too shaky to rely on. How sure can we be that nuclear deterrence won't fail? And what if it does fail?

The Bush administration made NMD its first national security priority upon coming into office. Defense Secretary Rumsfeld gave an initial statement of the administration's position at a February 2001 security conference in Munich, Germany:

> The deterrence of the Cold War— mutual assured destruction and the idea of massive retaliation—worked reasonably well during the Cold War. But the problems today are different. The demands are different. And we have an obligation to plan for these changing circumstances to make sure we are arranged—first and foremost—to dissuade rash and reckless aggressors from taking action or threatening action. And we know from history that weakness is provocative.
>
> No U.S. President can responsibly say that his defense policy is calculated and designed to leave the American people undefended against threats that are known to exist. And they do. Let there be no doubt. A system of defense need not be perfect; but the American people must not be left completely defenseless. It is not so much a technical question as a matter of a President's constitutional responsibility. Indeed, it is, in many respects, a moral issue.[47]

Three months later, in a speech at the National Defense University, President Bush elaborated further on the administration's plans and the underlying strategic view (see At the Source on page 394).

Three issues define the debate over NMD. One is about technological effectiveness. A 1998 report to the Pentagon revealed that only 4 out of 17 tests of a prototype NMD system were successful, and these were under the benign conditions of a planned test, wholly unlike the stressful conditions of actual combat and the "fog of war." Recent tests have been more successful, but still mixed. The technological challenges of this version of NMD are not as great as for the Reagan "Star Wars" system, which was based in space and was to provide a full national shield. Nevertheless they are formidable, and the margin of error is exceedingly small.

The second issue is cost. Experts estimate that more than $100 billion already have been spent on NMD research. In 1999 the Clinton administration and the Republican Congress agreed on an increase from $4 billion to $10 billion just for that year.[48] A report by the Congressional Budget Office put the estimated total NMD costs over the next fifteen to twenty-five years at as much as $238 billion.

> ► **At the Source** ◄
>
> ### PRESIDENT BUSH ON MISSILE DEFENSE
>
> ❝Unlike the Cold War, today's most urgent threats stem not from thousands of ballistic missiles in Soviet hands, but from a small number of missiles in the hands of [the world's least responsible] states—states for whom terror and blackmail are a way of life. . . . In such a world Cold War deterrence is no longer enough. . . . We need new concepts of deterrence that rely on both offensive and defensive forces. Deterrence can no longer be based solely on the threat of nuclear retaliation. Defenses can strengthen deterrence by reducing the incentive for proliferation.
>
> We need a new framework that allows us to build missile defenses to counter the different threats of today's world. To do so we must move beyond the constraints of the 30-year-old ABM Treaty. . . .
>
> Russia and the United States should work together to develop a new foundation for world peace and security in the 21st century. We should leave behind the constraints of an ABM Treaty that perpetuates a relationship based on distrust and mutual vulnerability. . . . Perhaps one day we can even cooperate on a joint defense. ❞
>
> Source: Excerpts from a speech delivered at the National Defense University, Washington, D.C., May 1, 2001. http://www.whitehouse.gov/news/releases/2001/05/20010501-1.0html

Third is strategic effectiveness. Even if it works technologically, will it contribute to security or set off "boomerang" effects from Russia, China, or others, leaving us less secure than we were before? These questions are not new; they were part of the Cold War–era debate over SALT I and the ABM Treaty (see Chapter 5). The answer then, expressed in the doctrine of mutual assured destruction, was that nuclear stability was more likely if both the United States and the Soviet Union did not have substantial missile-defense systems, so that each side knew that it could destroy the other. The Bush administration and other NMD proponents argue that this Cold War thinking is outdated. Their position seemed reinforced when the United States unilaterally abrogated the ABM Treaty and despite some initial expressions of discontent, President Putin went along. Concerns remain, though, whether this cooperation or even agreement to disagree will continue, or whether there still may be a boomerang effect in U.S.-Russia relations.

As for China, it is concerned both about the strategic balance and about proposals to provide theater NMD systems to Japan and Taiwan.

COUNTERPROLIFERATION Strategies for stopping the proliferation of weapons of mass destruction—nuclear, chemical, and biological—have two dimensions. One involves nonproliferation treaties and other multilateral efforts, as will be discussed in Chapter 8. The other involves *counterproliferation* policies, meaning efforts to counter the proliferation that treaties and international regimes have been unsuccessful in preventing. Counterproliferation strategies are a mix of military, diplomatic, and covert action as well as defensive measures such as anthrax and smallpox vaccination programs and development of suits and equipment to protect against chemical weapons.

The Iraq war was justified largely on counterproliferation grounds. We will disarm Saddam, President Bush repeatedly stated, because it is the only way to end his proliferation. As with other aspects of the Iraq war, the lessons for counterproliferation continue to be debated. Those who supported the war and who argue for potential attacks on other WMD proliferating countries and terrorist groups contend that the Iraq case shows how the kind of deterrence strategy that worked against the Soviet Union during the Cold War doesn't work against rogue states and terrorist groups. Since massive war efforts may not always be optimal, they press for the development of new weaponry including "bunker busters" that may themselves use nuclear warheads. Because such countries and terrorist groups were known to have built deep and well-fortified bunkers for command centers and WMD arsenals, this new generation of weapons is said to be needed as the offensive complement to NMD. Critics contend that this weaponry will be destabilizing, not stabilizing. Those against whom it is to be targeted will see it as an offensive threat, not just a defensive capacity. Critics also see the war-fighting scenario against proliferators as just as unrealistic as were nuclear war-fighting scenarios during the Cold War.

Defense Spending: How Much Is Enough?

One of the historical "great debates" (Chapter 3) and a recurring controversy during the Cold War, the question of defense spending levels is still with us. Defense budget cuts were the trend for the first decade or so of the post–Cold War era. From a peak of $304 billion in fiscal year 1989, the defense budget fell to $268 billion in fiscal year 1998, a 12 percent decline. Corrected for inflation, the drop was even sharper, at 30 percent. Over the last years of the Clinton administration the trend line shifted as defense spending started increasing again, although by small amounts. It was the war on terrorism that brought major increases. The fiscal year 2003 defense budget reached $386 billion, and continued large increases were projected.

Part of the debate is over how to interpret statistics such as these. By some measures spending seems too high, by others arguably too low. On the "more than enough" side, one comparison that is made is to Cold War defense budgets. The 2003 budget of $386 billion is more than double the defense budget in the early Reagan years ($185 billion in fiscal year 1982), one of the tensest points of the Cold War. The $439 billion projected for 2007 is almost ten times what the United States was spending in 1960, in the days when nuclear war was foreboding and Soviet-American competition was global. Another comparison is made to the defense budgets of other major powers. The U.S. defense budget is not just higher than any other country's, it is seven times higher than Russia's and eight times higher than China's. When it reached $400 billion in FY 2004 it was higher than the defense spending of the next fifteen nations combined.

Those on the "not enough" side have their own statistical interpretations. The Cold War comparisons need first of all to be corrected for inflation. When that is done, fiscal year 2003 spending is only 9 percent more than that of 1982, and 2007 spending is just 14 percent more than that of 1960. A further measure supporting this view is defense spending as a percentage of the total federal budget and of the national gross domestic product (GDP). Here we see actual declines: the fiscal year 1982 figures, for example, are 25 percent of the federal budget and 5.7 percent of GDP, whereas the fiscal year 2003 figures amount to only 18 percent of the federal budget and 3.5 percent of GDP.

Another part of the debate is over specific allocations within the defense budget. How much should be spent on new weapons? The need for maintaining technological supremacy for the American military is a point of consensus. But on how much spending is enough to achieve that, analysts disagree. Estimates vary from assessments of the $45 billion to $50 billion budgeted in 2002 for technology development as about $15 billion too little, to others that saw room for saving as much as $100 billion in weapons procurement and related areas. Congressional politics also enter in. One member of Congress slipped $250,000 into the defense budget for a study of a caffeinated chewing gum that might help sleep-deprived troops—and that is manufactured by a company in his district. Another added $5 million for retrofitting locks used on classified documents to meet stricter specifications—as manufactured (you guessed it!) by a company in his district.[49]

It is politically hard to reach consensus on these questions of how much to spend, especially during times of crisis and threat. We saw this during the

Cold War when these criticisms of defense spending often were squelched by fears of being labeled "soft on communism," even when the questions being asked were pragmatic ones. Recall from Chapter 1 that it took none other than President and former top World War II general Dwight Eisenhower to warn about the dangers (political as well as economic) of the "military-industrial complex." Some tried to label Eisenhower soft, but with his credentials it was pretty hard to do so. We see similar political dilemmas today in the context of the war on terrorism and concerns about being labeled "soft" on this threat. As one columnist put it during the 2002 budget buildup, Democrats fear "that they can't be for 'less' defense than Bush and be viable."[50]

Yet in strict policy terms the issues are seen as nothing short of ones of fundamental military transformation. The RMA has brought new missions with new technologies and new operational concepts. How are these new missions to be assessed? How are the new technologies to be harnessed? How should the armed services be organized and coordinated for this new era of warfare? How to cope with new issues such as information warfare and protecting cyberspace? As one study put it, transformation will "enable the U.S. military to retain its status as the world's best fighting force . . . but only if transformation is carried out wisely and effectively"[51]—much harder to do when politics gets in the way.

DOMESTIC BASE CLOSINGS   Another recurring politically difficult issue is that of closing domestic military bases. With the troop cutbacks that came with the end of the Cold War (from 2 million active-duty troops to about 1.4 million), many of the military bases in the United States no longer were needed. Yet these bases were important to the economics and communities of the cities and towns in which they were located. Many a member of Congress felt that, regardless of the rationale, he or she would not be re-elected if a base in his or her district were to be closed.*

One strategy that had been developed for earlier rounds of base closings was to appoint an independent commission that would make recommendations that Congress had to accept or reject in totality, with rules of debate preventing amendments.† This procedure helped individual members go along

---

*This was not as hard an issue for senators, because their constituencies are statewide and the impact of a base closing in a particular town is less politically intense than for members of the House of Representatives, who cover smaller pieces of political geography.

†The yes-or-no with no amendments also has been used as a procedure in trade policy; see the discussion in Chapter 9 about "fast-track" authority.

with the overall policy and at least partially shield themselves politically. Four rounds of closings—1988, 1992, 1993, and 1995—totaling 451 bases, including 97 major ones, were carried out largely in this manner. In 2001–2 the Bush administration pushed for creation of another commission and another round of base closings, so as to free up funds for the war on terrorism. Congressional opponents, though, reversed the argument, contending that the new emphasis on homeland security made it prudent to wait and see whether some bases might have renewed value. Economic recession was also a factor in the congressional opposition. The House again was the main obstacle: "There was almost no support for the idea in the House," according to Senate Armed Services Committee Chairman Carl Levin. The only compromise that could be reached was to delay any further round of closures until at least 2005. "What that means, very simply, is that the United States will continue to have 20 percent to 25 percent more bases than we need," Secretary of Defense Rumsfeld protested. "The money and the people that are devoted to that task cannot be devoted to something truly important with respect to the war on terrorism."[52]

The War on Terrorism

Up until September 11, 2001, the post–Cold War foreign policy agenda had a long list of issues but no single defining one like anti-communism served as during the Cold War. The war on terrorism became that defining issue for the Bush administration's foreign policy.

Osama bin Laden and his Al Qaeda terrorist network emerged in the 1990s. They were responsible for a number of terrorist attacks on the U.S. presence abroad, including the August 1998 bombings of the American embassies in Kenya and Tanzania and the October 2000 bombing of the naval warship USS *Cole* in a harbor in Yemen. Indeed, even before the September 11 attacks, arguments were being made that terrorism had to be given higher priority in U.S. foreign policy. Consider, for example, the report of the National Commission on Terrorism issued in June 2000:

> Terrorists attack American targets more often than those of any other country. America' pre-eminent role in the world guarantees that this will continue to be the case, and the threat of attacks creating massive casualties is growing. If the United States is to protect itself, if it is to remain a world leader, this nation must develop and continuously refine sound counterterrorism policies appropriate to the rapidly changing world around us.

> International terrorists once threatened Americans only when they were out-
> side the country. Today, international terrorists attack us on our own soil. . . .
> Terrorist attacks are becoming more lethal. Most terrorist organizations active
> in the 1970s and 1980s had clear political objectives. They tried to calibrate their
> attacks to produce just enough bloodshed to get attention for their cause, but not
> so much as to alienate public support. . . . Now, a growing percentage of terrorist
> attacks are designed to kill as many people as possible.[53]

This analysis and others like it were based in part on intelligence about bin
Laden and Al Qaeda and other terrorists, as well as being grounded in three
broader dynamics. First was terrorism as the "underside" of globalization. For
all the benefits of the rapid and widespread movement of people, money,
technology, and ideas, these trends also facilitated the operation of terrorists.
They too could move from one corner of the globe to another. They too could
communicate through the Internet. They too could visit various readily accessible Web sites and download information on various technologies, including
WMD. They too could move their money around electronically. Terrorists operated in other eras, but globalization was part of what makes the terrorist
threat that much greater today.

Second was the advantage that comes with being the offense and having
the element of surprise on one's side. Terrorism's "tactical advantages," as national security expert Richard Betts puts it, target right at "the soft underbelly
of American primacy." In some situations, depending on the balance of
forces and the nature of the warfare, the defense has the advantage. But with
terrorism, the advantage is always with the attacker. They have the "capacity
for strategic judo, the turning of the West's strength against itself. . . . Nine-
teen men from technologically backward societies did not have to rely on
homegrown instruments to devastate the Pentagon and World Trade Center.
They used computers and modern financial procedures with facility, and
they forcibly appropriated the aviation technology of the West and used it as
a weapon."[54] The openness of American society further complicates this, as
we will see later in this chapter in the discussion of the politics of homeland
security.

Third was the interconnection with many aspects of U.S. policy in the
Middle East and more broadly toward the Islamic world. These were areas
and relationships that had been conflict-ridden for the United States for
many years. Iran since the 1979 Islamic fundamentalist revolution; Iraq since
the 1990–91 Persian Gulf War; relations with Arab governments such as
Saudi Arabia and Egypt, which largely supported U.S. foreign policy but had
their own instabilities and opposition (bin Laden is Saudi, and two of his top

lieutenants are Egyptian); Islamic fundamentalism as it spread in many countries, including Pakistan and Lebanon; the failure to stay engaged in Afghanistan after the defeat of the Soviets in 1988; the Arab-Israeli conflict—these and other issues fed terrorism and turned it increasingly toward the United States as a principal target, while making strategizing against it an especially complicated task.

Still, it took the attacks on the World Trade Center and the Pentagon for the shift from *a* problem to *the* problem to occur. "We are at war," President Bush told the nation in announcing the military action against the Taliban regime and the Al Qaeda terrorist network in Afghanistan. And he didn't just mean Afghanistan; the struggle was global, and it was for the long term. It was not a classical war, but it was a war nevertheless. Other foreign policy issues had to be dealt with, but there was no higher priority for the Bush administration than the war on terrorism.

The Overall Bush Administration Strategy

The goal established by the Bush administration is to destroy, disrupt, and defeat Al Qaeda and other terrorists threatening U.S. security wherever they can be found. The overall strategy as developed by the Bush administration has four main components.

AMERICAN POWER   The war on terrorism requires that the United States draw more fully on its preponderance of power. It starts as a simple matter of self-defense. The United States has the power—the military power to destroy, disrupt, and defeat the enemy; the diplomatic power to ensure that other nations understand, as President Bush put it, that "you are either with us or against us."

The initial war in Afghanistan was as internationally consensual as wars get. The U.S. claim to be acting in self-defense was strong. The Taliban regime had been denied its country's seat in the United Nations, and only two countries in the world had granted it diplomatic recognition. It was among the world's worst repressors of women and worst offenders of human rights. Some aspects of the U.S. strategy were debated, but the right to use force in this situation was widely accepted by the international community.

Debate was much greater, though, over the Bush Doctrine of *pre-emptive use of force,* both as a general strategy and in the case of Iraq. Pre-emption means striking first based on credible evidence that the adversary is likely to attack you (see Chapter 6, At the Source on page 330). Deterrence doctrine is based on striking back, on the logic that the threat of second-strike capacity will stop an adversary from striking first. Although deterrence held up well during the Cold War, as a Bush administration official put it, "the nature of the enemy has changed, the nature of the threat has changed and so the response has to change. . . . In the world in which we live, it's not enough to deter. You need more capability, more flexibility, more nuanced options and choices."[55] Pre-emption might not be used often, but proponents argue that it needs to be there if deterrence and other anti-terrorism strategies fail. Does it really make sense to have to wait until terrorists use chemical, biological, or nuclear weapons to justify attacking them? Moreover, credible pre-emption could strengthen deterrence, letting an adversary know that if it even began to mount a threat it risked being attacked.[56] There are times, as National Security Adviser Rice put it, when "you can't wait to be attacked to respond."[57]

The Iraq war was the first major application of the Bush Doctrine. The rationale was the anticipatory pre-emptive one. Some allegations were made of Iraqi connections to Al Qaeda, but the main contention was that if Saddam were not soon disarmed of his weapons of mass destruction, and if he were not removed from power, the threat he posed would escalate from potential to actual. He was said to be close to completing development of nuclear weapons, and if we waited until he had these weapons, deterring or defeating him would be that much harder and riskier. There was evidence that he long had possessed, and still was believed to possess, chemical and biological weapons. And even if he hadn't consorted and conspired with bin Laden in the past, it was deemed inevitable that whatever their other differences, their anti-Americanism would bring them together. We needed to act now before it was too late.

COALITIONS OF THE WILLING   The Bush administration recognized that no matter how preponderant American power was, some aspects of the anti-terrorism strategy could not be achieved without multilateral cooperation. It wanted to be sure, though, that no international institution, no alliance, and no other country constrained American freedom of action. It wanted the collective action, legitimization, and other benefits that multilateralism brings without any impediments on the U.S. capacity to act unilaterally. In some respects, this worked for other countries as well, allowing them to be part of the overall coalition while deciding which particular policies and initiatives to sign on to. In other respects, though, there was inherent tension over just how far the United States could go on its own and how flexible a coalition can be and still be meaningfully called a coalition.

The global coalition initially forged after September 11 numbered over 170 countries. Not all joined the war effort in Afghanistan, but most if not all provided some form of support for some aspect of the war on terrorism. Economic sanctions were one example. Al Qaeda's financial network could not be disrupted without a comparably global cooperative effort. A number of countries around the world have joined in on enhanced enforcement efforts to crack the mix of sophisticated and traditional methods Al Qaeda uses for moving money around the world. Intelligence has been another area in which the United States (via the Central Intelligence Agency, the Federal Bureau of Investigation, and other American intelligence agencies) needs to work closely with counterparts in Europe, the Middle East, South Asia, and elsewhere to share information, coordinate actions, and take other steps to trace and counter terrorist cells and operations in their global network. In addition, on a more bilateral basis the Bush administration forged a new set of global military commitments. The post–Cold War trend had been toward reducing U.S. overseas military bases and military aid programs. Here, too, the war on terrorism caused a major policy shift. Afghanistan was Al Qaeda's principal base but not its only one; it had developed a global network of cells. Other terrorist groups not formally affiliated but sharing goals, tactics, and enemies were also operating in countries around the world. American military commitments were made to a number of these countries where the threat was deemed the greatest: the South and Central Asian front-line states surrounding Afghanistan (Pakistan, Uzbekistan, Tajikistan, and Kyrgyzstan), Southeast Asian states with large Muslim populations and known active Al Qaeda cells and similar groups (Indonesia, Malaysia, and the Philippines), Yemen (where the October 2000 Al Qaeda attack on the USS *Cole* had occurred), Qatar (where bases were built up for attacking Iraq) and other Middle Eastern states, and Georgia (the ex-Soviet state in the Caucasus, near where Al Qaeda operatives were active in Chechnya). The initial commitments were for military aid, training, and in some cases small numbers of U.S. troops. In some cases the commitments were made on a short-term basis; others were more open-ended.

The Iraq war put the coalition of the willing strategy to a tough test. The Bush administration was determined not to make its determination to go to war subject to the UN or NATO or any other international institutional constraint. It did mobilize over 40 countries in its coalition of the willing, but other than Britain no other major power was a member. The breadth of the coalition was deemed secondary to its being non-constraining. There even were some moves after the war to punish countries like France that had been the most unwilling. Yet there also were efforts to re-focus on economic sanctions, intelligence sharing, and other areas of the war on terrorism on which cooperation needed to be as broad as possible.

PRINCIPLES   The war on terrorism is not just about security; it also claims higher purposes. It is about principles as well as power. Just as the United States fought the Cold War to ensure democracy's triumph over the communist "evil empire," so it now must fight the war on terrorism to ensure the triumph of freedom over this era's forces of evil. From the beginning President Bush frequently used the language of "good," "evil," and "freedom." Bin Laden and the other terrorists were, in his words, "evildoers." Iraq, Iran, and North Korea were named in Bush's 2002 State of the Union speech as the three principal points on the "axis of evil." The war on terrorism in all its aspects was being fought to defeat evil and defend freedom: freedom for the Afghan women who had been so brutally repressed by the Taliban; freedom for the Iraqi people who needed to be liberated from Saddam Hussein; freedom for Americans to be able to live without the fear of terrorist attack; freedom for people everywhere to live without repression and fear. The Bush administration acknowledged that some of its new allies did not have very good human rights records themselves, but contended that improved human rights performance will be "an important byproduct of our alliance with them."[58]

Numerous political initiatives were taken to try to answer the "why do they hate us?" question. The U.S. strategy was premised on the belief that the problem was principally a communications one. The American "message" was solid, it just needed to get out more accurately and more widely. Charlotte Beers, a prominent advertising industry executive, was appointed undersecretary of state for public diplomacy and public affairs to take up this task. Among the initiatives taken to get the American message out were a new Arabic-language radio station, more engagement with moderate Islamic religious leaders, and other efforts to fare better in "the battle of ideas" that underlay and fed into much of the fundamentalism and anti-Americanism around the world.

HOMELAND SECURITY   More than ever before in its modern history, the September 11 attacks revealed the United States to be vulnerable right at home. Foreign policy in the past had been about U.S. involvements "over there": in the Middle East, in the Third World, in Europe, in Asia. Now the threat was "here," on this side of the oceans. Not since the bloodiest battles of the U.S. Civil War (1861–65) had as many Americans been killed in a single day. Not since the War of 1812, when the British attacked Washington, D.C., and burned the

White House, had America's own capital been attacked. Even Pearl Harbor was an attack on a military base, not on cities and civilian populations. Assuring the security of the American homeland became a crucial issue.

And an extremely complex one at that. Airport security was an obvious area for improvement. The anthrax letter-bombs that followed the World Trade Center attacks showed that one could be at risk in simply opening a letter at home. The United States has nearly 600,000 bridges, 170,000 water systems, 2,800 power plants (104 of them nuclear), 190,000 miles of interstate natural-gas pipelines, 463 skyscrapers, and innumerable shopping malls and sports stadiums that could be terrorist targets.[59] And nuclear waste sites. And harbors that every day receive millions of tons of shipping containers. And thousands of miles of border to patrol. Never before has the United States had to focus so much on security within its own borders. In doing so, however, it once again had to balance national security and civil liberties.

Debate over the Bush Strategy

It is hard to underestimate the threat the United States does face from global terrorism. Most experts agree that it is a question more of when than of if there will be an attempted WMD attack within the United States. There has been substantial debate, though, over whether the Bush war on terrorism is the optimal strategy for dealing with these threats.

USE-OF-FORCE DOCTRINE   The war against the Taliban and Al Qaeda ran into only limited opposition. To the extent that there was debate, it was over *how* the war should be fought more than *if* it should be fought. The doctrinal shift to pre-emption has been at the center of this debate. Will pre-emptive uses of force make the world safer or more dangerous? Three main points are raised by critics who pose this question.

Violation of International Law and Norms.   Article 51 of the UN Charter acknowledges the inherent right of states to act in self-defense but only "if an armed act occurs" and until the UN Security Council acts. Some would extend this to include situations in which the threat is so imminent as to be virtually certain, so long as the decision is made by the UN, not just an individual country. But the Bush pre-emption doctrine does not hold even to this standard of evidence, and is unilateral in its decision-making and action. The argument against the Bush doctrine, then, is in part ethical and juridical—about what is right and legal—and in part pragmatic—about how the weakening of laws and norms about the use of force in the name of today's security concern can become tomorrow's insecurity.

Questionable Efficacy. Legal and normative points aside, critics also are more skeptical that pre-emptive strikes can be counted on to work. To use force decisively when using it pre-emptively imposes an especially demanding requirement for reliable intelligence and especially careful planning for enemy countermoves and other contingencies including the enemy's own possible decision to act "pre-pre-emptively" and attack before you do. While some then would argue "I told you so" and claim justification, the net effect could end up being a self-fulfilling prophecy in which the targeted regime ends up defeated or removed but only after the threat that was to be prevented has already wreaked its havoc, perhaps with WMD. These concerns were not borne out in the Iraq war, although many critics were less than reassured that this meant they could be disregarded in other possible instances.

Dangerous Precedent. If the United States can take pre-emptive action in the name of its own security based on its own threat assessments and its own decision-making, then why can't other countries? Why can't India or Pakistan in their conflict? Israel or the Arab states in theirs? Russia in its near abroad? China against Taiwan? In any one of these or other cases, a state may genuinely see pre-emptive action as necessary in security terms, and could seize on the Bush Doctrine as a convenient rationalization, laying claim to the precedent for political cover. Either way the world could end up a more dangerous place.

MORE MULTILATERAL, LESS UNILATERAL   Most critics concur with a degree of unilateralism in American strategy. The balance they seek, though, has a stronger multilateral component. This in part is a matter of pragmatism: just as the terrorist threat has global reach, so too must the strategy used against it have comparable reach. The United States cannot on its own gather the intelligence needed, disrupt the financial transactions, block WMD acquisition, break up cells of operatives, establish surveillance over borders and the oceans, pay for the costs of winning the peace, and share other burdens and solve other problems central to the overall antiterrorism strategy. The coalitions can be flexible, with different nations playing varying roles, but they need to be strong and meaningful coalitions, to which the United States must be genuinely committed if it expects others to be. On this point many critics felt the Iraq war reinforced their position, that the fall-out from the disputes with key allies was affecting cooperation on other fronts of the war on terrorism.

While many of the other issues in the unilateralism-multilateralism debate do not have substantively direct links to the war on terrorism (e.g., the International Criminal Court, or the Kyoto global warming treaty), they have been part of the context. The Iraq dispute was taken by many to be part of a pattern in which the United States is shifting to what political scientist John Ikenberry calls "a new paradigm" of seeing itself "less bound to its partners and to global rules and institutions." This flies in the face of the lessons of the Cold War, when American power was enhanced by the "ability and willingness to exercise power within alliance and multinational frameworks." It also runs counter to world history, "step[ping] into the oldest trap of powerful imperial states: self-encirclement. When the most powerful state in the world throws its weight around, unconstrained by rules or norms of legitimacy, it risks a backlash. Other countries will bridle at an international order in which the United States plays only by its own rules. . . . [H]istory shows that powerful states tend to trigger self-encirclement by their own overestimation of their own power."[60]

WINNING THE PEACE   The United States cannot win this war unless it also wins the peace. Five sets of issues are key to this part of the strategy. First is stability in Afghanistan and Iraq. Full-fledged democracy is not likely, but the political systems must be sufficiently inclusive to have legitimacy among the country's various ethnic and other groups, the governments strong enough to keep the peace with the support of U.S. and multilateral peacekeeping forces and eventually on their own, and the economies rebuilt enough to bring a peace dividend to the Afghan and Iraqi people. Critics question whether the Bush administration has been as committed to winning the peace in either of these countries as it was to winning the wars.

Second are concerns that the new wave of global military commitments may be more part of the problem than the solution. The "ABT" (anybody but terrorists) rationale for alliances and commitments risks giving the United States bedfellows as strange as those brought out by the "ABC" (anything but communism) rationale used during the Cold War. Many of the governments now receiving military aid and hosting American bases in the name of the war on terrorism have questionable human rights records. Does this not contradict the principles-based claim of fighting the war on terrorism in the name of freedom? And while the initial commitments were small—limited numbers of troops, advisory and training roles, and only a few hundred million dollars— the risks of "mission creep" seemed high, with more money and larger roles and even more troops building up over time, just as in the Cold War's worst quagmires.

Third is the importance of achieving Arab-Israeli peace. It is likely true that even if the 2000 Camp David talks had brought about an Israeli-Palestinian peace agreement, bin Laden and Al Qaeda still would have launched the September 11 attacks. Their opposition is to Israel's very existence, not just to the terms of a deal but to any deal at all. Their anti-Americanism extends to other issues as well. Still, they and other terrorists exploit the Arab-Israeli conflict to build support for their cause. Arab-Israeli peace thus is a crucial component, and one for which the United States has had and continues to have a key peace-broker role to play (see Chapter 8).

Fourth is the importance of winning the battle of ideas in the Arab and Islamic worlds. Ultimately this is up to Arab and Islamic leaders themselves, who are rightly proud of their identities and their faith, and who do not want those who kill in the name of Islam to hijack their religion. But there is a role for U.S. policy to play in this effort. "America has a serious image problem," as a Council on Foreign Relations (CFR) task force concluded. "[S]tereotypes of Americans as arrogant, self-indulgent, hypocritical, inattentive, and unwilling to engage in cross-cultural dialogue are pervasive and deeply rooted. . . . Also at the root of these negative attitudes is Americans' perceived lack of empathy towards the pain, hardship and tragic plight of peoples throughout the developing world."[61] The Bush administration has increased its public diplomacy efforts, but not as much or in the ways most needed. As the CFR task force stressed, "the credibility of an American message will be enhanced when it does not appear unilateral, and when international legitimacy and consensus are sought for the principles being defended."[62]

Fifth is getting at the economic roots of the discontent that feeds and fosters radicalization. Here, too, the argument is a relative one. Although poverty and terrorism are not as directly linked as is sometimes claimed, poverty does provide a breeding ground for terrorism. "Justice and prosperity for the poor and dispossessed" are critical, as British prime minister Tony Blair put it, "so that people everywhere can see the chance of a better future through the hard work and creative power of the free citizen, not the violence and savagery of the fanatic."[63] Yet U.S. policies were seen by many as being too little and in some aspects making the problems even worse. In Pakistan, for example, at the same time that the United States was trying to build political support for the Musharraf regime and its pro-American tilt, newly enacted American restrictions on textile imports were costing jobs in an industry that accounts for 60 percent of Pakistan's industrial employment.[64] And even the doubling of U.S. foreign aid announced by the Bush administration in 2002 would still leave the United States last among major powers in the percentage of its GDP it spends on foreign aid.

In sum, the war on terrorism must be won, and military power is crucial for that. But the peace also must be won, and that requires due emphasis on other strategies and instruments of American power.

Security Threats from Other Nonstate Actors

In addition to terrorism, two other major security threats are posed by non-state actors.

Drug Wars

To the extent that the measure of a security threat is its impact on the everyday lives of the American people, illegal narcotics rank quite high. They have penetrated the nation's cities, schools, workplaces, and families. Although the war against drugs does have a "demand-side" domestic policy component, the "supply side" is largely a foreign policy problem. It tends to focus on Latin America, particularly Mexico, Colombia, Panama, Peru, and Bolivia. But the problem is virtually global: the "golden triangle" in southeast Asia of Burma, Thailand, and Laos; Afghanistan and Pakistan; former Soviet republics in central Asia; Lebanon and Syria; Nigeria.

Three principal strategies have been pursued to fight the international narcotics trade, and with only mixed results all around. One strategy of course has been to try to use diplomacy. The State Department has a special bureau dealing with international narcotics ("drugs and thugs," some call it), and the White House has its "drug czar," who coordinates efforts both within the U.S. government and with other countries. Diplomatic efforts go on all the time at working levels, and on occasion even at the head-of-state level. Such efforts include programs to provide assistance for drug eradication, crop substitution, and police training. One problem, though, has been concern about the reliability of diplomatic partners, as with Mexico in 1997, when the army general who headed the national drug-fighting agency was arrested for himself being on the payroll of the drug cartels. Another problem arises when diplomacy degenerates to finger-pointing, as with American accusations that Mexico or Colombia or some other supplier country isn't doing enough to stop the flow of drugs, and their countercharges that the United States isn't doing enough to curtail demand.

Another strategy is a form of economic sanctions known as *decertification*. Every year the State Department presents to Congress reports on every country known to be a source of drugs. If a country is deemed not to be doing enough against drugs, it can be "decertified," which means that it loses eligibility for a number of U.S. economic and trade-assistance programs. There have been some instances in which this coercive pressure ahs been effective, prompting countries to step up their anti-drug efforts to avoid decertification and countries that have been decertified to do more to regain eligibility for U.S. assistance. Some countries have reacted nationalistically against the whole process, seeing it as another demonstration of American arrogance— the very term "decertification" to some means the United States is putting itself in an overlord position. This also has led to charadelike and credibility-weakening situations in which the State Department has certified a country to avoid a diplomatic dispute even though its anti-drug record was highly questionable.

A third main strategy has been military. It is not just rhetoric when we speak of "drug wars." Some of the largest post–Cold War U.S. military assistance programs have been to the Colombian and other Latin American militaries for anti-drug operations. American military personnel have been stationed in Colombia, Peru, and elsewhere, in small but still significant numbers. There even have been U.S. military casualties. "This is not a one-night stand," said General Charles E. Wilhelm, commander of U.S. military forces in Latin American and the Caribbean. "This is a marriage for life."[65] Others, however, warn that these military commitments risk drawing the United States deeper into these countries' internal political conflicts. Colombia, where American military involvement has been the greatest, is a particular concern because of the interweaving of the drug war with a long-festering guerrilla war, and because of the Colombian military's history of human rights violations and other undemocratic practices that make them a questionable partner.

Global Crime Rings

"Most Americans still refuse to believe just how well-organized global crime has become," writes Senator John Kerry, a senior member of the Senate's main anti-crime subcommittee. "The new global criminal axis is composed of five principal powers in league with a host of lesser ones. The Big Five are the Italian Mafia, the Russian mobs, the Japanese *yakuza,* the Chinese triads and the Colombian cartels. They coordinate with smaller but highly organized gangs with distinct specialties in such countries as Nigeria, Poland, Jamaica and Panama." The threats have become so severe that they go well beyond "being exclusively in the realm of law enforcement; they also become a matter of national security."[66]

One of the reasons for this heightened concern about crime as a foreign policy issue is that, as a former head of the CIA warned, "international organized crime can threaten the stability of regions and the very viability of nations."[67] The annual income of many of these global crime rings exceeds the GDP of many a country; the United Nations estimates that international crime costs $750 billion a year. This gives criminals enormous economic power with the ability to, among other things, finance major weapons purchases for building formidable military arsenals of their own and providing plenty of money in bribes and kickbacks to public officials. It is the same basic pattern as with terrorists and drug lords—money and guns, both critical power resources, are more and more in the hands of nonstate actors.

Another reason for the heightened concern is that, while there long have been international dimensions to U.S. "domestic" crime, as with the Mafia, the international-domestic interconnection has become more pervasive. As former FBI Director Louis Freeh put it, whereas the FBI made its initial reputation after its founding in the 1920s by fighting "interstate crime," its future reputation depends on how effective it is against "transnational crime." The United States now is being "ravaged by foreign criminals originating in partial or complete sanctuaries abroad." In years past the FBI's "Ten Most Wanted" list consisted mostly of bank robbers, big-city racketeers, and kidnappers. In 1997 eighth of the ten fugitives on it were international criminals who had committed crimes in the United States. The FBI thus has vastly expanded its overseas role, from 70 special agents in 23 nations in 1994 to offices in 45 countries by early 2002. Its Moscow office, as one example, had 35 cases when it opened in 1994; by 1998 its caseload was up to 284.[68]

Foreign Policy Politics: Homeland Security and Politics with a New Enemy

September 11 transformed foreign policy politics no less than foreign policy strategy. For the first time since the end of the Cold War, there now was an Enemy. Not just a number of small-e enemies, or the possibility that a major one might emerge down the road: Osama bin Laden, Al Qaeda, and terrorism writ large constituted a capital-e Enemy.

The stakes now also were higher than perhaps at any point since the nuclear war scare of the Cuban missile crisis in 1962. The threat was here at home, not just out there. It could be targeted at average citizens in their daily lives, anywhere, anytime. As bad as the September 11 attack was, the next one could be much worse.

Initially, consistent with the historical pattern of "politics stopping at the water's edge" during crises and times of war, foreign policy politics again was characterized by broad domestic consensus. As discussed in Chapter 6, Congress overwhelmingly voted to support both the Afghanistan war and the Iraq war. Public opinion showed some differences, such as splits in the period leading up to the Iraq war over whether to work through the United Nations. Overall, though, it was strongly supportive of the war on terrorism.

This new political consensus had its foreign policy benefits, but it also raised difficult issues, just as previous consensuses had in the past.

National Security versus the Bill of Rights

As in the past, one of the toughest balances to strike is between national security and the Bill of Rights. How is security against terrorism to be made a priority in this new and threatening age while safeguarding the freedoms and rights on which the United States was founded and which have been fundamental to American democracy for more than 200 years?

These debates did not just split along standard liberal and conservative, Democratic and Republican lines. For example, William Safire, a noted conservative columnist and outspoken hawk on national security issues, warned about the dangers of greater government surveillance: "Is this the kind of world we want? The promise is greater safety; the tradeoff is government control of individual lives. Personal security may or may not be enhanced by this all-seeing eye and ear, but personal freedom will surely be sharply curtailed."[69] Yet Democrats in Congress voted in overwhelming numbers for the USA Patriot Act and other laws that prioritized the national security objective over the civil liberties one.

Two fundamental sets of questions lie at the heart of the various national security–civil liberties issues. First, what should the scope of the powers be? How much power is justified in the name of national security? Second, how is accountability in the exercise of those powers to be assured? How can checks and balances, provisions for judicial review, freedom of the press, and other political mechanisms be ensured?

DOMESTIC POWERS OF THE MILITARY AND INTELLIGENCE AGENCIES   In the aftermath of September 11, Americans began hearing much about a law called the Posse Comitatus Act of 1878. This law was passed during the Reconstruction era in reaction to President Ulysses S. Grant's use of federal troops to monitor elections in the former Confederate states. It prohibited the armed forces from engaging in police activities such as search, seizure, and arrest within the borders of the United States. In the century and a half since, this issue had rarely arisen. Even in World War II, domestic security against German and Japanese espionage and infiltration was maintained within these bounds. Now, though, given the nature of the terrorist threat, there was genuine debate about the military's role in homeland security.

One step was creation of the Northern Command. The American military is organized globally into regional commands: the Southern Command covers Latin America, the European Command covers NATO and Europe, the Central Command covers the Middle East and Central Asia, and the Pacific Command covers South and East Asia. Never before had there been a command structure to cover the United States or the rest of North America. As an organizational issue, the creation of the Northern Command generally was seen as necessary and enhancing. What role, though, would it play and what powers would it exercise? Could it fulfill its mission within the no-policing restrictions of the Posse Comitatus law? Should this law be changed?

Even more than for the military, debate intensified over the roles of the CIA, the FBI, and the rest of the intelligence community. Throughout the Cold War the CIA and the FBI operated largely independently, with the CIA charged with international intelligence and the FBI with the domestic realm. While this worked well in many respects and was consistent with civil liberties limitations on domestic intelligence, it also meant that the two agencies had little coordination and indeed developed bureaucratic rivalries. These contributed to the failures to prevent or warn against the September 11 attacks. One key issue, therefore, was to what extent and how to break down these bureaucratic barriers.

Another was about the scope and accountability of their power. How much power should the CIA and the FBI be granted? Should they be authorized, for example, to gather intelligence more widely and with fewer restrictions on wiretaps, search warrants, and undercover operations? If so, how was necessary operational secrecy to be preserved while assuring the accountability necessary for avoiding abuses like those of the past? The use of secret warrants by Attorney General John Ashcroft and the Justice Department increased 30 percent in 2002. And of the 1,228 times one was requested, the secret court in charge granted the warrant every time.[70] These and other practices fed questions about where the balance point was being struck between national security and civil liberties.

JUDICIAL PROCESSES   A number of issues have arisen regarding due process of the law.

Secrecy in the Courts.   Individuals suspected of terrorism have been arrested on immigration charges, and others have been arrested and detained as potential witnesses. The detentions were indefinite, and the cases were heard in secret. "The courtroom must be closed for these cases," said Judge Michael J. Creppy, the nation's top immigration judge. "No visitors, no family and no press." This secrecy even included "confirming or denying whether such a case is on the docket." Judge Gladys Kessler of the Federal District Court in Washington, D.C., saw it differently: "The court fully understands and appreciates that the first priority of the executive branch in a time of crisis is to ensure the physical security of its citizens. By the same token, the first priority of the judicial branch must be to ensure that our government always operates within the statutory and constitutional constraints which distinguish a democracy from a dictatorship."[71]

Military Tribunals.   Another controversy arose over decisions to try some terrorism suspects by military tribunals rather than civilian courts. One of the bases for the claim to the legitimacy of military tribunals was the *Ex Parte Quinn* Supreme Court decision during World War II. The president as commander-in-chief was said to have the authority "to seize and subject to disciplinary measures those enemies who in their attempt to thwart or impede our military effort have violated the law of war." The argument also was made that many of the terrorists were "unlawful combatants" and therefore not entitled to the protections of international law that the third Geneva Convention granted to regular prisoners-of-war. Critics contended both that U.S. law did limit the use of military tribunals and that the Geneva Conventions should and did apply. Duke University law professors Walter Dellinger and Christopher Schroeder acknowledged the constitutionality and historical precedents for some use of military tribunals but called for them to be "limited to extraordinary cases," for their jurisdiction to be "clearly and narrowly circumscribed," and for judicial review to ensure the necessary accountability.[72] Others made the case for the applicability of the Geneva Convention, including concern about precedents that others might use against American or allied soldiers.

FREEDOM OF THE PRESS   The freedom of the press issues raised by coverage within the United States of issues related to the war on terrorism in many respects were even more complex and difficult than the war reporting issues discussed in Chapter 6. The Persian Gulf, Afghanistan, and Iraq wars largely stayed "over there." World War II had an "in here" dimension because of German and Japanese espionage. But the sense of penetration of American society by the enemy in the war on terrorism is much greater. It can be exaggerated and misplaced, but it also is a very real concern. Should the press be restricted, for example, from breaking a story about an FBI operation aimed at an Al Qaeda cell in the United States? Perhaps such a cell planning to launch a biological weapons attack might escape or evade capture if it knew it was under surveillance. Yet what if the FBI were wrong and the suspects were innocent people? Breaking a story in such a situation could ensure that civil liberties are not violated, nor other unwarranted consequences inflicted on individuals and their families.

SECRET "SHADOW" GOVERNMENT: DANGER TO DEMOCRACY OR PRUDENT CONTINGENCY PLANNINGS?   An article in the *Washington Post* breaking the story of a secret "shadow government" that had been put in place post–September 11 in bunkers outside Washington caused quite a stir: "President Bush has dispatched a shadow government of about 100 senior civilian managers to live and work secretly outside Washington. . . . Its first mission, in the event of a disabling blow to Washington, would be to prevent collapse of essential government functions."[73] The feared "disabling blow" was an even more catastrophic terrorist attack, perhaps one using nuclear, chemical, or biological weapons. The "Continuity of Operations Plan" under which this was being done dated back to Cold War planning against nuclear war with the Soviet Union. Never during that era, though, had the plan been activated to this extent. And now it wasn't just for the immediate aftermath of September 11; the planning was being taken as "an indefinite precaution."[74]

The shadow government consisted of about 100 senior civilian managers from all the executive-branch departments and some major agencies. They lived and worked in these bunkers, 24 hours a day, for 90-day rotations, not allowed to tell their families anything other than that they were going on a business trip. This also appeared to have been where Vice President Cheney was when references were made to his being outside of Washington at an "undisclosed secure location." These officials would be the core group with which Vice President Cheney would work if a catastrophic emergency occurred. Their immediate tasks would be to ensure the carrying out of key government functions such as assuring the nation's food and water supplies, keeping transportation and telecommunications systems operating, responding to public health crises, and maintaining civil order. Later they also "would begin to reconstitute the government."[75]

The whole sense of secretiveness was understandable in some respects but also disturbing in a society used to openness. Given the historical pattern of abridgements of civil liberties in the name of national security, and in the context of the post–September 11 issues raised, might democratic procedures and practices be constricted even further under a more severe emergency? It was said that Congress and the Supreme Court had their own separate continuity plans, although on smaller scales and with major questions about whether it might be better to have representatives of these other two branches together with the executive branch under such an emergency. Or was this contingency planning prudent in the face of such a serious threat? Political analyst Norman Ornstein argued that the plan was "a start, but only a start." Continuity of government could not be left to "a group of unelected bureaucrats." Also needed was "a wholesale rethinking of issues of succession," including both provisions for selecting a new Congress and changes in presidential succession to include governors or others from outside Washington. This, in his view, would balance prudence with democratic assurance.[76]

DISTORTIONS OF DOMESTIC POLITICS   When national security becomes the overriding rationale, this can have distorting effects on domestic politics. For instance, the invocation of national security may be used as a rationale justifying policy choices for which its application is a real stretch. Take, for example, the claim made by President Bush that agricultural subsidies paid to American farmers to keep prices up was not just a farm policy or budget policy issue but a matter of national security: "This nation has got to eat," President Bush told a cheering crowd at the annual convention of the National Cattlemen's Beef Association in Denver, Colorado, at a time when Congress was considering a bill that would provide $172 billion in farm subsidies over ten years. "It's in our national security interests that we be able to feed ourselves. Thank goodness, we don't have to rely on somebody else's meat to make sure our people are healthy and well-fed."[77] Bush's political strategy aimed to trump the economic and budgetary arguments by invoking the national security rationale as a superceding justification. This is tried-and-true politics, but is it good policy? If eating beef is a matter of national security, then what isn't?

Another version of this pattern was the "pork-barreling" by Congress during the Iraq war of a bill intended primarily to pay for the war. The scene was described by a reporter: "The hour was late, the war in Iraq was raging, and members of the Senate simply wanted to pass the $80 billion bill to pay for the war and go home for the night." Before going home, though, various senators (Democrats and Republicans alike) inserted into the bill such pork-barrel projects and other special interest provisions as $3.3 million to fix a leaky dam in Vermont, a provision benefiting the Alaska salmon industry by allowing wild salmon to be labeled organic, $10 million in additional funds for a science research station at the South Pole, and $5 million for new police radio systems in Kentucky.[78]

A distorting effect that cuts even deeper to fundamental questions about democracy is the equating of dissent with disloyalty that comes when the domestic consensus is too restrictive. Manifesting national solidarity is one thing, the delegitimization of debate and dissent quite another. The war on terrorism has not produced repressive trends as dangerous to democracy as those of 1950s McCarthyism, but it has produced some worrisome political dynamics. In the immediate aftermath of the September 11 attacks, Attorney General Ashcroft accused critics of his domestic security policies of using tactics that "aid terrorists" and "give ammunition to America's enemies" by "erod[ing] our national unity."[79] A few months later, after Senate Democratic leader Tom Daschle criticized some of the Bush administration's anti-terrorism policies, even in the context of saying that some policies had been successful but others less so, he was attacked by Senate Republican leader Trent Lott: "*How dare* Senator Daschle criticize President Bush while we are fighting our war on terrorism, especially when we have troops in the field? He should not be trying to divide our country."[80] Had Senator Lott given specific substantive rebuttals of the Daschle criticisms, that would have been legitimate policy and political debate. It was the "how dare" notion that equated dissent with disloyalty.

OPEN SOCIETY   In a certain sense the openness of American society is a source of vulnerability. The very value that has been cherished for so long, the freedoms that come with being a democracy, are creating opportunities for terrorism. An Al Qaeda manual told its operatives that they could find much of the information and equipment they needed in libraries, magazines, shopping malls, and other everyday parts of American life. The September 11 hijackers visited the World Trade Center a number of times, going up with the throngs of tourists to the observation deck. They bought portable global-positioning-system equipment in electronics stores. They bought videotapes of the instrument panels of the jets they would hijack from toll-free phone numbers. They took their flight lessons in American flight schools.

But how can the vulnerabilities of openness be reduced without threatening the essence of American democracy and freedom? The war on terrorism has been called a war to preserve freedom. How is it to be fought so that freedom at home is not compromised, or worse? This is the essence of the tension between national security and the Bill of Rights, one that we have seen before in American history but that may well now pose even greater dilemmas and challenges.

The Department of Homeland Security and Executive-Branch Politics

The creation of a new Cabinet department charged with principal responsibility for homeland security was compared with the late-1940s creation of the national security state for the scope and significance of the changes in the foreign policy side of the executive branch (see Chapter 4). That was when, in response to the threat of the onset of the Cold War, the Defense Department, the CIA, the National Security Council, and other agencies were created. Now, with a new high-magnitude threat, the Department of Homeland Security (DHS) was established. It was huge, with 170,000 employees to start. It was complex, with pieces drawn from twenty-two agencies in eight other Cabinet departments, as well as newly created offices. It was far-reaching: homeland security in the context of terrorism and WMD threats encompassed border control (land, sea, and air), airplane and airport security, immigration, infrastructure protection (electric, communications, transportation), emergency public-health response and prevention, other public safety first responders, counterterrorism intelligence, and much more.

There was strong bipartisan support for creation of the DHS; even before the Bush administration made its proposal in June 2002 a number of bills had been introduced in Congress. Underlying the specific issues, this debate like others before has been about how best to achieve the five criteria for policy process rationality: adequate and timely information, thorough and incisive analysis, identification of a range of policy options, effective implementation strategies, and a feedback loop for evaluation and adaptation (see Chapter 2).

ORGANIZATIONAL STRUCTURE   One of the first decisions to be made was regarding which agencies to bring in to the DHS, and which to keep out. "One roof" was the argument for inclusiveness; bring them all together and they're more likely to work together. For example, border security had previously been divided between the Immigration and Naturalization Service, which was part of the Justice Department, the Customs Service, which was part of the Treasury Department, and the Animal and Plant Health Inspection Service, which was part of the Agriculture Department. Interagency problems of communication and coordination on border security, somewhat known prior to September 11, became all too well known in its wake. All of these were to be moved into the DHS.

Other agencies, though, had more "mixed missions"—some responsibilities related to homeland security and others not. The Coast Guard had border-security responsibilities but also non–homeland security responsibilities such as everyday search-and-rescue operations for recreational boaters. The Federal Emergency Management Agency (FEMA) is key to any emergency response to terrorism, but also to other emergencies such as hurricanes, earthquakes, and other natural disasters. The Plum Island Animal Disease Center was shifted from the Agriculture Department because of its relevance to biological warfare and defense, yet it still also had its traditional mission as "America's first line of defense against foreign animal diseases" of more familiar concern to farmers and ranchers, like hoof-and-mouth disease.[81] Some were concerned that moving these agencies into the DHS would take away from these and other responsibilities in ways that could take their own toll in loss of life, disruption, and damage.

Then there were the agencies not slated for inclusion in the DHS. While 22 agencies were being brought in, it was estimated that about 100 total agencies had some degree of homeland security responsibilities. Chief among those not being brought in were the FBI and the CIA. Both were deemed to need their independence. Yet both were especially key to the information and analysis criteria for policy process rationality. The DHS was given its own intelligence and threat-analysis division, but time would tell how well information-sharing and other coordination would work. One example of how poorly it worked, even just between the CIA and the FBI pre–September 11, was the CIA's failure to pass on to the FBI information it obtained from the Malaysian intelligence service, which had tapped an Al Qaeda meeting held in Kuala Lumpur in January 2000. This meeting included two of the September 11 hijackers, who got into the United States within days of this meeting, when the FBI and border agencies lacked critical information on their identities.

Congress's General Accounting Office (GAO) assessed the challenges facing DHS as "high risk" because of the complex management and bureaucratic tasks inherent in such a huge executive branch department.[82] Moreover, as big as it is, DHS still has to coordinate with other departments and agencies.

Despite being part of the same administration, in the world of administrative turf and budgets, competition and rivalry are part of the mix. As a Brookings Institution study warned, "interagency coordination led by Cabinet secretaries has seldom worked well in the past and it is not likely to do so now. The secretaries of Defense, Treasury, Justice, State, and [Health and Human Services] are unlike to defer to directives from another Cabinet agency that is a competitor for funds and presidential attention."[83]

ORGANIZATIONAL CULTURE AND HUMAN CAPITAL   Redrawing organizational charts also is at most a first step toward changing organizational cultures in ways that contribute to more effective performance. Routinization is part of the nature of bureaucracy: people get used to doing things a certain way. The FBI, for example, started to get fully computerized only in the 1990s, and even then there was resistance because of "a culture that preferred handwritten or typed reports." The software system was such a low priority that the FBI could not search its intelligence intercepts for multiple uses of terms such as "flight training school" or "hijack."[84]

Another problem of organizational culture was the risk aversion that had built up in the FBI and the CIA as a consequence of several decades of scandals, abuses, and failures. From agents in the field to mid-level bureaucrats in Washington to agency directors, the mindset tilted toward erring on the side of limited initiative. The challenge is to change this without reverting to an organizational culture in which intelligence agencies too readily use the ends of national security to justify means that may have too little regard for civil liberties and other aspects of the law, for this was what caused many of the scandals, abuses, and failures in the first place.

Beyond organizational charts and cultures, people matter most. Government in general has had a human capital problem in recent years. Public-sector careers are not nearly as attractive for current generations as for some past ones. The problem runs even deeper than just government. As a nation the United States is sorely lacking in language fluency and cultural familiarity relevant to many parts of the world, including the Arab and Islamic worlds. For example, as of October 2001, the American Translators Association had 2,217 members fluent in Spanish, 1,189 fluent in French, but only 120 fluent in Arabic, 21 fluent in Farsi (spoken in Iran), and 1 in Pashto (spoken in Afghanistan). It thus should not have been a total surprise to find out that an Al Qaeda message that "tomorrow is zero hour" was intercepted on September 10 but not translated until well after.[85]

CONGRESSIONAL OVERSIGHT   Congressional oversight can help assure accountability in the exercise of power, in the expenditure of public funds, and for overall performance standards. In these and other ways it is a crucial cog in the feedback loop for evaluation and adaptation of policy over time.

Yet it also can be problematic in any of three ways. *Too much* congressional oversight can become micromanagement, getting in the way of the expertise of agency officials and politicizing issues better left to the professional civil service. *Too little* congressional oversight can lead to abuses of power, corruption, and other dangers. *The wrong kind* of congressional oversight, such as when an executive department has to report to a proliferation of congressional committees, can make for a lack of clarity of accountability, conflicting directives from this and that committee chair, and other delays and inefficiencies in already complex processes. "The federal bureaucracy reports to and takes orders from Congress as well as the White House," the same Brookings study stated. "It would hardly do, then, to fix the problems that bedevil executive branch decision-making only to perpetuate roadblocks on Capitol Hill."[86]

PREVENTION AS WELL AS PROTECTION AND RESPONSE   Much of the mission of the DHS is geared to better protecting the nation against terrorism and better responding to terrorism if it occurs. Protection involves, among other things, tighter airport security to keep terrorists and bombs off airplanes, tighter border security to keep terrorists out of the country, the hardening of potential targets such as electric power plants and other critical infrastructure to make them more resistant to attack, and the development of biodefense vaccines and other health measures. All these things need to be in place prior to a terrorist attack and will matter if a terrorist attack is attempted. Response measures involve additional steps taken once a terrorist attack takes place: emergency first responders such as police, firefighters, and other public-safety officials; hospital and other public-health mobilization; emergency communications systems; and others.

And all of this has to be done all across the United States. This has put local communities, for so long so used to taking this type of security for granted, on the "front lines." "We've gone from being a local police officer who just worries about his local community," commented the deputy policy chief of a small town in Illinois, "to where you worry about international politics." In the state of Washington, the ferries that many commuters ride daily are sometimes accompanied by Coast Guard cutters with .50-caliber machine guns. In New York City "police officers are armed like assault troops" guarding bridges, tunnels, subway stations, museums, and many other places.[87]

Yet no matter how much money is spent and no matter how much effort is made, we can never know for sure just how well we are protected and how effectively we will respond until the event actually happens. We have to assume that terrorists are making their own plans in ways that we cannot thoroughly anticipate. We also cannot wish away the risk that what can go wrong often does go wrong.

This inherent uncertainty means two things. One is that prevention must also be part of the homeland security effort. Prevention entails reduction of the will, capability, and opportunity for terrorism. This task is even more formidable than protecting against and responding to terrorism's effects, not only for the foreign policy strategy reasons discussed earlier, but for foreign policy politics reasons, too. Bureaucracies are even worse at the anticipating and acting needed for prevention than they are at the reacting needed for protection and response. We saw this in the controversy over whether and what pre-September 11 warnings were available. Was there genuinely no way the government could have known that this or something like this was coming and could have acted to prevent it?

Second, ultimately what all this means is that homeland security is a question of the management and reduction of risk, not the elimination of risk. As much as one might like to achieve risk elimination, it simply is not possible. This is not a message that politicians of any party want to deliver. Speeches about fully assured security, and fingerpointing about who bears what responsibility for things not being achieved, are much more politically palatable. This works politically but makes the policy tasks all the more difficult.

Summary

The United States is the world's most powerful nation. It is number one in military might. Its nuclear arsenal is second to none. Its armed forces are the best trained and have the best military technology available. The United States also has the most active diplomacy, drawing on a broad range of strategies of statecraft. Yet it still faces formidable security challenges.

The end of the Cold War put the alignments and dynamics of major-power geopolitics in flux. U.S. relations with Russia have improved substantially from the Cold War, but uncertainties remain as to which scenario—Russia as friend, as great-power competitor, or as adversary—will prevail in the future. Relations with China continue to be debated between strategies of containment and those of engagement, each predicated on different assessments of the mix of common and competing interests. Relations with Cold War–era allies in western Europe and Japan remain generally positive but also are going through their own transitions. The major regional conflicts between India and Pakistan, between North and South Korea, and in the Middle East, carried over from the Cold War era, again have brought the world to crises a number of times, and have uncertain futures.

American military strategy is undergoing rethinking. Cold War–era strategies and doctrines need revising and updating, although not necessarily discarding. The core questions remain the same—how best to deter and defend against threats to the United States, its citizens, interests, and allies.

The war on terrorism has been the Bush administration's most defining issue. Terrorism is nothing new, but following the September 11 attacks it was posed not just as *a* problem but as *the* problem for American foreign policy. The Bush administration developed a multifaceted strategy, including a doctrine for the pre-emptive use of force and the most extensive expansion of American global military commitments since the early days of the Cold War. Both within the United States and internationally there has been much debate over the Bush strategy.

The threats from other nonstate actors such as drug lords and international criminals are also of a much greater scope and magnitude than in earlier eras. Bringing American power to bear against them in some respects can be even more difficult than against state-based actors.

The foreign policy politics of homeland security have been quite complex and contentious. Once again tensions and trade-offs have been posed between national security and civil liberties, as well as other aspects of American democracy. The creation of the Department of Homeland Security represented the most sweeping change in the foreign policy side of the executive branch in more than fifty years, raising a number of issues that remain to be worked out.

In sum, power still is at least part of the name of the game. What strategies, though, are the best for maximizing American power in ways that provide security for the United States, its allies, and its interests? How far can power be used, and how can it be used in ways consistent with the other three Ps of the national interest (peace, prosperity, principles)—that is the question we turn to in the next few chapters.

Notes

[1] Gail W. Lapidus, "Transforming Russia: American Policy in the 1990s," in *Eagle Rules? Foreign Policy and American Primacy in the Twenty-First Century,* ed. Robert J. Lieber (Upper Saddle River, N.J.: Prentice Hall, 2002), 108.

[2] Lapidus, "Transforming Russia," 108–09.

[3] Andrei Kozyrev, "Russia: A Chance for Survival," *Foreign Affairs* 71:2 (March–April 1992), 9–10.

[4] Dana Milbank and Sharon LaFraniere, "U.S., Russia Agree to Arms Pact," *Washington Post,* May 14, 2002, 1.

[5] Interview with Condoleezza Rice, Lehrer News Hour, May 13, 2002, 6 (transcript).

[6] Jane Perlez, "U.S. Scolds Russia for Plans to Resume Arms Sales to Iran," *New York Times,* March 15, 2001, A15.

[7] Patrick E. Tyler, "Moscow Says Remarks by U.S. Resurrect 'Spirit of Cold War'," *New York Times,* March 21, 2001.

[8] Lapidus, "Transforming Russia," 126.

[9] Speech by Russian National Security Adviser Sergei Ivanov at the Wehrkunde Security Conference, Munich, Germany, February 4, 2001.

[10] Jim Hoagland, "Three Miscreants," *Washington Post,* April 13, 2003, B7.

[11] Ivanov speech, Wehrkunde Security Conference, 2001.

[12] Cited in Stephen M. Walt, "Beyond Bin Laden: Reshaping U.S. Foreign Policy," *International Security* 26:2 (Winter 2001/02), 60.

[13] Robert Legvold, "The Three Russias: Decline, Revolution and Reconstruction," in *A Century's Journey: How the Great Powers Shape the World,* ed. Robert A. Pastor (New York: Basic Books, 1999), 188–89.

[14] Legvold, "The Three Russias," 189.

[15] Michel Oksenberg, "China: A Tortuous Path onto the World's Stage," in Pastor, *A Century's Journey,* 299.

[16] Senate Foreign Relations Committee, Confirmation Hearing, Secretary of State-designate Colin L. Powell, January 17, 2001, *www.state.gov/secretary,* 4.

[17] Richard Holbrooke, "A Defining Moment with China," *Washington Post,* January 2, 2002, A13.

[18] Aaron L. Friedberg, "11 September and the Future of Sino-American Relations," *Survival* 44:1 (Spring 2002), 36; Craig S. Smith, "China, in Harsh Crackdown, Executes Muslim Separatists," *New York Times,* December 16, 2001.

[19] James Dao, "New Pentagon Report Sees Rapid Buildup by China," *New York Times,* July 13, 2002, 4. See also U.S.-China Security Review Commission, *The National Security Implications of the Economic Relationship between the United States and China,* pursuant to Public Law 106-398, October 30, 2000, as amended (Washington, D.C.: U.S. Government Printing Office, 2002).

[20] Minxin Pei, "Beijing Drama: China's Governance Crisis and Bush's New Challenge," *Policy Brief 21* (November 2002), Carnegie Endowment for International Peace; Nicholas Eberstadt, "The Future of AIDS," *Foreign Affairs* 81:6 (November/December 2002).

[21] Minxin Pei, "Future Shock: The WTO and Political Change in China," *Policy Brief* 1 (February 2001), Carnegie Endowment for International Peace.

[22] Robert Kagan, "Power and Weakness," *Policy Review,* 113 (June 2002), 1.

[23] Nicole Gnesotto, "Reacting to America," *Survival* 44:4 (Winter 2002–03), 100, 102.

[24]Eurobarometer polls, cited in Frauke N. Bielka and Christian Tuschhoff, "Common Threats—Diverging Responses: Despite Similar Threat Perceptions Europeans and Americans Respond Differently to Terrorism," (unpublished paper, n.d.), and at *http://europa.eu.int/comm/public opinion/*

[25]Hans W. Maull, "Germany and the Use of Force: Still a 'Civilian Power'?" *Survival* 42:2 (Summer 2000), 56–80.

[26]U.S. Department of State, Bureau of East Asian and Pacific Affairs, "Fact Sheet: U.S.-Japan Security Relations," July 28, 1997.

[27]Peter Finn and Kathryn Tolbert, "Ex-Axis Powers Recast Foreign Military Roles," *Washington Post*, November 30, 2001, A34.

[28]Howard W. French, "Taboo against Nuclear Arms Is Being Challenged in Japan," *New York Times*, June 9, 2002, 1, 4.

[29]Bruce W. Jentleson, *With Friends like These: Reagan, Bush, and Saddam, 1982–1990* (New York: Norton, 1994).

[30]Ivo K. Daalder and Michael E. O'Hanlon, *Winning Ugly: NATO's War to Save Kosovo* (Washington, D.C.: Brookings Institution, 2000); Wesley K. Clark, *Waging Modern War: Bosnia, Kosovo and the Future of Combat* (New York: Public Affairs, 2001).

[31]Michael Cox, "American Power Before and After September 11: Dizzy with Success?" *International Affairs* 78:2 (2002), 290.

[32]Independent International Commission on Kosovo, *Kosovo Report: Conflict, International Response, Lessons Learned* (New York: Oxford University Press, 2000).

[33]Keith B. Richburg and William Branigin, "Attacks from Out of the Blue," *Washington Post*, November 18, 2001, A24; James Dao and Andrew C. Revkin, "A Revolution in Warfare," *New York Times*, April 16, 2002, D1, 4.

[34]Thomas E. Ricks, "Target Approval Delays Cost Air Force Key Hits," *Washington Post*, November 18, 2001, A1.

[35]David Johnston, Don Van Natta, Jr., and Judith Miller, "Qaeda's New Links Increase Threats from Global Sites," *New York Times*, June 16, 2002, A1.

[36]Drew Brown, "Commander: Afghan Mission May Last 2 Years," *Durham Herald-Sun*, September 21, 2002, A7.

[37]Matthew Brzezinski, "The Unmanned Army," *New York Times Magazine*, April 20, 2003, 38, 41.

[38]Thom Shanker, "Assessment of Iraq War Will Emphasize Joint Operations," *New York Times*, May 1, 2003, A10.

[39]George Liska, *Nations in Alliance: The Limits of Interdependence* (Baltimore: John Hopkins University Press, 1962), 12.

[40]Joseph Lepgold, "NATO's Post–Cold War Collective Action Problem," *International Security* 23: (Summer 1998), 84–85.

[41]David Abshire, "A Debate for 16 Parliaments," *Washington Post*, February 19, 1997, A21.

[42]Lepgold, "NATO's Post–Cold War Collective Action Problem," 81.

[43]Lepgold, "NATO's Post–Cold War Collective Action Problem," 91.

[44]Michael May, "Fearsome Security: The Role of Nuclear Weapons," *Brookings Review*, Summer 1995, 24.

[45]Jonathan Schell, "The Gift of Time: The Case for Abolishing Nuclear Weapons," *The Nation*, February 2–9, 1998.

[46]Schell, "The Gift of Time," 11–12.

[47]Speech by U.S. Defense Secretary Donald Rumsfeld at the Wehrkunde Security Conference, Munich, Germany, February 4, 2001.

[48]Dana Priest, "Cohen Says U.S. Will Build Missile Defense," *Washington Post,* January 21, 1999, A1, A10.

[49]Charles R. Babcock, "Pentagon Budget's Stealth Spending," *Washington Post,* October 13, 1998, A1, A4.

[50]Matt Miller, "Democrats and Defense," June 5, 2002, Tribune Media Services, Internet distribution, *mattino@att.net*

[51]Hans Binnendijk, "Introduction," in *Transforming America's Military,* ed. Hans Binnendijk (Washington, D.C.: National Defense University Press, 2002), xxxi.

[52]Robert Pear, "Deal to Close Bases Leaves Rumsfeld Disappointed," *New York Times,* December 14, 2001, A20.

[53]National Commission on Terrorism, *Countering the Changing Threat of International Terrorism,* report issued in 2001, available at www.fas.org/irp/threat/commission/html. On Osama bin Laden and other Islamic terrorist groups, see the "Holy Warriors" three-part series published by the *New York Times,* January 14–16, 2001.

[54]Richard K. Betts, "The Soft Underbelly of American Primacy: Tactical Advantages of Terror," *Political Science Quarterly* 117:1 (Spring 2002), 25.

[55]Thomas E. Ricks and Vernon Loeb, "Bush Developing Military Policy of Striking First," *Washington Post,* June 10, 2002, A1, A13.

[56]Barry R. Posen, "The Struggle against Terrorism: Grand Strategy, Strategy and Tactics," *International Security* 26:3 (Winter 2001/02), 39–55.

[57]David E. Sanger, "Bush to Formalize a Defense Policy of Hitting First," *New York Times,* June 17, 2002, A1, A6.

[58]Peter Slevin, "Some War Allies Show Poor Rights Records," *Washington Post,* March 5, 2002, A13.

[59]Betts, "Soft Underbelly of American Primacy," 30.

[60]G. John Ikenberry, "America's Imperial Ambition," *Foreign Affairs* 81:5 (September/October 2002), 58.

[61]Peter G. Peterson, "Public Diplomacy and the War on Terrorism," *Foreign Affairs* 81:5 (September/October 2002), 75–76; see the full report of the Independent Task Force on Public Diplomacy on the Council on Foreign Relations Web site, www.cfr.org.

[62]Peterson, "Public Diplomacy," 76.

[63]British Prime Minister Tony Blair, "Building a Strong International Community," October 2, 2001, www.britainusa.com.

[64]Keith Bradsher, "Pakistanis Fume as Clothing Sales to U.S. Tumble," *New York Times,* June 23, 2002, A3.

[65]Diana Jean Schemo, "Bogota Aid: To Fight Drugs or Rebels?" *New York Times,* June 2, 1998, A1, A12.

[66]Senator John Kerry, "Organized Crime Goes Global While the United States Stays Home," *Washington Post,* May 1, 1997, C1.

[67]Kerry, "Organized Crime."

[68]FBI Director Louis Freeh, testimony before the House Committee on International Relations, October 1, 1997, pp. 8, 10.

[69]William Safire, "The Great Unwatched," *New York Times,* February 18, 2002, A19.

[70]Eric Lichtblau and James Risen, "Broad Domestic Role Asked for CIA and Pentagon," *New York Times,* May 2, 2003, A8.

[71]Adam Liptak, Neil A. Lewis, and Benjamin Weiser, "After September 11, A Legal Battle on the Limits of Civil Liberty," *New York Times,* August 4, 2002, 1, 16; Linda Greenhouse, "The Imperial Presidency vs. the Imperial Judiciary," *New York Times,* September 8, 2002, WK 3.

[72]Walter Dellinger and Christopher H. Schroeder, "The Case for Judicial Review," *Washington Post,* December 6, 2001, A39.

[73]Barton Gelman and Susan Schmidt, "Shadow Government Is at Work in Secret," *Washington Post,* March 1, 2002, A1.

[74]Gelman and Schmidt, "Shadow Government."

[75]Gelman and Schmidt, "Shadow Government."

[76]Norman J. Ornstein, "Preparing for the Unthinkable: Bush's 'Shadow Government' Plan Is a Start—But Only a Start," *Wall Street Journal,* March 11, 2002. See www.continuityof government.org for information on the Continuity of Government Commission established by the American Enterprise Institute and the Brookings Institution.

[77]Mike Allen, "Bush Calls Farm Subsidies a National Security Issue," *Washington Post,* February 9, 2002, A4. The article also notes that the rural areas and business interests that stood to benefit the most from the farm subsidies were key Bush supporters in the 2000 presidential election.

[78]David Firestone, "Senate Rolls a Pork Barrel into War Bill," *New York Times,* April 9, 2002, A12.

[79]Neil A. Lewis, "Ashcroft Defends Antiterrorism Plans and Says Criticism May Aid Foes," *New York Times,* December 7, 2001, A1.

[80]Todd S. Purdum, "Democratic Leader Questions War Aims," *San Francisco Chronicle,* February 28, 2002, A20; Audrey Hudson, "Daschle Hits Execution of War," *Washington Times,* March 1, 2002, A1.

[81]Plum Island Animal Disease Center Website, *http://www.ars.usda.gov/plum/,* accessed May 11, 2003.

[82]U.S. Congress, General Accounting Office (GAO), *Department of Homeland Security: Major Management Challenges and Program Risks,* GAO-03-102, January 2003.

[83]Ivo H. Daalder et al., "Assessing the Department of Homeland Security," Brookings Institution, Washington, D.C., July 2002, 44.

[84]Patrick Tyler, "Feeling Secure, U.S. Failed to See Determined Enemy," *New York Times,* September 8, 2002, 19.

[85]Lynnley Browning, "Do You Speak Uzbek? Translators Are in Demand," *New York Times,* October 21, 2001, 4; Tyler, "Feeling Secure," 19.

[86]Daalder, et al., *Assessing the Department of Homeland Security,* 48.

[87]Jodi Wilgoren, "At One of 1,000 Front Lines in U.S., Local Officials Try to Plan for War," *New York Times,* June 19, 2002, A19; Timothy Egan, "Pacific Northwest Keeps Watch on Many Vulnerable Points," *New York Times,* March 25, 2003, B13; Richard Perez-Pena, "In New York, A Security Blanket with Holes," *New York Times,* March 23, 2003, B1, B10.

CHAPTER 8

Peace: Building a Post–Cold War World Order?

Introduction: Opportunities and Challenges of Peace-Building

Initial visions of the peace that was to follow the Cold War were in large part post–Cold War manifestations of International Institutionalism and an orientation more toward multilateralism than unilateralism. One key dimension of this approach, as discussed in Chapter 6, is an emphasis on the building of a system of international institutions, organizations, and regimes that provide the basis for cooperation among states to resolve tensions, settle disputes, and work together in ways that are mutually beneficial and, above all, to avoid war. Another key part is the peace-building and peace-brokering roles that the United States can play through its diplomacy and its use of military power for humanitarian interventions.

How much have international institutions achieved, and how much can they achieve, in building and maintaining a post–Cold War peace? How can the United States best play its peace-building and peace-brokering roles? What have been the main tensions between peace and the other national-interest objectives (power, prosperity, principles)? With these central questions in mind, this chapter examines

- the United Nations, and in particular UN peace operations;
- regional multilateral organizations in each of the world's major regions;
- nonproliferation regimes against weapons of mass destruction;

- ■ key peace-building policies of preventive diplomacy and humanitarian intervention; and
- ■ the U.S. peace-brokering role in general and as seen in three recent cases.

The record that comes through is mixed, showing strengths as well as weaknesses. We want to understand both the strengths and the weaknesses, the reasons for them, and the factors that affect them, so as to better assess the International Institutionalist paradigm and to be able to draw pertinent lessons for American foreign policy.

This chapter closes with a look at the foreign policy politics of peace-building through three pertinent cases: the UN and U.S. domestic politics, the congressional defeat in 1999 of the Comprehensive Test Ban Treaty, and the politics of humanitarian intervention.

The United Nations

8.1

The only way to effectively study the United Nations is to get beyond both the idealized views and the caricatures. Sweeping visions, such as that of Secretary of State Cordell Hull at the UN's founding in 1945, of cooperative and harmonious world government that would alleviate "the need for spheres of influence, alliances, balances of power," freeing the world from its "unhappy past," never were very realistic.[1] On the other hand, right-wing conspiratorial views of the UN plotting to take over the United States, including supposed sightings of UN "black helicopters" on secret maneuvers in the U.S. hinterland, are pretty far out, too.

Figure 8.1 sketches the main components of the United Nations. As an institution, the UN has three unique strengths. First is its *near-global membership*. At the UN's founding in 1945, there were only 51 members of the General Assembly. As of 2003 there are 191. The first major wave of growth came with decolonization and independence for the former European colonies in Africa. Between 1960 and 1962, the UN took in 27 new members, 23 of which were from Africa. Another surge came in the 1990s, a manifestation of the many new nations formed after the breakup of the Soviet Union (where one state became fifteen), Yugoslavia (where one became five) and Czechoslovakia (which divided into two states). Its inclusive membership makes the UN the one place where representatives of all the world's nation-states regularly meet. As Gareth Evans, a former Australian foreign minister, put it, "the world needs a center. . . . The United Nations is the only credible candidate."[2]

Second, the UN Security Council (UNSC) is vested, by the terms of the UN Charter, with "primary responsibility for the maintenance of international peace and security." UN advocates stress the "primary" responsibility wording. While not excluding the ways individual states retain some responsibility through their own foreign policies for their own security, they see the UNSC as having a crucial responsibility. Moreover, whereas other parts of the UN have only the power to make recommendations to member governments, decisions made by the UNSC are binding on member governments. Even though the UNSC does not always have the actual power to enforce its resolutions, these resolutions carry a *normative legitimacy* that no other institution can convey. The UNSC holds the international community's ultimate "seals of approval and disapproval."[3] Its resolutions are particularly important in legitimizing and mobilizing broad support for coercive measures against aggressors, human rights violators, or other offending states. This is evident in the use of economic sanctions, which have the greatest chance of getting multilateral support when authorized by the UNSC, as in such post–Cold War cases as the sanctions against Iraq, Haiti, Serbia, and Afghanistan. It is especially evident in justifying the use of military force, both for major wars (e.g., the Korean War, the Persian Gulf War, the Afghanistan War) and for peace operations (e.g., Somalia, Haiti, Bosnia). The 2002–03 debate over war with Iraq, in which the United States challenged the Security Council's role and went to war without full and final Security Council approval, was among the most contentious and divisive cases in UN history.

Third is the *scope of UN programs, geared to the full global agenda*, including not only peace, but also economic development, the environment, human rights, and public health. Although issues like the crises in Somalia, Bosnia, and Iraq get the most publicity, arguably the most meaningful work the UN does is in seeking, as stated in its Charter, "to employ international machinery for the promotion of the economic and social advancement of all peoples." It does this through specialized agencies and programs, some of which are shown in Figure 8.1.

For U.S. foreign policy, debates regarding the UN reflect the broader unilateralism-multilateralism debate laid out in Chapter 6. More specifically this debate focuses on three areas: the peace-power tension between the ways in which the UN can enhance American foreign policy and the ways in which it can limit U.S. prerogatives, questions about the UN's institutional

FIGURE 8.1 The United Nations System (partial listing)

PRINCIPAL ORGANS OF THE UNITED NATIONS

International Court of Justice

Security Council

General Assembly

Economic and Social Council

Trusteeship Council

Secretariat

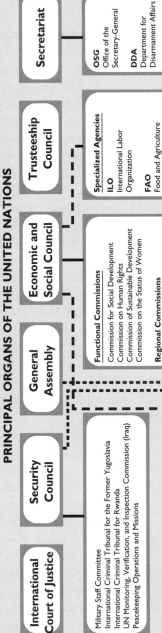

Military Staff Committee
International Criminal Tribunal for the Former Yugoslavia
International Criminal Tribunal for Rwanda
UN Monitoring, Verification, and Inspection Commission (Iraq)
Peacekeeping Operations and Missions

Programs and Funds

UNCTAD
United Nations Conference on Trade and Development

UNDCP
United Nations Drug Control Program

UNEP
United Nations Environment Program

UNDP
United Nations Development Program

UNFPA
United Nations Population Fund

UNHCR
Office of the United Nations High Commissioner for Refugees

UNICEF
United Nations Children's Fund

WFP
World Food Program

Other UN Entities

OHCHR
Office of the United Nations High Commissioner for Human Rights

UNU
United Nations University

Functional Commissions

Commission for Social Development
Commission on Human Rights
Commission of Sustainable Development
Commission on the Status of Women

Regional Commissions

Economic Commission for Africa (ECA)
Economic Commission for Europe (ECE)
Economic Commission for Latin America and the Caribbean (ECLAC)
Economic and Social Commission for Asia and the Pacific (ESCAP)
Economic and Social Commission for Western Asia (ESCWA)

Related Organizations

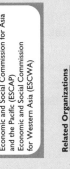

IAEA
International Atomic Energy Agency

OPCW
Organization for the Prohibition of Chemical Weapons

Specialized Agencies

ILO
International Labor Organization

FAO
Food and Agriculture Organization of the United Nations

UNESCO
United Nations Educational, Scientific, and Cultural Organization

WHO
World Health Organization

UNIDO
United Nations Industrial Development Organization

OSG
Office of the Secretary-General

DDA
Department for Disarmament Affairs

DPKO
Department of Peacekeeping Operations

United Nations Dept. of Public Information, DPI/2079/Add.1 (January 2002).

and programmatic effectiveness, and domestic political controversies evoked by the UN. The first two are addressed here, the third in the foreign policy politics section later in this chapter.

Peace and Power: Policy Enhancement versus Prerogative Encroachment

It is one thing to say that both the United States and the United Nations seek peace. The more difficult question from a U.S. perspective is whether their efforts toward peace are complementary and reinforcing, or whether they are in tension and pose trade-offs. To what extent does working with and through the UN enhance the U.S. capacity to achieve peace, directly or indirectly; to what extent does it encroach on the prerogatives of American power? Some argue that this is an arrogant question for Americans even to pose. Others see it as essential and justified by both the interests and the responsibilities of U.S. leadership.

The policy-enhancement argument has two aspects. One is that a strong and effective UN provides the crucial institutional infrastructure for building a post–Cold War order and thus indirectly enhances U.S. foreign policy and its national interest in peace. This argument goes back to the original vision of Franklin Roosevelt and other UN founders at the end of World War II, and to the lesson learned the hard way from the failure of the League of Nations. It continues to be articulated by the State Department, the Web site of which states that "engagement in the UN pays significant dividends to Americans in the form of a safer, more prosperous world." This argument implies that the UN should be judged on an overall, systemic basis rather than issue-by-issue asking whether the UN helped or hindered U.S. foreign policy in a particular instance.

While this is the approach many strong multilateralists take, a more explicitly self-interested argument about direct policy enhancement also is made to counter doubts about indirectness. Indeed the State Department gives much greater emphasis to this latter argument, supplementing its general engagement point with statements about how "the UN offers a unique forum *for advancing U.S. objectives*. . . . The multilateral system also provides a powerful platform *for advancing U.S. values and ideals*. . . . UN programs *serve U.S. objectives* by promoting free-market reform in the developing world. . . . The U.S. cannot rely solely on bilateral relations to *advance U.S. foreign policy objectives but must take advantage of [its] participation in the UN in order to influence other governments' opinions and policies*."[4]

The 1990–91 Persian Gulf War against Iraq was a strong example of both aspects of the policy-enhancement argument. Soon after Saddam Hussein's invasion of Kuwait in 1990 the UNSC imposed economic sanctions, condemned Iraq diplomatically, and took other measures to show that it was not just the United States but the broad international community that opposed Iraq's actions. As the crisis wore on and Saddam remained intransigent, the threat to use military force, initially made by the United States, was affirmed and enhanced by a UNSC resolution authorizing "all necessary means" to get Iraqi troops out of Kuwait, including the use of military force. So when Operation Desert Storm was launched in early 1991, it had the benefits of both UN legitimization and of the burden-sharing of twenty-seven coalition nations sending troops or providing other assistance. Yet both the military command for fighting the war and the diplomatic initiative for negotiating the terms of the peace were left to the United States.

This positive experience in the Persian Gulf War, along with the general aura of U.S. triumph at the end of the Cold War, led to a real bullishness about the UN. In January 1992 President George H.W. Bush joined other world leaders at the first-ever summit of the heads of state of UNSC members. The summit called for a major new study proposing "ways of strengthening . . . the capacity of the United Nations" for the new era.[5] The ensuing report by UN Secretary-General Boutros Boutros-Ghali, appropriately titled *An Agenda for Peace,* received a great deal of attention from the first Bush administration and then from the newly installed Clinton administration. Bill Clinton, his first UN ambassador Madeleine Albright, and other figures in this new administration went even further than their predecessors in stressing the enhancing effects and other benefits of an expanded role for the UN.

Then, however, came the crises in Somalia and Bosnia, and a sharp disillusionment with the UN within the United States. Among the issues raised by the failures of UN peacekeeping missions in these countries was the prerogative-encroachment one. Some of this criticism was unfair, inaccurate, and politically manipulated. Viewers of the movie *Black Hawk Down* know that the October 1993 debacle in Somalia in which 18 American soldiers were killed was more the fault of the Clinton administration than of the UN.[6] Some of the criticism, though, was valid. In Bosnia, for example, the "dual-key" arrangement, by which prior to the December 1995 Dayton accord the United States and NATO could not take military action without prior UN approval, undermined the credibility of the military threat and complicated military operations. The whole setup was "insane," Assistant Secretary of State Richard Holbrooke lamented in July 1995 when UN authorities wouldn't let NATO retaliate even when UN peacekeepers were taken hostage.[7]

The recurring crises with Iraq after the Gulf War also raised dissatisfaction with the UN role. Iraq had been kept under severe restrictions after the war had ended. A series of UNSC resolutions kept economic sanctions on Iraq, created the United Nations Special Commission on Iraq (UNSCOM), which had unprecedented authority for on-site inspection and other measures to force Iraq to eliminate its weapons of mass destruction, and took other steps to isolate and contain Iraq. The United States could have done little if any of this on its own. The UN's legitimacy was essential. But as Iraq challenged and defied the UN resolutions, the need to consult with the UN was one of the constraints on the U.S. capacity to take military action or exert its power in other ways. In February 1998 UN Secretary-General Kofi Annan mediated an agreement with Saddam Hussein that defused a looming crisis, but the agreement fell apart later in the year. As tensions mounted again in November 1998, and American bombers were within minutes (literally) of attacking Iraq, Saddam headed them off with a letter to Secretary-General Annan yet again pledging to cooperate. While many—including officials within his own administration—felt President Clinton still should have attacked, a primary reason that he did not was concern about a potential backlash at the UN. Iraq remained a problem, though, as Saddam did not live up to the deal struck with Secretary-General Annan.

The issue came to a head in 2002–03 when the Bush administration pushed for full-scale military action. The Bush administration had extensive internal debate as to whether to go to the UNSC for support. Those who favored doing so, such as Secretary of State Colin Powell, in effect made the policy enhancement argument, that having UNSC support would provide normative legitimacy as well as a broader coalition for burden sharing. Vice President Dick Cheney and Secretary of Defense Donald Rumsfeld opposed doing so because of what they viewed as the greater downside risks of prerogative encroachment. President Bush initially did go the UN route, getting a unanimous UNSC vote in November 2002 to pressure Iraq to comply with the UN weapons of mass destruction inspections and threatening military action if it did not. This consensus proved fleeting, though. Over the ensuing four months, tensions within the UNSC reached extraordinary levels as France, Russia, and others pushed back against the Bush administration's pressures for UNSC support for moving on to military action. The Bush administration ultimately decided to go to war without another UNSC vote. In part they claimed to actually have sufficient legitimacy based on past UNSC resolutions. In part they claimed they did not really need UNSC support since they viewed this as an act of self-defense within the Bush doctrine of pre-emption. They also knew they faced a veto by France and likely Russia in the Security Council.

Some analysts felt this actually was the way the Bush administration wanted it all along. In this view the administration had gone to the UN in the summer and fall 2002 just "to check off the box," calculating that the basis for taking unilateral military action would be strengthened after having at least tried the multilateral route. "We told you so," said those who all along had been skeptics of the UN and for whom the lack of action was not a surprise. Whichever analysis was more accurate, it was clear that the debate over Iraq had left the UN in much worse shape than it had been in a number of years.

EXPANSION OF THE SECURITY COUNCIL   An ongoing issue that also reveals this enhancement-encroachment tension is the debate over whether the UNSC should expand its number of permanent members.[8] The structure of the UNSC reflects the global balance of power as it was left by World War II: there are five permanent members—the United States, Russia (formerly the Soviet Union), Britain, France, and China (the Republic of China on Taiwan until 1971, and since then the People's Republic)—who in addition to their permanent seats also have the power to veto any UNSC action; and there are ten other UNSC seats, which rotate among countries for two-year terms and which do not carry the veto.

But for some, this World War II–era structure now seems outdated. Tremendous changes have taken place in the international system during the intervening decades. With this in mind, calls have been made for granting other countries permanent membership on the UNSC. What about Japan and Germany, some ask: given their great importance in global affairs and their rank as the second- and third-largest contributors to the UN budget, shouldn't they now have permanent seats? Should it be with or without the veto? And what about major Third World countries like Brazil, India, Nigeria, and South Africa, from regions that now get only rotating seats? Shouldn't their interests be represented by permanent seats? One of India's motivations for its May 1998 nuclear-weapons test was to express its dissatisfaction with its lack of progress toward a permanent UNSC seat despite being the second most populous country in the world and one of the most ancient civilizations. The same five nations that are the world's nuclear-weapons powers also are the UNSC permanent members. Now India, its leaders asserted, had nuclear weapons, and so now it also should receive the same status. Others contended that India's nuclear-weapons tests, carried out in defiance of the will of the international community, should instead weaken its claim to a UNSC permanent seat, because dangerous precedents would be set by condoning this path to permanent membership.

There had been some pressure to deal with the Security Council expansion issue in time for the UN's fiftieth anniversary in 1995. That didn't happen, and so the issue continues to brew, amid American ambivalence about the potential value of a larger and more representative Security Council on the one hand, and the concerns about encroachments on U.S. prerogatives on the other.

CREATION OF THE INTERNATIONAL CRIMINAL COURT   Following World War II, special international war-crimes tribunals were created to prosecute the Nazis (the Nuremberg trials) and Japanese military leaders. The UN General Assembly had considered creating a permanent international criminal court at various times since then, but no such action was taken. Nuremberg-like temporary war-crimes tribunals were set up in the 1990s to deal with atrocities committed during civil wars and ethnic conflicts in the former Yugoslavia and Rwanda. In their wake, proposals to create a permanent International Criminal Court (ICC) gained increasing support.

The ICC was approved at a UN conference held in Rome in mid-1998. Very few countries voted against it, but the United States was one of them. Originally the Clinton administration had supported the idea of an ICC, in large part because a permanent international court would potentially enhance U.S. foreign policy in cases against aggressors, gross violators of human rights, and rogue states. It backed off, though, in part for substantive reasons but mostly for political ones. The ICC struck the chords of anti-multilateralism and leeriness about international law in American politics. The treaty would have to be ratified by the U.S. Senate, and the anticipated vote count was coming up well short of the two-thirds majority needed. In December 2000, just before leaving office, Clinton finally did sign the Rome Treaty, albeit far too late for him to begin a ratification process in the Senate.

The George W. Bush administration was clear, quick, and blunt in its opposition to the ICC. Soon after taking office it announced that it was holding the treaty back and not sending it to the Senate. Then in May 2002 it officially rescinded the U.S. signature. The timing was deliberate: on April 11, 2002, the sixtieth country in the world had ratified the ICC treaty, the number necessary for the treaty to enter into force.

The U.S. debate on the ICC has largely fallen along the policy-enhancement vs. prerogative-encroachment lines. Proponents make three main arguments. First is that the ICC is the "missing link" in the international justice system that will help achieve "justice for all," and especially deal with perpetrators of genocide, war crimes, and other crimes against humanity. The existing

International Court of Justice in The Hague deals only with cases between states, not individuals. The ad hoc tribunals have had some impact but are subject to delays, uncertainties, and other deficiencies. The ICC also would claim jurisdiction when national criminal-justice institutions are unwilling or unable to act. "In the prospect of the International Criminal Court," stated Secretary-General Annan, "lies the promise of universal justice."[9]

Second, the ICC can help strengthen peace processes and conflict resolution. Negotiators try to bring to bear an array of policy instruments and incentives and disincentives in seeking cease-fires and peace settlements for conflicts that already are raging. Their hand is strengthened if they can provide assurances for all sides that once they have laid down their arms, justice will be even-handed. This means both prosecuting those whose actions warrant it, and protecting the innocent from vengeful and other politically charged prosecutions. Ideally, states should be able to create their own process of justice. In war-torn situations, though, that ideal often is not achievable, at least in the near term. As an international body the ICC has the standing and credibility to provide the necessary assurances and thus help move peace processes along.

Third, the existence of the ICC will deter future war criminals and other aggressors. To quote the UN: "Most perpetrators of such atrocities have believed that their crimes would go unpunished. . . . Once it is clear that the international community will no longer tolerate such monstrous acts without assigning responsibility and meting out appropriate punishment—to heads of State and commanding officers as well as to the lowliest soldiers in the field or militia recruits—it is hoped that those who would incite a genocide; embark on a campaign of ethnic cleansing; murder, rape and brutalize civilians caught in armed conflict; or use children for barbarous medical experiments will no longer find willing helpers. . . . Effective deterrence is a primary objective of the International Criminal Court."[10]

Opponents make their three main points along prerogative-encroachment lines. The first rejects the ICC's claim to jurisdiction over Americans on U.S. constitutional grounds. The U.S. Constitution is said to prohibit the U.S. government from consenting to judicial proceedings against American citizens by any courts other than American ones. As argued by John Negroponte, the Bush administration's ambassador to the United Nations, "an American judge has the legal and moral right founded in our Constitution and in democratic procedures to jail an American. But the International Criminal Court does not operate in the same democratic and constitutional context, and therefore does not have that right to deprive Americans of their freedom."[11]

Second is the concern about U.S. soldiers and diplomats, NGO workers, and others being subjected to politically motivated charges and prosecutions. "We're the ones who respond when the world dials 911," another opponent stated, "and if you want us to keep responding you should accommodate our views."[12] The Bush administration pushed this point in mid-2002 in threatening to end U.S. participation in the Bosnia peacekeeping mission unless an exemption was given ensuring that American soldiers and other U.S. citizens participating in those missions would not be subject under any conditions to ICC jurisdiction. It managed to get only a partial compromise, as even the British disputed both the necessity and the desirability of starting down a path of exceptions and exemptions. Yet the issue remained a fundamental one for ICC opponents. "The President of the United States is determined to protect our citizens—soldiers and civilians, peacekeepers and officials— . . . from unjust or politically motivated charges. . . . We do not believe the International Criminal Court contains sufficient safeguards to protect our nationals."

Third is a questioning of the claim to deterrence for the ICC. When so many perpetrators of ethnic cleansing and genocide never get charged, and when the prosecution of others takes so long, how strong a deterrent effect can there be? To deter those who would commit war crimes, the potential consequences of such actions have to be severe and probable. In the eyes of opponents, the ad hoc tribunals have not measured up, and the ICC is not likely to, either.

How Effective Is the UN?

A second debate regarding the UN deals with concerns about its effectiveness. How well do its programs and policies work? When it declares goals and objectives, how capable is it of achieving them? We consider these questions through three main areas of UN programs and policies.

ECONOMIC AND SOCIAL PROGRAMS   As noted earlier and seen in Figure 8.1, the UN has a wide array of economic and social programs. Although other UN departments and actions get more publicity, these programs are in many ways the most meaningful work the UN does. UNICEF (the United Nations Children's Fund), for example, is working to ensure that 90 percent of the world's children are immunized against diseases, to eradicate polio, to prohibit genital mutilation, to reduce child deaths from diarrhea by 50 percent, and to eliminate iodine-deficiency disorders. In late 1998 UNICEF, along with two other UN agencies, the World Health Organization (WHO) and the

UN Development Program (UNDP), plus the World Bank, launched a major new program to eradicate malaria, a scourge that kills one child every 30 seconds, and 3,000 children under five every day.

Other positive examples could be cited from among the many that exist. Not all UN socioeconomic development programs win such praise, however. For example, until reforms were initiated in the late 1990s at the WHO and former Norwegian prime minister Gro Harlem Brundtland was made its director-general, this "once-proud agency" had achieved "notoriety for bad management, a marked deterioration of its programs, and a measure of cronyism and favoritism verging on the corrupt."[13] Quite a few other UN programs have been hampered by excessive bureaucracy, corruption, and similar problems. Some reform has begun, and it clearly is needed. "While the United Nations is not the inefficient, incompetent body unfair critics depict it to be," wrote Yale professors Paul Kennedy and Bruce Russett, "it clearly requires a serious overhaul to prepare it for the years ahead."[14]

Another activity that has drawn both praise and criticism has been the numerous global conferences convened by the UN in the 1990s. Each was intended to focus attention and provide a launching pad for concerted action in an area of global concern: for example, the global environment was the topic of the 1992 Rio Earth Summit, population planning the focus of the 1994 Cairo conference, women's rights the topic of the 1996 Beijing conference, and sustainable development the focus of the 2002 Johannesburg conference. But these conferences have drawn mixed reviews. They have gotten credit for some achievements and for bringing important issues to the world's attention, but have also been criticized for being quite expensive, diverting the already limited funds available away from UN programs and policies, and for engaging at times more in politically charged rhetoric than in pragmatic policy.

A 1997 study by the Carnegie Commission on Preventing Deadly Conflict raised the question, "How expensive is the UN?" The commission's report provided some interesting comparisons. For example, the UN's core budget at that time was only $1.3 billion a year, which was almost $1 billion less than the annual budget for the city of Tokyo's fire department. Americans spend about $5.3 billion a year on spectator sports; the UN spends $4.6 billion on economic and social development. The entire UN system employs only about one-third as many people as McDonald's and less than Disneyland, Disney World and Euro Disney combined![15] These comparisons are not intended to justify waste or other problem areas, but they do help check common assumptions about the UN's size and resources.

HUMAN RIGHTS   The UN often is looked to as a defender of human rights. But one of the difficulties for the UN on human rights issues is the inherent tension between two norms, both of which are part of its Charter. One is the norm of *state sovereignty*. The state sovereignty norm stresses the rights and interests of the individual nation-states that constitute the membership of the UN. It is based on the principle that, as Professors Robert Art and Robert Jervis write, "no agency exists above the individual states with authority and power to make laws and settle disputes."[16] As stated in Article 2, Section 7, of the UN Charter, "nothing contained in the present Charter shall authorize the United Nations to intervene in matters which are essentially within the domestic jurisdiction of any state."

Yet other portions of the UN Charter manifest the norm of the *universality* of the rights of individuals, irrespective of the state in which they reside or whether threats to those rights come from foreign forces or their own governments. Article 3 affirms that "everyone has the right to life, liberty and the security of person"; Article 55 commits the UN to "promote . . . universal respect for, and observance of, human rights and fundamental freedoms"; Article 56 pledges all members "to take joint and separate action toward this end." In addition, documents such as the Universal Declaration of Human Rights, adopted by the UN General Assembly in 1948 by a unanimous vote, provide a sweeping affirmation of the "equal and inalienable rights of all members of the human family."

The argument here is that sovereignty not only confers rights on states, it also imposes responsibilities.[17] As UN Secretary-General Annan reminds us, "the [UN] Charter was issued in the name of 'the peoples', not the governments of the UN. . . . It was never meant as a license for governments to trample on human rights and human dignity. . . . The fact that a conflict is 'internal' does not give the parties any right to disregard the most basic rules of human conduct. . . . While paying full respect to state sovereignty, [we] assert the overriding right of people in desperate situations to receive help, and the right of international bodies to provide it."[18]

Another way of looking at this is as the tension between the traditional conception of state security and more recent articulations of "human security." The difference here is the unit of analysis. Is the principal concern with the security of states? If so, then the UN continues to think principally in terms of geographic units and to put its emphasis on preventing interstate war and other aggression. But if the principal concern is human security, then the emphasis shifts more to dealing also with the security of individuals from threats internal as well as external. To cite a UN report, "the concept of security has for too long been interpreted narrowly: as security of territory from external ag-gression. . . . Forgotten were the legitimate concerns of ordinary people who sought security in their daily lives."[19]

These inherent tensions complicate the UN's human rights role. The UN Commission on Human Rights reflects this tension; its operation has been characterized by a leading scholar as subject to "substantial political con-straints" and only "occasionally" effective.[20] States that violate the human rights of their peoples often are able to block or limit UN action against them, assisted by other repressive states that, while not involved in the case at hand, are concerned about precedents that might be used against them in the future.

This long-standing tension burst out in May 2001 when the United States lost its seat on the UN Human Rights Commission (UNHRC). This was the first time since the founding of the UNHRC in 1947, in which Eleanor Roo-sevelt played a leadership role, that the United States was not voted in as a member. The vote against the United States—which reportedly included U.S. friends and not just anti-American states—generally was seen as retribution for the U.S. refusal to pay its back dues (see below) as well as U.S. opposition to the International Criminal Court, the Land Mines treaty, the Kyoto global warming treaty, and other major UN initiatives. Whatever the arguments along these lines, the credibility of the UNHRC was severely undermined by the granting of seats to such major human rights offenders as Sudan, Pakistan, and Cuba. Human rights nongovernmental organizations (NGOs), while often critical of the United States on human rights issues, were quite harsh in their criticism of the commission for making itself "a rogues' gallery of human rights abusers."[21] The United States got its seat back the next year, but among the other members were such major human rights violators as China, Cuba, Libya, and Syria.

UN MILITARY PEACE OPERATIONS   Table 8.1 lists some of the more than 50 UN military peace operations since 1948. Whereas only 13 of these mis-sions were authorized prior to 1988, since 1988 more than 40 new missions have been undertaken. The number of UN troops shot up from 9,570 in 1988 to 73,393 in 1994; UN peacekeeping budgets went from $230 million to $3.6 billion.

Amid the controversies over its failures in Somalia and Bosnia in the early 1990s, the UN's past peacekeeping successes often get forgotten. Indeed, their record was so strong that the UN Peacekeeping Forces received the 1988 Nobel Peace Prize. These forces "represent the manifest will of the community

TABLE 8.1 Major United Nations Peacekeeping Operations, 1948–2003 (partial listing)

Year(s)	Mission	Location
1948–	UN Truce Supervision Organization (UNTSO)	Palestine
1949–	UN Military Observer Group in India and Pakistan (UNMOGIP)	India/Pakistan
1956–67	UN Emergency Force (UNEF I)	Egypt/Israel
1960–64	UN Operations in the Congo (ONUC)	Congo (Democratic Republic)
1964–	UN Peacekeeping Force in Cyprus (UNFICYP)	Cyprus
1978–	UN Interim Force in Lebanon (UNIFIL)	Lebanon
1988–90	UN Good Offices Mission in Afghanistan and Pakistan (UNGOMAP)	Afghanistan/Pakistan
1988–91	UN Iran-Iraq Military Observer Group (UNIIMOG)	Iran/Iraq
1989–90	UN Transition Assistance Group (UNTAG)	Namibia
1989–92	UN Observer Group in Central America (ONUCA)	Central America
1991–	UN Iraq-Kuwait Observation Mission (UNIKOM)	Iraq/Kuwait
1992–93	UN Transitional Authority in Cambodia (UNTAC)	Cambodia
1992–93	UN Operation in Somalia (UNOSOM I)	Somalia
1992–95	UN Protection Force (UNPROFOR)	Former Yugoslavia
1993–94	UN Observer Mission Uganda-Rwanda (UNOMUR)	Rwanda/Uganda
1993–95	UN Operation in Somalia (UNOSOM II)	Somalia
1993–96	UN Mission in Haiti (UNMIH)	Haiti
1995–99	UN Preventive Deployment Force (UNPREDEP)	Macedonia
1999–	UN Interim Administration Mission in Kosovo (UNMIK)	Kosovo
1999–	UN Mission in East Timor (UNMISET)	East Timor
1999–	UN Mission in the Democratic Republic of the Congo (MONUC)	Congo
1999–	UN Assistance Mission in Sierra Leone (UNAMSIL)	Sierra Leone

Source: United Nations Web site http://www.un.org/Depts/DPKO, accessed May 12, 2003.

of nations," the Nobel Committee's citation read. Through and because of them, the UN "has come to play a more central role in world affairs and has been invested with increasing trust."[22]

The recent peacekeeping record, though, has drawn more condemnations than commendations. Part of the UN's problem has been sheer overload. The huge number of operations going on simultaneously made for an enormous agenda, especially for an institution with so little of the military infrastructure of command and control, communications, intelligence, training, and logistics. Furthermore, the structure of decision-making authority often proved too slow and indecisive to either carry out complex and speedy military operations or convey credibility to an aggressor. This was the point Assistant Secretary of State Holbrooke was making in his lambasting of the dual-key UN/NATO command authority in Bosnia.

Additionally, all of these peace operations involved soldiers assembled on a temporary basis from the national armies of UN member countries. The original idea that the UN would have its own standing army of troops and officers assigned to it on an ongoing basis was never realized, as was discussed in Chapter 4. Each time there is need for a UN peace operation, it thus is necessary to assemble a new force. This adds to the problems of timely response, unit cohesiveness, and effective training.

The more fundamental problem, however, has been the difference in missions between peace*keeping* and peace *enforcing*. Most of the "first generation" UN successes had been on peacekeeping missions. In these situations the UN forces are brought in after the parties have agreed to the terms of peace, and with the consent of those parties, to ensure and facilitate the keeping of that peace. The peacekeepers' rules of engagement are neutral and impartial: to use force only for their own self-defense, and not to interfere in the internal affairs of the parties. But in Somalia and Bosnia the conflicts were still raging when UN troops landed. There was no peace to be kept; it had to be imposed and enforced. To the extent that the parties had reached any agreements, they were but partial ones—holding actions, gambits, even outright deceptions. In such situations the UN's limited rules of engagement do not work very well; neutrality and impartiality can let aggressors off the hook. Even a Nobel laureate method will not succeed when applied to purposes as fundamentally different as is peacekeeping from peace-making and peace-enforcing. By late 1995 even UN Secretary-General Boutros-Ghali was acknowledging that "[peace] enforcement is beyond the power of the UN. . . . In the future, if peace enforcement is needed it should be conducted by countries with the will to do it."[23]

The role of the UN in the post–Cold War era thus raises a number of important and continuing issues for U.S. foreign policy. The useful debates, however, are not about whether the United States should withdraw from, or turn its foreign policy over to, the UN. Rather they are about how strong an institution the UN is and can be, or cannot be, for building and maintaining peace.

Regional Multilateral Organizations

Article 52 of the UN Charter defines how regional multilateral organizations can complement and reinforce the UN's global role: "Nothing in the present Charter precludes the existence of regional arrangements or agencies for dealing with such matters relating to the maintenance of international peace and security as are appropriate for regional action provided that such arrangements or agencies are consistent with the Purposes and Principles of the United Nations." Many of today's major regional multilateral organizations were established during the Cold War era. In almost every case they have become increasingly important parts of the structure of peace in the post–Cold War era. There are three reasons why this has been generally true from region to region.

First, *the sources of instability now tend to be more regionally rooted than globally transmitted.* During the Cold War much of the world's instability was connected to the global geopolitics of bipolarity and the U.S.-Soviet rivalry. In the post–Cold war era, instability tends much more to be rooted in regional issues and rivalries. This has been true in the Balkans, in the Caucasus and other parts of the former Soviet Union, in Africa, in the Middle East, and elsewhere.

Second, *there is increasing recognition of the interconnection between regional security and domestic instability.* Ethnic conflicts, civil wars, and other conflicts that start out as internal problems can draw in regional states, spread across borders, set off massive refugee migrations, and create other general "contagion" effects that destabilize other parts of the region. Regional organizations thus have been making broader claims of legitimacy for intervening in domestic affairs in the name of regional security.

Third, given these regional roots and effects, it follows that *direct cooperation among the regional actors themselves is more crucial to peace and stability* than in the past, when the key actors usually were Washington and Moscow. On the one hand this means that countries and regions must confront long histories of rivalry and even hatred. On the other hand there can be common cultural ties, shared economic interests, and other relationships on which to try to build regional security institutions.

As with the United Nations, there is an ambivalence in U.S. foreign policy toward and with regional organizations. On the one hand, the United States is in the unique position of being a "member" in one way or another of almost every world region. Strengthening regional security has been the highest U.S. priority in Europe, where the United States is a member of NATO, its principal security alliance (discussed in Chapter 7) as well as of the Organization for Security and Cooperation in Europe. As a Western Hemisphere nation, the United States is a member of the Organization of American States. As a Pacific nation, it is a member of the Asia-Pacific Economic Cooperation forum and the Regional Forum of the Association of Southeast Asian Nations. The United States has been "sponsor" of efforts to create new regional multilateral institutions in the Middle East. Only in Africa, with the Organization for African Unity, has the U.S. role been less central, although even there it has been an important one.

On the other hand, two tensions similar to those with the UN have arisen. One is the policy enhancement–prerogative encroachment tension, by which American administrations are more eager to work through regional organizations when they enhance capacity to achieve U.S. policy objectives than when regional multilateralism encroaches on U.S. unilateral prerogatives. The other is the question of institutional effectiveness and whether and how regional organizations genuinely can fulfill the objectives they espouse.

We consider these issues as we discuss each of the major regional political-security organizations.

Europe: The Organization for Security and Cooperation in Europe

The Conference on Security and Cooperation in Europe (CSCE) was established in 1975 during détente as the only European institution with full East-West regional membership. With 35 members drawn from NATO, the Warsaw Pact, and the neutral states of Europe, its principal impact was through the Helsinki Final Act, the main parts of which established norms and principles for humans rights within and peaceful resolution of conflicts among member countries. For the most part the CSCE was just that, a "conference," which met from time to time as a forum for consultation and discussion. But when the East European revolutions came in 1989, it became clear in retrospect how important the CSCE had been in providing "a political platform and moral support for the champions of democratic change," such as Solidarity in Poland and Charter 77 in Czechoslovakia, that brought communism down.[24]

In the post–Cold War era, the CSCE expanded its membership to 55 states, enhanced its role, and changed its name. The name change, made in 1994 to the *Organization* for Security and Cooperation in Europe (OSCE), was intended to convey greater institutionalization. A primary motivation for institutionalizing has been the increased recognition of the link between regional security and the peaceful resolution of ethnic and other internal conflicts. These linkages were a major theme of the 1990 Charter of Paris for a New Europe, which established the first permanent organizations under the CSCE. "We are convinced," one provision of the charter reads, "that in order to strengthen peace and security among our states, the advancement of democracy and respect for and effective exercise of human rights are indispensable." The charter thus mandated "new forms of cooperation . . . in particular a range of methods for the peaceful settlement of disputes, including mandatory third-party involvement."

On this basis the OSCE has been taking on a greater role in "preventive diplomacy" and other political and diplomatic efforts at conflict management and conflict resolution. It does so through such structures as its Office for Democratic Institutions and Human Rights, which monitors elections, provides assistance in the drafting of constitutions and other laws, and promotes the development of civil society; the High Commissioner on National Minorities, which seeks to protect the rights of ethnic minorities, in part through the deployment of human rights observers; and third-party mediators and other diplomatic strategies for conflict resolution.

Its record thus far of preventing tensions and conflicts from leading to mass violence and ethnic war is a mixed one. One major study of the OSCE concludes that it can have the most success "in relatively low-level situations."[25] Consistent with this pattern, its 1990s successes include cases in which tensions had not yet crossed the Rubicon of widespread violence, and the OSCE gets a substantial share of the credit for keeping them relatively peaceful: in Estonia and Latvia, where explosive issues have arisen over withdrawal of Russian troops and human rights protections for Russian ethnic minorities; tensions between Hungary and Romania over treatment of their respective ethnic minorities; and in Macedonia, like Bosnia a former Yugoslav republic with deep ethnic splits, but which has managed to limit ethnic war. But in cases like Bosnia, Croatia, Kosovo, and Nagorno-Karabakh (an enclave with a large Armenian population that is geographically separate from but ruled by Azerbaijan that was mired in ethnic war from 1991–94, and has had a shaky truce since then), the conflicts ran too deep and had degenerated too much for the limited tools of the OSCE to accomplish much.[26]

U.S. support for the OSCE has been "relatively cool," observed Brown University professor Terry Hopmann. "Diplomats who have served in the U.S. Mission to the OSCE . . . have frequently expressed dismay at the low level of support given to their activities by senior officials in Washington."[27] The reasons largely have been the prerogative-encroachment and institutional-effectiveness ones. The OSCE often is seen as a competitor to NATO, yet it lacks NATO's military capacity and has a decision-making structure that is harder for the United States to dominate. While this is true, the very breadth of the OSCE's membership and mandate give its decisions and actions a legitimacy that NATO does not convey. Despite the problems of institutional effectiveness that have been noted, there also is evidence of success. Hopmann and other OSCE proponents see a chicken-and-egg problem of ineffectiveness being a function of low priority, and the possibilities of greater effectiveness if the United States and others were to make the OSCE a higher priority.

The Western Hemisphere: The Organization of American States

During the Cold War virtually all of U.S. policy toward Latin America, including creation of the Organization of American States (OAS) in 1948, was geared to the global containment strategy. The OAS largely was seen as being under the U.S. thumb. It dutifully supported the U.S. anticommunist interventions in Guatemala in 1954 and the Dominican Republic in 1965, and the expulsion of Cuba from its membership following Fidel Castro's revolution. With so many of its members being military dictatorships, the OAS could be seen as pro-democracy only if one accepted the "ABC" (anything but communism) definition of democracy.

With the Cold War over and anticommunism no longer the Western Hemisphere's organizing principle, and with all its member states now democracies (albeit some quite limited ones), in June 1991 the OAS adopted a resolution on its "Commitment to Democracy and the Renewal of the Inter-American System." Called the Santiago Resolution (the meeting took place in Santiago, Chile), this resolution was a first step toward the OAS's version of the OSCE's Charter of Paris. While including qualifiers about "due respect for the principle of nonintervention," it legitimized as grounds for

OAS intervention "the sudden or irregular interruption of the democratic political institutional process, or of the legitimate exercise of power by the democratically elected government in any of the Organization's member states." The measures to be considered included military intervention.

However, when the first test came a few months later in Haiti, the OAS took only limited action. It authorized some trade sanctions, but not even comprehensive ones. Memories of past U.S. interventions in Latin America were still too strong for it to authorize military force even against the brutal military regime in Haiti. (The UN eventually did.) The OAS did somewhat better in one of its next tests, which came in 1996 when the Paraguayan military attempted a coup. The OAS joined the United States in threatening diplomatic and economic sanctions, and it did so immediately and comprehensively. The coup was put down in an excellent example of how regional cooperation can be quite effective.

An attempted coup in Venezuela in April 2002 was a rare instance in which the OAS did not follow the U.S. lead. The coup was against Venezuelan president Hugo Chavez, an ex-military officer who had won the presidency in a free election but had governed in ways that alienated an increasing number of Venezuelans and also antagonized the United States. Whether or not the Bush administration explicitly or actively supported the coup against Chavez is a matter of debate; even if it did not, it certainly did nothing to oppose it and appeared to welcome it. While few Latin American leaders were very pro-Chavez, they also were leery of the anti-democratic precedent that the coup set, which could be "contagious" in the hemisphere. Just a few months earlier—in fact, coincidentally, on September 11, 2001—the OAS had approved its new Inter-American Democratic Charter, which built on the 1991 Santiago Resolution to further firm up the shared commitment of all member states to democracy. The OAS condemned "the alteration of the constitutional order" brought about by the coup in Venezuela and invoked its new Democratic Charter, which included threats to impose economic sanctions and perhaps take other actions. The United States voted for this measure but only after having lobbied to soften the language.

This was a striking example of the United States' being opposed and constrained within what for so long had been largely its own sphere of influence. The OAS was asserting itself as a stronger and more independent regional organization. It was acting at odds with U.S. policy preferences, claiming that its position was more consistent than the U.S. position with the core U.S. foreign policy goals of peace and principles.

Africa: The African Union

The Organization for African Unity (OAU) was established in 1963 as part of the struggle for decolonization. It originally had thirty-two members. Membership grew as more African nations became independent, and as secessionist movements created additional states. By 2002, when the OAU was replaced by the African Union (AU), there were 53 member states.

As in other regions, in Africa the threats are now far more from within than outside the region. Africa has paid a dear price at the hands first of European colonial powers and then of the Cold War superpowers. Although the legacies of both eras still are significant factors, the driving forces in so many of Africa's wars and so much of its instability are its own ethnic conflicts, anti-democratic and corrupt leaders, and interstate rivalries.

Given this colonial past, African nations have been especially sensitive to infringements on strict conceptions of state sovereignty. Yet this sensitivity has often been manipulated to protect dictatorial and corrupt leaders, thus working against the interests of Africa's peoples. In 1993, amid the ravages of wars in Somalia, Liberia, the Sudan, and other African countries, the OAU decided that it needed to take additional steps if it was to meet the demands of this new era to play a leadership role in helping forge peace and stability in Africa. The undeniability of the regional security consequences of conflicts traditionally considered domestic had reached the point that African leaders began to reassess traditional norms prohibiting external intervention for the purpose of preventing or managing domestic conflicts.[28]

The OAU thus established its "Mechanism for Conflict Prevention and Resolution," geared to multilateral interventions, both diplomatic and military. As with the OAS's Santiago document, this resolution still had significant qualifiers about "respect of sovereignty" and functioning "on the basis of consent and the cooperation of the parties to a conflict." While there were a few cases of successful OAU diplomatic initiatives, for the most part the OAU was constrained from having much impact. Other factors and responsibilities, including U.S. policy, contributed to the deadly conflicts that tore the continent, but the OAU bore its share of the blame as well.

The change from the OAU to the African Union in 2002 was a conscious effort by African leaders to strengthen their regional organization. The AU Charter went further than the OAU's had in establishing the right to intervene in member states in cases of genocide, war crimes, or gross violations of human rights. It called for the creation of an African army as a permanent regional multilateral peacekeeping force under the authority of a regional parliament. Member states also committed to allow free elections, to be monitored by AU election observers. Time will tell how robust the AU proves to be. One problem is financing: only 21 of the AU's 53 members had paid their dues when the new organization was first announced, and without funds, peacekeeping forces, election observers, and other initiatives are not possible. How committed member states' leaders will be when actual situations arise, and the AU wants to send its army or election observers in, also is uncertain. "What is worrying," a South African newspaper editorialized, "is that some of the leaders who will commit themselves to the AU's objectives are themselves dictators, murderers and thieves."[29]

Asia: The Association of Southeast Asian Nations

The Association of Southeast Asian Nations (ASEAN) was established in 1967 largely to promote economic cooperation among its members, which at that time were Indonesia, Malaysia, the Philippines, Singapore, and Thailand.* Security threats then largely arose from Cold War politics, and since most countries in ASEAN were U.S. allies, the United States took care of the region's security.

Here, too, the end of the Cold War meant a greater role for the regional organization in maintaining peace and security. Whereas ASEAN had held only three summits in its first twenty years of existence, it held four between 1992 and 2001. Yet ASEAN has two structural weaknesses in its regional peace and security role compared to other regional organizations. One is that the most powerful countries in the region are not full ASEAN members. Among Asian countries, that means China and Japan. The United States and Russia, both Pacific powers albeit not Asian countries, also are not members. Affiliated groupings have been established to provide forums for these powers to provide consultations, but this is not the same as full membership.

Second, ASEAN has not gone as far as the OSCE, the OAS, or the OAU in empowering itself to intervene on human rights and other internal issues of member states. In Myanmar (Burma), for example, where human rights violations have been rampant, ASEAN has refrained from imposing its own economic sanctions. This reflects a stricter conception of sovereignty as still prevalent in Asia, stressing the rights of states over the responsibilities.

---

*Today its membership also includes Brunei, Vietnam, Laos, Cambodia, and Myanmar (Burma).

The Middle East: The Multilateral Peace Process

As hard as the bilateral peace talks have been between Israel and its neighbors (specifically, the Palestinians and Syria), even reaching an agreement would not be sufficient to assure regional security in the Middle East. Regional security agreements and institutions need to be created, involving not just Israel and its immediate neighbors but a wider range of Arab states from the region. This is why the peace talks launched at the October 1991 Middle East peace conference in Madrid included multilateral as well as bilateral tracks. The multilaterals tracks were structured along five issue areas: regional economic development, water, environment, refugees, and arms control and regional security.

The Middle East regional multilateral negotiations largely broke down when the Israeli-Palestinian peace process was torn apart by the return to violence in 2000. Although only a few actual agreements had been reached compared to the past, when there was virtually no regional dialogue, this was significant progress in developing the bases for regional multilateralism. While it is hard to say when a multilateral peace process may resume, and when actual regional organizations including Arabs and Israelis will take shape, ultimately they will be necessary parts of regional peace and security.

In drawing lessons and implications from the 1990s, the Arms Control and Regional Security (ACRS) talks are of particular interest.[30] They did not involve all the states in the region—Iran, Iraq, and Libya were not invited to participate, and Syria and Lebanon boycotted them. But they did involve Israel and fourteen Arab states, including Egypt, Jordan, Saudi Arabia, Tunisia, and others, as well as the Palestinians. From 1992 to 1994, negotiations held under U.S. auspices made progress on some initial measures at a reasonably fast pace. There even were drafts of an "ACRS Declaration of Principles," including such pledges as to "refrain from the threat or use of force" and achieve "equal security for all," which in 1993–94 came very close to agreement. However, for a number of reasons, including both the Israeli-Palestinian problems and a worsening Israeli-Egyptian rivalry despite their peace treaty, the ACRS talks stalled well short of creating the hoped-for regional security institution. Moreover, the problem remained of what to do about states like Iran, Iraq, and Libya, which were not included in this process but posed security threats not just to Israel but also to other states in the region, especially with respect to weapons of mass destruction.

One of the important questions as we consider different regions is how much the regional security institutions in one region can serve as a model for those in another. The Middle East ACRS talks drew somewhat on the European experience with the CSCE. Some leaders, such as former Israeli prime minister Shimon Peres and former Jordanian crown prince Hassan, pushed for even more extensive emulation of Europe through a "Conference on Security and Cooperation in the Middle East" (CSCME). The Peres and Hassan proposals included similar sets of norms of peaceful resolution of conflict, similar proposals for cooperative security through arms control and other measures, and a number of other ideas drawn from the European experience. However, partly because of the difficulties in making further progress in the bilateral peace talks and partly because of doubts about whether something so closely based on the European model really fit the Middle East, the CSCME has remained more vision than reality.

No other region has developed its regional multilateral organizations as extensively as has Europe. But all the world's regions have made efforts toward this end, in recognition of the points made at the beginning of this section about the sources of instability being more regionally rooted than globally transmitted, the interconnectedness of regional security and domestic instability, and of potentially strong regional bases for cooperation. The United States is involved in important ways in all of them.

Nonproliferation Regimes

"International regimes" is the term used for combinations of norms, rules, and enforcement mechanisms set up by treaties and other agreements that seek to regulate key areas of international relations.[31] International regimes tend to be less formal organizationally than the UN and the regional organizations, but still can be said to be institutionalized to the extent that their norms, rules, and enforcement mechanisms are widely accepted.

Nonproliferation regimes are directed at preventing the spread of weapons of mass destruction (WMD), particularly nuclear, chemical, and biological weapons. Strengthening nonproliferation regimes has been a major goal for American foreign policy, because WMD proliferation threatens American security and interests in four areas: (1) a WMD attack directly on the United States; (2) an attack on U.S. forces overseas; (3) an attack on U.S. allies; and (4) the general threat to international peace and stability. While nonproliferation regimes have had some success, they also have had their limits and failures.

This has prompted some shift from this largely multilateral and diplomatic approach to more unilateral and coercive counterproliferation strategies, as discussed in Chapter 7, of using military force and other coercive means to seek to reverse proliferation that has occurred or is about to occur. We thus need to get a sense of what nonproliferation regimes have and have not achieved to be able to assess the policy choices we face for the future.

Nuclear Nonproliferation

Multilateral treaty efforts at preventing the proliferation of nuclear weapons began during the Cold War. In 1957, in one of the first major international nonproliferation agreements, the International Atomic Energy Agency (IAEA) was created to ensure that, as nations developed nuclear energy, it would be used only for peaceful purposes, such as nuclear power plants. In 1968 the UN General Assembly approved the nuclear Non-Proliferation Treaty (NPT), which entered into force in 1970. The NPT allowed the five states that already had nuclear weapons—the United States, the Soviet Union, Britain, France, and China—to keep them, but prohibited all other member states from acquiring or developing them. Despite these stringent restrictions, 185 countries have signed the treaty.

The original treaty stated that twenty-five years after coming into force, there would be a UN-sponsored conference to determine "whether the Treaty should be extended indefinitely, or for an additional fixed period or periods." When this conference was held in 1995, the decision was made to make the NPT permanent (the term used was "indefinite extension"). The Clinton administration was the principal force behind the success of that vote.

A persisting question, though, is how strong the nuclear nonproliferation regime actually is. North Korea brought the world to the brink of a major crisis in 1993–94 when intelligence reports showed that its ostensibly peaceful nuclear program was being used to develop nuclear weapons, despite North Korea's having signed the NPT. The United States negotiated an agreement that defused the crisis, but this agreement fell apart in 2002–03 amid revelations that North Korea had been cheating on it. There also have been other cases involving countries that never signed the NPT and are known or believed to have nuclear weapons. Israel, which does not admit to having nuclear weapons but is widely believed to have them, has maintained that its security concerns make it imprudent to sign the NPT. Then there are India and Pakistan, which in May and June 1998 defied the international community by conducting nuclear-weapons tests. This development was particularly alarming in light of the fact that these countries had already fought three wars against each other and tensions between them had spiraled into numerous crises. Now there was the added risk that the next war could go nuclear, as almost happened in the 2001–02 Kashmir crisis. Additionally, the example set when countries defy the nonproliferation regime without paying a significant price damages the regime's credibility.

Other weaknesses in the nonproliferation regime involve problems of verification and enforcement. It needs to be verified, not just assumed, that countries that have agreed to the NPT actually are abiding by their commitments. The IAEA is principally responsible for verifying countries' compliance. In the 1980s Iraq, despite being party to the NPT, managed to get around IAEA inspections and come close to bringing its nuclear-weapons programs to completion prior to the 1990–91 Persian Gulf War. (The Iraq case is discussed further later in this chapter.) Iran and Libya have been suspected of seeking to develop nuclear weapons despite being NPT signees. The problem of enforcement also pertains to the supplier end. There has been great concern, as discussed in Chapter 7, about "loose nukes" in Russia falling into the wrong hands. The United States has sought to counter this threat by creating an economic assistance program to pay for the destruction and deactivation of former Soviet missiles, by buying up the plutonium from the dismantled Russian nuclear weapons, and by employing out-of-work Russian nuclear scientists; the goal of these efforts is to reduce any incentives to sell these supplies and services to would-be proliferators.

The Comprehensive Test Ban Treaty (CTBT) is another key component of the nuclear nonproliferation regime. Efforts to limit nuclear testing began during the Cold War, most notably with the 1963 Limited Nuclear Test Ban Treaty. Negotiated by the United States, the Soviet Union, and the United Kingdom, and later signed on to by many other states, the Limited Test Ban Treaty prohibited nuclear testing in the atmosphere, underwater, and in outer space. These were the types of tests that created the most radioactive fallout. The ban was limited, though, still allowing underground testing and other exemptions. The CTBT is an effort to move further toward a total ban on nuclear testing.

The Clinton administration signed the CTBT in 1996, and brought the treaty to the U.S. Senate for ratification in 1999. But the Senate voted 48 to 51 against ratification. The CTBT defeat was compared to the defeat in 1919 of President Woodrow Wilson's League of Nations treaty. We will discuss the politics of the CTBT later in this chapter, but the key points here are the substantive arguments for and against the treaty.

Proponents stress the CTBT's contributions to international as well as U.S. national security by capping the destructiveness of the nuclear arsenals of existing nuclear weapons states, and as another constraint on proliferation of nuclear weaponry to additional states. They assess the provisions for monitoring, verification, and enforcement as providing the necessary assurances that the treaty will work in practice. Opponents contend that this capping is not consistent with U.S. national security interests, both because of concerns about the need for testing to ensure the reliability of existing weapons and because new nuclear weapons need to be developed to meet new threats. They also are skeptical of whether verification or other aspects of the treaty can really be made to work in practice.

As of mid-2003, 167 nations had signed the CTBT and 101 had ratified it. But the CTBT will come into force only when it is ratified by all 44 states deemed to be "nuclear capable." This is a larger group than just those that now have nuclear weapons. Approximately 10 of these nations had not ratified it, including the United States. The Bush administration opposes the treaty and thus has no plans to ask the Senate to reconsider it. CTBT proponents, though, remain active both in the United States and internationally.

A number of other issues also bear upon the strength of the nuclear nonproliferation regime. These include nuclear export controls, the Missile Technology Control Regime, and others, as summarized in the box on p. 455.

There is an argument in some policy and academic circles that at least some nuclear proliferation could strengthen peace.[32] One of the factors that kept the United States and the Soviet Union from engaging in direct war with each other during the Cold War, it is argued, was the possibility of escalation to nuclear war. Following such reasoning, some believe that war between India and Pakistan is less likely now that both have nuclear weapons, that although another Kashmir crisis might move them to the brink, the specter of escalation to the nuclear level would give them added incentive to de-escalate. While this type of argument is made by a number of prominent scholars, the prevailing view still stresses the risks and dangers of nuclear proliferation, and thus the need for as strong a nonproliferation regime as possible.

Chemical and Biological Weapons

Many view chemical and biological weapons as even scarier than nuclear ones. One reason is that chemical and biological weapons are less expensive to produce—the "poor man's nuclear weapon," some call them. Another is that the level of technology and military capability required for their use is much less sophisticated, and thus they are more accessible to terrorists. Americans

THE NPT AND OTHER KEY COMPONENTS OF THE NUCLEAR NONPROLIFERATION REGIME

Nuclear Nonproliferation Treaty (NPT): entered into force in 1970, extended indefinitely in 1995. Commits non–nuclear weapons states not to acquire or make nuclear weapons. Has 185 signatories; main holdouts are India, Pakistan, Israel, Brazil, and Cuba

Comprehensive Test Ban Treaty (CTBT): approved in 1996, bans all nuclear weapon test explosions; builds on earlier treaties such as the 1963 Limited Test Ban Treaty. Signed by 149 nations; main holdouts are India, Pakistan, and North Korea. The United States was the first to sign but in 1999 the Senate voted against ratification.

International Atomic Energy Agency (IAEA): international organization established in 1957 with principal responsibility for monitoring and verifying that nuclear energy is used for peaceful purposes and not weapons development

Nuclear Suppliers Group: informal group of nuclear supplier nations that maintains multilateral controls on nuclear-related exports

Zangger Committee: also part of multilateral nuclear export controls, maintains a "trigger list" of items that can be exported but for which the recipient state must comply with IAEA-supervised safeguards

Missile Technology Control Regime (MTCR): established in 1987, restricts exports of missiles that could carry nuclear weapons; members are states with missile technology and capacity, principally the United States, Russia, Britain, and France; among nonmembers is China.

Source: Zachary Davis and Carl Behrens, *Nuclear Nonproliferation Policy Issues in the 105th Congress,* Congressional Research Service (CRS) Issue Brief, Library of Congress, May 13, 1998.

experienced this in the weeks after the September 11 terrorist attacks, when anthrax-laden letter bombs made people fearful of even opening their mail. Even before this, there was the incident in Japan in 1995 in which a cult called Aum Shinrikyo unleashed a chemical-weapons attack on a busy subway train in Tokyo. The cult had intended to kill millions of people. Although the actual death toll was limited, as a *New York Times* headline put it, the "Japanese Cult's Failed Germ Warfare Succeeded in Alerting the World."[33] Investigation of the cult found a veritable arsenal of chemical weapons, as well as labs equipped to produce lethal germs and bacteria for biological weapons.

The first major anti–chemical weapons treaty, the Geneva Protocol, was negotiated in 1925. Its impetus was the battlefield use of chemical weapons (CW) in World War I by both sides. The Geneva Protocol prohibited the use of chemical weapons, although it did not prohibit their production or possession. Even so, chemical weapons were used subsequently, including by the Japanese in Manchuria in the 1930s, by Italy in Ethiopia in 1935, by Egypt in Yemen in the 1960s, by both Iran and Iraq in their 1980–88 war, possibly by the Soviets in Afghanistan in their 1979–88 war, and by Iraq against its own Kurdish population in 1988. Over the course of the Cold War both the United States and the Soviet Union built up large CW stockpiles. By the 1990s an estimated twenty other countries were believed to have chemical weapons.

The need for a new and stronger CW nonproliferation treaty was quite clear. The only other multilateral measure that had come into being was the Australia Group. Formed in 1984, and taking its name from the first meeting having been held at the Australian embassy in Paris, this was an organization of twenty Western states that shared intelligence and coordinated export controls to try to stem CW proliferation. As an informal group, not carrying the full weight of a treaty, and not fully multilateral, it had some impact, but limited. The United States and the Soviet Union had signed their own Chemical Weapons Destruction Accord in 1990, and this too represented some but still limited progress.

The main step came with the Chemical Weapons Convention (CWC). After many years of negotiations the CWC was completed in 1993 and came into force in 1997. As of mid-2003, 151 countries had signed and ratified the CWC. The CWC bans the development, production, acquisition, stockpiling, trade, and use of chemical weapons; it calls, in effect, for the total elimination of chemical weapons. As such it has been called "the most ambitious treaty in the history of arms control."[34] Compared to the NPT, the CWC is more far-reaching than the NPT in three main respects. First, it applies to all states—no exceptions, no previous possessors grandfathered in like the five major-power nuclear-weapons states in the NPT. By 2007 all states must have destroyed all their chemical weapons. Second, it has tougher and more intrusive enforcement provisions. It mandates short-notice, anytime, anywhere "challenge inspections" of sites where cheating is believed to be taking place. The Organization for the Prohibition of Chemical Weapons (OPCW) is the CWC's version of the IAEA, but has greater authority. Third, states that do not join the treaty face automatic trade sanctions. This was a primary reason why most of the U.S. chemical industry, while not overly welcoming the additional regulations imposed by the CWC, calculated that American companies had more to lose if the United States was not part of the treaty and therefore supported it during the Senate ratification debate.

The key tests of the CWC lie in whether these tough provisions work in practice. A number of countries still are suspected of retaining chemical weapons programs: as of 2002, according to the Carnegie Endowment for International Peace, these include China, Egypt, India, Iran, Iraq, Israel, Libya, North Korea, Pakistan, Sudan, and Syria. Questions still remain as to whether Russia will fully follow through with eliminating its arsenal of 40,000 metric tons of chemical weapons. As with Russian "loose nukes," the concern is not only about official Russian policy but also about terrorists and others getting access to the weapons complex.

There also are doubts about the effectiveness of the OPCW. Challenge inspections, as innovative as they are with the right they give to the OPCW to demand entry and access for inspections in a country suspected of violating the treaty had yet to be actually used in the first six years of the CWC regime. At least three factors have impeded their use. First, for all the high-minded rhetoric at the CWC signing ceremonies, member states have not followed through in meeting their budget commitments. Insufficient funding translates to inadequate technical and other professional expertise to ensure strong enforcement and verification. Second, the OPCW has had its own bureaucratic politics and inefficiencies with some allegations of corruption and incompetence against its original director. While each of these issues is managerially fixable, the third issue is the continuing ambivalence about challenge inspections as an abridgment of traditional conceptions of state sovereignty. As with human rights and other issues, strict sovereigntists raise concerns about abuses of this authority, while those stressing the responsibilities of states and the priority of international peace and security see such authority as essential for the CWC to have teeth and the OPCW to be effective as a monitoring, verification, and enforcement organization. Moreover, as with the NPT, the CWC deals with states but not with terrorists and other nonstate actors. They pose their own quite serious challenges.

Biological weapons (also called germ warfare) have met with even less nonproliferation progress. The Biological and Toxin Weapons Convention of 1972 purported to ban them totally (development, production, stockpiling, acquisition, trade, use), but it has been a very weak treaty. It has 162 signatories but its monitoring, verification, and enforcement provisions and mechanisms are much weaker than those of the CWC/OPCW and the NPT/IAEA. Many of the same countries thought likely to have CW programs also are suspected of harboring biological weapons (BW) programs. Concerns about Russia in this area are even greater than with CW, in part because of how extensive the Soviet-era BW programs were and how much secrecy shrouded them. Official acknowledgment of a BW program in Russia was not even made until 1992, and then the revelations were staggering: 1,500 metric tons of bubonic plague bacteria, 4,500 metric tons of anthrax, and more. And generally, the threat of terrorists using BW may be even greater than with other WMD.

Efforts to strengthen the BW treaty have not made much progress. Negotiations in mid-2001 broke up over whether the proposed changes in verification would be effective. The Bush administration contended that the treaty proposals would end up violating the confidentiality of the American pharmaceutical and biotechnology industries while doing little to detect treaty violations by states that were determined to develop BW. The debate in part reflected the even greater difficulties of dual-use distinctions—what is pharmaceutical or bioagricultural research, and what is the development of biological weapons can be tough to distinguish. It also was another manifestation of the Bush administration's limited belief in multilateral treaties as nonproliferation strategies. The administration did make alternative proposals of its own, but many viewed these as veiled efforts to block rather than reach agreement. The next scheduled round of multilateral negotiations is not until 2006.

Lessons of the Iraq Case

The case of Iraq demonstrates important lessons about the risks and dangers of not maintaining a strong overall nonproliferation regime.[35] These lessons actually go back well before the 2003 Iraq war or the 1990–91 Persian Gulf War to the 1980s. By the time he invaded Kuwait in August 1990, Saddam Hussein had assembled an astounding complex for developing the full WMD arsenal—nuclear, chemical, and biological weapons, and ballistic missiles. Where had he acquired this? Much of it from the West, including from the United States.

There definitely was some strategic logic in the U.S. "tilt" toward Iraq in its 1980–88 war with Iran, given the greater threat posed by Iran's Islamic fundamentalists led by Ayatollah Khomeini. But as noted in Chapter 7 the Reagan and first Bush administrations failed to see past the old adage, "the enemy of my enemy is my friend." The enemy of my enemy *may be* my friend, but he also may still be *my enemy, too.* Even after the Iran-Iraq War was over, thus lessening the strategic rationale, and amid reports of Saddam's having used chemical weapons against the Kurdish minority in Iraq, new licenses for dual-use technology exports were being granted by the United States. Later, following the Iraqi invasion of Kuwait, one former Reagan official would lament that "it would have been much better at the time of their use of poison gas [in 1988] if we'd put our foot down."[36] What was a dictator such as Saddam to think, when even the use of chemical weapons fell within the bounds of behavior that the United States considered tolerable? If this new relationship with the United States was not affected by an issue as salient as chemical warfare, then what would it be conditioned upon?

The first Bush administration continued this looseness on nonproliferation. It did so despite repeated warnings of what Saddam was up to. For example, a series of top-secret intelligence reports from the U.S. Defense Intelligence Agency and the CIA in mid-1989 provided extensive evidence that Saddam had developed a network of front companies across Europe and in the United States through which he was acquiring essential WMD technology. Nor was the United States alone in selling dual-use technologies to Iraq. Germany was far and away the biggest supplier. Britain also was a major one.

At the end of the Gulf War in February 1991, as part of the terms of his surrender, Saddam had to agree to allow UNSCOM into Iraq with unprecedented authority to search for and dismantle his WMD complexes. For a few years the UNSCOM inspectors were able to uncover a great deal, and some of what they found was quite shocking. Yet by around 1996–97 Saddam stepped up his obstruction of UNSCOM, playing cat-and-mouse with the inspectors, periodically kicking them out of the country, and precipitating repeated crises and tests of will with the UN, the United States, and the international community. It thus proved exceedingly difficult to undo the WMD threat that had been allowed to develop in Iraq. Indeed it took another war—and even then, the quick and decisive military victory notwithstanding, formidable challenges remained of winning the peace and ensuring a stable and non-aggressive successor government.

Land Mines and the Regime-Creating Role of NGOs

While not a WMD per se, anti-personnel land mines are included here because they exemplify a new and different pattern in the fight against weapons proliferation. The 1997 treaty banning land mines came about less because of independent decisions by governments than from the pressure brought by the International Campaign to Ban Landmines (ICBL), a network of approximately a thousand nongovernmental organizations (NGOs) from more than sixty countries. Moreover, the treaty has been signed by over 140 governments despite U.S. opposition.

Anti-personnel land mines, buried in the ground in fields and along roads where children and other innocent civilians accidentally trigger them, had been taking a huge toll in human life. Estimates were of twenty-six thousand people a year—five hundred per week—most of them civilians, being killed or maimed by land mines. An exact count of the number of land mines buried across the globe is impossible, but reliable estimates put the number at about 110 million. Although some demining efforts were going on, they could barely keep up with new mines being planted. And even if no new mines were planted, the demining rate was so slow that it would have taken 1,100 years![37]

Governments and the UN were concerned but were not acting expeditiously. The ICBL used a number of strategies to pressure countries to support the treaty. It documented the problem through numerous studies. It lobbied governments in Washington and other major capitals, and worked particularly closely with governments like Canada that were strong supporters. It worked through the UN. It used the media skillfully, as in the public display of veritable mountains of shoes (children's shoes especially) to symbolize those who had been killed by land mines. It also got support from celebrities, most notably Princess Diana.[38]

The main reason why the United States did not sign the land mine treaty was because of Pentagon concerns over risks to American troops, especially those still stationed along the demilitarized zone (DMZ) between North and South Korea. The Clinton administration was not entirely opposed to a land mine treaty, but it contended that until North Korea was ready to provide credible assurances that it would not attack South Korea, land mines would continue to be an essential part of the deterrence and defense posture along the DMZ. So, although not signing the treaty, the Clinton administration did initiate demining programs that the United States helped fund and carry out. The Bush administration has continued many of these programs while also refusing to sign the treaty.

Despite U.S. nonparticipation, the land mine treaty has been having real impact. Official trade in land mines has been brought to an end. Within the first few years, by late 2002, land mine production dropped from 55 known manufacturers to 14. More than 34 million mines have been destroyed in over

60 countries. But the problem of nonsignatories remains. Russia and China have also not signed, and of the estimated 230 million mines still estimated to exist, China accounts for 110 million, Russia 60–70 million, and the United States 11 million. Countries in major regional hot spots—India, Pakistan, Iraq, Iran, Israel, Egypt, Syria, Lebanon—also have not signed the treaty.[39]

When the Nobel Peace Prize for 1997 was announced, it went to Jody Williams, an American who was coordinator of the ICBL coalition. For this and other reasons the land mine campaign is serving as a model for NGOs concerned with other arms control and disarmament issues, such as an international campaign launched in 1998 targeted at assault rifles and other light weapons.

Ethnic and Other Deadly Conflicts

How to deal with the ethnic and other deadly conflicts that so marked—or, more to the point, marred—the first decade of the post–Cold War world has been another key dilemma for American power. Of the major conflicts shown in Map 8.1, the vast majority are fundamentally ethnic in nature. They involve humanitarian issues often more than geopolitical ones. As such they tend to be much less a matter of the sheer exertion of military force than the Persian Gulf and Iraq wars (see Chapter 7). They pose their own challenges both for the use of military force and for diplomacy.

Humanitarian Intervention

The question of when and where the United States should intervene militarily is especially difficult when the horrors of ethnic cleansing and genocide seem to urge action in the name of American principles, but involve areas that, as the U.S. ambassador to Somalia put it about that country, are "not a critical piece of real estate for anybody in the post–Cold War world." The argument was well framed in the "Mother Teresa" exchange of articles in *Foreign Affairs* by Michael Mandelbaum and Stanley Hoffmann. Mandelbaum argued that giving national-interest weight to humanitarian concerns is being "too much like Mother Teresa" and turns foreign policy into "social work." Hoffmann countered that the very distinction between interests and values is "largely fallacious," in that "a great power has an 'interest' that goes beyond strict national security concerns and its definition of world order is largely shaped by its values."[40]

Major Conflicts of the 1990s

Cambodia

East Timor

Kashmir

Tajikistan

Sindh

Sri Lanka

Azerbaijan

Afghanistan

Eritrea

Uganda

Rwanda

Burundi

Chechnya

Somalia

Democratic Republic of Congo (Zaire)

Georgia

Iraq

Kuwait

Moldova

Turkey

Yemen

Kosovo

Sudan

Croatia

Lebanon

South Africa

Bosnia

Chad

Nigeria

Angola

Algeria

Ghana

Liberia

Republic of Congo

Sierra Leone

Haiti

Colombia

Guatemala

Peru

El Salvador

Source: Carnegie Commission on Preventing Deadly Conflict, *Preventing Deadly Conflict: Final Report* (Washington, D.C.: Carnegie Commission on Preventing Deadly Conflict, 1997), p. 12. Used with permission.

THE LESSONS OF EXPERIENCE   The Clinton administration's mishandling of the 1993 Somalia intervention greatly exacerbated this debate. A much-ballyhooed report issued in 1994, *A National Security Strategy of Engagement and Enlargement* (the "En-En" strategy, to its critics), read more like a statement of when and why the United States *would not* intervene militarily than as a delineation of when and why it *would*.[41] When the administration did finally intervene in Haiti in 1994 and Bosnia in 1995 it pointed to these cases as evidence that it did have a guiding conception of when and how to use military force. In actuality, though, both of these cases were more negotiated, last-minute occupations than coercive, preventive interventions.

In Haiti, among other missteps, there had been the especially embarrassing incident in October 1993 of the U.S.S. *Harlan County* fleeing the Port-au-Prince harbor when met by demonstrators on the docks. In September 1994, President Clinton dispatched former president Jimmy Carter, Senator Sam Nunn, and then-retired general Colin Powell to Haiti as a last-ditch negotiating effort to avoid U.S. forces having to shoot their way onto the island. The Carter-Nunn-Powell mission succeeded in getting the Haitian military-coup leaders to step down, although, in large part because of the *Harlan County* and other credibility-sapping incidents, it wasn't until they were absolutely convinced that the American assault planes were in the air and naval forces on their way that the coup leaders agreed to go. The "invasion" thus became more of a peaceful landing and an agreed-upon temporary occupation.

In the Bosnia case, credit is due for the U.S.-led NATO peacekeeping mission begun in late 1995. About one-third of the sixty thousand NATO troops first sent to enforce the Dayton accord were American. And for all the killing that took place between 1991 and 1995, there has been very little since in Bosnia. Still there was a sense that the United States acted only when forced to do so, when most if not all other options had been exhausted, and only when the aggressor's defiance and disregard for the West had reached the brazen extremes that the Serbs' did. If it was then and only then that the United States would commit its military forces, this was not all that credibility-enhancing an example in the long run.

In Kosovo the United States and NATO acted sooner than they had in Bosnia, but still not soon or effectively enough to prevent massive killings and other violence. The threat of air strikes was made only in late 1998, many months after the first wave of Serbian aggression against the Kosovar Albanians and despite numerous warnings and calls for earlier preventive action. When the air campaign did get launched in March 1999, despite the massive tonnage dropped, the many sorties flown, and the number of physical targets hit, it was too little and too late to stop the full ethnic cleansing of Kosovo.

It remains to be demonstrated if and when the timing and strategies in cases involving ethnic conflicts and humanitarian issues may be different in the future.

REQUIREMENTS FOR A MORE EFFECTIVE STRATEGY   A number of factors are essential to an effective military intervention strategy for dealing with ethnic and other such conflicts. One is the need to bear in mind the distinction between the political and the genuinely humanitarian dimensions in humanitarian crises. Back in April 1991, when a deadly cyclone hit Bangladesh, killing 139,000 people and doing $2 billion worth of damage to this already impoverished country, and American military forces were sent to provide relief and help with reconstruction, this genuinely was a humanitarian intervention. But the starvation in Somalia, the outbreak of plague in Rwanda, the fears of annihilation of the Kurds in Iraq and the Muslims in Bosnia and Kosovo—all were *politically precipitated* humanitarian crises. This by no means diminishes the need for humanitarian relief to alleviate people's suffering, but it does point to important differences in how the mission needs to be defined, the forces structured, and the political and military components of the overall strategy woven together.

Another issue is what Professor Richard Betts has called the "delusion of impartiality."[42] Impartiality is pretty straightforward in genuinely humanitarian situations like the Bangladesh cyclone. So, too, in genuine peacekeeping situations, when both sides need to be confident that the international party will not take sides and assured that each will not be disadvantaged so long as it abides by the terms of the peace. It is when the parties are still in conflict, and the problem is peace-making or peace-enforcing, that impartiality is a delusion.* Impartiality in such cases would mean applying the same strictures to both sides, even if this leaves one side with significant military advantages over the other. It also would mean not coercing either side, irrespective of which one is doing more killing, seizing more territory, or committing more war crimes. "Such lofty evenhandedness may make sense for a judge in a court that can enforce its writ, but hardly for a general wielding a small stick in a bitter war."[43]

Instead the strategy must be "fair but firm." The parties to the conflict must know both that cooperation has its benefits and that noncooperation

---

*The distinction between peacekeeping and peace-making or peace enforcement will be expanded upon later in this chapter.

has its consequences. They must be assured that the benefits of cooperation will be fully equitable. And they must be convinced that the United States and any other international parties involved are prepared to enforce the consequences differentially, as warranted by who does and who does not cooperate. This does not mean that force must be used, but that it must be an option, and it must be seen by the parties as a credible one.

There also needs to be a questioning of the conventional wisdom of using force only as a last resort. Should genocide have to occur and force be used only then to end it, but not to try to prevent it in the first place? Force rarely if ever should be a first resort, but in some cases it may need to be an early and not just a last resort. This is the humanitarian intervention version of the debate over pre-emptive use of force. Indeed this debate already was going on before the Bush doctrine and the Iraq case drew so much attention. One of the lessons of cases like Bosnia and Rwanda was that it was extremely unrealistic to believe that vicious demagogues like Milosevic in the former Yugoslavia and the Hutu extremists in Rwanda will agree to peaceful methods of conflict resolution if they think they can achieve their goals militarily at costs they deem acceptable. Each situation will have to be analyzed to assess whether and how preventive military action or the threat thereof is likely to deter and not exacerbate oppression, but "preserving force as a last resort implies a lockstep sequencing of the means to achieve foreign policy objectives that is unduly inflexible and relegates the use of force to *in extremis* efforts to salvage a faltering foreign policy."[44]

Finally, there must be a more balanced assessment of the limits of air power. The utility of air power has been overestimated throughout the twentieth century; the Clinton administration apparently learned very little from this history.[45] It made more frequent use of air power than ever before in U.S. foreign policy, but with only limited success in transforming military might into political objectives. The Kosovo war was fought principally through air power, yet the Serbian ethnic cleansing went on. Most wars simply cannot be fought just from the air. Ground troops do carry risks, but they often are essential for results.

Preventive Statecraft

The basic logic of "preventive statecraft" seems unassailable: Act early to prevent disputes from escalating or problems from worsening.[46] Reduce tensions that if intensified could lead to war. Deal with today's conflicts before they become tomorrow's crisis. Preventive statecraft follows the same logic

8.2

as preventive medicine: Don't wait until the cancer has spread or the arteries are fully clogged. Or, as the auto mechanic says in a familiar television commercial, as he holds an oil filter in one hand and points to a seized-up car engine with the other, "Pay me now or pay me later."

Yet despite the unassailability of the basic logic, the post–Cold War track record thus far, both for the United States and for the rest of the international community, is very mixed. Too often we hear that nothing else could have been done, that nothing more or different was viable than the policies as pursued. But there are a number of bases for arguing that preventive statecraft could have worked, that deadly conflicts like those in Rwanda, Bosnia, and Kosovo could have been limited, if not prevented.

PURPOSIVE SOURCES OF ETHNIC CONFLICT   A starting point for understanding how and why preventive statecraft could have worked better involves the debate between "primordialist" and "purposive" theories of the sources of ethnic conflict. The primordialist view sees ethnicity as a fixed and inherently conflictual historical identity; thus the 1990s conflicts were primarily continuations of ones going back hundreds of years—e.g., "Balkan ghosts" going back to the fourteenth century, the Somali clan rivalries dating from the precolonial pastoral period, the medieval *buhake* agricultural caste system of Tutsi dominance over Hutu in what is now Rwanda. Yugoslavia was an "intractable problem from hell," as Secretary of State Warren Christopher put it, "tribal feuds, ancient hatreds, steeped in a history of bloodshed."[47]

If this were true, then it would be hard to hold out much hope for preventive statecraft. The histories, though, are not nearly so deterministic. A number of studies have shown that ethnic identities are much less fixed over time, and the frequency and intensity of ethnic conflict much more varying over both time and place than primordialist theory would have it. In Bosnia, for example, the ethnic intermarriage rate in 1991 was around 25 percent, and there were very few ethnically "pure" urban residents or ethnically homogeneous smaller communities. As a Bosnian Muslim schoolteacher put it, "we never, until the war, thought of ourselves as Muslims. We were Yugoslavs. But when we began to be murdered because we are Muslims things changed. The definition of who we are today has been determined by our killing."[48]

An alternative explanation of the sources of ethnic conflict is the "purposive" view. This view acknowledges the deep-seated nature of ethnic identifications and the corresponding animosities and unfinished agendas of vengeance that persist as historical legacies. But the purposive view takes a much less deterministic view of how, why, and if these identity-rooted tensions become deadly conflicts. It focuses the analysis on forces and factors that intensify and activate historical animosities into actions and policies reflecting conscious and deliberate choices for war and violence. The dominant dynamic is not the playing out of historical inevitability but, as another author put it, "the purposeful actions of political actors who actively create violent conflict" to serve their own domestic political agendas by "selectively drawing on history in order to portray [events] as historically inevitable."[49]

The conflicts thus were not strictly "intractable problems from hell." They were fed, shaped, manipulated, directed, and turned toward the purposes of leaders and others whose interests were served by playing the ethnic card.

MISSED OPPORTUNITIES   A second point in support of the potential of preventive statecraft is the strong evidence from a number of 1990s cases that the international community *did* have specific and identifiable opportunities to try to limit if not prevent these conflicts. But its statecraft was flawed, inadequate, or even absent. We cannot know for sure that conflict could have been prevented; this is what is called a "counterfactual argument," and its limits must be acknowledged.[50] Such arguments must be based on what genuinely was known and possible *at the time,* not just in retrospect—otherwise they would be vulnerable to the charge of "Monday-morning quarterbacking." Nevertheless the evidence in virtually every case is that different policies were possible, and such policies had plausible chances of positive impact.

In Somalia, for example, although "no amount of preventive diplomacy could have completely pre-empted some level of conflict," there is solid evidence of "a virtual litany of missed opportunities" implying "that timely diplomatic interventions at several key junctures might have significantly reduced, defused and contained that violence."[51] Similarly in Rwanda, a whole series of missed opportunities has been identified, beginning a few years before the April 1994 genocide and continuing up to its eve, when the Hutu-dominated military still was divided and "an important factor in their decision to act was the failure of the international community to respond forcefully to the initial killings in Kigali and other regions."[52] In the Bosnia case experts provide varying analyses as to what the most egregious international policies were (perhaps because the list from which to select is so long). But few disagree that there was a "failure to prevent what was preventable."[53] So, too, with Kosovo, on which numerous warnings had been sounded and many proposals made for preventive action, especially during 1998 when Serbian leader Slobodan Milosevic was launching his first wave of ethnic cleansing, and some even going back a number of years earlier.[54]

CASES OF SUCCESSFUL PREVENTIVE STATECRAFT   In addition to the failures that could have been successes, there were other cases that quite plausibly could have become deadly conflicts, but in which preventive statecraft worked. The former Yugoslav republic of Macedonia, which had its own quite significant ethnic tensions and vulnerabilities in the wake of the breakup of Yugoslavia but did not fall into mass violence, is a good example.[55] The Macedonia case has had two phases. The first was in 1993–95, in which analysts credit the maintenance of peace to the fact that an international presence was established early on the ground. The CSCE sent an observer mission headed by a skilled American diplomat and with a broadly defined mandate. A number of nongovernmental organizations also established themselves in Macedonia, both providing an early-warning system and helping establish conflict-resolution mechanisms and other multiethnic programs. Most significant was the actual deployment of a multinational military force before significant violence had been unleashed. This force included U.S. troops, which, despite their small number and their being confined to low-risk duties, "carry weight," as Macedonian President Kiro Gligorov stressed. "It is a signal to all those who want to destabilize this region."[56] The second phase in Macedonia came in 2001, when ethnic violence had begun to break out but a NATO force was deployed and U.S. and European diplomacy worked to prevent escalation.

Still, we must ask, even if preventive statecraft is doable, is it worth doing? It may be viable, but does it have sufficient value for the United States to justify the risks and the costs of undertaking it? Why not just wait and see, kick it down the road, and see if action really is necessary? If it were the case that the fires of ethnic conflicts, however intense, would just burn themselves up, and not threaten to spread regionally or destabilize more systematically, then in strict Realist terms one could argue that the United States could afford to just let them be. But we should realize by now that that is not always or even frequently the case.

Even though many of the ethnic conflicts of the 1990s did not involve inherently strategic locales, the damage to U.S. interests proved greater than anticipated as they escalated and spread. And whereas the costs of waiting tend to be assumed to be less than the costs of acting early, they have proven to be much greater than expected, arguably higher than those for preventive action would have been. For as difficult as preventive statecraft can be, the onset of mass violence transforms the nature of a conflict. A Rubicon gets crossed, on the other side of which resolution and even limitation of the conflict become much more difficult. The addition of revenge and retribution to other sources of tension plunges a conflict to a fundamentally different and more difficult depth. Foreign policy strategies that might have been effective at lower levels of conflict are less likely to be so amid intensified violence. The Croatia-Bosnia conflicts never were going to be easy to resolve, but after all the killings, the rapes, and the other war crimes, the tasks were vastly harder. So, too, in Rwanda, Somalia, and elsewhere where mass violence was not prevented.

For this and other reasons options do not necessarily stay open over time. A problem can get harder down that road to where it has been kicked. It thus is altogether Realist to act today rather than tomorrow. Moreover, the United States cannot not take a position. It follows from the earlier point about the purposive nature of these conflicts that, to the extent that the United States and other international actors can be expected to act (such as through military intervention or other measures such as economic sanctions and tough diplomacy) in ways that raise the costs and risks for ethnic leaders who would turn to mass violence, a moderating effect on these domestic actors' calculations is possible. If there is no such expectation, the calculation is left without a major constraint against turning to war and mass violence. Thus even "staying out" has an impact, especially when you are the most powerful country in the world. U.S. policy affects these conflicts one way or the other. The choice is how it will have its impact.

The United States as a Peace Broker

As we know, the United States' role as a peace broker goes back at least a century. President Theodore Roosevelt won the Nobel Peace Prize in 1906 for the brokering role he played in ending war between Russia and Japan. The Cold War era had many examples, including Secretary of State Henry Kissinger's "shuttle diplomacy" in the Middle East and President Jimmy Carter's Camp David Accord between Egypt and Israel. In the post–Cold War era the United States has played even more of a peace-broker role.

Historically and especially in our era, there are three principal reasons why the United States has been playing this role with such frequency. First are its *leadership responsibilities*. The sole surviving superpower may be too strong a term, but as the most powerful country in the world the United States has responsibilities to support and foster peace as much as possible. Sometimes this means acting on its own, unilaterally. At other times it means providing the leadership that is critical to forging multilateral efforts.

Second is its *acceptability to the parties in conflict.* During the Cold War the United States rarely was seen as a neutral broker. Now, though, even when it may be more allied with one side than the other (e.g., in the Middle East with Israel), it still tends to be seen by the parties involved as sufficiently balanced to play a brokering role. Furthermore, the United States is still the key to delivering the goods that the parties to the conflicts want and need, be they security guarantees or economic assistance. Here, too, it is not just what the United States itself provides directly, but its capacity to mobilize multilateral action and support.

Third is that *U.S. interests are at stake* in many of these conflicts. Peace-brokering is not altruism. It serves the interests of others, but it also serves U.S. foreign policy interests. These interests vary from case to case, as we will see, but they are there in almost every case.

It is one thing to seek to broker peace, however, and another to succeed at it. Many factors affect whether peace is achieved. In the following three cases we will analyze how the United States has played the peace broker role, and with what effectiveness.

Russia, Ukraine, and the Soviet Union's Nuclear Weapons, 1991–94

Among the consequences of the breakup of the Soviet Union in 1991 was that, where there had been a single nuclear-weapons power, there now were four: Russia, Ukraine, Belarus, and Kazakhstan. As the principal successor state to the Soviet Union, Russia had the principal claim to Soviet nuclear weapons. Deals were struck with Belarus and Kazakhstan to give up the old Soviet nuclear weapons left on their territories. But Ukraine was more reluctant.

There were a number of reasons for Ukraine's stance. Ukraine and Russia had a long history of rivalry and hostility. Ukraine had briefly been an independent nation (1917–19) before Soviet forces forcibly absorbed it into the Soviet Union. Now independent again, Ukraine was contesting a number of military and security issues with Russia in addition to the nuclear-weapons issue. Both countries also had their own antagonistic domestic politics, with extremist nationalists in Russia such as Vladimir Zhirinovsky threatening to reabsorb Ukraine, and Ukrainian nationalists in the Rada (its legislature) quite vitriolic in their anti-Russia rhetoric. Mixed in also were each country's concerns for its prestige. Nuclear weapons conferred international importance and status, and Ukraine was reluctant to give these up. It was, after all, the second-largest Soviet successor state, and was bigger and only slightly less populous than Britain or France, Europe's other nuclear powers.

U.S. INTERESTS   U.S. interests were at stake in a number of ways. Fear of a "Yugoslavia with nukes," of a country breaking up and potentially becoming embroiled in ethnic and other conflicts, only this time with nuclear weapons present, was high on everyone's list. Even short of that, the START I arms-control treaty just signed by Presidents George H.W. Bush and Mikhail Gorbachev after years of painstaking negotiations was at risk of being undermined. So, too, possibly with the global NPT, for if ex-Soviet republics other than Russia retained nuclear weapons, it would weaken the case against other countries elsewhere doing so.

LEADERSHIP AND ACCEPTABILITY TO THE PARTIES   Only the United States had the prestige and leverage to act as broker on such a major issue between such major countries. If Ukrainian president Leonid Kravchuk was to go against the anti-Russian nationalists, he needed to be able to assure his people that their security would not be threatened and also show that Ukraine gained something from the deal. Although not willing to grant the full security guarantees Ukraine wanted, the Clinton administration did provide some security assurances, took a number of steps to develop closer U.S.-Ukrainian bilateral relations, and helped get Russia to pledge to respect Ukraine's sovereignty and security. President Clinton visited Kiev, the Ukrainian capital, and President Kravchuk was invited to Washington. And in more concrete terms, Ukraine was given substantial sums of foreign aid, and special initiatives were taken to promote American trade with and investment in Ukraine.

In January 1994, after much negotiation, the Trilateral Agreement between the United States, Russia, and Ukraine was signed by Presidents Clinton, Yeltsin, and Kravchuk. And on June 1, 1996, the last nuclear weapon was removed from Ukraine. As President Clinton said that day, "in 1991 there were more than 4,000 strategic and tactical nuclear warheads in Ukraine. Today there are none . . . [a] historic contribution in reducing the nuclear threat."[57] U.S. peace-brokering had worked well.

Bosnia and the Dayton Accord, 1995

The Dayton accord ended the war in Bosnia. It was signed by the presidents of Bosnia, Croatia, and Serbia after negotiations led by the United States and held at a military base in Dayton, Ohio. In ending such a brutal war, the Dayton accord was an important success. Yet it came only after tens of thousands had been killed, and hundreds of thousands left as refugees by more than three years of the worst warfare in Europe since World War II.

U.S. LEADERSHIP   The United States did show leadership in bringing the parties together at Dayton. No other country had the power and prestige to be able to do this. Various UN peace initiatives had achieved various cease-fires, but not much more, and the cease-fires rarely lasted long. But it took a long time for the United States to actually undertake a major initiative. In 1991–92, when the wars in the former communist Yugoslavia were starting, the Bush administration largely held to the view that the conflicts were a European problem, and the western Europeans should be the ones to take the lead. Presidential candidate Bill Clinton was harshly critical of the Bush policy, and promised to be more assertive by, among other things, lifting the arms embargo against the Bosnian Muslims and launching air strikes against the Bosnian Serbs ("lift and strike"). But once in office, Clinton backed off, showing indecisiveness and succumbing to political concerns about the risks involved.

By mid-1995 the urgency of the situation no longer could be denied. The Bosnian Serbs had become so brash as to take several hundred UN peacekeepers hostage. Congress was threatening to cut off aid to the UN peacekeeping mission. This not only endangered what was left of any semblance of peacekeeping and humanitarian assistance, but threatened a crisis within NATO, because British and French troops were among the UN forces such abandonment would endanger. Then three top American officials were killed in Bosnia when their jeep hit a land mine. Realizing that there no longer was much of a middle option, that the choices now were give up or get serious, the Clinton administration finally asserted American leadership. NATO air strikes were launched against Bosnian Serbs, and with more firepower than the earlier "pinprick" strikes. Military support was given to the Croatian army for a major offensive against the Serbs. Economic sanctions were ratcheted up. And diplomacy was stepped up, culminating in the Dayton peace conference.

ACCEPTABILITY TO THE PARTIES   The United States had been the principal Western supporter of the Bosnian Muslims, so their leader, Alija Izetbegovic was more receptive to negotiations led by the United States than by others. So, too, with Croatia, which also had been receiving significant American military aid and assistance. U.S. relations with Serbia and its president, Slobodan Milosevic, had been more conflictual, but Milosevic knew that only Washington could lift the sanctions that were ravaging the Serbian economy and turn off the NATO air strikes against the Bosnian Serbs. This was another case in which the parties to the conflict knew that they needed to deal with the only country that could deliver.

U.S. INTERESTS   The question of interests was at the heart of the U.S. policy and political debate over Bosnia. Were the interests at stake sufficient to warrant the risks of involvement in the conflict? The initial answer from the Bush and early Clinton administrations was "no." Many other policy makers strongly disagreed, which is why Bosnia was such an intense political issue. As the war intensified, as it threatened to spread, as it set a dangerous precedent for other parts of Europe, as it split NATO, and as the horrors kept being shown on CNN, it became increasingly hard to deny that the United States had important interests at stake. These interests were well served by the peace, however limited and imperfect, that the Dayton accord brought.

The Middle East Peace Process

September 13, 1993. The lawn of the White House. Bright blue sky, warm with a touch of late-summer crispness in the air. On one side of President Clinton, Israeli prime minister Yitzhak Rabin; on the other side, Palestine Liberation Organization (PLO) chair Yasir Arafat. Sworn enemies, but there at the White House for a symbolic first handshake and to sign their first peace agreement, the Israeli-Palestinian Declaration of Principles (DOP).

"It is time to put an end to decades of confrontation and conflict," the DOP stated, "and strive to live in peaceful coexistence and mutual dignity and security and achieve a just, lasting and comprehensive peace" (see At the

Yitzhak Rabin and Yasir Arafat shake hands after signing the Israeli-Palestinian Declaration of Principles at the White House. (*AP/Wide World Photos*)

Source, p. 475). This document in itself was a historic breakthrough. Over the next few years other significant progress was made, including the signing of a full peace treaty between Israel and Jordan and a series of follow-on agreements between Israel and the Palestinians, including the 1998 Wye River agreement. The United States played the lead diplomatic role in all of these negotiations.

The 1990s progress toward peace was brutally overtaken by the violence that exploded in late 2000. It is, as we stated at the outset of this section, one thing to seek to broker peace and another to succeed at it. Amid all the uncertainties about the future, what is clear is the Middle East's need for peace-brokering and the United States' continuing central importance to any such efforts. We thus need to understand what the bases were for the U.S. peace-brokering role in the 1990s before considering why that role broke down and how it may play out in the future.

U.S. LEADERSHIP   One of the main reasons the Middle East peace process took off in the early 1990s was the transformed regional context caused by the double-barrel effects of the end of the Cold War and the U.S.-led victory in the Gulf War. Without the Soviet Union, Middle East "rejectionists" (those who reject peace with Israel) like the PLO were bereft of a superpower patron. In contrast, with its profound political victory in the Cold War and overwhelming military victory in the Gulf War, U.S. prestige was at an all-time high. Seeking to capitalize on this, the Bush administration called a Middle East peace conference for October 1991 in Madrid, Spain.* While the Soviet Union officially was the co-chair, it was clear that the main role lay with the United States.

The initial peace agreement Rabin and Arafat signed that day at the White House, the DOP, actually had been negotiated earlier during secret talks in Oslo, Norway. This led some to see the "Oslo agreement" as evidence that the U.S. role as Middle East peace broker had lessened. But this was too superficial an analysis. The personal role of Norwegian Foreign Minister Johan Jorgen Holst, who had built trust with both sides, definitely was an important factor in the decision to hold the talks in Oslo, and a good reminder that Americans do not have a monopoly on peace-brokering. Another factor was the need to conduct the talks somewhere where they would be out of the limelight, which

---

*The venue was symbolic because both Jews and Arabs (Moors) had been driven out of Spain in the fifteenth century during the Spanish Inquisition.

At the Source

ISRAELI-PALESTINIAN
DECLARATION OF PRINCIPLES (1993)

❝ The Government of the State of Israel and the Palestinian team (in the Jordanian-Palestinian delegation to the Middle East Peace Conference) (the 'Palestinian Delegation'), representing the Palestinian people, agree that it is time to put an end to decades of confrontation and conflict, recognize their mutual legitimate and political rights, and strive to live in peaceful coexistence and mutual dignity and security and achieve a just, lasting and comprehensive peace settlement and historic reconciliation through the agreed political process. . . . ❞

Accompanying letter from Palestine Liberation Organization (P.L.O.)
Chairman Yasir Arafat to Israeli Prime Minister Yitzhak Rabin

❝ Mr. Prime Minister,
The signing of the Declaration of Principles marks a new era in the history of the Middle East. In firm conviction thereof, I would like to confirm the following P.L.O. commitments:

The P.L.O. recognizes the right of the State of Israel to exist in peace and security. . . .

The P.L.O. renounces the use of terrorism and other acts of violence. . . . ❞

Accompanying letter from Prime Minister Rabin to Chairman Arafat

❝ Mr. Chairman,
In response to your letter of Sept. 9, 1993, I wish to confirm to you that in light of the P.L.O. commitments included in your letter the Government of Israel has decided to recognize the P.L.O. as the representative of the Palestinian people and commence negotiations with the P.L.O. within the Middle East peace process. . . . ❞

Source: Excerpts from "Declaration of Principles on Interim Self-Government Arrangements," Stockholm International Peace Research Institute, *SIPRI Yearbook 1994* (New York: Oxford University Press, 1994), appendix 3A.

would have been nearly impossible in the United States. Once the talks were completed, though, it was Washington where the signing ceremony took place. And the United States has played the major diplomatic role in the years since, in brokering the follow-on agreements and in trying to move the process along toward a comprehensive peace.

ACCEPTABILITY TO THE PARTIES IN CONFLICT   Israel long had held that it would not negotiate peace unless the United States played a key role in the process. It had, for example, rejected a number of UN-led initiatives because it believed the UN did not give sufficient consideration to Israeli security and other interests. The United States and Israel have had their differences, but one president after another, Republican and Democrat alike, has affirmed American support for Israel's security.

Prior to 1993 Arafat and the PLO considered the United States an enemy, and the United States condemned and opposed them as terrorists. But for a number of reasons those views had changed. For Arafat, although other world leaders had received him for many years, the invitation to the White House conferred a degree of legitimacy and status that could come only from Washington. The United States also was the key to unlocking international economic assistance, as for example with the two Donors Conferences, the first convened at the State Department within weeks of the 1993 DOP, at which $2.2 billion in economic assistance was pledged to the Palestinians by more than forty nations and international institutions such as the World Bank; and the second in December 1998 shortly after the Wye agreement, at which an additional $3 billion to $4 billion in aid was pledged to the Palestinians. Arafat also knew that if there ever were to be peace and independence for his people, only the United States could provide the combination of reassurance, persuasion, and pressure for Israel to agree.

U.S. INTERESTS   Cold War or post–Cold War, the interests the United States has at stake in the Middle East have been vital. No region has been more important to the American economy nor more capable of causing profound disruptions than the Middle East, because of its oil (prosperity). For this and other reasons the region remains geopolitically important (power). It has had more wars than any other region since 1945, and is home to the most ominous WMD proliferation threats (peace). It also has domestic political importance, given the influence both of the Jewish-American lobby and of the oil companies and other major corporations with commercial interests in the Arab world.

BREAKDOWN OF THE PEACE PROCESS Some critics of the Oslo strategy argue that it was fatally flawed in itself, that it had inherent weaknesses that ultimately proved too weak a basis for building peace. Others contend that the strategy was fundamentally sound but that it was poorly implemented over the course of the 1990s and at the July 2000 Camp David summit, which was supposed to bring the two sides to final agreement but broke up in disarray. Variants of these arguments dole out varying shares of responsibility to Israel, to Arafat and the Palestinians, to the Clinton administration, and to the George W. Bush administration. Which analysis is the more accurate affects not just understanding of what went wrong and why, but also has lessons to be learned and implications to be drawn for what should be done next. What is clear is the Middle East continues to be a region in great need of peace-brokering—and although the specifics may be different from those of the past, the U.S. role remains crucial.

Foreign Policy Politics:
The Politics of Peace-Building

Three issues provide insights into the U.S. domestic politics related to issues of peace-building: public opinion about the United Nations, the 1999 congressional defeat of the Comprehensive Test Ban Treaty, and executive-congressional relations and public opinion concerning humanitarian interventions.

The UN and U.S. Domestic Politics

GENERAL PATTERNS Figure 8.2 shows how strong U.S. public support was for the UN from the 1950s through the 1960s. This is consistent with the policy enhancement-prerogative encroachment analysis earlier in this chapter. In those years the UN's role was viewed by the American public as enhancing U.S. foreign policy. The UN generally supported U.S. positions during the Cold War. The strongest example of this support was in the Korean War, when the very same day that North Korea invaded South Korea, the UN Security Council ordered it to cease and withdraw, and then made the defense of South Korea a UN operation led by the United States and with troops from other

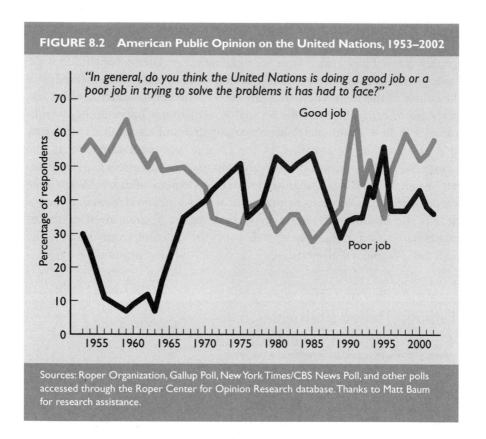

FIGURE 8.2   American Public Opinion on the United Nations, 1953–2002

"In general, do you think the United Nations is doing a good job or a poor job in trying to solve the problems it has had to face?"

Sources: Roper Organization, Gallup Poll, New York Times/CBS News Poll, and other polls accessed through the Roper Center for Opinion Research database. Thanks to Matt Baum for research assistance.

UN member countries.* On many other issues as well, a pro-U.S. tilt generally characterized UN decisions. Furthermore, people felt that the UN largely was effective in achieving its programmatic goals.

The "good job"/"poor job" lines first cross in Figure 8.2 in the early 1970s. The "poor job" view dominated public opinion through the mid-1980s. This was the period during which votes in the General Assembly often were critical of U.S. foreign policy and criticisms of UN inefficiencies and corruption mounted. The late 1980s–early 1990s turnaround was prompted initially by

---

*The Soviet Union was absent from the vote due to its boycott of the UNSC, stemming from the refusal of the Security Council to take China's seat away from the government of Chiang Kai-shek and give it to the People's Republic of China following the communist triumph in the Chinese civil war the previous October. Chiang's government had fled mainland China and had relocated on the island of Formosa (Taiwan).

peacekeeping successes in Afghanistan and elsewhere, and then especially by the 1990–91 Persian Gulf War.

The "poor job" gap reopened in reaction to Somalia and Bosnia. In August 1995 only 35 percent of Americans rated the UN positively, while 56 percent rated it negatively. Polls began to even out again in 1996 as the situation in Bosnia improved and the UN got credit at least for agreeing to let NATO take charge. Other factors, such as internal reforms and the election of a new secretary-general, Kofi Annan, also helped the "good job" rating recapture a majority. Indeed, no doubt to the dismay of many of the UN's most ardent congressional critics, a separate 1995 poll by the Times-Mirror Center for the People and the Press asking about favorable and unfavorable views of a number of different political institutions showed that 67 percent of the American public gave a favorable rating to the UN but only 53 percent to the U.S. Congress. And in a Gallup poll a few months later asking about who has "too much power," 63 percent of Americans said the Internal Revenue Service and 62 percent the advertising industry, but only 21 percent the UN.[58] Still, part of the political problem is that those who are anti-UN—the segment of the public we characterized as "antagonistics" in Chapter 7—tend to be the most vocal and active, at times violently so.

American public opinion stayed steadily supportive of the UN until the controversies of the 2003 Iraq war. Initially polls showed a strong preference for using military force with UN authorization rather than unilaterally. But as the crisis escalated the public tilted toward the Bush administration's view of the United Nations as obstructionist and even anti-American. A February 2003 *Washington Post*/ABC News poll showed 72 percent favoring military force even if the United Nations opposed it.[59]

Yet even amidst the controversy over Iraq there were signs that the American public was not falling back into a more generalized and lasting disillusionment with the UN. For UN supporters this was a hopeful albeit far from certain sign.

U.S. DEBT TO THE UN   A highly politically contentious domestic debate about the UN has been over repayment of the back dues the United States owes to the UN. The United States had been withholding some of its dues in protest against UN policies with which it disagreed and also as leverage to push for reform of the UN bureaucracy. The UN is financed through formulas that vary the contributions of member nations principally according to their size and wealth. For many years the U.S. contributed 25 percent of the regular UN budget, the highest share of any individual country. Although the precise amounts were disputed, most estimates put the U.S. arrears at over $1.5 billion by early 1999. The "Richest Deadbeat" was how a *New York Times* headline described the situation. The United States was in a group of countries whose debts were so high that they risked losing their votes in the General Assembly—countries such as Bosnia, Cambodia, Congo, Iraq, Somalia, Togo, and Yugoslavia. The policy effects of this debt were quite real. For example, when Yugoslav Serb attacks on ethnic Albanians in Kosovo began intensifying in mid-1998, the UN reaffirmed its arms embargo against Yugoslavia. But the UN's lack of funds made enforcement of the embargo very difficult.

Congress, not the president, has the final say on repaying the U.S. debt, because Congress has the power of the purse. Thus congressional critics have been well positioned on this issue. Their points to some extent are serious and substantive, raising concerns about the need for UN reform. Yet the issue has also been highly political. In 1998, for example, conservatives in Congress attached an anti-abortion clause to the UN funding bill, specifying that funds from the United States could not be used for any UN program that facilitated or provided abortions. Even American allies were outraged. "It's preposterous," the Dutch ambassador to the UN stated, that the United States should try to set conditions for what it is obligated to pay under international law. "It's as simple as that."[60]

A compromise was reached in the last weeks of the Clinton administration that partially settled these issues. The deal was largely negotiated between UN Ambassador Richard Holbrooke and Senator Jesse Helms (R-N.C.), with some late intervention by media mogul Ted Turner. The U.S. contribution to the UN's administrative budget was reduced from 25 percent to 22 percent. This still was the highest share for any single country, although it now was not that much more than Japan's (19.6 percent) and was less than the shares of the four major European countries combined (Germany 9.8 percent, France 6.5 percent, the United Kingdom 5.6 percent, and Italy 5.1 percent, for a total of 27 percent). The U.S. share of the costs of UN peacekeeping operations was to be cut from 31 percent to 26.5 percent by the end of 2002 and eventually to 25 percent. In exchange, Congress began paying part of the U.S. arrears. Ted Turner's role was in providing $34 million to help offset costs to countries that now were having to increase their UN payments—a highly unusual situation in which a private citizen intervened directly to help work out an international dispute among governments.

Yet this did not totally resolve the issue, for the UN and congressional critics still differed on the exact amount of the arrears owed. The shift from the Clinton to the Bush administration reduced pressure from the executive branch for further compromise. Meanwhile, other countries, including some U.S. allies, were critical of the new dues structure. For example, the European Union countries together were paying more than the new U.S. dues level, yet their combined GDP was less than that of the United States.

U.S. TROOPS UNDER FOREIGN COMMAND　The question of whether U.S. troops should be placed under non-American command was the hottest issue raised by the Somalia and Bosnia experiences. The dominant perception in the United States of the Somalia debacle was that it was caused principally by the failures of UN commanders, and American soldiers paid the price with their lives. In fact, the decision to launch the commando operations that resulted in American deaths was made without the knowledge of the UN force commander. The political pressure after U.S. soldiers were killed was so high that the Clinton administration retreated, not only withdrawing U.S. troops from Somalia but also changing its policy on whether U.S. troops would serve under foreign command. Just a few months earlier the administration had been reported to be leaning toward putting American troops under UN commanders "on a regular basis." But in the wake of Somalia it issued a major policy statement that "the United States does not support a standing UN army nor will it earmark specific military units for participation in UN operations."[61]

While there is plenty to debate on this issue, it is not the case that U.S. troops have never served under foreign command. U.S. troops served under foreign command in World Wars I and II, and in some successful Cold War–era UN peacekeeping operations. It still can be argued that these were mostly exceptional and high-stakes situations, with more vital U.S. interests at stake than in most post–Cold War situations. But the historical record at least should be clear.

Congressional Defeat of the Comprehensive Test Ban Treaty, 1999

The defeat of the CTBT in the Senate ratification process brought many comparisons to the 1919 defeat of the League of Nations treaty. It also was seen in the contemporary context as a victory for unilateralism over multilateralism. The dynamics of the debate were driven in part by the substantive differences over whether the CTBT served the national interest, and in part by politics.

In signing the CTBT in 1996, President Clinton called it "the longest-sought, hardest-fought prize in arms control history."[62] He sent it to the

Senate for ratification in September 1997. But it stayed bottled up in the Senate Foreign Relations Committee for almost two years. Republicans had the majority in the Senate and controlled the key committees. Senator Helms, a strong CTBT opponent, used his powers as chair of the Foreign Relations Committee to block the scheduling of hearings on the treaty. In July 1999, all 45 Senate Democrats issued a joint statement calling on Helms to hold hearings and allow the treaty to go to the floor for a full Senate vote. Helms still refused. Senator Byron Dorgan (D-N.D.) turned to another Senate procedural tactic, threatening to filibuster on the Senate floor and block any other votes from being taken on any other issues. He would put himself on the Senate floor "like a potted plant," Dorgan said. "I am sorry if I am going to cause some problems around here with the schedule. But frankly, as I said, there are big issues and there are small issues. This is a big issue. And I am flat tired of seeing small issues around this chamber every day in every way, when the big issues are bottled up in some committee and the key is held by one or two people."[63]

On the Republican side, Senator Jon Kyl (R-Ariz.) had been engaged in legislative maneuvering of his own. He had lined up 42 of the 55 Republican senators as against the treaty. This was four more than the one-third needed, according to the Constitution's special provision for treaty ratification. Kyl had done this quietly, without the Clinton administration or Senate Democrats getting wind of it. At that point, working with Senate Majority Leader Trent Lott (R-Miss.), Kyl "made an offer that the Democrats would find hard to refuse." Through what in legislative procedure is called a unanimous consent agreement (used for bringing a bill to the Senate floor quickly), they offered to bring the CTBT right to the floor within a week, even without committee hearings. The Democrats were in a bind. They thought this might be too quick, not allowing enough time for getting supportive expert testimony in hearings, activating pro-CTBT public opinion, or stepping up lobbying efforts by the Clinton administration on Capitol Hill. But as one staff aide said, "We would have looked stupid demanding hearings, demanding a vote, and then complaining about the process."[64]

The hearings that were held included experts on both sides of the issue. Among the most influential testimony was that from the directors of the Sandia and Lawrence Livermore National Laboratories, where much of the nuclear weapons testing was done. The weapons-lab directors had issued a pro-CTBT statement the previous year, expressing their view that computerized testing and other aspects of the "stockpile stewardship program" still permitted by the CTBT would suffice. But during the congressional hearings their testimony conveyed greater doubt and uncertainty. "Had the directors learned something . . . that made them more nervous about the adequacy of the stockpile program? Maybe they were just being typical scientists, unwilling to say that anything is 100 percent certain. . . . It is also possible that, on the contrary, they were shrewd politicians, men who understood that the treaty was going down, that the majority party on Capitol Hill was against it, and that they needed to be on the right side of the issue."[65]

All along public opinion was largely pro-CTBT, as much as 70–80 percent supportive. But this was an issue on which the general public was less influential than issue activists. No senator was brought by general public pressures over to the pro-treaty side from a position of being opposed or undecided. Vice President Al Gore tried to make the CTBT a campaign issue in the 2000 presidential election, but it did not have political legs.

Although the Clinton administration pushed hard at the end, many pro-CTBT senators and activists were critical of the administration for doing too little for so long. The final vote was 48 in favor, 51 opposed; ratification would have required 67 votes in favor. President Clinton blamed the defeat on "politics, pure and simple." He also had in mind the fallout from the congressional efforts to impeach him over the Monica Lewinsky scandal. Majority Leader Lott maintained that "it was not about politics; it was about the substance of the treaty, and that's all it was."[66] Undoubtedly both foreign policy strategy and foreign policy politics came into play. Debate over the CTBT was part of the broader debate between unilateralism and multilateralism. It also was a manifestation of the fundamental constitutional design of separate institutions sharing powers, spiced and shaped by partisan politics.

The Politics of Humanitarian Intervention

PENNSYLVANIA AVENUE FUMBLING   War-powers tensions between the president and Congress have been even more difficult than usual with regard to humanitarian interventions. Somalia was Bill Clinton's first war-powers issue, and it was a disaster. The original troop commitment had been made by President George H.W. Bush in December 1992, with the mission defined largely as a short-term humanitarian one of relief from starvation (Operation Provide Comfort). The troops were sent by executive action, outside the procedures of the War Powers Resolution (WPR), although with strong bipartisan support. The Clinton administration later would be criticized for keeping the troops in and taking on the broader mission of "nation-building." Had it withdrawn the troops according to the original schedule, however, the risk of reversion to chaos was high. In this regard the administration's mistake may have been less taking on the broader mission per se than not paying enough attention to the requirements of a more effective strategy, and not sufficiently consulting with Congress and bringing it in to have some "co-ownership" for the policy.

Once the policy started to go badly, and especially in October 1993 when eighteen American soldiers were killed, and one dead soldier was ignominiously dragged through the streets of the capital city, Mogadishu, a political firestorm was set off on Capitol Hill, on the airwaves, and with the general public. Within hours the president felt he had no choice but to get on television with a hastily prepared speech promising to withdraw the American troops. Whether this was the right decision, and whether the mistake was not having withdrawn the troops sooner or not having made a more concerted effort to accomplish the mission, the picture conveyed to the world was of an American political system still fumbling the war power.

The September 1994 Haiti intervention went better, but actually was a close call. Had the Carter-Nunn-Powell mission not succeeded in persuading the Haitian military to step down, and had the invasion brought casualties, the outcry on Capitol Hill likely would have been deafening. Other than the Congressional Black Caucus and some other liberal Democrats who had been pushing for military action, most others in Congress were nonsupportive if not outright opposed to a Haiti intervention. Moreover, the Clinton administration had not bothered to come to Congress, despite the consultation clause of the WPR, not even for a resolution like the one Bush got for the Persian Gulf War.

The usual presidentialist claim of the demands of a crisis situation was not very convincing in this case, given all the advance planning and the fact that the Clinton administration had gone to the UN Security Council almost two months earlier for an "all necessary means" resolution authorizing the intervention. The real reason for not consulting Congress was that the administration was afraid it would lose. In the end, and yet again, the ambiguities of the WPR and the reluctance of Congress to act on its own allowed the president to go his own way, with plenty of criticism but few biting procedural constraints.

The politics of the deployment of U.S. troops to Bosnia as part of IFOR following the Dayton accord largely adhered to the same pattern. The president was not stopped from deploying the troops, but he was not exactly supported in doing so, either. The House did pass a resolution that was at best a mixed message; it stated support for the troops themselves but "disowned the deployment decision."[67] The Senate resolution was more supportive, but it too contained far more caveats, criticisms, and reservations than presidents usually get when putting American troops on the ground. Moreover, to get even this Clinton had to state that the deployment was only for one year. Yet it was clear from the outset that this was an unrealistic timetable. Indeed, a year later the president announced that, although he would make some cuts in numbers, the American troops needed to stay in Bosnia another year. Another year later came yet another extension; this one was left more open-ended. Congress criticized, and passed various measures affecting the deployment at the margins, but didn't stop them.

In the Kosovo case as well there was neither strong and explicit congressional support nor a concerted effort to stop the military action. When a few House members pushed to have at least some formal legislative action, whether a declaration of war or an invocation of the provisions and procedures of the WPR, they garnered little support.

The pattern in these cases, and one likely to hold in other humanitarian intervention cases, is of a Congress more divided and more critical of presidential action than in cases like the 2001 Afghanistan and 2003 Iraq wars, in which there was a much stronger and more evident argument that America's own security was being more directly threatened. Still, though, Congress stopped short in all of these humanitarian intervention cases from blocking presidential action. In Somalia it reacted to the Mogadishu debacle, as it likely would to other instances of apparent failed and flawed strategy. But there has yet to be a case in which a president determined to make a commitment in the name of humanitarian intervention has been voted down by Congress.

These cases, even more than the Afghanistan and Iraq war cases, show how the war-powers issue still is unresolved, and full of potential for further interbranch conflict. The immediate political costs and constraints have been contained, but only by deferring the central issue—indeed, the most central issue any democracy must grapple with—for yet another day.

PUBLIC OPINION ON THE USE OF MILITARY FORCE   During the early Cold War the public generally was willing to support the use of military force. In Chapter 5 we saw how, as part of the "Vietnam trauma," public support for the use of force became extremely weak. Starting in the 1980s and then in the 1990s, the pattern became more mixed, with public support having increased for the use of force for certain objectives but not for others. The picture we get is of a public that is neither as trigger-happy as during parts of the Cold War, nor as gun-shy as in the wake of Vietnam; the American public has become "pretty prudent."[68]

Behind these trends we can see three general patterns. First, public support tends to be greatest when the principal policy objective for which force is being used is to coerce *foreign policy restraint* on an aggressor threatening the

United States, its citizens, or its interests. The Persian Gulf War is an example. When the first deployments were made to Saudi Arabia, public-opinion polls registered in the range of 60–70 percent support, which was higher than support for Vietnam ever was. Polls also showed that public support was not strictly dependent on expectations of low casualties. In one poll posing hypothetical questions about possible casualties, only at the level of ten thousand or more deaths did support fall significantly—but even then at 60 percent this was still something much less than an antiwar movement. Belief in the importance of the objective of restraining aggression provided at least some tolerance for the risks of casualties.

Second, the public tends to be least supportive of military force when the principal objective is to engineer *internal political change* in another country's government. The low levels of support for aiding the Nicaraguan contras in the 1980s are one example. Haiti in the 1990s is another: only about 35 percent of Americans supported the military intervention when it was launched in September 1994. Even with the halo effect of the casualty-free occupation, approval ratings only went up to about 45 percent. The public still had doubts about using force to remake a government.[69] In the Afghanistan and Iraq cases, even with the regime change intent of removing the Taliban and Saddam Hussein governments, the link between the nature of these regimes and their aggressive policies caused the American public to perceive these cases largely in terms of the foreign policy restraint objective. This perception of internal political change as a means to the ends of foreign policy restraint was a key reason that public support was so much higher than in cases like Nicaragua in the 1980s when as hard as the Reagan administration tried, it could not convincingly make the link between the nature of the Sandinista regime and clear and present dangers to American security.

Third are *humanitarian interventions,* for which public support tends to fall in between. In Somalia, for example, which started out as the veritable "pure" humanitarian intervention case, initial polls showed 70 percent support or higher. However, as perceptions of the mission changed to "nation-building"—i.e., internal political change—public support dropped to 47 percent, and then to 35 percent when the American soldiers were killed. This was indicative of the much lower public tolerance for casualties when the objective was remaking governments rather than restraining aggression. Then when, six months later, the Rwandan genocide began, the "Somalia effect" worked against getting involved in a conflict that was strikingly similar, and to many seemed more protracted and dangerous. On the other hand it was difficult not to be moved by the killing and suffering shown on television. Post-

Rwanda support for humanitarian intervention did come back up, although not as high as pre-Somalia. The humanitarian objective explains why support for the use of ground troops was higher than many expected in the early stages of the Kosovo war. The American public was not eager to send ground forces in, but it was willing to do so given the nature of the principal policy objectives.

This basic pattern of what the public is and is not inclined to support does have an underlying logic based on conceptions of legitimacy and calculations of *efficacy*. On the first point, using force to restrain aggression has a much stronger normative claim than does trying to remake governments. Humanitarian intervention falls in between, with some situations so dire that claims to legitimacy can be made even if the intervention is within a state and without the consent of the state's government. As to prospects for effectiveness, foreign policy restraint objectives have the inherent advantage of being more readily translatable into an operational military plan. Internal political change objectives, however, tend to require strategies more political in nature and less suitable to an operational military plan. Humanitarian interventions fall in between on this point as well; they usually have discrete missions and objectives but are difficult to keep from crossing over into state-building.

Other factors may also come into play in any particular case. Multilateral support and burden-sharing is one; the public often wants to know that other countries are also bearing some of the risks and costs.* The reactions of congressional leaders, newspaper editorialists, television pundits, and other elites are also a factor. Fundamentally, though, the American public is hardly eager to use military force, but is not invariably opposed to it. It still lacks lots of information, and may not even be able to find the relevant places on a map, but it manages to show "good judgment in the use of resources" and "caution and circumspection as to danger and risk"—exactly how the dictionary defines "prudence."

Summary

The end of the Cold War did not mean the end of war. If there is to be a broad and enduring peace, it needs to be built. This chapter has focused on key international institutions and key roles for U.S. foreign policy in such efforts.

---

*This can cut both ways, however, as with the strong opposition to U.S. troops serving under foreign command as discussed earlier in this chapter.

With regard to the United Nations, it is essential to get beyond both the idealized views that underemphasize the limits and problems the UN does have as a global institution, and the caricatures and castigations that certain groups and political figures too often propagate. Arguments about whether the United States should withdraw from, or turn its foreign policy over to, the UN really are straw men. The substantively important debates are on questions concerning how strong an institution the UN is and can be for building and maintaining peace. These debates bear especially on U.S. foreign policy on issues such as human rights, peace operations, and global social and economic development.

A second main set of players in building peace comprises the increasingly important regional organizations. Because instability, conflict, and threats of war now tend to be much more regionally rooted than globally transmitted, regional organizations like the OSCE, the AU, and others need to play more important roles than in the past. This is being recognized in almost every region of the world, albeit with varying rates of progress. Here, too, the American foreign policy interest is in the potential for policy enhancement and complementarity between what the United States can do through its own initiatives and what can be better done through collective or coordinated action. Yet as with the UN, regional organizations also bring up issues of prerogative encroachment and conflicting interests.

Nonproliferation regimes are less formal institutions but ones that address some of the post–Cold War era's most dangerous threats. A balanced perspective is especially important with regard to such an ominous issue. On the one hand, back in the 1960s predictions claimed that as many as fifteen to twenty states would acquire nuclear weapons. Today, even counting suspected ones, the actual figure is probably fewer than ten. The NPT is in large part responsible for these numbers' being so low. The CWC also represents significant nonproliferation progress. Yet WMD threats remain, and in some respects are growing worse, both from certain states and from the risks of WMD terrorism.

The United States also has key direct roles to play in peace-building. Preventive diplomacy has a strong logic of acting early before ethnic and other conflicts get worse. To be effective, though, it must meet requisites that are easier to invoke than to implement. Humanitarian interventions also pose tough choices, as many of the deadly conflicts in the 1990s demonstrated.

Claims of success for U.S. peace-brokering at times are overblown, just as blame for failures sometimes gets exaggerated. Issues like the Middle East peace process continue to pose complex policy challenges and engender debates over what U.S. policy should be. Whatever the strategy, both the U.S. interests at stake and the needs of a post–Cold War peace make the U.S. role as peace broker a crucial one. This was evident in the cases discussed herein.

The foreign policy politics of peace-building are a mix of continuity with and change from past patterns. On issues like the United Nations and humanitarian intervention overall, American public opinion is more internationalist than it is often given credit for. Domestic constraints are there, but they are more flexible than many contend, more potentially malleable to presidential leadership. Activist constituencies often have disproportionate impact, as on the debate over the CTBT. The UN dues issue, the CTBT debate, and various humanitarian intervention cases also have been shaped by the age-old constitutional "invitation to struggle" along Pennsylvania Avenue.

In sum, the International Internationalist paradigm and the policies that follow from it have been and will continue to be integral to post–Cold War American foreign policy. There is great potential for going further in building a post–Cold War peace; there also are formidable challenges.

Notes

[1] Quoted in Thomas J. Paterson, J. Gary Clifford, and Kenneth J. Hagan, *American Foreign Relations: A History since 1895* (Lexington, Mass.: D.C. Heath, 1995), 243–44.

[2] Quoted in Michael N. Barnett, "Bringing in the New World Order: Liberalism, Legitimacy, and the United Nations," *World Politics* 49:4 (July 1997), 541.

[3] Barnett, "Bringing in the New World Order," 543.

[4] U.S. Department of State, Bureau of International Organization Affairs, "Fact Sheet: United Nations" (November 26, 2002), available at www.state.gov (emphasis added), accessed May 12, 2003.

[5] Boutros Boutros-Ghali, *An Agenda for Peace* (New York: United Nations, 1992), 1.

[6] Mats R. Berdahl, "Fateful Encounter: The United States and UN Peacekeeping," *Survival* 36 (Spring 1994).

[7] Cited in Bruce W. Jentleson, "Who, Why, What and How: Debates over Post–Cold War Military Interventionism," in *Eagle Adrift: American Foreign Policy at the End of the Century,* ed., Robert J. Lieber (New York: Longman, 1997), 63–64.

[8] Bruce Russett, ed., *The Once and Future Security Council* (New York: St. Martin's, 1997).

[9] Kofi Annan, "Rome Statute of the International Criminal Court: Overview," http://www.un.org/law/icc/general/overview.htm, accessed May 10, 2003.

[10] "Rome Statute of the International Criminal Court: Overview."

[11] This and other parts of the arguments of opponents draw principally on Ambassador Negroponte's statement of July 12, 2002, and the State Department Fact Sheet on the International Criminal Court, May 6, 2002, both available at www.state.gov.

[12] Thomas W. Lippman, "America Avoids the Stand," *Washington Post,* July 26, 1998, C1, C4.

[13] "No Third Term at the U.N.," *Washington Post,* May 2, 1997, A18.

[14]Paul Kennedy and Bruce Russett, "Reforming the United Nations," *Foreign Affairs* 74:5 (September/October 1995), 50–71; Independent Working Group on the Future of the United Nations, *The United Nations in Its Second Half Century* (New York: Ford Foundation, 1995).

[15]Carnegie Commission on Preventing Deadly Conflict, *Preventing Deadly Conflict: Final Report* (Washington, D.C.: Carnegie Commission, 1997), 135.

[16]Robert J. Art and Robert Jervis, *International Politics: Enduring Concepts and Contemporary Issues,* 3d ed. (New York: HarperCollins, 1992), 2.

[17]Francis M. Deng, Sadikel Kimaro, Terrence Lyons, Donald Rothchild, and I. William Zartman, *Sovereignty as Responsibility: Conflict Management in Africa* (Washington, D.C.: Brookings Institution Press, 1996); Bruce W. Jentleson, "Preventive Diplomacy: Analytic Conclusions and Policy Lessons," in *Opportunities Missed, Opportunities Seized: Preventive Diplomacy in the Post–Cold War World,* ed. Jentleson (Lanham, MD.: Rowman and Littlefield, 1999).

[18]Kofi Annan, "Intervention," Ditchley Foundation Lecture 35, reprinted as "Supplement to the Ditchley Conference Reports 1997/98," 2, 4–5.

[19]United Nations Development Program (UNDP), *Human Development Report, 1994* (New York: Oxford University Press, 1994), 22.

[20]Jack Donnelly, "Humanitarian Intervention and American Foreign Policy: Law, Morality and Politics," in *Human Rights in the World Community: Issues and Actions,* eds. Richard P. Claude, and Burns H. Weston (Philadelphia: University of Pennsylvania Press, 1992), 63.

[21]Barbara Crossette, "For First Time, U.S. Is Excluded from U.N. Human Rights Panel," *New York Times,* May 4, 2001, A1, A13.

[22]Jentleson, "Who, Why, What and How," 55.

[23]John M. Goshko, "Balkan Peacekeeping Exposes Limits of UN, Boutros-Ghali Says," *Washington Post,* October 10, 1995, A21.

[24]"From CSCE to OSCE: Historical Retrospective," OSCE Web site, http:/www.osceprag. cz/info/facts/history.htm, accessed September 23, 1998.

[25]Abram Chayes and Antonia Handler Chayes, eds., *Preventing Conflict in the Post-Communist World: Mobilizing International and Regional Organizations* (Washington, D.C.: Brookings Institution Press, 1996), 10.

[26]P. Terrence Hopmann, "Building Security in Post–Cold War Eurasia: The OSCE and U.S. Foreign Policy," *Peaceworks* 3 (Washington, D.C.: U.S. Institute of Peace, 1999); and chapters in Jentleson, ed., *Opportunities Missed, Opportunities Seized.*

[27]Hopmann, "The OSCE and U.S. Foreign Policy," 41.

[28]Edmond J. Keller, "Transnational Ethnic Conflict in Africa," in *The International Spread of Ethnic Conflict: Fear, Diffusion, and Escalation,* ed. David A. Lake and Donald Rothchild (Princeton: Princeton University Press, 1998), 275–92.

[29]*The Sunday Times of Johannesburg,* cited in Rachel L. Swarns, *Washington Post,* "A Hint of the Coming Battle for Africa's Future," July 9, 2002, A3.

[30]Bruce W. Jentleson, *The Middle East Arms Control and Regional Security (ACRS) Talks: Progress, Problems and Prospects,* Policy Paper 26, University of California Institute on Global Conflict and Cooperation, September 1996; Joel Peters, *Pathways to Peace: The Multilateral Arab-Israeli Peace Talks* (London: Royal Institute of International Affairs, 1996).

[31]Stephen D. Krasner, ed., "International Regimes," special edition of *International Organization* 36:2 (Spring 1982); Andreas Hasenclever, Peter Mayer, and Volker Rittberger, *Theories of International Regimes* (New York: Cambridge University Press, 1997).

[32]See Scott D. Sagan and Kenneth N. Waltz, *The Spread of Nuclear Weapons: A Debate* (New York: Norton, 1995).

[33]*New York Times,* May 26, 1998, A1.

[34]Joseph Cirincione, *Deadly Arsenals: Tracking Weapons of Mass Destruction* (Washington, D.C.: Carnegie Endowment for International Peace, 2002), 396.

[35]Bruce W. Jentleson, *With Friends Like These: Reagan, Bush and Saddam, 1982–1990* (New York: Norton, 1994).

[36]Quoted in Jentleson, *With Friends Like These,* 93.

[37]Richard Price, "Reversing the Gun Sights: Transnational Civil Society Targets Land Mines," *International Organization* 52:3 (Summer 1998), 618.

[38]Price, "Reversing the Gun Sights."

[39]*Land Mine Monitor Report 2002,* www.icbl.org/lm/2002/findings.html.

[40]Quoted in Jentleson, "Who, Why, What and How: Debate over Post–Cold War Military Intervention," 52; Michael Mandelbaum, "Foreign Policy as Social Work," *Foreign Affairs* 75:1 (January/February 1996), 16–32; Stanley Hoffman, "In Defense of Mother Theresa: Morality in Foreign Policy, *Foreign Affairs* 75:2 (March/April 1996), 172–75.

[41]President William J. Clinton, *A National Security Strategy of Engagement and Enlargement* (Washington, D.C.: U.S. Government Printing Office, 1994).

[42]Richard K. Betts, "The Delusion of Impartial Intervention," *Foreign Affairs* 73:6 (November/December 1994), 20–33.

[43]Betts, "The Delusion of Impartial Intervention," 25.

[44]Bruce W. Jentleson, *Coercive Prevention: Normative, Policy and Political Dilemmas, Peaceworks* 35 (Washington, D.C.: U.S. Institute of Peace, 2000); Jane E. Holl, "We the People Here Don't Want No War: Executive Branch Perspectives on the Use of Force," in *The United States and the Use of Force in the Post–Cold War Era: A Report by the Aspen Strategy Group* (Queenstown, Md.: Aspen Institute Press, 1995), 124 and *passim.*

[45]See, for example, Robert A. Pape, *Bombing to Win: Air Power and Coercion* (Ithaca, N.Y.: Cornell University Press, 1996).

[46]This section draws on Bruce W. Jentleson, ed., *Opportunities Missed, Opportunities Seized.*

[47]Robert D. Kaplan, *Balkan Ghosts: A Journey through History* (New York: St. Martin's, 1993); Bruce W. Jentleson, "Preventive Diplomacy: A Conceptual and Analytic Framework," in Jentleson, ed., *Opportunities Missed, Opportunities Seized.*

[48]Chris Hedges, "War Turns Sarajevo Away from Europe," *New York Times,* July 28, 1995, A4.

[49]V.P. Gagnon, "Ethnic Nationalism and International Conflict: The Case of Serbia," *International Security* 19:3 (Winter 1994–95). The Carnegie Commission for Preventing Deadly Conflict in its *Final Report* makes its own strong statement of the purposive view: "Mass violence invariably results from the deliberately violent response of determined leaders and their groups to a wide range of social, economic and political conditions that provide the environment for violent conflict, but usually do not independently spawn violence" (p. 39).

[50]Philip Tetlock and Aaron Belkin, *Counterfactual Thought Experiments in World Politics: Logical, Methodological and Psychological Perspectives* (Princeton: Princeton University Press, 1997).

[51]Kenneth Menkhaus and Louis Ortmayer, "Somalia: Missed Crises and Missed Opportunities," in Jentleson, ed., *Opportunities Missed, Opportunities Seized,* 212–13, 233.

[52]Astri Suhrke and Bruce Jones, "Preventive Diplomacy in Rwanda: Failure to Act or Failure of Actions?" in Jentleson, ed., *Opportunities Missed, Opportunities Seized,* 259.

[53]Susan Woodward, "Costly Disinterest: Missed Opportunities for Preventive Diplomacy in Croatia and Bosnia and Herzegovina, 1985–1991," in Jentleson, ed., *Opportunities Missed, Opportunities Seized,* 139; Woodward, *Balkan Tragedy: Chaos and Dissolution after the Cold War* (Washington, D.C.: Brookings Institution Press, 1995).

[54]United States Institute of Peace, "Kosovo: Escaping the Cul-de-Sac," Special Report, July 1998.

[55]Michael Lund, "Preventive Diplomacy for Macedonia, 1992–1998: From Containment to Nation-Building," in Jentleson, ed., *Opportunities Missed, Opportunities Seized,* 173–208.

[56]Michael G. Roskin, "Macedonia and Albania: The Missing Alliance," *Parameters* (Winter 1993–94), 98.

[57]James E. Goodby, "Preventive Diplomacy for Nuclear Nonproliferation in the Former Soviet Union," in Jentleson, ed., *Opportunities Missed, Opportunities Seized.*

[58]Shoon Kathleen Murray, Louis Klarevas, and Thomas Hartley, "Are Policymakers Misreading Public Views towards the United Nations?" paper presented at the 38th Annual Convention of the International Studies Association, Toronto, Canada, March 1997, 6.

[59]Roper Center polls at roperweb.ropercenter.uconn.edu, accessed July 7, 2003, and *Washington Post* polls at www.washingtonpost.com, accessed May 25, 2003.

[60]Steven Lee Myers, "Plan to Pay Off UN Dues Stalls," *New York Times,* May 21, 1997, A1, A8.

[61]Cited in Jentleson, "Who, Why, What and How," 62–63.

[62]Terry L. Deibel, "The Death of a Treaty," *Foreign Affairs* 81:5 (September/October 2002), 142–61.

[63]Deibel, "Death of a Treaty," 147.

[64]Deibel, "Death of a Treaty," 150.

[65]Deibel, "Death of a Treaty," 158.

[66]Deibel, "Death of a Treaty," 158.

[67]Pat Towell and Donna Cassata, "Congress Takes Symbolic Stand on Troop Deployment," *Congressional Quarterly Weekly Report,* December 16, 1995, 3817.

[68]This section draws on Bruce W. Jentleson, "The Pretty Prudent Public: Post–Vietnam American Public Opinion on the Use of Military Force," *International Studies Quarterly* 36:1 (March 1992), 49–74; Bruce W. Jentleson and Rebecca L. Britton "Still Pretty Prudent: Post–Cold War American Opinion on the Use of Military Force," *Journal of Conflict Resolution* 42:4 (August 1998), 395–417.

[69]What about Panama, 1989, the question might be asked, when polls showed over 80 percent support for the overthrow of the dictator General Manuel Noriega? Although this was a case of using force for internal political change, these polls all were taken after the fact and really reflected the "halo effect" of quick success. More telling are polls taken in the months prior to the invasion which showed only 32 percent support.

9 *Prosperity: The Globalization Agenda*

Introduction: American Foreign Policy in an Era of Globalization

We live in an age of globalization. The profound changes in the international political economy stand with the end of the Cold War bipolarity, the war on terrorism, the politics of identity causing ethnic and related wars, and the struggles to spread democracy as driving forces of this new era. Our focus in this chapter is on the challenges posed for U.S. foreign policy in its pursuit of prosperity amid the complex and powerful forces of globalization.

The first section of this chapter looks at the overall debate over globalization. Next are three issue areas of major importance to American foreign policy: international trade and the World Trade Organization; international finance and the International Monetary Fund; and sustainable development, including global poverty, AIDS and other global public health issues, and global environmental issues. The foreign policy politics section includes two subsections, one on the role of nongovernmental organizations (NGOs) and other aspects of the politics of globalization, and one on the making of U.S. trade policy.

The Globalization Debate

So what is globalization anyway? What's so new and different about it? Is it a good thing or a bad thing? These and related questions can be addressed initially in terms of the dynamics, dimensions, and dilemmas of globalization.

The basic *dynamic* of globalization is the increasing interconnectedness of the world across nation-state boundaries—an interconnectedness that affects governments, businesses, communities, and people in a wide range of policy areas. Many definitions of globalization have been offered, each with its own emphases (see Perspectives on page 495). They all focus on the fact that, although there have been other historical periods in which trade and investment have grown and nations have become more interdependent, the dynamic driving contemporary globalization is unique in that it is "wider," "deeper," and "faster." By "wider" we mean that it stretches beyond just the largest and richest countries of North America, Europe, and Asia to increasingly include countries and peoples in all corners of the globe. By "deeper" we stress the "thickness" of networks of interaction, that economic, cultural, and other interactions are not just individualized exchanges of goods, ideas, and the like but are more ongoing and interwoven with a greater "density" of interrelationship. The speed with which these interactions happen is remarkable, whether it involves a few computer keystrokes that move billions of dollars from one side of the world to the other, or the instantaneous movement of news via cable and satellite telecommunications.

What also makes today's era of globalization unique are its many *dimensions*. The economic dimension is arguably the most fundamental. We see this reflected in international trade in two respects. One is its extensiveness, the sheer quantity of trade. Trade now accounts for over 30 percent of U.S. gross domestic product (GDP), almost double what it was thirty years ago. Imports are much more prevalent in the purchasing patterns of the average American consumer, be it a major purchase like an automobile or everyday items like clothing. And exports are increasingly important sources of jobs. One study found that exporting companies had almost 20 percent faster employment growth and were 9 percent less likely to go out of business than companies that did not export.[1] As for monetary policy, whereas in the past decisions by the Federal Reserve Board were based almost exclusively on domestic economic factors such as inflation and unemployment, now much greater attention is paid to the value of the dollar relative to that of other major currencies, to the impact of financial crises in other countries on U.S. growth rates, and to other international economic factors. In these and other ways globalization has been both raising the salience of foreign economic policy and making the line between it and domestic economic policy less and less distinct.

The other key pattern in international trade is its organization and nature. "It is not just how much countries trade with each other that is important," one globalization expert wrote, "but also the way in which this trade is

PERSPECTIVES

DEFINING GLOBALIZATION

While there are a lot of similarities in kind between the previous era of globalization (pre–World War) and the one we are now in, what is new today is the degree and intensity with which the world is being tied together into a single globalized marketplace. What is also new is the sheer number of people and countries able to partake of this process and be affected by it. . . . This new era of globalization, compared to the one before it, is turbocharged.

Thomas L. Friedman, *The Lexus and the Olive Tree*

Globalization is not new, but the present era has distinctive features. Shrinking space, shrinking time and disappearing borders are linking people's lives more deeply, more intensely, more immediately than ever before.

United Nations Development Program,
"Globalization with a Human Face"

Globalism is a state of the world involving networks of interdependence at multicontinental distances. These networks can be linked through flows and influences of capital and goods, information and ideas, people and force, as well as environmentally and biologically relevant substances (such as acid rain or pathogens).

Robert O. Keohane and Joseph S. Nye, Jr.,
Governance in a Globalizing World

[Globalization is] the closer integration of the countries and peoples of the world which has been brought about by the enormous reduction of costs of transportation and communication, and the breaking down of artificial barriers to the flow of goods, services, capital, knowledge, and (to a lesser extent) peoples across borders.

Joseph E. Stiglitz, *Globalization and Its Discontents*

[Globalization is] the interdependent infrastructure of global open economies, societies and technologies.

Maryann Cusimano Love, *Beyond Sovereignty*
(*Continued on page 496*)

(Defining Globalization   *Continued from page 495)*
Sources: Thomas L. Friedman, *The Lexus and the Olive Tree: Understanding Globalization* (New York: Farrar, Straus, Giroux, 1999), xv; United Nations Development Program (UNDP), "Globalization with a Human Face," in UNDP, *Human Development Report 1999* (New York: Oxford University Press, 1999), 1; Robert O. Keohane and Joseph S. Nye, Jr., "Introduction," in Joseph S. Nye, Jr., and John D. Donahue, eds., *Governance in a Globalizing World* (Washington, D.C.: Brookings Institution Press, 2000), 2; Joseph E. Stiglitz, *Globalization and Its Discontents* (New York: Norton, 2002), 9; and Maryann Cusimano Love, "Preface," in Maryann Cusimano Love, ed., *Beyond Sovereignty: Issues for a Global Agenda* (Toronto: Wadsworth, 2002), xv.

structured: what goods and services are traded, and between whom they are traded."[2] About one-fourth to one-third of world trade is *intra-firm*—i.e., between divisions of the same global corporation located in different countries, rather than between different companies in different countries. As an example, truck axles are shipped from a General Motors (GM) plant in Detroit to a GM affiliate in Brazil. These count as a trade transaction between the two countries (U.S. export, Brazilian import), yet "the goods never leave the corporate 'boundaries' of GM."[3] The trade is between countries yet within a corporation that is organized on a global basis. For the United States, intra-firm trade accounts for more than 33 percent of exports and more than 40 percent of imports. Another large component of trade takes place on an *intra-industry* basis—i.e., within the same industry even if not within the same firm. Computers are an example: U.S.-based companies like Dell contract with companies in India, Taiwan, Mexico, and elsewhere to produce parts and software. They are not part of the same firm, but they are part of the same industry. This facet of international trade is not totally new, but its extent is much greater than in the past, making for depth and thickness of globalized economic relationships that are qualitatively different from past trade patterns.[4] Thus the trade policy challenges posed in this new era are even more complex than in earlier eras.

   A similar dynamic is evident in international finance. One prominent investment banker drew attention in the late 1990s to the widening gap between the "awesome force of the global financial marketplace" and the more limited reach of the policies of national governments and international institutions like the International Monetary Fund (IMF).[5] With many more countries having market economies than ever before, and given how drastically new technology has reduced intracorporate costs of running distant operations, major multinational corporations (MNCs) have a much wider range of choices about where to build a new factory or make other foreign direct investments. Bankers, money managers, stockbrokers, and other international financiers don't just have Wall Street, London, Frankfurt, and Tokyo, but also Hong Kong, Moscow, Brasilia, and many other of the world's proliferated stock markets, currency markets, and other investment exchanges from which to choose. Whatever their choices, it takes just the click of a computer mouse to move huge sums of money instantly-often over $1 trillion going from one country to another in a single day. Although market-based principles dictate that private investors should be free to make such decisions, one of the main purposes both of U.S. policy and of international economic institutions has been to provide a degree of governance against instabilities, inequities, and other imperfections.

Another key dimension of globalization involves telecommunications technology. News regularly moves instantaneously, 24/7, from one end of the world to the other, be it through the BBC (British Broadcasting Company), CNN (Cable News Network), the Arab satellite network Al Jazeera, or others in this growth industry. The Internet provides an even more widespread communications link that, even with the developing world on the other side of the "digital divide" and much less networked in, is putting all types of information at the fingertips of more and more people. The Internet also demonstrates how globalization can be both a positive force and a negative one. The openness it provides and the way in which it undermines governmental monopolies on information can impose a check against dictators, who might be more likely to repress their people if they knew they could keep it quiet. Yet the Internet also facilitates such problems as terrorism: the terrorists who plotted the World Trade Center attacks communicated with each other from Internet cafés around the world and even from American public libraries.

Globalization also has an important social and cultural dimension involving the flow of ideas, customs, and people. This is more of a multidirectional flow than many Americans realize. American products, music, movies, and other cultural influences can be found in almost every corner of the globe. Want a McDonald's hamburger? You'll find one in most every major city in the world. Walk around a small village in Latin America or the Middle East and you'll see people wearing Michael Jordan T-shirts or New York Yankees baseball caps or other American clothing. In turn, American culture is much more diverse than ever before. The restaurant listings in the telephone book of almost any American city reveal how many more ethnic restaurants are listed today than existed twenty years ago. More and more video stores specialize in foreign-language movies. School calendars for a high school in the Washington, D.C., area are now written in Spanish and Vietnamese as well as in English.

While driven in part by economics and communications, this cultural dimension especially reflects immigration patterns. It is the movement of peoples that in the long run may be the most profound dimension of globalization. We saw in Chapter 6 how U.S. immigration patterns changed over the course of the twentieth century, with the most dramatic shift in immigration coming from Latin America (which accounted for 4 percent of total immigration in 1920, but 50 percent in 1996) and from Asia (which grew from 1 percent to 27 percent over the same time period). Western Europe is also becoming much more ethnically heterogeneous due to increased immigration, especially from Africa, South Asia, and the Arab world. Other parts of the world have also seen substantial population shifts, as in Africa, where they have been largely the consequence of refugees fleeing ethnic wars and famines.

All of this poses a number of major policy *dilemmas.* Although each of these policy dilemmas has its own details and specific issues, in the broadest sense all are manifestations of the challenges of "governance" amid globalization. Global governance is not the same thing as global government. The latter term usually refers to ideas about making the United Nations and other international institutions into full governing structures, along with some sort of global constitution. That kind of withering of the nation-state is highly unlikely. *Global governance* is a broader and more flexible concept:

> Governance does not mean mere government. It means the framework of rules, institutions and established practices that set limits and give incentives for the behavior of individuals, organizations and firms.
>
> Governance signifies a diverse range of cooperative problem-solving arrangements, state and nonstate, to manage collective affairs. . . . It takes place through "laws, norms and architectures," not necessarily the field of action of governments alone but rather in association with one another, with multinational bodies, with corporate and sometimes academic research entities and NGOs. Such collective activity, structured or improvised, produces governance, sometimes without governmental activity.[6]

Even with this distinction between global governance and global government, the issue of sovereignty is raised by these new arrangements. Although sensitive and controversial, this issue is unavoidable. The complex dynamics and multiple dimensions of globalization lay bare the ways in which states are not as insulated or self-contained as traditional conceptions of state sovereignty presume. Whereas in Chapter 8 the issue was how much the international community could choose to intervene militarily and diplomatically in states without violating their sovereignty, here it is less a matter of intervention by other countries or international institutions than penetration of states by economic and other globalized forces. Prognostications about the "withering of the nation-state" may be overstated, but the powerful forces of globalization belie traditional conceptions of state sovereignty.

For a while in the 1990s there was a sense that the global governance agenda really was not that complex, that a ready and largely standard formula could be followed to maximize international trade and stabilize international finance to the benefit of all, and that the rest of the globalization agenda would benefit accordingly. Dubbed the "Washington consensus,"* the basic formula held that countries should give the highest priority to reducing barriers to international trade and investment, cutting their own government spending, reducing government regulations, promoting privatization, and taking other steps to gain the greater economic efficiency and competitiveness that would promote economic growth. Joseph Stiglitz, a former top Clinton administration and World Bank official and a co-winner of the 2001 Nobel Prize in economics, defines the Washington Consensus as follows:

> According to the Washington Consensus, growth occurs through liberalization, "freeing up" markets. Privatization, liberalization and macrostability are supposed to create a climate to attract investment, including from abroad. This investment creates growth. Foreign business brings with it technical expertise and access to foreign markets, creating new employment possibilities. Foreign companies also have access to sources of finance, especially important in those developing countries where local financial institutions are weak.[7]

This strategy relied largely on the "magic of the marketplace," tracing back to Adam Smith and his conception of the "invisible hand" by which growth would be maximized and all would benefit accordingly. In practice, though, the magic was not there as much or for as many as advertised. In the United States and other industrialized countries, labor groups and others saw themselves as "losers" in the game of globalization, while others were "winners." In many developing countries, both intrasocietal inequalities and the

---

*So called because of its ideological and programmatic roots in both the Clinton administration and the two Washington, D.C.-based international economic institutions, the International Monetary Fund (IMF) and the World Bank.

North-South income gap in the international system were seen as widening; worse, as the boom of the 1990s faded, a number of countries plunged into deep economic crises. This led to calls for "globalization with a human face":

> Inequality between countries has increased. The income gap between the fifth of the world's people living in the richest countries and the fifth in the poorest was 74 to 1 in 1997, up from 60 to 1 in 1990 and 30 to 1 in 1960. . . . Markets are neither the first nor the last word in human development. Many activities and goods that are critical to human development are provided outside the market—but these are being squeezed by the pressures of global competition. . . . When the market goes too far in dominating social and political outcomes, the opportunities and rewards of globalization spread unequally and inequitably—concentrating power and wealth in a select group of people, nations and corporations, marginalizing the others.[8]

Adding to the dilemma, all of these issues must compete for priority on the U.S. foreign policy agenda, especially since September 11, 2001. Writing in the mid-1990s, Thomas Friedman, the *New York Times* Pulitzer Prize–winning columnist, argued that "globalization is not the only thing influencing events in the world today, but to the extent that there is a North Star and a worldwide shaping force, it is this system."[9] Indeed on this and other issues we have discussed while the "September 10" foreign policy agenda was quite a full and pressing one, the war on terrorism has made it much harder to keep focus and priority on that agenda, as a matter both of relative priority and of 4 Ps trade-offs on some key issues of trade and sustainable development.

In sum, globalization is neither wholly positive nor wholly negative. It simply *is*. Policies can shape it, but they cannot stop or reverse it. The world is too interconnected to be disconnected. But the range of policy dilemmas also cannot be left to the ostensible "magic" of the marketplace. The globalization agenda will pose ever more complex and pressing policy challenges for American foreign policy.

International Trade

The year 1971 was the first year since 1893 that the United States ran a balance-of-payments deficit. Since then the American trade balance has been in surplus only twice, in 1973 and 1975 (see Table 9.1). The trade deficit first exceeded $100 billion in 1984. Since 1998 the trade deficit has shot up to record levels, as the table indicates.

TABLE 9.1	The U.S. Trade Balance, 1960–2002 (in millions of dollars)		
	Exports	Imports	Trade balance
1960	25,940	22,432	3,508
1970	56,640	54,386	2,254
1971	59,677	60,979	−1,302
1980	271,834	291,241	−19,407
1985	289,070	410,950	−121,880
1990	535,233	616,093	−80,860
1995	794,433	890,821	−96,338
1996	852,120	953,963	−101,843
1997	934,980	1,042,745	−107,765
1998	932,670	1,099,612	−166,933
1999	957,146	1,219,383	−262,238
2000	1,064,239	1,442,920	−378,681
2001	998,022	1,356,312	−358,290
2002	971,665	1,407,341	−435,676

Sources: U.S. Census Bureau, Foreign Trade Division, Foreign Trade Statistics, www.census.gov/foreign-trade/statistics/historical/gands.pdf accessed March 31, 2003.

The trade deficit goes up when the growth in the value of American exports does not keep up with the growth in the value of American imports. A number of factors contribute to this dynamic. Export growth is principally affected by three factors: economic growth rates in other countries and their consequent overall demand for goods and services, including for American exports; the openness of other countries' markets; and the competitiveness of American exporters against foreign domestic producers and other exporters. Import growth is affected by its own three factors: U.S. economic growth rates and the consequent overall demand for goods and services from both domestic and foreign producers; the openness of American markets; and the competitiveness of American domestic producers against foreign producers selling in American markets. Thus, for example, the 1997–2000 jump in the U.S. trade deficit was driven in large part by the discrepancy between the global recession following the 1997 Asian financial crisis and the continuing American domestic economic boom. The drop in the trade deficit in 2001 came about despite a decline in U.S. exports, because of a larger decline in U.S. imports due to recession at home. In 2002 imports went up, but exports kept going down.

Most economists and other analysts don't see a small-to-moderate U.S. trade deficit as a major problem, arguing that trade deficits actually help the world economy since they put more dollars in international circulation and the dollar serves as the principal transaction and reserve currency for world trade. Nevertheless, when the U.S. trade deficit runs over $300 billion and $400 billion, more concern gets expressed as to whether the signs indicate a structural and not just cyclical weakening of the American trade position.

What countries does the United States trade with? Figure 9.1 shows us, and also shows both change and continuity in American trade partners over the past two decades. The share of U.S. trade with western Europe has decreased slightly over those decades, although the Europeans still account for the largest regional share. Overall trade with the East Asia–Pacific region was about the same, but now fully 7 percent of it is with China, which does not even appear on the 1980 pie chart. Trade went up substantially with Canada and Mexico, a result of the North American Free Trade Agreement (NAFTA) having passed in 1993. Falling oil prices largely explain the relative declines in trade with both the Middle East and Africa (Algeria and Nigeria are major African oil producers).

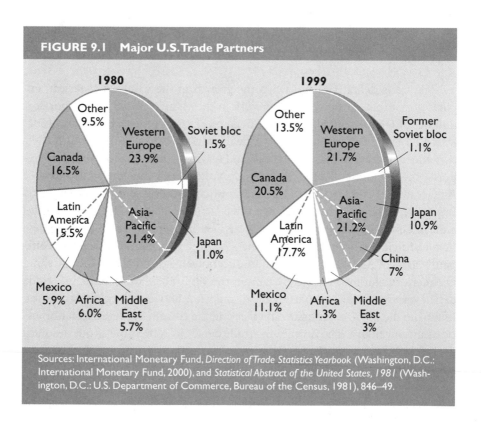

FIGURE 9.1   Major U.S. Trade Partners

1980

- Other 9.5%
- Western Europe 23.9%
- Soviet bloc 1.5%
- Canada 16.5%
- Latin America 15.5%
- Asia-Pacific 21.4%
- Japan 11.0%
- Mexico 5.9%
- Africa 6.0%
- Middle East 5.7%

1999

- Other 13.5%
- Western Europe 21.7%
- Former Soviet bloc 1.1%
- Canada 20.5%
- Asia-Pacific 21.2%
- Japan 10.9%
- Latin America 17.7%
- China 7%
- Mexico 11.1%
- Africa 1.3%
- Middle East 3%

Sources: International Monetary Fund, *Direction of Trade Statistics Yearbook* (Washington, D.C.: International Monetary Fund, 2000), and *Statistical Abstract of the United States, 1981* (Washington, D.C.: U.S. Department of Commerce, Bureau of the Census, 1981), 846–49.

TABLE 9.2   U.S. Dependence on Oil Imports as a Percentage of Total Oil Consumption, 1973 and 2002

Source of Oil	1973	2002
Imports	20%	45%
OPEC countries	13%	21%
Persian Gulf OPEC countries	5%	11%

Sources: Department of Energy, Energy Information Administration, *International Energy Annual 1988* (Washington, D.C.: U.S. Department of Energy, 1989), 31; www.census.gov/foreign-trade/PressRelease/current_press_release/exh3s.pdf, accessed December 10, 2002.

However, as Table 9.2 shows, U.S. dependence on imported oil has grown greater since 1973, the year that the first OPEC (Organization of Petroleum Exporting Countries) oil crisis hit. Despite the United States' having gone through one oil crisis after another—the 1979 OPEC crisis set off by the Iranian Revolution followed on the 1973 one, and there was another brief scare in 1990–91 during the Persian Gulf War—imports grew from about 20 percent of total U.S. oil consumption to 45 percent. And within that the shares for OPEC as a whole and for the Persian Gulf OPEC countries both almost doubled. Falling oil prices have made this oil dependence less costly economically, but it nevertheless poses serious issues for U.S. energy and economic security.

The Uruguay Round, the WTO, and the Doha Round

The 1994 Uruguay Round trade agreement was the transition from the General Agreement on Tariffs and Trade (GATT) to the *World Trade Organization* (WTO).* The WTO was designed as a significantly stronger multilateral institution than GATT had been. One aspect of this strengthening is its formalization as an institution. Whereas GATT always was more of a set of agreements than an international institution per se, the WTO has full legal standing and is very much a formal organization, with more than five hundred employees at its headquarters in Geneva, Switzerland. The WTO is also more inclusive than

---

*As with previous rounds of multilateral trade negotiations, this one was named for the locale (country or city) in which the negotiations were initiated.

was its predecessor. As of 2003, 146 countries were members of the WTO (accounting for over 90 percent of world trade), with many other countries in the process of applying for membership.

The Uruguay Round agreement also was significant in going further than previous GATT agreements had in two respects. One was the extension of free-trade policies to additional economic sectors. Whereas the GATT principally had covered trade in industrial and manufactured goods, the Uruguay Round also included agreements on trade in services (e.g., banking, insurance, some investment areas), intellectual property (e.g., movies, books, computer software, other inventions), and agriculture. The term "GATT" still is used to refer to the trade agreements covering industrial goods; it has now been supplemented by the GATS, General Agreement on Trade in Services; TRIPS, Trade Related Aspects of Intellectual Property Rights; and TRIMs, Trade Related Investment Measures. The free-trade provisions on agriculture are still limited but quite significant since, as one noted authority put it, "never before had there been anything more than token trade liberalization in this politically 'untouchable' sector."[10] And in the years since the Uruguay Round, additional agreements have been reached covering telecommunications and information technology equipment as well as further liberalization of financial services. All of these are areas in which American exporters are highly competitive and thus stand to gain from trade liberalization.

A second strengthening of the WTO trade regime is in its greater coverage of nontariff barriers (NTBs). Originally the GATT treaties dealt primarily with lowering tariffs. Since tariffs were the main barrier to trade, this made sense for a time. But as tariffs came down, some countries increasingly resorted to means other than tariffs for protecting their domestic markets from import competition—e.g., burdensome requirements for import licensing, special regulations and standards harder for imports to meet than for domestic products, quiet collusion among businesses, and cumbersome customs inspections. GATT did start to deal with NTBs in its 1979 Tokyo Round agreement, but the Uruguay Round went much further. Japan long has been the most egregious user of NTBs, and the United States was particularly interested in opening up Japanese markets. However, there is another side to this issue: The United States also has its own policies and practices that other countries see as NTBs.

One of the issues that has been the most controversial within the United States has been the greater regulatory authority given to the WTO. In the past the GATT secretariat could play an advisory and facilitative role in resolving trade disputes, but it lacked authority to impose a settlement. The WTO, by contrast, has been given dispute-settlement authority that is binding. Initial rulings by its panels can be appealed, at which point the final decision is made by a vote of the full membership. Each country has one vote, irrespective of its size. This is like the UN General Assembly, and quite different from other international economic institutions such as the IMF and the World Bank, where voting is proportional to a country's financial contribution. For the United States this means that, whereas it gets about an 18 percent vote in the IMF and the World Bank, in the WTO its vote counts no more than that of any other country.

Some WTO rulings have been made in favor of the United States, and some have been against. For example, among its early rulings, in 1997 the WTO supported the U.S. position that a European Union law restricting imports of beef with hormone residues was not based on science as claimed but rather was a disguised restriction on trade inconsistent with global trade rules and unfairly discriminating against American beef exports. On the other hand in 2003 the WTO ruled against the United States in a case brought by the European Union regarding steel tariffs enacted by the Bush administration in 2002.

In general, proponents of a strong dispute-settlement process believe that in the end it is beneficial because it adds to the sense of order that is critical for the growth of global trade. If American exporters are being treated unfairly, they now have a better chance of making their case on its merits to the WTO (a neutral third party) and having the dispute resolved in their favor. However, critics fear that any such benefits are outweighed by other countries' using and abusing the system against the United States, taking advantage of a forum in which the rules provide power in numbers. These critics would prefer the older way of doing things, whereby American power and status could be brought to bear, be it explicitly or implicitly, to help resolve trade disputes in the United States' favor. Moreover, in some of the other powers given to the WTO, such as the new "trade policy review mechanism," which for the first time subjects national trade policies to systematic and regular review, critics see the fostering of a global bureaucracy prone to inefficiencies and threatening American sovereignty. Proponents, on the other hand, see the WTO as a needed administrative and regulatory body for an age of such extensive trade interdependence.

In late 2001, two years after an earlier effort to begin a new round of global trade negotiations failed amid massive anti-globalization protests at the WTO summit in Seattle, the Doha Round of trade negotiations (named for the capital of Qatar) was launched. The Doha Declaration released at the first meeting stressed the overall free trade goal of "maintain[ing] the process of reform and liberalization of trade policies." Within that it pledged "to ensure that developing countries, and especially the least developed among them, secure a share of the growth of world trade commensurate with their needs of economic development." It also affirmed "sustainable development," and not just economic growth, as defining the scope of the agenda. The particulars of the Doha negotiating agenda pick up where the 1994 Uruguay Round left off: further reductions in tariffs and NTBs, further reduction of subsidies and other barriers to agricultural trade, further liberalization of trade in services (GATS), follow-on work on TRIMs, some key TRIPs measures including on pharmaceuticals and the global AIDS crisis, and issues involving trade and the environment, electronic commerce, and technology transfer, among others. January 1, 2005, was set as the deadline for reaching agreement.*

The George W. Bush administration came into office heralding itself as strongly supportive of free trade, but its record on this issue has been mixed. On the one hand it has made a proposal for the elimination of tariffs on manufactured goods by 2015. As announced by U.S. Trade Representative Robert Zoellick, this proposal would increase world income by $832 billion a year, almost two-thirds of which would go to developing countries. It would include consumer goods such as shoes and toys as well as industrial goods such as machinery. On the other hand, in 2002 the administration raised tariffs on steel to protect the American steel industry against imports from the European Union, Russia, Brazil, East Asia, and other lower-cost producers. There was no question that the American steel industry had been hit hard: more than one-third of the companies in the U.S. steel industry had gone into bankruptcy, 20 percent of domestic steel production capacity had been shut down, and more than 70,000 workers had lost their jobs. But questions were raised about whether higher tariffs were the optimal policy response, whether they were allowable under WTO rules, and whether such actions amount to hypocrisy on the part of the free-trade-preaching United States.

Similar debate has arisen over agricultural trade. In 2002 the Bush administration and Congress increased subsidies to American agriculture by $180 billion over the next decade. Although proponents claim that these subsidies fulfill a necessary economic need on the part of American farmers, critics see subsidies as a major hit on the U.S. budget deficit and a significant barrier to

---

*You can keep up with progress on the Doha Round through the Web sites of the WTO (www.wto.org), the U.S. Trade Representative (www.ustr.gov), and various NGOs and industry association groups also listed in our Web site Bibliography.

developing countries' efforts to compete in global markets. To be sure, the United States is far from the only offender. The European Union, Japan, and other developed countries have even heftier agricultural subsidies. All told, the developed world pays out over $300 billion a year in agricultural subsidies, which is seven times greater than what it gives out in foreign aid for economic development. By one estimate, a 40 percent reduction in agricultural protectionism on the part of developed countries would increase the world's real income by $60 billion per year.[11] Echoing the contrast between its far-reaching tariff-reduction proposal and its particular actions on steel tariffs, the Bush administration has put an ambitious proposal on the WTO table to reduce and eventually eliminate agricultural subsidies. Its argument is akin to that used to defend an arms race: as long as its competitors are "armed" with their agricultural subsidies, the United States will stay armed, but it will "disarm" if others also will. Critics, however, question how serious the Bush administration is about its WTO proposal.

THE FREE TRADE AREA OF THE AMERICAS   Another major issue on the U.S. trade agenda is the creation of the hemisphere-wide Free Trade Area of the Americas (FTAA). The proposed FTAA would build on the North American Free Trade Agreement (NAFTA), worked out in 1991–93 among the United States, Canada, and Mexico. The goal of creating an FTAA was set at the first Summit of the Americas, held in 1994 during the Clinton administration. It was reaffirmed at the April 2001 Summit of the Americas held in Quebec City, Canada. January 2005 was set as the deadline for reaching a full FTAA agreement.* A first step was taken in late 2002 with the signing of a free trade agreement between the United States and Chile.

The European Union (EU) remains the most extensive example of such regional economic integration. The FTAA will not go as far as the EU has, but it does seek to give countries in the Americas lower barriers for trading and investing with each other than will be given to countries from other regions. This kind of regional trade agreement is consistent with the overall WTO global system, so long as the barriers for those outside the region are no higher than those that characterize the WTO overall.

Like the WTO negotiations, the FTAA talks have been quite controversial. The 2001 Quebec City summit was marked by protests akin to those at the 1999 WTO summit in Seattle. These anti-globalization pressures led President

---

*The progress of the FTAA negotiations can be tracked via the same Web sites listed in the preceding footnote.

Bush to shift from earlier positions and state that "our commitment to open trade must be matched by a strong commitment to protecting our environment and improving labor standards."[12] An agreement was reached in Quebec City to create a special committee to foster dialogue with and input from NGOs and other representatives of civil society, making the FTAA "the first major trade negotiation where such a group has been established at the outset of the negotiations."[13]

Geo-Economics: Friends as Foes?

> The methods of commerce are displacing military methods—with disposable capital in lieu of firepower, civilian innovation in lieu of military-technical advancement, and market penetration in lieu of garrisons and bases. . . . It is true, of course, that, under whatever name, "geo-economics" has always been an important aspect of international life. In the past, however, the outdoing of others in the realm of commerce was overshadowed by strategic priorities and strategic modalities. . . . Now, however, as the relevance of military threats and military alliances wanes, geo-economic priorities and modalities are becoming dominant in state action.[14]

It is telling that this quotation is from a noted Cold War military strategist, Edward Luttwak. Luttwak does qualify his conception of geo-economics, noting that it does not mean that "World Politics is . . . about to give way to World Business," in the sense of private-sector MNCs and banks supplanting states as the key actors in international relations.[15] But it is a scenario of states competing with each other all the more to benefit from and influence the economic activities and choices of major corporations and banks in order to ensure states' own national economic positions.

And it is western Europe and Japan, the very countries that were the principal U.S. allies during the Cold War, that are now cast as the United States' principal competitors, and even potential adversaries. It isn't so much that economic tensions and conflicts with these countries are totally new. Quite a few trade disputes have erupted in the past, such as the 1960s "chicken wars" with western Europe over frozen chicken imports, or the 1970s "textile wrangle" and then the 1970s–80s Toyota-smashing auto wars with Japan. But as long as the common enemy of the Soviet Union lurked, these and other economic disputes were subordinated to the shared security interests of the Cold War. With the Soviet threat gone, though, relations have been opened to more divergence of interests, competition, and, at times, reinforcing cycles of resentment.

Japan in particular came to be seen as a potential economic adversary. A mid-1990s public-opinion poll found that 62 percent of Americans viewed economic competition from Japan as a "critical threat" to the United States.[16] Nor was this just some emotional reaction among the mass public. The challenge from Japan "is a real one," wrote one noted American strategist, citing the modified Clausewitz axiom that "economics is the continuation of war by other means."[17] These concerns were not just about the general trade balance, but were also about growing American dependence on Japan for technologies such as semiconductors that are key to the advanced weapons and communications systems on which American military might rests. Could the United States be sure, the nightmare question started to be asked, that in some future crisis when there might be disagreement, Japan wouldn't try to pressure the United States by embargoing semiconductors or other militarily vital technologies? As Japan fell back into its own economic problems starting in the late 1990s, these questions became less pressing. The underlying geo-economics, though, remained, and it may re-emerge as economic cycles run their course.

With the Europeans, both trade competition and conflicts have an even longer history and a more contentious current agenda. U.S.-European differences over agricultural trade were one of the issues that held up completion of the Uruguay Round in 1994. Incidents of economic espionage and "walls that have ears," as recounted in Perspectives on p. 510, have exacerbated existing tensions. Although this account is of French economic espionage against the United States, the spying also has gone in the other direction; in one incident France expelled an American embassy official on economic espionage grounds. Major differences have also arisen over economic sanctions, especially when the United States has tried to punish European countries and companies for not going along with U.S. policies.

Still, concerns along these lines shouldn't become alarmist. The United States, western Europe, and Japan continue to share a fundamental consensus on the mutual benefits of the global free-trade system. Compliance with its rules is still the norm on all sides. When one or another trade dispute has brought the parties too close to the abyss of trade wars, they have shown the ability to find compromises and other working agreements. Moreover, broader foreign policy and security considerations still glue the alliance together and remind all parties that power and peace interests have not gone away and at times must be weighed against the benefits of opening another Toys 'R Us or selling more cellular phones. Finally, some argue that, while it is true that Japan and others don't play by strict free-market rules, focusing too

PERSPECTIVES
PERSPECTIVES
PERSPECTIVES

"ECONOMIC SUMMIT SUBPLOT: DO FRENCH WALLS HAVE EARS?"

LYON, France, June 29—As *Air Force One* descended the other night for the opening of the 22nd annual summit meeting of the world's biggest industrial nations, a security agent gathered the small army of Cabinet members and aides accompanying President Clinton and delivered a clear warning.

Enjoy the two- and three-star restaurants, he said, and the fine Beaujolais. But bring all your documents with you—not only classified material, but anything that sheds new light on Washington's economic strategies.

"He just wanted to remind us that this is France we're visiting," one of Mr. Clinton's economic aides said during the summit meeting. "When it comes to economic espionage, no one is any better".....

And more than ever before, wherever trade negotiators go, it is widely assumed that bugs, miniature video cameras and tapped telephones are there to greet them....

"We've certainly held summits in places where we've had a problem," he said.

It's not just summit meetings. Ms. Barshefsky [the U.S. trade representative] visited Beijing two weeks ago to discuss Washington's accusations of piracy of software music and videos. When American security agents swept her room, others in the Administration say, they found so much electronic gear they started to laugh. How did she deal with it?

"I got dressed fast," Ms. Barshefsky said.

Surveillance is a two-way street, of course. Only last year the French caught the Central Intelligence Agency station in Paris trying to steal a variety of economic secrets, from the details of the French position on global trade talks to a host of other matters. They expelled several agents and the station chief. The incident led to a major internal investigation within the C.I.A., not only because of the embarrassment, but because the United States Ambassador in Paris, Pamela Harriman, had been kept in the dark about the operation until the arrests.

(*Continued on page 511*)

("**Economic Summit Subplot**" *Continued from page 510*)

And last year in Geneva, American intelligence was working hard to discover up-to-the-minute details of Japan's position on a tense set of negotiations about selling more American cars and auto parts in Japan. When news of that operation leaked several months later, the Japanese felt compelled to feign shock and issue a protest. The Administration asked the Federal Bureau of Investigation to conduct an investigation— not of the espionage itself, but of how the word of it got out. . . .

Such back-room talks over chips or the proper powers of the World Trade Organization lack the drama of the arms control negotiations of the 80's and almost never involve issues of life or death. That is one reason American intelligence agencies are so reluctant to dive fully into the economic espionage business.

But they know they have little choice: one study after another about the future of intelligence identifies economic threats—from a rising China, a resurgent Japan, a European Union that begins to act truly like a union—as a major challenge of the next decade, along with fighting terrorism and drugs.

Source: David E. Sanger, "Economic Subplot: Do French Walls Have Ears?" *New York Times,* July 1, 1996, pp. A1, D2. Copyright © 1996 by The New York Times. Reprinted by permission.

much on retaliation diverts attention and resources from what the United States can and must do in its own domestic policy to maintain international competitiveness. Policies to promote the development and commercialization of new technologies, improve the educational system, and other such "self-help" measures are more essential to the U.S. geo-economic position than anything Japan or the European Union could or should do.

International Finance

U.S. goals for the international financial system remain fundamentally the same as when the system was set up at the end of World War II: help provide the monetary and financial stability necessary for global economic growth and particularly for the growth of international trade; avoid the monetary versions of economic nationalism and protectionism that lead countries to compete more than cooperate; and in these and other ways contribute to international peace and stability. The system as designed continues to be grounded in free-market principles but with sufficient international management and regulation to prevent or at least correct the imperfections of market forces. This management is carried out primarily through the multilateral institutional structure of the International Monetary Fund (IMF) with the United States in a lead role, and with Japan and western Europe also playing key roles.

But although the goals remain largely unchanged, the complexities and controversies inherent in achieving them have increased substantially. We see these dynamics and dilemmas in the recurring international financial crises of the second half of the 1990s, and in U.S. policy debates about the IMF and the future of international financial and monetary policy.

1990s Financial Crises

The world economy was wracked beginning in the mid-1990s by a chain of financial crises in Asia and Latin America. The first of these crises hit Mexico in 1995. The Mexican peso collapsed, losing almost half its value in less than a month. In this crisis as well as the others, primary responsibility lay with the national government itself. In the Mexican case a peasant uprising in the state of Chiapas, scandals involving the ruling PRI party, and doubts about the new government of President Ernesto Zedillo fed a climate of political instability. The problems of the Mexican economy were largely homegrown, the result of inefficient policies, government corruption, and profligate spending on imports. News that these problems were more severe than realized was the catalyst that pushed the peso into its plunge and set the crisis off.

A key factor making the crisis as bad as it was was the problem of "hot money"—short-term investments in stocks, bonds, and currencies seeking quick returns. Such investments are held by investors ready and able to shift these funds from one country to another at the slightest doubt about the rate of return. Hot money had been surging into Mexico, so much so that it was second only to China in the amount of foreign investment entering the country between 1990 and 1994. When the worse-than-expected economic news broke, on top of the concerns about political stability, both Mexican and foreign investors rushed their funds out of Mexican financial markets.

The Mexican crisis hit home for the United States. The success of NAFTA was at stake, just a year after the hard-fought political battle to pass the agreement. Concerns were raised about "contagion" effects spreading to other countries in the Western Hemisphere. In putting together a financial rescue package the Clinton administration faced substantial congressional opposition, which claimed that the proposed rescue plan was misusing American taxpayers' money to "bail out" Mexico and Wall Street. The administration therefore resorted to a bit of an end-run to provide much-needed aid to Mexico by drawing on the president's discretionary authority to meet an economic emergency without additional congressional legislation. Working with the IMF the administration put together a package of credits worth $50 billion, of which about $20 billion came from the United States.

At one level this was a success story: Mexico got its economy stabilized and growing again. It paid the credits back to the United States ahead of schedule. The U.S. Treasury even made a $500 million profit from the interest. The United States and the IMF showed the capacity for financial crisis management. But questions remained about crisis prevention. Why hadn't there been an earlier response, before the situation became a crisis? The top U.S. official at the IMF criticized the organization for failing to provide early warning, for not being "on top of" deteriorating economic conditions and not having "expressed more concern about the trend and urged Mexican authorities to be cautious in monetary policy."[18] Others criticized the United States for itself not being sufficiently attuned to the economic and political problems of its neighbor and trade partner. Furthermore, although the end run around Congress had worked this time, the overall issue of the IMF remained unresolved in Pennsylvania Avenue diplomacy. And, as we would soon see, the hot money problem was still there in other national and international markets.

The Asian financial crisis that struck in mid-1997 involved not just one country but a number of them. It started in Thailand and spread to Indonesia and South Korea. All had been success stories, "Asian tigers," exemplars of the newly industrialized countries that the United States hailed in the 1970s and 1980s as proof that capitalism worked better than socialism or other forms of statism. But the underside of East Asian capitalism, with its speculative investments, cronyism and corruption, overconsumption of imports, and excessive debt, now burst the bubbles. This crisis proved much less controllable than the Mexican one. In the last half of 1997 the Thai, Korean, and Indonesian stock markets fell by 33–45 percent. Their currencies (the baht, won, and rupiah, respectively) fell by even larger percentages. In all three cases overall growth of GDP was negative, meaning their economies were shrinking and massive numbers of working- and middle-class families were losing their jobs and most of their savings.

U.S. interests were affected in a number of ways by this crisis. American banks and mutual funds were heavily invested in Asian markets. American companies had factories, fast-food restaurants, computer programming, and other major investments at risk. American exporters lost some of their fastest-growing markets, accounting for a big chunk of the growth in the 1998–2000 trade deficit. And politically all three countries were U.S. allies. In Indonesia the government of President Suharto fell; this had the potential to be a positive change, given Suharto's thirty-two-year-long corrupt and authoritarian rule, but the immediate effect was to cause more chaos and rising political violence. There also was continuing concern about the spread of the crisis to Japan, which was already having serious economic problems that, if worsened, could spiral the crisis dangerously downward.

Then two other major countries, Russia and Brazil, joined the list of financial crisis victims. The Russian crisis hit in late 1998; the ruble had tumbled by 282 percent by December 1998 and 324 percent by May 1999. Even though there was less foreign investment at stake in Russia than in the Mexican and Asian cases, the Russian crisis had a "last straw" effect on investor psychology and set off a sharp drop on Wall Street, with the Dow Jones industrial average plummeting more than 20 percent. Suddenly the crisis was brought home to average Americans, as they watched their retirement funds, college savings for their children, and other nest eggs shrink with each passing day. The stock market restabilized later in 1998 only to have Brazil—another heralded economic success story, the world's eighth-largest economy, and a potential contagion to other parts of Latin America—go into financial crisis in early 1999. Two years later it was Argentina, albeit less as a direct contagion from Brazil and more as a manifestation of its own extensive fiscal and financial problems.

In the Asian, Russian, Brazilian, and Argentinean cases IMF rescue packages were put together, but they were less effective than in the Mexican case. There were a number of reasons for this, among which were greater doubts than before about both U.S. and IMF policy.

Policy Debates over the IMF

When a country faces financial crisis, the IMF usually makes credits and other support available, but also insists that the recipient state agree to tight fiscal policies, outright austerity measures, and economic reforms as a condition of receiving the IMF assistance. To the IMF, overspending, inefficiency, corruption, and other economic ineptitude is what gets countries into financial fixes, and unless major reforms are put in place any added money likely will be wasted. In the 1995 Mexican peso crisis, for example, the IMF conditioned its financing on Mexican agreement to implement stringent fiscal and monetary policies and take other steps to stabilize the exchange rate and reform the economy. This is the financial piece of the Washington consensus discussed earlier. Too much government regulation and spending are seen as the problem, and greater deregulation of banks and other financial markets are considered key to the solution. These and other policy guidelines are established as "conditionalities" that must be met for a country to receive IMF loans and credits. The IMF then disburses the financing in "tranches" at designated intervals, conditional on compliance and performance.

Two quite different critiques are offered of the IMF formula. One is that the Washington Consensus had it wrong.[19] It overvalued the benefits of freeing markets up and overassumed that what was good for capital would be good for developing world economies. It relied too much on "one size fits all" and did not tailor strategies to different national political and economic contexts and structures. It also was too quick to cut employment, health, and other government services that provided a safety net for those most in need. In these and other ways, the medicine is too harsh; in the name of saving the patient it risks killing him. Here are countries already in serious crisis and the immediate effect of IMF austerity is to ratchet up unemployment, push up the prices of food and other staples, and cut way back on the social safety net governments can provide. There has to be a better way to get reform, it is argued, a more graduated approach that still has room for necessary social services.

The other critique believes that the IMF's readiness to bail countries out when they get in financial trouble creates a version of the classic problem of a "moral hazard." This means that in the name of providing help, incentives for the very behavior and actions that are to be encouraged are in fact reduced by showing that, if things get bad enough, someone else will step in to reduce the risks and lower the costs. Might the very success of the 1995 bailout of Mexico have led the Thai, Korean, and Indonesian governments to think that they could continue on their profligate and corrupt ways, for is real trouble hit, the IMF would be there for them, too? Perhaps U.S. banks and mutual funds felt the same false sense of security. States and others in similar situations are more likely to learn and change their ways, this argument claims, if they have to pay the price of their mistakes.

Another level of the debate goes to the very viability of the IMF as the principal multilateral institution for managing the international financial system. Here, too, we get two quite contrasting sets of arguments. One view is that the IMF is not powerful enough, and that a much stronger international financial institution needs to be created, possibly a global central bank modeled after the U.S. Federal Reserve. International rules and norms also need to be changed to allow countries, as a French official put it, "to bring the Frankenstein of deregulated global financial markets under control."[20] This could include policies such as capital controls, long prohibited as inconsistent with free markets and unfettered capital flows, but now advocated by some in at least their partial form as a necessary check on the extraordinary power that markets wield.

Others, such as former treasury secretary Robert Rubin, concurred on the need for change but questioned whether such sweeping new proposals would not end up creating a host of their own problems. Instead they have been pushing for reforms to strengthen the IMF in a more step-by-step manner. Among their proposals are policies requiring greater "transparency," that is, more disclosure of financial information to the IMF both by banks and other private-sector actors and by national governments; new powers for the IMF to act preventively before a full financial crisis hits; and increases in the funds available to the IMF.

Further compounding this debate are broader shifts in international monetary power. Although the United States still is unquestionably the world's strongest financial power, Europe is seeing its relative financial power increase. With the European Union having developed a common currency (the euro), this is likely to be even truer in the years to come as the euro competes with the dollar as the currency of choice for international transactions and national financial reserves. As Joan Spero and Jeffrey Hart write, "although the United States is still necessary, it is not sufficiently powerful to fulfill its earlier role. . . . In a world in which monetary power is more widely dispersed, management will depend not on the preferences of a dominant power but on the negotiations of several key powers."[21]

Sustainable Development

Sustainable development has been defined as a policy approach that "meets the needs of the present without compromising the ability of future generations to meet their own needs." Its conception of "needs of the present" has two main elements: an emphasis on issues of global inequality and "the essential needs of the world's poor, to which overriding priority should be given"; and a broadening of the agenda beyond just the economic aspects of development to also include issues of "human development" and "human security" such as AIDS and other global public health crises, hunger and nutrition, and education and literacy. "The real wealth of a nation is its people," states a major UN report. "And the purpose of development is to create an enabling environment for people to enjoy long, healthy and creative lives. This simple but powerful truth is too often forgotten in the pursuit of material and financial wealth."[22]

The other key part of the definition of sustainable development is its reference to future generations—a reference that is particularly relevant when it comes to the global environment. Can it really be considered development in the positive sense of the term if the economic growth rates achieved today come as a result of overexploitation and despoliation of natural resources that will impose major costs and serious risks on future generations? Just as the first part of the definition of sustainable development broadens our conception, this second part gives it a longer-term time frame. All told, the conception calls for policy-makers to look beyond immediate pocketbook concerns, to look down the road and across the planet. Across the planet at poverty and the dire conditions in which billions of people live. Down the road to future generations for whom we are but stewards of the environment and creators of policies that have lasting legacies.

9.2

Poverty and the Human Condition

Although there were some economic-development success stories during the Cold War, overall not a lot of progress was made in reducing Third World poverty, in either absolute or relative terms. One of the most telling absolute measures is the World Bank's "human development index," which quantifies the quality of life for people around the world by tabulating income data (per capita GDP), basic nutrition, access to clean water and health services, life expectancy, adult literacy rates, and other indicators of the human condition. As of the late 1990s, of 123 developing countries, only 19 made the "high" human development category, while 68 were in the "medium" and 36 in the "low" category. "Low" human development meant an average real GDP per capita of $1,269 per year or less, life expectancy of 57 years or less, only 68 percent or less of the population with access to such basic needs as clean water, and an adult literacy rate of less than half the population.[23]

The most telling relative measure is the widening of the income gap between North and South. Whereas in 1960 about 70 percent of global income went to the richest 20 percent of countries, by 1990 this was up to 83 percent. Put another way, the ratio of the richest to the poorest had gone from 30:1— itself enormously unequal—to 64:1. Despite the end of the Cold War and other developments that seemed propitious for progress against Third World poverty and social ills, this overall trend continues. For every country that has had its per capita income go up in the 1990s, there are almost three that had it go down. The map on p. 522, showing regions and countries drawn according to income, shows how disproportional global income distribution continues to be.

Moreover, the intra-country income gap between the "haves" and the "have-nots" has been getting wider. In Latin America the income share of the richest 20 percent of the population now is more than 50 percent, while the poorest 20 percent receive only about 5 percent of their nations' income. One in three people in the region lives on less than $2 a day. Nor is the situation any better in economic-growth "success" stories like China, where the progress that was made in the 1980s in reducing poverty leveled off in the 1990s, leaving more than 25 percent of the population, some 350 million people, living on less than $1 a day.

Others of the '90s success stories have come crashing down. One major example is Brazil. Its president in the 1990s, Fernando Enrique Cardoso, was seen by many as epitomizing the ostensibly newly emerging Third World consensus in favor of capitalism. Back in the 1970s, as Professor Cardoso, he was the co-author of *Development and Underdevelopment in Latin America*, a leading book critiquing capitalism and favoring more socialistic policies that was used in college courses around the world. Yet as president of Brazil he was the champion of policies favoring private foreign investment, reducing the role of the state in the economy, and other strongly pro-capitalist and free-market measures. The initial popularity of these policies got him elected and re-elected. However, when the 1999 financial crisis hit Brazil, Cardoso's popularity fell and many began questioning whether free market-ism really was the optimal economic strategy. Over the next few years this went beyond questioning to widespread disillusionment among Brazilians culminating in the presidential election victory in 2002 of Luis Inacio Lula da Silva, a labor leader and globalization critic who had never even come close in three previous tries at the presidency. While Lula did moderate his positions somewhat this time around, the thrust remained one that was more akin to Professor Cardoso than President Cardoso.

Others on the world scene also have raised their voices on behalf of the world's poor. Pope John Paul II, in a speech to the UN General Assembly, put much of the blame on the developed world—and by implication particularly the United States—for its "consumerist culture," its "unjust criteria in the distribution of resources and production," and its politics "to safeguard special interest groups." UN Secretary-General Kofi Annan, in a speech to the 1999 World Economic Forum, a conclave of the world's leading government officials and international business leaders, warned that until and unless people in poor countries can gain confidence in the global economy, it "will be fragile and vulnerable—vulnerable to backlash from all the '-isms' of our post–Cold War world: protectionism, populism, nationalism, ethnic chauvinism, fanaticism and terrorism." The key to gaining that confidence, he stressed, is to break away from the idea that the choice is only "between a global market driven . . . by calculations of short-term profit and one which has a human face."[24]

Some of this goes back to trade issues and the declining terms of trade between the industrialized, technology-driven economies of the North and the raw materials–based economies of the South. Spero and Hart show that between 1965 and 1991 the average terms of trade deteriorated almost 50 percent for the poorest Third World countries and about 30 percent for those considered middle-income developing countries.[25] In other words, the poorest countries were getting half as much value for their exports to the developed world, in terms of the prices they could charge compared to the prices they had to pay; middle-income countries were getting only about 70 percent value compared to 1965.

The challenge for Lula in Brazil and for other proponents of alternative policies goes back to our earlier discussion of the overall globalization debate and how to shape it but not fall back into trying to stop it. Another finding made by Spero and Hart is a very strong correlation between economic growth rates and "outward" rather than "inward" national economic policies—i.e., policies open to foreign trade and investment rather than closed off through import substitution, expropriation of foreign investment, and the like. The difference was almost twofold between the 8–9 percent average growth rate for those Third World countries most outwardly oriented, and 3–4 percent for those most inward oriented.[26]

The need to attract foreign capital also remains. The fact is that with U.S. and other sources of foreign aid still so limited, foreign investors will continue to be the major source of the capital that developing countries need. Inflows of private capital into developing countries surged from a mere $18.4 billion in 1987 to $225 billion in 1996. Things leveled off and even dropped some amid recent crises. And it may be that more common ground emerges on which foreign investors and developing countries can work out terms and conditions more consistent with sustainable development. Still developing countries know that they will continue to have to pay attention to the credo, as Thomas Friedman put it, "Don't mess with Moody's," referring to the investor service that establishes the credit ratings for companies and now for countries: "In the 1960s the most important visitor a developing country could have was the head of AID [the Agency for International Development], the U.S. agency that doled out foreign aid. In the 1970s and '80s the most important visitor a developing country could have was from the IMF to help restructure its economy. In the 1990s the most important visitor a developing country can have is from Moody's Investors Service Inc."[27]

Overpopulation, World Hunger, and Global Public Health

The *global population problem* has grown worse.[28] World population is now about 6.3 billion. Population growth in the 1990s was the fastest in the 250 years that such measurements have been taken. In 1800, world population was 1 billion. It took 125 years to reach 2 billion (1925). It then took 35 years to reach 3 billion (1960). Since then the intervals have been 14 years (4 billion, 1974), 13 years (5 billion, 1987), and 12 years (6 billion, 1999). Not only is the sheer size of these numbers a problem in itself, but more than 90 percent of this population growth is in the Third World. Contrast the map on p. 522, showing the world drawn proportional to population distribution, with the map on p. 523, based on income distribution. In part the situation in the income-distribution map is caused by that in the population-distribution one: rapid population growth means that economic growth rates must be even higher to register positive on a per capita basis. Nevertheless, the two maps together provide a graphic indication of global inequality.

The Bush administration reverted back to the old Reagan policy of making American aid to international population planning heavily contingent on the UN's and other multilateral agencies' abiding by U.S. prohibitions on funding abortion. Even though Congress had appropriated $34 million for the UN Population Fund, the Bush administration froze the money. It equated such foreign aid that might be used directly or indirectly to support abortions in other countries to the debate over federal funding for abortion within the United States. China's "one-child per family" policies, which include forced abortions and involuntary sterilization, were a partial reason for these stipulations, but the broader context was an externalization of America's own domestic politics on abortion and the Bush administration's desire to support a key issue on the conservative agenda. Others in the world rejected as a matter of principle such an effort to apply one's own domestic policies (and politics) to the rest of the world. They also opposed it on substantive grounds. The UN Population Fund limited its work in China to counties where the one-child policy is no longer enforced, and more generally audited its budget so as not to spend any American money on China programs. Yet the withholding of the $34 million, which represented 13 percent of the agency's budget, threatened a wide global impact: "2 million unwanted pregnancies, 800,000 induced abortions, 4,700 maternal deaths and 77,000 infant and child deaths."[29] Similar issues arose in December 2002 at the regional Asian and Pacific Population Conference, where the Bush administration pushed its anti-abortion positions but was rebuffed by votes of 31 to 1 and 32 to 1 on key resolutions.[30]

Hunger also remains a huge problem around the world. A 2003 report by the World Health Organization (WHO) pointed to hunger as the leading cause of death in the world. Close to one billion people, it is estimated, are chronically undernourished—that's one out of every six humans. The problem, though, is less one of food production than of food distribution. Mid-1970s predictions of falling food supplies have been proven wrong by advances in agricultural sciences and technology. But for a number of reasons, including declining foreign aid, other financial problems, the ravages of wars, and political actions by many Third World governments, the world's food does not reach the people who need it the most.

GLOBAL AIDS   Another increasingly controversial global issue is the spread of *AIDS*. The figures are staggering. More than 42 million people worldwide are infected with HIV. This is more than 50 percent higher than was predicted at the beginning of the 1990s. In 2002 about 3 million people died of AIDS, and 5 million became newly infected (see Dynamics of Choice on page 524).

More than two-thirds of those infected are in sub-Saharan Africa. In the country of Botswana, 36 percent of all adults are infected. In the Republic of South Africa the figure is about 22 percent. In India the total numbers are not as great but the growth rate of new cases is alarmingly high. Russia also now has an alarmingly high AIDS growth rate, as does China. It is truly, as the UN Joint Program on HIV/AIDS (UNAIDS) has called it, "a global epidemic."

At one level the policy challenge is a global public health one, and at that a twofold challenge of both prevention and treatment. Those who have already contracted the disease must be provided with treatment. At the same time education and access to health care must be improved and other measures taken to prevent the further spread of AIDS.

Increasingly, two other dimensions also are being recognized. The AIDS crisis also has a security dimension, in that states in which it is so widespread also risk being destabilized politically. Obviously this threatens the people of those states; it also can pose security threats to American interests when these

Global Population Patterns

Japan 126

Philippines 72

China 1,215

Vietnam 75

Indonesia 197

Bangladesh 122

Thailand 60

AUSTRALIA

ASIA

Iran 63

Russian Federation 148

India 945

Pakistan 134

Ethiopia 58

Turkey 63

Ukraine 51

AFRICA

EUROPE

Germany 82

Egypt 59

Nigeria 115

United Kingdom 59

France 58

Italy 57

Brazil 161

NORTH AMERICA

CENTRAL AMERICA

SOUTH AMERICA

United States 265

Mexico 93

1996
World Population =
5,754,000,000

Note: All figures in millions.

Source: World Bank, 1998 World Development Indicators (Washington, D.C.: World Bank, 1998), 42–44.

Global Income Distribution

1997 World GDP = $28.2 trillion

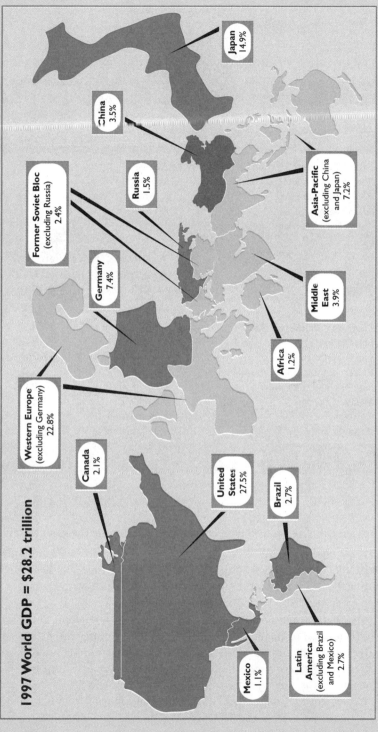

Japan 14.9%

China 3.5%

Asia-Pacific (excluding China and Japan) 7.2%

Former Soviet Bloc (excluding Russia) 2.4%

Russia 1.5%

Germany 7.4%

Middle East 3.9%

Africa 1.2%

Western Europe (excluding Germany) 22.8%

Canada 2.1%

United States 27.5%

Brazil 2.7%

Mexico 1.1%

Latin America (excluding Brazil and Mexico) 2.7%

Note: The *World Development Report* does not include o has no data for Iran, Iraq, Bahrain, Kuwait, and Qatar. GDP figures included from those countries are from the following years: 1991 (Iran, Kuwait, Bahrain, Qatar), 1992 (Iraq).

Source: World Bank, *World Development Report: Knowledge for Development, 1998/99* (Oxford: Oxford University Press, 1999), 212; *World Statistical Pocketbook* (New York: United Nations, 1995), 85–86, 114, 150.

DYNAMICS OF CHOICE

The AIDS Crisis

GLOBAL CRISIS

People living with HIV/AIDS	42 million
People newly infected in 2002	5 million
AIDS deaths in 2000	3.1 million
AIDS deaths overall	27.4 million

REGIONAL PATTERNS

Region	Number of current HIV/AIDS cases	Percentage of total world cases
Sub-Saharan Africa	29.4 million	70.0
South and Southeast Asia	6.0 million	14.3
Latin America	1.5 million	3.6
North America	1.0 million	2.4
Eastern Europe and Central Asia	1.2 million	2.8
East Asia and the Pacific	1.2 million	2.8
Western Europe	0.7 million	1.4
Caribbean	0.44 million	1.0
Australia and New Zealand	0.015 million	<1.0

Source: UNAIDS (www.unaids.org).

states are U.S. friends and allies or when they become the kind of failed states in which anarchy reigns and terrorism can find safe haven. This point was made and concern raised about AIDS and other global infectious diseases in a landmark 2000 study by the Central Intelligence Agency:

> The persistent infectious disease burden is likely to aggravate and, in some cases, may even provoke economic decay, social fragmentation, and political destabilization in the hardest hit countries in the developing and former communist worlds. . . .
>
> The infectious disease burden will weaken the military capabilities of some countries—as well as international peacekeeping efforts—as their armies and recruitment pools experience HIV infection rates ranging from 10 to 60 percent. . . .

Infectious diseases are likely to slow socioeconomic development in the hardest hit developing and former communist countries and regions. This will challenge democratic development and transitions and possibly contribute to humanitarian emergencies and civil conflicts.

Infectious disease-related embargoes and restrictions on travel and immigration will cause friction among and between developed and developing countries.[31]

The spread of AIDS also threatens economic development. How can a country succeed in economic development when it is losing such large numbers of citizens, often at the most productive stages of their working lives? As UN Secretary-General Kofi Annan stated in a speech to the African summit on HIV/AIDS,

> Disease, like war, is not only a product of underdevelopment. It is also one of the biggest obstacles preventing our societies from developing as they should. This is especially true of HIV/AIDS, which takes its biggest toll among young adults—the age group that normally produces most, and has the main responsibility for rearing the next generation. That is why AIDS has become not only the primary cause of death on this continent, but our biggest development challenge.[32]

Even more immediate are the added costs of dealing with the ravaging consequences; consider, for example, the thousands of children orphaned by AIDS, 92 percent of whom are in Africa.

Secretary-General Annan called for an increase in global AIDS spending to $7–10 billion a year. Compared to current levels of spending this would amount to a major increase; on the other hand it would still equal only about 1 percent of total world military spending. The United States increased its global AIDS spending by almost 80 percent between 2001 and 2003, yet this still only amounted to $1.3 billion, with only $200 million for the global AIDS fund. In his 2003 State of the Union address President Bush set the goal even higher at $15 billion over the next five years, of which $10 billion would be in new commitments. This still falls short of the goals set by Secretary-General Annan. To be sure, it is not just an issue for U.S. policy. Other countries also have obligations to meet. The UN has been working to better coordinate its various agencies working in this area, such as UNICEF and the World Health Organization. Governments in countries with high HIV/AIDS rates such as South Africa also need to develop more effective policies. Major pharmaceutical companies are grappling with their pricing of AIDS drugs, and balancing private intellectual property rights and the rights of afflicted nations and peoples to affordable life-saving health care is a major issue in the current WTO

Doha trade round. Private foundations, led by the Gates Foundation (Bill Gates), have been providing substantial funding for treatment and prevention programs. A truly global and high priority effort is required, on which the United States as well as the United Nations are being looked to for leadership.

Nor is AIDS the only global public health crisis. Tuberculosis still kills over two million people every year, malaria another one million. Since 1973 over 30 new diseases have emerged, including SARS (severe acute respiratory syndrome) and the West Nile virus. Twenty old diseases, believed to have been wiped out, have re-emerged. While some of these hit the United States directly, the greatest impact continues to be in the developing world. Among the most challenging policy questions raised by these and other global public health issues is the "10/90" inequality: that is, that 90 percent of investments in health care go toward diseases that primarily affect the 10 percent of the world population in the richer and more developed countries, whereas only 10 percent of health care investments go toward diseases that primarily affect the other 90 percent in the world's poorer and less developed countries.

U.S. FOREIGN AID POLICY   Views of American foreign aid policy vary widely. Consider on the one hand the positive claims made by the Bush administration:

- The United States leads the world in official development assistance ($11 billion);
- It leads the world in humanitarian assistance and food aid ($2.5 billion);
- It gives the most in charitable donations to developing countries ($4 billion);
- It imports the most from developing countries ($449 billion);
- It invests the most private capital in developing countries ($36 billion annual average, 1997–2000).[33]

On the other hand, domestic and foreign critics raise a number of points. One is that the sheer size of the American economy explains statistics such as these when taken as absolute numbers. They argue that the United States fares more poorly on relative measures. It falls well short, for example, of the international standard of foreign aid budgets equaling 0.7 percent of a country's GDP. Critics also take issue with the criteria the United States has tended to use in deciding to which countries to allocate its foreign aid. Officially, of course, U.S. policy always has favored Third World economic development. But in reality, for virtually the entire Cold War this goal was a much lower priority than global containment. This is evident when you consider who received the bulk of U.S. Cold War foreign aid: geopolitically strategic countries like South Vietnam in the 1960s and 1970s, Israel and Egypt since the late 1970s, and El Salvador in the 1980s. It also was evident in the much greater sums spent on military aid than on economic aid.

With the Cold War over, some hoped that more of U.S. foreign aid would be redirected to economic development. Instead, during the 1990s the United States used the end of the Cold War as a rationale to cut back on rather than reallocate its foreign aid. In inflation-adjusted terms the decline has been close to 50 percent. U.S. aid to Central America, for example, fell from $226 million a year in the 1980s to $26 million in 1997. The politics here was predictable in some respects but paradoxical in others. One poll found that 75 percent of the American public believed that too much was spent on foreign aid, and only 4 percent thought that too little was spent (17 percent thought things were about right). But whereas most people thought that foreign aid accounted for 15 percent of the federal budget, the actual figure is less than 1 percent.[34] One set of follow-up questions asked respondents how much of the federal budget *should* be spent in foreign aid, and got the extraordinarily high answer of about 13 percent. Yet when the question was phrased differently—"Now imagine that the U.S. spends 1 percent of the federal budget on foreign aid. Would you feel that this is too little, too much or about right?"—46 percent said it was "about right," and only 34 percent considered it "too little." This is better than the 75 percent "too much" and 4 percent "too little" of the original poll cited, but nevertheless gives some pause.

In March 2002 the Bush administration announced a new foreign aid strategy in the form of what it called the Millennium Challenge Account. This represented the largest increase in U.S. foreign aid in decades, with proposed increases in core assistance to developing countries of 50 percent over three years, reaching an additional $5 billion by fiscal year 2006. Much of this increase was to go into the Millennium Challenge Account and would be allocated based on assessments of how committed governments were to economic and political reform. The strategy was to have "aid linked to sound policies," to ensure that countries receiving aid were rooting out corruption, investing in health care and education, and fostering private enterprise and entrepreneurship. "The Millennium Challenge Account recognizes that economic development assistance can be successful only if it is linked to sound policies in developing countries. . . . [I]n countries where poor public policy dominates, aid can harm the very citizens it is meant to help—crowding out private investment and perpetuating failed policies."[35]

On this issue many NGOs and others usually critical of Bush administration policies have been largely supportive. The Center for Global Development, a Washington-based NGO, praised the Millenium Challenge Account proposal as "very positive." It concurred with the emphasis on conditioning aid on good governance and sound economic policies. It called the balance between criteria set by the United States and greater emphasis on recipient countries' developing their *own* "business plans" as "revolutionary change in U.S. foreign assistance."[36] This NGO and others did stress, however, that many details of the plan remained to be worked out, details that ultimately would affect how much the policy lived up to initial expectations. There also was concern that the poorest of the poor nations would not be able to meet the criteria and still be left outside the reach of the program despite their need.

THE WORLD BANK   The World Bank continues to be the principal multilateral institution for fighting global poverty. Over the years it has achieved many successes but also been plagued by a number of failures and controversies. In the current era it faces a number of key policy dilemmas. As with the WTO and the IMF, many critics are disillusioned with the World Bank's advocacy of the Washington Consensus. As one former World Bank official has written, "To argue that developing countries need market-friendly policies, stable macroeconomic environments . . . open and transparent capital markets and equity-based corporate structures with attention to modern shareholder values is to say that you will be developed when you are developed. It is the old debate about inputs and outputs, where everything that development brings has become a necessary input to achieving it."[37]

Debate is also swirling over the World Bank's commitment to sustainable development. The bank long was seen by environmentalists as among the worst offenders, and much in need of "greening" in its policies and programs. Since the mid-1990s it has taken a number of steps in this direction. Critics have also pointed to the need to pay more attention to corruption, political repression, and other domestic political issues in recipient countries. Traditionally the World Bank claimed to be apolitical, that its decisions were economic ones to be made on economic criteria and whose success was to be evaluated based on growth rates and other hard economic data. By the mid-1990s, though, the World Bank had begun to shift its stand, based on the strong evidence that good government is a necessary part of sound economic development. This evidence was reinforced in 1997–99 by cases like Indonesia, a formerly vaunted success story that was then undermined in large part by massive corruption.

A further issue also is a political one, albeit at the level of the donor countries and the extent to which they should be allowed to attach political conditions to their lending and voting.* In theory, as a multilateral economic development institution the World Bank is supposed to be detached from the politics of the international agenda. Yet the United States, its biggest donor, has also been the country most inclined to make political linkages and attach conditions to its funding. Some of this has been initiated by presidents, some imposed by Congress. Back when the U.S. voting share in the World Bank was over 40 percent, it was much easier for the United States to impose its position. But with its voting share less than 20 percent now and without the bloc strength of the Cold War alliances, other countries are both more willing and more able to oppose the United States on these issues. Moreover, the United States now also needs to be concerned about precedents; in the future other countries might also seek to impose political conditions on World Bank lending and be able to get 51 percent of the vote despite U.S. opposition.

Global Environmental Issues

In his best-selling book *Earth in the Balance,* then-senator Al Gore honed in on the global environment as "the central organizing principle of civilization." Gore was critical of "violations of our stewardship" as manifested in such global environmental problems as ozone depletion and global warming.[38] Although Gore, other U.S. and international leaders, and environmental NGOs succeeded in raising the priority given to global environmental issues both in U.S. policy and globally, resulting in some important treaties and other progress, the global environmental policy agenda remains a full one.

In general analytic terms, global environmental issues pose four types of policy difficulties. First, they constitute a classic "collective action" problem. Collective action problems are those in which all would benefit by taking joint action to deal with a problem, and all suffer from not doing so, but collective action is impeded by each waiting for the other to act first or by lack of agreement on what should be done. It is the essence of interdependence that all countries will suffer if global warming, ozone depletion, and other global

---

*Like in the IMF but unlike in the UN General Assembly, voting in the World Bank is not "one country, one vote" but is proportional to the size of a country's financial contribution. In past decades the U.S. share was more than 40 percent. As the relative share of U.S. funding has declined, so too has the U.S. voting share, now down to under 20 percent.

environmental problems grow worse, and that all countries therefore have interests in ensuring that they do not. But it is the essence of the problem of global governance that taking such action is so difficult.

Second, environmental issues raise the fundamental tradeoff between short-term and long-term gain. As with other issues we have discussed, global environmental issues require acting today, paying the costs today, for benefits that will be reaped only many years from now. Nor is the need to act today absolutely self-evident. The danger is not yet clear and present, the world not yet in crisis. With global warming, for example, although some changes in weather patterns have been felt, the severe effects of climate change really won't hit until well into the future. Yet if the international community waits until then to act it will be too late. The same short-term/long-term dynamic holds for species and biodiversity preservation, stopping desertification, curtailing air and water pollution, and addressing other environmental issues. To the old axiom that "all politics is local" can be added that "all politics are short-term."

Third, issues of North-South equity further complicate global environmental negotiations. For example, on global warming, developing countries claim a right to higher ceilings on industrial emissions. They base their claim both on economic grounds that poor countries cannot afford more sophisticated emissions-scrubbing technologies, and on the historical-justice argument that developed countries did more than their share of polluting when they were developing during the nineteenth and early twentieth centuries. You had your turn, the argument goes; it's our turn now. Moreover, the developing countries argue, the problem is largely one of the developed world's making.

Fourth is the problem of enforcement. As in other policy areas, once multilateral agreements are reached, norms affirmed, and actions mandated, how to ensure fulfillment and compliance? Most treaties and other agreements do call for sanctions or other penalties and consequences for states that do not meet their obligations, but these are not always enforced. Special multilateral bodies can be created, but as a practical matter such bodies have very limited authority and power. For example, following the 1992 Earth Summit in Rio de Janeiro, Brazil, the UN created a Commission on Sustainable Development. Ten years later, though, at the Johannesburg, South Africa, World Summit on Sustainable Development, even the UN's own statements acknowledged how little this commission had achieved and the need to "recharge" and "revitalize" it.[39]

This analytic context helps explain both the scope and the limits of progress by the United States and the international community on global environmental issues. The beginnings of an infrastructure of treaties and other global environmental agreements has been created: for example, the 1987 Montreal Protocol on ozone depletion, the 1992 Rio Treaty on biodiversity, the 1994 UN Law of the Sea treaty, and the 1997 Kyoto global warming treaty. But only the Montreal Protocol has been approved by the U.S. Congress.

These issues, and those that will succeed them, are crucial because of the range of U.S. interests affected. By presenting them in the context of the U.S. national interest in prosperity, the conventional formulation of economics vs. environment is rejected. Of course environmental protection is more expensive than allowing water pollution, air pollution, and excess use of nonrenewable resources to be treated as "externalities." This is not an open-ended justification for excess regulation and undue economic burdens, but also is not a rationalization for a private company's treating a cost borne by society as an externality. This is the essence of the concept of sustainable development. Moreover, there are profits to be made, jobs to be created, and export markets to be gained in the emerging industry of environmental-protection equipment and technology. And not all solutions are high tech: take Ben and Jerry's Rain Forest Crunch ice cream, which is made from Brazilian rain-forest nuts specially imported so as to create a market incentive for preserving the rain forest.

Environmental issues also merge with broader U.S. foreign policy concerns about political stability and security (peace). Environmental scarcity and degradation have been sources of conflict and violence in a number of wars, both recent and historical. They also further complicate the tasks of building strong and democratic states, not just in the Third World but everywhere. The environment is an issue for Russia, where for decades pollution standards for industries were close to nil, where entire bodies of water like the Aral Sea were totally destroyed, where nuclear and other wastes were disposed of with much too little precaution. It also is an issue for China, five of whose largest cities are among the most polluted in the world, and where numerous other environmental problems continue to grow worse.

The complicated interweaving of domestic and foreign policy issues with the global environment is evidenced by the U.S. position on the *1997 Kyoto global warming treaty* (named for the city in Japan where key negotiations took place). The Kyoto treaty aims to address how "greenhouse gases" emitted by industrial and other forms of pollution are causing dangerous increases in average global temperatures (i.e., global warming), which could have catastrophic consequences for the global environment. Global warming is not just a "green" concern; it could have ripple effects that could cause major economic disruptions, resource wars, massive refugee flows, and other political, economic, and security crises. Key provisions of the Kyoto treaty set legally binding limits on the emission of greenhouse gases. Following the "your turn, our turn" argument noted earlier, most of the cuts in emissions were to be borne by the United States and other developed, industrialized countries. The treaty is to come into force when ratified by at least 55 countries and when the group of ratifiers represents 55 percent of the world's emissions. As of the end of 2002, the requisite number of countries had ratified the treaty, but the 55 percent emissions target had not been met, in large part because of U.S. refusal to ratify the treaty.

The Clinton administration signed the treaty in 1997 but held back on submitting it to the Senate for ratification out of fear that the treaty would not garner the 2/3 majority needed to pass. The Bush administration did not even try this straddle; it simply opposed the treaty. Early on National Security Adviser Condoleezza Rice was reported to have told a meeting of European ambassadors that the Kyoto treaty was "dead on arrival."[40] President Bush described it as "fatally flawed," "unrealistic," and "not based on science."[41] Yet over 175 other nations have signed the treaty.

On the question of scientific evidence, a major new report issued in February 2001 by the UN Intergovernmental Panel on Climate Change, co-chaired by Harvard University scientist James J. McCarthy and widely considered the most authoritative environmental panel in the world, provided strong evidence that the threat was even worse than previously thought (see At the Source on page 533). While some scientists still question the validity and reliability of reports like this one, such skeptics are becoming fewer and fewer. And the forecasts are becoming grimmer and grimmer. Estimates of average temperature increases over this century have been raised from a minimum of 2.7 degrees to a staggering 10.4 degrees. Nor are the dire effects only in the future: already, the costs from climate-related natural disasters have gone up from an annual average loss of $4 billion per year in the 1950s to $40 billion in 1999.

A related study issued around the same time focused on the melting of the world's glacial ice caps. "The seemingly indestructible snows of [Mount] Kilimanjaro that inspired Ernest Hemingway's famous short story," one *New York Times* lead editorial warned, "may well disappear in the next 15 years."[42] The warning from the 700 scientists who conducted the study was even more dire: "Projected climate changes during the 21st century have the potential to lead to future large-scale and possible irreversible changes in Earth systems resulting in impacts at continental and global scales."[43] For any Americans who might try to take comfort in this being relevant only to mountains in Asia or glaciers

REPORT ON GLOBAL WARMING

- An increasing body of research gives a collective picture of a warming world and other changes in the climate system.
- Globally the 1990s were the warmest decade since 1861 and 1998 the warmest year.
- Snow and ice covers have decreased.
- Global average sea level has risen and ocean heat content has increased.
- While some natural processes are at work, the main source of the problem is emission of greenhouse gases and aerosols due to human activities.

Source: United Nations, *Report of Working Group I of the Intergovernmental Panel on Climate Change,* January 2001, available at www.ipcc.ch.

at the North and South Poles, the report went on to stress how the interlinking chain of global climate also could increase droughts in the American Midwest, hurricanes along the Atlantic and Gulf of Mexico coasts, and floods in the Pacific Northwest, and could have many other destructive effects on American life, the American economy, and the American environment.

The other key point made by these reports was further evidence that these climate problems are man-made. One of the disputes among scientists has been over how much of global warming and other climate change is attributable to natural processes, which may run through self-equilibrating cycles over time, and how much is the result of excessive use of oil and other fossil fuels, industrial pollution, wasteful consumption patterns, and other non-inevitable human and societal practices. The evidence was stronger than ever in support of the latter analysis: that this is not happening *to* us but is being done *by* us. On a positive note, this also means that we can correct the problems we have been creating—but only through major policy shifts.

It was in this context that the Bush administration's denouncing of the Kyoto treaty and loosening of Clinton-era limitations on carbon dioxide pollution were met with such strong reactions internationally and domestically.

Critics not only question the Bush skepticism about the scientific evidence but draw the comparison to the much looser standard used for national missile defense, about which there have been even greater doubts about technological feasibility, yet policy has proceeded full speed ahead. They also see the Bush approach to concerns about another energy crisis—emphasizing more oil production rather than more conservation or alternative energy sources—as part of the problem, not a solution. Although the Bush administration did come forward with its own policy proposals to combat global warming, it has encountered widespread doubts about whether this is a serious effort at better policy or an attempt at a legitimizing cover for seeking to gut the Kyoto treaty.

Part of the policy dilemma for the global community, though, is that effective policy is unachievable without U.S. participation. The United States produces almost one-fourth of all the greenhouse gases in the world, making it by far the world's largest polluter, both in total quantity and on a per capita basis. The average American consumes twice as much energy as the average European. It is true that the Kyoto treaty can go into effect as soon as 55 countries that together account for 55 percent of worldwide carbon dioxide emissions ratify it. But getting to these levels will be that much harder without the United States. Thus, on this issue as well as on others involving major multilateral treaties, the United States continues to have the power and position to impede if not block multilateralism.

Foreign Policy Politics: The New Politics of Globalization and the Old Politics of Trade

We see elements of both the old and the new in the foreign policy politics of issues focused on in this chapter. The new is manifested by the much expanded and more influential role that NGOs play; the old in the basic historical pattern of free trade vs. protectionism being played out yet again in the making of U.S. trade policy.

NGOs and the Politics of Globalization

Simply saying the word "Seattle" to a trade policy specialist signifies the new politics of globalization. The reference is not just to the city that is the home of Bill Gates, Microsoft, and Starbucks; it is to Seattle as the "ground zero" where anti-globalization protest politics first emerged as a major political force during the November 1999 WTO summit there. Whether one thinks this is a good thing or a bad thing, trade policy politics have been redefined since Seattle, both in the United States and globally. At every major international economic meeting since then, the anti-globalization movement has disrupted the proceedings and sought to redefine the agenda through mass demonstrations.

Three principal traits characterize the anti-globalization movement as a political force. One is the form of its political action. In the past, protest politics has been associated more with other areas of foreign policy—the anti-Vietnam movement of the 1970s, or the nuclear freeze and anti-apartheid movements of the 1980s. Traditional trade policy politics largely worked through legislative and executive-branch lobbying, and through election campaign contributions and support. Although these "insider" and campaign activities continue, taking to the streets in Seattle, Quebec, and elsewhere represents a new form of political action in the realm of trade policy.

Second, a host of new groups has gotten involved in the policy-making process. Labor unions, corporations, and other economic interest groups continue to play major roles, of course. But environmental groups, human rights groups, public health groups, and other political issue groups have become actively engaged to a much greater extent than in the past. Whereas in the past the main issues in trade negotiations were tariffs and nontariff barriers, the agenda now almost always includes labor standards, environmental impact, and other such issues; the broad social and political agenda has become increasingly interconnected with the international economic agenda.

Third, this trend is not exclusively an American phenomenon. Many of the NGOs involved are based in western Europe, in Russia and the former Soviet bloc countries, or in many developing countries. The transnational links that have been developed in some ways resemble the transnational network that formed to promote the land mines treaty discussed in Chapter 8. Those networks use the Internet for communication, and use professional media strategies and target prominent international meetings for maximum news coverage. They seek change not just on a national, policy by policy basis, but through multilateral forums and global agreements.

The political impact of the anti-globalization movement was evident at the 2001 Summit of the Americas. In his major speech at the summit, President Bush tempered his pure free-trade leanings with the additional statement that "our commitment to open trade must be matched by a strong commitment to protecting our environment and improving labor standards." Lori Wallach, a leader of the anti-globalization movement, remarked, "You could have dialed 911 when I heard what Bush said. I needed to be resuscitated"—although she added that although Bush's statement "show[ed] the political shift, now we've got to see the policy shift."[44]

The anti-globalization movement also has engendered negative reactions, and not just from pure free traders. The violence and vandalism that have marred many of these protests, much of which has been precipitated by anarchists and related groups, has had some discrediting effect. There also is a distinction, as a key Democratic member of Congress put it, between trying to "stop" globalization and trying to "shape" it. "Those who come across as trying to stop globalization aren't winning," said Representative Sander Levin (D-Mich.), whose district includes major auto plants and large numbers of autoworkers. "But for those—and I'm among them—who think you must shape it, there is some progress."[45]

A study by scholars Margaret Keck and Kathryn Sikkink has provided important insights into how NGOs work and what makes them effective.[46] Keck and Sikkink stressed four sets of factors. First is "information politics" and the ability of NGOs to serve as alternative sources of credible information and to use the Internet and other information technologies for timely and targeted communication of that information. National governments and international institutions no longer have an exclusive position as the sources of the "facts" and other key information about the issues of the day. Many NGOs produce their own studies, issue their own policy papers, and conduct their own press briefings. The key for them is to ensure their reputations for credibility and not overstate or misstate their case.

Second is "symbolic politics," meaning "the ability to call upon symbols, actions or stories that make sense of a situation that is frequently far away."[47] NGOs have mastered the art of politics as theater, and global politics as global theater. They have been adept at getting celebrity endorsements, staging events for the media that dramatize issues, and otherwise tapping symbols as well as the substance of issues.

Third is "leverage politics," by which in addition to generally using information and tapping symbols, NGOs target the actors and institutions that are the greatest points of leverage on a particular issue. On some issues this may be the United States; on other issues it may be another country's government; on yet other issues, the UN, the WTO, the IMF, the World Bank, or other international institutions may be the most ideal targets. NGOs' own global networks can give them the reach and flexibility for exercising this leverage.

Fourth is "accountability politics." We have seen throughout this chapter the lag between the global reach of so many policy areas and the still-limited grasp of political structures and processes for global governance. NGOs have positioned themselves as "the voice of the people" on many issues, as the ostensible vehicles for representing the interests and views of constituencies outside the "global bureaucracies" of the WTO and other international institutions or the board rooms of global corporations.

This claim to being the vehicle for accountability is one of the main reasons why NGOs often are seen as the "good guys" in the politics of globalization. Yet, although this often is true, it is not always the case. NGOs are not strictly high-minded altruistic actors. They have their own interests, including competition with other NGOs for prominence or funding. One recent study showed how "organizational insecurity, competitive pressures, and fiscal uncertainty" have become increasingly common among NGOs.[48] Nor are they always effective in carrying out the goals to which they claim to aspire. In some instances their impact has been counterproductive and opportunistic.

The politics of globalization, then, like politics in general, is all the more interesting when we analyze it, rather than just make assumptions about who is having what impact for what reasons and in what ways.

Making U.S. Trade Policy: Process and Politics

Trade policy has been among the more politically contentious issue areas of post-Cold War U.S. foreign policy. The old free-trade consensus is not dead, but it has eroded and fractured. More Americans see themselves as either winners or losers; the latter sentiment feeds neo-protectionism. There is a sense, especially among labor unions and other workers, of "breaking the postwar bargain," as professor Ethan Kapstein put it, that "just when working people need the nation-state as a buffer against the world economy, it is abandoning them."[49] Manufacturing employment in the United States has been falling, and those who find new jobs often do so at much lower pay. Although this jobs shift is not solely due to trade competition, it often tends to be seen heavily in those terms.

Politics arises in each of three key areas in the making of U.S. trade policy: executive-branch negotiation and congressional approval of treaties and other trade agreements; the promotion of American exports and foreign investments; and the regulation of imports. Dynamics of Choice on p. 538 indicates the major executive-branch agencies involved in each of these areas.

TRADE AGREEMENTS   The executive branch agency that takes the lead in conducting trade negotiations is the U.S. Trade Representative (USTR). The

DYNAMICS OF CHOICE

The Making of U.S. Trade Policy

Policy area	Key executive-branch agencies
Negotiating trade agreements	U.S. Trade Representative (USTR) Commerce Department State Department, Bureau of Economic Affairs Agriculture Department Environmental Protection Agency (EPA)
Export promotion	U.S. Export-Import Bank Overseas Private Investment Corporation (OPIC) Trade and Development Agency (TDA) State Department Agriculture Department
Administrative trade remedies	U.S. International Trade Commission (ITC) Commerce Department Federal Trade Commission Labor Department

office of the USTR was first established in 1962 and in the years since has grown in importance; the USTR now holds rank as an ambassador and a member of the president's Cabinet. Depending on the issue area, other executive-branch actors may also be part of the negotiating team: the Commerce Department on issues relating to industrial goods and technology, or the Agriculture Department on agricultural trade. The State Department may also be involved through its Bureau of Economics, Business, and Agricultural Affairs. On issues that may affect the environment, the Environmental Protection Agency (EPA) plays a role.

When trade agreements take the form of treaties, they require ratification by two-thirds of the Senate. Although the House of Representatives has no formal role in treaties, it usually finds a way to be involved—often through legislation providing the funds needed for treaty implementation, because all appropriations bills are required by the Constitution to originate in the House. Trade agreements that are not formal treaties require approval by both chambers, although only by simple majority votes.

NAFTA was a major political test in U.S. trade policy, one that showed broader patterns in post–Cold War trade politics.[50] A big protectionist push was made by NAFTA opponents, led by billionaire businessman Ross Perot, who at the time was riding high as an independent candidate in the 1992 presidential election and as a national protest figure. The liberal wing of the Democratic Party and the neo-isolationist wing of the Republican Party also were part of the anti-NAFTA coalition. As they saw it, jobs would be lost as American companies closed factories and moved south to Mexico for its cheap labor, weak environmental regulations, and other profits-enhancing benefits.

NAFTA was originally signed in 1992 by President George H.W. Bush. President Clinton pushed it through congressional approval, and did so with a coalition drawing much more support from Republicans than from Democrats (see Dynamics of Choice on page 540). In the end the margin of victory, 61 to 38 in the Senate and 234 to 200 in the House, was larger than expected. Although this amounted to a choice for free trade over protectionism, it also has to be noted that the decision was not based strictly on the policy merits of the case—there was plenty of wheeling and dealing, as senators and representatives linked their votes to related trade issues, to other pet projects, and even to invitations to White House dinners.

By 1997, though, trade policy politics had shifted sufficiently against trade agreements that the Clinton administration was unable to get Congress to renew its fast-track trade treaty–negotiating authority. *Fast-track authority* was first established in the 1970s (see Chapter 5) as a way of keeping trade agreements from being amended to death or unduly delayed in Congress. It got its name from the guarantee that any trade agreements the president negotiates and submits to Congress under this authority will receive expedited legislative consideration within ninety days, and under the special procedural rule that the vote be "up or down," yea or nay—i.e., no amendments are allowed. Proponents saw this special procedure as having been key to the success of trade agreements over the previous two decades, as it precluded Congress from excessively delaying or amending agreements already negotiated with other countries. Opponents, though, claimed that without some amending, trade agreements go too far in picking winners and forsaking losers. The immediate effect of the loss of fast-track authority was to set back the Clinton administration's efforts to build from NAFTA to a hemispheric

DYNAMICS OF CHOICE

The Congressional Vote on NAFTA, 1993

	Yea	Nay
House of Representatives		
Democrats	102	157
Republicans	132	43
Total	234	200
Senate		
Democrats	27	28
Republicans	34	10
Total	61	38

Free Trade Area of the Americas. The broader effect was to delay initiation of a new round of global trade talks, because the credibility of U.S. leadership was undermined when the president could not show sufficient political strength at home to regain fast-track authority.

In 2001–2 the Bush administration and fast-track supporters mounted another effort to renew fast-track authority. Part of their strategy was a lesson in political semantics: "Fast-track" authority became "trade promotion" authority. Whereas the original name, with its connotation of moving quickly and not getting bogged down, had once been an advantage, it now seemed to connote a process that moved too fast and allowed too little opportunity for input. "Trade promotion" seemed to convey something that more people could support, something seemingly less political. It passed this time, by a solid margin in the Senate but only by a very close vote in the House.

EXPORT PROMOTION   The opening of markets through trade treaties and agreements does not ensure that American exporters will be the ones that win the major sales. Nor is it purely a matter of economic competitiveness. All major industrial countries have government policies to promote the exports of their companies, although such efforts are subject to rules, established by the GATT and furthered by the WTO, as to what is permissible. The 1979 GATT agreement included restrictions on the use of *subsidies,* which are special payments and other methods governments use to reduce exporters' costs so as to make their goods more price-competitive in international markets. These restrictions were strengthened and expanded in the 1994 WTO agreement. Still, plenty of room exists for export-promotion programs seeking a competitive edge.

As of the early 1990s the United States lagged behind its major Western economic competitors in export promotion. One Clinton administration study estimated that the United Kingdom spent $1.50 on export promotion for every $1 billion worth of nonfarm exports, and France $1.01, but the United States only $.33.[51] To change this imbalance, more funding was provided to certain export-promotion executive-branch agencies, such as the Export-Import Bank of the United States, which provides credit and other financing for foreign customers to buy American exports; the Trade and Development Agency, which helps American companies put together business plans and feasibility studies for new export opportunities; and the Overseas Private Investment Corporation, which provides insurance and financing for foreign investments by U.S. companies that will create jobs back home and increase exports. Even though agricultural exports account for less than 10 percent of American exports, the Agriculture Department gets more than 50 percent of the export-promotion budget, reflecting interest-group politics and the power of farm constituencies.

The State Department also has increased its role in export promotion as part of its post–Cold War retooling. "For a long time secretaries of state thought of economics as 'low policy' while they dealt only with high science like arms control," Secretary of State Warren Christopher stated in 1995. "I make no apologies for putting economics at the top of our foreign policy agenda."[52] As part of their training before assuming their embassy posts, U.S. ambassadors now go through a course titled "Diplomacy for Global Competitiveness." Once in their posts, as described in *Newsweek,* the U.S. ambassador to South Korea "hosted an auto show on the front lawn of his residence, displaying Buicks and Mercurys like a local used-car huckster"; the U.S. ambassador to India "won a contract for Cogentrix, a U.S. power company, with what he calls 'a lot of hugging and kissing' of Indian officials"; and the U.S. ambassador to Argentina "called in Argentine reporters to inform them that he was there as the chief U.S. lobbyist for his nation's businesses."[53]

ADMINISTRATIVE TRADE REMEDIES   Administrative trade remedies are actions by executive-branch agencies in cases in which relief from import competition is warranted under the rules of the international trading system.

From early on GATT had an "escape clause" that allowed governments to provide temporary relief to industries seriously injured by import competition that resulted from lower tariffs. GATT also provides "anti-dumping" provisions against a foreign supplier that exports goods at less than fair value. In such cases the importing country can impose an additional duty equal to the calculated difference between the asking price and the fair-market price. In cases involving unfair subsidies provided by a foreign government, the importing country can impose "countervailing duties," also according to an equalizing calculation. The U.S. government also provides "trade adjustment assistance" (TAA), special economic assistance to companies, workers, and communities hurt by import competition, which is supposed to help them adjust by either becoming more competitive or shifting to new industries. TAA programs are the province of the Department of Labor.

The U.S. agency that administers escape clause, anti-dumping, and countervailing duty cases in the International Trade commission (ITC). The ITC is an independent regulatory agency with six members, evenly divided between Republicans and Democrats, all appointed by the president (subject to Senate confirmation). Its ability to decide its cases objectively rather than politically is further aided by the seven-year length of the members' terms. The Commerce Department is also involved in anti-dumping and countervailing duty cases. Headed as it is by a member of the president's Cabinet, it is more political, but unless the ITC concurs, Commerce alone cannot provide import relief.

These administrative trade remedies also provide a good example of how Congress can shape policy through legislative crafting. Take the escape clause remedies. The 1962 Trade Expansion Act set the criteria for escape clause relief as imports being the "major cause" of the injury suffered by an industry. This meant *greater* than all the other causes combined, a difficult standard to meet. The 1974 Trade Act changed "major" to "substantial," which meant that the injury from imports now has only to be *equal* to any of the other individual factors, a much less stringent criterion on which the ITC must base its rulings.[54]

A reverse example involved the Federal Trade Commission (FTC), another independent regulatory agency, and a recent case involving the "Made in the U.S.A." label.* In 1997 the FTC announced that it was lowering the standard required for a product to be considered made in the United States from its being "all or virtually all" made of American parts by American labor,

---

*The FTC's name is a bit deceptive. It deals primarily with fair advertising, consumer protection, economic competition, and other aspects of domestic commerce and "trade."

to allowing the label when 75 percent of the product met these standards. Reaction was strong from labor unions and their congressional supporters, who saw this as taking away an incentive for industries to invest and create jobs at home. The FTC was forced to back down.

Summary

As with the other main issue areas of U.S. foreign policy, the post–Cold War international political economy poses complex policy choices amid dynamic patterns of change. Globalization has many aspects, and as stressed at the outset of this chapter is not inherently or exclusively a positive or negative force. Two things are certain, however. One is that globalization has made foreign economic and social policy issues more salient than in the past: we now hear much less "low politics" denigration of foreign economic policy issues compared to political-military ones. The other is that achieving foreign economic and social policy objectives is more complex and difficult now than when the United States enjoyed greater international economic dominance.

In some respects, despite all the changes, the international political economy has stayed remarkably stable. In trade, international finance, and development the three principal multilateral institutions (the World Bank, the IMF, and the WTO) continue to play central roles. Liberal norms and rules of open markets and nondiscrimination continue to define the game. Over the course of the 1990s many countries have adopted a capitalist economic system in full or in part. Communist command economies, African socialism, Latin American nationalist statism, and other alternative economic models largely were discredited and abandoned. It didn't seem to matter who the leader or what the country was, the speech was likely to be rich in rhetoric about free markets, free enterprise, and the other virtues of capitalism.

Yet by the latter years of the decade people came to realize that what we are seeing is not just the triumph but also the testing of capitalism on a world scale. More and more questions have been raised and doubts expressed about capitalism's flaws and failures. Some of the problems have involved corruption, as in Russia with the millions siphoned off by the "klepto-capitalists," and in East Asia, where "crony capitalism" had run rampant. Some involved the failure of capitalism to produce its promised "rising tide that lifts all boats." Not only has inequality among countries grown worse, but equity gaps within many countries also widened, in both the developed and the developing worlds. Capitalism is not about to be abandoned, but there is an increasing desire to search for modifications, adaptations, and possibly alternatives.

For U.S. policy this poses challenges in each of the three main economic policy areas: trade, international finance, and sustainable development. Free and fair trade is seen as ever more crucial to U.S. prosperity. This needs to be achieved, though, in the dual context of the WTO at the international level, and increasingly contentious domestic trade politics. In international finance and international development, questions are being raised about the classical free market-ism the United States espouses as its overall strategy and international political-economic ideology. Where is the balance to be struck between markets' virtues and their imperfections and instabilities? What are the lessons of the 1990s financial crises that will help U.S. policy, the IMF, and others do a better job at financial crisis prevention and management? Even when global growth was going strong, its rising tide did not lift all boats: poverty deepened for billions of people. We know quite a bit about what doesn't work for development but still too little about what does, especially for sustainable development and responsible stewardship of the human condition and the global environment.

All told, the questions, issues, and policy choices posed by efforts to promote U.S. interests in prosperity are yet another area in which the new era and the new century present both challenges and opportunities for U.S. foreign policy.

Notes

[1]J. David Richardson and Karin Rindal, *Why Exports Matter: More!* (Washington, D.C.: Institute of International Economics and the Manufacturing Institute, 1996), 1.

[2]Wolfgang E. Reinicke, *Global Public Policy: Governing without Government?* (Washington, D.C.: Brookings Institution Press, 1998), 24.

[3]Reinicke, *Global Public Policy,* 25.

[4]Robert Keohane and Joseph Nye use the term "thickness" in their "Introduction" in Joseph S. Nye, Jr. and John D. Donahue, *Governance in a Globalizing World* (Washington, D.C.: Brookings Institution Press, 2000), 1–41.

[5]Roger C. Altman, "The Nuke of the 1990s," *New York Times Magazine,* March 1, 1998, 34.

[6]United Nations Development Program (UNDP), *Human Development Report 1999* (New York: Oxford University Press, 1999), 276.

[7]Joseph Stiglitz, *Globalization and Its Discontents* (New York: Norton, 2002), 67.

[8]UNDP, *Human Development Report 1999,* 266–69.

[9]Thomas L. Friedman, *The Lexus and the Olive Tree* (New York: Farrar, Straus and Giroux, 1999), xviii.

[10]Stephen D. Cohen, "General Agreement on Tariffs and Trade," in Bruce W. Jentleson and Thomas G. Paterson, eds., *Encyclopedia of U.S. Foreign Relations* (New York: Oxford University Press, 1997), Vol. 2, 207.

[11]"The Hypocrisy of Farm Subsidies," *New York Times,* December 1, 2002, 8; "Plowing Up Subsidies," *Foreign Policy* 133 (November–December 2002), 30–32.

[12]Paul Blustein, "Protests a Success of Sorts," *Washington Post,* April 23, 2001, A11.

[13]U.S. Trade Representative, "Overview of the FTAA Process," www.ustr.gov/FTAA, accessed November 30, 2002.

[14]Edward Luttwak, "From Geo-Politics to Geo-Economics," *National Interest* 20 (Summer 1990), 17, 20.

[15]Luttwak, "From Geo-Politics to Geo-Economics," 19.

[16]John E. Rielly, ed., *American Public Opinion and U.S. Foreign Policy, 1994* (Chicago: Chicago Council on Foreign Relations, 1995), 21.

[17]Samuel P. Huntington, "America's Changing Strategic Interests," *Survival* 33:1 (January/February 1991), 8–10.

[18]Karin Lissakers, quoted in John M. Berry and Clay Chandler, "Fast Currency Trades Feed Fears of a Crisis," *Washington Post,* April 17, 1995, A13.

[19]See, for example, Stiglitz, *Globalization and Its Discontents.*

[20]Jean-Paul Fitoussi, quoted in Roger Cohen, "Redrawing the Free Market," *New York Times,* November 14, 1998, A17, A19.

[21]Joan E. Spero and Jeffrey A. Hart, *The Politics of International Economic Relations* (New York: St. Martin's, 1997), 44.

[22]World Commission on Environment and Development, *Our Common Future* (New York: Oxford University Press, 1987), 43; UNDP, *Human Development Report 1999,* 265.

[23]World Bank, *Human Development 2002* (New York: Oxford University Press, 2002), Table 5.

[24]Secretary-General Kofi Annan, "Markets for a Better World," speech at the World Economic Forum, Davos, Switzerland, January 1998, UN Press Release SG/SM/6448.

[25]Spero and Hart, *Politics of International Economic Relations,* 219.

[26]Spero and Hart, *Politics of International Economic Relations,* 233.

[27]Thomas L. Friedman, "Don't Mess with Moody's," *New York Times,* February 22, 1995, A19.

[28]Alene Gelbard, Carl Haub, and Mary M. Kent, *World Population beyond Six Billion* (Washington, D.C.: Population Reference Bureau, 1999).

[29]Barbara Crossette, "UN Agency on Population Blames U.S. for Cutbacks," *New York Times,* April 6, 2002, A8.

[30]James Dao, "Over U.S. Protest, Asian Group Approves Family Planning Goals," *New York Times,* December 18, 2002, A7.

[31]Central Intelligence Agency, *The Global Infectious Disease Threat and Its Implications for the United States,* National Intelligence Estimate 99-17D (January 2000), available at www.cia.gov/cia.publications/nie/report/nie99-17d.html.

[32]UN Secretary-General Kofi Annan, speech to the African Summit on HIV/AIDS, Tuberculosis and Other Infectious Diseases, Abuja, Nigeria, April 26, 2001, available at www.unaids.org.

[33]U.S. Agency for International Development (USAID), "Millennium Challenge Account Update," June 3, 2002, available at www.usaid.gov/press/releases/2002/fs_mcs.htm. Figures are for 2001 unless otherwise noted.

[34]Steven Kull and I. M. Destler, *Misreading the Public: The Myth of a New Isolationism* (Washington, D.C.: Brookings Institution Press, 1999), 113-33.

[35]USAID, "Millennium Challenge Account Update."

[36]Steve Radelet, "Initial Reactions to the Announcement of the MCA," Center for Global Development, December 18, 2002, available at www.cgdev.org.

[37]Jessica Einhorn, "The World Bank's Mission Creep," *Foreign Affairs* 80:5 (September/October 2001), 31.

[38]Al Gore, *Earth in the Balance* (Boston: Houghton Mifflin, 1992).

[39]"UN Taking First Steps towards Implementing Johannesburg Outcome," September 23, 2002, www.johannesburgsummit.org.

[40]Cited in Alan Sipress, "Aggravated Allies Waiting for U.S. to Change Its Tune," *Washington Post,* April 22, 2001, A4.

[41]Chris Woodford, "Global Warming," *World at Risk: A Global Issues Sourcebook* (Washington, D.C.: Congressional Quarterly Press, 2002), 261.

[42]"A Global Warning to Mr. Bush," *New York Times,* February 26, 2001, A18.

[43]Eric Pianin, "UN Report Forecasts Crises Brought on by Global Warming," *Washington Post,* February 20, 2001, A6.

[44]Paul Blustein, "Protests a Success of Sorts," *Washington Post,* April 23, 2001, A11.

[45]Blustein, "Protests a Success."

[46]Margaret E. Keck and Kathryn Sikkink, *Activists beyond Borders: Advocacy Networks in International Politics* (Ithaca, N.Y.: Cornell University Press, 1998).

[47]Keck and Sikkink, *Activists beyond Borders,* 16.

[48]Alexander Cooley and James Ron, "The NGO Scramble: Organizational Insecurity and the Political Economy of Transnational Action," *International Security* 27 (Summer 2002), 5–39.

[49]Ethan B. Kapstein, "Workers and the World Economy," *Foreign Affairs 75:3* (May/June 1996), 16.

[50]Frederick W. Mayer, *Interpreting NAFTA: The Science and Art of Political Analysis* (New York: Columbia University Press, 1998).

[51]Bruce Stokes, "Team Players," *National Journal,* January 7, 1995, 18.

[52]Michael Hirsh and Karen Breslau, "Closing the Deal Diplomacy: In Clinton's Foreign Policy, the Business of America Is Business," *Newsweek,* March 6, 1995, 34.

[53]Stokes, "Team Players," 10–11.

[54]I. M. Destler, *American Trade Politics,* 2d ed. (Washington, D.C.: Institute of International Economics, 1992), 142–43.

10 *Principles: The Coming of a Democratic Century?*

Introduction: Democracy and the U.S. National Interest

Democracy was sweeping the world—at least it seemed that way in the heady days of the late 1980s and early 1990s. The Berlin Wall, one of the Cold War's starkest symbols, had fallen. The Soviet Union itself crumbled. Nelson Mandela, a political prisoner of apartheid for almost thirty years, was released from prison and within a few years was elected president of a post-apartheid South Africa. Military and Marxist governments fell in Latin America. All over the globe we seemed to be witnessing "the end of history," as Francis Fukuyama termed it, not just the end of the Cold War but "the universalization of Western liberal democracy as the final form of human government."[1] The first Bush administration and then the Clinton administration minced few words in hailing the U.S. role in turning the tide of history.

As the 1990s went on, however, we also witnessed horrors and inhumanity on scales that many had hoped were part of the past. Ethnic cleansing in Bosnia was followed by genocide in Rwanda. Terror tore societies apart. Human rights were further trampled in China and elsewhere. It seemed, as Samuel Huntington responded to Fukuyama, that "so long as human beings exist, there is no exit from the traumas of history."[2] Huntington's own "clash of civilizations" theory, in which "the great divisions among humankind" with their deep cultural and historical roots demarcate "the battle lines of the future," offered a much bleaker view.[3] Still others spoke of "the coming anarchy," global chaos, failed states, and the like.[4]

547

Nelson Mandela raises his fist in triumph as he celebrates his release after twenty-seven years of imprisonment in South Africa. (*AP/Wide World Photos*)

Consequently, on the eve of what was being foreseen as the "democratic century," the record was much more mixed, the policy choices facing the United States more complicated, and the global future of democracy more uncertain than it seemed in those heady days of 1989–91.

In this chapter we first want to take stock of *the status and prospects of global democracy and human rights,* assessing both the progress that has been made and the problems that have been encountered in regions and countries of particular concern to U.S. foreign policy. The next three sections involve relationships between principles and the other three core national interest objectives: *principles-peace* and the debate over "democratic peace" theory and

A Rwandan boy passes the bodies of those killed in the violent clashes between the Hutu and Tutsi ethnic groups. (*Betty Press/Woodfin Camp/PNI*)

its claim that democracies do not fight wars against each other; *principles-power,* and the tensions and trade-offs often posed; and *principles-prosperity,* focusing on the use of economic sanctions.

We then assess the *policy strategies for promoting democracy and protecting human rights,* linking these to some of the literature on democratization and political development, and focusing on U.S. policy along with some discussion of the UN, other international actors, and nongovernmental organizations. The chapter's final section examines the foreign policy politics of economic sanctions, as exemplified by the case of the anti-apartheid sanctions against South Africa.

Global Democracy and Human Rights: Status and Prospects

As we survey the status of democracy and human rights in the world, we need to take into account the successes, the limits and setbacks, and the uncertainties that remain.

Post–Cold War Democratic Success Stories

Looking at the overall global democracy scorecard in Table 10.1, we can see how widespread democracy has become. Of 193 countries and other territories, 145 are ranked as democracies (76 percent). This is a much higher number and much higher percentage than in the 1980s. Today's figures include 42 countries that have made a transition to democracy since 1989 (marked in Table 10.1 in **bold**), and only 5 countries that slipped from democracy to non-democracy (marked in *italics* in Table 10.1).*

Among the new democracies is much of the former Soviet bloc. Nine of these countries—the Czech Republic, Estonia, Hungary, Latvia, Lithuania,

---

*These data are based on surveys done by Freedom House, a New York–based nongovernmental organization. The key criteria used as measures of democracy and freedom are political rights and civil liberties. Freedom House's definition of democracy is "a political system in which the people choose their authoritative leaders freely from among competing groups and individuals," freedom as "the opportunity to act spontaneously in a variety of fields outside the control of the government and other centers of potential domination."

TABLE 10.1   The Status of Global Democracy

Democracies (145)

(a) Free (86)

Andorra	El Salvador	Mali	Saint Vincent &
Argentina	**Estonia**	Malta	the Grenadines
Australia	Fiji	Marshall Islands	Samoa
Austria	Finland	Mauritius	San Marino
Bahamas	France	Micronesia	**Sao Tome &**
Barbados	Germany	Monaco	**Principe**
Belgium	Greece	**Mongolia**	**Slovakia**
Belize	Grenada	Namibia	**Slovenia**
Benin	Guyana	Nauru	Solomon Islands
Bolivia	**Hungary**	Netherlands	South Africa
Botswana	Iceland	New Zealand	Spain
Bulgaria	India	Norway	Sweden
Canada	Ireland	**Palau**	Switzerland
Cape Verde	Israel	**Panama**	Taiwan
Chile	Italy	Papua New	Thailand
Costa Rica	Jamaica	Guinea	Trinidad & Tobago
Cyprus	Japan	Peru	Tuvalu
Czech Republic	Kiribati	Philippines	United Kingdom
Denmark	Korea, South	**Poland**	United States
Dominica	**Latvia**	Portugal	Uruguay
Dominican	Liechtenstein	**Romania**	Vanuatu
Republic	**Lithuania**	Saint Kitts-Nevis	
Ecuador	Luxembourg	Saint Lucia	

(b) Partly free (59)

Albania	**East Timor**	Madagascar	Montenegro
Antigua &	**Ethiopia**	**Malawi**	**Seychelles**
Barbuda	**Gabon**	Malaysia	Sierra Leone
Armenia	**Georgia**	Mexico	Singapore
Azerbaijan	Ghana	**Moldova**	Sri Lanka
Bangladesh	Guatemala	Morocco	Suriname
Bosnia &	**Guinea Bissau**	**Mozambique**	Tanzania
Herzegovina	**Haiti**	Nepal	**Togo**
Brazil	Honduras	**Nicaragua**	Tonga
Burkina Faso	Indonesia	**Niger**	Turkey
Central African	Jordan	Nigeria	Uganda
Republic	Kuwait	Paraguay	**Ukraine**
Colombia	**Kyrgyzstan**	Peru	Venezuela
Comoros	**Lesotho**	**Russia**	Zambia
Côte d'Ivoire	Liberia	Senegal	Zimbabwe
Croatia	**Macedonia**	Serbia and	

(Continued on page 551)

Table 10.1   The Status of Global Democracy   *(Continued)*

Nondemocracies (not free) (48)

Afghanistan	Congo (Demo-	Korea, North	*Swaziland*
Algeria	cratic Republic	Laos	*Syria*
Angola	of)	Lebanon	Tajikistan
Bahrain	Cuba	Libya	*Tunisia*
Belarus	Djibouti	Maldives	Turkmenistan
Bhutan	Egypt	Mauritania	United Arab Emi-
Brunei	Equatorial Guinea	Myanmar (Burma)	rates
Burundi	Eritrea	Oman	Uzbekistan
Cambodia	*Gambia*	*Pakistan*	Vietnam
Cameroon	Guinea	Qatar	Yemen
Chad	Iran	Rwanda	
China	Iraq	Saudi Arabia	
Congo (Republic	Kazakhstan	Somalia	
of)	Kenya	Sudan	

Note: Bold indicates post-1989 democracy. Italics indicate shift from democracy to non-democracy since 1989.
Sources: Freedom House, *Freedom in the World: The Annual Survey of Political Rights and Civil Liberties,* 2000-01 (New Brunswick, N.J.: Transaction Publishers, 2002), and www.freedom-house.org, accessed on March 28, 2003.

Poland, Romania, Slovakia, and Slovenia—make it into the "free" category; Russia and 11 others—Albania, Armenia, Azerbaijan, Bosnia & Herzegovina, Croatia, Georgia, Kyrgyzstan, Macedonia, Moldova, Serbia and Montenegro and Ukraine, to "partly free." Belarus, Kazakhstan, Tajikistan, Turkmenistan, and Uzbekistan are noncommunist but still not free.

Also included as democracies are all the countries of Latin America except Cuba. This, too, is a major historical shift. Panama, Nicaragua, and Haiti are the three Latin American countries that have become democracies since 1989. Going back just a few more years, such other countries as El Salvador, Honduras, Argentina, Chile, Brazil, Ecuador, Paraguay, and Peru also were not democracies. Indeed almost every Latin American country has had a military coup at least once in the twentieth century. Now, though, there are some signs that Latin American militaries have become more accepting of the principles of civilian control and the illegitimacy of the military playing an active role in politics. A scene at the second Conference of Defense Ministers of the Americas held in Argentina in 1996 was illustrative: "The civilian cabinet ministers in their business suits were in the front row. Almost all of the generals with their epaulets and medals and gold trim were relegated to the back—a vivid reminder that the balance of power has clearly shifted to the civilians."[5]

In Africa the most remarkable case is South Africa. The apartheid system had ensured the white minority's total control of the government and the economy, and had condemned the black majority to oppression, injustice, and poverty—indeed, later revelations pointed to torture and assassination plots against black leaders ordered by government officials. Yet by 1994 Nelson Mandela, a former political prisoner, had been elected president of South Africa. Black majority rule was established, with protections for white minority rights. And although the transition to democracy is far from over, and not everything has gone perfectly, it is not hard to imagine a more violent and undemocratic path that South Africa could have taken to this point.

Limits and Uncertainties

There are quite a few cases and countries, though, on the other side of the scale: 48 countries in Table 10.1, or about 25 percent of the world. Moreover, tremendous uncertainties remain as to whether the gains made in many new democracies will be consolidated and institutionalized. History is replete with democratic revolutions that failed—the February 1917 revolution in Russia, for example, which was trumped by Vladimir Lenin and the Bolsheviks, or the 1920s and 1930s Weimar Republic in Germany, which elected as chancellor one Adolf Hitler.

To be sure, the problems and setbacks that feed pessimism have to be kept in perspective—after all, who believed that the early 1990s successes were possible even just a few years before they occurred? The lesson that endures despite the fading euphoria is that positive political change is always possible. This is a main reason why theories like Huntington's clash of civilizations are too deterministic, as if states, their leaders, and their people can only play out the civilizational script as already inscribed over the centuries, and cannot shape their societies, their political systems, and their values in an evolving way.
10.

Yet so, too, does there need to be a tempering of Fukuyama's end-of-history optimism on the other side. It takes nothing away from the successes achieved thus far to acknowledge that to declare democracy is not the same as to consolidate and institutionalize it. Democracy can be said to be consolidated and institutionalized when governing regimes can change, but the political system itself remains stable. The political change that does occur must be within the bounds of a constitutional order and peaceful, with little or limited
10.2

political violence. This is the challenge facing so many of the newly democratic countries.

The following sections will examine trends and patterns in key states and regions.

AFRICA   Almost half of the countries in Africa are still nondemocracies. Many have been torn by civil wars and genocidal killings—e.g., Angola, Liberia, Somalia, Rwanda, Burundi, the Democratic Republic of Congo (the former Zaire), and others. There is no doubt that some of Africa's problems are the legacies of the Cold War, when the United States readily supported dictators friendly to its cause, and the Soviet Union supported various Afro-Marxist-Leninist regimes. The European colonial powers (France, Britain, and Belgium, especially) also bear a substantial share of responsibility for their disregard of tribal and ethnic divisions in drawing country boundaries as they were withdrawing from their colonial empires. But to acknowledge the degree of Western responsibility is not to dismiss the responsibility of Africa's own leaders, whose rivalries, repression, and corruption have taken their toll on their own people.[6]

Note also needs to be made of South Africa, for amid the peacefulness of its post-apartheid transition and other aspects of its democratic success, there also have been some worrying signs. Crime rates in South Africa are extremely high: an average of 53.4 murders per 100,000 people in the late 1990s, compared to an international average of 5.5; an estimated 500 crime syndicates operating in the country; a crime-solving rate of only 23 percent; and only 3.6 percent of perpetrators imprisoned. Economically even before the global recession hit, in 1997–98 South Africa's per capita gross domestic product (GDP) grew only 2 percent, well below the rate needed to even come close to meeting expectations for economic progress and narrowing of the racial inequality gap. And the AIDS crisis tears at the social fabric of this nation which has been such an inspiration to so much of the world.

THE MIDDLE EAST   The very low percentage (about 25 percent) of Arab-Muslim countries that are even partly free democracies seems at least somewhat consistent with Huntington's "clash of civilizations" analysis. "Western ideas of individualism, liberalism, constitutionalism, human rights, equality, liberty, the rule of law, democracy, free markets, the separation of church and state, often have little resonance in Islamic societies," Huntington contends.[7] Saudi Arabia and most of the other Persian Gulf Arab states are monarchies or sheikdoms. Others, such as Syria, Libya, and Iraq, are dictatorships. Egypt has elections, but not free ones, and Egyptian president Hosni Mubarak has been in power for over two decades. Of Arab countries, only Morocco, Jordan, and Kuwait get a partly free rating.[8]

The relation of Islamic fundamentalism to human rights and democratization is particularly controversial. "Democracy is irrelevant to Islam and Islam is superior to democracy," is how one noted scholar assesses the political dogma common to Islamic fundamentalist leaders. "Their notion of the 'rule of law' refers to the unalterable law of Islam," hardly a basis for social tolerance or political pluralism.[9] In a number of instances where militants have come to power, domestic repression has been of totalitarian reach, seeking to regulate virtually all aspects of society and individual conduct in accordance with fundamentalist interpretations of the Koran. An "ends-justify-the-means" logic is often used to justify terrorism, assassinations, and other political violence.

Others point to signs of nonfundamentalist political Islam emerging, "a new generation of Islamic thinkers and parties ... seeking to harmonize imaginatively Islam's injunctions with democracy's imperatives."[10] These observers see the possible emergence of an Islamic version of democracy, maintaining cultural authenticity and roots in Islam while also adopting more of the political pluralism, democratic accountability, and strong civil society characteristic of Western democracies. Arab countries in which these "Islamic perestroika" trends have been identified include Algeria, Egypt, Morocco, Tunisia, Libya, Jordan, and Qatar. How strong these trends will become and whether they will spread more broadly remains to be seen. But they are there, and too often missed in Western analyses that focus too singularly on Islamic fundamentalism.

In this regard Iran poses some of the most significant and intriguing uncertainties. The 1978–79 Islamic fundamentalist revolution led by Ayatollah Ruhollah Khomeini that overthrew the shah established a theocratic state. Elections were held in the years that followed and a president and parliament existed, but the principal governing authority rested with the religious "supreme leader"—Khomeini until his death in 1989, and then Ayatollah Khamenei, his successor. Then in 1997, in a surprise result, the presidential election was won by Mohammad Khatami, a more moderate proreform *mullah* (religious leader) over the candidate favored by the theocrats. Khatami's victory came about largely because of strong support among women and youth (the voting age is sixteen) and other groups within Iranian society favoring liberalization. Tensions between the moderates and the fundamentalists grew even more intense. Elections in early 2000 produced a strong reformist majority in the *majlis* (parliament), setting off a fundamentalist backlash including the shutting down of newspapers and a wave of political killings. This dynamic was fueled further by President Khatami's re-election in 2001, and both the pressures towards reform and the counter repression mounted by the fundamentalists.

The Freedom House data on which Table 10.1 is based list Iran as a nondemocracy. The basis for this is the fact that, elections notwithstanding, the Iranian constitution still vests key powers in unelected religious authorities. The ranking thus fits based on the criteria Freedom House has used, but the democratizing undercurrents in Iran are stronger and more swirling than in many other countries listed with it as nondemocracies. Some of these involve the Iranian student movement and its emergence as potentially "the leading engine for political reform," potentially comparable to student movements in major historical world revolutions (see Perspectives on page 556).

RUSSIA   What Russia has achieved in transitioning from almost a century of authoritarian communism to democracy is not to be underestimated. Very few people anywhere predicted that Russia would have had such a peaceful transition. A bicameral representative legislature was put in place, and the Duma (the lower house of the legislature) in particular was given a major role in governing. Russia's new constitution has held up despite a number of crises. Free elections have been held at the local, provincial, and national level, including in 2000 the election of Vladimir Putin as the new president succeeding Boris Yeltsin—the first democratic succession in Russian history.

Still Russia's road has been anything but straight and smooth as it has moved from the initiation of democracy toward its consolidation and institutionalization.

An early and graphic example of this challenge came in October 1993. Yeltsin, who led the anti-Soviet revolution and became the first president of Russia, was pushing hard for political and economic reform. His main opposition was coming from the Duma, where the communists and other hard-line and antireform political parties had sufficient strength to block many of these reforms. Amid political deadlock Yeltsin resorted to a military attack on the parliament building. The juxtaposition of the same man who in August 1991 defiantly stood on Soviet army tanks, personifying the democratic revolution, now commanding Russian army tanks in an attack on the national legislature captured the dilemmas of democratization. This posed a difficult policy choice for the Clinton administration: Although Clinton was strongly supportive of Yeltsin, a military attack on an elected legislature was not exactly an exemplary practice of democracy.

PERSPECTIVES
PERSPECTIVES
PERSPECTIVES

IRAN'S STUDENT REVOLUTIONARIES

TEHRAN, July 6—A forceful student movement is replacing President Mohammad Khatami as the leading engine for political reform in Iran. Activists at the country's vibrant, overflowing universities say their calls for change are gathering momentum and they are preparing to put delicate issues like renewing relations with the United States to a public vote for the first time.

Unlike Mr. Khatami, who has twice been elected president but has been stymied in his quest for change by the still-powerful conservative clerics and their supporters, the students are not patient, polite or at all ready to settle for the status quo. . . .

Students were a powerhouse of revolution from Bolshevik Russia to Tiananmen Square and Eastern Europe in 1989 and in Iran's own Islamic revolution ten years earlier. . . .

In today's Iran, students derive strength from numbers. There are 1.7 million in a country of 65 million where two-thirds of the population is under 30. The closed, state-run economy, combined with corruption and mismanagement, has prevented the development necessary to give everyone jobs. Officials predict six million will be jobless in 2004. . . .

"They want more freedom in their private and social lives," [Mohsen Sazgara, a reformist politician and former journalist] added. "They are fed up with the state's interference, telling them what to do. They want to be able to integrate into the global culture, have a democratic system and be sure that there will be jobs in the future."

Ahmad Faraji, a student who was jailed for two weeks, said: "We still do not reject Mr. Khatami and his reform movement but believe they are not enough. We think change should be from the bottom up; society must act more forcefully and participate in the process of change by finding its voice to criticize."

Source: Nazila Fathi, "Iran's Students Step Up Reform Drive," *New York Times,* July 7, 2002, 6.

Nor did the political tensions subside. The communists and other hard-liners kept posing challenges. They gained additional seats in the Duma in the December 1993 elections and then in 1995 won the largest block of seats of any political party. In the 1996 presidential elections Yeltsin was re-elected, but the communist candidate Gennadi Zyuganov made a strong showing.

Yeltsin also faced growing discontent arising from the deepening economic crisis. The transition from the Soviet command economy to market-based capitalism initially proved to be a "great leap backward."[11] Russian GDP fell below that of countries such as Mexico, Brazil, and Indonesia. The standard of living for the average Russian was lower in 2000 than it had been in 1990. Forty percent of the population was living below the poverty line. Government employees, Russian army soldiers, and others went months without receiving paychecks. Social services were cut back dramatically in the name of fiscal responsibility. Corruption was rampant, "robber-baron capitalism" creating a new economic elite of billionaires. In 1998 a major financial crisis was set off as the Russian government defaulted on its debt, the ruble (Russian currency) collapsed, and investment plummeted.

Yeltsin's own behavior added to the problems. He always had been mercurial, now he became even more unpredictable and unstable. His bouts with alcoholism became more frequent and more evidently interfered with policy. On December 31, 1999, Yeltsin announced his resignation as president and appointed Putin as his successor. At first this appointment was on a provisional basis, but in March 2000 Putin was elected with slightly over 50 percent of the vote (the communist Zyuganov again was the leading challenger, with 29 percent).

Putin abated some of the drift of Yeltsin's last years by strengthening the state in ways that, as reported in the *New York Times* "managed to produce a measure of order and even modest prosperity that his embattled predecessor [Yeltsin] could only dream of."[12] Yet the question, as the *Times* went on to say, "is where a strong state ends and a strongman begins." Putin himself is a former KGB (the Soviet spy agency) agent. As president he has been once again strengthening the KGB's successor agencies, reversing the breakup into separate agencies that Yeltsin began and giving their leaders more power within the Kremlin and a mandate for stepping up internal security measures. "I see only one aim in re-uniting all the security services into one large monster," stated noted dissident Sergei Kovalev. "The creation of a more authoritarian state."[13] A similar warning came from Senator Joseph Lieberman (D-Conn.): "Russia's leaders [are being] tempted now to turn back towards authoritarianism."[14]

Lieberman focused on the crackdown on freedom of the press as another major area of concern. Newspapers and television stations have been shut down for criticizing the Putin government. Their owners have been arrested and forced into exile. In 2000, sixteen journalists were killed and seventy-three attacked, many of them badly beaten. The Committee to Protect Journalists, a major free-press NGO, named Putin to their list of the "ten worst enemies of the press" in 2001.[15]

Thus without dismissing the democratization achievements that Russia has made, questions remain about their sustainability. Elections have been held, but the overall pattern is what Stanford professor Gail Lapidus calls "electoralism with authoritarian institutions and values; democratic consolidation remains a distant goal."[16] Broader questions also remain as to whether, if political and economic conditions do not get better, the Russian people may turn to a "strongman" leader, whether military or ultranationalist or some other antidemocrat.

CHINA   Whereas Russia exemplifies the problems involved in the transition from communism to democracy, China demonstrates problems associated with seeking to maintain communism and resist the transition to democracy. It is, as Professor Edward Friedman put it, "the only major surviving communist dictatorship."[17]

The overall dilemma China faces is how to combine economic liberalization, modernization, and opening to the global economy with continuation of a closed, repressive, nondemocratic political system. The strategy since China began its economic opening over twenty years ago under the leadership of Deng Xiaoping has been based on the populace's being sufficiently satisfied with the economic benefits that it remains politically quiescent. But even when economic growth was booming, this strategy was not totally successful. The 1989 Tiananmen Square protests for greater democratization and human rights, for example, reached such a crescendo that the Chinese government crushed them militarily, killing many protesters and arresting large numbers in what came to be known as the Tiananmen Square massacre. Moreover, in recent years economic growth has been slowing, and the rising standard of living experienced by many Chinese during the 1980s and early 1990s has stalled. Then there are the 800 million peasants who largely have been left out of the benefits even when economic growth has been rapid. Total unemployment estimates range as high as 100 million. Some analysts see Chinese membership in the World Trade Organization (WTO) as holding "long-term promise" but bringing "unprecedented economic and political challenges" in the short term, potentially setting off "future shock" that could "increase the pains of reform and pressures on the government."[18]

The forces of globalization also have been both economic boon and political threat for China. The technologies that U.S. and other foreign investment have brought into the country have been essential to economic growth and modernization. But global technology also has aspects that pressure for political opening, such as the Internet. In March 2001, indicative of its fear of how the Internet was undermining its monopoly on the flow of politically relevant information, the Chinese government arrested a young computer whiz while he was "on his way back from his grandmother's funeral," without any apparent cause other than that he was known to have the skills to be able to "run circles around Beijing's Internet fire walls."[19] Soho.com, China's main Internet portal, posted the notice that "topics which damage the reputation of the state" are forbidden. It went on to warn that "if you are a Chinese national and willingly choose to break these laws, Soho.com is legally obliged to report you to the Public Security Bureau."[20]

Human rights pressures also are likely to increase. Amnesty International and Human Rights Watch, the two major human-rights NGOs, both rate China as among the world's worst human rights violators. These groups cite numerous cases involving individual dissidents, as well as the Falun Gong, the partly religious and partly political movement that has been prominent for a number of years.

Another set of issues showing the roadblocks to democratization involve national and ethnic groups seeking greater autonomy from the central government in Beijing and possibly secession from China. Tibet is the most prominent such case.

LATIN AMERICA   Any complacency brought on by the spread of democracy in the 1990s has been shaken by the instabilities of the current decade. Venezuela had an attempted coup in 2002 and further instability in 2003. Argentina had five presidents within two months in late 2001. Ecuador and Peru have been shaken by their own economic and political instabilities. Honduras and Nicaragua slid from free to partly free in the Freedom House rankings. And concerns have been mounting about Brazil, the region's largest country.

As a general pattern, these instabilities have two principal sources. One is the continued weakness of political institutions. As assessed by one prominent analyst, "severe deficiencies mark political life—weak capacity and performance of government institutions, widespread corruption, irregular and often arbitrary rule of law, poorly developed patterns of representation and participation, and large numbers of marginalized citizens."[21]

Second is the limits and failures of globalization. There is much debate, as discussed in Chapter 9, over the extent to which the recent economic problems of many developing countries are being caused by their own governments' policy blunders or are inherent in the dynamics of globalization. Whatever the case, Latin America has been hit hard. It long has been the region with the greatest inequalities in the distribution of wealth among social classes. Although there has been some growth of middle classes, Latin American economies still tend to be dominated by wealthy elites with large impoverished masses of urban poor and rural *campesinos* (peasants). In Mexico, for example, the richest 10 percent of the population controls 41 percent of the country's wealth, while the share of the bottom half of the population is only 16 percent, an even wider gap than in the 1980s; as of the mid-1990s, according to UN and World Bank figures, the number of Mexicans living in extreme poverty had increased from 17 million to 22 million.

During the Cold War Latin America was one of the regions in which socialism had its greatest appeal as a popular movement. Although socialism itself may not re-emerge, the question remains of whether other competing ideologies and political models may emerge. In their fundamentals, socialism and communism were efforts to address the problem of social, political, and economic inequality. Although these particular remedies largely failed, the core problem of inequality remains—indeed, income gaps and disparities in wealth have been growing wider in many societies around the world. If democracy and capitalism do not more effectively deal with these fundamental problems, it stands to reason that other ideologies will be articulated and other political models advanced with at least the promise of doing so. This could develop in ways compatible with democracy, or could destabilize democracy. Given Latin America's history, the possibility of popular unrest pulling the military out of the barracks and back into politics cannot be dismissed; in the early 1960s, for example, a democratizing wave then gaining force was swept away by a string of military coups.

Latin America is also plagued by its infamous drug cartels. In Colombia the drug cartels have assassinated government officials who sought to crack down on them, including supreme court justices and a popular presidential candidate; their leaders even continue to run their businesses from jail (see Perspectives on p. 561). Mexico and Panama are among the other Latin American countries that must cope with the reality that "narco-democracies" cannot remain democracies for very long.

PERSPECTIVES
PERSPECTIVES
PERSPECTIVES

"COLOMBIA SAYS DRUG BARONS THREATEN, BRIBE CONGRESS FROM JAIL"

BOGOTA, Colombia, Dec. 18 — The Colombian Congress wound up one of its most controversial sessions today amid growing evidence that jailed leaders of the Cali cocaine cartel continue to use bribes and threats to seek legislation favoring their interests....

The revelations stirred national and international outrage. Facing U.S. economic sanctions and a public outcry over the vote, President Ernesto Samper led a successful government lobbying effort to revive the bill in a conference committee. It was passed on Monday.

"It would have been better if the Congress had voted to pass the bill out of conviction and not pressure, but they passed it," said Enrique Santos Calderon, a political analyst. "For the first time, business groups, the [Roman Catholic] church, the international community and media all reacted against the national disgrace, and it was too much pressure even for the cartels."

But the cartels may not remain passive in the face of defeat. On Monday and Tuesday, two car bombs were set off—one in Cali and one in the northern city of Monteria—killing five people. Car bombs have long been a favorite instrument of terror of the drug cartels, and police blamed them for the attacks.

Although Colombians are accustomed to the interference of the drug barons, the brazenness of their recent efforts caused alarm and, for the first time, brought public acknowledgment from the government that traffickers continue to operate from prison cells.

Chief prosecutor [former General Alfonso] Valdivieso, in an interview, called the cartel's ability to reach beyond prison walls "terrifying."

"We will have to make greater efforts to keep the prisons from being a mockery, a place of privilege where the criminals can continue to carry out crimes," he said.

GLOBAL HUMAN RIGHTS   The overall global human rights situation also is an area in which the limits of progress are quite evident. Some sense of the scope and horror of the persecution and killing that continue around the world is conveyed in one of Amnesty International's recent annual global human rights reports (see Perspectives on p. 561). Thousands of people have been killed without legal due process (extrajudicial executions). Thousands of others were subjected to torture, detained without trial, or held as political prisoners or prisoners of conscience. More than 140,000 people have "disappeared," presumably at the hands of governments and for political reasons. The items listed in the box are just excerpts from a report that runs over three hundred pages.

Serious questions thus remain about the future of democracy and human rights around the world. There is reason for optimism, but also some basis for pessimism and much uncertainty. It is very important to take a long-term view of developments in this area. In the United States' own history it took 11 years after declaring independence to develop a workable constitution (the first version, the Articles of Confederation, failed). It took 89 years for slavery to be abolished. It took 144 years until women gained the right to vote. It was 188 years until full constitutional protections were guaranteed to all citizens. Thus we cannot expect full and uninterrupted democratization in only a decade among the world's nascent democracies.

Principles and Peace: The Democratic Peace Debate

According to the theory of the democratic peace, the United States should support the spread of democracy not just because it is the right thing to do, but also because history demonstrates that democracies do not fight wars against fellow democracies; thus it is in the U.S. interest to support democratization in order to reduce the risks of war. The theory does not claim that democracies don't go to war at all. They have, and they do—against nondemocracies. But they don't, and they won't, it is argued, against other democracies. This is the tenet of the democratic peace paradigm that right makes for might, that the world is a safer and a better place to the extent that democracy spreads. For American foreign policy, the promotion of democracy thus is said to have the added value of serving objectives of peace as well as of principles.

The Clinton administration made democratic peace theory central to its foreign policy. "Democracies do not attack each other," President Clinton

PERSPECTIVES
PERSPECTIVES

PERSPECTIVES

THE STATUS OF GLOBAL HUMAN RIGHTS

Extrajudicial executions

Thousands of extrajudicial executions or possible extrajudicial executions were reported in 63 countries, including Bahrain, Burundi, Colombia, India, Russia, and Rwanda.

Disappearances

The fate of more than 140,000 people in 49 countries who disappeared in recent years remains unknown. Many of those, in countries including Burundi, Rwanda, Colombia, Iraq, Sri Lanka, and Turkey, may have subsequently been killed.

Torture or ill treatment

At least 10,000 detainees were subjected to torture or ill treatment, including rape, in 114 countries, including Yugoslavia, Indonesia (including East Timor), Iran, Mexico, and Sudan. More than 4,500 people died as a result of torture in custody or inhuman prison conditions in 54 countries including Egypt, Kenya, Myanmar (Burma), and Turkey.

Prisoners of conscience

Prisoners of conscience or possible prisoners of conscience were held in 85 countries, including Bosnia & Herzegovina, China, Kenya, Peru, and Tunisia.

Unfair trials

A reported 27 countries, including China, Colombia, Nigeria, Saudi Arabia, and Yugoslavia, imprisoned people after unfair trials.

Detention without charge or trial

Forty-three countries, including Azerbaijan, India, Israel (and the occupied territories), areas under the jurisdiction of the Palestinian Authority, Paraguay, and Rwanda, held a total of more than 46,000 people without charging them with any crime.

Human-rights abuses by armed opposition groups

Armed opposition groups committed abuses, including torture, hostage-taking, and deliberate and arbitrary killings, in 41 countries, including Afghanistan, Algeria, Colombia, Sierra Leone, and the United Kingdom.

Source: Amnesty International, *1997 Annual Report* (New York: Amnesty International, 1997).

declared in his 1994 State of the Union address, so therefore "ultimately the best strategy to ensure our security and to build a durable peace is to support the advance of democracy elsewhere."[22] Clinton's advisers coined the term "enlargement," playing off the old Cold War "containment," to refer to the spread of global democracy and the U.S. interests thus served. As laid out in a major Clinton administration policy statement, "all of America's strategic interests—from promoting prosperity at home to checking global threats abroad before they threaten our territory—are served by enlarging the community of democratic and free-market nations. Thus, working with new democratic states to help preserve them as democracies committed to free markets and respect for human rights is a key part of our national security strategy."[23] Ensuring the success of democracy was thus posed as a pragmatic and not just an idealistic goal, serving peace as well as principles.

Is this theory valid? Let's examine the main arguments and evidence first from proponents and then from critics of the theory.

Democratic Peace Theory

Proponents of the democratic peace theory make the sweeping claim that "the absence of war between democratic states comes as close to anything we have to an empirical law in international relations."[24] The empirical evidence as they present it indeed is impressive:

- Democracies have not fought any wars against each other in the entire period of world history since 1815. This encompasses 71 interstate wars involving nearly 270 participants.
- Since the end of World War II democracies have been only one-eighth as likely as nondemocracies to threaten to use military force against another democracy, and only one-tenth as likely to even use limited force against each other.
- Democracies have fought numerous wars against nondemocracies, however, including World War I, World War II, and numerous wars during the Cold War.[25]

The central tenets of the democratic peace paradigm and their logic and philosophical basis, although very often associated with President Woodrow Wilson in the history of U.S. foreign policy, can be traced all the way back to the eighteenth-century European political philosopher Immanuel Kant and his book *Perpetual Peace*. The basic argument has three components: the

constraints imposed by democratic political systems, the internationalization of democratic norms, and the bonds built by trade.

DOMESTIC POLITICAL CONSTRAINTS We already have seen how, historically, going to war has been one of the recurring great debates in American
politics. Kant, who was writing before there even was a United States of
America with its own constitution and foreign policy, made his argument
with reference to democracies generally. If "the consent of the citizenry is required in order to decide that war should be declared," he wrote, "nothing is
more natural than that they would be very cautious in commencing such a
poor game. . . . But, on the other hand, in a constitution which is not republican, and under which the subjects are not citizens, a declaration of war is the
easiest thing to decide upon, because war does not require of the ruler . . . the
least sacrifice of the pleasure of his table, the chase, his country houses, his
court functions and the like."[26] Kant also stressed, though, that these constraints were less likely vis-à-vis nondemocracies, toward which mass publics
were more prone to being aroused by crusade-like appeals. Democracies' willingness to go to war against nondemocracies and their unwillingness to go to
war against each other thus follow the same domestic political logic.

INTERNATIONALIZATION OF DEMOCRATIC NORMS All democracies,
no matter what their particular representative structure, must practice compromise and consensus-building in their domestic politics and policy. Their
watchwords need to be tolerance and trust, and the essence of a successful
democratic system is managing if not resolving conflicts and tensions within
society in lawful and peaceful ways. As Michael Doyle, whose articles were
among the first to advance the democratic peace thesis, states, democracies,
"which rest on consent, presume foreign republics to also be consensual, just,
and therefore deserving of accommodation."[27] Nondemocracies, in contrast,
as another author puts it, "are viewed *prima facie* as unreasonable, unpredictable."[28] There is a rational logic here, not just ideology. It makes sense not
to go to war against a country that you are confident won't move quickly to
war against you. But going to war may become the rational choice if you fear
the other may seek to strike pre-emptively or by surprise.

BONDS OF TRADE The combination of this spirit of political commonality
and the common tendency of democracies to have free-market economic systems also leads them to develop trade and other economic relations with one
another. "The 'spirit of commerce,'" in Kant's term, in turn becomes another

factor inhibiting war. The same idea also is found in the work of such other eminent political philosophers as Montesquieu, who wrote of "the natural effect" of trade as being "to bring about peace," and John Stuart Mill, who went even further in seeing the expansion of international trade in the mid-nineteenth century as "rapidly rendering war obsolete."[29] The basic ideas are that as trade develops there becomes more to lose from going to war, and in any event that war would be against people who are no longer strangers. This is said to be especially true today, given how international interdependence now encompasses not just trade but investment, finance, and many other economic interconnections.

Critiques and Caveats

Four main arguments have been made by those who question the democratic peace theory.

SPURIOUS RELATIONSHIP?   Some scholars question whether there really is a strong relationship between states' forms of government and the likelihood of their going to war against each other. These critics contend that on two counts the claim for this causal link is "spurious," meaning not valid because of methodological problems. One is a definitional point about how both "democracy" and "war" are defined by democratic peace theorists, and the resulting criteria for including or excluding cases. These critics examined the empirical data going back to 1815 and cited a number of cases in which they say democratic peace proponents inaccurately excluded some conflicts that involved democracies vs. democracies, or miscategorized countries that fought wars as nondemocracies when they should be considered democracies.[30] Among the historical examples cited are the American Civil War and Finland's siding with the Axis powers in World War II. Applying the theory to the contemporary context is problematic: so many of today's wars are ethnic conflicts, civil wars, and other intrastate conflicts, yet the democratic peace theory principally addresses classical interstate wars.

A second methodological criticism is that democratic peace theorists confuse correlation with causality, mistakenly emphasizing the nature of the domestic political system as the cause of peaceful relations rather than a Realist calculation that cooperation served national interests better than conflict. For example, with regard to the claim that the United States, Western Europe, and Japan didn't fight wars with each other from 1945–91 because they are democracies, critics argue that the more important factor was these countries' shared security interests based on the Cold War and the common threat from the Soviet Union. There also are a number of historical cases of "near-miss" crises in which democracies almost did go to war against each other, but didn't for reasons that had more to do with assessments of their interests than with the other side's being a democracy. These include two crises between the United States and Great Britain in the nineteenth century, as well as some others.[31]

The dynamics of democracy, producing as they sometimes do openings for demagoguery and enemy-bashing, also can exacerbate tensions. During the Cold War in the United States wariness about being branded "soft on communism" fed involvement in Vietnam and elsewhere. In Russia in the 1990s the Duma has been a bastion of aggressive nationalism. In India in 1998 the Hindu nationalist Bharatiya Janata Party went ahead with nuclear tests as one of its first actions on coming to power, while virtually all other political parties in the country were reluctant for domestic political reasons to oppose the tests. In Pakistan the political pressure on Prime Minister Nawaz Sharif and his party to counter with nuclear tests of its own was irresistible.

TRADE AND PEACE?   A second point raises doubts about how much trade actually inhibits war. On the eve of World War I, Sir Norman Angell, the foremost heir to the Kant-Montesquieu-Mill tradition, diagnosed war as "a failure of understanding" that could be corrected by the kind of mutual familiarity and interchange bred by international commerce. Yet the fact that Germany was Britain's second leading trade partner didn't stop the two countries from going to war. There are other historical cases as well in which high levels of economic interdependence did not prevent war. Moreover, high levels of trade surely do not prevent other political and diplomatic conflicts. U.S.-European and U.S.-Japanese relations provide numerous examples.

AGGRESSIVE TENDENCIES OF DEMOCRATIZING STATES   Third, and more in the way of a qualifying caveat than straight criticism, is that even if one accepts that mature democracies may not fight with each other, states that are still undergoing democratization and are not yet stable democracies may actually be even *more* aggressive and warlike than stable nondemocracies. These transition periods are notoriously unstable, as elites and other groups compete for political influence, and as the general public struggles with the economic difficulties of transitions, the disorientation of political change, and an uncertain future. They thus are quite susceptible to "belligerent nationalism" as a rallying cry and diversion from domestic problems. As political

scientists Edward Mansfield and Jack Snyder put it, "elite groups left over from the ruling circles of the old regime, many of whom have a particular interest in war and empire, vie for power and survival with each other and with new elites representing rising democratic forces. Both old and new elites use all the resources they can muster to mobilize mass allies, often through nationalistic appeals, to defend their positions and to stake out new ones. However, like the sorcerer's apprentice, these elites typically find that their mass allies, once mobilized, are difficult to control. When this happens, war can result from nationalist prestige strategies that hard-pressed leaders use to stay astride their unmanageable political coalitions."[32]

POWER, NOT JUST AUTOMATIC PEACE   The fourth point is derived from the ways in which the George W. Bush administration's approach to global democratization differs from the Clinton administration's. The Bush administration also has stressed its commitment to global democracy, to principles as a core U.S. national interest objective. Its national security strategy reflects some democratic peace logic in committing to "extend the peace by encouraging free and open societies on every continent." But there is less confidence that democracy will succeed in key countries around the world without support from American power. Nor is there as much of an assumption that new democracies will be peace-like without some pressure from American power. Thus the Bush strategy stresses not just helping democracy spread but creating "a balance of power" that favors democracy and ensures that the tendencies to be peace-like do get manifested.[33]

Principles and Power: Tensions and Trade-Offs

As we have seen throughout this book, American foreign policy repeatedly has been faced with tensions and trade-offs between considerations of power and principle. They were there in pre–Cold War history; they were there during the Cold War; and they are with us in this new era.

Rwanda and the National Interest

The 1994 genocide in Rwanda, in which mass murders were carried out while the United States and the rest of the international community did very little, was "a failure of international will—of civic courage—at the highest level."[34]

Professor Michael Barnett, who then was working at the U.S. Mission to the United Nations, pulls no punches in his account:

> In one hundred days, between April 6 and July 19, 1994, [Hutu extremists] murdered roughly eight hundred thousand individuals [Tutsis, who were the rival ethnic group, and Hutu moderates]. . . . And unlike the Nazis who used modern industrial technology to accomplish the most primitive of ends, the perpetrators of the Rwandan genocide employed primarily low-tech and physically demanding instruments of death that required an intimacy with their victims. The genocide was executed with a brutality and sadism that defy imagination. Eyewitnesses were in denial. They believed that the high-pitched screams they were hearing were wind gusts, that the packs of dogs at the roadside were feeding on animal remains and not dismembered corpses, that the smells enveloping them emanated from spoiled food and not decomposing bodies.[35]

Yet despite knowing the horrors that were transpiring, neither the United States nor the United Nations nor any other country or international institution took any significant action. People working in the State Department then recall being told to be sure not to use the word "genocide" because doing so could invoke obligations under the international genocide treaty to take action, and the Clinton administration did not want to get significantly involved.

Worse, this was a situation in which there had been a chance for preventive diplomacy and intervention. The UN did have a peacekeeping force on the ground, the UN Assistance Mission in Rwanda (UNAMIR), stemming from a previous period of Hutu-Tutsi ethnic conflict. It was small and had a limited mandate. But its commander, Major General Romeo Dallaire of Canada, had learned from informants months prior to the genocide about what was being planned. All he needed to prevent it, he said, was about five thousand more troops and a more robust mandate allowing his forces to take more proactive and concerted action. This was not like asking for a Persian Gulf War–size force of hundreds of thousands. But General Dallaire's request was denied.

The Clinton administration had a strong voice in this pattern of inaction. While others, including the UN and major European nations also bore responsibility, had the United States spoken out and pushed for action it is likely that the UN would have acted or that, as in other cases, a coalition of nations could have been put together. But the Rwanda crisis came just months after the October 1993 debacle in Somalia, and the Clinton administration balked at confronting potential domestic political opposition. It expressed its empathy, but largely contended that the U.S. national interest was not sufficiently at stake.

As far as principles are concerned, it is hard to think of a more compelling purpose than prevention of genocide. In Kosovo, where the United States led the NATO intervention in 1999, principles and power were largely complementary. The intervention was intended both to stop ethnic cleansing and to ensure stability in Europe (a vital region) and the credibility of NATO (a vital alliance). Are values alone, then, not a sufficient basis for U.S. intervention or other concerted action? That position has the strength of avoiding overcommitment or always being called upon as the "global 911." But it qualifies if not undermines the claim that the United States genuinely and consistently stands for principles. This trade-off can be debated, but it cannot be denied. There have been other episodes, and undoubtedly there will be more. The principles-power tension thus will remain an issue for U.S. foreign policy in dealing with ethnic and other deadly conflicts.

From ABC to ABT?

In Part I of this book we saw a number of cases during the Cold War in which American foreign policy sided with nondemocratic but anticommunist regimes, still claiming to be true to its principles through the "ABC" (anything but communist) definition of Third World democrats. In the contemporary context of the war on terrorism, are we moving towards an "ABT"—anybody but terrorists—definition?

Consider Pakistan. General Pervez Musharraf came to power in a military coup there in 1999. The Clinton administration opposed the Musharraf coup as a violation of democratic principles, and imposed economic sanctions on the country. The Bush administration largely continued this policy until the September 11, 2001, terrorist attacks. At that point, power considerations strongly overrode principles; the United States needed close relations with Pakistan to fight the war in Afghanistan, to try to break up Al Qaeda, and to try to capture Osama bin Laden. Musharraf also came to be seen as the best bet for blocking Islamic fundamentalists and other anti-American forces from gaining ground within Pakistan.

Although the government Musharraf forced out was democratic, independent analysts acknowledged that "Pakistanis broadly welcomed [Musharraf's] overthrow of what was widely perceived as a corrupt civilian government."[36] His own popularity, though, fell. When the first post-coup legislative elections were held in October 2002, opposition groups fared better than Musharraf's political party. Among the opposition groups who did well were Islamic fundamentalist parties that were anti-American and called for the imposition of Islamic law.

Some argued that the United States was only feeding into anti-Americanism by being so supportive of Musharraf. His dictatorial rule had contributed to the political strength of his opponents. The previous spring he had called a referendum seeking support for staying in power beyond the period he had promised at the time of his coup. He got the positive vote he wanted but by a smaller margin than expected and amid widespread accusations of a rigged referendum. While going ahead with the October 2002 legislative elections, he circumscribed them by maintaining his right as president to dismiss the legislature and amend the constitution. By being so pro-Musharraf, and by not pushing him to be more genuinely democratic, the United States was both inconsistent with its own principles and risking a boomerang effect against its power interests.

The counterargument saw the anti-American nature of much of the Pakistani opposition as all the more reason for supporting Musharraf. If the Islamic fundamentalist parties were to come to power, it was argued, they were unlikely to stick by democracy once in power. Moreover, the security interests at stake could not be underestimated in the wake of September 11. This was the war on terrorism's theater of origin. If American power did not continue to be effectively asserted here, the whole war on terrorism could be lost and American security seriously endangered. From this perspective, therefore, the ABT case was seen as both consistent with principles and also giving power its due.

Pakistan is not the only country over which this debate has been playing out. The war on terrorism has brought U.S. military aid and other forms of cooperation to a number of other governments with questionable democratic credentials and human rights records. Many of these have been Central Asian states also bordering Afghanistan: Uzbekistan, Tajikistan, Turkmenistan, and Kyrgyzstan. Of these, only Kyrgyzstan makes it even to the "partly free" list in Table 10.1. All have their own Islamic fundamentalist movements known or suspected of being anti-American and linked to Al Qaeda or other global terrorist networks. Here, too, the Bush administration has both stressed the overriding importance of power considerations and claimed a degree of consistency with principles—by making comparisons to the alternatives and by pointing to military-training programs and other cooperation as ways to help infuse greater respect for democracy and human rights.

In sum, just as the ABC debate was central to Cold War policies, so too is the ABT debate central to our current era.

Principles as Power: Soft Power's Significance

The term "soft power" captures how American principles encompass more than just idealism and altruism. *Soft power,* as defined by Professor Joseph Nye, is based less on coercion and traditional measures of power than on intangible assets such as cultural attraction, political values, and societal strengths that others admire.[37] This is not a strictly new phenomenon; historically the United States and other major powers always have tried to use their reputations and ideologies as sources of power. But it is more important in the post–Cold War world, when power has become "less fungible, less coercive and less tangible."[38] It is part of how "right" can make for "might," how principles can be a source of power.

In 1990, on becoming the president of postcommunist Czechoslovakia, Vaclav Havel quoted Thomas Jefferson as the inspiration for the ideals for which he stood, indeed for which he had gone to jail as a political prisoner during the communist years (see Chapter 6, *Perspectives,* p. 298). American power certainly played a role in bringing down the Soviet empire, and the pursuit of greater prosperity and the attractiveness of capitalism over communism also were important factors. Yet here was the leader of the Czechoslovak "Velvet Revolution," a name reflecting the peacefulness with which its country's communism was brought down, stressing not these material factors but the principles for which the United States stood as the basis for his greatest gratitude.

Yet it was just a year earlier that Chinese students protesting for greater democracy built a replica of the Statue of Liberty in Tiananmen Square. This was quite extraordinary for a number of reasons, including that China is a country that tends to look within its own culture and history for models. It was this very sense of respect and admiration for American principles that made it all the more consequential when, in the wake of the Tiananmen Square massacre and mass arrests, the United States put priority on geopolitical (power) and economic (prosperity) considerations in its relations with the Chinese government. In not standing by the Chinese students, the United States was seen by many as not standing up for its own principles.

The crucial policy choice from a soft-power perspective is not so much whether the United States still can claim to be truer to democratic values than other major powers, but whether it lives up to the standards to which it lays claim for itself. It is one thing to pursue a power-politics foreign policy if the state doing so makes limited claims to standing for some set of values greater than self-interest. But if such claims are made, then it is more problematic.

The soft-power concept provides important perspective for understanding this issue not just as Democratic Idealism but also in terms of how power may be less well served than often is claimed. The issue is not about purity, but about contradiction.

Concerns about soft power also point us to how U.S. domestic policy has indirect foreign policy effects. In 1957, when the segregationist governor of Arkansas was blocking integration of the public schools, one of the reasons President Eisenhower sent in the National Guard was concern about how the U.S. record of segregation would undermine the mantle of principles in foreign policy. It was harder to sustain the claim to stand for freedom in foreign policy if it was not being lived up to in the United States' own domestic policy.

The Realist scholar Hans Morgenthau emphasized this point. The Cold War struggle ultimately will not be determined by military strength or diplomatic maneuvering, he wrote in 1967 with particular reference to Vietnam, but "by the visible virtues and vices of their [the U.S. and Soviet] respective political, economic and social systems. . . . It is at this point that foreign policy and domestic politics merge. . . . The United States ought to again concentrate its efforts upon creating a society at home which can again serve as a model for other nations to emulate."[39]

Soft power also provides a perspective on how the war on terrorism is fought out on the domestic front. In Chapter 7 we discussed the difficulties of striking a balance between national security and civil liberties. The point there was the importance of taking seriously the security imperatives of the terrorist threat while avoiding the damage done to the rights of individual citizens and the American democratic system. The point here is that when national security too readily and too thoroughly trumps civil liberties, American credibility is weakened in the eyes of other governments and peoples. If the United States is not true to its professed standards and values within its own borders, it is harder to sustain the values dimension of its claim to global leadership. To be sure, the United States would have to go a long way before it even approached the hypocrisy of a bin Laden. But American leadership and authority are based not just on assertions of holding to higher political values than others in the world, but also on being as true to American values as the United States claims to be. Thus the treatment of Arab Americans and others of the Muslim faith in the United States affects the dynamics of anti-Americanism in the Middle East and elsewhere in the Islamic world.

In a broad sense some of America's severe social problems also come into play when questions of soft power arises. "In most Asian eyes," Kishore

Mahbubani of Singapore has written, "the evidence of real social decay in the United States is clear and palpable": a 560 percent increase in violent crime since 1960, and a total of 10,567 people killed by handguns in just one year (1990) compared to just 87 in Japan; increases since 1960 of greater than 400 percent in out-of-wedlock births, and more than 200 percent in teenage suicides; a 50 percent increase in hunger since 1985; schools in which the main problems have changed, according to a survey of teachers, from rather innocuous acts such as talking out of turn, chewing gum in class, and making noise to assault, robbery, rape, drug abuse, alcohol abuse, and pregnancy.[40] The American media are depicted as having become overly aggressive, too muckraking, and too sensationalist, and emanating a self-righteous self-image that leads them "to undermine public confidence in virtually every public institution, while leaving their own powers neither checked nor balanced by any countervailing institution." Overall, and quite provocatively, the question is posed as to whether "in working so hard to increase the scope of individual freedom within their society, Americans have progressively cut down the thick web of human relations and obligations that have produced social harmony in traditional societies. . . . Is there *too much freedom* in American society?"[emphasis added][41]

Without doubt, critiques such as this have some elements of ideological America-bashing. But some of the points raised also are made by critics within the United States. Any nation that allows its social problems to mount—its educational system to decline, its once-great cities to decay, its crime rate to shoot up, its race relations to fester—risks having its claim to moral leadership increasingly questioned around the world.

Principles and Prosperity: The Economic Sanctions Debate

One area in which principles-prosperity tensions and trade-offs have come up with great frequency in recent years has been the use of economic sanctions. While not the only purpose for which economic sanctions are used, democracy promotion and human rights protection have been among their main purposes. As such, policy-makers must decide whether to impose limits on economic relations with other countries (trade, investment, loans, foreign aid) to try to force internal political changes.

Key Cases

The case most often cited as a success was the 1980s anti-apartheid sanctions against South Africa, a mix of U.S., UN, and European measures.[42] Other factors also contributed to ending apartheid, but sanctions get a substantial share of the credit. We will study this case in depth later in this chapter in our look at the U.S. domestic politics of sanctions.

Back in Chapter 1 we highlighted the debate over economic sanctions against China following the 1989 Tiananmen Square massacre. Other issues came into play, but mostly this debate was about the tensions and trade-offs between, on the one hand, the economic interests at stake in trade with and investment in China, and, on the other, the defense of human rights as a fundamental American principle. The first Bush administration imposed only limited sanctions on China, stopping short of revoking China's main economic benefit, most-favored-nation (MFN) status. Despite Bill Clinton's harsh criticism of this policy during his 1992 presidential campaign as coddling "the butchers of Beijing," once in office the Clinton administration imposed only limited additional sanctions and also did not revoke MFN. Both administrations claimed that they were not abandoning principles, that other pro–human rights steps were being taken, but most analysts and observers saw this as a choice of economic interests over principles.

Another prominent case involved Haiti. In 1991 the Haitian military staged a coup, overthrowing the democratically elected government of President Jean-Bertrand Aristide. The first Bush administration again imposed only limited sanctions. This time, however, the Clinton administration significantly increased the sanctions, including working through the UN for a multilateral oil embargo. The sanctions had limited efficacy, though, and it took a U.S. military intervention in September 1994 to bring Aristide back to power.

The Haiti case demonstrated the "political gain–civilian pain" dilemma, in which sanctions risk hurting most those they seek to help.[43] Sanctions hit Haiti so hard that per capita GDP fell 25 percent, unemployment leapt to 60–70 percent, and inflation rose to 60 percent, all in a country that already was the poorest in the Western Hemisphere. When sanctions were first imposed, the Haitian people generally supported them, showing a willingness to bear some costs in the expectation that the military regime and its supporters would be brought down. Instead, in large part because the sanctions were so poorly enforced and targeted, the coup leaders bore so few of the costs that in Creole (the Haitian language), *anbago,* the word for "embargo," gave way to *anba gwo,* meaning "under the heels of the rich and powerful."[44]

As analysts we need to ask whether the Haiti case is proof that "sanctions don't work," as many critics contend as a general rule, or whether this is a "false negative" in which sanctions could have worked had they been implemented differently. The plausibility of the question is based primarily on the sanctions' having been imposed partially and incrementally rather than comprehensively and decisively. Haiti was the epitome of a target state vulnerable to economic sanctions: a small country with a weak economy, dependent on the United States for almost 70 percent of its trade, and pretty conducive to sanctions enforcement given its mostly island geography. But the initial Bush administration sanctions were very limited ones. Even when the Clinton administration moved to more comprehensive sanctions, it did so in an on-off fashion. In June 1993 it stepped up the sanctions to include a ban from U.S. ports on all foreign ships doing business with Haiti, froze the financial assets in U.S. banks of coup leaders, and pushed the oil embargo through the UN. The decision soon after by the coup leaders to agree to terms for ending the coup indicated the stepped-up sanctions were working. But the Clinton administration moved too quickly to re-loosen the sanctions. Intended as a carrot, the easing of sanctions backfired and allowed the coup leaders to stockpile oil and take other steps to bolster their anti-sanctions defense, after which they abrogated the agreement. Noted sanctions analysts Kimberly Ann Elliott and Gary Hufbauer make the case that tighter and quicker sanctions, especially financial ones, could have worked. "Carefully crafted financial sanctions, swiftly applied, might have captured the attention of the economic elite, without whose support the military would not [have been] able to rule. The Haitian elite keeps little of its wealth in Haiti and enjoys spending time and money in the United States. A global assets freeze, coupled with a travel ban, would have hit primarily that class."[45]

The sanctions imposed on Iraq in the 1990s are another example of sanctions that did not work as well as intended, although the reasons for their ineffectiveness are more complicated. These sanctions had a broad range of objectives, including the military ones of preventing Saddam Hussein from importing technology and materials for building weapons of mass destruction, as well as the overall goal of trying to undermine Saddam's regime economically so as to bring about regime change without military intervention or covert action.

This case, too, poses the political gain–civilian pain dilemma. The Iraqi people suffered tremendously. In late 1996 UNICEF (the UN Children's Fund) estimated that 4,500 children under the age of 5 were dying in Iraq every month. A UN Food and Agriculture Organization report in 1997 found food shortages and malnutrition in Iraq to have become ever more "severe and chronic."[46] Yet all along, going back to the first UN sanctions against Iraq in 1990, provisions were offered to allow for humanitarian relief with the caveat that the UN would control the funds to ensure that Saddam Hussein did not divert them for weapons of mass destruction or other such purposes. Moreover, while blaming the United States and the international community for the suffering of the Iraqi people, Saddam kept managing to find funds to build and refurbish his multiple presidential palaces and to secretly import military equipment and technology. This does not relieve U.S. policy from concern for the humanitarian issues, but it does reveal the complexity of the policy choices and policy effects.

Do Sanctions Work?

The evidence from these and many other cases is that sanctions have worked in some ways and in some cases but not others.[47] The sanctions literature reflects this mixed assessment. "It would be difficult to find any proposition in the international relations literature more widely accepted," wrote Professor David Baldwin in the mid-1980s, "than those belittling the utility of economic techniques of statecraft."[48] One recent article was straightforwardly titled "Why Economic Sanctions Do Not Work."[49] Baldwin's statement as quoted above, however, was a critical one, from which he went on to question whether sanctions are held to an "analytical 'double standard' . . . prone to accentuate the negative and downplay the positive aspects of such measures."[50] Other studies also have concluded that sanctions have worked and can work more often than is often acknowledged.

Among the factors that affect whether sanctions work, one of the most important is the extent to which the sanctions are multilateral. If other countries serve as alternative trade partners for the target state, sanctions can have little or no impact. Alternative trade partners also can have a political effect by significantly reducing the credibility that sanctions convey. This works in different ways depending on whether the alternative partner is an ally or an adversary of the state initiating the sanctions, but either way it can have an important impact.

Another factor is the extent to which the target state has the economic capacity to defend itself against the sanctions. For example, Rhodesia (now Zimbabwe), which despite in the 1960s–70s becoming the first country to be hit with sanctions by the full United Nations, had sufficient domestic industrial capacity to substitute for most of the embargoed goods and ride the sanctions out for more than ten years. In other cases economic self-defense is not possible economy-wide, but the governing regime and supportive elites can lessen sanctions' effect on themselves through black markets, sanctions-busting, and other profiteering, as was seen in Iraq and Haiti in the 1990s.

Third is whether sanctions are a good "fit" with the foreign policy objectives being pursued. One of the recurring problems in U.S. policy is that sanctions often are turned to as a default option, based more on the constraints on other options than on careful analysis of sanctions themselves. "When in doubt, impose sanctions" assumes that there is nothing to lose by doing so, but in fact sanctions often can end up net negative for the United States, whether through misfiring and missing the regime but hitting the populace, or backfiring and hurting American exporters more than foreign regimes, or weakening rather than buttressing American credibility when the results fall well short of the threats.

What makes sanctions particularly vexing for U.S. post–Cold War policy is that the broad economic, strategic, and political systemic changes do not cut strictly one way or the other. They have created what has been called the "vulnerability-viability paradox." On the one hand, target states are now more vulnerable to sanctions in three respects. First, in economic terms, while the impact of globalization does vary, few if any countries have been able to stay sufficiently insulated or isolated as not to be vulnerable to the economic disruptions set off by sanctions. Whereas the impact of Cold War–era sanctions on nations' gross national products averaged less than 2 percent, a number of the 1990s cases involved double-digit effects. Second is the increased willingness of the United Nations to use its sanctions authority, broadening the coalition and establishing legitimacy in ways only the UN can. There were only two cases of UN-mandated sanctions prior to 1990, but since then there have been more than ten. Third, because democratization has opened up more countries' political systems, groups whose interests are at risk are in more of a position to bring political pressure for policy change to avoid or end sanctions.

On the other hand, other aspects of these same systemic trends have made the political viability of sanctions more problematic. Economically, the greater economic vulnerability of countries has been part of the reason for the sanctions-induced humanitarian crises. Strategically, although it is true that the UN has used sanctions more recently than in the past, at times they have been watered down or delayed by various countries. The United States also has had major disputes with western Europe in cases like Iran and Cuba, where the allies see their geopolitical as well as economic interests differently.

As to the democratization trend, many of the regimes against which sanctions have been used have not been part of it (Iraq, Serbia, and Cuba, for instance).

In sum, the issue of sanctions involves both policy choice and policy design. Which of the national interest objectives, principles or prosperity, is to be given priority? And if the policy choice is for sanctions, how to design the strategy so that it achieves its objectives?

Policy Strategies for Promoting Democracy and Protecting Human Rights

In this section we discuss the major international actors involved in democracy promotion and human rights protection, the strategies for achieving these objectives, and the effectiveness of these strategies.

Who: Key International Actors

The array of actors involved in promoting democratization may be broader than in any other area of foreign policy. The box on p. 580 provides an illustrative listing, in four main categories.

U.S. GOVERNMENT   The lead U.S. agency for democracy promotion is the Agency for International Development (AID). Since the end of the Cold War, AID has broadened its "development" mission to increasingly include political as well as economic development. AID runs some programs directly, and also provides funding to nongovernmental organizations (NGOs). The National Endowment for Democracy receives funds from Congress and AID and channels them principally to four NGOs (see the discussion of NGOs below).

The State Department is involved principally through its Bureau of Democracy, Human Rights, and Labor. It also manages programs such as the Fulbright scholarships and other educational and cultural-exchange programs. Additional roles are played by almost every Cabinet department: the Pentagon works on civil-military relations, the Justice Department helps develop the rule of law, the Education Department conducts literacy training, the Commerce Department promotes free enterprise. The U.S. Congress also is involved, with its numerous legislative-exchange programs for legislators and their staffs from newly democratizing countries. Local governments participate too, through programs like "Sister Cities," linking people at the grassroots

KEY ACTORS IN THE PROMOTION OF DEMOCRACY (PARTIAL LIST)

U.S. government
Agency for International Development (AID)
National Endowment for Democracy (NED)
U.S. Department of State, Bureau of Democracy, Human Rights, and Labor
U.S. Departments of Defense, Justice, Education, Commerce
U.S. Congress
State governments

International organizations
UN Commission on Human Rights
UN Electoral Assistance Units
International Court of Justice
International Institute for Democracy and Electoral Assistance
Organization for Security and Cooperation in Europe (OSCE)
Organization of American States (OAS)
African Union (AU)

Other governments
European Union (EU)
Swedish International Development Authority
Norwegian Agency for Development

Nongovernmental organizations (NGOs)
National Democratic Institute for International Affairs
International Republican Institute
Free Trade Union Institute
Center for International Private Enterprise
Foundation for a Civil Society
German political party *stiftungs*
Westminster Foundation for Democracy (United Kingdom)
International Center for Human Rights and Democratic Development (Canada)
Ford, Asia, Soros Foundations
American Bar Association, Central and East European Law Initiative
Amnesty International
Human Rights Watch

level across the United States to other cities around the world.* Some also take other initiatives, as did Dayton, Ohio, the city where the accord ending the Bosnian war was negotiated in 1995, in developing its own city-to-city contacts with Sarajevo, the capital of Bosnia (see Perspectives, p. 582).

INTERNATIONAL ORGANIZATIONS   The United Nations is involved in promoting democracy in a number of ways. The first time the UN was given a role in monitoring elections and helping build democratic political institutions was in 1989 in Namibia, a territory in Africa previously under UN trusteeship. Since then the UN's electoral assistance and observer missions have been sent to numerous states. Its Commission on Human Rights provides a forum for human rights issues to be raised. The International Court of Justice, based in The Hague in the Netherlands, exercises some capacity to enforce international law. The UN High Commissioner for Refugees (UNHCR) seeks to provide protection and relief for populations displaced by war, repression, or natural disasters.

The Organization for Security and Cooperation in Europe (OSCE) has been the most active of regional multilateral organizations. It has sent election observers, conflict resolution teams, and other missions to a number of member countries. The Organization of American States (OAS), which had tolerated if not condoned military coups in the past, amended its charter in 1992 to suspend member states in which democratic governments are overthrown. Its 2001 Inter-American Democratic Charter further strengthened the OAS's commitment to and role in protecting and promoting democracy. The 2002 Venezuela case manifested this commitment in action and not just words. The new African Union (AU) has committed to playing a more active regional democracy role than had its predecessor, the Organization of African Unity. An important cross-regional organization is the International Institute for Democracy and Electoral Assistance (International IDEA), set up in 1995 by fourteen governments including India, South Africa, Spain, the Scandinavian countries, and others.

OTHER GOVERNMENTS   The European Union (EU) long has made democracy a precondition for membership. This created an incentive for countries like Greece, Spain, and Portugal to democratize in the 1970s and 1980s, and does so

---

*Davis, California, for example, is a sister city with three foreign cities: Uman, Ukraine; Rutillo Grande, El Salvador; and Qufu, China.

PERSPECTIVES
PERSPECTIVES
PERSPECTIVES

"DAYTON KEEPS FORGING NEW BOSNIAN LINKS"

SARAJEVO, Dec. 11 — Jan Vargo and Martha Lampe, two middle-aged women from Dayton, Ohio, never thought they would find themselves sitting in a snow-covered trench in the hills overlooking Sarajevo. The real-estate agent and owner of a string of child care centers had never given much thought to the war in Bosnia. "All the names were so strange and I couldn't figure out who were the good guys and who were the bad guys," said Lampe.

But after their Midwestern industrial city was chosen as the site for the Bosnian Peace Talks last year, Vargo and Lampe, like many Daytonians, began to show concern for the fate of the country. This week, they joined a group of 35 Daytonians who visited the Bosnian capital and found themselves taking a tour of the city's former front line with a demobilized soldier in the Bosnian army.

The travelers from Dayton—who included the mayor, the editor of the Dayton Daily News, several City Council members, an 81-year-old retired minister and an 18-year-old student—were part of a cultural exchange organized by the Friendship Force, a nonprofit organization in Atlanta. . . .

Chris Sanders, 67, a volunteer with the Dayton Art Institute, met with Sarajevo museum curators and said she plans to help raise money for them. Jan Rudd, 62, a volunteer at Dayton's women's health clinic, met with women's organizations here and plans to organize links with women's groups in Dayton. Andrew Bosworth, the deputy director of international programs at the University of Dayton, met with Sarajevo University officials and local high school officials in an effort to organize student exchanges. And Mike Turner, Dayton's 36-year-old mayor, put together a Dayton-Balkans business directory and is planning to return in March with a delegation of Dayton business executives. He said he also hopes to make Sarajevo Dayton's sister city.

Source: Stacy Sullivan, "Dayton Keeps Forging New Bosnian Links," *Washington Post,* December 12, 1996, A47.

today for the former communist countries seeking EU membership. The EU also has programs similar to the AID ones to provide direct democracy assistance. A number of countries also run their own bilateral democracy programs. The Scandinavian countries are widely regarded as world leaders in this area.

NGOs   NGOs often receive government or UN funding, but maintain significant independence in their democracy programs. In the United States, based on a model adapted from Germany, where each major political party has run international democracy-promotion programs since the 1950s, the four NGOs that get most of the National Endowment for Democracy funding are the Democratic Party's National Democratic Institute for International Affairs, the Republican Party's International Republican Institute, the AFL-CIO's Free Trade Union Institute, and the U.S. Chamber of Commerce's Center for International Private Enterprise. Another major U.S.-based NGO is the Foundation for a Civil Society. Britain has the Westminster Foundation for Democracy, Canada its International Center for Human Rights and Democratic Development.

Other NGOs active in building and supporting democracy include private nonprofit foundations such as the Ford, Soros, and Asia Foundations; professional associations such as the American Bar Association and its Central and Eastern Europe Law Initiative (ABA-CEELI); and groups with their own global networks of offices such as Amnesty International and Human Rights Watch.

How: Key Strategies

Along with this identification of the "who" is the question of "how." To be sure, there is no single, one-size-fits-all strategy for democracy promotion. The foreign policy challenge for the United States as well as other international actors is to determine the right fit and right mix for different countries with different sets of problems, and to pursue those strategies with the right combination of international actors.

This generally involves five main objectives: facilitating free and fair elections; helping build strong and accountable political institutions; strengthening the rule of law; protecting human rights; and helping cultivate a robust civil society.

FACILITATING FREE AND FAIR ELECTIONS   *International electoral assistance and monitoring* often provides the most reliable assurance that elections in newly democratizing countries will be free and fair. The mere presence of American and other international observers can deter electoral fraud or detect attempted fraud. One major example is the 1986 presidential election in the Philippines. Then-dictator Ferdinand Marcos tried to steal the election in order to keep himself in power. But a bipartisan U.S. congressional observer team was there as witness to the fraud. Marcos initially was able to convince President Reagan back in Washington that there was "fraud on both sides." But when Reagan made this statement, Senator Richard Lugar (R-Ind.), head of the U.S. observer team, was in a position to state that "the President was misinformed." Senator Lugar was able to come to his own conclusion in part because, since 1983, when Marcos had assassinated opposition leader Benigno Aquino, some U.S. aid to the Philippines had been channeled to Catholic Church and human rights groups for purchasing computers and other equipment that gave them the technical capacity to independently count the votes. Marcos ended up having no choice but to concede the election to Corazon Aquino, wife of the assassinated opposition leader, and to flee the country.[51]

Another example is the February 1990 election in Nicaragua, the first free election in that country's history. An election-observer team, headed by former president Jimmy Carter and including a number of Latin American former presidents, monitored the voting processes. As the election returns were coming in, and it became clear that Sandinista President Daniel Ortega was going to lose to challenger Violeta Chamorro, word spread in Managua that Ortega and the Sandinistas might not accept the results. Because of both his pro–human rights record as U.S. president and the conflict resolution and humanitarian assistance work he had been doing as an ex-president, Jimmy Carter had a great deal of credibility with both sides in the Nicaraguan election and more generally in the eyes of the world. Carter shuttled between Ortega's headquarters and Chamorro's, and told Ortega in no uncertain terms that he would be declaring the elections as having been free and fair, and would oppose any move not to abide by their results. Ortega felt that he had little choice but to back off and accept the results. A crisis was averted, and Nicaragua started on the path to democracy.

On the other hand there have been a number of less successful cases. In Belarus and Armenia, two former Soviet republics, fraud occurred despite the presence of OSCE election-observer teams. The OSCE responded by not certifying the fairness of the elections, and OSCE member countries did impose some sanctions and penalties, but the results stood nevertheless. In Cambodia UN observers helped ensure the fairness of elections, but power struggles continued, civil war resumed, and coups were launched.

Critical forms of electoral assistance also need to be provided prior to the actual election day. *Voter education programs* help prepare populaces that may rarely or never have had a genuinely free and fair election to participate effectively. In Bangladesh, for example, AID support for voter-education programs run by NGOs helped ensure a 74 percent turnout in the 1996 parliamentary elections, the largest in Bangladesh's history (U.S. turnout in midterm congressional elections is about 34 percent). Special targeted efforts increased the voting rate of women, only 45 percent in 1991, to 80 percent.[52]

Political parties need to be built, either to fill the void or to replace old, undemocratic parties. Effective parties are essential for channeling and coalescing groups and individuals within society in ways that help make for organized and peaceful political processes. Helping countries create and strengthen democratic political parties involves everything from training in membership recruitment to fund-raising, public-opinion polling, message development, candidate selection systems, grassroots organizing, and, yes, even making campaign commercials. This is an area in which the National Endowment for Democracy and its Democratic and Republican Party partners are very involved, as are the German party-based democracy-promotion *stiftungs*.

BUILDING STRONG AND ACCOUNTABLE POLITICAL INSTITUTIONS

Although democratic revolutions often are personality driven, with people mobilizing around a charismatic leader, long-term stable democracy requires strong and accountable *political institutions*. The democratization literature stresses three main sets of reasons why political institutionalization is important.[53] The first concerns maintenance of political stability. Political systems that have built strong political institutions are less dependent on and less vulnerable to the fate or whims of a particular governing regime. The stronger the political institutions, the better they can withstand the ups and downs of a governing regime's popularity, and the better they can stand up to any extra-constitutional challenges that a leader or regime may attempt, particularly those that would use or threaten force and violence for political change. This is particularly important vis-à-vis the military, as democracies with strong democratic institutions are better able to resist coups and maintain civilian control of the military.

The second set of reasons concerns representativeness. Political systems with strong political institutions are more likely to convey a sense of genuine choice, competition, and accountability. People need to feel that the system has integrity irrespective of whether their favored candidates win an election. This means believing in the fairness of the electoral process and feeling assured that civil liberties and minority rights will be guaranteed. Strong institutions help ensure a level of confidence in the rules of the game.

Third is effective governance. The instability that comes with weak institutions makes the steadiness and follow-through that governing requires very difficult to achieve. In contrast, well-institutionalized democracies are more capable of governing effectively because, as democracy scholar Larry Diamond writes, "they have more effective and stable structures for representing interests and because they are more likely to produce working legislative majorities or coalitions that can adopt and sustain policies."[54]

A main area for democratic institution-building is strengthening *legislatures*. To fulfill their representative functions legislatures must also develop other professional and institutional capacities to carry out such tasks as designing committee systems, developing the legal and technical expertise for drafting legislation, computerizing legislative operations, communicating and servicing constituencies, and building up research and library support systems. The U.S. Congress has developed a number of training and exchange programs with legislatures in newly democratizing countries, as have the parliaments and assemblies of a number of west European countries.

Another key area is *civil-military relations*. This is where the Pentagon has been playing an important role. A main example is the NATO Partnership for Peace (PFP) program, which has had the objective not only of fostering military cooperation but also the inculcation by Western NATO militaries in their ex-communist counterparts of the principles of civilian control of the military. Related to this are various training and education programs for military officers, as at the George C. Marshall Center for Security Studies, linked to NATO and based in Germany, with what William J. Perry, secretary of defense in the Clinton administration, characterized as a "democratic defense management" curriculum.[55]

Local government programs are the focus of a number of AID initiatives. An official AID document stressed the reasons for this focus: "Decentralization shifts responsibility for decision-making to the leadership and the citizens most directly affected. Fiscal decentralization helps improve local finances, enabling local officials to better provide for their constituencies. Improvements in service delivery build public confidence in democratic processes. Accordingly, they reinforce citizen participation."[56] Among the programs cited were aid to a fishermen's association in the Philippines seeking to ban commercial trawlers from local waters, the creation of a national mayors's association in Bulgaria, and a petition drive in Mozambique to help small farmers get titles to their lands.

Another main need has been for *anti-corruption initiatives.* Corruption undermines democratization both by siphoning off scarce resources in largely poor countries, and in an even more fundamental sense by deeply delegitimizing those in power and potentially the political system itself. It is hard enough to convince a long-suffering people that the benefits of democratization will take time, that they must hang in there and make individual sacrifices for the collective good. But if those who govern and their friends and associates are enriching themselves, the disillusionment and anger among the people are not hard to understand. In Russia, for example, corruption became so endemic in the 1990s that economic privatization was dubbed *prikhvatizatsiya* (literally, "grabification"). There are few things that can more quickly and widely delegitimize a new government than corruption. One NGO called Transparency International was formed for the express purpose of fighting corruption. Each year it issues a list ranking countries by their levels of corruption and uses these and other strategies for pressuring countries to enact anti-corruption reforms.

In this regard and in many others, the accountability provided by a *free press* is crucial. Yet this also tends to be an area in which democratizing countries have limited experience and are in need of outside assistance. The Vienna-based International Press Institute (IPI), another NGO, has played an important role in this effort. With membership of about 2,000 leading editors, publishers, broadcasting executives, and journalists in more than eighty countries, the IPI runs training programs and conferences for journalists from ex-communist and other newly democratizing countries. It also publishes a monthly magazine and an annual report monitoring press freedom.[57] Journalists also need protection against repression and assassinations targeted against them. In 2002, according to the New York–based Committee to Protect Journalists, 11 journalists were killed and 118 in 22 different countries were jailed. China was the worst offender, followed by Nepal, Turkey, Burma, and Eritrea.

STRENGTHENING THE RULE OF LAW   The "rule of law" means that citizens are protected by a strong constitution and other legal guarantees against both arbitrary acts by the state and lawless acts by other citizens. A wide range of programs and initiatives are needed in this regard. They include assistance in the very drafting of a constitution, as well as in writing other legal codes. Courts may lack the most basic infrastructures of trained judicial reporters, computers for compiling jury lists, "bench books" for how to conduct jury trials, and the like. Law schools often need to have their curriculums overhauled. Police forces need to be trained. Special initiatives may be needed to help women, minorities, and the disadvantaged. Broad education programs on the very principle of the rule of law as the basis for justice need to be undertaken.

The American Bar Association's Central and East European Law Initiative (CEELI) is a good example. The ABA is the principal association of lawyers in the United States. Through CEELI it has been seeking to provide legal expertise to countries emerging from communism on constitutional law, judicial restructuring, criminal law, commercial law, environmental law, gender-related issues, and other legal areas. CEELI also has created partnerships linking law schools in the region with American law schools. The box on p. 589 lists some of the CEELI programs in Russia as illustrations. Note how these cover quite a range of topics, including how trials by jury are supposed to work, advocacy training for defense lawyers, a resource manual for commercial law, consumer rights protection, legal ethics, sexual harassment, domestic violence, criminal legal procedures such as pre-trial detention and plea bargaining, natural resource management, and bankruptcy law.

Another challenge is reckoning with the past, or what is often called *transitional justice*.[58] Many newly democratizing societies are emerging from pasts that can only be characterized as horrific: El Salvador, with its decade of civil war, right-wing "death squads," and guerrilla violence; Cambodia, where the Khmer Rouge left hundreds of thousands dead in the "killing fields"; South Africa, with generations of discrimination, oppression, and killings under the apartheid system; Chile and Argentina, freed from the torture, arbitrary arrests, and *desaparecidos* (the disappeared ones) under military dictatorships; Hungary, where property-rights claims must be adjudicated against confiscations not only made in the communist era but going back to the Nazi occupation.

The transitional-justice dilemma pulls between retribution and moving on.[59] Many countries have granted amnesties for past political crimes as part of a reconciliation process. In South Africa the government of Nelson Mandela set up a process stressing amnesty in return for truth about the past. The South African "truth commission" heard startling and disturbing revelations from former high-level government officials admitting their roles in assassinations, attacks on unarmed protesters, and other heinous acts. Truth was being revealed, and overall it seemed that in the South African case it was contributing to national healing. In Guatemala, however, where the 1996 Law of National Reconciliation ending more than thirty years of civil war included a sweeping amnesty, some critics derided it as a "piñata of forgiving, of forgetting the human toll of the war they share responsibility for inciting."[60] And the human

CEELI PROGRAMS IN RUSSIA

Legal profession reform and continuing legal education
1993: Workshop for lawyers of the Moscow Regional Collegium of Advocates to publicize and discuss Russia's new jury trial legislation
1995: Jury trial workshops for defense attorneys, including interactive training techniques and videotaping and critiquing of each attorney's performance
1997: Launch of program for commercial-law training
1997: Grants for programs on consumer-rights protection

Legal education
1993: Established law faculty training program to bring law professors to U.S.
1996: Established legal specialist program to assist Russian law schools in developing clinical, legal writing, and other innovative programs

Women's legal issues
1995: Workshop on sexual harassment, domestic violence, and women's rights law
1997: Assistance for parliamentary hearing on "International Cooperation on the Trafficking in Women and Children"
1998: Grants for pro bono representation of women who are victims of sexual violence

Judicial reform
1993: Provided computers and other equipment for compiling jury lists and organizing trials to courts in nine regions in which jury trials were being started
1997: Workshop on judicial independence

Criminal law reform
1996: Workshops on such topics as pre-trial detention, plea bargaining, search and seizure, discovery, and investigating and prosecuting organized crime

Source: Web site of the American Bar Association, http://www.abanet.org/ceeli, accessed on November 15, 1998.

toll continued: in April 1998 a Roman Catholic bishop was bludgeoned to death in Guatemala City two days after having issued a scathing report on human rights abuses by the army, the government, and paramilitary units.

An interesting and precedent-challenging case arose in 1998–99 over charges of human rights violations by former Chilean dictator General Augusto Pinochet. Pinochet's rule, which lasted from 1973 to 1990, was notorious for brutal human rights violations. Part of the transitional justice agreement made in 1990 when democratic rule was restored in Chile was amnesty for Pinochet; in fact, he was made a senator for life. But it wasn't only Chileans who were killed, tortured, and abducted under Pinochet; some foreigners were as well. When Pinochet traveled to London in October 1998 for medical attention at a British hospital, a judge in Spain invoked international law to demand that he be extradited to Spain to face trial for the killing of Spanish citizens who had been residing in Chile.

The Pinochet case went back and forth. In August 2000 Pinochet was placed under house arrest in Chile. In December he was released under a ruling by the Chilean Supreme Court. In January 2001 the case was reinstated by the investigating judge. In March the case was upheld but only with some of the toughest charges dismissed. In July an appeals court ruled the aging Pinochet mentally unfit to stand trial. The following July this ruling was upheld by the Chilean Supreme Court.

This ruling ended the case but not the debate. The principle raised by the Pinochet case was that of *universal jurisdiction*. One issue was whether a violator of human rights like Pinochet could be tried by the courts of a country other than his own and on grounds inconsistent with the laws of his own country, based on charges of harm done to the other country's citizens.

The other key issue was whether ex-leaders still were protected by the principle of "sovereign immunity" from legal action in the courts of another country (as distinct from the jurisdiction of the International Criminal Court, discussed in Chapter 8). Chilean government officials argued that other governments should not interfere, that this was their business, part of their effort "to re-establish peace in a country where friends and former enemies can coexist." Samuel Pisar, a distinguished French international lawyer and himself a survivor of the Nazi death camps, hailed Pinochet's arrest as manifesting the "almost universal clamor today that those who commit crimes against humanity must be pursued to the ends of the world, wherever and whenever they can be found, and brought to justice."[61] Former U.S. secretary of state Henry Kissinger was among the staunchest critics, warning that we "must not allow legal principles to be used as weapons to settle political scores" and that "historically, the dictatorship of the virtuous has often led to inquisitions and even witch hunts."[62]

PROTECTING HUMAN RIGHTS   At the Source on p. 592 lists the major internationally recognized human rights as delineated in one or more of three principal documents signed under the auspices of the United Nations: the 1948 Universal Declaration of Human Rights; the 1966 International Covenant on Economic, Social, and Cultural Rights; and the 1966 International Covenant on Civil and Political Rights.

There are a number of means by which the United States tries to use its leverage in bilateral relations with governments that violate human rights: these include diplomatic démarches, public denunciations, economic sanctions, and other political measures. The United States also is the only country to issue its own country-by-country human rights reports. The practice was started in the late 1970s during the Carter administration and came to be required by a law passed by Congress.

Recent administrations' human rights policies have differed in the emphasis and focus given to human rights violations. The Carter administration went further than its predecessors in focusing on human rights violations by governments that, while pro-American, were authoritarian and repressive—e.g., Antonio Somoza in Nicaragua, the shah of Iran. The Reagan administration put its focus on communist regimes such as the Soviet Union, Cuba, and post-Somoza Marxist Nicaragua. For the first Bush and the Clinton administrations, with the Cold War over and the war on terrorism not yet begun, there was less of a pattern along pro- or anti-American lines. The pattern came back in the second Bush administration, though, with its emphasis on the "axis of evil" and other states that support terrorism. Other human rights violators are not ignored, but the emphasis is on those that link most closely to the anti-Americanism of global terrorism.*

The United Nations has numerous entities that deal with human rights, some of which were listed in the box on p. 580. The UN Commission on Human Rights, which drafted the Universal Declaration of Human Rights and other human rights covenants, is the main UN forum in which human rights issues are raised. Its Subcommission on the Prevention of Discrimination and the Protection of Minorities makes recommendations on and conducts investigations of issues dealing with the prevention of discrimination and the

---

*Check the State Department website, http://www.state.gov, for the most recent human rights reports.

At the Source

PRINCIPAL INTERNATIONALLY RECOGNIZED HUMAN RIGHTS

Drawn from the Universal Declaration of Human Rights; the International Covenant on Economic, Social, and Cultural Rights; and the International Covenant on Civil and Political Rights

66 Equality of rights without discrimination
Life
Liberty and security of person
Protection against slavery
Protection against torture and cruel and inhuman punishment
Equal protection of the law
Access to legal remedies for rights violations
Protection against arbitrary arrest or detention
Hearing before an independent and impartial judiciary
Presumption of innocence
Freedom of movement and residence
Freedom to seek asylum from persecution
Freedom of thought, conscience, and religion
Freedom of opinion, expression, and the press
Freedom of assembly and association
Political participation
Special protections for children
Education
Self-determination
Humane treatment when detained or imprisoned
Protection against arbitrary expulsion of aliens
Protection against advocacy or racial or religious hatred
Protection of minority culture 99

Source: Jack Donnelly, "State Sovereignty and International Intervention: The Case of Human Rights," in Gene M. Lyons and Michael Mastanduno, eds, *Beyond Westphalia? State Sovereignty and International Intervention* (Baltimore: Johns Hopkins University Press, 1995), 117.

protection of ethnic, racial, and linguistic minorities. The UNHCR is responsible for protecting refugees fleeing persecution, conflict, and widespread human rights violations, and promoting just resolution of refugee crises.

The UN also convenes special conferences, as with the 1993 World Conference on Human Rights in Vienna, attended by 171 states. The declaration agreed to at this conference stated that "human rights and fundamental freedoms are the birthright of all human beings; their protection and promotion is the first responsibility of governments."[63] Two years later the UN World Conference on Women was held in Beijing, focusing particularly on women's rights. This conference's "platform for action" advocated changing laws and practices that discriminate against or oppress women.

In addition, since 1946 the standing International Court of Justice (ICJ) located in The Hague has been the principal judicial organ of the UN. Although the ICJ is an important institution, the limits of its power mirror some of the limits on the UN generally with regard to human rights. Back in April 1993, when the Bosnian war was still raging, the ICJ ruled that Serbia should stop its ethnic cleansing. A few months later, though, on an appeal from Serbia, the ICJ had to acknowledge that the means of enforcing its ruling were beyond the scope of its jurisdiction. This was indicative of the normative tension in the UN's authority between universality and sovereignty, as discussed in Chapter 8, and a problem that has carried over with the newly established International Criminal Court (ICC).

NGOs such as Amnesty International and Human Rights Watch play such an important role in human rights advocacy that they are often referred to as the "conscience" of governments. Unbound by trade-offs with other foreign policy objectives and less inhibited by the formalities of traditional diplomacy, human rights NGOs can be more vocal and assertive than governments or multilateral organizations. Their impact often is quite substantial in terms of both influencing official policy and initiating their own direct efforts. Indeed, Amnesty International won the Nobel Peace Prize in 1977. Since then, with the Internet and faxes and other advanced communications making it both more difficult for repressive governments to hide their human rights violations and easier for advocacy groups to communicate with their own global networks of activists, the NGO role in human rights advocacy has grown even more significant.

CULTIVATING CIVIL SOCIETY   A strong civil society is one that has lots of what Harvard scholar Robert Putnam calls "social capital"—a public-spiritedness and community involvement that goes beyond just voting. It entails other forms of civic engagement, a sense of "reciprocity and coopera-tion," and a shared ethic among citizens of being "helpful, respectful and trustful towards one another, even when they differ on matters of sub-stance."[64] The statement of goals by Dialog, a community outreach NGO in Poland, well captures what is meant by civil society: "to encourage citizens to respond actively to problems that concern them; and, through such re-sponses, to build—or rebuild—a civil society. A society in which ordinary citizens trust each other, organize voluntarily to achieve common ends, ex-pect local government to respond to their needs, and participate generally in the public life of the community."[65]

In many newly democratizing societies decades of dictatorship and even longer historical traditions of authoritarianism have left little base on which to build such practices and values. Particularly in states so recently torn by ethnic cleansing, genocide, and other bitter and violent societal rending, con-ceptions of trust and common goals can seem altogether alien. Yet it is in these very cases that cultivation of the values and practices of civil society is all the more essential, for as the British political scientist Richard Rose states, "the construction of trustworthy political institutions is more likely to hap-pen from the bottom up than the top down."[66] Elections won't work, politi-cal institutions won't be stable, and the rule of law won't become ensconced unless the basic civic values of nonviolent resolution of political differences, tolerance for societal differences, and commitment to some level of political engagement provide a societal foundation.

Thus while policies geared to helping develop civil society are much less dramatic than election monitoring, much less visible than legislative ex-changes, and much less noticeable than human rights advocacy, they are no less essential over the long term. Illustrative programs and policies include the National Endowment for Democracy's funding for a new high school civics curriculum in Russia, training of newly elected village committee members on effective local governance in China, civic and voter education initiatives by youth NGOs in Slovakia, public-advocacy training and assistance for a local association of small farmers seeking formal titles to their land in Mozam-bique, and training community leaders to become conflict mediators in Colombia.

What: Assessing Effectiveness

Enough time has now passed that assessments of the effectiveness of post–Cold War democracy promotion are beginning to come in.[67] These assessments have been decidedly mixed. While the figures back in Table 10.1 do show an overall positive trend, a striking number of countries have become less democratic and seem "stuck in a twilight zone of tentative commitment, illiberal practices and shallow institutionalization."[68] Some take an even more critical view. "The effects of democracy promotion programs," Thomas Carothers of the Carnegie Endowment for International Peace concluded, "are usually modestly positive, sometimes negligible and occasionally negative." Carothers ran through many of the major program areas:

- Rule of law: "What stands out about U.S. rule-of-law assistance since the mid-1980s is how difficult and often disappointing such work is. . . . Most of the projects launched with enthusiasm—and large budgets—. . . have fallen far short of their goals."
- Legislative assistance: "The record is riddled with disappointment and failure. . . . All too often [programs] have barely scratched the surface in feckless, corrupt, patronage-ridden parliaments. . . .
- Civil society: "Democracy promoters are starting to learn . . . just how inflated their expectations have been and how limited their capabilities to produce broad-scale change really are."[69]

In each of these areas he does also make some positive points: that rule-of-law programs have "help[ed] push the issue onto the agenda of governments . . . [which] in the long run may prove an important contribution"; that there are some important cases in which legislative aid "has helped make possible significant improvement" (citing Poland, the Czech Republic, Hungary, El Salvador, and the Philippines); and "various lines of positive evolution" and "more sophisticated programming" in civil society efforts. And in his conclusions he stresses that his analysis does not mean that "democracy aid does not work or is futile," that it is "a useful element of American foreign aid and foreign policy that is gradually gaining coherence, one that is rarely of decisive importance but usually more than a decorative add-on."[70]

Seven key lessons can be drawn from recent experience. First is that the difficulties of promoting democracy do not take away from the importance of doing so. The principles "P" is vital to the U.S. national interest both as a matter of being true to the values for which Americans claim to stand, and as a manifestation of "soft power" and the precept that right also can make for might. U.S. foreign policy needs to be more realistic and less romantic about what effective democracy promotion requires, to re-assess but not reduce the commitment to democracy promotion.

Second, the emphasis on consolidation and institutionalization is the right one. "American foreign policymakers should indeed view the democratic consolidation of post-transition countries as a legitimate foreign policy objective," as *Foreign Affairs* editor Gideon Rose argued, "and their most important democracy-related policy challenge over the next decade."[71] Free and fair elections remain crucial to this effort, but they are not enough by themselves. Many countries have managed to hold elections that qualify as free and fair, but only barely, without becoming "liberal democracies" in terms of also allowing civil liberties, free press, and other basic freedoms and democratic practices.[72] Strong and accountable political institutions do need to be built; the rule of law does need to be strengthened; human rights do need to be protected; civil society does need to be cultivated—but by learning the lessons of what worked and what did not over the past decade, and why.

Third is the "no blueprints" caveat. There has been too much transposing of the U.S. model to the rest of the world, as if one size fits all. Any political system must have its local roots, connecting it to its nation's history, culture, economic system, and political dynamics. Indeed, there are many aspects of the model that the U.S. democratic political system succeeds in spite of, not because of. There also are lessons to be learned from other Western democracies, not just the United States. Strong criticisms have been launched at the consultants who fly in to a democratizing country, put on their "made-in-American" PowerPoint presentations, and then head out to the next destination. Local ideas need to be tapped and local leaders need to be engaged in ways that adapt and apply general democratization strategies to particular national contexts.

Fourth is the importance of working with other countries and within international institutions whenever possible. This includes both the United Nations and regional multilateral organizations such as the OSCE and the OAS.

Fifth is the importance of long-term perspectives. The U.S. democratic system was not built in a few years or few decades; it is an ongoing process, and indeed still an imperfect one. So while measurable impact has to be there, markers need to be set that allow for short- and medium-term assessment but also for a longer-term approach. One of the studies noted earlier points to the not fully tangible "enhancing [of] the resources, skills, techniques, ideas and legitimacy of civil society organizations, civic education efforts, the mass media" and other local actors as one of the main contributions of democracy-promotion programs.[73] Another concurs, stressing that "many of the most important results of democracy promotion are psychological, moral, subjective, indirect and time-delayed."[74]

Sixth is the need to start thinking again about democratization as not just a political dynamic but also an economic one. This partially harks back to the 1950s and 1960s, when democratization strategies were linked to socioeconomic development. In the 1990s, U.S. foreign aid for democracy promotion went up substantially, but in part at the cost of a decline in economic development aid. Yet to try to build democracy without tackling problems of poverty, the concentration of economic power, and related social inequalities is "to float on the surface of current politics, never affecting the broader structural tides beneath."[75] This serves as another example of continuity amid change as we look at American foreign policy over time, and as a link among the 4 Ps—in this instance, principles and prosperity.

Finally, and most important, while our focus has been on U.S. and other international policies and strategies, ultimately the key to successful democratization and well-protected human rights lies with *the leaders and peoples themselves.* The example of Nelson Mandela in South Africa shines above all. Here was a man who was held as a political prisoner for 27 years but who did not do unto his old enemies as they had done to him. As president, Mandela displayed extraordinary statesmanship and ruled in a spirit of reconciliation, not retribution. No wonder Mandela won the Nobel Peace Prize, along with F. W. de Klerk, the last white president of South Africa, who led the move to bring apartheid down from within. Other cases are less historically dramatic but also involve leaders and groups opting for peaceful and democratic transitions over their own narrow self-interests. When the opposite choice is made, though, the effects are devastating. One of the main paths to ethnic conflict in recent years has been when leaders foment political violence, when they play to and play up the historical roots of hatreds, and seek to mobilize groups around these divisions rather than seek reconciliation.

Another important characteristic of leaders is their ability to make the often difficult transition from leader of a revolutionary movement to leader of a government. Revolutionary leaders need to inspire their people, lead them to the barricades with bold rhetoric and defiance, project a persona larger than life, and often keep political power highly concentrated in their own hands and those of a small inner circle. But governing requires creating nascent political institutions, delivering services, building an economy, accepting accountability, and opening up processes for greater access and representation. The differences between the skills and dispositions required by these two roles are one of the reasons why great revolutionary leaders often are less successful when it comes to governing. This was an issue for Yasir Arafat as the Israeli occupation of Gaza and the West Bank started coming to an end: Arafat had trouble making the transition from revolutionary and terrorist to the president of an incipient independent state responsible for delivering on policies for the day-to-day betterment of his people and for leading the way in building Palestinian democracy. Boris Yeltsin, too, whose defiant leadership on top of the tanks facing down the August 1991 anti-Soviet military coup was crucial, showed substantial limitations as president of Russia.

Foreign Policy Politics: Economic Sanctions and the South Africa Case

Earlier in this chapter we discussed prosperity-principles tensions and other aspects of foreign policy strategy with economic sanctions as a principal example. Here we focus on economic sanctions from the standpoint of foreign policy politics.

The baseline for presidential-congressional relations on cases of economic sanctions is the provision of the Constitution granting Congress the power "to regulate commerce with foreign nations." Sanctions are like tariffs in this respect (although one is more politically motivated and the other more economically motivated), but both constitute regulation of international trade. Presidents do have some powers to impose sanctions granted through the International Economic Emergency Powers Act and other legislation. Executive-branch politics is also often in evidence: different departments and agencies have different perspectives and interests at stake, for in bureaucratic politics, where you stand depends on where you sit.

All five types of interest groups in our interest group typology from Chapter 2 may exert pressure in sanctions cases: economic interest groups, based on their trade and investment interests; identity groups, motivated by their ethnic, racial, national, religious, and other links to targeted countries; political issue groups, including many NGOs engaged in democracy promotion and human rights protection; state and local governments, drawing on their purchasing power, pension funds, and other economic levers to pursue their own sanctions; and foreign governments, through contracts with Washington, D.C., law firms, public relations firms, and other lobbyists. The press and media may also be engaged, depending on the salience and drama of the case. The extent to which public opinion is activated varies in similar ways.

Of all the recent sanctions cases, the 1985–86 anti-apartheid sanctions against South Africa stand out as an example in which the foreign policy politics was especially intense and for our purposes very instructive.[76] Ever since 1948, South Africa had been governed by a system called "apartheid." Technically meaning "separatehood," the apartheid system gave the white minority superiority over the black African majority. The black majority was denied meaningful political participation, relegated to economic inequality, confined to living in designated areas, and repressed overall. The apartheid system was viewed as the most unequal and racist in the world.

Prior to the mid-1980s, the United States had done little to oppose or seek to change the apartheid system. The Kennedy administration had imposed an arms embargo (i.e., economic sanctions on military weapons). The Carter administration had signed on to the United Nations arms embargo and added some other selected sanctions. The Reagan administration shifted back in the other direction: Secretary of State Al Haig spoke of "old friends . . . who are getting together again."[77] By 1984 American exports of aircraft, computers, communications equipment, and other military-related goods had increased 100 percent over Carter administration levels.

But things grew worse in South Africa. Anti-apartheid protests so intensified that President P. W. Botha declared a state of emergency, cracking down against political demonstrations, school boycotts, labor stoppages, and rent strikes. His regime arrested key black leaders, including the leaders of the largest black political movement, the African National Congress (ANC). These leaders joined the imprisoned Nelson Mandela, the ANC leader who had been arrested and held in prison since the early 1960s. By late 1985, as the situation became increasingly violent, the reported death toll was more than three people every day.

The anti-apartheid movement in the United States responded to these events with a political impact greater than that of any protest movement since the Vietnam War. It was led by TransAfrica, a small political issue group that until then was not all that well known. TransAfrica came up with the very effective initial strategy of dramatizing the issue and demonstrating outrage by having political leaders and celebrities protest at the South African embassy in Washington, D.C., in ways that would intentionally get them arrested. By mid-December 1985 the "celebrity arrests" included American civil rights leaders, Hollywood movie stars, religious leaders of many faiths, and fifteen members of Congress. This public protest in turn led to greater press coverage; before long the average American "was gaining an unprecedented awareness of South Africa."[78] Public opinion was strongly opposed to apartheid. College campuses became seized with this issue. Teach-ins, demonstrations, and other manifestations of student activism were somewhat reminiscent of activities on campuses during the Vietnam era.

The principal policy issue was whether to impose economic sanctions and, if so, how comprehensive to make those sanctions. Some proposals included sanctioning all U.S. trade and investment in South Africa. American companies had extensive economic interests in South Africa. The United States was South Africa's leading trade partner, supplying 15 percent of its imports, including 70 percent of its computer equipment, 45 percent of its oil, and 33 percent of its cars. Imports from South Africa were only 8 percent of total U.S. imports but included 75 percent of the U.S. supply of chromium, vital for manufacturing stainless steel and aircraft engines; 67 percent of the platinum, used in automobile catalytic converters, fertilizer, explosives, and purified glass; and $140 million in diamonds. In terms of investments, about 350 American firms had operations in South Africa, including 57 of the Fortune 100 companies. American banks had about $7.5 million in loans out to South African companies. It thus was no surprise that most of the American business community opposed sanctions.

In Congress, the strong support from Democrats for an anti-apartheid sanctions bill was no surprise. The support that started to come from Republicans was. The Republican Reagan administration was opposed to sanctions, as Republicans in Congress long had been. But a group of young conservative House members saw this issue as one that could be politically beneficial in broadening the party's popular base. "South Africa has been able to depend on conservatives in the United States . . . to treat them with benign neglect," said Representative Vin Weber (R-Minn.), a leader of this group. "We served notice that, with the emerging generation of conservative leadership, that is not going to be the case."[79] Senator Richard Lugar (R-Ind.), chair of the Senate Foreign Relations Committee, also became a supporter of at least some sanctions. Lugar was generally seen as a moderate on foreign policy issues, and was emerging through this and other issues as a more prominent foreign policy figure.

The Anti-Apartheid Act of 1985 was approved by huge margins, 380 to 48 in the House and 80 to 12 in the Senate, despite continued opposition from the Reagan administration. When the White House threatened to veto the bill, Weber and Lugar were among those warning the White House that on this issue the two-thirds majorities needed for veto override would be there, with many Republicans as part of them.

Congress still had to go through the final steps of a conference committee to work out differences between the House and Senate bills, and then bring that bill to final votes in both chambers. The Reagan administration took advantage of this delay to shift tactics. It issued an executive order imposing its own sanctions, which were more than it had previously favored but less than those mandated by the congressional bills. Party loyalty prevailed at that point, and the House and Senate Republicans blocked final passage of the congressional bills.

But the issue was taken up again the following year. In May 1986 Democrats in the House introduced a new bill, the Comprehensive Anti-Apartheid Sanctions Act, which called for even more extensive sanctions. This bill was approved on the floor with an amendment by Representative Ron Dellums (D-Calif.), not only prohibiting new investments by American companies in South Africa but also requiring disinvestment (i.e., selling off of existing investments). The Senate then passed its own bill that went further than the 1985 Reagan executive order but not as far as the House bill. Lugar kept the Senate coalition together amid opposition to any sanctions bill from conservatives such as Jesse Helms (R-N.C.) and pressure from liberals such as Edward Kennedy (D-Mass.) to make the Senate bill as tough as the House one.

Largely on the basis of a commitment by Senator Lugar to stand by the bill even if President Reagan vetoed it, House Democratic leaders agreed to bypass the negotiations of a conference committee and accept the Senate version of the bill. President Reagan did veto it. But by votes of 313 to 83 in the House and 78 to 21 in the Senate, well beyond the necessary two-thirds majorities, the veto was overridden and the Comprehensive Anti-Apartheid Sanctions Act became law.

This was the first foreign policy veto override since President Richard Nixon's veto in 1973 of the War Powers Resolution. It showed how politically strong the anti-apartheid forces had become. All along, groups like TransAfrica had been keeping up their pressure, as had businesses and other interests on the other side. State and local governments were coming out against apartheid, passing their own versions of sanctions through prohibitions on purchases from and investments in American companies doing business with South Africa. Public opinion showed ever larger majorities in favor of sanctions. Campuses stayed active. Meanwhile, the press and television kept covering the South African government's violent and repressive tactics.

In this case the foreign policy politics were strong enough to push the government to give priority to principles over prosperity. The anti-apartheid sanctions case offers lessons and implications helpful for understanding the foreign policy politics of other sanctions cases, as well as other democracy promotion and human rights protection cases.

Summary

Will the twenty-first century be a democratic one? This is the question with which we began this chapter. The reasons why the answer still is uncertain should now be clear.

The falls of communism, apartheid, military dictatorships, and other forms of repression during the 1990s constituted historic progress in the spread of democracy and human rights around the world. Yet there were limits and uncertainties to this progress, especially in regions like Africa and the Middle East, and a long list of human rights violations in all too many countries. The long-term trend depends on whether the political, social, economic, and other challenges to democratic consolidation and institutionalization are met.

This trend is of importance to the United States for a number of reasons. Democracy and individual freedom are the essence of the principles to which American foreign policy has long laid claim. They also further the U.S. interest in peace. The relationship posited by the democratic peace theory is a strong one, albeit not as simple or unequivocal as often portrayed.

Democracy promotion and human rights protection also can create tensions and trade-offs with considerations of power and prosperity. This has come up repeatedly in our discussion, in this chapter and throughout the book, with other power-principles and prosperity-principles dilemmas. Yet the complementarities are more frequent and more significant than is often recognized.

Policies for promoting democracy and protecting human rights thus require serious and extensive attention. Key roles are played by a number of other international actors and by NGOs, but as partners with and complements to, not substitutes for, the United States. These policy strategies are varied; all require ongoing commitments. They pose a number of difficult policy choices, for devising effective strategies and for providing sufficient funding and other resources.

The ancient Athenians, often credited with one of the earliest democracies, chose as their patron the goddess Athena. Athena herself was said to have sprung forth from the head of Zeus, the god of gods. Democracy, however, cannot just spring forth. It must be built, painstakingly, continuously, by those who want it for their own political systems and by those whose foreign policy is served by its global spread.

Notes

[1] Francis Fukuyama, "The End of History?" *The National Interest* 16 (Summer 1989), 3–4.

[2] Samuel P. Huntington, "No Exit—The Errors of Endism," *The National Interest* 17 (Fall 1989), 10.

[3] Samuel P. Huntington, "The Clash of Civilizations?" *Foreign Affairs* 72:3 (Summer 1993), 22.

[4] Robert D. Kaplan, "The Coming Anarchy?" *Atlantic Monthly* 273 (February 1994), 44–46; Chester A. Crocker and Fen Osler Hampson with Pamela Aall, eds., *Managing Global Chaos: Sources of and Responses to International Conflict* (Washington, D.C.: U.S. Institute of Peace Press, 1996); I. William Zartman, ed., *Collapsed States: The Disintegration and Restoration of Legitimate Authority* (Boulder, Colo.: Westview, 1995).

[5] Gabriel Escobar, "A Nod to Civilian Ascendancy," *Washington Post,* October 14, 1996, A23.

[6] See, for example, Donald Rothchild, *Managing Ethnic Conflict in Africa: Pressures and Incentives for Cooperation* (Washington, D.C.: Brookings Institution Press, 1997); David R. Smock, ed., *Making War and Waging Peace: Foreign Intervention in Africa* (Washington, D.C.: U.S. Institute of Peace Press, 1993); and Keith B. Richburg, *Out of America: A Black Man Confronts Africa* (New York: Basic Books, 1997).

[7] Huntington, "The Clash of Civilizations?" 40.

[8] On Arab democratization more generally, see John L. Esposito and John O. Voll, *Islam and Democracy* (New York: Oxford University Press, 1996); Yehudah Mirsky and Matt Ahrens, eds., *Democracy in the Middle East: Defining the Challenge* (Washington, D.C.: Washington Institute for Near East Policy, 1993); Saad Eddin Ibrahim, "The Troubled Triangle: Populism, Islam and Civil Society in the Arab World," *International Political Science Review,* 19 (October 1998), pp. 357–72; Augustus Richard Norton and Farhad Kazemi, eds., *Civil Society in the Middle East* (Leiden: Brill, 1994–95).

[9] Martin Kramer, "Where Islam and Democracy Part Ways," in Mirsky and Ahrens, eds., *Democracy in the Middle East,* 32, 34.

[10] Ray Takeyh, "The Lineaments of Islamic Fundamentalism," *World Policy Journal,* Winter 2001–2, 59–67.

[11] Gail Lapidus, "Transforming Russia: American Policy in the 1990s," in Robert J. Lieber, ed., *Eagle Rules? Foreign Policy and American Primacy in the Twenty-First Century* (Upper Saddle River, N.J.: Prentice-Hall, 2002), 120.

[12] Michael Wines, "Russia's Latest Dictator Goes by the Name of Law," *New York Times,* January 21, 2001, Section 4, p. 3.

[13] Mark Franchetti, "Putin Resurrects Spectre of KGB," *Sunday Times* (London), February 4, 2001, web.lexis-nexis.com.

[14] Speech by Senator Joseph I. Lieberman at the Wehrkunde security conference, Munich, Germany, February 4, 2001.

[15] Ellen Mickiewicz, *Changing Channels: Television and the Struggle for Power in Russia* (New York: Oxford University Press, 1997); Kathy Lally, "Battle over Free Press Intensifies in Russia," *Baltimore Sun,* February 3, 2001, 1A; "A Moscow Media Magnate Urges a Definition of Limits for Russia," *New York Times,* May 4, 2001.

[16] Lapidus, "Transforming Russia," 117.

[17] Edward Friedman, "Lone Eagle, Lone Dragon? How the Cold War Did Not End," in Lieber, *Eagle Rules?* 195.

[18]Minxin Pei, "Future Shock: The WTO and Political Change in China," *Policy Brief* 1 (February 2001), Carnegie Endowment for International Peace.

[19]Elisabeth Rosenthal, "China Detains and Isolates Liberal Computer Whiz," *New York Times*, April 21, 2001, A3.

[20]Tom Malinowski, "China's Willing Censors," *Washington Post*, April 20, 2001, A25.

[21]Thomas Carothers, "Democracy without Illusion," *Foreign Affairs* 76:1 (January/February 1997), 89.

[22]Bill Clinton, "State of the Union Address," *New York Times*, January 26, 1994, A17.

[23]"A National Security Strategy of Engagement and Enlargement," reprinted in *America's Strategic Choices*, ed. Michael E. Brown et al. (Cambridge, Mass.: MIT Press, 1997), 319.

[24]Jack S. Levy, "Domestic Politics and War," in *The Origin and Prevention of Major Wars*, ed. Robert I. Rotberg and Theodore K. Rabb (Cambridge, U.K.: Cambridge University Press, 1989), 88.

[25]See, for example, Bruce Russett, *Grasping the Democratic Peace* (Princeton: Princeton University Press, 1993); John Owen, "How Liberalism Produces Democratic Peace," *International Security* 19:2 (Fall 1994), 87–125; Melvin Small and J. David Singer, "The War Proneness of Democratic Regimes," *Jerusalem Journal of International Relations* 1 (Summer 1976), 50–69.

[26]Immanuel Kant, "Perpetual Peace," cited in Michael W. Doyle, "Kant, Liberal Legacies, and Foreign Affairs," in *Debating the Democratic Peace*, ed. Michael E. Brown et al. (Cambridge, Mass.: MIT Press, 1997), 24–25.

[27]Doyle, "Kant, Liberal Legacies, and Foreign Affairs," 49.

[28]Owen, "How Liberalism Produces Democratic Peace," 96.

[29]Cited in Bruce W. Jentleson, "The Political Basis for Trade in U.S.-Soviet Relations," *Millennium: Journal of International Studies* 15 (Spring 1986), 27.

[30]David E. Spiro, "The Insignificance of the Liberal Peace," *International Security* 19:2 (Fall 1994) 50–86.

[31]Henry S. Farber and Joanne Gowa, "Politics and Peace," *International Security* 20:2 (Fall 1995), 123–46; Christopher Layne, "Kant or Cant: The Myth of the Democratic Peace," *International Security* 19:2 (Fall 1994) 5–49.

[32]Edward D. Mansfield and Jack Snyder, "Democratization and the Danger of War," *International Security* 20:1 (Summer 1995), 7.

[33]George W. Bush, *National Security Strategy for the United States, 2002*, http://www.whitehouse.gov/nsc, 1.

[34]International Commission on Intervention and State Sovereignty (ICISS), *The Responsibility to Protect* (Ottawa, Canada: International Development Research Centre, 2001), 1.

[35]Michael Barnett, *Eyewitness to a Genocide: The United States and Rwanda* (Ithaca: Cornell University Press, 2002), 1. See also Samantha Power, *"A Problem from Hell": America and the Age of Genocide* (New York: Basic Books, 2002), ch. 10.

[36]David Rohde, "Pakistani Fundamentalists and Secular Opponents of Muhsarraf Do Well in Election," *New York Times*, October 11, 2002, A8.

[37]Joseph S. Nye, Jr., *Bound to Lead: The Changing Nature of American Power* (New York: Basic Books, 1990); and Joseph S. Nye, Jr., *The Paradox of American Power: Why the World's Only Superpower Can't Go It Alone* (New York: Oxford University Press, 2002).

[38]Nye, *Bound to Lead*, 188.

[39]Hans J. Morgenthau, cited in Michael J. Smith, "Ethics and Intervention," *Ethics and International Affairs* 1989 (no. 3), 8.

[40]Kishore Mahbubani, "The United States: 'Go East, Young Man,'" *Washington Quarterly* 17:2 (Spring 1994), 6 and *passim*.

[41]Mahbubani, "Go East, Young Man," 7, 9.

[42]This section draws on a study I did for the National Academy of Sciences, National Research Council, Commission on Behavioral and Social Sciences and Education, Committee on International Conflict Resolution. See Bruce W. Jentleson, "Economic Sanctions and Post–Cold War Conflicts: Challenges for Theory and Policy," in *International Conflict Resolution after the Cold War*, ed. Paul C. Stern and Daniel Druckman (Washington, D.C.: National Academy Press, 2000), 123–77.

[43]Thomas G. Weiss, David Cortright, George A. Lopez, and Larry Minear, eds., *Political Gain and Civilian Pain: Humanitarian Impact of Economic Sanctions* (Lanham, Md.: Rowman and Littlefield, 1997).

[44]Claudette Antoine Werleigh, "The Use of Sanctions in Haiti: Assessing the Economic Realities," in *Economic Sanctions: Panacea or Peacebuilding in the Post–Cold War World?* ed. David Cortright and George Lopez (Boulder, Colo.: Westview, 1995), 169.

[45]Kimberley Ann Elliott and Gary Clyde Hufbauer, "'New' Approaches to Economic Sanctions," in *U.S. Intervention Policy for the Post–Cold War World*, ed. Arnold Kanter and Linton F. Brooks (New York: Norton, 1994), 153–54.

[46]Eric Hoskins, "The Humanitarian Impact of Economic Sanctions and War in Iraq," in *Weiss, Political Gain and Civilian Pain*.

[47]Jentleson, "Economic Sanctions and Post–Cold War Conflicts;" Richard N. Haass, ed., *Economic Sanctions and American Diplomacy* (Washington, D.C.: Brookings Institution Press, 1998); Cortright and Lopez, *Economic Sanctions: Panacea or Peacebuilding*; Richard N. Haass and Meghan L. O'Sullivan, eds., *Honey and Vinegar: Incentives, Sanctions and Foreign Policy* (Washington, D.C.: Brookings Institution Press, 2000); Meghan L. O'Sullivan, *Shrewd Sanctions: Economic Statecraft and State Sponsors of Terrorism* (Washington, D.C.: Brookings Institution Press, 2003).

[48]David A. Baldwin, *Economic Statecraft* (Princeton: Princeton University Press, 1985), 57.

[49]Robert A. Pape, "Why Economic Sanctions Do Not Work," *International Security*, 22:2 (Fall 1997), 90–136.

[50]Baldwin, *Economic Statecraft*, 144.

[51]Bruce W. Jentleson, "Discrepant Responses to Falling Dictators: Presidential Belief Systems and the Mediating Effects of the Senior Advisory Process," *Political Psychology* 11 (June 1990), 377–80.

[52]U.S. Agency for International Development (AID), *Agency Performance Report 1997*, available at http://www.info.usaid.gov/democracy/, accessed September 29, 1998, 37–39.

[53]Larry Diamond, *Promoting Democracy in the 1990s: Actors and Instruments, Issues and Imperatives* (Washington, D.C.: Carnegie Commission for Preventing Deadly Conflict, 1995), 40–48.

[54]Diamond, "Promoting Democracy in the 1990s," 41.

[55]William J. Perry, "Defense in an Age of Hope," *Foreign Affairs* 79:6 (November/December 1996), 69–70.

[56]AID, *Agency Performance Report 1997*, 42.

[57]Adam Feinstein, "Fighting for Press Freedom," *Journal of Democracy* 6 (January 1995), 159–68.

[58]Neil J. Kritz, ed., *Transitional Justice: How Emerging Democracies Reckon with Former Regimes* (Washington, D.C.: U.S. Institute of Peace Press, 1995).

[59]Among the sources on transitional justice see the three-volume study *Transitional Justice: How*

Emerging Democracies Reckon with Former Regimes (Washington, D.C.: U.S. Institute of Peace Press, 1995).

[60]Francisco Goldman, "In Guatemala, All Is Forgotten," *New York Times,* December 23, 1996, A13.

[61]Genaro Arriagada, "Beyond Justice," *Washington Post,* October 25, 1998, C7; Charles True-heart, "Pinochet Case Signifies Cries for Retribution," *Washington Post,* October 25, 1998, A21.

[62]Henry Kissinger, *Does America Need a Foreign Policy? Toward a Diplomacy for the 21st Century* (New York: Simon and Schuster, 2001), 273, 275. As secretary of state in the Nixon administration, Kissinger played a central role in U.S. policy toward Chile, including opposition to the Salvador Allende government and support for the Pinochet coup.

[63]United Nations, World Conference on Human Rights, June 14–25, 1993, *Report,* A/CONF.157/24 (Part I).

[64]Robert D. Putnam, *Making Democracy Work: Civic Traditions in Modern Italy* (Princeton: Princeton University Press, 1993), 176. This section draws on an outstanding paper written by Sarah Schroeder, one of my students in Fall 1996, "How Should the United States Support Democracy Consolidation in Haiti? The Relationship between Civil Society and Political Institutions."

[65]Cited in Diamond, *Promoting Democracy in the 1990s,* 56–57.

[66]Richard Rose, "Rethinking Civil Society: Postcommunism and the Problem of Trust," *Journal of Democracy* 5 (July 1994), 29.

[67]Gideon Rose, "Democracy Promotion and American Foreign Policy: A Review Essay," *International Security* 25:2 (Winter 2000–01), 186–203.

[68]Larry Diamond, *Developing Democracy: Toward Consolidation* (Baltimore, Md.: Johns Hopkins University Press, 1999), 20.

[69]Thomas Carothers, *Aiding Democracy Abroad: The Learning Curve* (Washington, D.C.: Carnegie Endowment for International Peace, 1999), 308, 171, 182, 251.

[70]Carothers, *Aiding Democracy Abroad,* 171, 182, 249–50, 347.

[71]Rose, "Democracy Promotion and American Foreign Policy," 198.

[72]Fareed Zakaria, *The Future of Freedom: Illiberal Democracy at Home and Abroad* (New York: W.W. Norton, 2003).

[73]Diamond, *Developing Democracy,* 272.

[74]Carothers, *Aiding Democracy Abroad,* 340.

[75]Rose, "Democracy Promotion and American Foreign Policy," 200.

[76]This section draws on Bruce W. Jentleson, "American Diplomacy: Around the World and Along Pennsylvania Avenue," in *A Question of Balance: The President, the Congress and Foreign Policy,* ed. Thomas E. Mann (Washington, D.C.: Brookings Institution Press, 1990), 146–200; and Bruce W. Jentleson, ed., *Perspectives on American Foreign Policy: Readings and Cases* (New York: Norton, 2000), chap. 2, and the Kennedy School of Government (Harvard University) case study "The United States and South Africa: The Anti-Apartheid Sanctions Debate of 1985," by Pamela Varley for Gregory Treverton (1989).

[77]Cited in Jentleson, "American Diplomacy," 157.

[78]Jentleson, *Perspectives,* 42.

[79]Cited in Jentleson, *Perspectives,* 42.

Readings for Part II American Foreign Policy in the Twenty-First Century: Choices and Challenges

Unilateralism

6.1

CHARLES KRAUTHAMMER

The Unipolar Moment Revisited

In late 1990, shortly before the collapse of the Soviet Union, it was clear that the world we had known for half a century was disappearing. The question was what would succeed it. I suggested then that we had already entered the "unipolar moment." The gap in power between the leading nation and all the others was so unprecedented as to yield an international structure unique to modern history: unipolarity.

*　*　*

Unipolarity After September 11, 2001

There is little need to rehearse the acceleration of unipolarity in the 1990s. Japan, whose claim to power rested exclusively on economics, went into economic decline. Germany stagnated. The Soviet Union ceased to exist, contracting into a smaller, radically weakened Russia. The European Union turned inward toward the great project of integration and built a strong social infrastructure at the expense of military capacity. Only China grew in strength, but coming from so far behind it will be decades before it can challenge American primacy—and that assumes that its current growth continues unabated.

The result is the dominance of a single power unlike anything ever seen. Even at its height Britain could always be seriously challenged by the next greatest powers. Britain had a smaller army than the land powers of Europe and its navy was equaled by the next two navies combined. Today, American military spending exceeds that of the next *twenty* countries combined. Its navy, air force and space power are unrivaled. Its technology is irresistible. It is dominant by every measure: military, economic, technological, diplomatic, cultural, even linguistic, with a myriad of countries trying to fend off the inexorable march of Internet-fueled MTV English.

American dominance has not gone unnoticed. During the 1990s, it was mainly

From *The National Interest* 70 (Winter 2002/03), 5–17.

China and Russia that denounced unipo-larity in their occasional joint commu-niqués. As the new century dawned it was on everyone's lips. A French foreign minis-ter dubbed the United States not a super-power but a hyperpower. The dominant concern of foreign policy establishments everywhere became understanding and liv-ing with the 800-pound American gorilla.

And then September 11 *heightened* the asymmetry. It did so in three ways. First, and most obviously, it led to a demonstra-tion of heretofore latent American mili-tary power. Kosovo, the first war ever fought and won exclusively from the air, had given a hint of America's quantum leap in military power (and the enormous gap that had developed between American and European military capabilities). But it took September 11 for the United States to unleash with concentrated fury a fuller display of its power in Afghanistan. Being a relatively pacific, commercial republic, the United States does not go around looking for demonstration wars. This one was thrust upon it. In response, America showed that at a range of 7,000 miles and with but a handful of losses, it could de-stroy within weeks a hardened, fanatical regime favored by geography and climate in the "graveyard of empires." . . .

Second, September 11 demonstrated a new form of American strength. The cen-ter of its economy was struck, its aviation shut down, Congress brought to a halt, the government sent underground, the coun-try paralyzed and fearful. Yet within days the markets reopened, the economy began its recovery, the president mobilized the nation, and a united Congress immedi-ately underwrote a huge new worldwide campaign against terror. The Pentagon started planning the U.S. military response even as its demolished western façade still smoldered.

America had long been perceived as in-vulnerable. That illusion was shattered on September 11, 2001. But with a demonstra-tion of its recuperative powers—an econ-omy and political system so deeply rooted and fundamentally sound that it could spring back to life within days—that sense of invulnerability assumed a new character. It was transmuted from impermeability to resilience, the product of unrivaled human, technological and political reserves.

The third effect of September 11 was to accelerate the realignment of the cur-rent great powers, such as they are, behind the United States. In 1990, America's principal ally was NATO. A decade later, its alliance base had grown to include for-mer members of the Warsaw Pact. Some of the major powers, however, remained uncommitted. Russia and China flirted with the idea of an "anti-hegemonic al-liance." Russian leaders made ostentatious visits to pieces of the old Soviet empire such as Cuba and North Korea. India and Pakistan, frozen out by the United States because of their nuclear testing, remained focused mainly on one another. But after September 11, the bystanders came call-ing. Pakistan made an immediate strate-gic decision to join the American camp. India enlisted with equal alacrity, offering the United States basing, overflight rights and a level of cooperation unheard of during its half century of Nehruist genu-flection to anti-American non-alignment.

Russia's Putin, seeing both a coincidence of interests in the fight against Islamic radicalism and an opportunity to gain acceptance in the Western camp, dramatically realigned Russian foreign policy toward the United States. (Russia has already been rewarded with a larger role in NATO and tacit American recognition of Russia's interests in its "near abroad.") China remains more distant but, also having a coincidence of interests with the United States in fighting Islamic radicalism, it has cooperated with the war on terror and muted its competition with America in the Pacific.

* * *

The American hegemon has no great power enemies, an historical oddity of the first order. Yet it does face a serious threat to its dominance, indeed to its essential security. It comes from a source even more historically odd: an archipelago of rogue states (some connected with transnational terrorists) wielding weapons of mass destruction.

The threat is not trivial. It is the single greatest danger to the United States because, for all of America's dominance, and for all of its recently demonstrated resilience, there is one thing it might not survive: decapitation. The detonation of a dozen nuclear weapons in major American cities, or the spreading of smallpox or anthrax throughout the general population, is an existential threat. It is perhaps the only realistic threat to America as a functioning hegemon, perhaps even to America as a functioning modern society.

* * *

The Crisis of Unipolarity

Accordingly, not one but a host of new doctrines have come tumbling out since September 11. First came the with-us-or-against-us ultimatum to any state aiding, abetting or harboring terrorists. Then, pre-emptive attack on any enemy state developing weapons of mass destruction. And now, regime change in any such state.

The boldness of these policies—or, as much of the world contends, their arrogance—is breathtaking. The American anti-terrorism ultimatum, it is said, is high-handed and permits the arbitrary application of American power everywhere. Pre-emption is said to violate traditional doctrines of just war. And regime change, as Henry Kissinger has argued, threatens 350 years of post-Westphalian international practice. Taken together, they amount to an unprecedented assertion of American freedom of action and a definitive statement of a new American unilateralism.

To be sure, these are not the first instances of American unilateralism. Before September 11, the George W. Bush Administration had acted unilaterally, but on more minor matters, such as the Kyoto Protocol and the Biological Weapons Convention, and with less bluntness, as in its protracted negotiations with Russia over the ABM treaty. The "axis of evil" speech of January 29, however, took unilateralism to a new level. Latent resentments about American willfulness are latent no more. American dominance, which had been tolerated if not welcomed, is now producing such irritation and hostility in once friendly quarters, such as Europe, that some suggest we have arrived at the end of the opposition-free grace period that America had enjoyed during the unipolar moment.[1]

* * *

Realism and the New Unilateralism

The basic division between the two major foreign policy schools in America centers on the question of what is, and what should be, the fundamental basis of international relations: paper or power. Liberal internationalism envisions a world order that, like domestic society, is governed by laws and not men. Realists see this vision as hopelessly utopian. The history of paper treaties—from the prewar Kellogg-Briand Pact and Munich to the post–Cold War Oslo accords and the 1994 Agreed Framework with North Korea—is a history of naiveté and cynicism, a combination both toxic and volatile that invariably ends badly. Trade agreements with Canada are one thing. Pieces of parchment to which existential enemies affix a signature are quite another. They are worse than worthless because they give a false sense of security and breed complacency. For the realist, the ultimate determinant of the most basic elements of international life—security, stability and peace—is power.

Which is why a realist would hardly forfeit the current unipolarity for the vain promise of goo-goo one-worldism. Nor, however, should a realist want to forfeit unipolarity for the familiarity of traditional multipolarity. Multipolarity is inherently fluid and unpredictable. Europe practiced multipolarity for centuries and found it so unstable and bloody, culminating in 1914 in the catastrophic collapse of delicately balanced alliance systems, that Europe sought its permanent abolition in political and economic union. Having abjured multipolarity for the region, it is odd in the extreme to then prefer multipolarity for the world.

Less can be said about the destiny of unipolarity. It is too new. Yet we do have the history of the last decade, our only modern experience with unipolarity, and it was a decade of unusual stability among all major powers. It would be foolish to project from just a ten-year experience, but that experience does call into question the basis for the claims that unipolarity is intrinsically unstable or impossible to sustain in a mass democracy.

I would argue that unipolarity, managed benignly, is far more likely to keep the peace. Benignity is, of course, in the eye of the beholder. But the American claim to benignity is not mere self-congratulation. We have a track record. Consider one of history's rare controlled experiments. In the 1940s, lines were drawn through three peoples—Germans, Koreans and Chinese—one side closely bound to the United States, the other to its adversary. It turned into a controlled experiment because both states in the divided lands shared a common culture. Fifty years later the results are in. Does anyone doubt the superiority, both moral and material, of West Germany vs. East Germany, South Korea vs. North Korea and Taiwan vs. China?

*   *   *

The form of realism that I am arguing for—call it the new unilateralism—is clear in its determination to self-consciously and confidently deploy American power in pursuit of those global ends. Note: global ends. There is a form of unilateralism that is devoted only to narrow American self-interest and it has a name, too: It is called isolationism. Critics of the new unilateralism often confuse it with isolationism because both are prepared to unashamedly exercise American power. But isolationists *oppose* America acting as a unipolar power not because they disagree with the unilateral means, but because they deem the ends far too broad. Isolationists would abandon the larger world and use American power exclusively for the narrowest of American interests: manning Fortress America by defending the American homeland and putting up barriers to trade and immigration.

The new unilateralism defines American interests far beyond narrow self-defense. In particular, it identifies two other major interests, both global: extending the peace by advancing democracy and preserving the peace by acting as balancer of last resort. Britain was the balancer in Europe, joining the weaker coalition against the stronger to create equilibrium. America's unique global power allows it to be the balancer in every region. We balanced Iraq by supporting its weaker neighbors in the Gulf War. We balance China by supporting the ring of smaller states at its periphery (from South Korea to Taiwan, even to Vietnam). Our role in the Balkans was essentially to create a microbalance: to support the weaker Bosnian Muslims against their more dominant neighbors, and subsequently to support the weaker Albanian Kosovars against the Serbs.

Of course, both of these tasks often advance American national interests as well. The promotion of democracy multiplies the number of nations likely to be friendly to the United States, and regional equilibria produce stability that benefits a commercial republic like the United States. America's (intended) exertions on behalf of pre-emptive non-proliferation, too, are clearly in the interest of both the United States and the international system as a whole.

*   *   *

When I first proposed the unipolar model in 1990, I suggested that we should accept both its burdens and opportunities and that, if America did not wreck its economy, unipolarity could last thirty or forty years. That seemed bold at the time. Today, it seems rather modest. The unipolar moment has become the unipolar era. It remains true, however, that its durability will be decided at home. It will depend largely on whether it is welcomed by Americans or seen as a burden to be shed—either because we are too good for the world (the isolationist critique) or because we are not worthy of it (the liberal internationalist critique).

The new unilateralism argues explicitly and unashamedly for maintaining unipolarity, for sustaining America's unrivaled dominance for the foreseeable future. It could be a long future, assuming we successfully manage the single greatest threat, namely, weapons of mass destruction in the hands of rogue states. This in itself will require the aggressive and confident application of unipolar power rather than falling back, as we did in the 1990s, on paralyzing multilateralism. The future of the unipolar era hinges on whether America is governed by those who wish to retain, augment and use unipolarity to advance not just American but global ends, or whether America is governed by those who wish to give it up—either by allowing unipolarity to decay as they retreat to Fortress America, or by passing on the burden by gradually transferring power to multilateral institutions as heirs to American hegemony. The challenge to unipolarity is not from the outside but from the inside. The choice is ours. To impiously paraphrase Benjamin Franklin: History has given you an empire, if you will keep it.

Note

[1] A Sky News poll finds that even the British public considers George W. Bush a greater threat to world peace than Saddam Hussein. The poll was conducted September 2–6, 2002.

Multilateralism

What is the International Community? This article is excerpted from a cover story in Foreign Policy magazine presenting a range of definitions offered by UN Secretary-General Kofi Annan and others of what is meant by "the international community"

Kofi A. Annan: Problems Without Passports

Ours is a world in which no individual, and no country, exists in isolation. All of us live simultaneously in our own communities and in the world at large. Peoples and cultures are increasingly hybrid. The same icons, whether on a movie screen or a computer screen, are recognizable from Berlin to Bangalore. We are all consumers in the same global economy. We are all influenced by the same tides of political, social, and technological change. Pollution, organized crime, and the proliferation of deadly weapons likewise show little regard for the niceties of borders; they are problems without passports and, as such, our common enemy. We are connected, wired, interdependent.

Such connections are nothing new. Human beings have interacted across planet Earth for centuries. But today's globalization is different. It is happening more rapidly. It is driven by new engines, such as the Internet. And it is governed by different rules, or in too many cases, by no rules at all. Globalization is bringing more choices and new opportunities for prosperity. It is making us more familiar with global diversity. However, millions of people around the world experience globalization not as an agent of progress but as a disruptive force, almost hurricanelike in its ability to destroy lives, jobs, and traditions. Many have an urge to resist the process and take refuge in the illusory comforts of nationalism, fundamentalism, or other isms.

Faced with the potential good of globalization as well as its risks, faced with the persistence of deadly conflicts in which civilians are primary targets, and faced with the pervasiveness of poverty and injustice, we must identify areas where collective action is needed—and then take that action to safeguard the common, global interest. Local communities have fire departments, municipal services, and town councils. Nations have legislatures and judicial bodies. But in today's globalized world, the institutions and mechanisms available for global

From *Foreign Policy 132* (September–October 2002), 28–47.

action, not to mention a general sense of a shared global fate, are hardly more than embryonic. It is high time we gave more concrete meaning to the idea of the international community.

What makes a community? What binds it together? For some it is faith. For others it is the defense of an idea, such as democracy. Some communities are homogeneous, others multicultural. Some are as small as schools and villages, others as large as continents. Today, of course, more and more communities are virtual, as people, even in the remotest locations on earth, discover and promote their shared values through the latest communications and information technologies.

But what binds us into an international community? In the broadest sense, there is a shared vision of a better world for all people as set out, for example, in the founding charter of the United Nations. There is a sense of common vulnerability in the face of global warming and the threat posed by the spread of weapons of mass destruction. There is the framework of international law, treaties, and human rights conventions. There is equally a sense of shared opportunity, which is why we build common markets and joint institutions such as the United Nations. Together, we are stronger.

Some people say the international community is only a fiction. Others believe it is too elastic a concept to have any real meaning. Still others claim it is a mere vehicle of convenience, to be trotted out only in emergencies or when a scapegoat for inaction is needed. Some maintain there are no internationally recognized norms, goals, or fears on which to base such a community. Op-ed pages and news reports refer routinely to the "so-called international community," as if the term does not yet have the solidity of actual fact. I believe these skeptics are wrong. The international community does exist. It has an address. It has achievements to its credit. And more and more, it is developing a conscience.

When governments, urged by civil society, work together to realize the long-held dream of an International Criminal Court for the prosecution of genocide and the most heinous crimes against humanity, that is the international community at work for the rule of law. When an outpouring of international aid flows to victims of earthquakes and other disasters, that is the international community following its humanitarian impulse. When rich countries pledge to open more of their markets to poor-country goods and decide to reverse the decade-long decline in official development assistance, that is the international community throwing its weight behind the cause of development. When countries contribute troops to police cease-fire lines or to provide security in states that have collapsed or succumbed to civil war, that is the international community at work for collective security.

Examples abound of the international community at work, from Afghanistan and East Timor to Africa and Central America. At the same time, there are important caveats. Too often the international community fails to do what is needed. It failed to prevent genocide in Rwanda. For too long it reacted with weakness and hesitation to the horror of ethnic cleansing in the former Yugoslavia. The international community has not done enough to help Africa at a time when Africa needs it most and stands to benefit most. And in a world of unprecedented wealth, the international community allows nearly half of all humanity to subsist on $2 or less a day.

For much of the 20th century, the international system was based on division and hard calculations of realpolitik. In the new century, the international community can and must do better. I do not suggest that an era of complete harmony is within reach. Interests and ideas will always clash. But the world can improve on the last century's dismal record. The international community is a work in progress. Many strands of cooperation have asserted themselves over the years. We must now stitch them into a strong fabric of community—of international community for an international era.

Sadako Ogata: Guilty Parties

Those of us thinking about global public policy have brooded over the meaning of the term "international community." Personally, I avoid invoking it because the term seems too amorphous both conceptually and in practice. And yet I find it widely used as if it represents a reality that no one dares question. But does the international community actually exist? If so, what does it really represent?

It seems clear that the term does not stand for any specific geographic area or population group. Arguably, the United Nations—the most universal international organization with 190 member states— is the closest embodiment of the international community. True, when the United Nations aspires to eradicate poverty, promote disarmament, or protect the environment, its efforts are often perceived as expressing the position or wishes of the international community. In this sense, when a multilateral agency pursues what might be widely considered as the common good, such an effort tends to be enshrined in international community terms. As a concept, then, the international community comes to life more on account of the substance to which it aspires rather than the entity it represents.

* * *

In my decade (1991–2000) as the United Nations High Commissioner for Refugees, my constant goal was to build global consensus for the protection of refugees—that is, of those individuals fleeing religious, ethnic, or political persecution at the hands of their own states or by groups engaged in internal conflicts. The principle of refugee protection is enshrined in the Convention Relating to the Status of Refugees, which entered into force in 1954. Although the number of signatories to the convention increased from 104 when I took office to 141 today, I nonetheless faced great difficulties seeking to ensure that states lived up to the provisions of the convention, even regarding the acceptance of people in desperate flight.

I sought to enlist governments and the global public for support in my efforts, insisting that borders be kept open, asking that asylum seekers' claims be fairly examined, and soliciting funds to cover victims' needs. But obtaining a positive response was never easy. The international community did not seem to exist even in the face of human tragedies. Indeed, this community only emerged when human crises hit the international media, when scenes of misery—whether involving the Kurds, the Rwandans, or the Kosovars—flashed across living room television screens in the developed world. Such episodes taught me the crucial role of the media in transforming specific humanitarian causes to more generally shared concerns.

Ultimately, the international community does exist, but only as a potential source of power, to promote common cause or legitimize common action. It is essentially a virtual community. However, the international community can be brought to life in response to vital callings, with conscious or unconscious inputs. It thus represents a useful conceptual tool that political leaders, activists, and the media can deploy to move policy thinking closer to what might be construed as the common good. Why not, then, mobilize greater efforts for building the real international community?

Arjun Appadurai: Broken Promises

The international community is neither international nor a community. It is not international because, as a moral idea, it does not exist in any recognizable organizational form. It is not a community because it has little to do with social relations, spatial intimacy, or long-term moral amity. Yet there is something compellingly real about this misnamed object. That reality lies in its moral promise.

The moral promise of the idea of the international community rests on a moral premise and a wish. Sometime in the period after the birth of the League of Nations, and fortified by the ascendance of the idea of human rights in the international order after World War II, a decisive shift took place away from the notion that relations between nations were fundamentally premised on power and interest and toward the idea that all nations could form some sort of genuine moral system on a planetary scale. The emergence of the United Nations and its affiliated agencies was the main expression of this shift. Ever since, a deep battle has raged between these two visions of politics beyond the nation—one fundamentally realist and instrumental, the other moral and moralistic. The international community is today less a social fact and more a way to remind nation-states of the common humanity of their citizens and of the essential decencies that must guide relations between nations. It is the single strongest slogan of the liberal value of empathy at a distance, the idea that makes everyone feel obliged to recognize the suffering and needs of all human beings.

The social expression of this moral slogan is, of course, not completely ephemeral. It appears in a web of relations and institutions defined by those nations springing directly from the democratic revolutions of the 18th century—along with their direct supporters outside this original set—and those international organizations that either came out of the League of Nations or the Bretton Woods consensus. But for most of the world, the international community is less a community than a club for the world's wealthiest nations, notably those in North America and Western Europe, which have combined relatively strong democratic polities with high standards of living for the bulk of their citizens.

Thus, as a social and political reality, the international community does not inspire any real sense of ownership among the poorer 80 percent of the world's population. And even among the upper 20 percent, it remains a network for a relatively small group of politicians, bureaucrats, and interventionist opinion makers. Yet its political exclusiveness is not its most difficult challenge.

The central problem is that the international community today is a Westphalian form struggling to remain the ruling authority in an era of increasingly transnational loyalties, regional polities, and global economic regimes. Each of these trends is bad news for polities, economies, and societies conceived in national terms. Diasporic affiliations and mobile, media-linked communities of migrants are redrawing the relationships of location and affiliation. Sri Lankan Tamils, Kurds, Chinese emigrants, Indian techno-coolies, each in their own way, owe their allegiance to multiple forms of citizenship. Their mental geography is surely no longer Westphalian. In this sense, these communities mimic the global market, which is now strikingly beyond the regulative capabilities of most nation-states. Even a nation as wealthy as the United States no longer escapes the net of the global economy, if nothing else because its run-

away financial engine can hardly function wholly within the confines of the U.S. national economy. More generally, both on the street and in the chambers of the technocrats, the fraught debates about an institution such as the World Trade Organization are more than indicators of resistance to reform or of anti-Americanism in many quarters. They are symptoms of the impossibility of constructing new global organizations on an international conceptual foundation.

A certain vision of internationalism is therefore coming to an end. The world needs global organizations and transnational arenas for citizenship and sovereignty. The exclusivity of the international community is not just one more chapter in the story of how wealthy nations have always behaved—carving up the world in the names of their own civilizing missions. Rather, the challenge for the international community is to transform itself into an instrument of global governance. This objective cannot be achieved by stretching the current liberal vision of international law and a common humanity to accommodate more countries and points of view. Rather, new ideas about global governance are a prerequisite for tackling the problem of inclusion.

So, what of the premise and promise of the international community, as primarily a landscape of conscience more than a political or legal formation? Those who today speak on behalf of the international community must tackle the following challenges: Can notions of global equity, peace, and freedom remain regulated by the relations between nations, when markets, migrants, and money have all slipped substantially beyond the control of the nation-state? Can the world continue to behave as if covenants between nations exhaust the limits of what happens with air, water, land, and all other biological resources, when the fate of the environment is clearly affected by transnational processes, interests, and profit-making strategies? Can the world continue to behave as if nations are the most significant receptacles of large-scale loyalty in a world where various forms of religious, moral, and political affiliations are plainly transnational in scope? And finally, can the world rely on any sort of international force to bring peace when it is increasingly clear that wars have become an affair of everyday life and of civil society itself in many countries?

If the answers to these questions are not built on a new cultural architecture that recognizes that global politics are not just international politics by another name, the international community—with its moral promise—may well be reduced to an exclusive club or a museum devoted to memories of Westphalia.

The Media and Foreign Policy

WARREN P. STROBEL

The Media and U.S. Policies Toward Intervention: A Closer Look at the "CNN Effect"

With the rise of "real-time" television in the 1980s, the growth of Ted Turner's 24-hour-a-day Cable News Network (CNN), and the deployment of news media technologies that can transmit video signals to and from virtually anywhere on the planet, government officials, legislators, media professionals, and scholars have voiced growing concern that journalists are exercising an irresistible control over western foreign policy.[1] It is said that dramatic images of starving masses, shelled populations, or dead American soldiers spark ill-considered public demands for action from elected officials. These temporary emotional responses may conflict with the more considered judgment of foreign policy officials, forcing them to take action that will soon have to be reversed or modified.

While the term "CNN effect" has numerous definitions and includes a range of phenomena, at heart it is understood to be a loss of policy control on the part of government policymakers.[2] CNN, it is said,

makes, or at least exercises inordinate influence on, policy. * * *

This essay argues that these concerns, while understandable in the light of recent international changes, are misplaced. The CNN effect is grossly exaggerated, operating in few, if any, of the cases where it is most commonly cited. The media's effect on foreign policy is far more complex than the CNN-effect label would suggest, and far more dependent on the policy actions of government officials themselves than is seen to be the case. It is true that U.S. government policies and actions regarding international conflict are subject to more open public review than previously in history. But policymakers retain great power to frame events and solicit public support—indeed, CNN at times increases this power. Put another way, if officials do not have a firm and well-considered policy or have failed to communicate their views in such a way as to garner the support of the American people, the news media will fill this vacuum (often by giving greater

From *Managing Global Chaos: Sources of and Responses to International Conflict,* Chester A. Crocker and Fen Osler Hampson with Pamela Aall, eds. (Washington, D.C.: U.S. Institute of Peace Press, 1996), 357–76.

time and attention to the criticism or policy preferences of its opponents). In this regard, little has changed since Daniel Hallin, studying the reporting of the Vietnam War, an era of much less sophisticated media technology, concluded that the news media's impact is intimately related to the consensus of society as a whole.[3] What *has* changed is the speed with which the news media can expose such gaps.

This analysis will examine the CNN effect as it applies to prospective or actual U.S. interventions in what are now called peace operations or operations other than war.[4] My conclusions are based on more than 100 interviews conducted during 1994–1995 with four main groups: senior policymakers from the Bush and Clinton administrations; military spokespersons and other U.S. officers (primarily from the Army and Marine Corps); print, radio, and television journalists, primarily from U.S. news organizations; and personnel from the United Nations, other international governmental organizations (IGOs), and nongovernmental organizations (NGOs). The findings can be summarized as follows:

- Graphic televised images hold no power to force U.S. policymakers to intervene in a civil conflict where there is no clear national interest.
- There seems to be an inverse relationship between the power of images on policymakers and the presumed costs of intervention. (At the time of the decision, the costs of U.S. action in Somalia appeared to be low.)

- Images do add to the pressures on policymakers to address humanitarian aspects of a crisis, but the news media are not the agenda-setters they are often portrayed to be. Government relief officials, other relief agencies, and U.S. lawmakers play key roles in drawing news media attention to such suffering.
- Because public and media pressures are not specific, policymakers often react with what might be called a minimalist response, attempting to signal more of a policy change than has actually taken place.
- There is evidence that the power of televised images to provoke emotional responses is diminishing as conflict and humanitarian need become ubiquitous features of the post–Cold War era, at least as portrayed on television.
- Media reports have a greater impact when executive branch policy is in flux or is poorly articulated.
- The prevalence of real-time media reports often contracts the policymaking process, giving officials less time before they must respond publicly. But this does not mean the media automatically determine policy outcomes.

In short, the CNN effect does not exist in many places where it is said to be found, and even where its traces can be detected, they are exaggerated, working only in combination with other factors.

* * *

Stepping Back

* * *

The overarching U.S.-Soviet struggle provided a context within which administration officials could explain their policies to the news media and, in turn, helped the news media explain to readers and viewers the significance of complex and far-off events. The news media were more supportive than is usually remembered of U.S. foreign policy aims during the Cold War. Until the 1968 Tet offensive, the television networks and prestige newspapers such as the *New York Times* largely agreed with the White House's claim of the strategic importance of South Vietnam. Journalists such as the *Times'* David Halberstam criticized the means, not the ends.[5]

The end of the Cold War has deprived American administrations of a ready context in which to explain their policies and crated a sort of meta-vacuum. This, the media have filled using their own professional ideology, which puts a high premium on crisis, drama, and unfilled humanitarian needs.[6]

* * *

Somalia: Who Set the Agenda?

Because it is widely accepted that television images of starving civilians, especially children, forced President George H. W. Bush to dispatch U.S. military forces to Somalia in the fall of 1992, this is a good place to begin a more detailed examination of the news media's impact on U.S.

intervention policy. This analysis challenges that widely held belief on three counts. First, the levels of television coverage were incompatible with the types of pressure usually associated with the CNN effect: Sharp increases in the levels of television reporting tended to *follow* administration actions, rather than precede them. Second, the television coverage (and other media attention) that did take place was almost always a result, not of media initiative and agenda-setting, but of deliberate and successful attempts by others to stir up media interest in Somalia in order to move policy. These "others" were a loose coalition of U.S. government relief officials, interested members of Congress, and representatives of NGOs and IGOs. Their efforts highlight the growing role in particular of nongovernmental or supragovernmental bodies in international relations.[7] Finally, interviews with numerous Bush administration officials made it clear that they intervened in Somalia largely because they expected it to be an exercise with low costs and high political benefit. Simultaneously, President Bush was wrestling with the question of a potential U.S. intervention in the former Yugoslavia, which senior officials agreed would require tens of thousands of U.S. ground troops. Somalia was chosen partly because it was easier and would relieve pressure for action in the Balkans.

Even a cursory look at patterns of coverage of Somalia by the three U.S. broadcast television networks and by CNN raises questions about the impact of these media on the decision to intervene in Somalia. President Bush's first major decision regarding Somalia, one that "created an activist consensus in the national security bureaucracy where none had existed earlier,"[8] was to begin an airlift of emergency food supplies to drought-affected areas in Somalia and northern Kenya. This decision was announced August 14, 1992, although it had been made two days earlier. Prior to August 14, there were only fifteen network evening news stories in 1992 that mentioned Somalia; six of them were merely fleeting glimpses of Somalia's plight as part of one-minute or forty-second "round-ups" of news from around the world. CNN coverage patterns were roughly similar, with the exception of a burst of coverage in May stemming from a single correspondent's ten-day visit to Somalia. Once the airlift decision was announced, television coverage jumped to unprecedented levels, remaining relatively high in September, and then almost vanishing in October, no doubt overshadowed by the upcoming 1992 presidential election. Rather than television bringing U.S. troops and airplanes to Somalia in the first place, it was Bush's policy action that attracted increased media attention, with dozens of journalists descending on the country to report on the airlift. Of course, once there, they sent back more reports about the horrible conditions in the countryside. This pattern was repeated in November, prior to Bush's November 25 decision to launch Operation Restore Hope, the dispatch of nearly 30,000 U.S. troops to guard relief supplies. Somalia returned to television's agenda in mid-November, but it was Bush's decision that sparked the most intense media coverage.

* * * Nonetheless, once the images of starvation appeared on American television screens, they did have some further effect. Secretary of State James A. Baker III asked the rhetorical question of whether Bush would have dispatched troops to Somalia in December 1992 absent those images: "We probably wouldn't have," he concluded.[9] The next question is why they had an impact. The answer seems to be that senior Bush administration officials all believed that the Somalia intervention would be low in costs, especially casualties, and high in benefit. One of those benefits was to ease the simultaneous pressure the administration was feeling in the fall of 1992 to engage in a potentially much more costly intervention: the former Yugoslavia. Baker; his successor, Lawrence Eagleburger; and Brent Scowcroft, National Security Adviser to George H. W. Bush, all used virtually the same words: There was an easy consensus within the administration on doing something about Somalia.[10] In other words, the images from Somalia operated only on a narrow portion of the spectrum of national security concerns: a humanitarianism crisis that seemed to be an "easy fix."

* * *

In summary, the case most often held up as an example of the CNN effect—Somalia—falls apart under close examination. It was not the media that set the agenda in the fall of 1992, but the Bush administration itself, the Congress, and relief officials in and out of government. The horrible images did have an effect, but a narrow one. Reflecting on the experience, [Assistant Secretary of State Robert]

Gallucci said that pictures "don't come anywhere near" forcing an introduction of U.S. ground troops when it is known they will be in harm's way.

"When you're short of that, then the pictures are very useful in getting people to focus on it as a basis for humanitarian support." For anything more than that, "it's gotta answer the question, Why us?" It is to these limits of media power that we now turn our attention.

Bosnia: The Limits of Images' Power

*   *   *

* * * [T]here were two points at which news media pressure for intervention [in Yugoslavia] were at their most intense. The first was in August 1992, with the revelations, first by Gutman in *Newsday* and then on Britain's Independent Television Network (ITN), of the murder and gross mistreatment of Bosnian Muslims in Serb-run concentration camps. The second, the televised bloody aftermath of the February 1994 "marketplace massacre" in Sarajevo, will be examined in a moment.

Gutman's Pulitzer Prize–winning reports in *Newsday* and the vivid ITN images of emaciated men behind barbed wire, recalling as they did the Holocaust, caused an emotional reaction around the world. In the United States, journalists, lawmakers, and other politicians—including presidential candidate Bill Clinton—demanded action to stop the abuses. Yet by this time, the Bush administration had looked at the question of intervention in the former

Yugoslavia, and determined it was an abyss that would draw in thousands of U.S. ground troops for an indefinite period (Clinton would later come to this same conclusion). Two factors about this policy decision are important in determining why the media had so little effect: The decision was firmly held, and it was shared by all the senior members of Bush's national security team. As Warren Zimmermann, the last U.S. ambassador to Yugoslavia, put it: "It wouldn't have mattered if television was going 24 hours around the clock with Serb atrocities. Bush wasn't going to get in."[11] Eagleburger used virtually identical language, saying: "Through all the time we were there, you have to understand that we had largely made a decision we were not going to get militarily involved. And nothing, including those stories, pushed us into it. . . . I hated it. Because this was condoning—I won't say genocide—but condoning a hell of a lot of murder. . . . It made us damn uncomfortable. But this was a policy that wasn't going to get changed no matter what the press said."[12]

In other words, while it was difficult for policymakers not to respond to the news media reports and the outcry that they engendered, they decided it would be even more costly to respond. Politically, however, the Bush administration could not afford to be seen as doing nothing or as uncaring. On August 6, 1992, the day the ITN videotape aired, Bush demanded that the Serbs open the camps to international access. A week later, with U.S. support, the UN Security Council passed Resolution 770, demanding outside access to the camps and authorizing member states to use "all measures necessary" (that is, force) to ensure humanitarian relief supplies were delivered. The news media reports also played a role in the establishment of the first war crimes tribunals in Europe since World War II. While some things had changed on the surface, U.S. policy remained largely the same, defined by Bush's August 7 statement that the United States would not intervene with force. Bush recalled Vietnam, saying, "I do not want to see the United States bogged down in any way into some guerilla warfare. We lived through that once." Resolution 770 never was fully implemented.

This lack of real policy change was further confirmed in interviews with officials and reporters. Scowcroft said, "We did some marginal things, but there was a real consensus—and I think probably an unshakable consensus—to make a real difference . . . would require an American or NATO intervention that we did not see justified." Foreign Service officer George Kenney, who on August 25 publicly resigned to protest the lack of substantive U.S. action, said that government concern with the media "only extended to the appearance of maintaining we were behaving responsibly," while in reality refusing further entanglement in the Balkans. I asked journalist Roy Gutman, who actively tried to raise the alarm within the U.S. government once he had confirmed atrocities were taking place, for his assessment of his reports' impact. He curled two fingers in the symbol for a zero. "Really," he said. "What you had is a lot of reaction to reports, but never any policy change."[13] This is the minimalist response.

* * *

Real-Time Intervention: The Sarajevo Market Massacres

Another facet of the loss of policy control associated with the idea of a CNN effect is the ability of modern news media to transmit graphic images almost instantaneously. This speed, it is said, overwhelms the traditional policymaking structures, forcing decisions that might not otherwise be made, perhaps before all the facts are in.

A good example of the impact of real-time media reports on intervention decisions is the gruesome footage of the February 5, 1994, "marketplace massacre," in which a mortar shell fired by an unknown party (but almost certainly Bosnian Serbs) landed in a crowded marketplace in Sarajevo, killing 68 people and horribly wounding nearly 200 others. In the aftermath of the attack and the public outcry, the United States abandoned its hands-off policy toward the Balkan conflict. It led NATO in issuing an ultimatum to the Bosnian Serbs to remove their heavy weapons from around Bosnia's capital (an extension of this threat would lead to NATO's first use of offensive force in Europe in its history) and established the five-nation "Contact Group," giving new momentum to the search for a diplomatic solution to the conflict. Sarajevens enjoyed a bit of normalcy after nearly two years of siege.

This clearly seems to be a case where videotaped images led the United States into, or at least toward, intervention. But while the images did have an impact, it was not the simple cause-effect one that this glance at events would indicate. At the time of the shelling, the United States already was moving toward a more active role in the Balkans, for reasons that included intense pressure from France and U.S. concern that the inability to affect the conflict was eroding the Atlantic alliance and American leadership. On February 4, the day *before* the shelling, Secretary of State Warren Christopher proposed that the United States lead a new diplomatic effort, combined with the threat of using force.[14] "I am acutely uncomfortable with the passive position we are now in, and believe that now is the time to undertake a new initiative," he wrote in a letter to Defense Secretary William Perry and National Security Adviser Anthony Lake.[15] "We had a real sense that we didn't have a Bosnia policy that was going anywhere," said a senior State Department official. Before the shelling, "We had already made the psychological determination [about] the direction we wanted to go." This official was in a series of meetings on fashioning a new policy toward Bosnia when the mortar attack occurred—and recalled worrying that the new policy would be seen, incorrectly, as an instant response to the massacre.[16]

This is not to say that the bloody images had no impact; media reports actually had three effects. First, according to White House spokesperson Michael McCurry, they galvanized and accelerated the decision-making process. "The impact of the marketplace bombing . . . was to force there to be a response much quicker than the U.S. government" routinely produces one, McCurry said.[17] Second, it provided ammunition for those, such as Christo-

pher, who had been arguing in administration councils for action. Third, it provided a moment of increased public attention to Bosnia that made it easier for the administration to explain a more robust policy. "It was a short window. We took advantage of it. We moved the policy forward. And it was successful," said McCurry's predecessor, Dee Dee Myers.[18]

In summary, rather than forcing the Clinton administration into doing something (undertaking an intervention) that it did not want to do, the images from Sarajevo helped the administration take a step that some of its senior members were arguing for. The images had an impact because the structure they affected—Clinton Administration foreign policy—was itself in flux.

* * *

Perhaps the clearest lesson here is that, in an age of instant, 'round-the-clock television news, foreign policy leadership remains both possible and necessary—perhaps even more necessary than before. * * * There seems little doubt that CNN and its brethren have made leadership more difficult. Numerous officials spoke of the temptation to respond to dramatic video images and the intense public outcry that often can accompany them. These calls can be resisted, but at a political price. If policy is not well anchored, the temptation to respond to the calculation of the moment can be overwhelming. CNN, in particular, gives opponents of policy—whether in the U.S. Congress or in the streets of Mogadishu—a platform to make their views known instantly, thus complicating the life of today's policy-maker. Television feeds on conflict, whether political or physical, emphasizing the challenge to policy. * * *

* * *

Nonetheless, while it is neither possible nor advisable to suppress all challenges to policy, this paper has found a clear inverse relationship between leadership and news media impact. When policy is well grounded, it is less likely that the media will be able to shift officials' focus. When policy is clear, reasonably constant, and well communicated, the news media follow officials rather than lead them—by the rules of "objectivity," they can do nothing else.[19] * * *

In sum, the awesome powers of communication technology at the news media's disposal have not had as dramatic an impact on this critical aspect of foreign policy as it might seem at first glance. Each of the cases revealed how other, abiding factors played a central role in the decision about whether or not to intervene. These factors included the real potential costs in U.S. blood and treasure; the credibility of the United States on the international scene; the future of important alliances; and the goals and benefits of the proposed mission itself. Journalists have had an impact on the decision about whether or not the United States will send its men and women into combat for a long time, as the case of the Yellow Press, McKinley, and the Spanish-American War shows. They still have an impact—and for the same reasons. What technology per se has changed is the pressures of time. If government of-

ficials allow others to dominate the debate, if they fail to communicate their policies and build support, if those policies fail, the news media will reflect all this, and officials will soon find that the impact of the media can be very real—and blindingly swift—indeed.

While the news media have made modern governance more difficult and more risky, Kennan's fears about the obsolescence of official prerogatives are exaggerated at best. Policymakers retain the power to set the agenda, to make policy choices and to lead. To do so, they need a sophisticated understanding, not simplistic descriptions, of the news media's complex role.

Notes

[1]For our purposes, "real-time" means not only images that are broadcast as they are occurring (that is, live) but also those that reach policymakers and other audiences within twenty-four hours of the event. See Nik Gowing, *Real-Time Television Coverage of Armed Conflicts and Diplomatic Crises: Does it Pressure or Distort Foreign Policy Decisions?* Working paper 94-1, Joan Shorenstein Barone Center on the Press, Politics, and Public Policy, Harvard University, Cambridge, Mass., June 1994.

[2]Steven Livingston and Todd Eachus, "Humanitarian Crises and U.S. Foreign Policy: Somalia and the CNN Effect Reconsidered," *Political Communication* 12, no. 4 (October–December 1995): 415–416.

[3]Daniel Hallin, *The "Uncensored War": The Media and Vietnam* (Berkeley: University of California Press, 1986).

[4]"Peace operations" is the term employed by the Clinton administration in its May 1994 policy declaration, where it was defined as "the entire spectrum of activities from traditional peacekeeping to peace enforcement aimed at defusing and resolving

international conflicts." "Operations other than war" (OOTWs), as used by the U.S. military, is somewhat broader, encompassing such activities as drug interdiction and relief missions such as those conducted in Bangladesh (Operation Sea Angel) or south Florida (Hurricane Andrew).

[5]Hallin, *The "Uncensored War."*

[6]*The Media and Foreign Policy in the Post–Cold War World* (New York: Freedom Forum Media Studies Center, 1993).

[7]Livingston and Eachus, "Humanitarian Crises"; and Eric V. Larson, *U.S. Casualties in Somalia: The Media Response and the Myth of the "CNN Effect"* (draft), RAND, Santa Monica, Calif., March 1995, p. 69.

[8]Herman J. Cohen, "Intervention in Somalia," *The Diplomatic Record 1992–1993* (Boulder, Colo.: Westview Press, 1994), pp. 62–63.

[9]Telephone interview with Baker, September 11, 1995.

[10]Interviews: Baker, September 11, 1995; Eagleburger, February 1, 1995; and Scowcroft, February 27, 1995.

[11]Interview with Zimmermann, June 8, 1995.

[12]Eagleburger interview.

[13]Scowcroft interview; interview with Kenney, January 26, 1995; and interview with Gutman, January 31, 1995.

[14]Elizabeth Drew, *On The Edge: The Clinton Presidency* (New York: Simon and Schuster, 1994).

[15]Elaine Sciolino and Douglas Jehl, "As U.S. Sought a Bosnia Policy, the French Offered a Good Idea," *New York Times,* February 14, 1994, p. A1.

[16]Background interview, February 3, 1995.

[17]Interview with McCurry, May 15, 1995 (at the time of the event, McCurry was State Department spokesperson).

[18]Interview with Myers, February 27, 1995.

[19]Hallin, *The "Uncensored War."*

United States vs. Western Europe?

7.1

Robert Kagan

Power and Weakness

It is time to stop pretending that Europeans and Americans share a common view of the world, or even that they occupy the same world. On the all-important question of power—the efficacy of power, the morality of power, the desirability of power—American and European perspectives are diverging. Europe is turning away from power, or to put it a little differently, it is moving beyond power into a self-contained world of laws and rules and transnational negotiation and cooperation. It is entering a post-historical paradise of peace and relative prosperity, the realization of Kant's "Perpetual Peace." The United States, meanwhile, remains mired in history, exercising power in the anarchic Hobbesian world where international laws and rules are unreliable and where true security and the defense and promotion of a liberal order still depend on the possession and use of military might. That is why on major strategic and international questions today, Americans are from Mars and Europeans are from Venus: They agree on little and understand one another less and less. And this state of affairs is not transitory—the product of one American election or one catastrophic event. The reasons for the transatlantic divide are deep, long in development, and likely to endure. When it comes to setting national priorities, determining threats, defining challenges, and fashioning and implementing foreign and defense policies, the United States and Europe have parted ways. . . .

Today's transatlantic problem, in short, is not a George W. Bush problem. It is a power problem. American military strength has produced a propensity to use that strength. Europe's military weakness has produced a perfectly understandable aversion to the exercise of military power. Indeed, it has produced a powerful European interest in inhabiting a world where strength doesn't matter, where international law and international institutions predominate, where unilateral action by powerful nations is forbidden, where all nations regardless of their strength have equal rights and are equally protected by commonly agreed-upon international rules of behavior. Europeans have a deep interest in devaluing and eventually eradicating the

From *Policy Review* 113 (June 2002).

brutal laws of an anarchic, Hobbesian world where power is the ultimate determinant of national security and success.

This is no reproach. It is what weaker powers have wanted from time immemorial. It was what Americans wanted in the eighteenth and early nineteenth centuries, when the brutality of a European system of power politics run by the global giants of France, Britain, and Russia left Americans constantly vulnerable to imperial thrashing. It was what the other small powers of Europe wanted in those years, too, only to be sneered at by Bourbon kings and other powerful monarchs, who spoke instead of *raison d'état*. The great proponent of international law on the high seas in the eighteenth century was the United States; the great opponent was Britain's navy, the "Mistress of the Seas." In an anarchic world, small powers always fear they will be victims. Great powers, on the other hand, often fear rules that may constrain them more than they fear the anarchy in which their power brings security and prosperity.

This natural and historic disagreement between the stronger and the weaker manifests itself in today's transatlantic dispute over the question of unilateralism. Europeans generally believe their objection to American unilateralism is proof of their greater commitment to certain ideals concerning world order. They are less willing to acknowledge that their hostility to unilateralism is also self-interested. Europeans fear American unilateralism. They fear it perpetuates a Hobbesian world in which they may become increasingly vulnerable. The United States may be a rela-

tively benign hegemon, but insofar as its actions delay the arrival of a world order more conducive to the safety of weaker powers, it is objectively dangerous.

* * *

Important as the power gap may be in shaping the respective strategic cultures of the United States and Europe, it is only one part of the story. Europe in the past half-century has developed a genuinely different perspective on the role of power in international relations, a perspective that springs directly from its unique historical experience since the end of World War II. It is a perspective that Americans do not share and cannot share, inasmuch as the formative historical experiences on their side of the Atlantic have not been the same.

Consider again the qualities that make up the European strategic culture: the emphasis on negotiation, diplomacy, and commercial ties, on international law over the use of force, on seduction over coercion, on multilateralism over unilateralism. It is true that these are not traditionally European approaches to international relations when viewed from a long historical perspective. But they are a product of more recent European history. The modern European strategic culture represents a conscious rejection of the European past, a rejection of the evils of European *machtpolitik*. It is a reflection of Europeans' ardent and understandable desire never to return to that past. Who knows better than Europeans the dangers that arise from unbridled power politics, from an excessive reliance on military force, from policies produced by national egoism and ambition, even from balance of power and *raison d'état*? As German Foreign Minister Joschka Fischer put it in a speech outlining his vision of the European future at Humboldt University in Berlin (May 12, 2000), "The core of the concept of Europe after 1945 was and still is a rejection of the European balance-of-power principle and the hegemonic ambitions of individual states that had emerged following the Peace of Westphalia in 1648." The European Union is itself the product of an awful century of European warfare.

* * *

The transmission of the European miracle to the rest of the world has become Europe's new *mission civilisatrice*. Just as Americans have always believed that they had discovered the secret to human happiness and wished to export it to the rest of the world, so the Europeans have a new mission born of their own discovery of perpetual peace.

Thus we arrive at what may be the most important reason for the divergence in views between Europe and the United States. America's power, and its willingness to exercise that power—unilaterally if necessary—represents a threat to Europe's new sense of mission. Perhaps the greatest threat. * * * Such American action represents an assault on the essence of "postmodern" Europe. It is an assault on Europe's new ideals, a denial of their universal validity, much as the monarchies of eighteenth- and nineteenth-century Europe were an assault on American republican ideals. Americans ought to be the first to understand that a threat to one's beliefs can be as frightening as a threat to one's physical security.

As Americans have for two centuries, Europeans speak with great confidence of the superiority of their global understanding, the wisdom they have to offer other nations about conflict resolution, and their way of addressing international problems. But just as in the first decade of the American republic, there is a hint of insecurity in the European claim to "success," an evident need to have their success affirmed and their views accepted by other nations, particularly by the mighty United States. After all, to deny the validity of the new European idealism is to raise profound doubts about the viability of the European project. If international problems cannot, in fact, be settled the European way, wouldn't that suggest that Europe itself may eventually fall short of a solution, with all the horrors this implies?

* * *

Perhaps it is not just coincidence that the amazing progress toward European integration in recent years has been accompanied not by the emergence of a European superpower but, on the contrary, by a diminishing of European military capabilities relative to the United States. Turning Europe into a global superpower capable of balancing the power of the United States may have been one of the original selling points of the European Union—an independent European foreign and defense policy was supposed to be one of the most important byproducts of European integration. But, in truth, the ambition for European "power" is something of an anachronism. It is an atavistic impulse, inconsistent with the ideals of postmodern Europe, whose very existence depends on the rejection of power politics. Whatever its architects may have intended, European integration has proved to be the enemy of European military power and, indeed, of an important European global role.

* * *

Can Europe change course and assume a larger role on the world stage? There has been no shortage of European leaders urging it to do so. Nor is the weakness of EU foreign policy today necessarily proof that it must be weak tomorrow, given the EU's record of overcoming weaknesses in other areas. And yet the political will to demand more power for Europe appears to be lacking, and for the very good reason that Europe does not see a mission for itself that requires power. Its mission is to oppose power. It is revealing that the argument most often advanced by Europeans for augmenting their military strength these days is not that it will allow Europe to expand its strategic purview. It is merely to rein in and "multilateralize" the United States. "America," writes the pro-American British scholar Timothy Garton Ash in the *New York Times* (April 9, 2002), "has too much power for anyone's good, including its own." Therefore Europe must amass power, but for no other reason than to save the world and the United States from the dangers inherent in the present lopsided situation.

The Bush Doctrine

Excerpts from the Bush Administration's
National Security Strategy for the United States (2002)

The United States of America is fighting a war against terrorists of global reach. The enemy is not a single political regime or person or religion or ideology. The enemy is terrorism—premeditated, politically motivated violence perpetrated against innocents.

In many regions, legitimate grievances prevent the emergence of a lasting peace. Such grievances deserve to be, and must be, addressed within a political process. But no cause justifies terror. The United States will make no concessions to terrorist demands and strike no deals with them. We make no distinction between terrorists and those who knowingly harbor or provide aid to them.

The struggle against global terrorism is different from any other war in our history. It will be fought on many fronts against a particularly elusive enemy over an extended period of time. Progress will come through the persistent accumulation of successes—some seen, some unseen.

* * *

The nature of the Cold War threat required the United States—with our allies and friends—to emphasize deterrence of the enemy's use of force, producing a grim strategy of mutual assured destruction. With the collapse of the Soviet Union and the end of the Cold War, our security environment has undergone profound transformation.

But new deadly challenges have emerged from rogue states and terrorists. None of these contemporary threats rival the sheer destructive power that was arrayed against us by the Soviet Union. However, the nature and motivations of these new adversaries, their determination to obtain destructive powers hitherto available only to the world's strongest states, and the greater likelihood that they will use weapons of mass destruction against us, make today's security environment more complex and dangerous.

For centuries, international law recognized that nations need not suffer an attack before they can lawfully take action to defend themselves against forces that present an imminent danger of attack. Legal scholars and international jurists often conditioned the legitimacy of preemption on the existence of an imminent

From George W. Bush, *National Security Strategy for the United States (2002)*, http:www.whitehouse.gov/nsc

threat—most often a visible mobilization of armies, navies, and air forces preparing to attack.

We must adapt the concept of imminent threat to the capabilities and objectives of today's adversaries. Rogue states and terrorists do not seek to attack us using conventional means. They know such attacks would fail. Instead, they rely on acts of terror and, potentially, the use of weapons of mass destruction—weapons that can be easily concealed, delivered covertly, and used without warning.

The targets of these attacks are our military forces and our civilian population, in direct violation of one of the principal norms of the law of warfare. As was demonstrated by the losses on September 11, 2001, mass civilian casualties is the specific objective of terrorists and these losses would be exponentially more severe if terrorists acquired and used weapons of mass destruction.

The United States has long maintained the option of preemptive actions to counter a sufficient threat to our national security. The greater the threat, the greater is the risk of inaction—and the more compelling the case for taking anticipatory action to defend ourselves, even if uncertainty remains as to the time and place of the enemy's attack. To forestall or prevent such hostile acts by our adversaries, the United States will, if necessary, act preemptively.

The United States will not use force in all cases to preempt emerging threats, nor should nations use preemption as a pretext for aggression. Yet in an age where the enemies of civilization openly and actively seek the world's most destructive technologies, the United States cannot remain idle while dangers gather. We will always proceed deliberately, weighing the consequences of our actions.

Bush Doctrine Critique

7.3

G. John Ikenberry

America's Imperial Ambition

The Lures of Preemption

In the shadows of the Bush administration's war on terrorism, sweeping new ideas are circulating about U.S. grand strategy and the restructuring of today's unipolar world. They call for American unilateral and preemptive, even preventive, use of force, facilitated if possible by coalitions of the willing—but ultimately unconstrained by the rules and norms of the international community. At the extreme, these notions form a neoimperial vision in which the United States arrogates to itself the global role of setting standards, determining threats, using force, and meting out justice. It is a vision in which sovereignty becomes more absolute for America even as it becomes more conditional for countries that challenge Washington's standards of internal and external behavior. It is a vision made necessary—at least in the eyes of its advocates—by the new and apocalyptic character of contemporary terrorist threats and by America's unprecedented global dominance. These radical strategic ideas and impulses could transform today's world order in a way

that the end of the Cold War, strangely enough, did not.

* * *

A New Grand Strategy

For the first time since the dawn of the Cold War, a new grand strategy is taking shape in Washington. It is advanced most directly as a response to terrorism, but it also constitutes a broader view about how the United States should wield power and organize world order. According to this new paradigm, America is to be less bound to its partners and to global rules and institutions while it steps forward to play a more unilateral and anticipatory role in attacking terrorist threats and confronting rogue states seeking WMD [weapons of mass destruction]. The United States will use its unrivaled military power to manage the global order.

* * *

Imperial Dangers

Pitfalls accompany this neoimperial grand strategy, however. Unchecked U.S. power,

From *Foreign Affairs* 81:5 (September–October 2002), 44–60.

shorn of legitimacy and disentangled from the postwar norms and institutions of the international order, will usher in a more hostile international system, making it far harder to achieve American interests. The secret of the United States' long brilliant run as the world's leading state was its ability and willingness to exercise power within alliance and multinational frameworks, which made its power and agenda more acceptable to allies and other key states around the world. This achievement has now been put at risk by the administration's new thinking.

*   *   *

The specific doctrine of preemptive action poses a related problem: once the United States feels it can take such a course, nothing will stop other countries from doing the same. Does the United States want this doctrine in the hands of Pakistan, or even China or Russia? After all, it would not require the intervening state to first provide evidence for its actions. The United States argues that to wait until all the evidence is in, or until authoritative international bodies support action, is to wait too long. Yet that approach is the only basis that the United States can use if it needs to appeal for restraint in the actions of others. Moreover, and quite paradoxically, overwhelming American conventional military might, combined with a policy of preemptive strikes, could lead hostile states to accelerate programs to acquire their only possible deterrent to the United States: WMD. This is another version of the security dilemma, but one made worse by a neoimperial grand strategy.

Another problem follows. The use of force to eliminate WMD capabilities or overturn dangerous regimes is never simple, whether it is pursued unilaterally or by a concert of major states. After the military intervention is over, the target country has to be put back together. Peacekeeping and state building are inevitably required, as are long-term strategies that bring the UN, the World Bank, and the major powers together to orchestrate aid and other forms of assistance. This is not heroic work, but it is utterly necessary. Peacekeeping troops may be required for many years, even after a new regime is built. Regional conflicts inflamed by outside military intervention must also be calmed. This is the "long tail" of burdens and commitments that comes with every major military action.

When these costs and obligations are added to America's imperial military role, it becomes even more doubtful that the neoimperial strategy can be sustained at home over the long haul—the classic problem of imperial overstretch. The United States could keep its military predominance for decades if it is supported by a growing and increasingly productive economy. But the indirect burdens of cleaning up the political mess in terrorist-prone failed states levy a hidden cost. Peacekeeping and state building will require coalitions of states and multilateral agencies that can be brought into the process only if the initial decisions about military intervention are hammered out in consultation with other major states. America's older realist and liberal grand strategies suddenly become relevant again.

A third problem with an imperial grand strategy is that it cannot generate the cooperation needed to solve practical problems at the heart of the U.S. foreign policy agenda. In the fight on terrorism, the United States needs cooperation from European and Asian countries in intelligence, law enforcement, and logistics. Outside the security sphere, realizing U.S. objectives depends even more on a continuous stream of amicable working relations with major states around the world. It needs partners for trade liberalization, global financial stabilization, environmental protection, deterring transnational organized crime, managing the rise of China, and a host of other thorny challenges. But it is impossible to expect would-be partners to acquiesce to America's self-appointed global security protectorate and then pursue business as usual in all other domains.

The key policy tool for states confronting a unipolar and unilateral America is to withhold cooperation in day-to-day relations with the United States. One obvious means is trade policy; the European response to the recent American decision to impose tariffs on imported steel is explicable in these terms. This particular struggle concerns specific trade issues, but it is also a struggle over how Washington exercises power. The United States may be a unipolar military power, but economic and political power is more evenly distributed across the globe. The major states may not have much leverage in directly restraining American military policy, but they can make the United States pay a price in other areas.

Finally, the neoimperial grand strategy poses a wider problem for the maintenance of American unipolar power. It steps into the oldest trap of powerful imperial states: self-encirclement. When the most powerful state in the world throws its weight around, unconstrained by rules or norms of legitimacy, it risks a backlash. Other countries will bridle at an international order in which the United States plays only by its own rules. The proponents of the new grand strategy have assumed that the United States can single-handedly deploy military power abroad and not suffer untoward consequences; relations will be coarser with friends and allies, they believe, but such are the costs of leadership. But history shows that powerful states tend to trigger self-encirclement by their own overestimation of their power. Charles V, Louis XIV, Napoleon, and the leaders of post-Bismarck Germany sought to expand their imperial domains and impose a coercive order on others. Their imperial orders were all brought down when other countries decided they were not prepared to live in a world dominated by an overweening coercive state. America's imperial goals and modus operandi are much more limited and benign than were those of age-old emperors. But a hard-line imperial grand strategy runs the risk that history will repeat itself.

Bring in the Old

Wars change world politics, and so too will America's war on terrorism. How great states fight wars, how they define the stakes, how they make the peace in its aftermath—all give lasting shape to the international system that emerges after the guns fall silent. In mobilizing their societies for battle, wartime leaders have tended to describe the military struggle as more than simply the defeat of an enemy. Woodrow Wilson sent U.S. troops to Europe not only to stop the kaiser's army but to destroy militarism and usher in a worldwide democratic revolution. Franklin Roosevelt saw the war with Germany and Japan as a struggle to secure the "four great freedoms." The Atlantic Charter was a statement of war aims that called not just for the defeat of fascism but for a new dedication to social welfare and human rights within an open and stable world system. To advance these visions, Wilson and Roosevelt proposed new international rules and mechanisms of cooperation. Their message was clear: If you bear the burdens of war, we, your leaders, will use this dreadful conflict to usher in a more peaceful and decent order among states. Fighting the war had as much to do with building global relations as it did with vanquishing an enemy.

Bush has not fully articulated a vision of postwar international order, aside from defining the struggle as one between freedom and evil. The world has seen Washington take determined steps to fight terrorism, but it does not yet have a sense of Bush's larger, positive agenda for a strengthened and more decent international order.

This failure explains why the sympathy and goodwill generated around the world for the United States after September 11 quickly disappeared. Newspapers that once proclaimed, "We are all Americans," now express distrust toward America. The prevailing view is that the United States seems prepared to use its power to go after terrorists and evil regimes, but not to use it to help build a more stable and peaceful world order. The United States appears to be degrading the rules and institutions of international community, not enhancing them. To the rest of the world, neoimperial thinking has more to do with exercising power than with exercising leadership.

In contrast, America's older strategic orientations—balance-of-power realism and liberal multilateralism—suggest a mature world power that seeks stability and pursues its interests in ways that do not fundamentally threaten the positions of other states. They are strategies of co-option and reassurance. The new imperial grand strategy presents the United States very differently: a revisionist state seeking to parlay its momentary power advantages into a world order in which it runs the show. Unlike the hegemonic states of the past, the United States does not seek territory or outright political domination in Europe or Asia; "America has no empire to extend or utopia to establish," Bush noted in his West Point address. But the sheer power advantages that the United States possesses and the doctrines of preemption and counterterrorism that it is articulating do unsettle governments and people around the world. The costs could be high. The last thing the United States wants is for foreign diplomats and government leaders to ask, How can we work around, undermine, contain, and retaliate against U.S. power?

Rather than invent a new grand strategy, the United States should reinvigorate its older strategies, those based on the view that America's security partnerships are not simply instrumental tools but critical components of an American-led world political order that should be preserved. U.S. power is both leveraged and made more legitimate and user-friendly by these partnerships. The neoimperial thinkers are haunted by the specter of catastrophic terrorism and seek a radical reordering of America's role in the world. America's commanding unipolar power and the advent of frightening new terrorist threats feed this imperial temptation. But it is a grand strategic vision that, taken to the extreme, will leave the world more dangerous and divided—and the United States less secure.

The United Nations

8.1

KOFI A. ANNAN

'We the Peoples'

We need to remind ourselves why the United Nations exists—for what, and for whom. We also need to ask ourselves what kind of United Nations the world's leaders are prepared to support, in deeds as well as words. Clear answers are necessary to energize and focus the Organization's work in the decades ahead. It is those answers that the Millennium Summit must provide.

Of course, the United Nations exists to serve its member States. It is the only body of its kind with universal membership and comprehensive scope, and encompassing so many areas of human endeavour. These features make it a uniquely useful forum—for sharing information, conducting negotiations, elaborating norms and voicing expectations, coordinating the behaviour of states and other actors, and pursuing common plans of action. We must ensure that the United Nations performs these functions as efficiently and effectively as possible.

The United Nations is more than a mere tool, however. As its Charter makes clear, the United Nations was intended to introduce new principles into international relations, making a qualitative difference to their day-to-day conduct. The Charter's very first Article defines our purposes: resolving disputes by peaceful means; devising cooperative solutions to economic, social, cultural and humanitarian problems; and broadly encouraging behaviour in conformity with the principles of justice and international law. In other words, quite apart from whatever practical tasks the United Nations is asked to perform, it has the avowed purpose of transforming relations among states, and the methods by which the world's affairs are managed.

Nor is that all. For even though the United Nations is an organization of states, the Charter is written in the name of "we the peoples". It reaffirms the dignity and worth of the human person, respect for human rights and the equal rights of men

From Millennium Report of the Secretary-General of the United Nations, 'We the Peoples': The role of the United Nations in the 21st Century (March 2002), www.un.org.

and women, and a commitment to social progress as measured by better standards of life, in freedom from want and fear alike. Ultimately, then, the United Nations exists for, and must serve, the needs and hopes of people everywhere.

* * *

When it was created more than half a century ago, in the convulsive aftermath of world war, the United Nations reflected humanity's greatest hopes for a just and peaceful global community. It still embodies that dream. We remain the only global institution with the legitimacy and scope that derive from universal membership, and a mandate that encompasses development, security and human rights as well as the environment. In this sense, the United Nations is unique in world affairs.

We are an organization without independent military capability, and we dispose of relatively modest resources in the economic realm. Yet our influence and impact on the world is far greater than many believe to be the case—and often more than we ourselves realize. This influence derives not from any exercise of power, but from the force of the values we represent; our role in helping to establish and sustain global norms; our ability to stimulate global concern and action; and the trust we enjoy for the practical work we do on the ground to improve people's lives.

The importance of principles and norms is easily underestimated; but in the decades since the United Nations was created, the spreading acceptance of new norms has profoundly affected the lives of many millions of people. War was once a normal instrument of statecraft; it is now universally proscribed, except in very specific circumstances. Democracy, once challenged by authoritarianism in various guises, has not only prevailed in much of the world, but is now generally seen as the most legitimate and desirable form of government. The protection of fundamental human rights, once considered the province of sovereign states alone, is now a universal concern transcending both governments and borders.

* * *

The United Nations plays an equally important, but largely unsung, role in creating and sustaining the global rules without which modern societies simply could not function. * * * Indeed, it is impossible to imagine our globalized world without the principles and practice of multilateralism to underpin it. An open world economy, in the place of mercantilism; a gradual decrease in the importance of competitive military alliances coupled with a Security Council more often able to reach decisions; the General Assembly or great gatherings of states and civil society organizations addressing humanity's common concerns— these are some of the signs, partial and halting though they may be, of an indispensable multilateral system in action.

Taking a long-term view, the expansion of the rule of law has been the foundation of much of the social progress achieved in the last millennium. Of course, this remains an unfinished project, especially at the international level, and our efforts to deepen it continue. Support for the rule of law would be enhanced if countries signed and ratified international treaties and conventions. Some decline to do so for reasons of substance, but a far greater number simply lack the necessary expertise and resources, especially when national legislation is needed to give force to international instruments.

* * *

If the international community were to create a new United Nations tomorrow, its make-up would surely be different from the one we have. In 2000, our structure reflects decades of mandates conferred by Member States and, in some cases, the legacy of deep political disagreements. While there is widespread consensus on the need to make the United Nations a more modern and flexible organization, unless Member States are willing to contemplate **real structural reform,** there will continue to be severe limits to what we can achieve.

When the scope of our responsibilities and the hopes invested in us are measured against our resources, we confront a sobering truth. The budget for our core functions—the Secretariat operations in New York, Geneva, Nairobi, Vienna and five regional commissions—is just $1.25 billion a year. That is about 4 percent of New York City's annual budget—and nearly a billion dollars less than the annual cost of running Tokyo's Fire Department. Our resources simply are not commensurate with our global tasks.

* * *

The purposes and principles of the United Nations are set out clearly in the Charter, and in the Universal Declaration of Human Rights. Their relevance and capacity to inspire have in no way diminished. If anything they have increased, as peoples have become interconnected in new ways, and the need for collective responsibility at the global level has come to be more widely felt. The following values, which reflect the spirit of the Charter, are—I believe—shared by all nations, and are of particular importance for the age we are now entering:

FREEDOM.   Men and women have the right to live their lives and raise their children in dignity, free from hunger and squalor and from the fear of violence or oppression. These rights are best assured by representative government, based on the will of the people.

EQUITY AND SOLIDARITY.   No individual and no nation must be denied the opportunity to benefit from globalization. Global risks must be managed in a way that shares the costs and burdens fairly. Those who suffer, or who benefit least, are entitled to help from those who benefit most.

TOLERANCE.   Human beings must respect each other, in all their diversity of faith, culture and language. Differences within and between societies should be neither feared nor repressed, but cherished.

NON-VIOLENCE.   Disputes between and within nations should be resolved by peaceful means, except where use of force is authorized by the Charter.

RESPECT FOR NATURE. Prudence should be shown in handling all living species and natural resources. Only so can the immeasurable riches we inherit from nature be preserved and passed on to our descendants.

SHARED RESPONSIBILITY. States must act together to maintain international peace and security, in accordance with the Charter. The management of risks and threats that affect all the world's peoples should be considered multilaterally.

. . .

In applying these values to the new century, our priorities must be clear.

First, we must spare no effort to free our fellow men and women from the abject and dehumanizing poverty in which more than 1 billion of them are currently confined. Let us resolve therefore:

- To halve, by the time this century is 15 years old, the proportion of the world's people (currently 22 percent) whose income is less than one dollar a day.
- To halve, by the same date, the proportion of people (currently 20 percent) who are unable to reach, or to afford, safe drinking water.
- That by the same date all children everywhere, boys and girls alike, will be able to complete a full course of primary schooling; and that girls and boys will have equal access to all levels of education.
- That by then we will have halted, and begun to reverse, the spread of HIV/AIDS.
- That, by 2020, we will have achieved significant improvement in the lives of at least 100 million slum dwellers around the world.
- To develop strategies that will give young people everywhere the chance of finding decent work.
- To ensure that the benefits of new technology, especially information technology, are available to all.
- That every national government will from now on commit itself to national policies and programmes directed specifically at reducing poverty, to be developed and applied in consultation with civil society.

At the international level, the more fortunate countries owe a duty of solidarity to the less fortunate. Let them resolve therefore:

- To grant free access to their markets for goods produced in poor countries—and, as a first step, to be prepared, at the Third United Nations Conference on the Least Developed Countries in March 2001, to adopt a policy of duty-free and quota-free access for essentially all exports from the least developed countries.
- To remove the shackles of debt which currently keep many of the poorest countries imprisoned in their poverty—and, as first steps, to implement the expansion of the debt relief programme for heavily indebted poor countries agreed last

year without further delay, and to be prepared to cancel all official debts of the heavily indebted poor countries, in return for those countries making demonstrable commitments to poverty reduction.

■ To grant more generous development assistance, particularly to those countries which are genuinely applying their resources to poverty reduction.

■ To work with the pharmaceutical industry and other partners to develop an effective and affordable vaccine against HIV; and to make HIV-related drugs more widely accessible in developing countries.

At both the national and international levels, private investment has an indispensable role to play. Let us resolve therefore:

■ To develop strong partnerships with the private sector to combat poverty in all its aspects.

Extreme poverty in sub-Saharan Africa affects a higher proportion of the population than in any other region. It is compounded by a higher incidence of conflict, HIV/AIDS and many other ills. Let us resolve therefore:

■ That in all our efforts we will make special provision for the needs of Africa, and give our full support to Africans in their struggle to overcome the continent's problems.

For my part, I have announced four new initiatives in the course of this report:

■ A Health InterNetwork, to provide hospitals and clinics in developing countries with access to up-to-date medical information.

■ A United Nations Information Technology Service (UNITeS), to train groups in developing countries in the uses and opportunities of information technology.

■ A disaster response initiative, "First on the Ground", which will provide uninterrupted communications access to areas affected by natural disasters and emergencies.

■ A global policy network to explore viable new approaches to the problem of youth employment.

Second, we must spare no effort to free our fellow men and women from the scourge of war—as the Charter requires us to do—and especially from the violence of civil conflict and the fear of weapons of mass destruction, which are the two great sources of terror in the present age. Let us resolve therefore:

■ To strengthen respect for law, in international as in national affairs, in particular the agreed provisions of treaties on the control of armaments, and international humanitarian and human rights law. I invite all governments that have not done so to sign and ratify the various conventions, covenants and treaties which form the central corpus of international law.

- To make the United Nations more effective in its work of maintaining peace and security, notably by
  -Strengthening the capacity of the United Nations to conduct peace operations.
  -Adopting measures to make economic sanctions adopted by the Security Council less harsh on innocent populations, and more effective in penalizing delinquent rulers.
- To take energetic action to curb the illegal traffic in small arms, notably by
  -Creating greater transparency in arms transfers.
  -Supporting regional disarmament measures, such as the moratorium on the importing, exporting or manufacturing of light weapons in West Africa.
  -Extending to other areas—especially post-conflict situations—the "weapons for goods" programmes that have worked well in Albania, El Salvador, Mozambique and Panama.
  -To examine the possibility of convening a major international conference to identify ways of eliminating nuclear dangers.

Third, we must spare no effort to free our fellow men and women, and above all our children and grandchildren, from the danger of living on a planet irredeemably spoilt by human activities, and whose resources can no longer provide for their needs. Given the extraordinary risks humanity confronts, let us resolve:

- To adopt a new ethic of conservation and stewardship; and, as first steps:
  -To adopt and ratify the Kyoto Protocol, so that it can enter into force by 2002, and to ensure that its goals are met, as a step towards reducing emissions of greenhouse gases.
  -To consider seriously incorporating the United Nations system of "green accounting" into national accounts.
  -To provide financial support for, and become actively engaged in, the Millennium Ecosystem Assessment.

Finally, we must spare no effort to make the United Nations a more effective instrument in the hands of the world's peoples for pursuing all three of these priorities—the fight against poverty, ignorance and disease; the fight against violence and terror; and the fight against the degradation and destruction of our common home. Let us resolve therefore:

- To reform the Security Council, in a way that both enables it to carry out its responsibilities more effectively and gives it greater legitimacy in the eyes of all the world's peoples.
- To ensure that the Organization is

given the necessary resources to carry out its mandates.

■ To ensure that the Secretariat makes best use of those resources in the interests of all Member States, by allowing it to adopt the best management practices and technologies available, and to concentrate on those tasks that reflect the current priorities of Member States.

■ To give full opportunities to non-governmental organizations and other non-state actors to make their indispensable contribution to the Organization's work.

•   •   •

I believe that these priorities are clear, and that all these things are achievable if we have the will to achieve them. For many of the priorities, strategies have already been worked out, and are summarized in this report. For others, what is needed first is to apply our minds, our energies and our research budgets to an intensive quest for workable solutions.

No state and no organization can solve all these problems by acting alone. Nor however, should any state imagine that others will solve them for it, if its own government and citizens do not apply themselves wholeheartedly to the task. Building a twenty-first century safer and more equitable than the twentieth is a task that requires the determined efforts of every state and every individual. In inspiring and coordinating those efforts, a renewed United Nations will have a vital and exalting role to play.

Realism of Preventive Diplomacy

BRUCE W. JENTLESON

Coercive Prevention
Normative, Political, and Policy Dilemmas

For all that has been proclaimed about the importance of preventive diplomacy, the reality of international action falls far short. While the first decade of the post–Cold War era did have some preventive successes, it was more marked (or marred) by missed opportunities.[1] Even in such "success" cases as Kosovo and East Timor, whatever may have been achieved was achieved only *after* mass killings, only *after* scores of villages were ravaged, only *after* hundreds of thousands were left as refugees. Yes, these conflicts were stopped from getting worse—but they already were humanitarian tragedies.

Is this the best we can do? I think not. To be sure, one can never be certain that policy X would have worked in this situation or policy Y in that situation. But nor should one simply accept assertions that nothing else could have been done, that nothing more or different was viable than the policies as pursued. Although such know-our-limits thinking often goes under the guise of realism, we must ask what is so realistic about trying to put societies back together after they have been devastated? Where is the strategic wisdom in continually doing so little for so long that the "realistic" choices end up being between a bad option and a worse one?

* * *

We have to confront the question—at least from a U.S. perspective—of whether it is worth doing. This is the realist critique, that much of the 1990s' agenda has been "social work" or other such internationalist idealism that, however morally commendable, fails the basic realist calculus of interests (too low), costs (too high), and options (too few).[2]

* * *

Interests Underestimated

It is agreed that few if any of the ethnic and other intrastate conflicts of the past decade have implicated U.S. "vital interests." War between major powers has not been a major risk. An attack on the homeland has not been threatened. Oil or other economically strategic resources have not been at stake. What the former U.S. ambassador to

From United States Institute of Peace, *Peaceworks 35* (Washington, D.C.: U.S. Institute of Peace, 2000)

Somalia said about the country, that it just was "not a critical piece of real estate for anybody in the post–Cold War world," has applied elsewhere as well.[3] Kosovo could be argued to have partly and indirectly impinged on vital interests such as European security, but it was a stretch to call Kosovo a vital interest.

This assessment tends to undervalue the interests at stake in such cases in three respects. First, such an assessment is *too static.* Although it may be true that many of these issues and places have limited intrinsic importance, the more the conflicts intensify the more important the issues and places often become. Initial assessments of intrinsic interests at stake often fail to account for the dynamics of spread and escalation by which the risks to the interests of outside parties become greater. Spread and escalation occur through various combinations of direct "contagion" caused by physical movement of refugees and weapons to other countries in the region, demonstration effects that even without direct contact activate and escalate other conflicts, and other modes of conflict diffusion.[4] * * * Former assistant secretary of state for Africa Chester Crocker makes the point even more strongly, arguing that it simply "is not possible to compartmentalize the globe and wall off the strategic slums. Regional crises exist, they worsen when left unattended, and they have a way of imposing themselves on the Western agenda."[5] Thus the paradox is that even though many of these conflicts do not start out involving inherently strategic locales, the damage to major power and other international interests often proves greater than anticipated because the assessment of the conflict's limited importance results in inaction or inadequate action. This is not to reverse totally the assessment of interests as limited in such cases, but rather to open up the question for analysis rather than assumption.

Second is that the policy decision must be based not just on how important interests are in an absolute sense, but on the *proportionality* of the commitment involved relative to the importance of the interests. Thus a stronger case may be made when the interests at stake are of limited importance but the intervention requires only a proportionally limited-scale commitment to be effective, than when a medium-importance interest is at stake abut a disproportionately large commitment is required. It is more important whether ends and means match than what the absolute value of the ends are.

Third, the realists' insistence that interests but not values must be the basis for policy decisions creates a false dichotomy. "The distinction between interests and values," as Stanley Hoffmann argues, "is largely fallacious . . . a great power has an 'interest' in world order that goes beyond strict national security concerns and its definition of world order is largely shaped by its values."[6] Such thinking cannot go so far as to become "a universalist humanitarian impulse," which, as Richard Haass notes, "would surely qualify as a case of what Paul Kennedy defines as 'imperial overstretch.'" But as Haass acknowledges, "not acting entails real costs, not only for the innocent people who lose their homes or lives or both, but also for America's image in the world."[7] As for those who then raise the question of values inconsistency, and ask why preventive strategies are attempted here but not there, the answer is that to bring values in is not to knock interests out, that relative assessments still need to be made so as to strike a balance and avoid omni-interventionism. How interests and values aggregate is thus an assessment to be made, not an assumption to be set.

Costs Overestimated

In a sense policymakers are no different from most people in putting greater weight on immediate costs than on anticipated ones. It always seems easier to pay tomorrow rather than today—thus the success of credit cards, thus the failures of conflict prevention. There is the added probability calculus that perhaps the costs won't have to be paid, the bill won't come due, if the issue peters out or at least self-limits. But the bills have been coming due, and when they have it has been with the equivalent of exorbitant interest and late fees. One study estimated that the costs of conflict prevention to outside powers in the Bosnia case would have been $33.3 billion, compared with the estimated $53.7 billion that the peacekeeping and post conflict peacebuilding actually cost. Similar disproportions were extrapolated for other cases: for example, $5 billion costs for the Haiti conflict compared with the $2.3 billion estimate for conflict prevention; $7.3 billion compared with $1.5 billion for Somalia; and in a case of successful prevention, Macedonia, $0.3 billion costs for prevention compared with $15 billion had the conflict even reached intermediate intensity let alone higher levels.[8] Time and again, the costs of waiting proved to be much greater than expected, and almost certainly more than those for preventive action would have been.

The less quantifiable aspect of costs involves the credibility of major powers and international institutions. Credibility is not just about resolve but also about judgment and the capacity to discern when major interests are at stake and when they are not. When international actors appear to lack the judgment to discern that their interests are at stake and/or the will to act when they are, the credibility of the actors suffers.

Options Narrowed

A former Croatian militiaman reflected on his own killing of seventy-two civilians and command of a death camp. "The most difficult thing is to ignite a house or kill a man for the first time," he stated, "but afterwards even this becomes routine."[9] The addition of revenge and retribution to other sources of tension plunges a conflict down to a fundamentally different and more difficult depth. Certain international strategies that may have been effective at lower levels of conflict are less likely to be so amid intensified violence. When that happens a Rubicon is crossed, the other side of which resolution and even limitation of the conflict become much more difficult.

Part of this is the classic problem for statecraft that the more extensive the objectives, the greater and usually more coercive are the strategies needed to achieve them. Preventing a conflict from escalating to violence is a more limited objective than ending violence once it has begun.[10] Another aspect is that the capacity of domestic leaders to build "conflict constituencies" is that much greater when they have retribution and revenge to invoke.[11]

Options thus do *not* necessarily stay open over time; the problem often gets harder down that road to where it has been kicked. In some respects it is no wonder that the Bosnia peacekeeping force has had to be so large for so long. The Kosovo peacekeeping force likewise is unlikely to be withdrawn anytime soon (other than in failure). So when we then turn around and find military readiness problems for the U.S. Army as a consequence of these large-scale, drawn-out deployments, the key implication is not that the commitments should not have been made in the first place but rather that earlier action should have been taken when the options were greater. Nor should it be a surprise that the political and civic aspects also have taken longer, cost more, and succeeded less than promised. Putting these societies back together is, as Bill Zartman has put it, like "putting humpty-dumpty together again."[12]

* * *

Furthermore, in considering their options, international actors need to realize that while they may profess neutrality, by limiting their involvement to humanitarian rescue or simply staying out, there is no "nonposition" in the sense of no impact one way or the other. If one party to the conflict assesses that it has the advantage in military power and other means of violence, so long as the other side cannot count on international assistance to balance and buttress, it should be no surprise that war becomes the option of choice. In other instances, the choice of war is at least in part a preemptive one. War is less a consequence of outright aggressive intentions than a manifestation of the "security dilemma" in which warfare breaks out from mutual insecurities and fears of vulnerabilities that credible international action could have assuaged. In these and other ways, the parties to the conflict take into account what action international actors are likely to take.

In sum, even on its own terms, the realist critique of conflict prevention does not hold up. The interests at stake are greater than asserted; it is the costs of waiting, more than the costs of acting early, that are so high; and the available options narrow over time. It is conflict prevention, not inaction, that is the more realistic strategy.

* * *

One of the main problems for coercive prevention, given the intrastate nature of the vast majority of post–Cold War conflicts, is the persistent prevalence of the norm of *sovereignty as rights* over the norm of *sovereignty as responsibility*.

* * *

With regard to the 1945–90 period, many point to Article 2 (7) of the UN Charter as the embodiment of sovereignty as rights: "Nothing contained in the present Charter shall authorize the United Nations to intervene in matters which are essentially within the domestic jurisdiction of any state." To the extent that this was true for that period, it was because of the functionality of the sovereignty-as-rights interpretation. Especially in the context of anticolonialism and the Cold War, sovereignty strict constructionism had a strong rationale as an organizing principle for maintaining international peace and for establishing the basic legal equality of states. Also in these contexts the affirmation of the rights of states was viewed as largely consistent with the rights of the individuals within those states to self-determination and to live free from external repression or worse.

* * *

Thus, during the Cold War the international community could maintain some claim to the norm of sovereignty as rights even if the major powers acted differently. Yet even then there was a degree of relatively. For while strict constructionists are quick to cite Article 2 (7), numerous other portions of the UN Charter as well as other sources provide normative legitimacy and legal basis for the competing conception of "sovereignty as responsibility.[13]

This emphasis on the responsibilities that come with sovereignty is founded at the most fundamental level on a conception of the individual, not the state, as the "right and duty bearing unit in international society." States have the responsibility "at the very least," as Francis Deng, Bill Zartman, Don Rothchild, and colleagues argue, of "ensuring a certain level of protection for and providing the basic needs of the people."[14] It is to be stressed that the rights and responsibilities conceptions of sovereignty are not dichotomous, but rather mark out a continuum along which there are gradations and conditionalities.[15]

* * *

The UN Charter, as Secretary-General Kofi Annan has put it, "was issued in the name of 'the peoples', not the governments of the United Nations. . . . The Charter protects the sovereignty of peoples. It was never meant as a license for governments to trample on human rights and human dignity. Sovereignty implies responsibility, not just power."[16] This also comes through in such other provisions of the UN Charter as Article 3, affirming that "everyone has the right to life, liberty and the security of person"; Article 55 that commits the United Nations to "promote . . . universal respect for, and observance of, human rights and fundamental freedoms"; and Article 56 that pledges all members "to take joint and separate action" toward this end. Even Article 2 (7) needs to be qualified, according to Secretary-General Annan, with "the important rider that this principle shall not prejudice the application of enforcement measures under Chapter VII. In other words, even national sovereignty can be set aside if it stands in the way of the Security Council's overriding duty to preserve international peace and security."[17] Further affirmations of the responsibilities of sovereignty are manifested in the Genocide Convention, the Universal Declaration of Human Rights, and other international covenants that make no distinction on whether the offender is a foreign invader or one's own government.

* * *

In sum, however the who question is worked out, given the intrastate nature in whole or in part of the vast majority of major post-Cold War conflicts, the central point is the need for a conception of sovereignty that also reflects the responsibilities that come with the rights. The scope of a state's right to sovereign authority is not unconditional or normatively superior to the right to security of the polity. Until and unless this conception of sovereignty as responsibility gains greater international legitimacy, international conflict prevention strategies will continue more often than not to be too little, too late[18]

Notes

[1]That these were missed opportunities, and not just unpreventable occurrences, is strongly corroborated in the study I edited for the Carnegie Commission on Preventing Deadly Conflict, *Opportunities Missed, Opportunities Seized: Preventive Diplomacy in the Post–Cold War World* (Lanham, Md.: Rowman and Littlefield, 1999).

[2]Michael Mandelbaum, "Foreign Policy as Social Work," *Foreign Affairs* 75 (January–February 1996), 16–32.

[3]*Washington Post,* September 4, 1995, A43.

[4]Stuart Hill and Donald Rothchild, "The Contagion of Political Conflict in Africa and the World," *Journal of Conflict Resolution* 30 (December 1986): 716–735; Stuart Hill, Donald Rothchild, and Colin Cameron, "Tactical Information and the Diffusion of Peaceful Protests," in *The International Spread of Ethnic Conflict; Fear, Diffusion, and Escalation,* ed. David A. Lake and Donald Rothchild (Princeton, N.J.: Princeton University Press, 1998). 61–88.

[5]Chester A. Crocker, "A Poor Case for Quitting: Mistaking Incompetence for Interventionism," *Foreign Affairs* 79 (January–February 2000): 184.

[6]Stanley Hoffmann, "In Defense of Mother Theresa: Morality in Foreign Policy," *Foreign Affairs* 75 (March–April 1994): 172; see also Hoffmann, "The Politics and Ethics of Military Intervention," *Survival* (winter 1995–96): 29–51.

[7]Richard N. Haass, "What Do We Do with American Primacy?" *Foreign Affairs* 78 (September–October 1999): 45.

[8]Michael E. Brown and Richard N. Rosecrance, eds., *The Costs of Conflict: Prevention and Cure in the Global Arena* (Lanham, Md.: Rowman and Littlefield, 1999), 225.

[9]Chris Hedges, "Croatian's Confession Describes Torture and Killing on a Vast Scale," *New York Times,* September 5, 1997, A1.

[10]Thomas C. Schelling, *Arms and Influence* (New Haven, Conn.: Yale University Press, 1966); Alexander L. George and William E. Simons, eds., *The Limits of Coercive Diplomacy,* 2d ed. (Boulder, Colo.: Westview Press, 1994); Alexander L. George, *Forceful Persuasion* (Washington, D.C.: United States Institute of Peace Press, 1991).

[11]Ken Menkhaus and Louis Ortmayer, "Somalia: Misread Crises and Missed Opportunities," in Jentleson, *Opportunities Missed, Opportunities Seized.*

[12]I. Williams Zartman, "Putting Humpty-Dumpty Together Again," in *The International Spread of Ethnic Conflict: Fear, Diffusion, and Escalation,* ed. David A. Lake and Donald Rothchild (Princeton, N.J.: Princeton University Press, 1998).

[13]For development of this concept, see Francis M. Deng, Sadikei Kimaro, Terence Lyons, Donald Rothchild, and I. William Zartman, *Sovereignty as Responsibility: Conflict Management in Africa* (Washington, D.C.: Brookings Institution, 1996).

[14]Ibid., 28.

[15]James N. Rosenau, "Sovereignty in a Turbulent World," in *Beyond Westphalia: State Sovereignty and International Intervention,* ed. Gene M. Lyons and Michael Mastanduno (Baltimore: Johns Hopkins University Press, 1995), 195.

[16]Kofi Annan, "Intervention," Ditchley Foundation Lecture 35, 1998, 2. See also Annan, *Report of the Secretary-General on the Work of the Organization,* September 1999.

[17]Annan, "Intervention."

[18]For views that concur on some points and disagree on others with my discussion here, see the papers from the Pugwash Study Group on Intervention, Sovereignty, and International Security (Pugwash Meeting no. 252, December 1999), available at http://www.pugwash.org

Free Trade vs. Protectionism

GARY BURTLESS, ROBERT Z. LAWRENCE, ROBERT E. LITAN,
AND ROBERT J. SHAPIRO

Globaphobia

The fate of the U.S. economy has become increasingly linked with the economies of other nations for two reasons. One is well known and is, in fact, the result of deliberate policy. Since the end of the World War II, nations around the world, led by the United States, have been steadily lowering trade barriers—in recent cases, unilaterally. Average tariffs imposed by high-income countries like the United States have dropped from over 40 percent to just 6 percent, while barriers to services trade have come down. Many countries have negotiated free trade agreements with their neighbors.

The other force behind globalization is one over which politicians have little or no control: the continuing progress of technology. Faster and bigger airplanes move people and goods more quickly and cheaply. The cost of communication, fueled by a revolution in computer and materials technologies, continues to plummet. Although most investment stays at home, large pools of liquid capital nonetheless flow around the world at a quickening pace in search of the best returns, as the Asian currency crisis of late 1997 vividly demonstrated.

Whatever the reasons behind it, globalization has aroused concern and outright hostility among some in the United States. Both were much in evidence in the fall of 1997, during the tense debate in Congress over the extension of "fast-track" trade negotiating authority for the president and in the ultimate decision to postpone a vote on the issue until some time in 1998. Critics of globalization are not limited to well-known figures in the three major political parties—Patrick Buchanan, Richard Gephardt, and Ross Perot. Opinion surveys show that at least half of the American population believes that "globalization"—whatever people assume the term means—does more harm than good and that expanded trade will lead to lower wages for American workers.

From *Globaphobia: Confronting Fears about Open Trade* (Washington, D.C.: Brookings Institution, 1998), chapter 1.

653

These views no doubt help to explain why many polls show most Americans opposed to new free trade agreements. A similar, if not greater, degree of hostility to world economic integration is common in Europe.

We have written this book to demonstrate that the fear of globalization—or "globaphobia"—rests on very weak foundations. * * * In the pages that follow, we argue that the surface appeal of globaphobia has nonetheless led many American voters and policymakers astray in a number of respects.

First, the United States globalized rapidly during the golden years before 1973, when productivity and wages were growing briskly and inequality was shrinking, demonstrating that living standards can advance at a healthy rate while the United States increases its links with the rest of the world. In any event, it is useful to keep in mine that the U.S. economy is no more globalized today—measured by the share of trade in its total output—than it was *before World War I.*

Second, even though globalization harms some American workers, the protectionist remedies suggested by some trade critics are, at best, short-term palliatives and, at worst, harmful to the interests of the broad class of workers that they are designed to help. Sheltering U.S. firms from imports may grant some workers a short reprieve from wage cuts or downsizing. But protection dulls the incentives of workers and firms to innovate and stay abreast of market developments. As a result, its benefits for individual workers and firms are often temporary. Indeed, protection invites

foreign exporters to leap trade barriers by building plants in this country—as foreign manufacturers of automobiles, automobile parts, film, and other products have done. We are not criticizing this result: the United States has a strong national interest in attracting foreign investors, who typically bring technologies and management practices that ultimately yield higher wage and living standards for U.S. workers. But the movement to the United States of foreign companies and their plants simply underscores how erecting barriers to imports is often fools' gold for those who believe that protection will permanently shelter jobs or the profits of employers.

Third, erecting new barriers to imports also has an unseen boomerang effect in depressing exports. This is one of the most important, but least understood, propositions that we discuss in this book. While higher barriers to imports can temporarily improve the trade balance, this improvement would cause the value of the dollar on world exchange markets to rise, undercutting the competitive position of U.S. exports and curtailing job opportunities for Americans in export industries. Moreover, by increasing the costs of inputs (whether imported or domestic) that producers use to generate goods and services, protection further damages the competitive position of U.S. exporters. This is especially true in high-tech industries, where many American firms rely on foreign-made parts or capital equipment. The dangers of protection are further compounded to the extent it provokes retaliation by other countries. In that event, some Americans who work in exporting industries would lose their jobs, both directly and because higher barriers abroad would induce some of our exporting firms to move their plants (and jobs) overseas. In short, protection is not a zero-sum policy for the United States: it is a *negative sum* policy.

Fourth, globaphobia distracts policymakers and voters from implementing policies that would directly address the major causes of the stagnation or deterioration in the wages of less-skilled Americans. *The most significant problem faced by underpaid workers in the United States is not foreign competition. It is the mismatch between the skills that employers increasingly demand and the skills that many young adults bring to the labor market.* For the next generation of workers, the problem can be addressed by improvements in schooling and public and private training. The more difficult challenge is faced by today's unskilled adults, who find themselves unable to respond to the help wanted ads in daily newspapers, which often call for highly technical skills. It is easy to blame foreign imports for low wages, but doing so will not equip these workers with the new skills that employers need. The role of government is to help those who want to help themselves; most important, by maintaining a high-pressure economy that continues to generate new jobs, and secondarily, by facilitating training and providing effective inducements to displaced workers to find new jobs as rapidly as possible.

Fifth, Americans in fact have a vested interest in negotiating additional reductions of overseas barriers that limit the market for U.S. goods and services. These barriers typically harm the very industries in which America leads the world, including agriculture, financial services, pharmaceuticals, aircraft, and telecommunications. The failure of Congress to grant the president fast-track negotiating authority sends an odd and perverse message to the rest of the world. The United States, which once led the crusade for trade liberalization, now seems to have lost faith in the benefits of trade. Over time, this loss of faith may give ammunition to opponents of free trade in other countries, not only in resisting further trade liberalization but in imposing new barriers.

Sixth, it cannot be stressed too heavily that open trade benefits consumers. Each barrier to trade raises prices not only on the affected imports but also on the domestically produced goods or services with which they compete. Those who would nonetheless have the United States erect barriers to foreign goods—whether in the name of "fair trade," "national security," or some other claimed objective—must face the fact that they are asking the government to tax consumers in order to achieve these goals. And Americans must decide how willing they are to pay that tax. By contrast, lowering barriers to foreign goods delivers the equivalent of a tax cut to American consumers, while encouraging U.S. firms to innovate. The net result is higher living standards for Americans at home.

Finally, to ensure support for free trade, political leaders must abandon the argument traditionally used to advance the cause of trade liberalization: that it will generate *more* jobs. Proponents of freer trade should instead stick with the truth. Total employment depends on the overall macroeconomic environment (the willingness and capacity of Americans to buy goods and services) not on the trade balance (which depends on the difference between the amounts that Americans save and invest). We trade with foreigners for the same reasons that we trade among ourselves: to get better deals. Lower trade barriers in other countries mean *better* jobs for Americans. Firms in industries that are major exporters pay anywhere from 5 to 15 percent more than the average national wage. The "price" for gaining those trade opportunities—reducing our own trade barriers—is one that Americans should be glad to pay.

In spite of the enormous benefits of openness to trade and capital flows from the rest of the world and notwithstanding the additional benefits that Americans would derive from further liberalization, it is important to recognize that open borders create losers as well as winners. Openness exposes workers and company owners to the risk of major losses when new foreign competitors enter the U.S. market. Workers can lose their jobs. This has certainly occurred in a wide range of industries exposed to intense foreign competition—autos, steel, textiles, apparel, and footwear. Indeed, the whole point of engaging in trade is to shift resources—capital and labor—toward their most productive uses, a process that inevitably causes pain to those required to shift. In some cases, workers are forced to accept permanent reductions in pay, either in the jobs they continue to hold in a trade-affected industry or in new jobs they must

take after suffering displacement. Other workers, including mainly the unskilled and semiskilled, may be forced to accept small pay reductions as an indirect effect of liberalization. Indeed, the job losses of thousands of similar workers in traded goods industries may tend to push down the wages of *all* workers—even those in the service sector—in a particular skill category.

We acknowledge that these losses occur, though their size is vastly exaggerated in media accounts and the popular imagination. Nonetheless, we believe the nation has both a political and a moral responsibility to offer better compensation to the workers who suffer sizable losses as a result of trade liberalization. In the final chapter we spell out a detailed program for doing so. Decent compensation for the workers who suffer losses is easily affordable in view of the substantial benefits the country enjoys as a result of open trade. Liberal trade, like technological progress, mainly creates winners, not losers. Among the big winners are the stockholders, executives, and workers of exporting firms such as Boeing, Microsoft, and General Electric, as well as Hollywood (whose movies and television shows are seen around the world). There are many millions of more modest winners as well, including the workers, retirees, and nonworking poor, who benefit from lower prices and a far wider and better selection of products.

One problem in making the case for open borders is that few of the winners recognize the extent of the gains they enjoy as a result of free trade. The losses suffered by displaced workers in the auto, apparel, or shoemaking industries are vividly portrayed on the nightly news, but few Americans realize that cars, clothes, and shoes are cheaper, better made, or more varied as a result of their country's openness to the rest of the world. Workers who make products sold outside the United States often fail to recognize how much their jobs and wages depend on America's willingness to import as well as its capacity to export. People contributing to a pension fund seldom realize that their returns (and future pensions) are boosted by the fund's ability to invest overseas, and almost no borrower understands that the cost of a mortgage or car loan is lower because of America's attractiveness to foreigners as a place to invest their money. All of these benefits help improve the standard of living of typical Americans, and they can be directly or indirectly traced to our openness. They are nearly invisible to most citizens, however; certainly far less visible than the painful losses suffered by workers who lose their jobs when a factory is shut down.

*   *   *

Globalization and Global Inequality

9.2

UNITED NATIONS DEVELOPMENT PROGRAM

Globalization with a Human Face

"The real wealth of a nation is its people. And the purpose of development is to create an enabling environment for people to enjoy long, healthy and creative lives. This simple but powerful truth is too often forgotten in the pursuit of material and financial wealth." Those are the opening lines of the first *Human Development Report,* published in 1990. This tenth *Human Development Report*—like the first and all the others—is about people. It is about the growing interdependence of people in today's globalizing world.

Globalization is not new, but the present era has distinctive features. Shrinking space, shrinking time and disappearing borders are linking people's lives more deeply, more intensely, more immediately than ever before.

More than $1.5 trillion is now exchanged in the world's currency markets each day, and nearly a fifth of the goods and services produced each year are traded. But globalization is more than the flow of money and commodities—it is the growing interdependence of the worlds' people. And globalization is a process integrating not just the economy but culture, technology and governance. People everywhere are becoming connected—affected by events in far corners of the world.

*　*　*

Globalization offers great opportunities for human advance—but only with stronger governance.

*　*　*

Today's globalization is being driven by market expansion—opening national borders to trade, capital, information—outpacing governance of these markets and their repercussions for people. More progress has been made in norms, standards, policies and institutions for open global markets than for people and their rights. And a new

From United Nations Development Program *Human Development Report 1999* (New York: Oxford University Press, 1999).

commitment is needed to the ethics of universalism set out in the Universal Declaration of Human Rights.

Competitive markets may be the best guarantee of efficiency, but not necessarily of equity. Liberalization and privatization can be a step to competitive markets—but not a guarantee of them. And markets are neither the first nor the last word in human development. Many activities and goods that are critical to human development are provided outside the market—but these are being squeezed by the pressures of global competition. There is a fiscal squeeze on public goods, a time squeeze on care activities and an incentive squeeze on the environment.

When the market goes too far in dominating social and political outcomes, the opportunities and rewards of globalization spread unequally and inequitably—concentrating power and wealth in a select group of people, nations and corporations, marginalizing the others. When the market gets out of hand, the instabilities show up in boom and bust economies, as in the financial crisis in East Asia and its worldwide repercussions, cutting global output by an estimated $2 trillion in 1998–2000. When the profit motives of market players get out of hand, they challenge people's ethics—and sacrifice respect for justice and human rights.

The challenge of globalization in the new century is not to stop the expansion of global markets. The challenge is to find the rules and institutions for stronger governance—local, national, regional and global—to preserve the advantages of global markets and competition, but also to

provide enough space for human, community and environmental resources to ensure that globalization works for people—not just for profits. Globalization with:

- *Ethics*—less violation of human rights, not more.
- *Equity*—less disparity within and between nations, not more.
- *Inclusion*—less marginalization of people and countries, not more.
- *Human security*—less instability of societies and less vulnerability of people, not more.
- *Sustainability*—less environmental destruction, not more.
- *Development*—less poverty and deprivation, not more.

The opportunities and benefits of globalization need to be shared much more widely.

Since the 1980s many countries have seized the opportunities of economic and technological globalization. Beyond the industrial countries, the newly industrializing East Asian tigers are joined by Chile, the Dominican Republic, India, Mauritius, Poland, Turkey and many others linking into global markets, attracting foreign investment and taking advantage of technological advance. Their export growth has averaged more than 5% a year, diversifying into manufactures.

At the other extreme are the many countries benefiting little from expanding markets and advancing technology—Madagascar, Niger, the Russian Federation, Tajikistan and Venezuela among them.

These countries are becoming even more marginal—ironic, since many of them are highly "integrated," with exports nearly 30% of GDP for Sub-Saharan Africa and only 19% for the OECD. But these countries hang on the vagaries of global markets, with the prices of primary commodities having fallen to their lowest in a century and a half. They have shown little growth in exports and attracted virtually no foreign investment. In sum, today, global opportunities are unevenly distributed—between countries and people.

If global opportunities are not shared better, the failed growth of the last decades will continue. More than 80 countries still have per capita incomes lower than they were a decade or more ago. While 40 countries have sustained average per capita income growth of more than 3% a year since 1990, 55 countries, mostly in Sub-Saharan Africa and Eastern Europe and the Commonwealth of Independent States (CIS), have had declining per capita incomes.

* * *

Inequality has been rising in many countries since the early 1980s. In China disparities are widening between the export-oriented regions of the coast and the interior: the human poverty index is just under 20% in coastal provinces, but more than 50% in inland Guizhou. The countries of Eastern Europe and the CIS have registered some of the largest increases ever in the Gini coefficient, a measure of income inequality. OECD countries also registered big increases in inequality after the 1980s—especially Sweden, the United Kingdom and the United States.

Inequality between countries has also increased. The income gap between the fifth of the world's people living in the richest countries and the fifth in the poorest was 74 to 1 in 1997, up from 60 to 1 in 1990 and 30 to 1 in 1960. In the nineteenth century, too, inequality grew rapidly during the last three decades, in an era of rapid global integration: the income gap between the top and bottom countries increased from 3 to 1 in 1820 to 7 to 1 in 1870 and 11 to 1 in 1913.

By the late 1990s the fifth of the world's people living in the highest-income countries had:

- 86% of world GDP—the bottom fifth just 1%.
- 82% of world export markets—the bottom fifth just 1%.
- 68% of foreign direct investment—the bottom fifth just 1%.
- 74% of world telephone lines, today's basic means of communication—the bottom fifth just 1.5%.

* * *

Globalization is creating new threats to human security—in rich countries and poor.

One achievement of recent decades has been greater security for people in many countries—more political freedom and stability in Chile, peace in Central America, safer streets in the United States. But in the globalizing world of shrinking time, shrinking space and disappearing borders, people are confronting new threats to human security—sudden and hurtful disruptions in the pattern of daily life.

Financial volatility and economic insecurity. The financial turmoil in East Asia in 1997–99 demonstrates the risks of global financial markets. Net capital flows to Indonesia, the Republic of Korea, Malaysia, the Philippines and Thailand rocketed in the 1990s, reaching $93 billion in 1996. As turmoil hit market after market, these flows reversed overnight—with an outflow of $12 billion in 1997. The swing amounted to 11% of the precrisis GDPs of these countries. Two important lessons come out of this experience.

First, the human impacts are severe and are likely to persist long after economic recovery.

Bankruptcies spread. Education and health budgets came under pressure. More than 13 million people lost their jobs. As prices of essentials rose sharply, real wages fell sharply, down some 40–60% in Indonesia. The consequences go deeper—all countries report erosion of their social fabric, with social unrest, more crime, more violence in the home.

* * *

Second, far from being isolated incidents, financial crises have become increasingly common with the spread and growth of global capital flows. They result from rapid buildups and reversals of short-term capital flows and are likely to recur. More likely when national institutions regulating financial markets are not well developed, they are now recognized as systemic features of global capital markets. No single country can withstand their whims,

and global action is needed to prevent and manage them.

* * *

Health insecurity. Growing travel and migration have helped spread HIV/AIDS. More than 33 million people were living with HIV/AIDS in 1998, with almost 6 million new infections in that year. And the epidemic is now spreading rapidly to new locations, such as rural India and Eastern Europe and the CIS. With 95% of the 16,000 infected each day living in developing countries, AIDS has become a poor person's disease, taking a heavy toll on life expectancy, reversing the gains of recent decades. For nine countries in Africa, a loss of 17 years in life expectancy is projected by 2010, back to the levels of the 1960s.

Cultural insecurity. Globalization opens people's lives to culture and all its creativity—and to the flow of ideas and knowledge. But the new culture carried by expanding global markets is disquieting. As Mahatma Gandhi expressed so eloquently earlier in the century, "I do not want my house to be walled in on all sides and my windows to be stuffed. I want the cultures of all the lands to be blown about my house as freely as possible. But I refuse to be blown off my feet by any." Today's flow of culture is unbalanced, heavily weighted in one direction, from rich countries to poor.

* * *

Such onslaughts of foreign culture can put cultural diversity at risk, and make people fear losing their cultural identity. What is needed is support to indigenous and national cultures—to let them flourish alongside foreign cultures.

* * *

Environmental insecurity. Chronic environmental degradation—today's silent emergency—threatens people worldwide and undercuts the livelihoods of at least half a billion people. Poor people themselves, having little choice, put pressure on the environment, but so does the consumption of the rich. The growing export markets for fish, shrimp, paper and many other products mean depleted stocks, less biodiversity and fewer forests. Most of the costs are borne by the poor—though it is the world's rich who benefit most. The fifth of the world's people living in the richest countries consume 84% of the world's paper.

Political and community insecurity. Closely related to many other forms of insecurity is the rise of social tensions that threaten political stability and community cohesion. Of the 61 major armed conflicts fought between 1989 and 1998, only three were between states—the rest were civil.

Globalization has given new characteristics to conflicts. Feeding these conflicts is the global traffic in weapons, involving new actors and blurring political and business interests. In the power vacuum of the post–cold war era, military companies and mercenary armies began offering training to governments—and corporations. Accountable only to those who pay them, these hired military services pose a severe threat to human security. . . .

Despite the potential for development, the Internet poses severe problems of access and exclusion. Who was in the loop in 1998?

- *Geography divides.* Thailand has more cellular phones than Africa. South Asia, home to 23% of the world's people, has less than 1% of Internet users.
- *Education is a ticket to the network high society.* Globally, 30% of users had at least one university degree.
- *Income buys access.* To purchase a computer would cost the average Bangladeshi more than eight years' income, the average American, just one month's wage.
- *Men and youth dominate.* Women make up just 17% of the Internet users in Japan, only 7% in China. Most users in China and the United Kingdom are under 30.
- *English talks.* English prevails in almost 80% of all Websites, yet less than one in 10 people worldwide speaks it.

This exclusivity is creating parallel worlds. Those with income, education and—literally—connections have cheap and instantaneous access to information. The rest are left with uncertain, slow and costly access. When people in these two worlds live and compete side by side, the advantage of being connected will overpower the marginal and impoverished, cutting off their voices and concerns from the global conversation.

* * *

Global technological breakthroughs offer great potential for human advance and for eradicating poverty—but not with today's agendas.

Liberalization, privatization and tighter intellectual property rights are shaping the path for the new technologies, determining how they are used. But the privatization and concentration of technology are going too far. Corporations define research agendas and tightly control their findings with patents, racing to lay claim to intellectual property under the rules set out in the agreement on Trade-Related Aspects of Intellectual property Rights (TRIPS).

Poor people and poor countries risk being pushed to the margin in this proprietary regime controlling the world's knowledge:

- In defining research agendas, money talks, not need—cosmetic drugs and slow-ripening tomatoes come higher on the priority list than drought-resistant crops or a vaccine against malaria.
- From new drugs to better seeds, the best of the new technologies are priced for those who can pay. For poor people, they remain far out of reach.
- Tighter property rights raise the price of technology transfer, blocking developing countries from the dynamic knowledge sectors. The TRIPS agreement will enable multinationals to dominate the global market even more easily.

- New patent laws pay scant attention to the knowledge of indigenous people. These laws ignore cultural diversity in the way innovations are created and shared—and diversity in views on what can and should be owned, from plant varieties to human life. The result: a silent theft of centuries of knowledge from some of the poorest communities in developing countries.
- Despite the risks of genetic engineering, the rush and push of commercial interests are putting profits before people.

* * *

National and global governance have to be reinvented—with human development and equity at their core.

None of these pernicious trends—growing marginalization, growing human insecurity, growing inequality—is inevitable. With political will and commitment in the global community, they can all be reversed. With stronger governance—local, national, regional and global—the benefits of competitive markets can be preserved with clear rules and boundaries, and stronger action can be taken to meet the needs of human development.

Governance does not mean mere government. It means the framework of rules, institutions and established practices that set limits and give incentives for the behavior of individuals, organizations and firms. Without strong governance, the dangers of global conflicts could be a reality of the 21st century—trade wars promoting national and corporate interests, uncontrolled financial volatility setting off civil conflicts, untamed global crime infecting safe neighbourhoods and criminalizing politics, business and the police.

With the market collapse in East Asia, with the contagion to Brazil, Russia and elsewhere and with the threat of a global recession still looming, global governance is being re-examined. But the current debate is:

- Too narrow, limited to the concerns of economic growth and financial stability and neglecting broader human concerns such as persistent global poverty, growing inequality between and within countries, exclusion of poor people and countries and persisting human rights abuses.
- Too geographically unbalanced, dominated by the largest economies—usually the G-7, sometimes just the G-1, and only occasionally bringing in the large newly industrializing countries. Most small and poor developing countries are excluded, as are people's organizations.

Nor does the debate address the current weaknesses, imbalances and inequities in global governance—which, having developed in an ad hoc way, leaves many gaps.

- Multilateral agreements have helped establish global markets without considering their impacts on human development and poverty.
- The structures and processes for global policy-making are not representative. The key economic structures—the IMF, World Bank, G-7, G-10, G-22, OECD, WTO—are dominated by the large and rich countries, leaving poor countries and poor people with little influence and little voice, either for lack of membership or for lack of capacity for effective representation and participation. There is little transparency in decisions, and there is no structured forum for civil society institutions to express their views.
- There are no mechanisms for making ethical standards and human rights binding for corporations and individuals, not just governments.

In short, stronger national and global governance are needed for human well-being, not for the market.

*   *   *

NGOs

Margaret E. Keck and Kathryn Sikkink

Transnational Networks in International Politics: An Introduction

World politics at the end of the twentieth century involves, alongside states, many nonstate actors that interact with each other, with states, and with international organizations. These interactions are structured in terms of networks, and transnational networks are increasingly visible in international politics. Some involve economic actors and firms. Some are networks of scientists and experts whose professional ties and shared causal ideas underpin their efforts to influence policy.[1] Others are networks of activists, distinguishable largely by the centrality of principled ideas or values in motivating their formation.[2] We will call these *transnational advocacy networks.*

Advocacy networks are significant transnationally and domestically. By building new links among actors in civil societies, states, and international organizations, they multiply the channels of access to the international system. In such issue areas as the environment and human rights, they also make international resources available to new actors in domestic political and social struggles. By thus blurring the boundaries between a state's relations with its own nationals and the recourse both citizens and states have to the international system, advocacy networks are helping to transform the practice of national sovereignty.

* * *

Major actors in advocacy networks may include the following: (1) international and domestic nongovernmental research and advocacy organizations; (2) local social movements; (3) foundations; (4) the media; (5) churches, trade unions, consumer organizations, and intellectuals; (6) parts of regional and international intergovernmental organizations; and (7) parts of the executive and/or parliamentary branches of governments. Not all these will be present in each advocacy network. Initial research suggests, however, that international and domestic NGOs play a central role in all advocacy networks, usually initiating actions and pressuring more powerful actors to take positions. NGOs introduce new ideas, provide information, and lobby for policy changes.

From *Activists Beyond Borders: Advocacy Networks in International Politics* (Ithaca, N.Y.: Cornell University Press, 1998), chapter 1.

Groups in a network share values and frequently exchange information and services. The flow of information among actors in the network reveals a dense web of connections among these groups, both formal and informal. The movement of funds and services is especially notable between foundations and NGOs, and some NGOs provide services such as training for other NGOs in the same and sometimes other advocacy networks. Personnel also circulate within and among networks, as relevant players move from one to another in a version of the "revolving door."

Relationships among networks, both within and between issue areas, are similar to what scholars of social movements have found for domestic activism.[3] Individuals and foundation funding have moved back and forth among them. Environmentalists and women's groups have looked at the history of human rights campaigns for models of effective international institution building. Refugee resettlement and indigenous people's rights are increasingly central components of international environmental activity, and vice versa; mainstream human rights organizations have joined the campaign for women's rights. Some activists consider themselves part of an "NGO community."

* * *

Advocacy networks are not new. We can find examples as far back as the nineteenth-century campaign for the abolition of slavery. But their number, size, and professionalism, and the speed, density, and complexity of international linkages among them has grown dramatically in the last three decades. As Hugh Heclo remarks about domestic issue networks, "If the current situation is a mere outgrowth of old tendencies, it is so in the same sense that a 16-lane spaghetti interchange is the mere elaboration of a country crossroads."[4]

We cannot accurately count transnational advocacy networks to measure their growth over time, but one proxy is the increase in the number of international NGOs committed to social change. Because international NGOs are key components of any advocacy network, this increase suggests broader trends in the number, size, and density of advocacy networks generally.

* * *

Transnational advocacy networks appear most likely to emerge around those issues where (1) channels between domestic groups and their governments are blocked or hampered or where such channels are ineffective for resolving a conflict, setting into motion the "boomerang" pattern of influence characteristic of these networks; (2) activists or "political entrepreneurs" believe that networking will further their missions and campaigns, and actively promote networks; and (3) conferences and other forms of international contact create arenas for forming and strengthening networks. Where channels of participation are blocked, the international arena may be the only means that domestic activists have to gain attention to their issues. Boomerang strategies are most common in campaigns where the target is a state's domestic policies or behavior; where a campaign seeks broad procedural change involving dispersed actors, strategies are more diffuse.

Political Entrepreneurs

Just as oppression and injustice do not themselves produce movements or revolutions, claims around issues amenable to international action do not produce transnational networks. Activists—"people who care enough about some issue that they are prepared to incur significant costs and act to achieve their goals"[5]—do. They create them when they believe that transnational networking will further their organizational missions—by sharing information, attaining greater visibility, gaining access to wider publics, multiplying channels of institutional access, and so forth. For example, in the campaign to stop the promotion of infant formula to poor women in developing countries, organizers settled on a boycott of Nestlé, the largest producer, as its main tactic. Because Nestlé was a transnational actor, activists believed a transnational network was necessary to bring pressure on corporations and governments.[6] Over time, in such issue areas, participation in transnational networks has become an essential component of the collective identities of the activists involved, and networking a part of their common repertoire. The political entrepreneurs who become the core networkers for a new campaign have often gained experience in earlier ones.

The Growth of International Contact

Opportunities for network activities have increased over the last two decades. In addition to the efforts of pioneers, a proliferation of international organizations and conferences has provided foci for connections. Cheaper air travel and new electronic communication technologies speed information flows and simplify personal contact among activists.[7]

Underlying these trends is a broader cultural shift. The new networks have depended on the creation of a new kind of global public (or civil society), which grew as a cultural legacy of the 1960s.[8] Both the activism that swept Western Europe, the United States, and many parts of the third world during that decade, and the vastly increased opportunities for international contact, contributed to this shift. With a significant decline in air fares, foreign travel ceased to be the exclusive privilege of the wealthy. Students participated in exchange programs. The Peace Corps and lay missionary programs sent thousands of young people to live and work in the developing world. Political exiles from Latin America taught in U.S. and European universities. Churches opened their doors to refugees, and to new ideas and commitments.

Obviously, internationalism was not invented in the sixties. Religious and political traditions including missionary outreach, the solidarity traditions of labor and the left, and liberal internationalism have long stirred action by individuals or groups beyond the borders of their own state. While many activists working in advocacy networks come out of these traditions, they tend no longer to define themselves in terms of these traditions or the organizations that carried them. This is most true for activists on the left who suffered disillusionment from their groups' refusal to address seriously the concerns of women, the environment, or human rights violations in eastern bloc countries. Absent a range of options that in earlier decades would have competed for their commitments, advocacy and activism through either NGOs or grassroots movements became the most likely alternative for those seeking to "make a difference."

* * *

How Do Transnational Advocacy Networks Work?

Transnational advocacy networks seek influence in many of the same ways that other political groups or social movements do. Since they are not powerful in a traditional sense of the word, they must use the power of their information, ideas, and strategies to alter the information and value contexts within which states make policies. The bulk of what networks do might be termed persuasion or socialization, but neither process is devoid of conflict. Persuasion and socialization often involve not just reasoning with opponents, but also bringing pressure, arm-twisting, encouraging sanctions, and shaming. * * *

* * *

Our typology of tactics that networks use in their efforts at persuasion, socialization, and pressure includes (1) *information politics,* or the ability to quickly and credibly generate politically usable information and move it to where it will have the most impact; (2) *symbolic politics,* or the ability to call upon symbols, actions,

or stories that make sense of a situation for an audience that is frequently far away;[9] (3) *leverage politics,* or the ability to call upon powerful actors to affect a situation where weaker members of a network are unlikely to have influence; and (4) *accountability politics,* or the effort to hold powerful actors to their previously stated policies or principles.

* * *

Information Politics

Information binds network members together and is essential for network effectiveness. Many information exchanges are informal—telephone calls, E-mail and fax communications, and the circulation of newsletters, pamphlets and bulletins. They provide information that would not otherwise be available, from sources that might not otherwise be heard, and they must make this information comprehensible and useful to activists and publics who may be geographically and/or socially distant.[10]

* * *

Nonstate actors gain influence by serving as alternate sources of information. Information flows in advocacy networks provide not only facts but testimony—stories told by people whose lives have been affected. Moreover, activists interpret facts and testimony, usually framing issues simply, in terms of right and wrong because their purpose is to persuade people and stimulate them to act. How does this process of persuasion occur? An effective frame must show that a given state of affairs is neither natural nor accidental, identify the responsible party or parties, and propose credible solutions. These aims require clear, powerful messages that appeal to shared principles, which often have more impact on state policy than advice of technical experts. An important part of the political struggle over information is precisely whether an issue is defined primarily as technical—and thus subject to consideration by "qualified" experts—or as something that concerns a broader global constituency.

* * *

Networks strive to uncover and investigate problems, and alert the press and policymakers. One activist described this as the "human rights methodology"—"promoting change by reporting facts."[11] To be credible, the information produced by networks must be reliable and well documented. To gain attention, the information must be timely and dramatic. Sometimes these multiple goals of information politics conflict, but both credibility and drama seem to be essential components of a strategy aimed at persuading publics and policymakers to change their minds.

* * *

Symbolic Politics

Activists frame issues by identifying and providing convincing explanations for powerful symbolic events, which in turn become catalysts for the growth of networks. Symbolic interpretation is part of the process of persuasion by which networks create awareness and expand their constituencies. Awarding the 1992 Nobel Peace Prize to Maya activists Rigoberta Menchú and the UN's designation of 1993 as the Year of Indigenous Peoples heightened public awareness of the situation of indigenous peoples in the Americas. Indigenous people's use of 1992, the 500th anniversary of the voyage of Columbus to the Americas, to raise a host of issues well illustrates the use of symbolic events to reshape understandings.[12]

* * *

Leverage Politics

Activists in advocacy networks are concerned with political effectiveness. Their definition of effectiveness often includes some policy change by "target actors" such as governments, international financial institutions like the World Bank, or private actors like transnational corporations. In order to bring about policy change, networks need to pressure and persuade more powerful actors. To gain influence the networks seek leverage (the word appears often in the discourse of advocacy organizations) over more powerful actors. By leveraging more powerful institutions, weak groups gain influence far beyond their ability to influence state practices directly. The identification of material or moral leverage is a crucial strategic step in network campaigns.

Material leverage usually links the issue to money or goods (but potentially also to votes in international organizations, prestigious offices, or other benefits). * * *

* * *

Although NGO influence often depends on securing powerful allies, their credibility still depends in part on their ability to mobilize their own members and affect public opinion via the media. In democracies the potential to influence votes gives large membership organizations an advantage over nonmembership organizations in lobbying for policy change; environmental organizations, several of whose memberships number in the millions, are more likely to have this added clout than are human rights organizations.

Moral leverage involves what some commentators have called the "mobilization of shame," where the behavior of target actors is held up to the light of international scrutiny. Network activists exert moral leverage on the assumption that governments value the good opinion of others; insofar as networks can demonstrate that a state is violating international obligations or is not living up to its own claims, they hope to jeopardize its credit enough to motivate a change in policy or behavior. The degree to which states are vulnerable to this kind of pressure varies, and will be discussed further below.

Accountability Politics

Networks devote considerable energy to convincing governments and other actors to publicly change their positions on issues. This is often dismissed as inconsequential change, since talk is cheap and governments sometimes change discursive positions hoping to divert network and public attention. Network activists, however, try to make such statements into opportunities for accountability politics. Once a government has publicly committed itself to a principle—for example, in favor of human rights or democracy—networks can use those positions, and their command of information, to expose the distance between discourse and practice. This is embarrassing to many governments, which may try to save face by closing that distance.

* * *

Domestic structures through which states and private actors can be held accountable to their pronouncements, to the law, or to contracts vary considerably from one nation to another, even among democracies. The centrality of the courts in U.S. politics creates a venue for the representation of diffuse interests that is not available in most European democracies.[13] It also explains the large number of U.S. advocacy organizations that specialize in litigation. * * *

Under What Conditions Do Advocacy Networks Have Influence?

To assess the influence of advocacy networks we must look at goal achievement at several different levels. We identify the following types or stages of network influence: (1) issue creation and agenda setting; (2) influence on discursive positions of states and international organizations; (3) influence on institutional procedures; (4) influence on policy change in "target actors" which may be states, international organizations like the World Bank, or private actors like the Nestlé Corporation; and (5) influence on state behavior.

Networks generate attention to new issues and help set agendas when they provoke media attention, debates, hearings, and meetings on issues that previously had not been a matter of public debate. Because values are the essence of advocacy networks, this stage of influence may require a modification of the "value context" in which policy debates takes place. The UN's theme years and decades, such as International Women's Decade and the Year of Indigenous Peoples, were international events promoted by networks that heightened awareness of issues.

Networks influence discursive positions when they help persuade states and international organizations to support international declarations or to change stated domestic policy positions. The role environmental networks played in shaping state positions and conference declarations at the 1992 "Earth Summit" in Rio de Janeiro is an example of this kind of impact. They may also pressure states to make more binding commitments by signing conventions and codes of conduct.

The targets of network campaigns frequently respond to demands for policy change with changes in procedures (which may affect policies in the future). The multilateral bank campaign is largely responsible for a number of changes in internal bank directives mandating greater NGO and local participation in discussions of projects. It also opened access to formerly restricted information, and led to the establishment of an independent inspection panel for World Bank projects. Procedural changes can greatly increase the opportunity for advocacy organizations to develop regular contact with other key players on an issue, and they sometimes offer the opportunity to move from outside to inside pressure strategies.

A network's activities may produce changes in policies, not only of the target states, but also of other states and/or international institutions. Explicit policy shifts seem to denote success, but even here both their causes and meanings may be elusive. We can point with some confidence to network impact where human rights network pressures have achieved cut-offs of military aid to repressive regimes, or a curtailment of repressive practices. Sometimes human rights activity even affects regime stability. But we must take care to distinguish between policy change and change in behavior; official policies regarding timber extraction in Sarawak, Malaysia, for example, may say little about how timber companies behave on the ground in the absence of enforcement.

We speak of stages of impact, and not merely types of impact, because we believe that increased attention, followed by changes in discursive positions, make governments more vulnerable to the claims that networks raise. (Discursive changes can also have a powerfully divisive effect on networks themselves, splitting insiders from outsiders, reformers from radicals.) A government that claims to be protecting indigenous areas or ecological reserves is potentially more vulnerable to charges that such areas are endangered than one that makes no such claim. At that point the effort is not to make governments change their position but to hold them to their word. Meaningful policy change is thus more likely when the first three types or stage of impact have occurred.

* * *

Issue Characteristics

Issues that involve ideas about right and wrong are amenable to advocacy networking because they arouse strong feelings, allow networks to recruit volunteers and activists, and infuse meaning into these volunteer activities. However, not all principled ideas lead to network formation, and some issues can be framed more easily than others so as to resonate with policymakers and publics. * * *

* * *

As we look at the issues around which transnational advocacy networks have organized most effectively, we find two issue characteristics that appear most frequently: (1) issues involving bodily harm to vulnerable individuals, especially when there is a short and clear causal chain (or story) assigning responsibility; and (2) issues involving legal equality of opportunity. The first respond to a normative logic, and the second to a juridical and institutional one.

* * *

Actor Characteristics

However amenable particular issues may be to strong transnational and transcultural messages, there must be actors capable of transmitting those messages and targets who are vulnerable to persuasion or leverage. * * *

Target actors must be vulnerable either to material incentives or to sanctions from outside actors, or they must be sensitive to pressure because of gaps between stated commitments and practice. Vulnerability arises both from the availability of leverage and the target's sensitivity to leverage; if either is missing, a campaign may fail.

* * *

Notes

[1]Peter Haas has called these "knowledge-based" or "epistemic communities." See Peter Haas, "Introduction: Epistemic Communities and International Policy Coordination," *Knowledge, Power and International Policy Coordination,* special issue, *International Organization* 46 (Winter 1992), pp. 1–36.

[2]Ideas that specify criteria for determining whether actions are right and wrong and whether outcomes are just or unjust are shared principled beliefs or values, Beliefs about cause-effect relationships are shared casual beliefs, Judith Goldstein and Robert Keohane, eds., *Ideas and Foreign Policy: Beliefs, Institutions, and Political Change* (Ithaca: Cornell University Press, 1993), pp. 8–10.

[3]See John D. McCarthy and Mayer N. Zald, "Resource Mobilization and Social Movements: A Partial Theory," *American Journal of Sociology* 82:6 (1977): 1212–41. Myra Marx Feree and Frederick D. Miller, "Mobilization and Meaning: Toward an Integration of Social Psychological and Resource Perspectives on Social Movements," *Sociological Inquiry* 55 (1985): 49–50; and David S. Meyer and Nancy Whittier, "Social Movement Spillover," *Social Problems* 41:2 (May 1994): 277–98.

[4]Hugh Heclo, "Issue Networks and the Executive Establishment," in *The New American Political System,* ed. Anthony King (Washington, D.C.: American Enterprise Institute, 1978). p. 97.

[5]Pamela E. Oliver and Gerald Marwell, "Mobilizing Technologies for Collective Action," in *Frontiers in Social Movement Theory*, ed. Aldon D. Morris and Carol McClurg Mueller (New Haven: Yale University Press, 1992), p. 252.

[6]See Kathryn Sikkink, "Codes of Conduct for Transnational Corporations: The Case of the WHO/UNICEF Code," *International Organization* 40 (Autumn 1986): 815–40.

[7]The constant dollar yield of airline tickets in 1995 was one half of what it was in 1966, while the number of international passengers enplaned increased more than four times during the same period. Air Transport Association home page, June 1997, http://www.airtransport.org/data/traffic.htm. See James Rosenau, *Turbulence in World Politics* (Princeton: Princeton University Press, 1990), pp. 12, 25.

[8]See Sidney Tarrow, "Mentalities, Political Cultures, and Collective Action Frames: Constructing Meanings through Action," in *Frontiers in Social Movement Theory*, p. 184.

[9]Alison Brysk uses the categories "information politics" and "symbolic politics" to discuss strategies of transnational actors, especially networks around Indian rights. See "Acting Globally: Indian Rights and International Politics in Latin America," in *Indigenous Peoples and Democracy in Latin America*, ed. Donna Lee Van Cott (New York: St. Martin's Press/Inter-American Dialogue, 1994), pp. 29–51; and "Hearts and Minds: Bringing Symbolic Politics Back In," *Polity* 27 (Summer 1995): 559–85.

[10]Rosenau, *Turbulence*, p. 199, argues that "as the adequacy of information and the very nature of knowledge have emerged as central issues, what were once regarded as the petty quarrels of scholars over the adequacy of evidence and the metaphysics of proof have become prominent activities in international relations."

[11]Dorothy Q. Thomas, "Holding Governments Accountable by Public Pressure," In *Ours by Right: Women's Rights as Human Rights*, ed. Joanna Kerr (London: Zed Books, 1993), p. 83. This methodology is not new. See, for example, David H. Lumsdaine, *Moral Vision*, in *International Politics: The Foreign Aid Regime* (Princeton: Princeton University Press, 1993), pp. 187–88, 211–13.

[12]Brysk, "Acting Globally."

The Triumph of Democracy

10.1

FRANCIS FUKUYAMA

The End of History?

In watching the flow of events over the past decade or so, it is hard to avoid the feeling that something very fundamental has happened in world history. The past year has seen a flood of articles commemorating the end of the Cold War, and the fact that "peace" seems to be breaking out in many regions of the world. Most of these analyses lack any larger conceptual framework for distinguishing between what is essential and what is contingent or accidental in world history, and are predictably superficial. If Mr. Gorbachev were ousted from the Kremlin or a new Ayatollah proclaimed the millennium from a desolate Middle Eastern capital, these same commentators would scramble to announce the rebirth of a new era of conflict.

And yet, all of these people sense dimly that there is some larger process at work, a process that gives coherence and order to the daily headlines. The twentieth century saw the developed world descend into a paroxysm of ideological violence, as liberalism contended first with the remnants of absolutism, then bolshevism and fascism and finally an updated Marxism that threatened to lead to the ultimate apocalypse of nuclear war. But the century that began full of self-confidence in the ultimate triumph of Western liberal democracy seems at its close to be returning full circle to where it started: not to an "end of ideology" or a convergence between capitalism and socialism, as earlier predicted, but to an unabashed victory of economic and political liberalism.

The triumph of the West, of the Western *idea*, is evident first of all in the total exhaustion of viable systematic alternatives to Western liberalism. In the past decade, there have been unmistakable changes in the intellectual climate of the world's two largest communist countries, and the beginnings of significant reform movements in both. But this phenomenon extends beyond high politics and it can be seen also in the ineluctable spread of consumerist Western culture in such diverse contexts as the peasants' markets and

From *National Interest,* 16 (Summer 1989).

color television sets now omnipresent throughout China, the cooperative restaurants and clothing stores opened in the past year in Moscow, the Beethoven piped into Japanese department stores, and the rock music enjoyed alike in Prague, Rangoon, and Tehran.

What we may be witnessing is not just the end of the Cold War, or the passing of a particular period of postwar history, but the end of history as such: that is, the end point of mankind's ideological evolution and the universalization of Western liberal democracy as the final form of human government. This is not to say that there will no longer be events to fill the pages of *Foreign Affairs*'s yearly summaries of international relations, for the victory of liberalism has occurred primarily in the realm of ideas or consciousness and is as yet incomplete in the real or material world. But there are powerful reasons for believing that it is the ideal that will govern the material world *in the long run*. To understand how this is so, we must first consider some theoretical issues concerning the nature of historical change.

* * *

Have we in fact reached the end of history? Are there, in other words, any fundamental "contradictions" in human life that cannot be resolved in the context of modern liberalism, that would be resolvable by an alternative political-economic structure? If we accept the idealist premises laid out above, we must seek an answer to this question in the realm of ideology and consciousness.

Our task is not to answer exhaustively the challenges to liberalism promoted by every crackpot messiah around the world, but only those that are embodied in important social or political forces and movements, and which are therefore part of world history. For our purposes, it matters very little what strange thoughts occur to people in Albania or Burkina Faso, for we are interested in what one could in some sense call the common ideological heritage of mankind.

In the past century, there have been two major challenges to liberalism, those of fascism and of communism. The former[1] saw the political weakness, materialism, anomie, and lack of community of the West as fundamental contradictions in liberal societies that could only be resolved by a strong state that forged a new "people" on the basis of national exclusiveness. Fascism was destroyed as a living ideology by World War II. This was a defeat, of course, on a very material level, but it amounted to a defeat of the idea as well. What destroyed fascism as an idea was not universal moral revulsion against it, since plenty of people were willing to endorse the idea so long as it seemed the wave of the future, but its lack of success. After the war, it seemed to most people that German fascism as well as its other European and Asian variants were bound to self-destruct. There was no material reason why new fascist movements could not have sprung up again after the war in other locales, but for the fact that expansionist ultranationalism, with its promise of unending conflict leading to disastrous military defeat, had completely lost its appeal. The ruins of the Reich chancellory as well as the atomic bombs dropped on Hiroshima and Nagasaki killed this ideology on the level of consciousness as well as materially, and all of the proto-fascist movements spawned by the German and Japanese examples like the Peronist movement in Argentina or Subhas Chandra Bose's Indian National Army withered after the war.

The ideological challenge mounted by the other great alternative to liberalism, communism, was far more serious. Marx, speaking Hegel's language, asserted that liberal society contained a fundamental contradiction that could not be resolved within its context, that between capital and labor, and this contradiction has constituted the chief accusation against liberalism ever since. But surely, the class issue has actually been successfully resolved in the West. As Kojève (among others) noted, the egalitarianism of modern America represents the essential achievement of the classless society envisioned by Marx. This is not to say that there are not rich people and poor people in the United States, or that the gap between them has not grown in recent years. But the root causes of economic inequality do not have to do with the underlying legal and social structure of our society, which remains fundamentally egalitarian and moderately redistributionist, so much as with the cultural and social characteristics of the groups that make it up, which are in turn the historical legacy of premodern conditions. Thus black poverty in the United States is not the inherent product of liberalism,

but is rather the "legacy of slavery and racism" which persisted long after the formal abolition of slavery.

* * *

If we admit for the moment that the fascist and communist challenges to liberalism are dead, are there any other ideological competitors left? Or put another way, are there contradictions in liberal society beyond that of class that are not resolvable? Two possibilities suggest themselves, those of religion and nationalism.

The rise of religious fundamentalism in recent years within the Christian, Jewish, and Muslim traditions has been widely noted. One is inclined to say that the revival of religion in some way attests to a broad unhappiness with the impersonality and spiritual vacuity of liberal consumerist societies. Yet while the emptiness at the core of liberalism is most certainly a defect in the ideology—indeed, a flaw that one does not need the perspective of religion to recognize[2]—it is not at all clear that it is remediable through politics. Modern liberalism itself was historically a consequence of the weakness of religiously-based, societies which, failing to agree on the nature of the world's nationalist movements do not have a political program beyond the negative desire of independence *from* some other group or people, and do not offer anything like a comprehensive agenda for socioeconomic organization. As such, they are compatible with doctrines and ideologies that do offer such agendas. While they may constitute a source of conflict for liberal societies, this conflict does not arise from liberalism itself so much as from the fact that the liberalism in question is incomplete. Certainly a great deal of the world's ethnic and nationalist tension can be explained in terms of peoples who are forced to live in unrepresentative political systems that they have not chosen.

While it is impossible to rule out the sudden appearance of new ideologies or previously unrecognized contradictions in liberal societies, then, the present world seems to confirm that the fundamental principles of socio-political organization have not advanced terribly far since 1806. Many of the wars and revolutions fought since that time have been undertaken in the name of ideologies which claimed to be more advanced than liberalism, but whose pretensions were ultimately unmasked by history. In the meantime, they have helped to spread the universal homogenous state to the point where it could have a significant effect on the overall character of international relations.

* * *

The passing of Marxism-Leninism first from China and then from the Soviet Union will mean its death as a living ideology of world historical significance. For while there may be some isolated true believers left in places like Managua, Pyongyang, or Cambridge, Massachusetts, the fact that there is not a single large state in which it is a going concern undermines completely its pretensions to being in the vanguard of human history. And the death of this ideology means the growing "Common Marketization" of international relations, and the diminution of the likelihood of large-scale conflict between states.

This does not by any means imply the end of international conflict *per se*. For the world at that point would be divided between a part that was historical and a part that was post-historical. Conflict between states still in history, and between those states and those at the end of history, would still be possible. There would still be a high and perhaps rising level of ethnic and nationalist violence, since those are impulses incompletely played out, even in parts of the post-historical world. Palestinians and Kurds, Sikhs and Tamils, Irish Catholics and Walloons, Armenians and Azeris, will continue to have their unresolved grievances. This implies that terrorism and wars of national liberation will continue to be an important item on the international agenda. But large-scale conflict must involve large states still caught in the grip of history, and they are what appear to be passing from the scene.

The end of history will be a very sad time. The struggle for recognition, the willingness to risk one's life for a purely abstract goal, the worldwide ideological struggle that called forth daring, courage, imagination, and idealism, will be replaced by economic calculation, the endless solving of technical problems, environmental concerns, and the satisfaction of sophisticated consumer demands. In the post-historical period there will be neither art nor philosophy, just the perpetual caretaking of the museum of human history. I can feel in myself, and see in others around me, a powerful nostalgia for the time when history existed. Such nostalgia, in fact, will continue to fuel competition and conflict even in the post-historical world for some time to come. Even though I recognize its inevitability, I have the most ambivalent feelings for the civilization that has been created in Europe since 1945, with its north Atlantic and Asian offshoots. Perhaps this very prospect of centuries of boredom at the end of history will serve to get history started once again.

Notes

[1] I am not using the term "fascism" here in its most precise sense, fully aware of the frequent misuse of this term to denounce anyone to the right of the user.

"Fascism" here denotes any organized ultranationalist movement with universalistic pretensions—not universalistic with regard to its nationalism, of course, since the latter is exclusive by definition, but with regard to the movement's belief in its right to rule other people. Hence Imperial Japan would qualify as fascist while former strongman Stoessner's Paraguay or Pinochet's Chile would not. Obviously fascist ideologies cannot be universalistic in the sense of Marxism or liberalism, but the structure of the doctrine can be transferred from country to country.

[2] I am thinking particularly of Rousseau and the Western philosophical tradition that flows from him that was highly critical of Lockean or Hobbesian liberalism, though one could criticize liberalism from the standpoint of classical political philosophy as well.

Ongoing Threats to Democracy

10.2

SAMUEL P. HUNTINGTON

The Clash of Civilizations?

The Next Pattern of Conflict

World politics is entering a new phase, and intellectuals have not hesitated to proliferate visions of what it will be—the end of history, the return of traditional rivalries between nation states, and the decline of the nation state from the conflicting pulls of tribalism and globalism, among others. Each of these visions catches aspects of the emerging reality. Yet they all miss a crucial, indeed, a central, aspect of what global politics is likely to be in the coming years.

It is my hypothesis that the fundamental source of conflict in this new world will not be primarily ideological or primarily economic. The great divisions among humankind and the dominating source of conflict will be cultural. Nation states will remain the most powerful actors in world affairs, but the principal conflicts of global politics will occur between nations and groups of different civilizations. The clash of civilizations will dominate global politics. The fault lines between civilizations will be the battle lines of the future.

*　*　*

The Nature of Civilizations

During the cold war the world was divided into the First, Second and Third Worlds. Those divisions are no longer relevant. It is far more meaningful now to group countries not in terms of their political or economic systems or in terms of their level of economic development but rather in terms of their culture and civilization.

What do we mean when we talk of a civilization? A civilization is a cultural entity. Villages, regions, ethnic groups, nationalities, religious groups, all have distinct cultures at different levels of cultural heterogeneity. The culture of a village in southern Italy may be different from that of a village in northern Italy, but both will share in common Italian culture that distinguishes them from German villages. European communities, in turn, will share cultural features that distinguish them from Arab or Chinese communities. Arabs, Chinese and Westerners, however, are not part of any broader cultural entity. They constitute civilizations. A civilization is thus the highest cultural grouping of people and the broadest level of cultural

From *Foreign Affairs* 72:3 (Summer 1993).

identity people have short of that which distinguishes humans from other species. It is defined both by common objective elements, such as language, history, religion, customs, institutions, and by the subjective self-identification of people. People have levels of identity: a resident of Rome may define himself with varying degrees of intensity as a Roman, an Italian, a Catholic, a Christian, a European, a Westerner. The civilization to which he belongs is the broadest level of identification with which he intensely identifies. People can and do redefine their identities and, as a result, the composition and boundaries of civilizations change.

*   *   *

Why Civilizations Will Clash

Civilization identity will be increasingly important in the future, and the world will be shaped in large measure by the interactions among seven or eight major civilizations. These include Western, Confucian, Japanese, Islamic, Hindu, Slavic-Orthodox, Latin American and possibly African civilization. The most important conflicts of the future will occur along the cultural fault lines separating these civilizations from one another.

Why will this be the case?

First, differences among civilizations are not only real; they are basic. Civilizations are differentiated from each other by history, language, culture, tradition and, most important, religion. The people of different civilizations have different views on the relations between God and man, the individual and the group, the citizen and the state, parents and children, husband and wife, as well as differing views of the relative importance of rights and responsibilities, liberty and authority, equality and hierarchy. These differences are the product of centuries. They will not soon disappear. They are far more fundamental than differences among political ideologies and political regimes. Differences do not necessarily mean conflict, and conflict does not necessarily mean violence. Over the centuries, however, differences among civilizations have generated the most prolonged and the most violent conflicts.

Second, the world is becoming a smaller place. The interactions between peoples of different civilizations are increasing; these increasing interactions intensify civilization consciousness and awareness of differences between civilizations and commonalities within civilizations. North African immigration to France generates hostility among Frenchmen and at the same time increased receptivity to immigration by "good" European Catholic Poles. * * *

The interactions among peoples of different civilizations enhance the civilization-consciousness of people that, in turn, invigorates differences and animosities stretching or thought to stretch back deep into history.

Third, the processes of economic modernization and social change throughout the world are separating people from long-standing local identities. They also weaken the nation state as a source of identity. In much of the world religion has moved in to fill this gap, often in the form of movements that are labeled "fundamentalist."

Such movements are found in Western Christianity, Judaism, Buddhism and Hinduism, as well as in Islam. In most countries and most religions the people active in fundamentalist movements are young, college-educated, middle-class technicians, professionals and business persons. The "unsecularization of the world," George Weigel has remarked, "is one of the dominant social facts of life in the late twentieth century." The revival of religion, "la revanche de Dieu," as Gilles Kepel labeled it, provides a basis for identity and commitment that transcends national boundaries and unites civilizations.

Fourth, the growth of civilization-consciousness is enhanced by the dual role of the West. On the one hand, the West is at a peak of power. At the same time, however, and perhaps as a result, a return to the roots phenomenon is occurring among non-Western civilizations. Increasingly one hears references to trends toward a turning inward and "Asianization" in Japan, the end of the Nehru legacy and the "Hinduization" of India, the failure of Western ideas of socialism and nationalism and hence "re-Islamization" of the Middle East, and now a debate over Westernization versus Russianization in Boris Yeltsin's country. A West at the peak of its power confronts non-Wests that increasingly have the desire, the will and the resources to shape the world in non-Western ways.

* * *

Fifth, cultural characteristics and differences are less mutable and hence less easily compromised and resolved than political and economic ones. In the former Soviet Union, communists can become democrats, the rich can become poor and the poor rich, but Russians cannot become Estonians and Azeris cannot become Armenians. In class and ideological conflicts, the key question was "Which side are you on?" and people could and did choose sides and change sides. In conflicts between civilizations, the question is "What are you?" That is a given that cannot be changed. And as we know, from Bosnia to the Caucasus to the Sudan, the wrong answer to that question can mean a bullet in the head. * * *

Finally, economic regionalism is increasing. The proportions of total trade that were intraregional rose between 1980 and 1989 from 51 percent to 59 percent in Europe, 33 percent to 37 percent in East Asia, and 32 percent to 36 percent in North America. The importance of regional economic blocs is likely to continue to increase in the future. On the one hand, successful economic regionalism will reinforce civilization-consciousness. On the other hand, economic regionalism may succeed only when it is rooted in a common civilization.

* * *

As people define their identity in ethnic and religious terms, they are likely to see an "us" versus "them" relation existing between themselves and people of different ethnicity or religion. The end of ideologically defined states in Eastern Europe and the former Soviet Union permits traditional ethnic identities and animosities to come to the fore. Differences in culture and religion create differences over policy issues, ranging from human rights to immigration to trade and commerce to the environment. Geographical propinquity gives rise to conflicting territorial claims from Bosnia to Mindanao. Most important, the efforts of the West to promote its values of democracy and liberalism as universal values, to maintain its military predominance and to advance its economic interests engender countering responses from other civilizations. Decreasingly able to mobilize support and form coalitions on the basis of ideology, governments and groups will increasingly attempt to mobilize support by appealing to common religion and civilization identity.

The clash of civilizations thus occurs at two levels. At the micro-level, adjacent groups along the fault lines between civilizations struggle, often violently, over the control of territory and each other. At the macro-level, states from different civilizations compete for relative military and economic power, struggle over the control of international institutions and third parties, and competitively promote their particular political and religious values.

* * *

The West Versus the Rest

The West is now at an extraordinary peak of power in relation to other civilizations. Its superpower opponent has disappeared from the map. Military conflict among Western states is unthinkable, and Western military power is unrivaled. Apart from Japan, the West faces no economic challenge. It dominates international political and security institutions and with

Japan international economic institutions. Global political and security issues are effectively settled by a directorate of the United States, Britain and France, world economic issues by a directorate of the United States, Germany and Japan, all of which maintain extraordinarily close relations with each other to the exclusion of lesser and largely non-Western countries. Decisions made at the U.N. Security Council or in the International Monetary Fund that reflect the interests of the West are presented to the world as reflecting the desires of the world community. The very phrase "the world community" has become the euphemistic collective noun (replacing "the Free World") to give global legitimacy to actions reflecting the interests of the United States and other Western powers.[1] * * *

Differences in power and struggles for military, economic and institutional power are thus one source of conflict between the West and other civilizations. Differences in culture, that is basic values and beliefs, are a second source of conflict. V. S. Naipaul has argued that Western civilization is the "universal civilization" that "fits all men." At a superficial level much of Western culture has indeed permeated the rest of the world. At a more basic level, however, Western concepts differ fundamentally from those prevalent in other civilizations. Western ideas of individualism, liberalism, constitutionalism, human rights, equality, liberty, the rule of law, democracy, free markets, the separation of church and state, often have little resonance in Islamic, Confucian, Japanese, Hindu, Buddhist or Orthodox cultures. Western efforts to propagate such ideas produce instead a reaction against "human rights imperialism" and a reaffirmation of indigenous values, as can be seen in the support for religious fundamentalism by the younger generation in non-Western cultures. The very notion that there could be a "universal civilization" is a Western idea, directly at odds with the particularism of most Asian societies and their emphasis on what distinguishes one people from another. Indeed, the author of a review of 100 comparative studies of values in different societies concluded that "the values that are most important in the West are least important worldwide."[2] In the political realm, of course, these differences are most manifest in the efforts of the United States and other Western powers to induce other peoples to adopt Western ideas concerning democracy and human rights. Modern democratic government originated in the West. When it has developed in non-Western societies it has usually been the product of Western colonialism or imposition.

The central axis of world politics in the future is likely to be, in Kishore Mahbubani's phrase, the conflict between "the West and the Rest" and the responses of non-Western civilizations to Western power and values.[3] Those responses generally take one or a combination of three forms. At one extreme, non-Western states can, like Burma and North Korea, attempt to pursue a course of isolation, to insulate their societies from penetration or "corruption" by the West, and, in effect, to opt out of participation in the Western-dominated global community. The costs of this course, however, are high, and few states have pursued it exclusively. A second alternative, the equivalent of "band-wagoning" in international relations theory, is to attempt to join the West and accept its values and institutions. The third alternative is to attempt to "balance" the West by developing economic and military power and cooperating with other non-Western societies against the West, while preserving indigenous values and institutions; in short, to modernize but not to Westernize.

* * *

The Confucian-Islamic Connection

The obstacles to non-Western countries joining the West vary considerably. They are least for Latin American and East European countries. They are greater for the Orthodox countries of the former Soviet Union. They are still greater for Muslim, Confucian, Hindu and Buddhist societies. Japan has established a unique position for itself as an associate member of the West: it is in the West in some respects but clearly not of the West in important dimensions. Those countries that for reason of culture and power do not wish to, or cannot, join the West compete with the West by developing their own economic, military and political power. They do this by promoting their internal development and by cooperating with other non-Western countries. The most prominent form of this cooperation is the Confucian-Islamic connection that has emerged to challenge Western interests, values and power.

* * *

Implications for the West

This article does not argue that civilization identities will replace all other identities, that nation states will disappear, that each civilization will become a single coherent political entity, that groups within a civilization will not conflict with and even fight each other. This paper does set forth the hypotheses that differences between civilizations are real and important; civilization-consciousness is increasing; conflict between civilizations will supplant ideological and other forms of conflict as the dominant global form of conflict; international relations, historically a game played out within Western civilization, will increasingly be de-Westernized and become a game in which non-Western civilizations are actors and not simply objects; successful political, security and economic international institutions are more likely to develop within civilizations than across civilizations; conflicts between groups in different civilizations will be more frequent, more sustained and more violent than conflicts between groups in the same civilization; violent conflicts between groups in different civilizations are the most likely and most dangerous source of escalation that could lead to global wars; the paramount axis of world politics will be the relations between "the West and the Rest"; the elites in some torn non-Western countries will try to make their countries part of the West, but in most cases face major obstacles to accomplishing this; a central focus of conflict for the immediate future will be between the West and several Islamic-Confucian states.

This is not to advocate the desirability of conflicts between civilizations. It is to set forth descriptive hypotheses as to what the future may be like. If these are plausible hypotheses, however, it is necessary to consider their implications for Western policy. These implications should be divided between short-term advantage and long-term accommodation. In the short term it is clearly in the interest of the West to promote greater cooperation and unity within its own civilization, particularly between its European and North American components; to incorporate into the West societies in Eastern Europe and Latin America whose cultures are close to those of the West; to promote and maintain cooperative relations with Russia and Japan; to prevent escalation of local inter-civilization conflicts into major inter-civilization wars; to limit the expansion of the military strength of Confucian and Islamic states; to moderate the reduction of Western military capabilities and maintain military superiority in East and Southwest Asia; to exploit differences and conflicts among Confucian and Islamic states; to support in other civilizations groups sympathetic to Western values and interest; to strengthen international institutions that reflect and legitimate Western interests and values and to promote the involvement of non-Western states in those institutions.

In the longer term other measures would be called for. Western civilization is both Western and modern. Non-Western civilizations have attempted to become modern without becoming Western. To date only Japan has fully succeeded in this quest. Non-Western civilizations will continue to attempt to acquire the wealth, technology, skills, machines and weapons that are part of being modern. They will also attempt to reconcile this modernity with their traditional culture and values. Their economic and military strength relative to the West will increase. Hence the West will increasingly have to accommodate these non-Western modern civilizations whose power approaches that of the West but whose values and interests differ significantly from those of the West. This will require the West to maintain the economic and military power necessary to protect its interests in relation to these civilizations. It will also, however, require the West to develop a more profound understanding of the basic religious and philosophical assumptions underlying other civilizations and the ways in which people in those civilizations see their interests. It will require an effort to identify elements of commonality between Western and other civilizations. For the relevant future, there will be no universal civilization, but instead a world of different civilizations, each of which will have to learn to coexist with the others.

Notes

[1] Almost invariably Western leaders claim they are acting on behalf of "the world community." One minor lapse occurred during the runup to the Gulf War. In an interview on "Good Morning America," Dec. 21, 1990, British Prime Minister John Major referred to the actions "the West" was taking against Saddam Hussein. He quickly corrected himself and subsequently referred to "the world community." He was, however, right when he erred.

[2] Harry C. Triandis, *The New York Times*, Dec. 25, 1990, p. 41, and "Cross-Cultural Studies of Individualism and Collectivism," Nebraska Symposium on Motivation, vol. 37, 1989, pp. 41–133.

[3] Kishore Mahbubani, "The West and the Rest," *The National Interest*, Summer 1992, pp. 3–13.

Democratic Peace?

10.3

EDWARD D. MANSFIELD AND JACK SNYDER

Democratization and the Danger of War

One of the best-known findings of contemporary social science is that no democracies have ever fought a war against each other, given reasonably restrictive definitions of democracy and of war.[1] This insight is now part of everyday public discourse and serves as a basis for American foreign policymaking. President Bill Clinton's 1994 State of the Union address invoked the absence of war between democracies as a justification for promoting democratization around the globe. In the week following the U.S. military landing in Haiti, National Security Adviser Anthony Lake reiterated that "spreading democracy . . . serves our interests" because democracies "tend not to abuse their citizens' rights or wage war on one another."[2]

It is probably true that a world where more countries were mature, stable democracies would be safer and preferable for the United States. However, countries do not become mature democracies overnight. More typically, they go through a rocky transitional period, where democratic control over foreign policy is partial, where mass politics mixes in a volatile way with authoritarian elite politics, and where democratization suffers reversals. In this transitional phase of democratization, countries become more aggressive and war-prone, not less, and they do fight wars with democratic states.

The contemporary era shows that incipient or partial democratization can be an occasion for the rise of belligerent nationalism and war.[3] Two pairs of states—Serbia and Croatia, and Armenia and Azerbaijan—have found themselves at war while experimenting with varying degrees of partial electoral democracy. Russia's poorly institutionalized, partial democracy has tense relationships with many of its neighbors and has used military force brutally to reassert control in Chechnya; its electorate cast nearly a quarter of its votes for the party of radical nationalist Vladimir Zhirinovsky.

This contemporary connection between democratization and conflict is no coincidence. Using the same databases that are typically used to study the democratic peace, we find considerable statistical evidence that democratizing states are

---

From *International Security* 20:1 (Summer 1995), 5–38.

more likely to fight wars than are mature democracies or stable autocracies. States like contemporary Russia that make the biggest leap in democratization—from total autocracy to extensive mass democracy—are about twice as likely to fight wars in the decade after democratization as are states that remain autocracies. However, reversing the process of democratization, once it has begun, will not reduce this risk. Regimes that are changing toward autocracy, including states that revert to autocracy after failed experiments with democracy, are also more likely to fight wars than are states whose regime is unchanging.

Moreover, virtually every great power has gone on the warpath during the initial phase of its entry into the era of mass politics. Mid-Victorian Britain, poised between the partial democracy of the First Reform Bill of 1832 and the full-fledged democracy of the later Gladstone era, was carried into the Crimean War by a groundswell of belligerent public opinion. Napoleon III's France, drifting from plebiscitary toward parliamentary rule, fought a series of wars designed to establish its credentials as a liberal, popular, nationalist type of empire. The ruling elite of Wilhelmine Germany, facing universal suffrage but limited governmental accountability, was pushed toward World War I by its escalating competition with middle-class mass groups for the mantle of German nationalism. Japan's "Taisho democracy" of the 1920s brought an era of mass politics that led the Japanese army to devise and sell an imperial ideology with broad-based appeal.[4] In each case, the combination of incipient democratization and the material resources of a great power produced nationalism, truculence abroad, and major war.

Why should democratizing states be so belligerent? The pattern of the democratizing great powers suggests that the problem lies in the nature of domestic political competition after the breakup of the autocratic regime. Elite groups left over from the ruling circles of the old regime, many of whom have a particular interest in war and empire, vie for power and survival with each other and with new elites representing rising democratic forces. Both old and new elites use all the resources they can muster to mobilize mass allies, often through nationalist appeals, to defend their threatened positions and to stake out new ones. However, like the sorcerer's apprentice, these elites typically *find* that their mass allies, once mobilized, are difficult to control. When this happens, war can result from nationalist prestige strategies that hard-pressed leaders use to stay astride their unmanageable political coalitions.[5]

The problem is not that mass public opinion in democratizing states demonstrates an unvarnished, persistent preference for military adventure. On the contrary, public opinion often starts off highly averse to war. Rather, elites exploit their power in the imperfect institutions of partial democracies to create *faits accomplis,* control political agendas, and shape the content of information media in ways that promote belligerent pressure-group lobbies or upwellings of militancy in the populace as a whole.

Once this ideological connection between militant elites and their mass constituents is forged, the state may jettison electoral democracy while retaining nationalistic, populist rhetoric. As in the failure of Weimar and Taisho democracy, the adverse effects of democratization on war-proneness may even heighten after democracy collapses. Thus, the aftershock of failed democratization is at least one of the factors explaining the link between autocratization and war.

*   *   *

How Democratization Causes War

Why are democratization and autocratization associated with an increased chance of war? What causal mechanism is at work?* Based on case studies of four great powers during their initial phases of democratization, we argue that threatened elites from the collapsing autocratic regime, many of whom have parochial interests in war and empire, use nationalist appeals to compete for mass allies with each other and with new elites. In these circumstances, the likelihood of war increases due to the interests of some of the elite groups, the effectiveness of their propaganda, and the incentive for weak leaders to resort to prestige strategies in foreign affairs in an attempt to enhance their authority over diverse constituencies. Further, we speculate that transitional regimes, including both democratizing and autocratizing states, share

some common institutional weaknesses that make war more likely. At least in some cases, the link between autocratization and war reflects the success of a ruling elite in using nationalist formulas developed during the period of democratization to cloak itself in populist legitimacy, while dismantling the substance of democracy. In explaining the logic behind these arguments, we draw on some standard theories about the consequences of different institutional arrangements for political outcomes.

We illustrate these arguments with some contemporary examples and with cases drawn from four great powers at early stages in the expansion of mass political participation: mid-Victorian Britain, the France of Napoleon III, Bismarckian and Wilhelmine Germany, and Taisho Japan. *   *   *

Democratic versus Democratizing Institutions

Well-institutionalized democracies that reliably place ultimate authority in the hands of the average voter virtually never fight wars against each other. Moreover, although mature democracies do fight wars about as frequently as other types of states, they seem to be more prudent: they usually win their wars; they are quicker to abandon strategic overcommitments; and they do not fight gratuitous "preventive" wars.[6] Explanations for these tendencies focus variously on the self-interest of the average voter who bears the costs of war,

---

*Editor's Note: Autocratization is shifting away from democracy toward autocracy or other nondemocratic rule.

the norms of bargaining and conflict resolution inherent in democracy, the moderating impact of constitutional checks and balances, and the free marketplace of ideas.[7]

However, these happy solutions typically emerge only in the very long run. In the initial stages of expanding political participation, strong barriers prevent the emergence of full-fledged democratic processes and the foreign policy outcomes associated with them. The two main barriers are the weakness of democratic institutions and the resistance of social groups who would be the losers in a process of full-fledged democratization.

Popular inputs into the policymaking process can have wildly different effects, depending on the way that political institutions structure and aggregate those inputs.[8] It is a staple of political science that different institutional rules—for example, proportional representation versus single-member districts, or congressional versus executive authority over tariffs—can produce different political outcomes, even holding constant the preferences of individual voters. In newly democratizing states, the institutions that structure political outcomes may allow for popular participation in the policy process, but they way they channel that input is often a parody of full-fledged democracy. As Samuel Huntington has put it, the typical problem of political development is the gap between high levels of political participation and weak integrative institutions to reconcile the multiplicity of contending claims.[9] In newly democratizing states without strong parties, independent courts, a free press,

and untainted electoral procedures, there is no reason to expect that mass politics will produce the same impact on foreign policy as it does in mature democracies.

* * *

COMPETITIVE MASS MOBILIZATION In a period of democratization, threatened elite groups have an overwhelming incentive to mobilize allies among the mass of people, but only on their own terms, using whatever special resources they still retain. These have included monopolies of information (e.g., the German Navy's unique "expertise" in making strategic assessments); propaganda assets (the Japanese Army's public relations blitz justifying the invasion of Manchuria); patronage (British Foreign Secretary Palmerston's gifts of foreign service postings to the sons of cooperative journalists); wealth (Krupp steel's bankrolling of mass nationalist and militarist leagues); organizational skills and networks (the Japanese army's exploitation of rural reservist organizations to build a social base); and the ability to use the control of traditional political institutions to shape the political agenda and structure the terms of political bargains (the Wilhelmine ruling elite's deal with the Center Party, eliminating anti-Catholic legislation in exchange for support in the Reichstag on the naval budget).[10]

* * *

Ideology takes on particular significance in the competition for mass support.

New participants in the political process may be uncertain of where their political interests lie, because they lack established habits and good information, and are thus fertile ground for ideological appeals. Ideology can yield particularly big payoffs, moreover, when there is no efficient free marketplace of ideas to counter false claims with reliable facts. Elites try out all sorts of ideological appeals, depending on the social position that they need to defend, the nature of the mass group that they want to recruit, and the type of appeals that seem plausible in the given political setting. A nearly universal element in these ideological appeals is nationalism, which has the advantage of positing a community of interest that unites elites and masses, thus distracting attention from class cleavages.

Nationalist appeals have often succeeded even though the average voter was not consistently pro-war or pro-empire.

* * *

Implications for Policy

In light of these findings, it would be hard to maintain a naive enthusiasm for spreading peace by promoting democratization. Pushing nuclear-armed great powers like Russia or China toward democratization is like spinning a roulette wheel, where many of the potential outcomes are likely to be undesirable. However, in most cases the initial steps on the road to democratization will not be produced by the conscious policy of the United States, no matter what that policy may be. The roulette wheel is already spinning for Russia, and perhaps China, regardless of what the West does. Moreover, reversals of democratization are nearly as risky as democratization itself. Consequently, the international community needs a strategy not so much for promoting or reversing democratization as for managing the process in ways that minimize its risks and facilitate smooth transitions.

What might be some of these mitigating conditions, and how might they be promoted? The association of democratization with war is probabilistic. Democratization can lead either to war or to peace, depending on a variety of factors, such as the incentives facing the old elites during the transition process, the structure of the marketplace of foreign policy ideas, the speed and thoroughness of the democratic transition, and the character of the international environment in which democratization occurs. Some of these features may be subject to manipulation by astute democratic reformers and their allies in the international community.

One of the major findings of scholarship on democratization in Latin America is that the process goes most smoothly when elites that are threatened by the transition, especially the military, are given a "golden parachute."[11] Above all, they need a guarantee that if they relinquish power they will not wind up in jail. The history of the democratizing great powers broadens this insight. Democratization was least likely to lead to imprudent aggression in cases where the old elites saw a reasonably bright future for themselves in the new social order. British aristocrats, for example, had more of their wealth invested in commerce and industry than they did in agriculture, so they had many interests in common with the rising middle classes. They could face democratization with relative equanimity. In contrast, Prussia's capital-starved, small-scale Junker landholders had no choice but to rely on agricultural protection and military careers.

In today's context, finding benign, productive employment for the erst-while Communist *nomenklatura*, military officer corps, nuclear scientists, and smoke stack industrialists ought to rank high on the list of priorities. Policies aimed at giving them a stake in the privatization process and subsidizing the conversion of their skills to new, peaceful tasks in a market economy seem like a step in the right direction. According to some interpretations, Russian Defense Minister Pavel Grachev was eager to use force to solve the Chechen confrontation in order to show that Russian military power was still useful and that increased investment in the Russian army would pay big dividends. Instead of pursuing this reckless path, the Russian military elite needs to be convinced that its prestige, housing, pensions, and technical competence will rise if and only if it transforms itself into a western-style military, subordinate to civilian authority and resorting to force only in accordance with prevailing international norms. Moreover, through old elites need to be kept happy, they also need to be kept weak. Pacts should not prop up the remnants of the authoritarian system, but rather create a niche for them in the new system.

A top priority must also be placed on creating a free, competitive, yet responsible marketplace of ideas in the newly democratizing states. Most of the war-prone democratizing great powers had pluralistic public debates, but the terms of these debates were skewed to favor groups with money, privileged access to the media of communication, and proprietary control over information, ranging from historical archives to intelligence about the military balance. Pluralism is not enough. Without an even playing field, pluralism simply creates the incentive and opportunity for privileged groups to propound self-serving myths, which historically have often taken a nationalist turn. One of the rays of hope in the Chechen affair was the alacrity with which Russian journalists exposed the true costs of the fighting and the lies of the government and the military about it. Though elites should get a golden parachute in terms of their pecuniary interests, they should be given no quarter on the battlefield of ideas. Myth-making should be held up to the utmost scrutiny by aggressive journalists who maintain their credibility by scrupulously distinguishing fact from opinion and tirelessly verifying their sources. Promoting this kind of journalistic infrastructure is probably the most highly leveraged investment that the West can make in a peaceful democratic transition.

Our research offers inconclusive results about the wisdom of speed and thoroughness in transitions to democracy. On the one hand, we found that states making the big jump from autocracy to democracy were much more war-prone than those moving from autocracy to anocracy. This would seem to favor a strategy of limited goals. On the other hand, the experience of the former Communist states suggests that those that have gone farthest and fastest toward full democracy are less nationalistic and less involved in militarized quarrels. This is a question that needs more research.

Finally, what kind of ruling coalition emerges in the course of democratization depends a great deal on the incentives that are created by the international environment. Both Germany and Japan started on the path toward liberal, stable democratization in the mid-1920s, encouraged in part by abundant opportunities for trade and investment from the advanced democracies and by credible security treaties that defused nationalist scaremongering in domestic politics. But when the international supports for free trade and democracy were yanked out in the late 1920s, their liberal coalitions collapsed. Especially for the case of contemporary China, whose democratization may occur in the context of sharply expanding economic ties to the West, the steadiness of the Western commercial partnership and security presence is likely to play a major role in shaping the incentives of proto-democratic coalition politics.

In the long run, the enlargement of the zone of stable democracy will probably enhance the prospects for peace. But in the short run, there is a lot of work to be done to minimize the dangers of the turbulent transition.

Notes

[1] Michael Doyle, "Liberalism and World Politics," *American Political Science Review*, Vol. 80, No. 4 (December 1986), pp. 1151–1169; Bruce Russett, *Grasping the Democratic Peace* (Princeton: Princeton University Press, 1993). For skeptical views, see David E. Spiro, "The Insignificance of the Liberal Peace," *International Security*, Vol. 19, No. 2 (Fall 1994), pp. 50–86; and Christopher Layne, "Kant or Cant: The Myth of the Democratic Peace," *International Security*, Vol. 19, No. 2 (Fall 1994), pp. 5–49. They are rebutted by Bruce Russett, "The Democratic Peace: 'And Yet It Moves'," *International Security*, Vol. 19, No. 4 (Spring 1995), pp. 164–175.

[2] "Transcript of Clinton's Address," *New York Times*, January 26, 1994, p. A17; Anthony Lake, "The Reach of Democracy: Tying Power to Diplomacy," *New York Times*, September 23, 1994, p. A35.

[3] Zeev Maoz and Bruce Russett, "Normative and Structural Causes of the Democratic Peace, 1956–1986," *American Political Science Review*, Vol. 87, No. 3 (September 1993), pp. 630, 636; they note that newly created democracies, such as those in Eastern Europe today, may experience conflicts, insofar as their democratic rules and norms are not adequately established. See also Russett, *Grasping the Democratic Peace*, p. 134, on post-Soviet Georgia.

[4] Asa Briggs, *Victorian People*, rev. ed. (Chicago: University of Chicago, 1970), chaps. 2–3; Geoff Eley, *Reshaping the German Right* (New Haven: Yale University Press, 1980); Alain Plessis, *De la fête impériale au mur des fédérés, 1852–1871* (Paris: Editions du seuil, 1973), translated as *The Rise and Fall of the Second Empire, 1852–1871* (Cambridge: Cambridge University Press, 1985); Jack Snyder, *Myths of Empire: Domestic Politics and International Ambition* (Ithaca: Cornell University Press, 1991), chaps. 3–5.

[5] Hans Ulrich Wehler, *The German Empire, 1871–1918* (Dover, N.H.: Berg, 1985); Jack S. Levy, "The Diversionary Theory of War: A Critique," In Manus Midlarsky, ed., *Handbook of War Studies* (Boston: Unwin-Hyman, 1989), pp. 259–288.

[6]David Lake, "Powerful Pacifists," *American Political Science Review,* Vol. 86, No. 1 (March 1992), pp. 24–37; Snyder, *Myths of Empire,* pp. 49–52; Randall Schweller, "Domestic Structure and Preventive War: Are Democracies More Pacific?" *World Politics,* Vol. 44, No. 2 (January 1992), pp. 235–269.

[7]Russett, *Grasping the Democratic Peace;* Miles Kahler, "Introduction," in Miles Kahler, ed., *Liberalization and Foreign Policy* (forthcoming); Jack Snyder, "Democratization, War, and Nationalism in the Post-Communist States," in Celeste Wallander, ed., *The Sources of Russian Conduct after the Cold War* (Boulder: Westview, forthcoming).

[8]Kenneth Shepsle, "Studying Institutions: Some Lessons from the Rational Choice Approach," *Journal of Theoretical Politics,* Vol. 1, No. 2 (April 1989), pp. 131–147.

[9]Samuel Huntington, *Political Order in Changing Societies* (New Haven: Yale University Press, 1968).

[10]Snyder, *Myths of Empire,* pp. 103, 140–141, 205; Louise Young, "Mobilizing for Empire: Japan and Manchukuo, 1930–1945," Ph.D. dissertation, Columbia University, 1992.

[11]On the importance of bargaining with and co-opting old elites (giving them incentives, a "golden parachute," to depart from power), see the literature summarized in Doh Chull Shin, "On the Third Wave of Democratization: A Synthesis and Evaluation of Recent Theory and Research," *World Politics,* Vol. 47, No. 1 (October 1994), pp. 135–170, esp. 161–163.

Web Bibliography

The following Web sites provide useful sources for further reading and student research. They are intended as a supplement to other library sources.

Research and Polling

Americans and the World: www.americans-world.org

Gallup Poll: www.gallup.com

Program on International Policy Attitudes: www.pipa.org

Roper Center for Public Opinion Research: www.ropercenter.uconn.edu

News Sources

British Broadcasting Corporation: news.bbc.co.uk

Economist: www.economist.com

Cable News Network: www.cnn.com

Financial Times: news.ft.com

New York Times: www.nytimes.com

Washington Post: www.washingtonpost.com

Journals

Foreign Affairs: www.foreignaffairs.org

Foreign Policy: www.foreignpolicy.com

International Security: mitpress.mit.edu/isec

National Interest: www.nationalinterest.org

World Policy Journal: www.worldpolicy.org/journal/index.html

U.S. Government

Centers for Disease Control and Prevention: www.cdc.gov

CDC site on terrorism: www.bt.cdc.gov

Central Intelligence Agency: www.cia.gov

Federal Bureau of Investigation: www.fbi.gov

U.S. Agency for International Development: www.usaid.gov

U.S. Commission on National Security for the 21st Century: www.nssg.gov

U.S. Congress: www.congress.gov

U.S. Department of Commerce: www.doc.gov

U.S. Department of Defense: www.defenselink.mil

U.S. Department of Homeland Security: www.dhs.gov

U.S. Department of State: www.state.gov

U.S. Department of Treasury: www.ustreas.gov

U.S. Environmental Protection Agency: www.epa.gov

U.S. General Accounting Office: www.gao.gov

U.S. House of Representatives: www.house.gov

U.S. International Trade Commission: www.usitc.gov

U.S. Office of National Drug Control Policy: www.whitehousedrugpolicy.gov

U.S. Senate: www.senate.gov

U.S. Trade Representative: www.ustr.gov

White House: www.whitehouse.gov

Think Tanks and Research Organizations

Brookings Institution: www.brookings.org

Carnegie Endowment for International Peace: www.ceip.org

Center for Defense Information: www.cdi.org

Centre for Defense and International Security Studies: www.cdiss.org

Center for Strategic and Budgetary Assessments: www.csbaonline.org

Center for Strategic and International Studies: www.csis.org

Columbia International Affairs Online (comprehensive source for theory and research in international affairs): www.ciaonet.org

Council on Foreign Relations: www.cfr.org

Federation of American Scientists Chemical and Biological Weapons

Arms Control Program: www.fas.org/bwc

Global Security: www.globalsecurity.org

Henry L. Stimson Center: www.stimson.org

Heritage Foundation: www.heritage.org

Institute for Defense and Disarmament Studies: www.idss.org

Institute for International Economics: www.iie.com

International Development Network: www.idn.org

International Development Research Centre: www.idrc.ca

International Institute for Strategic Studies: www.iiss.org

National Policy Association: www.npal.org

Pacific Research Institute Center for Environmental Studies: www.pacificresearch.org/centers/ces/index.html

RAND: www.rand.org

Terrorism Research Center: www.terrorism.com

U.S. Institute for Peace: www.usip.org

Washington Institute for Near East Policy: www.washingtoninstitute.org

Nongovernmental Organizations and Associations

Amnesty International: www.amnesty.org

AFL-CIO: www.aflcio.org

Center for Global Development: www.cgdev.org

Doctors Without Borders: www.msf.org

Federation of International Trade Associations: www.fita.org

Freedom House: www.freedomhouse.org

Global Exchange: www.globalexchange.org

Global Policy Forum: www.globalpolicy.org

Global Trade Watch: www.citizen.org/trade

Greenpeace: www.greenpeace.org

Human Rights Watch: www.hrw.org

International Alert: www.international-alert.org

International Campaign to Ban Landmines: www.icbl.org

International Crisis Group: www.crisisweb.org

International Institute for Democracy and Electoral Assistance: www.idea.int

National Association of Manufacturers: www.nam.org

National Endowment for Democracy: www.ned.org

One World: www.oneworld.net

Refugees International: www.refugeesinternational.org

Transparency International: www.transparency.org

U.S. Chamber of Commerce: www.uschamber.com

International Government Organizations

African Union (formerly the Organization for African Unity): www.africa-union.org

Association of Southeast Asian Nations: www.aseansec.org

Commission on Global Governance: www.cgg.ch

Economic Community of West African States (ECOWAS): www.ecowas.int

European Union: europa.eu.int

Free Trade Area of the Americas: www.ftaa-alca.org

Group of 77 (promotes the economic goals of developing nations): www.g77.org

International Atomic Energy Agency: www.iaea.org/worldatom

International Criminal Court: www.un.org/law/icc

International Monetary Fund: www.imf.org

Interpol: www.interpol.int

Non-Aligned Movement (a forum for developing countries): www.nam.gov.za

North Atlantic Treaty Organization (NATO): www.nato.int

Organization of American States: www.oas.org

Organization for the Prohibition of Chemical Weapons: www.opcw.org

Organization for Security and Cooperation in Europe: www.osce.org

United Nations: www.un.org

UN Commission on Human Rights: www.unhcr.ch

UN Commission on Trade and Development: www.unctad.org

UN Department of Peacekeeping: www.un.org/Depts/dpko/dpko/home.shtml

UN Environmental Programme: www.unep.org

UN Intergovernmental Panel on Climate Change: www.ipcc.ch

UN Programme on HIV/AIDS: www.unaids.org

World Bank: www.worldbank.org

World Health Organization: www.who.org

World Trade Organization: www.wto.org

Foreign Governments (a selected list)

China: www.china.org.cn/english/

France: www.premierministre.gouv.fr/en

Germany: eng.bundesregierung.de/frameset/index.jsp

India: goidirectory.nic.in

Israel: www.info.gov.il/eng/mainpage.asp

Mexico: www.mexonline.com/mexagncy.htm

Nigeria: www.nigeria.gov.ng

North Korea: www.korea-dpr.com

Pakistan: www.pak.gov.pk

Russian Federation: www.gov.ru

United Kingdom (England, N. Ireland, Scotland, Wales): www.ukonline.gov.uk

Credits

Index